PROCEEDINGS OF THE FORTY-SIXTH COLLOQUIUM ON THE LAW OF OUTER SPACE

INTERNATIONAL INSTITUTE OF SPACE LAW
OF THE
INTERNATIONAL ASTRONAUTICAL FEDERATION

29 SEPTEMBER – 3 OCTOBER 2003
BREMEN, GERMANY

AIAA

Published and Distributed by
AMERICAN INSTITUTE OF AERONAUTICS AND ASTRONAUTICS

ISBN
1-56347-673-8

Printed in the U.S.A.

INTRODUCTION

BY
N. JASENTULIYANA
PRESIDENT

The coordination and regulation of space activities by law is important in order to promote international cooperation and avoid conflicting claims and competition which would jeopardize beneficial uses of space for the benefit of the international community.

For its part, during the year 2003, the International Institute of Space Law (IISL), which is composed of members representing over 40 countries distinguished for their contribution to space law, continued its activities aimed at contributing to a better understanding and application of space law.

Scholarly work by specialists was encouraged through the Institute's annual colloquium and its regional and sponsored meetings. It is gratifying that several young scholars are now presenting papers at the colloquium and the Diederiks-Verschoor Award for the best paper presented at the colloquium by a new participant aimed at encouraging young scholars was further enhanced by the addition this year of a cash award. The Institute is grateful to the donors for the generous contributions made to enhance the award as well as the Eilene Galloway Award for the Best Written Brief and the Sterns and Tennen Award for the Best Oralist in the annual Manfred Lachs Moot Court Competition which is organized to popularize space law among university students.

2003 Manfred Lachs Moot Court Competition was once again a resounding success with increasing number of universities participating in the competition particularly from the Asia Pacific region which joined the competition recently. The continued participation of the Judges from the International Court of Justice (ICJ) to judge the world finals of the moot competition enhances its prestige and the Institute is grateful to the judges for their kind participation.

In continuing its research efforts, the Institute, through an open ended working group was engaged in working out a text of a statement to be posted on its website relating to Property Rights on the Moon and Celestial Bodies. In view of recent public and media interest on the subject the Institute felt it should rally distinguished specialists among its membership to provide guidance on the subject by way of such a statement on the property rights on the Moon and Celestial Bodies.

Recognizing the interdisciplinary nature of space activities, the Institute organized a Plenary Event at the annual International Astronautical Congress (IAC) in Bremen on the subject of "Space Business: Emerging Profitability in Space", with a view to providing Lawyers, Managers, and Scientists the opportunity to discuss various facets of the subject. We are grateful to the CEOs and other senior managers from space industry and organizations that participated as panelists to make the IISL Plenary a very successful IAC event.

Due to SARS the regional meeting planned for Beijing was postponed and will now be held in April 2004. It will serve as another forum for scholarly and practical discussions particularly in new areas of concern to space law relating to commercial uses of space technology, trade issues, insurance, financing asset protection and export control.

The Institute is grateful to its members for the cooperation and support they give to make its work a success. Prime among them is our indefatigable Secretary, Tanja Masson-Zwaan who in spite of having to relocate to different countries during the year (Singapore, France and Holland) and her many professional and family responsibilities, worked tirelessly to make the work of the Institute a success. Our hard working Treasurer Frans Von der Dunk and several of the Directors have worked through out the year, spending many hours on the internet to provide their advice, guidance and support to the work of the Institute.

The Institute is also grateful for the generous support provided by the German Space Agency DLR and EADS Space Transportation along with the University of Bremen in sponsoring the Annual IISL Dinner and the Manfred Lachs Moot Court Competition. We are particularly indebted to Prof. Jane Smith of the University of Bremen who coordinated the local arrangements and whose commitment was critical in obtaining the support for the Institute's activities in Bremen.

The Institute is grateful to its members who gave their time generously to prepare the Institute's reports and proceedings, operate it's web site, organize the regional Moot Competitions, draft the Moot Court case, judge the briefs and regional and semi-final competitions, act as speakers at Institute organized meetings, represent the Institute at various international meetings, and assist the Institute in various other ways.

We also continued our close cooperation with the United Nations and the European Center for Space Law (ECSL) as described in the annex below.

With out the strong support and encouragement of those I have referred to here, the Institute could not have carried out its numerous tasks so successfully in the year 2003, and I look forward to their continued cooperation in making the work of the Institute even more meaningful in the years ahead.

Annex: General Information

Background

The International Institute of Space Law (IISL) was founded by the International Astronautical Federation (IAF) in 1960. The IISL replaced the Permanent Committee on Space Law which the IAF had created in 1958 under the chairmanship of Andrew G. Haley. Since 1958, the IISL has held annual colloquia on space law in many nations. The IISL presently has elected individual and institutional members from over 40 countries, who are distinguished for their contributions to space law development. While a component of the IAF, the IISL is authorized to function autonomously in accordance with its Statutes. The purposes and objectives of the Institute include the cooperation with appropriate international organizations and national institutions in the field of space law, the carrying out of tasks for fostering the social science aspects of astronautics, space travel and exploration, the organization of meetings and colloquia on juridical and sociological aspects of the space sciences, and the publication of proceedings, reports and other publications. Each year, the Institute publishes a report of the Standing Committee on the Status of International Agreements Relating to Activities in Outer Space, headed by Dr. A. Terekhov.
The financial resources of the Institute are derived from membership dues, research grants, remuneration received from the sale of its publications, and donations received from individuals, associations, institutions, foundations, and other organizations with interests in the development of law governing space activities.

IISL and the United Nations

IISL members have been appointed by the International Astronautical Federation as Official Observers to annual sessions of the United Nations (UN) Committee on the Peaceful Uses of Outer Space and its Legal Subcommittee. In addition, the IISL has, like in past years, prepared a report on legal developments under contract with the UN, to be published in the annual Highlights in Space Report, and provides yearly reports on its activities to the Legal Subcommittee.

In 2004, the IISL will again co-organize a symposium for the delegates and staff of the Legal Subcommittee session; the Coordinator of the program is Ms. Tanja Masson-Zwaan. The symposium will deal with *New Developments and the Legal Framework covering the Exploitation of the Resources of the Moon.*

46th IISL Colloquium

The 46th IISL Colloquium was held from from 29 Sept. to 3 Oct. 2003 in Bremen, Germany. Around 60 papers were presented, and sessions were held on the following topics:

Session 1: Legal Aspects of Applications and Private Space Activities; Chairmen: Maurice Andem and Hermann Ersfeld; Rapporteur:Philippe Achilleas

Session 2: Space Treaties, Law and Policies and Telecommunication Issues; Chairmen: Lesley Jane Smith and Peter Van Fenema; Rapporteur: Martha Mejia-Kayser

Session 3: Space Law and International Security Chairmen: John B. Gantt and Yuri Kolossov; Rapporteur: Liara Covert

Session 4: Space Traffic Management and Navigation; Chairmen: José Monserrat Filho and Lubos Perek; Rapporteur: Sylvia Ospina

Session 5: New Issues Relating to Nuclear Power Sources; Chairmen: Stephan Hobe and Marcia Smith; Rapporteur: Gerardine Goh

The IISL also held a successful Plenary Event on "Space Business: Emerging Profitability in Space", at which the following speakers expressed their views: Stéphane Chenard, Executive Vice-President of Euroconsult in France, Wilfried Bornemann, Director, Navigation & Constellations of Astrium Earth Observation, Navigation & Science in Germany, Dr M.G. Chandrasekhar of World Space, Roscoe Moore III, President of PeerSat Inc. in the USA, Robert Z. Dalal, Chief Executive Officer of Space Imaging Inc. in the USA, Ramin Khadem, Chief Financial Officer of Inmarsat Ventures plc in the UK, and K. R. Sridhara Murthi, Executive Director of Antrix Corporation Ltd. in India. The panel was coordinated by Jim Keravala and the IISL President.

IISL Publications

The Proceedings of the Bremen Colloquium will be published by the AIAA.

The Institute is currently preparing an update of its space law bibliography, an index of papers published in its Proceedings. A first volume of this book came out in 1996 with the kind support of the UN Office for Outer Space Affairs, which is again instrumental in this effort.

Manfred Lachs Space Law Moot Court Competition

The World Finals of the 12th Manfred Lachs Space Law Moot Court Competition were held during the Bremen Colloquium. Preliminary Rounds had previously been held in Europe, the USA and the Asia-Pacific. Three Judges of the ICJ judged the Finals: H.E. Judge Guillaume, H.E. Judge Koroma and H.E. Judge Vereshchetin.
The results of the world finals were as follows:

Winner: University of Auckland, New Zealand (Jesse Wilson and Isaac Hikaka)

Runner up: Georgetown University Law Center, Washington DC, USA (Petra Vorwig and Amanda Shafer)

2nd runner up: University of Bremen, Germany Deirdre Ní Chearbhaill and Kamlesh Gungaphul)

Eilene M. Galloway Award for Best Written Brief: University of Bremen

Sterns and Tennen Award for Best Oralist: Petra Vorwig, Georgetown University

The finals were held at the Landgericht of Bremen. A Reception and Dinner were hosted after the finals in the restaurant 'Ratskeller. Around 200 guests attended. The dinner was sponsored by EADS Space Transportation and DLR, to whom IISL is most grateful.

A report on the competition, the case and the finalists' briefs are published in this volume. The competition will be held for the 13th time in Vancouver, Canada, in October 2004.

Awards

A Distinguished Service Award was presented to Dr Kai-Uwe Schrogl (DLR) during the IAF Banquet.

Ms Joann Clayton-Townsend also received an award *in absentia.*

The Dr. I.H.Ph. Diederiks-Verschoor Award was given for the 3rd time in Bremen, to Ms Gerardine Goh of Singapore for her paper "TINTALLE - kindling International Security with Space Law". In total, 6 papers had been submitted. Prof Fernandez Brital provided the medal.

V. Space Law Conference Beijing

The Chinese Institute of Space Law (CISL) will host the next regional conference in Beijing, China, from **25-27 April 2004.** The Conference had to be postponed last year because of SARS. The Conference is sponsored by the China National Space Administration; the Ministry of Science and Technology; the Chinese Academy of Sciences; and the China Aerospace Science and Technology Corporation.

The programme has been updated and slightly revised, and has been posted on the IISL and IAF websites. The Conference will focus on the following sessions-topics: (1) National Space Programmes, Policies and Legislation in Asia; (2) Trade Issues, including Insurance, Financing, Asset protection, Export controls; (3) Use of GNSS and benefits for the Asian Region; (4) Commercial Use of Space, including Launching; (5) Protection of Developing Countries' Interests, including Access to Space, and (6) Remote Sensing & Telecommunications. Special keynote lectures will address the Development and Future of Aerospace Technology in China, and the Development of Satellite and Manned Space Flight in China.

47th IISL Colloquium

The 47th Colloquium of the IISL will be held in Vancouver, Canada, from 4-8 Oct. 2004. The following sessions are scheduled:

Session 1: New developments in National Space Legislation

The session will focus on new developments at the level of national space legislation, dealing with such issues as the involvement of private entities, the regulatory and/or participatory roles of governments, and the impact of international co-operation at the domestic level. Papers should specifically address developments regarding further implementation of existing national space legislation, and initiatives to establish new national space legislation.

Chairmen: Dr. Frans von der Dunk, The Netherlands, and (tbc).

Rapporteur: Dr. Patrick Salin, Canada.

Session 2: International Law and Practice of Agreements on Cooperation regarding Space Activities

Since the adoption by the UN General Assembly of the Declaration on International Cooperation of 1996, a large practice has developed as to cooperative agreements, also involving developing states. Papers should focus on multilateral and bilateral agreements formalizing cooperation amongst governments and space agencies. Regarding multilateral agreements, authors could address for instance those regarding telecommunications, the ISS (including the MoU's at the level of space agencies) or GNSS (Navigation Systems). Regarding bilateral agreements they could focus on agreements relating to specific space projects, for instance regulating the use of spaceports by foreign governments and operators (Alcantara, Bajkonour) or on the use of remote sensing data: Landsat, Envisat, SPOT, RadarSat.

Chairmen: Mr. Marco Ferrazzani, ESA/Italy and Mr Paul Fauteux, Canada
Rapporteur: Ms Macha Ejova, Russia

Session 3: A General Convention on Space Law?

Papers should consider aspects of the desirability or otherwise of the elaboration of a general convention to codify existing space law, the questions of procedure and substance that would arise, and the possible progressive development of space law through such an instrument.
Chairmen: Prof. Dr. Ram Jakhu, Canada, and Dr Lucy Stojak, ISU/Canada
Rapporteur: Dr. A.A. Golrounia, Iran

Sessions 4 and 5: Other Legal Matters

Papers may address all other legal matters.
Authors are specifically invited to address recent developments in the field of Commercialization and Privatization of Space Activities
Chairmen: Dr. Sylvia Ospina, Colombia and Dr Pierre Nadeau, Canadian Space Agency, Canada.
Rapporteur tbd

The topics of sessions 4 and 5 will be determined after all abstracts have been revicwcd.

Manfred Lachs Space Law Moot Court Competition

The 13th Manfred Lachs Space Law Moot Court Competition will be held in Vancouver. The case for 2004 is on the moot court website, www.spacemoot.org

Regional rounds will be held in Europe, North America and the Asia Pacific. It is expected that Canada and Mexico will join the North American round.

The **Official Rules** of the moot court have been updated and revised, the new rules are available on the IISL website.

Dr. I.H.Ph. Diederiks-Verschoor Award

All authors will receive an invitation to apply for this Award with their instructions package. This year, in addition to the prestigious medal, the winner will also get a money prize of 500 Euros.

VII. 48th IISL Colloquium

The 48th Colloquium on the law of outer space will be held during the IAF Congress in Fukuoka, Japan, from 16 - 21 October 2005. The session topics for this colloquium will de decided in the Spring of 2004.

Elections 2002

Board of Directors:

Two new members of the Board of Directors were elected: Prof. Jonathan Galloway (Lake Forrest College, Illinois, USA) and Mr K.R. Sridhara Murthi (ISRO/Antrix Corp., India).

Ms. Marcia Smith was elected as Vice-President, In September 2003, Ms. Smith was presented with the 2003 Women in Aerospace Lifetime Achievement Award.

Several other Directors and Officers were re-elected for a new term of three years. Prof. N.M. Matte (Canada) and Dr. He Qizhi (China) were elected as **Honorary Director**.

Members:

The following members were elected in 2003:

Institutional member

International Center for Space Law
Prof. Dr. N. Malysheva, Deputy Director
Tereshchenkivska str. 2
01004 Kiev, UKRAINE
T 380(44) 235 4952
F 380(44) 235 7813
E islc@priocom.com.ua

Individual members

Dr. Ciro Arevalo
Dep. Ambassador of the Embassy and Permanent Mission of Colombia
Embassy of Colombia
Stadiongasse 6
A-1010 Vienna, AUSTRIA
T 43-1 405 7146
F 43-1 408 8303
E ciroarevalo1@yahoo.com

Mr. Jürgen Cloppenburg
Institute of Air and Space Law
Albertus-Magnus Platz
D-50923 Cologne, GERMANY
T 49- 221 470 2988
F 49- 221 470 4968
E juergen.cloppenburg@uni-koeln.de

Dr. Michael Gerhard
DLR
Linder Höhe
D-50923 Cologne, GERMANY
T 49-2203 601 2942
F 49-2203 601 2893
E michael.gerhard@dlr.de

Ms. Gerardine Meishan Goh
c/o 59 Puay Hee Avenue
SINGAPORE 348160
T 65 63 82 24 38
E vysionary@hotmail.com

Ms. Jana K. Hettling, LL.M
Institute of Air and Space Law
Albertus Magnus Platz
D-50923 Cologne, GERMANY
T 49-221 470 2988
F 49-221 470 4968
E jana.hettling@uni-koeln.de

Mr. Ken Hodgkins
Deputy Director, Office of Space and Advanced Technology
US Department of State, SA-23
Washington DC 20520, USA
T 1-202 663 2398
F 1-202 663 2402
E hodgkinskd@state.gov

Mr. Jean-François Mayence
Advisor & Official Representative, legal affairs & international relations
Office for Scientific, Technical & Cultural Affairs - Space Dept.
Rue de la Science 8
1000 Brussels, BELGIUM
T 32-2 238 3517
F 32-2 230 5912
E maye@belspo.be

Ms. Kristina Moll
Institute of Air and Space Law
Albertus Magnus Platz
D-50923 Cologne, GERMANY
T 49-221 470 6211
F 49-221 470 4968
E kristina.moll@uni-koeln.de

Mr. Sethu Nandakumar
130 Sir Henry Parkes Rd
Coventry CV5 6BJ
UNITED KINGDOM
T 44-079 868 19810
E sethu_nand75@yahoo.co.uk

Mr. Thomas Reuter
Institute of Air and Space Law
Albertus Magnus Platz
D-50923 Cologne, GERMANY
T 49-221 470 6211
F 49-221 470 4968
E thomas.reuter@uni-koeln.de

Ms. Sagee Sasikumar
Faculty Member, Hidayattullah National Law Univ.
Civil Lines, Near RAj Bhavan,
Raipur (C.G.) - 492001, Chhattisgarh, INDIA
E sagee@hnluraipur.com

Prof. Dr. Lesley-Jane Smith
Professor of German and Int'l Economic & Comparative Law
University of Bremen, Faculty of Law
GW 1, Universitätsallee
D-28359 Bremen, GERMANY
T 49-421 218 2247
F 49-421 218 3403
E ljsmith@barkhof.uni-bremen.de

Mr. Yun Zhao
Lecturer, City Univ. of Hong Kong
School of Law
Tat Chee Avenue 83, Kowloon
HONG KONG
T 852-2788 7387
F 852-2788 7530
E lwzhao@cityu.edu.hk

Photos from the 46th Colloquium on the Law of Outer Space

▲ Bremer Dom

◀ Group photo of attendants at annual IISL Dinner in the Ratskeller.

▼ The Mayor of Bremen greets Judge and Madame Guillaume.

▼ Secretary Tanja Masson-Zwaan, Treasurer Frans von der Dunk and president Jasentuliyana.

▼ Manfred Lachs moot court semi-finals, the team of Bremen University and University of Auckland and their coaches, and Judges Dr. Ribbelink, Prof. Hobe and Ms. Smith.

▲ N. Jasentuliyana presents the IISL Distinguished Service Award to Dr. Kai-Uwe Schrogl.

◀ IAF President Marcio Barbosa and the IAF Board of Trustees.

▲ IISL President N. Jasentuliyana with Dr. and Mrs. Fasan and Mr. and Mrs. Love.

Treasurer Frans ▶ von der Dunk, Vice President Marcia Smith. ICJ Judge Koroma, Patricia Sterns, Jeffrey Maclure.

Dr. and Mrs. Perek. ▶

◀ Dr. Marietta Benkoe and Berndt Schmidt-Tedd presenting an hommage to Mrs. Eilene Galloway, accepted on her behalf by her son Prof. Jonathan Galloway.

▲ The finalists and Judges with IISL President N. Jasentuliyana.

Prof. Isabella Diederiks- ▶ Verschoor, IISL President Emeritus, with Dr. Yun Zhao of Hong Kong.

▲ Dr. Tennen, Mrs. and Dr. Fasan, Dr. Ramirez de Arellano

◀ Moot Court World Finals at Landgericht in Bremen; University of Auckland team on left, Georgetown University School of Law team on right.

TABLE OF CONTENTS

SPACE TREATIES, LAW AND POLICIES AND TELECOMMUNICATION ISSUES

SPACE LAW AND INTERNATIONAL SECURITY

SPACE TRAFFIC MANAGEMENT AND NAVIGATION

NEW ISSUES RELATING TO NUCLEAR POWER SOURCES

SESSION REPORTS

IISL/ECSL SPACE LAW SYMPOSIUM 2003, HELD ON THE OCCASION OF THE 42ND SESSION OF THE LEGAL SUBCOMMITTEE OF UNCOPUOS

ADDENDA

Session 1:
LEGAL ASPECTS OF APPLICATIONS AND PRIVATE SPACE ACTIVITIES

Chairmen: Maurice N. Andem, Finland
Hermann Ersfeld, Germany

Rapporteur: Philippe Achilleas, France

COOPERATION, CONFLICT AND COMPETITION IN SPACE LAW

Jonathan F. Galloway
Professor of Politics, Emeritus
Lake Forest College
Lake Forest, IL 60045
USA
galloway@lfc.edu
Member, IISL, IAA, AIAA

Abstract

Cooperation is a major theme of international space law but the law and history also recognize the existence of competition and conflict. What are the trend lines in terms of promoting collective goods, commercialization and new military uses of space? An overview of selected major laws and policies combined with a theoretical examination of game theory (zero-sum and non-zero sum games) will enable us to obtain an overall understanding of the space age and the choices that space lawyers and policymakers face in the future.

Game Theory

One way to understand the development of the law of outer space is to employ game theory. Game theory helps us to understand the dynamics and logic of cooperation, conflict and competition. For those of us interested in and committed to the progressive development of space law, it pays to understand historical situations in which we can expect more cooperation and creative competition and then distinguish those from scenarios in which there will likely be conflict and destructive competition.

There are two sorts of games - zero sum and non-zero sum. In zero-sum games there is a winner and a loser. An example would be chess, or, in the real world a war such as that pictured by Thucydides in the Melian Dialogue.[1] The Cold War could be seen as a bipolar zero-sum game which the United States won and the Soviet Union lost. It is clear that military conflicts are most susceptible to the logic of a zero-sum dynamic in which there is a winner and a loser.[2]

In a non-zero sum game, there can be winners and losers. In a win-win game, both sides win. This can be the case with commercial competition if one accepts the notion of Adam Smith's invisible hand and the magic of the market. A game in which all sides lose would be cutthroat commercial competition in which there are trade wars such as occurred during the Great Depression. Another example is a "game," or is it a tragedy humans play with nature vis-à-vis treating the atmosphere as a place to dump industrial pollutants.

One hopes that over time players will learn to play non-zero sum games in which the participants all come out ahead. This is the theme of Robert Wright's book, *Nonzero: The Logic of Human Destiny*[3] in which he argues that "...on balance, over the long run, non-zero sum situations produce more positive sums than negative sums, and more mutual benefit than parasitism."[4] Wright sees the current age of globalization as one "in which relations among nations grow more non-zero-sum year by year (as) the natural outgrowth of several billion years of unfolding non-zero sum logic."[5] Wright puts himself on the side of progress in evolution and in human history. He associates his thinking with that of Francis Fuguyama's *The End of History and the Last Man*[6] and against that of Stephen Jay Gould who sees humankind as an outgrowth of random evolution, a "momentary cosmic accident."[7] However, Wright stops his analysis at earth and is not concerned with continuing his logic to include the solar system and the cosmos. If he took this leap, he would no doubt concern himself with the thinking of humankind as a spacefaring and galactic civilization.[8] In this way the logic of human destiny would go to low-earth orbit, the geostationary orbit, Lagrange points, the moon, Mars and beyond.

Cooperation

Let us examine and assess mankind's movement into space as an example of the logic and experience of cooperation. After the space age began on October 4, 1957 with the orbiting of SPUTNIK, the United States was caught in a competitive prestige race with the USSR but rather than let this race deteriorate into a zero-sum game, the National Aeronautics and Space Act of 1958 committed the U.S. to, inter alia, "peaceful purposes for the benefit of all mankind."[9] The U.S. is to be "a leader" (not "the" leader) in "The conduct of peaceful activities."[10] Furthermore, there is to be "cooperation by the United States with other nations and groups of nations in work done pursuant to this Act and in the peaceful application of the results thereof."[11] Section 205 of the NASA statutue states "the Administration, under the foreign policy guidance of the President, may engage in a program of international cooperation in work done pursuant to this Act, and in the peaceful application of the results thereof, pursuant to agreements made by the President with the advice and consent of the Senate."

It is clear that if one major player in a game is committed to cooperation there is going to be a lot of cooperation as there has been in law and in programs.[12] The prime example in international law is the Outer Space Treaty of 1967 which commits states, inter alia, to explore space "for the benefit and in the interests of all countries," to desist from "national appropriation by claim of sovereignty, by means of use or occupation, or by any other means," and "to undertake not to place in orbit around the Earth any objects carrying nuclear weapons or any other kinds of weapons of mass destruction."[13] Then there are four other space treaties that have come out of the United Nations - the Agreement on the Rescue of Astronauts,[14] the Liability Convention,[15] the Registration Convention[16] and the Moon Agreement[17] plus the five principles adopted by the General Assembly.[18] There are numerous national laws. Furthermore, in fact there are a plethora of international and global institutions and programs devoted to cooperation in the peaceful uses of outer space. Among these are the UN Committee on the Peaceful Uses of Outer Space, the ITU, the WMO, and the International Space Station.[19]

While there has undoubtedly been much positive cooperation in developing the peaceful uses of outer space both in law and practice some commentators see cooperation as a side game while the real players are playing "for real;" i.e., they are playing a zero-sum game.

Conflict

It is possible that we are at the end point of a zero-sum game in which there has been one winner for all time - the United States. To advocates of American Empire this is indeed the case.[20] The outcome of the Cold War and the events since seem to point to a permanent American hegemony in terms of military power, economic wealth and cultural outreach. Because there is no other player, the "game" is over and the law is basically what the U.S. says it is or how it interprets existing treaties. In this vein, Everett C. Dolman updates the Halford Mackinder thesis as follows - "Who controls low-Earth orbit controls near-Earth space. Who controls near-Earth space dominates Terra. Who dominates Terra determines the destiny of humankind."[21]

Advocates of a zero-sum conflict view the Outer Space Treaty not as ushering in an era of cooperation for the human species but as an intermission, a period of détente in a win-lose encounter. The players or actors in the game even engaged in "a perverse competition of who could out-cooperate whom."[22] Since the United States won the game, i.e, the Cold War, the U.S. is now set to dominate space. According to these commentators, the United States should renounce the Outer Space Treaty and claim sovereignty over parts of space.[23] It should dominate economically and militarily rather than cooperate.[24]

In short, Robert Wright's vision of human progress is a dream and an illusion. Realpolitik - now Astropolitik - is the underlying reality of world politics as indicated by the U.S. withdrawal from the ABM Treaty, the plan to build new nuclear weapons, etc.[25] According to Dolman we actually need to emphasize conflict in order to realize the ultimate perfection of humankind as a multiplanetary species.[26] The logic here must be the logic of MacKinder, Mahan and Social Darwinism.

Some students of strategic power see it as only part of the game. The real game is a three dimensional chess game. Joseph S. Nye, Jr. sees world politics as a three-dimensional chess game. "The top board is unipolar," while "The middle economic board is multipolar," and "the bottom board of transnational relations that cross borders outside the control of governments has a widely dispersed structure of power."[27] In this type of "chess game," the United States cannot play bipolar chess. It can choose to dominate militarily; play in a competitive market economically; and recognize the power of non-state actors and forces transnationally. Since the latter two games take up most of international relations, a great power or superpower concentrates on the first at its own peril. Military power has less leverage among great powers than in previous epochs. Now states should concentrate on win-win scenarios and non-zero sumness rather than win-lose, zero-sum conflicts. If states do not do this they are in danger of winning Pyrrhic victories resulting in lose-lose outcomes.

Nye advises the U.S. to be less unilateral and more multilateral, as is fitting given international law and treaty commitments. The U.S. has a national interest in keeping world commons secure. What are these commons? Nye mentions the seas, the climate, endangered species, outer space and the virtual commons of cyberspace.[28] Yet the U.S. is stepping back from providing leadership as a collective good. It has withdrawn its signature from the International Criminal Court; not ratified the Comprehensive Test Ban Treaty; withdrawn from the Anti-Ballistic Missile Treaty; refused to enter the Kyoto Protocol; and taken some moves against free trade.[29] Playing world politics as if it is a zero-sum game which has ended in hegemony is myopic from the point of view of history. We may expect the United States to have its day in the sun - perhaps a long unipolar moment - but it will end. Other forces and powers tend to make the system multipolar.[30] For space law, this means that the principles of consensus-building in international fora such as the UN, UNISPACE and the ITU will be very relevant and vital.

Competition

In game theory, competition can result in both sides winning or both sides losing. The hope is that most commercial competition will result - through the workings of market forces - in an ever bigger pie. Otherwise, cutthroat competition either within or between nations will result in everyone losing. Robert Wright sees the Prisoners' Dilemma game as a non-zero sum game in which through learning behavior, i.e., playing the game over and over both sides can win.[31] This has happened in lab experiments and in history.[32]

Given the history of the Space Age, we can expect more and more commercial competition. In the beginnings, there were very few commercial competitors and they were heavily subsidized and regulated by governments. Now there are many more and many government ventures have been partly or wholly privatized. In U.S. law, there has been a push towards privatization since the Communications Satellite Act of 1962 and more recently with the 1998 Commercial Space Act.[33] Even international organizations - viz INTELSAT and INMARSAT have been privatized.[34] But for true capitalism to occur in outer space, there must not only be privatization on earth but property rights in space. "However, in common law countries such as the United States, legal theory dictates that the government must have sovereignty over territory before it can confer title on its citizens."[35] Thus there can be no real property rights in outer space due to Article II of the Outer Space Treaty. On the other hand, Wayne White contends that "jurisdictional authority under the Outer Space Treaty provides most of the protections traditionally associated with property rights."[36] And James E. Dunstan argues that "customary international law, consistent with the Outer Space Treaty, has come to develop a regime for property use that is compatible with private investment."[37] The evidence he uses to support this thesis is the practice of states vis-à-vis owning moon rocks, controlling frequency spectrum and orbital slots, doing business on Mir, and providing for property rights on the International Space Station. Dunstan argues that real property rights are not necessary because their functional equivalent already exists.

This is related to the argument Sterns and Tennen make when they say, "The corpus juris spatialis, and the Outer Space

Treaty in particular, contain several provisions which recognize and promote the role of private entities in space." [38] Sterns and Tennen make clear that "claims of fee simple ownership of space property are unnecessary and ineffective to protect private interests from interference." What exists to protect space commerce are national licensing regimes which are compatible with Articles VI and IX of the Outer Space Treaty.

So capitalism in space already exists and it is growing in terms of commercial space businesses in communications satellites, remote sensing, GPS, weather satellites and even space tourism. Still, space entrepeneurship is in its infantile stage because of the high costs of launch (about $10,000 a lb.) and because the public perception exists that space is a purview of governments and not the private sector. If these two factors can be changed, then the new frontier will truly witness a new millennium.

In the meantime, are we witnessing positive change and progressive evolution through the workings out of the logic of non-zero sumness as Robert Wright argues? It appears that we are in terms of the increasing cooperation and in the promise of commerce in space. Yet, caution and prudence should lead us to withhold final judgment given the plans for new military programs in space.

Prospect?

Ultimate non-zero-sumness will arrive when humanity becomes a multiplanetary species[39] and when we recognize ourselves more as humankind rather than conflictual subsets of our species. Previously evolution and natural selection made our species fit for earth or what Carl Sagan called that Pale Blue Dot, but for our species to survive, conscious acts of will, intelligence and wisdom will require us, as Tsiolkowsky said, to leave the cradle. In this new environment, we may colonize Mars and build space cities, but we will require legal and political regimes and constitutions to make the journey worthwhile. Not only will astronauts be the envoys of all mankind, but so will lawyers, politicians, businessmen, scientists and engineers. The altruism built into our biology through evolution will enable us to cooperate in making this journey.

[1] Thucydides, *The Peloponessian War* (New York; Penquin, 1954), Book V, pp. 400-408.
[2] Thomas C. Schelling, *The Strategy of Conflict* (Cambridge: Harvard University Press, 1960).
[3] (New York: Vintage, 2001)
[4] Wright, p. 6.
[5] Wright, p. 7.
[6] (New York: Avon Books, 1992).
[7] Wright (p. 15 and p. 267). Gould, *Wonderful Life* (New York: Norton, 1989).
[8]Robert Zubrin, *Entering Space: Creating a Spacefaring Civilization* (New York: Putnam, 1999).
[9] 72 Stat. 426-438 (July 29, 1958); 42 U.S.C. 2451.
[10]Sec. 102 (5).

[11] Sec. 102 (7).
[12] Eilene Galloway, "International Institutions to Ensure Peaceful Uses of Outer Space," in Nandasiri Jasentuliyana, ed., *Space Law: Development and Scope* (Westport, CT: Praeger, 1992).
[13] Treaty on Principles Governing the Activities of States in the Exploration and Use of Outer Space, Including the Moon and other Celestial Bodies (1967). 18 UST 2410; TIAS 6347; 610 UNTS 205. See articles I, II & IV.
[14] Space (1968). 19 UST 7570; TIAS 6599; 672 UNTS 119.
[15] Convention on International Liability for Damage Caused by Space Objects (1976). 24 UST 2389; TIAS 762; 961 UNTS 187.
[16] Convention on Registration of Objects Launched Into Outer Space (1976). 28 UST 695; TIAS 589480; 1023 UNTS15.
[17] Agreement Governing the Activities of States on the Moon and Other Celestial Bodies (1984). 18 ILM 1434; 1363 UNTS 3.
[18]

a. Declaration of Legal Principles Governing the Activities of States in the Exploration and Use of Outer Space

b. Principles Governing the Use by States of Artificial Earth Satellites for International Direct Television Broadcasting

c. Principles Relating to Remote Sensing of the Earth from Outer Space

d. Principles Relevant to the Use of Nuclear Power Sources in Outer Space

e. Declaration on International Cooperation in the Exploration and Use of Outer Space for the Benefit and in the Interest of All States, Taking into Particular Account the Needs of Developing Countries

[19] For annual assessments see the UN series, "Highlights in Space: Progress in Space Science, Technology and Applications, International Cooperation and Space Law."
[20] Robert D. Kaplan, *Warrior Politics* (New York: Random House, 2002).
[21] Everett C. Dolman, *Astropolitik: Classical Geopolitics in the Space Age* (London: Frank Cass, 2002). p. 8. Dolman is a professor at Maxwell Air Force Base.
[22] Ibid.
[23] Dolman, pp. 140-141.
[24] Dolman, pp. 151, 173. Also, see James W. Canan, "Iraq and the Space Factor," *Aerospace America* (August, 2003), pp. 32-36.
[25] John Mearsheimer, *The Tragedy of Great Power Politics* (New York: W. W. Norton, 2002).
[26] Dolman, p. 182.
[27] *The Paradox of American Power - Why the World's Only Superpower Can't Go It Alone* (New York: Oxford University Press, 2002). p. 140.
[28] Ibid., p. 145.
[29] Ibid., 205 et passim.
[30] Charles Kupchan, *The End of the American Era* (New York: Alfred A. Knopf, 2003).
[31] Wright, op. cit., p. 57.
[32] Robert Axelrod, *The Evolution of Cooperation* (New York: Basic Books, 1984).
[33] See "United States Space Law" http://www:spacebizstation.com/uslaw.html
[34] David Sagar, "The Privatization of INMARSAT," *Proceedings of the Forty-First Colloquium on the Law of Outer Space* (AIAA, 1999), pp. 205-223. Jonathan F. Galloway, "Privatizing An International Cooperative? The Case of Intelsat," *Proceedings of the Thirty-Ninth Colloquium on the Law of Outer Space* (AIAA, 1997), pp. 144-150.

[35] Wayne White, "The Legal Regime for Private Activities in Outer Space," chap. 6 in Edward L. Hudgins, ed., *Space: The Free-Market Frontier* (Washington, DC:" CATO Institute, 2002), pp. 83-111, 84.
[36] Ibid.
[37] James E. Dunstan, "Toward a Unified Theory of Space Property Rights: Sometimes the Best Way to Predict the Weather is to Look Outside," chap. 16 in Hudgins, op. cit., pp. 225-226.
[38] P. M. Sterns and L. I. Tennen, "Privateering and Profiteering on the Moon and Other Celestial Bodies: Debunking the Myth of Property Rights in Space," *Proceedings of the Forty-Fifth Colloquium on the Law of Outer Space* (AIAA, 2003), 56-67, 57.
[39] Ramiro Iglesias, *The Route Towards Cosmic Man* (Mexico, D.F.: Noriega, 1999).

IAC-03-IISL.1.04

PROTECTING THE SPACE ENVIRONMENT

Sergio Marchisio*

Vice Chairman, European Centre for Space Law
Institute for International Legal Studies, CNR
University of Rome "La Sapienza", Italy
marchisio@isgi.cnr.it

ABSTRACT

The basic legal framework for the protection of the space environment is supplied by space law, by environmental law, and more generally by international law at large, which also applies to space activities. The effectiveness of environmental protection requires the application of both primary and secondary rules, the former establishing states rights and obligations, and the latter dealing with the consequences arising from breaches of primary rules, or damage caused by state activities. The substantial norms of space law on environmental protection have been, in the main, conceived from an Earth oriented-perspective; some of them, however, serve as a legal basis for maintaining the space environment. On the other hand, no secondary rule can be found in space law which specifically concerns the legal consequences of environmental damage to outer space. Integration of the applicable substantial norms can be derived from the application of international principles and rules on sustainable development. As for secondary norms, we can resort to the general principles of international law on state responsibility for wrongful acts, and to the principles concerning state liability for damage caused by ultra-hazardous activities. These latter are, however, not so consolidated in international law. State practice also contributes to defining the legal regime. However, there is need for further development. This can be achieved through international co-operation in adopting technical norms and recommended standards, a task that could be appropriately managed by the Legal Subcommittee of the United Nations Committee for Peaceful Uses of Outer Space (UNCOPUOS).

1. THE PROTECTION OF THE SPACE ENVIRONMENT AND THE EVOLUTION OF INTERNATIONAL ENVIRONMENTAL LAW

The subject of the protection of the space environment has largely been addressed in recent years, although interest in the topic seems to be lower currently than in the past. It has to be said, however, that pollution of outer space and the increasing presence of man-made debris were been considered by jurists initially as a potential nuisance to operational satellites, rather than a potential threat to the conservation of the space environment itself.[1]

It remains that space activities are *per se* ultra-hazardous activities, which may be harmful to both the space and the terrestrial environment, two aspects that are strictly intertwined. After the report adopted by the UNCOPUOS Scientific and Technical Subcommittee (STSC) in 1999,[2] we can say that the peril of debris is a major risk factor for the space environment, especially in Low Earth Orbits (LEOs) and in the geo-stationary orbit, limited resources where debris accumulation is becoming particularly worrying.[3]

The legal doctrine has considered this issue with the utmost attention and the Proceedings of the annual Colloquia organized by the International Institute of Space Law (IISL) of the International Astronautical Federation are an inestimably valuable source of knowledge in this respect. Professor Lyall's paper presented at the 1999 Colloquium outlined that the rules of law, both national and international, aimed at protecting the terrestrial environment had developed remarkably, but, other than some general principles, few of them were readily transposable to the space environment.[4]
Is this conclusion still valid? I believe that some lessons have to be learnt by looking at the evolution of international environmental law which may also be helpful in protecting the space environment.

2. THE APPLICABILITY OF PRIMARY AND SECONDARY RULES OF INTERNATIONAL LAW

Following the motto *repetita iuvant*, I would like to restate two preliminary points.
Firstly, Article III of the 1967 Outer Space Treaty (OST) establishes that activities related to the exploration and use of outer space are to be carried out in accordance with international law. Therefore, applicable law includes not only the specific rules of international space law but also the rules of international law, whether their nature be customary, conventional or other, which are applicable to space activities.
Secondly, in dealing with this matter, it is useful to keep in mind that we have primary and secondary norms of international law: the former are substantial or material rules of international law, imposing rights and obligations of environmental protection upon states; the latter are instrumental rules concerning consequences arising from the breach of primary rules establishing international obligations (rules on responsibility) or concerning the legal consequences of damage attributable to states under international law (rules on liability).
The effectiveness of environmental protection obviously requires the application of both primary and secondary rules.

3. THE PROTECTION OF THE SPACE ENVIRONMENT IN SPACE LAW

3.1. The "Earth Oriented" Perspective

So said, it is commonly understood that the main problem in dealing with this matter lies on the one hand, in the scarcity of primary norms of international law which impose clear obligations upon states carrying out space activity and, on the other hand, in the weakness of secondary norms of a customary nature applicable to environmental damage to space.
The explanation is given that the major "environmentalist" concern in space treaties has been, at the moment of their negotiation and conclusion, the so-called "back-contamination" resulting from the introduction of extra-terrestrial substances. This point of view is shared by several norms contained in the five space Treaties. We can mention, on this point, Article IX of the OST setting out the obligation to avoid, in the exploration of outer space "adverse change in the environment of the Earth resulting from the introduction of extraterrestrial matter"; and Article II of the 1972 Liability Convention, concerning the absolute liability of states to pay compensation for the damage their space objects cause on Earth.[5] As for the codes of conduct elaborated by the UNCOPUOS Legal Subcommittee (LSC) and adopted by the General Assembly (GA) of the United Nations, mention must be made of the Principles relating to the use of nuclear power sources in outer space adopted by the 1992 GA resolution 47/68, which deals with the safe use of nuclear power sources in

outer space particularly in order to avoid the risk of re-entry of radioactive material to the Earth (principle 5).[6]

The view that the norms of space law on environmental protection deal with the matter from an Earth-oriented perspective is, therefore, correct. In my opinion, however, this circumstance cannot be overestimated. There is in fact a clear link between Earth pollution from the space and planetary contamination, because the source of the former can, at the same time, be the source of the latter.

I do recognize, however, that we are concerned here with a more general problem, i.e. the protection of the space environment *per se*.

3.2. Maintaining the Space Environment *per se*

Beside the limitation resulting from the "Earth-oriented perspective", some norms of international law serve as a basis for a legal regime of protection of the space environment as such. According to Article 1 of the OST, "the exploration and use of outer space shall be carried out for the benefit and in the interest of all countries, and shall be the province of all mankind". A contextual interpretation shows that this norm is aimed at protecting not only the freedom of any state to carry out space activities without suffering harmful interference by others, but also at safeguarding the cosmic environment as an essential element of this freedom. Contamination of the space environment being one of the major threats to the freedom of outer space, the protection of the space environment has to be considered as an integral part - not a limit - of space activities. Then comes Article IX of the OST, which, after mentioning the principles of co-operation, mutual assistance and of due regard to the interests of all states, sets forth the proviso that states shall "pursue studies in outer space, including the Moon and other celestial bodies, and conduct exploration of them so as to avoid their harmful contamination". This norm clearly imposes upon states conducting space exploration activities, the obligation of avoiding harmful contamination of outer space and the Earth's orbits, which are an integral part of the space environment. It also establishes a duty of consultation upon states that "have reason to believe" that their planned activities, or experiments could produce potentially harmful interference with activities of other states. As is known, the establishment of the said consultation mechanism was a result of the early "environmentalist" concerns expressed by the Consultative Group on Potentially Harmful Effects established in 1962 by the Committee on Space Research (COSPAR) of the International Council of Scientific Unions.[7]

As regards the 1979 Moon Agreement, Article 7, para. 1, elaborates fully more in comparison with previous space treaties, by explicitly considering the risk of lunar contamination and imposing upon states the duty to take measures to prevent the disruption of the existing balance of its environment.[8]

4. INTEGRATION DERIVING FROM RULES OF INTERNATIONAL ENVIRONMENTAL LAW

4.1. The Principle of Sustainable Development

These primary norms of international space law are integrated by rules and principles on environmental protection of general scope, which have developed greatly in recent years.[9] These rules and principles are contained in multilateral treaties, in acts of soft law, such as the GA declarations of principles, but are often evidence of general practices accepted as law in the sense of Article 38 of the Statute of the International Court of Justice (ICJ).

Now, in the judgment of 25 November 1997 on the case of *Projected Dam of Gabcikovo-Nagymaros*, the Court stated that the principle of sustainable development had to be applied, as a legal principle, in the context of the obligations of the riparian states of the Danube river to not allow that the flow of water be altered, after the project's completion, by harmful activities and work.[10]

In para. 140 of this decision, the ICJ explicitly makes reference to existing norms of international law in the field of environmental protection, and among them specifically to a well consolidated principle of general international law, which provides a duty of control and preventive action.

The Court goes further towards recognizing "new norms and new standards" affirmed by a large number of instruments that tend to reconcile economic development with the protection of the environment.

4.2. The Duty to Prevent Environmental Damage

The duty of control and preventive action is implied in the traditional principle 2 of the 1992 Rio Declaration on environment and development, restating principle 21 of the 1972 Stockholm Declaration. Beside the sovereign right of states to exploit their resources pursuant to their environmental and developmental policies, there is a responsibility – that is to say an obligation – to ensure that activities within their jurisdiction or control do not cause damage to the environment of other states or of areas beyond the limits of their national jurisdictions. The same concept was expressed by the ICJ in its advisory opinion on the *Legality of the Threat or Use of Nuclear Weapons*: "the existence of a general obligation of states to ensure that activities within their jurisdiction and control respect the environment of other states or of areas beyond national jurisdiction is now part of the corpus of international law relating to the environment".[11]

This responsibility also covers, indeed, outer space as an area beyond national jurisdiction, as a *res communis omnium* or common space of the international community as a whole. And space activities are paradigmatic of that kind of activity which must remain under the jurisdiction or control of a given state according to Article VI of the OST.

The obligation of preventive action to avoid potential damage to outer space as a whole has to be fulfilled also, and principally, by developing environmental laws and requirements within national space legislations. States have to exercise due diligence in planning and performing their space activities and in framing and enforcing their laws and regulations in the space field. In this area, we must take into account that the precautionary approach, according to which when there are threats of "serious or irreversible damage" to the environment, lack of scientific certainty cannot be invoked by states in order to postpone preventive measures (principle 15 of the Rio Declaration), has gained increasing relevance in international law, in the European Union Law, and in national legislation.

4.3. The Duty to Inform

In this legal framework, the duty to inform also plays an important role. Information is recognized as a prerequisite for effective national and international environmental management, protection and co-operation. In international law, the information duty is mostly envisaged from an Earth-oriented perspective (principles 18 and 19 of the Rio Declaration, which relate to terrestrial environment). This is also true for access to environmental information, as is clearly shown by the Convention of the United Nations Economic Commission for Europe (UNECE) concerning access to information, public participation in decision-making and access to justice in environmental matters (Aarhus, 1998).[12]

As for space law, specific provisions on the duty to inform and the duty of consultation are contained in the last part of Article IX of the OST, which makes reference to activities in outer space which would cause potentially harmful interference; and in Article XI of the same Treaty concerning the information which has to be given to the Secretary-General of the United Nations, as well as to the public and the international scientific community.

Moreover, Article IV of the 1975 Registration Convention has had, in my opinion, an application environmentally oriented, in a functional sense. This point will be better highlighted by the examination of state practice on the registration of space objects and related information, which the COPUOS LSC will start considering from 2004.

4.4. Other Environmental Principles and Criteria

It is true, in the end, that many principles and rules that have been developed more explicitly within international environmental law are, at least implicitly, of growing relevance also in international space law. Even the debated principle of common but differentiated responsibility affirmed in the Rio Declaration merits attention in taking into account the needs of developing countries.[13] The principle could be considered, in fact, a more specific application of two general principles wich are found in international space law: that of international co-operation, and that according to which space activities have to be carried out for the benefit and in the interests of all countries, irrespective of their degree of economic or scientific development (Articles I and IX of the OST). Indeed, many bilateral and multilateral agreements concerning joint participation of developed and developing countries in space programmes take into account, in establishing the rights and obligations of the contracting parties , their differing degrees of economic development and of scientific and technical knowledge.[14]

Moreover, a lesson which can be learned from the application of environmental treaties and principles is that any international environmental regime requires the participation of the private sector to be viable. Industry has been associated as a core component in the functioning of the regime applicable to the protection of the ozone layer within the framework of the 1985 Vienna Convention, the subsequent Montreal Protocol, and its technical annexes and amendments, which have led to the trading off and phasing out of dangerous substances that deplete the ozone layer.[15]

Therefore, space law is not the only branch of international law where private sector participants have earned a major role in ensuring the effectiveness of applicable legal regimes.

It is my habit to see the glass half-full, rather than half-empty, so, I think that the abovementioned stipulations, even if they probably fail to set completely clear obligations, do pave the way for identifying the existing legal regime which protects the space environment.

5. DEVELOPMENTS IN STATE PRACTICE

It has been often said that international space law is a law without practice: claims for compensation are rare and there are no disputes.

This is true on the one hand, but, on the other, we have a very conspicuous practice of the space-faring states from which we can deduct, if not yet a consolidated *opinio iuris*, a clear tendency toward the recognition of the imperative of space environment protection. The main evidence of legal obligation is to be found in current practice of states and a rough idea of state practice can be gathered from concrete behaviour and action rather than from more classical sources.

Now, it seems that this practice shows a growing tendency not only toward consciousness of the problem but also toward tackling it, by behaving to protect, to the maximum possible extent, the space environment and by trying to avoid harmful contamination. In this regard, we may mention the application of the recommendation contained in the 2002 GA resolution 57/116 calling for the continuation of national research on space debris and the safety of nuclear-powered satellites; the conduct and procedures adopted by space-faring countries to effectively minimize the creation of space debris; the application of Article IV of the Registration Convention and state practice on the re-entry of space objects, like the MIR manned orbital station and its "safe and controlled" descent from orbit, or like the Beppo-sax Italian satellite's destruction and splash down into the Pacific Ocean on April 29, 2003 following a procedure of voluntary notification to potentially affected states; and finally, NASA's Galileo nuclear-powered spacecraft, deliberately destroyed by disintegrating it at high altitude within Jupiter's atmosphere "to eliminate the chance of an unwanted impact with Jupiter's moon Europe".[16]

As for the contribution of the scientific community, we may recall the COSPAR Planetary Protection Policy, aimed at providing acceptable guidelines which can be generally adopted by states to avoid contamination in their space exploration.[17]

Finally, mention has to be made of national legislation, as a part of relevant state practice. Regarding this point, the UK Outer Space Act of 1986, Section 5, includes among the conditions that might be imposed on private operators for them to obtain a license for their space activities, the requirement that their operations be conducted in such a way as to prevent contamination of outer space or adverse changes to the environment of the Earth.[18]

6. THE LACK OF SECONDARY NORMS

But the feeling still remains that the substantial legal regime for space protection is not well defined and needs to be improved from a *de lege ferenda* point of view.

This conclusion is also true as far as the secondary norms are concerned. The special regime of international responsibility and absolute/strict liability set forth in Articles VI and VII of the OST and in the 1972 Convention does not provide any mechanism for claiming compensation for environmental planetary damage.

Also, if we look at the current situation of general international law, we can see that absolute/strict liability for harmful consequences of internationally lawful activities is not reflected yet by specific customary norms. It is well known that the Draft Articles on prevention of transboundary harm from hazardous activities adopted by the International Law Commission (ILC) in 2001 confirms such a conclusion.[19]

The only secondary rules of general international law applicable to the protection of the space environment are, therefore, the norms on state responsibility for wrongful acts, according to which every breach of an international legal obligation entails state responsibility and creates a further obligation to make reparation. This regime is mentioned, in my interpretation, in the last phrase of Principle XIV of the 1986 GA resolution 41/65 on remote sensing, according to which the application of the strict liability regime to remote sensing is without prejudice to the applicability of the

norms of international law on state responsibility for remote sensing activities.
Now, the critical point is the concept of "injured state". In fact, in the case of violation of an obligation concerning the protection of the space environment, which state is entitled to invoke the responsibility of the violator state? This is a rather controversial issue. According to Article 42 of the Draft Articles on state responsibility for internationally wrongful acts adopted by the ILC in 2001, a state is entitled as an "injured state" to invoke the responsibility of another state, if *a*) the obligation breached is owed to him individually; or *b*) the obligation is owed to a group of states, or the international community as a whole, and the breach of the obligation specially affects that state, within the group or the international community. These criteria clearly identify the state entitled to invoke the responsibility as a state whose rights and interests are directly affected by an internationally wrongful act. In addition, according to Article 48 of the Draft Articles, any state *other than an injured state* is entitled to invoke the responsibility if "*a*) the obligation breached is owed to a group of states including that state and is established for the protection of a collective interest of the group; or *b*) the obligation breached is owed to the international community as a whole".[20] Therefore, Article 48 entitles a state which is not directly affected by the breach of an obligation to invoke the responsibility, if that obligation is established for the protection of *a collective interest*, or is owed *to the international community as a whole*. Is this criterion applicable to the damage to the space environment when there has been a breach of legal obligations?
This is an open question. It is evident, however, that the protection of the outer space environment is inherently linked with the concept of outer space as an intergenerational trust of the international community as a whole. In fact, the principle of exploration and use of space as the province of humankind contains, even implicitly, the concept of intergenerational equity, which is at the core of international law in the field of sustainable development and environmental protection.[21] Intergenerational equity transcends spatial dimensions by viewing international law from an inter-temporal perspective, linking the present to the future. It can therefore address the question whether harm to areas beyond national jurisdiction can be averted or recompensed where potential or actual harm occurs to the space environment. The task ahead lies in translating widely expressed concern for future generations into normative obligations.
But this is a more general task of progressive development of international law.

7. INTERNATIONAL CO-OPERATION TO LIMIT SPACE DEBRIS AND OTHER HARMFUL EFFECTS

The *de lege ferenda* point of view is very intriguing, but rather difficult. I think that in the short term, a more pragmatic approach has to be taken.
The United Nations has paid great attention to the necessity of protecting space environment. Thanks to the COPUOS action, progress has been made in the area of international co-operation to limit space debris or other harmful effects of space activities. Following the adoption of the 1999 Report on space debris, the STSC has continued its consideration of the item in accordance with the work plan adopted at its 38th Session. The Inter-Agency Debris Coordination Committee (IADC) has adopted and presented the Space Debris Mitigation Guidelines, based on a consensus among the Committee members[22]. The STSC has requested and encouraged all member states to study these proposals and to provide their comment before 2004.

This constitutes a solid body of work, which could also form the basis for the LSC to address this item. Until now, the LSC has only been able to discuss the space debris issue on a very general level. Some COPUOS members, like Brazil and the Czech Republic, put forward a proposal to consider the issue of the legal aspects of space debris within the Subcommittee, while France recently proposed that the LSC embark on the negotiation of a declaration of principles on the subject. Others are of the opinion that such a step would not be constructive at the present time, the fastest way of reducing the space debris being for space-faring nations to immediately implement on a voluntary basis the measures contained in the IADC Guidelines.[23]

This consideration brings me to my last point, which is the role of the LSC in this field. Some years ago, in 1999, during the Perugia Colloquium on "International Organization and Space Law", Dr. Jasentuliyana put forward the idea of the drafting by both COPUOS Subcommittees, on an ordinary functional basis, of international recommendations and standards.[24] As the experience of some specialized institutions shows, real drive can come from the so called technical norms. We may recall the recommended standards and practices of the International Civil Aviation Organization (ICAO), adopted in the form of annexes to the constituent Treaty following an opting-out procedure; the *Codex Alimentarius*, a joint system of the Food and Agricultural Organization (FAO) and of the World Health Organization (WHO) for deciding food standards and fair practices in food trade, which has been adopted by acceptance by member states (full acceptance, target acceptance, and acceptance with specific deviations); the regulatory frameworks of the WHO and, finally, the technical annexes to a number of environmental treaties, like the 1987 Montreal Protocol on substances depleting the ozone layer, based on an opt-out mechanism.

I think that this proposal should be revitalized, in order to allow the LSC to consider an international regulatory framework applicable to space debris for an orderly, reliable and safe environment for beneficial space activities.

---

[1] Cfr. Reijnen, B.C.M., de Graaff, W., *The Pollution of Outer Space, in Particular of the Geostationary Orbit. Scientific, Policy and Legal Aspects*, Dordrecht-Boston-London, 1989, p. 38 ff. See also Gorove, S., *Developments in Space Law. Issues and Policy*, Dordrecht-Boston-London, 1991, 164 ff.

[2] Committee on the Peaceful Uses of Outer Space, Report of the Scientific and Technical Subcommittee on the Work of its Thirty-sixth Session, UNGA doc. A/AC.105/719, 18 March 1999.

[3] Cfr. Courteix, S., *La pollution de l'espace extra-atmosphérique par les débris spatiaux*, "Mankind and the Environment. What rights for the twenty-first century?", Paris, 1998, pp. 563-581. See also Frankle, E.A., *International Regulation of Orbital Debris*, "IISL Proceedings", 2000, p. 369 ff.

[4] Lyall, F., *Protection of the Space Environment and Law*, "IISL Proceedings", 1999, p. 472 ff.

[5] See, generally, Reijnen, B., *The United Nations Treaties Analysed*, Utrecht, 1992, p. 122 ff. and p. 184 f.

[6] See Courteix, S., *The Legal Regime of Nuclear Power Satellites: a Problem at the Cross-Roads of Nuclear Law and Space Law*, "IISL Proceedings", 1991, p. 117 ff.

[7] Cfr. Cheng, B., *Studies in International Space Law*, Oxford, 1997, p. 256 f.

[8] On the "parallel line" between Article 7 of the Moon Agreement and Article 145 of the United Nations Convention on the Law of the Sea concerning protection of the marine environment, see Baslar, K., *The Concept of the Common Heritage of Mankind in International Law*, The Hague-Boston-London, 1998, p. 174 f.

[9] Cfr. Abeyratne, R.I.R., *Use of Nuclear Power Sources in Outer Space and its Effect on Environmental Protection*, "Journal of Space Law", 1997 p. 17 ff., at pp. 24-26.

[10] "International Legal Materials", 1998, p. 162. See also *Symposium: The Case Concerning the Gabcikovo-Nagymaros Project*, in "Yearbook of International Environmental Law", 1997, pp. 3-50,

and SANDS, P., *International Courts and the Concept of "Sustainable Development"*, "Max Planck Yearbook of United Nations Law", 1999, pp. 389-405.

[11] I.C.J., *Reports*, 1996, p. 226 ff.

[12] See generally Leme Machado, P.A., *Information and Participation: Required Instruments for the Improvement of Environmental Rights*, "Environmental Policy and Law", No. 4, 1997, pp. 285-288, and more specifically Stec, S., Casey-Lefkowitz, *The Aarhus Convention: an Implementation Guide*, Economic Commission for Europe, United Nations, New York-Geneva, 2000.

[13] According to Principle 7 of the Rio Declaration "the developed countries acknowledge the responsibility that they bear in the international pursuit of sustainable development in view of the pressure their societies place on the global environment and of the technologies and financial resources they command".

[14] See, for example, the Italy-Kenya agreements on the San Marco-Malindi station. Cfr. Ferrajolo, O., *Launch and Tracking Stations: the San Marco-Malindi Case*, "Outlook on Space Law over the Next 30 Years", The Hague-London-Boston, 1997, pp. 273-284, at p. 283 f.

[15] On the ozone layer's legal regime see Nanda, V.P., Pring, G., *International Environmental Law and Policy for the 21st Century*, Ardsley, N.Y., 2003, p. 239 ff.

[16] See "Le Monde", September 20, 2003, p. 27.

[17] The text of the document on a revised and consolidated planetary protection policy, adopted by the COSPAR Council on 20 October 2002 can be downloaded at http://www.cosparhq.org/scistr/PPPPolicy.htm.

[18] Cfr. Close, R., *Overview of the Outer Space Act and the UK Licensing Framework*, Paper presented at the first UK Conference on "The Impact of Space Debris on the Private Commercial Operator", held on 9th November, 2001 at Inmarsat, London.

[19] Report of the International Law Commission on the Work of its Fifty-third Session, Official Records of the General Assembly, Fifty-sixth Session, Supplement No. 10 (A/56/10), chp.V.E.1.

[20] Cfr. Crawford, J., *The International Law Commission's Articles on State Responsibility. Introduction, Text and Commentaries*, Cambridge, 2002, p. 254 ff. and p. 276 ff.

[21] See the classical contribution by WEISS, *Our Rights and Obligations to Future Generations*, "American Journal of International Law", 1990, pp. 198-207.

[22] IADC Space Debris Mitigation Guidelines, IADC-02-01, 15 October 2002.

[23] Committee on the Peaceful Uses of Outer Space, Report of the Scientific and Technical Subcommittee on its Fortieth Session, Held in Vienna from 17 to 28 February 2003, UNGA doc. A/AC.105/804, 5 March 2003.

[24] Jasentuliyana, N., *Strengthening International Space Law – The Role of the United Nations*, "International Organisations and Space Law. Proceeding of the Third ECSL Colloquium", Noordwijk, The Netherlands, 1999, p. 87 ff. See also Perek, L., *Maintaining the Space Environment*, Discussion Paper presented at the Technical Forum of UNISPACE III, IISL Workshop on Space Law of the 21st Century, Session 8, July 23, 1999.

PLANETARY PROTECTION IN PUBLIC INTERNATIONAL LAW*

*Dr. jur. Ulrike M. Bohlmann***
European Space Agency, Legal Department,
8-10, rue Mario Nikis, 75038 Paris Cedex 15, France,
Tel. +33 (0) 1 53 69 72 79, Fax +33 (0) 1 53 69 76 71,
Ulrike.Bohlmann@esa.int

Abstract

More and more exciting missions are planned or are already on their way to explore our solar system. One of the driving forces behind these missions is the desire to search for life beyond the Earth. Basic ethical considerations lead to the conviction that the protection of the space environment including these potentially existing forms of life is a goal in itself. More specifically and from a more practical point of view, it is essential to prevent the contamination of celestial bodies with Earth organisms that might be taken there by scientific missions. This paper aims at giving an overview over the existing international rules relevant to the subject of planetary protection and their legal value. Furthermore, some recommendations as to possible future developments, especially in the European and international context, are elaborated.

I. Introduction

On 2nd June 2003, ESA launched the Mars Express spacecraft, Europe's first space-craft to the Red Planet. It carries seven instruments that perform remote sensing of Mars and a lander, Beagle 2, which will perform in-situ investigations of the surface, using geo-chemical, exobiological, and atmospheric parameters. Mars Express is also designed to look for signs of past or present life.

The question what Mars Express is going to find, inspires imagination. If it is going to find traces of life, questions emerge as to where this life might come from - whether it is Martian life or Terrestrial contamination left by earlier visitors - what the characteristics of this life might be, and to what kind of protection it might be entitled.

More generally, in a time where the number of missions that are planned in carried out to study our solar system increases constantly and where sample return mission become conceivable, the issue of environmental aspects of these space activities, the protection of the environment of our solar system comes to the forefront of concern. This concern has been conceptualised under the catchword of "planetary protection".

** The views expressed are purely personal and do not necessarily reflect those of the European Space Agency.

In essence, the notion of planetary protection, as it is currently understood and as it is also at the basis of this paper, is the activity that seeks to prevent the biological cross contamination of solar system bodies, especially those that may (or do) harbour living entities[2]. Thus, it has a two-fold orientation: it encompasses protection against forward contamination, e.g. the contamination of the extra-terrestrial environment with terrestrial organisms, and protection against backward contamination, e.g. the contamination of the Earth by extra-terrestrial organisms.

II. The current legal framework with regard to planetary protection

Several sets of legal instruments, several sources and guidelines may be cited in connection with the subject matter: The classical outer space law as incorporated in the international space law treaties has its' role to play as well as the planetary protection guidelines developed by COSPAR, national policies based thereupon or also the more general international environmental law.

1. Relevant provisions of the Outer Space Treaty

The most important provision of the Outer Space Treaty, OST,[3] in this context is the second sentence of Article IX, which stipulates, "States Parties to the Treaty shall pursue studies of outer space, including the Moon and other celestial bodies, and conduct exploration of them so as to avoid their harmful contamination and also adverse changes in the environment of the Earth resulting from the introduction of extra-terrestrial material and, where necessary, shall adopt appropriate measures for this purpose."

Since the main terms, like "harmful contamination" and "adverse changes", are not defined, the factual side of the provision remains rather ambiguous. Furthermore, the nature and extent of the "appropriate measures" to be adopted by the States Parties to the Treaty remain at the sole discretion of the respective Party. Hence, the provision heavily lacks specificity. It is not self-executing, but requires additional rule making. Its effect as such is minimal[4]. This becomes even more evident, when having a look at the following sentence of Article IX: "If a State Party has reason to believe that an activity or experiment planned by it or its nationals in outer space, including the Moon and other celestial bodies, would cause potential harmful interference with activities of other States Parties in the exploration and use of outer space, including the Moon and other celestial bodies, it shall undertake appropriate international consultations before proceeding with any such activity or experiment." Accordingly, it is only in case of potential harmful interference with activities of other States that States Parties shall undertake consultations. The issue of environmental integrity of outer space on the other hand has not been considered important enough to endow it with even this quite weak protection of "undertaking

2 United Nations, Highlights in Space 2001, p. 140. "Solar system bodies" can be defined as all the celestial bodies physically located in our solar system. Celestial bodies in a legal sense are commonly understood to be all natural objects in Outer Space, including their eventual gaseous coronas, see for example: *W. v. Kries/ B. Schmidt-Tedd/ K.-U. Schrogl*, Grundzüge des Raumfahrtrechts – Rahmenbestimmungen und Anwendungsgebiete, 2002, p. 17.

3 Treaty on Principles Governing the Activities of States in the Exploration and Use of Outer Space, including the Moon and Other Celestial Bodies, opened for signature 27 January 1966, entered into force 10 October 1967, 610 United Nations Treaty Series (UNTS) 205.

4 See also *A. McCloud*, Space Pollution, in: IISL 1987, pp 142, 143.

appropriate international consultations" as foreseen by Article IX 3rd sentence.[5]

2. Relevant Provisions of the Liability Convention

Article II of the Liability Convention[6] stipulates, "A launching State shall be absolutely liable to pay compensation for damage caused by its space object on the surface of the Earth or to aircraft in flight." Article III goes on to stipulate "In the event of damage being caused elsewhere than on the surface of the Earth to a space object of one launching State or to persons or property on board such a space object of another launching State, the latter shall be liable only if damage is due to its fault or the fault of persons for who, it is responsible."

Thus, should a space object cause damage, which in Article I (a) of the Convention is defined as meaning for the purposes of the Convention "loss of life, personal injury or other impairment of health; or loss of or damage to property of States or of persons, natural or juridical, or property of international intergovernmental organisations", on the surface of the Earth a victim State Party to the Convention does not have to prove fault, the launching State is absolutely liable. This also comprises damage caused by the introduction of extra-terrestrial material, so-called back-contamination. However, international liability under the Liability Convention does not address any kind of environmental damage outside of the Earth.

3. Relevant provisions of the Moon Treaty

The Moon Treaty[7], the provisions of which also apply to other celestial bodies within the solar system other than the Earth, and the respective orbits or trajectories around them, elaborates a bit more on the principles regarding the protection of the extra-terrestrial environment. This is probably also due to the period in which it was written. In the late 1970s, environmental considerations were becoming a global concern.

According to its Article 7.1 "In exploring and using the Moon, States Parties shall take measures to prevent the disruption of the existing balance of its environment, whether by introducing adverse changes in that environment, by its harmful contamination through the introduction of extra-environmental matter or otherwise. States Parties to the Treaty shall also take measures to avoid harmfully affecting the environment of the Earth through the introduction of extra-environmental matter or otherwise." Thus, issues of forward and

---

5 *Reijnen* argues that it is more the spirit of the OST, as articulated in its Article I stipulating that, the exploration and use of outer space, including the Moon and other celestial bodies, shall be carried out for the benefit and in the interests of all countries, and not the wording of its actual provisions that forms the basis for the protection of outer space against contamination, since the major benefits and interests are best served by an unpolluted outer space (*G.C.M. Reijnen*, Environmental Pollution of Outer Space, in particular of the geo-stationary orbit, in: IISL 1987, pp. 155). Given the fact that also Article I OST was not intended to specifically protect the environmental integrity of outer space (See also *P.M. Sterns, L.I. Tennen*, Principles of Protection of the Outer Space Environment in the Corpus Iuris Spatialis, in: IISL 1987, pp.172), this argumentation seems too far-reaching. In any case, we can state that the primary objective of protection of these provisions of the OST is the human exploration and use of outer space, human space activities and not an intrinsic value of the outer space environment.

6 Convention on International Liability for Damage Caused by Space Objects, opened for signature 29 March 1972, entered into force 1 September 1972, 961 UNTS 187.

7 Agreement Governing the Activities of States on the Moon and Other Celestial Bodies, opened for signature 18 December 1979, entered into force 11 July 1984, 1363 UNTS 3.

backward contamination are addressed, but once again, we can state with *Williamson*[8], that there is good intention, but unfortunately, the definitions are missing. Anyway, we can assert as already elaborated by *P.M. Sterns and L.I. Tennen*[9] that the language of the Moon Treaty clarifies, that harmful contamination is but one means of disruption of the natural environment of celestial bodies. For the first time in space law, the existing balance of the extra-terrestrial environment becomes the focus.

The third paragraph of Article 7 of the Moon Treaty is also of interest in this context. It stipulates "States Parties shall report to other States Parties and to the Secretary-General concerning areas of the Moon having a special scientific interest in order that, without prejudice to the rights of other States Parties, consideration may be given to the designation of such areas as international scientific preserves, for which special protective arrangements are to be agreed upon in consultation with the competent bodies of the United Nations." This provision is quite interesting, since it foresees the possibility – even though not mandatory – to establish zones of special protection on celestial bodies, but once again, the potential establishment of these international preserves is driven by scientific interest only and not by the recognition of an intrinsic value of the extra-terrestrial environment as such.

Another novelty with regard to the principles of international environmental law and space law can be found in the Moon Treaty: the second sentence of its Article 4.1 which stipulates "Due regard shall be paid to the interests of present and future generations [...]" evokes for the first time in the - admittedly short - history of space law the principle of intergenerational equity, which is part of the more general concept of sustainability.

The last provision of the Moon Treaty, we want to mention in this paper is Article 5.3, which formulates: "In carrying out activities under this Agreement, States Parties shall promptly inform the Secretary General, as well as the public and the international scientific community, of any phenomena they discover in outer space, including the Moon, which could endanger human life or health, as well as any indication of organic life." The most interesting aspect of this provision is the fact that States Parties are not only obliged to inform the other State Parties and the Secretary General but also the public and the international scientific community.

However, since the Moon Treaty has received only ten ratifications and five additional signatures[10], its force and value is – contrary to the Outer Space Treaty and the Liability Convention[11] - rather limited; no customary value can be attributed to its regulations and it is only binding upon its States Parties.

4. The COSPAR Planetary Protection Policy

COSPAR, the Committee on Space Research, was established in October 1958 by the International Council of Scientific Unions, ICSU, to continue the co-operative

8 *M. Williamson*, Protection of the Space Environment under the Outer Space Treaty, IISL 1997, pp 296.

9 *P.M. Sterns, L.I. Tennen*, Principles of Protection of the Outer Space Environment in the Corpus Iuris Spatialis, in: IISL 1987, pp.172.

10 Status as of 1 January 2003, A/AC.105/C.2/ 2003/CRP.5.

11 The Outer Space Treaty has been ratified by 98 States, and signed by an additional 27, Status as of 1 January 2003, A/AC.105/C.2/ 2003/CRP.5, it is regarded as having a universal customary value; The same applies to the Liability Convention, that has been ratified by 82 States, signed by an additional 25 States and the rights and obligations of which have been accepted by two international organisations, Status as of 1 January 2003, A/AC.105/C.2/ 2003/CRP.5.

programmes of rocket and satellite research undertaken during the International Geophysical Year (1957 – 1958). COSPAR's objectives are to promote on an international level scientific research in space, with emphasis on the exchange of results, information and opinions, and to provide a forum, open to all scientists, for the discussion of problems that may affect scientific space research. It is an interdisciplinary scientific committee concerned with scientific research and defines itself as a non-political organisation. Its activities with regard to scientific programmes have a consultative and co-ordinating character.

COSPAR's Panel on Planetary Protection is concerned with biological interchange in the conduct of solar system exploration, including possible effects of contamination of planets other than the Earth, and of planetary satellites within the solar system by terrestrial organisms, on the one hand, and contamination of the Earth by materials returned from outer space carrying potential extraterrestrial organisms, on the other hand. The primary objectives of the Panel within COSPAR are to develop, maintain, and promulgate planetary protection knowledge and policy, and plan to prevent the harmful effects of such contamination, and through symposia, workshops, and topical meetings at COSPAR Assemblies to provide an international forum for exchange of information in this area.

At the second session of its 34th meeting, the COSPAR Council adopted a revised and consolidated planetary protection policy[12]. In addition to providing specific guidelines, the policy recommends that COSPAR members provide information to COSPAR within a reasonable time not to exceed six months after launch about the procedures and computations used for planetary protection for each flight and again within one year after the end of a solar-system exploration mission about the areas of the target(s) which may have been subject to contamination.

The COSPAR Planetary Protection Policy is intended for the reference of space-faring nations, both as an international standard on procedures to avoid organic-constituent and biological contamination in space exploration, and to provide accepted guidelines in this area to guide compliance with the wording of this UN Space Treaty and other relevant international agreements. It bases itself on the policy statement by *DeVincenzi* et al. of 1983: "Although the existence of life elsewhere in the solar system may be unlikely, the conduct of scientific investigations of possible extraterrestrial life forms, precursors, and remnants must not be jeopardized. In addition, the Earth must be protected from the potential hazard posed by extraterrestrial matter carried by a spacecraft returning from another planet. Therefore, for certain space mission/ target planet combinations, controls on contamination shall be imposed, in accordance with issuances implementing this policy."

This new Planetary Protection Policy develops further the direction already taken by COSPAR in 1964, when the approach of absolute pre-launch sterilisation proved to be unobtainable and, consequently, a policy of probabilistic avoidance of contamination was adopted.[13]

The five categories for target body/mission type combinations and their respective suggested ranges of requirements are the following:

[12] The text of this policy can be downloaded at: <http://www.cosparhq.org/scistr/PPPPolicy.htm>

[13] For additional information, see: *G. Schwehm* Planetary Protection in: *K. H. Böckstiegel* (ed.) Environmental Aspects of Activities in Outer Space – Proceedings of an international colloquium, Cologne May, 16 – 19, 1988, pp 61.

Category I includes any mission to a target body, which is not of direct interest for understanding the process of chemical evolution or the origin of life. No protection of such bodies is warranted and no planetary protection requirements are imposed by the COSPAR Planetary Protection Policy.

Category II missions comprise all types of missions to those target bodies where there is significant interest relative to the process of chemical evolution and the origin of life, but where there is only a remote chance that contamination carried by a spacecraft could jeopardize future exploration. The requirements are for simple documentation only. Preparation of a short planetary protection plan is required for these flight projects primarily to outline intended or potential impact targets, brief Pre- and Post-launch analyses detailing impact strategies, and a Post-encounter and End-of-Mission Report which will provide the location of impact if such an event occurs. Solar system bodies considered to be classified as Category II are listed in the Appendix to the COSPAR Planetary Protection Policy, and include Comets, Carbonaceous Chondrite Asteroids, Jupiter, Saturn, Uranus, Neptune, Pluto/ Charon and Kuiper-Belt Objects.

Category III missions comprise certain types of missions (mostly flyby and orbiter) to a target body of chemical evolution and/or origin of life interest or for which scientific opinion provides a significant chance of contamination, which could jeopardize a future biological experiment. Requirements will consist of documentation (more involved than Category II) and some implementing procedures, including trajectory biasing, the use of cleanrooms during spacecraft assembly and testing, and possibly bioburden reduction. Although no impact is intended for Category III missions, an inventory of bulk constituent organics is required if the probability of impact is significant. Category III specifications for selected solar system bodies are set forth in the Appendix to this document. Solar system bodies considered to be classified as Category III also are listed in the Appendix to the COSPAR Planetary Protection Policy and include Mars and Europa.

Category IV missions comprise certain types of missions (mostly probe and lander) to a target body of chemical evolution and/or origin of life interest or for which scientific opinion provides a significant chance of contamination, which could jeopardize future biological experiments. Requirements imposed include rather detailed documentation (more involved than Category III), including a bioassay to enumerate the bioburden, a probability of contamination analysis, an inventory of the bulk constituent organics and an increased number of implementing procedures. The implementing procedures required may include trajectory biasing, cleanrooms, bioload reduction, possible partial sterilization of the direct contact hardware and a bioshield for that hardware. Generally, the requirements and compliance are similar to Viking, with the exception of complete lander/probe sterilisation. Category IV specifications for selected solar system bodies are set forth in the Appendix to the COSPAR Planetary Protection Policy. Solar system bodies considered to be classified as Category IV also are listed in the Appendix and include Mars and Europa.

Category V missions comprise all Earth-return missions. The concern for these missions is the protection of the terrestrial system, the Earth and the Moon. (The Moon must be protected from back contamination to retain freedom from planetary protection requirements on Earth-Moon travel.) For solar system bodies deemed by scientific opinion to have no indigenous life forms, a subcategory "unrestricted Earth return" is defined. Missions in this subcategory have planetary protection requirements on the outbound phase only, corresponding to the category of that phase (typically Category I or II). For all other Category V missions, in a subcategory defined as "restricted Earth return," – including Mars and Europa - the highest degree of concern is expressed by the absolute prohibition of destructive impact upon return, the need for containment throughout the return phase of all returned hardware which directly contacted the target body or unsterilised material from the body, and the need for containment of any unsterilised sample collected and returned to Earth. Post-mission, there is a need to conduct timely analyses of the unsterilised sample collected and returned to Earth, under strict containment, and using the most sensitive techniques. If any sign of the existence of a nonterrestrial replicating entity is found, the returned sample must remain contained unless treated by an effective sterilising procedure. Category V concerns are reflected in requirements that encompass those of Category IV plus a continuing monitoring of project activities, studies and research (i.e., in sterilisation procedures and containment techniques).

Obviously, the COSPAR Planetary Protection Policy is a very consistent and highly developed system of recommendations by an independent and international body of scientists with a high reputation in the field. However, COSPAR is a non-government organisation that is not endowed with institutionalised authority and although it is the continuous policy of many actors in the space field to comply with COSPAR's recommendations, these are not legally binding but their quality amounts more to a moral kind of obligation.

Another quality of the COSPAR Planetary Protection Policy is that, by the setting of standards, it influences the national planetary protection policies. The most prominent example is probably the NASA Policy Directive NPD 8020.7E, Biological Contamination Control for Outbound and Inbound Planetary Spacecraft[14], and its implementing procedures and guidelines contained in 8020.12B, Planetary Protection Provisions for Robotic Extraterrestrial Missions[15].

NPD 8020.7E rephrases the above-cited COSPAR policy statement and adopts it as the basis for the NASA policy. NPG 8020.12B implements this policy in detail by listing the general planetary protection requirements applicable to the different categories of missions and goes on to affirm that specific requirements will be determined by the NASA Planetary Protection Officer in accordance with NPG 8020.12B and under the NASA accepted policy guidelines of COSPAR and in consultation with the Space Studies Board of the National Research Council. The very detailed and elaborated NASA Planetary Protection Guidelines are intended to apply not only to NASA missions but also to the flight of NASA instruments or experiments on non-NASA spacecrafts. However, the quality of these policies and guidelines remains that of a national, internal document that is not binding internationally. According to the NASA Planetary Protection Officer, *J. Rummel*, the policy is based on the desire to preserve extraterrestrial environments for the science opportunities[16].

---

14 The text can be downloaded at: <http://planpro.jpl.nasa.gov/npd80207.html>.

15 The text can be downloaded at: < http://nodis3.gsfc.nasa.gov/library/displayAll.cfm?Internal_ID=N_PG_8020_012B_&page_name=all>.

16 Cited after *L. Woodmansee*, If Life exists on Mars, our robotic probes may have brought it there, <http://www.spacedaily.com/news/life-01zg1.html >; See also *J. Rummel*, Planetary exploration in the time of astrobiology: Protecting against biological contamination, in: Proceedings of the National Academy of Sciences, available at: <http://www.pnas.org>.

5. International Environmental Law

When addressing international environmental law, the most prominent texts to cite are the so-called Stockholm[17] and Rio[18] Declarations.

The UN Conference on the Human Environment, that was held from 5 – 15 June 1972 in Stockholm, was the first universal conference of States that tackled questions of international environmental protection. Delegations from 114 States[19] participated and numerous international institutions and non-governmental organisations were represented. One of the main outputs of the Conference was the Stockholm Declaration that states the common convictions of the participants in 26 principles. Of peculiar interest in our context is Principle 21, that – clearly following the Trail Smelter Arbitration[20] - states "States have, in accordance with the Charter of the United Nations and the principles of international law, the sovereign right to exploit their own resources pursuant to their own environmental policies, and the responsibility to ensure that activities within their jurisdiction or control do not cause damage to the environment of other States or of areas beyond the limits of national jurisdiction." Thus, also the environment of outer space as one of the areas beyond the limits of national jurisdiction, is protected by this principle, in other words: The Stockholm Conference was convinced of the responsibility of States to ensure that activities within their jurisdiction or control do not cause damage to the outer space environment. This protection, however, is weakened by the reference to a State's own environmental policy.[21]

The United Nations General Assembly Resolution 2996 (XXVII) 1972 asserts that Principle 21 [and 22] of the Stockholm Declaration 'lay down the basic rules governing the matter'. 112 States voted in favour of this resolution, none opposed, the then Eastern Bloc States abstained on Res. 2996, but have supported subsequent treaties recognising the normative character of Principle 21. With minor changes – a reference to national developmental policies was added – the principle was repeated in Principle 2 of Rio Declaration and Article 3 of the Convention on Biological Diversity[22], so that – although the Stockholm Declaration has not a binding character – at least Principle 21 may be regarded as reflecting customary international law.

Principle 15 of the Rio Declaration, elaborates further on the so-called precautionary approach by stating "In order to protect the environment, the precautionary approach shall be widely applied by States according to their capabilities. Where there are threats of serious or irreversible damage, lack of full scientific certainty shall not be used as a reason for postponing cost-effective measures to prevent environmental degradation." Thus, there is an international obligation of diligent prevention and control. This obligation arises when there is a foreseeability of harm, in the sense of an objectively determined risk. Risk can be defined as encompassing both a low probability of causing disastrous harm and a high

17 Declaration of the United Nations Conference on the Human Environment, adopted in Stockholm on 16 June 1972, 11 ILM 1416 (1972).

18 Declaration of the United Nations Conference on Environment and Development, adopted in Rio de Janeiro on 12 August 1992, 31 ILM 874 (1992).

19 The States of the then Eastern Bloc were not represented.

20 3 Reports of International Arbitral Awards pp 1903 (1949).

21 For more details, see *P. Birnie/ A. Boyle*, International Law and the Environment, 2nd ed. 2002, pp 109.

22 31 ILM 818 (1992), opened to signature on 22 May 1992 and entered into force on 29 December 1993.

probability of causing significant harm[23], thereby taking into consideration both the magnitude and the probability of harm. This international obligation comprises also a duty to enquire potential dangers of a planned activity. The question, to what extent a risk of damage to the environment, including the extra-terrestrial environment, a risk that can never be excluded totally, is socially acceptable, remains to be answered in each single case after a careful risk assessment.

The legal significance of the precautionary approach as embedded in Principle 15 of the Rio Declaration is best described by *P. Birnie* and *A. Boyle*[24]: it has a legally important core on which there is international consensus – this is proven by its use by national and international courts, by international organisations and in treaties[25]. This essence is that in performing their obligations of environmental protection states cannot rely on scientific uncertainty to justify a lack of action when there is enough evidence to establish the possibility of a risk of serious harm, even if there is as yet no proof of harm. This also applies to activities that might be dangerous to the extraterrestrial environment.

Another text of international environmental law that is of particular interest to the area of planetary protection is the Convention on Biological Diversity[26]. According to its Article 4, subject to the rights of other States, and except as otherwise expressly provided in the Convention, the provisions of it apply, in relation to each Contracting Party in the case of processes and activities, regardless of where their effects occur, carried out under the jurisdiction or control of a Contracting Party, within the area of its national jurisdiction or beyond the limits of national jurisdiction. Thus, it is also applicable to outer space activities.

Article 8 (h) of the Convention provides "Each Contracting Party shall, as far as possible and as appropriate prevent the introduction of, control or eradicate those alien species which threaten ecosystems, habitats or species". "Ecosystem" is defined as a dynamic complex of plant, animal and micro-organism communities and their non-living environment interacting as a functional unit and "Habitat" as the place or type of site, where an organism or population naturally occurs, Article 2 of the Convention. Accordingly, the issues of forward and backward contamination are dealt with by the Convention, the potentially harmful introduction of species that are foreign to a given environment, be it terrestrial or extra-terrestrial, is to be prevented, or at least controlled or eradicated. This obligation is, however, limited to "as far as possible and as appropriate".

III. Some thoughts on the development of the law: So far and beyond ?

The short overview of public international law that is relevant to planetary protection issues under II, shows also the influence a new kind of thinking in ethical and environmental terms has had on the development of the law.

The early texts, like the Outer Space Treaty and the Liability Convention, base themselves on anthropocentric and geocentric values, the protection of the

---

23 See Article 2 of the International Law Commission's Draft Convention on the Prevention of Transboundary Harm from Hazardous Activities, 2001, the text can be downloaded under: <http://www.un.org/law/ilc/texts/prevention/preventionfra.htm>.

24 International Law and the Environment, 2nd ed. 2002, pp 120.

25 For examples see: *P. Birnie/ A. Boyle*, International Law and the Environment, 2nd ed. 2002, pp 118.

26 The Convention was opened to signature on 22 May 1992 and entered into force on 29 December 1993, 31 ILM 818 (1992).

extra-terrestrial environment found its reason in the preservation of scientific opportunities. The COSPAR Planetary Protection Policy and the relevant NASA Policy Directive based upon it follow along the same lines. The Moon Treaty, then, elaborates further on the balance of the extra-terrestrial environment, and mentions for the first time in space law the principle of intergenerational equity, which is one of the main subjects of modern international environmental law based on the Rio Declaration and which is geared at the avoidance of irreversible harm. Nevertheless, also the Moon Treaty lays the emphasis on the scientific interest, for which international preserves might be established and not an intrinsic value of the extra-terrestrial environment. The idea to conserve species and their habitat for their own value and not just as resources exploitable by man is still relatively young; steps of a shift of the anthropocentric to an eco-centric or bio-centric ethical approach, that attributes value to all life as part of an ecosystem or to all life as such, have taken place in the framework of the Convention on Biological Diversity. The further steps to a cosmo-centric ethic that recognises the intrinsic value of the extra-terrestrial environment and of its existing balance have not been taken, yet. In that context, we can only underline what has already been written by *I. Almár*, that it would be highly desirable to extend the attitudes of environmentalists' movements also to the extraterrestrial environments.[27]

IV. Steps to take

Several ways would allow strengthening the position of the extraterrestrial environment ranging from raising the public's awareness of the issue to supporting the work done by expert groups, such as COSPAR. Furthermore, each public actor in the field of space activities should reflect the concerns of planetary protection and develop a corresponding policy, be it on a national or on a regional basis.

All this, however, can only be complementary to the development of an internationally binding legal instrument. Given the universality of the issue, obviously, the best forum to work on a suitable text is COPUOS. The work done by COSPAR is invaluable in that context and it should be made use of to the largest extent possible. Furthermore, it would be useful not to content oneself with vague principles and intentions, but to also include supervisory mechanisms and efficient procedures in case of non-compliance.

Such a legal instrument might help to avoid scenarios as the well known one *H. G. Wells* evoked in his famous "War of the Worlds", the terrestrial and the extraterrestrial environment are worth some serious thoughts.

27 *I. Almár*, Protection of the lifeless environment in the solar system, IISL 2002, p 438.

IAC-03-IISL.1.07

THE SPACE SHUTTLE COLUMBIA AND THE LEGAL HIGH FRONTIER: POSSIBLE CLAIMS AND DEFENSES

Charles R. Lucy, Esq.,
Law Offices of Holland & Hart, LLP
Colorado Springs, Colorado, U.S.A.
(clucy@hollandhart.com)

Skip Smith, Esq.*
Law Offices of Sherman & Howard, LLP
Colorado Springs, Colorado, U.S.A.
(ssmith@sah.com)

ABSTRACT

When a major aerospace accident occurs, attention immediately focuses on causation to determine safety of flight issues. A secondary, but equally important, determination focuses on the question of liability. Such was the case in the wake of the space shuttle Columbia accident on February 1, 2003. The recently published Columbia Accident Investigation Report provides a roadmap for the safe return to flight of the space shuttle program, but also raises interesting liability questions. This paper attempts to address those issues as they relate to international law and the domestic law of the United States. Those laws raise difficult barriers to would-be claimants and pose serious questions for the assessment of liability in future cases.

*Member, IISL

INTRODUCTION

The recent release of the Columbia Accident Investigation Board (CAIB) report on August 26, 2003,[1] culminates a painful but necessary step in the return of NASA to manned space flight. Director O'Keefe has vowed to move forward by adopting the report as a blueprint for the safe and successful resumption of space shuttle operations.[2] However, while NASA looks forward, there are many problems from the past that remain unresolved, including the thorny issues surrounding a regrettable, but preventable disaster. These issues are further complicated because they involve overlapping considerations of international law under the Liability Convention, the substantive laws of the United States, including the Federal Tort Claims Act (FTCA) and the Federal Employees Compensation Act (FECA), and the myriad tort laws of up to 50 local state jurisdictions. This article will examine these legal cross currents and outline the legal hierarchy that may ultimately lead to their resolution.

THE COLUMBIA ACCIDENT INVESTIGATION BOARD REPORT

As might be expected, the CAIB report contains an exhaustive analysis of the physical and organizational causes of the Columbia crash. It describes in almost prosaic terms the anatomy of a disaster:

The physical cause of the loss of Columbia and its crew was a breach in the Thermal Protection System on the leading edge of the left wing. The breach was initiated by a piece of insulating foam that separated from the left bipod ramp of the External Tank and struck the wing in the vicinity of the lower half of Reinforced Carbon-Carbon panel 8 at 81.9 seconds after launch. During re-entry, this breach in the Thermal Protection System allowed superheated air to penetrate the leading-edge insulation and progressively melt the aluminum structure of the left wing, resulting in a weakening of the structure until increasing aerodynamic forces caused loss of control, failure of the wing, and breakup of the Orbiter.[3]

The problem of foam separation was well known to NASA officials prior to STS 107.[4] According to the CAIB report, foam loss occurred on more than 80% of the shuttle missions for which imagery was available to make such a determination.[5] In addition, foam loss similar to that which was observed during Columbia's last launch occurred in almost 10% of the observable cases.[6] These losses were tolerated by NASA despite design specifications precluding the shedding of debris during launch and pre-launch operations.[7] This phenomenon occurred so frequently that by the time of STS 107, it was regarded as a turnaround, or maintenance event, rather than a safety of flight issue.[8]

Various theories were advanced for this problem, from cryopumping[9] to cryoingestion[10] to subsurface defects[11] but no serious actions were taken to correct the problem. Only belatedly did NASA contractors attempt a limited effort to harden the Thermal Protection System to withstand greater impacts,[12] a solution designed to treat the symptom and not the disease.

The block of foam that separated from Columbia's external fuel tank on January 16, 2003 was 21 to 27 inches long, 12 to 18 inches wide and weighed approximately 1.67 pounds.[13] It struck Columbia's left wing in a tumbling motion at a relative speed of 400 to 600 miles per hour,[14] causing the damage that would lead to calamity on February 1, 2003. Unfortunately, the CAIB report was unable to isolate a single causative factor for this event:

Analysis of numerous separate variables indicated that none could be identified as the sole initiating factor of bipod foam loss. - The Board therefore concludes that a combination of several factors resulted in bipod foam loss.[15]

Specifically, the CAIB found:

Negligence on the part of NASA, Lockheed Martin, or United Space Alliance workers does not appear to have been a factor.[16]

In the Board's view, NASA's organizational culture and structure had as much to do with this accident as the External Tank foam.[17] That culture led to overconfidence on the part of NASA officials that resulted in an acceptance of risk as a cost of doing business without any meaningful analysis of the cumulative impact of those risks.[18] More tragically, that culture resulted in a failure to assess the extent of damage to the shuttle before its fateful re-entry.[19] In fact, the CAIB report documents no fewer than eight missed opportunities to do so.[20]

In the final analysis, and despite the Board's assertion that no one factor caused the debris impact problem, there is plenty of blame to go around for Columbia's catastrophic failure. One member of the CAIB, Brigadier General Duane Deal, felt so strongly about the safety issues uncovered during the Board's investigation that he issued his own "minority report"[21] which is certain to fuel additional controversy and potential litigation. Even the CAIB report itself hints at a certain tension bubbling just below the surface of the investigation when it refers to speculation by NASA scientists that foam installation defects attributable to private industry caused the foam separation which led to Columbia's end.[22] It is against this ominous background that an analysis of legal liability must take place.

THE INTERNATIONAL FRAMEWORK

The obvious starting point for any analysis of legal liability for the Columbia disaster is the Convention on International Liability for Damage Caused by Space Objects.[23] That document was negotiated for the purpose of creating:

...international rules and procedures concerning liability for damage caused by space objects and to ensure, in particular, the prompt payment under the terms of [the] Convention of a full and equitable measure of compensation to victims of such damage...[24]

Article I of the Convention provides a broad definition of damage to include loss of life, personal injury and property damage, and goes on to define a space object to include its component parts as well as the launch vehicle and the parts thereof[25]. Article II then states the well-known principle of the Convention that:

A launching state shall be absolutely liable to pay compensation for damage caused by its space object on the surface of the earth or to aircraft flight.[26]

Article III of the Convention then goes on to discuss liability for space collisions, placing liability upon a launching state only if its object strikes another space object due to its fault.[27]

The Convention carves out a large exception concerning liability in Article VII, exempting damage caused by space objects of a launching state to its own nationals or to foreign nationals participating in the operation of the space object.[28] This provision effectively bars recovery under the Convention by any of the seven astronauts aboard Columbia, including Israeli Colonel Ilan Ramon. Also exempted would be anyone on the ground in the Columbia flight path over Texas and Louisiana who came in contact with shuttle debris or experienced damage as a result of falling components. Thus, it appears that the only persons who would be able to file a claim under the Liability Convention would be non-U.S. citizens on the ground. While they still have time to file a claim under the Convention within its one-year statute of limitations,[29] the probabilities are remote that anyone will actually avail themselves of this international remedy.

REMEDIES UNDER U. S. LAW

If the international framework for recovery by U. S. plaintiffs is bleak, the picture under U. S. domestic law is not much better, at least with respect to Columbia's crew and their families. Although the Congress has established an elaborate compensation scheme for federal employees injured in the line of duty, including military personnel, that largesse comes with a price. That price tag is a virtual immunity from liability for the negligent acts of the federal government. Thus while the Federal Tort Claims Act,[30] provides for a limited waiver of federal sovereign immunity, that waiver does not apply to federal employees in general under the Federal Employees Compensation Act,[31] or to military personnel in particular under the Supreme Court doctrine enunciated in Feres v. United States.[32] In Feres, the Supreme Court held that a member of the armed forces could not sue the federal government for personal injuries, death, or property loss sustained "incident to service".[33] The latter term equates roughly to being in the line of duty, although a soldier need not be "on duty" for Feres to apply. The Court pointed to a number of reasons for this rule, including the peculiar and special relationship between the Government and members of its armed forces, the disadvantages faced by a soldier contemplating litigation, and the safety net of compensation and benefits available to members of the armed forces through such agencies as the Department of Veteran's Affairs.[34] Essentially, the same rule applies to federal civilian employees under FECA, which is their exclusive remedy for personal injury and death claims.[35] In a subsequent decision, the Supreme Court barred a government contractor sued by a service member from cross-claiming against the government for indemnification, Stencel Aero Engineering Corp v. United States.[36] This latter case effectively sealed the last chink in the armor of federal sovereign immunity against any and all liability claims arising from the injury or death of federal employees caused by the negligent acts of their employer.

The effect of the preceding discussion is that the heirs of USAF Colonel Rick Husband, Navy Commander William McCool, USAF Lieutenant Colonel Michael Anderson and Navy Captains Laurel Clark and David Brown would be barred from suing the federal government under the Feres doctrine, and NASA employee Kalpana Chawla would be barred by FECA. Ironically, the only shuttle passenger who might not be barred under the FTCA would be Israeli Colonel Ilan Ramon. However, as discussed below, he would face the same hurdles confronting non-federal employees who may have suffered debris-related damage/injuries on the ground. Another possible complication in this case would be the existence of a Status of Forces Agreement between the United States and Israel, which could preclude recovery by his surviving family members.

As mentioned above, the FTCA would apply to those injured by falling/fallen debris, including those participating in the recovery effort, assuming they are not employed by the federal government.[37] For these plaintiffs (and Colonel Ramon), the FTCA opens the door to possible liability claims, assuming that an administrative claim has first been filed within two years[38] and that any number of exceptions do not apply. Chief among these is the discretionary function exception, which provides that the FTCA's waiver of sovereign immunity does not apply to:

Any claim...based upon the exercise or performance or the failure to exercise or perform a discretionary function or duty on the part of a federal agency or an employee of the Government, whether or not the discretion involved be abused.[39]

This discretionary function exception to the waiver of sovereign immunity under the FTCA requires planning, rather than operational level activity,[40] and a demonstration by the federal government that (1) the function involved an element of choice and was not mandated by regulation, statute or policy requiring a particular course of action and (2) the discretionary nature of the function is of a kind that the exception was designed to shield.[41] Needless to say, the discretionary function exception to the FTCA can (and does) provide an exceptionally large loophole through which the federal government can escape liability under the Act. In addition, it is hard to imagine a more discretionary governmental function than space flight or the operation of a spacecraft such as the space shuttle. Notwithstanding, there is one other avenue of recovery that may not require a prospective plaintiff to rebut a discretionary function claim by the government if negligence of a government contractor can be demonstrated. Even this avenue of recovery has become difficult to pursue due in part to the same discretionary function exception discussed above.

THE CIVILIAN CONTRACTOR DEFENSE

For many years, federal employee plaintiffs were able to obtain some relief from the limitations of the FTCA and FECA by suing civilian contractors who created the dangerous condition or instrumentality that led to their death or injury. However, that avenue of recovery was narrowed substantially in Boyle v. United Technologies Corp.[42] In that case, the Supreme Court found a limited immunity for government contractors under the discretionary function exception of the FTCA:

Liability for design defects in military equipment cannot be imposed, pursuant to state law, when (1) the United States approved reasonably precise specifications; (2) the equipment conformed to those specifications; and (3) the supplier warned the United States about the dangers in the use of the equipment that were known to the supplier but not to the United States.[43]

The Boyle Court explained its reasoning in the following terms:

...It makes little sense to insulate the Government against financial liability [under the FTCA] for the judgment that a particular feature of military

equipment is necessary when the Government produces the equipment itself, but not when it contracts for the production.[44]

The presence of a significant federal interest in the program that initiated the contracting activity has been suggested as a fourth element of Boyle.[45] While this fourth "requirement" should be more properly understood in the context of whether federal law should pre-empt state law in a particular procurement context,[46] it was clear that the Boyle Court was concerned about the impact of state tort lawsuits on the national defense.

In arriving at its decision, the Court implicitly recognized that the government contractor defense would not apply to commercial, off the shelf, items for which there was no government input.[47] The active participation of a contractor in the design process, however, would not preclude assertion of the defense, especially where the design selection reflected a "significant policy judgment" by the government.[48] In the view of at least one commentator, this could apply to every situation in which design specifications are incorporated into a government contract.[49] That same commentator observed that the defense would apply to any person injured by a defective product purchased by the government, and that it would not be limited strictly to defense related products.[50]

In the years since Boyle was decided, however, the question as to whether the government contractor defense applies to non-defense, as well as defense, contractors remains unresolved.[51] Obviously, such a determination could be significant, since NASA is a non-DOD, civilian agency of the federal government.[52] While noting that the federal circuits are split on the issue, several commentators have argued persuasively that the defense should not be extended beyond noncommercial military products.[53] They point to the Boyle Court's reference to "military equipment" in its holding and note the majority's concern that state tort law will be used to "second guess" military decisions and that defense contractors will raise their prices to the government in order to cover their increased liability.[54] The Court may have also signaled a reluctance to extend Boyle in its decision in Hercules, Inc. v. United States.[55] In that case, certain contractors involved in making Agent Orange for the Department of Defense sought to apply the government contractor defense through an implied indemnification theory.[56] However, the Court refused to extend the defense that far and, as in Stencel Aero, preserved the immunity of the United States from collateral attack by civilian contractors found to be liable to civilian plaintiffs.[57]

In addition to the non-DOD argument discussed above, various theories have been suggested to circumvent the holding in Boyle. The most obvious involve a frontal assault on the three pronged test enunciated in Boyle.[58] Frankly, these may be the most productive avenues of attack for a prospective plaintiff, especially where the government specification is not precise or the contractor deviates from that specification in a way that is not approved by the government. However, if the government accepts a known deviation, the contractor may again escape liability.[59] This may be of great significance in the Columbia disaster where NASA accepted a known problem with foam separation without seeking meaningful corrections from the manufacturer. In addition, as the federal procurement system leans more and more toward the purchase of commercial, off the shelf items, the defense could lose some of its vitality. Still, it is hard to procure tanks, aircraft and submarines, including their components, off the shelf. Thus, Boyle will probably retain its potency with respect to many government procurement actions.

Some commentators have suggested asserting liability under state tort law requirements that impose a duty to warn potential users of hazardous products.[60] However, one wonders how such warnings would be of any utility when combined with the inherently dangerous instrumentalities of war or space flight. At least one court has noted that a military member injured in a weapon system failure could hardly have refused to use the system based upon some hypothetical safety warning on the device.[61] Other courts, however, have allowed plaintiffs to prove their case.[62]

Commentators have also suggested asserting claims based on a failure by the manufacturer to incorporate obvious safety features into a design.[63] The trade-offs implicit in the production of any complex piece of equipment such as the space shuttle, however, involve precisely the kinds of discretionary decisions that the FTCA and Boyle were designed to protect. In fact, the Boyle Court itself recognized "...the trade-off between greater safety and greater combat effectiveness."[64]

THE FUTURE

While the CAIB report provides a comprehensive roadmap for the recovery of the space shuttle program, it also opens some interesting possibilities for recoveries of another kind. These include monetary awards from personal injury lawsuits based upon negligent space shuttle design issues, the negligent manufacture of shuttle components, and failure to comply with government-furnished specifications.

As discussed above, there are many hurdles that must be overcome before a successful lawsuit can be maintained, assuming that any of these circumstances can be proven. In the final analysis, however, all parties recognize that space flight is an inherently dangerous activity. In this regard, Congress has seen fit to provide for the indemnification of users of space vehicles, including the space shuttle, for death, bodily injury or property loss/damage to the extent that such claims are not compensated by the liability insurance of the user.[65] In fact, United Space Alliance, which is a joint venture formed by Lockheed and Boeing to conduct space shuttle maintenance and launch operations, has such an indemnity agreement in place.[66] It should also be noted that the families of the victims themselves may be reluctant to sue out of a sense of loyalty and respect.[67] And Congress may step in directly, having set a compensation precedent in the wake of the September 11, 2001 terrorist attack on the World Trade Center towers. Whatever the source, there will be compensation for the families of the brave crew of Columbia, not necessarily because it's legal, but because it's the right thing to do. However, the most meaningful way to "compensate" the Columbia crew and their families will be NASA's safe and responsible return to manned space flight in the near future.

3130397_1.DOC

Notes

[1] Columbia Accident Investigation Board Report, Volume 1, August 2003 [hereinafter cited as CAIB Report].
[2] *Aviation Week and Space Technology*, Vol. 159, No. 9, September 1, 2003, p. 22.
[3] CAIB Report, *supra*, at 49.
[4] *Id.* at 121. STS 107 is the mission designation for Columbia's 28th, and final, flight.
[5] *Id.* at 53.
[6] *Id.*
[7] *Id.* at 122.
[8] *Id.* at 130.
[9] *Id.* at 53. "Cryopumping" involves the freezing/liquification of air that seeps beneath the foam and is trapped in voids at or near the surface of the liquid oxygen and liquid hydrogen tanks. After launch, as propellant levels decrease and aerodynamic heating occurs, the trapped air can boil away or evaporate, building up pressure beneath the foam. This rapid increase in subsurface pressure could cause the foam to break away from the External Tank.
[10] *Id.* "Cryoingestion" involves the same fluid mechanics as "cryopumping" except that the fluid involved is gaseous nitrogen which may seep from the intertank, which is filled with nitrogen during tanking operations.
[11] *Id.* at 52-53.
[12] *Id.* at 130. The material used to improve impact resistance of space shuttle tiles suffers from a higher thermal conductivity than normal tiles and is therefore of limited utility.
[13] *Id.* at 59; *Aviation Week and Space Technology*, *supra*, at 23.
[14] CAIB Report at 59-60.
[15] *Id.* at 55.
[16] *Id.* at 53.
[17] *Id.* at 177.
[18] *Id.* at 139.
[19] *Id.* at 169.
[20] *Id.* at 140.
[21] CAIB Report, Appendix.
[22] CAIB Report at 52. Similar concerns were expressed at the factory that built the fuel tanks in question, Garcia, Kidwell and Greene, *Michoud Space Center to Come Under Scrutiny in Shuttle Probe*, The Miami Herald, February 16, 2003.
[23] U.N. Convention on International Liability for Damage Caused by Space Objects, March 29, 1972, 961 U.N.T.S. 187 (entered into force September 1, 1972) [hereinafter cited as Liability Convention].
[24] Liability Convention, Preamble.
[25] *Id.* at Article I.
[26] *Id.* at Article II.
[27] *Id.* at Article III.
[28] *Id.* at Article VII.
[29] *Id.* at Article X.
[30] 28 U.S.C. §§ 1291, 1346(b) and (c), 1402(b), 2401(b), 2402, and 2671-80.
[31] 5 U.S.C. §§ 8101-8193.
[32] 340 U.S. 135 (1950).
[33] *Id.* at 146.
[34] Id. at 143, 145.
[35] 5 U.S.C. 8116. The same rule applies for non-appropriated fund employees under the Longshore and Harbor Workers' Compensation Act, 5 U.S.C. § 8173; 33 U.S.C. §§ 910-50.
[36] 431 U.S. 666 (1977).
[37] An interesting problem is presented by the various volunteers who participated in the search and recovery effort in that their volunteer status may or may not confer rights (and bar recovery) under FECA. The receipt of these so-called "gratuitous" services by the federal government must generally be approved in advance and include a waiver of any right to compensation. The ban on the receipt of volunteer services has numerous exceptions, including emergency situations involving the safety of human life or the protection of property, 31 U.S.C. § 1342.
[38] 28 U.S.C. §§ 2675 and 2401(b).
[39] 28 U.S.C. § 2680(a).
[40] Dalehite v. United States, 346 U.S. 15, 42 (1953).
[41] Black Hills Aviation, Inc. v. United States, 34 F.3d 968 (10th Cir. 1994).
[42] 487 U.S. 500 (1988).
[43] *Id.* at 512.
[44] *Id.*
[45] Wagner, *Note: Tate v. Boeing Helicopters: Government Contractors Increasingly At Risk Despite the Government Contractor Defense*, 23 N. Ky. L. Rev. 377, 384 (Spring 1996).

[46] Loy, *Note: The Government Contractor Defense: Is It a Weapon Only for the Military?*, 83 Ky. L.J. 505, 512 (1994).
[47] *See*, Cantu and Young, *The Government Contractor Defense: Breaking the Boyle Barrier*, 62 Alb. L. Rev. 403, 421.
[48] Boyle, *supra*, at 513.
[49] Nash & Cibinic, *The Government Contractor Defense: The Supreme Court Expands Protection*, 2 N&CR ¶48 (August 1988).
[50] *Id.*
[51] Seidelson, *From Feres v. United States to Boyle v. United Technologies Corp.: An Examination of Supreme Court Jurisprudence and a Couple of Suggestions*, 32 Duq. L. Rev.219, 264 (Winter, 1994).
[52] 42 U.S.C. § 2472.
[53] Loy, *supra*; Townsend, *Comment: Ambulance Chasers Beware: Carley v. Wheeled Coach and the Questionable Expansion of the Government Contractor Defense*, 78 Minn. L. Rev. 1545 (June, 1994).
[54] Loy, *supra*, at 514-515.
[55] 516 U.S. 417 (1996)
[56] *Id.*
[57] *Id.*
[58] *See*, Cantu and Young, *supra*.
[59] Landgraf v. McDonnell Douglas Helicopter Co., 993 F.2d 558 (6th Cir. 1993). In effect, acceptance of the deviation by the government constitutes a de facto conformance with the specification.
[60] Wagner, *supra*, at 386.
[61] Quiles v. Sikorsky Aircraft, 84 F. Supp. 2d 154 (D. Mass. 1999).
[62] Oliver v. Oshkosh Truck Corp., 96 F.3d 992 (7th Cir. 1996).
[63] Wagner, supra, at 401-404.
[64] Boyle, supra, at 511. The Boyle Court, however, did hint that under the right circumstances a state requirement for certain safety features not in conflict with federal specifications might not trigger pre-emption under Boyle. *Id.* at 509.
[65] 42 U.S.C. 2458b.
[66] Berman, *The Legal Cleanup: Lawyers Consider Issues Stemming From Crash of Space Shuttle Columbia*, 89 A.B.A.J. 19 (August, 2003).
[67] Johnson, *Shuttle Contractors May Face Liability Suits; But Contract and Court Ruling Could Prevent Repeat of Challenger's $10 Million in Settlements*, The Washington Post, February 4, 2003, p. El.

LEGAL PARAMETERS OF SPACE TOURISM

Lesley Jane Smith[(1)] & Kay-Uwe Hörl[(2)]

[(1)] *Prof. Dr., LL.M, Hanse Law School, Bremen, Germany, ljsmith@barkhof.uni-bremen.de*
[(2)] *D.C.L. & LL.M. (McGill), EADS Astrium GmbH, 81663 Munich, Germany, Kay.Uwe.Hoerl@astrium.eads.net*

ABSTRACT

The commercial concept of space tourism raises important legal issues not specifically addressed by first generation rules of international space law. The principles established in the nineteen sixties and seventies were inspired by the philosophy that exploration of space was undertaken by and for the benefit of mankind. Technical developments since then have increased the potential for new space applications, with a corresponding increase in commercial interest in space. If space tourism is to develop, legal and regulatory mechanisms should take into account changes in perception about space travel and its control.

This paper briefly traces the generational transition from manned flights with astronauts to new cooperative space projects which could become a realistic platform for space tourism. It demonstrates where regulation is necessary and highlights current international structures in the moves toward furthering space tourism as a viable, regulated, even if exclusive, market.

INTRODUCTION

Space tourism – although in its infancy – is a reality[1]. The past two years have been witness to the ascent of the first two non-professional "space tourists". Space tourism may, however, be less than it appears. Generally it is limited to sub-orbital activities such as gravitational experiences with parabolic flights or training packages with astronaut-like preparation[2]. Although it rarely takes place in space at all, the term is not a misnomer. Adventure tourism is a growth market and the opportunities available at present merely serve to nourish the client crave for "real" space tourism.

Nevertheless, despite the two genuine tourists referred to subsequently in this paper, space activities to date have taken only about 400 people into space[3]. More adventure-inspired people would travel into space if it were to become an affordable exercise. Interest in space travel will rise as it decreases in cost and this has not remained unnoticed. Work is already underway on the development and construction of flight elements for space tourists. After initial market evaluation, EADS Space Transportation GmbH carried out feasibility studies for a space hotel. It is now developing a six-passenger, re-usable transport vehicle, dubbed "Hopper"[4]. These efforts may eventually lead to the "space-coaster", a vehicle capable of carrying up to 12 amateur travellers that could take space tourism into a new era[5].

Nevertheless, discussions about passenger vessels such as the space coaster reinforce the need for an assessment as to what, if any, regulatory provisions governing space activities and applications can or do apply to these new forms of (ad)venture. It is for this very reason that space tourism poses a challenge to the regulatory community at international and national level. Space law, as an intermix of treaty and customary principles of international law, and to a certain extent, national regulation, is progressively interrelated with various other branches of private law, as a result of increasing commercialisation and presence of the private sector in space.

After briefly discussing the current interaction and approach of the private and public sector in space tourism (I), this paper focuses on the legal and policy considerations that determine its viability from a substantive point of view (II). It identifies those areas where steps could and should be taken to propel space tourism into the realms of legally regulated space activity (III). It concludes by summarising conceivable structural developments (IV).

I. CURRENT APPROACH

The immediate success *in tourist terms* of the space missions undertaken by Dennis Tito (USA, aged 60) on 6 May 2001, followed by Mark Shuttleworth (South Africa, aged 28) is based on two significant factors. *Firstly*, both individuals were in such favourable financial circumstances as to be able to afford to fund their travel. While the exact sums themselves are irrelevant, it is important to note that they are beyond the reach of any average tourist. *The second*, and possibly *most significant*, factor was the form of transport used for the missions. Both space tourists were taken aboard the Soyuz taxi to the International Space Station (ISS). The Soyuz taxi is currently the only operational vehicle that meets the accepted criteria for passenger transportation, in this case, to the ISS. Furthermore, the ISS is currently the only realistic destination for such periods of human life in space. The limited capacity of states and private companies at present to provide alternative space transport and life facilities means that today development of the tourist sector is effectively linked to the use of Soyuz. This in turn is of immediate relevance to the Russian space programme[6].

The tourist voyages mentioned were also of *regulatory* importance: Tito and Shuttleworth acted as a personal interface in a sphere traditionally regulated with a very different objective in mind[7]. Space tourism is a side-product of what began as an exercise between nation states to regulate objectives of principle, under the auspices of UNCOPOUS, such as non-appropriation but peaceful exploration of outer space and its celestial bodies, international responsibility of launching states for activities in outer space, alongside centralising the UN Secretary General's role as coordinator and disseminator of information on a state's activities in outer space[8]. The Outer Space Treaty 1967 outlines clear principles of cooperation and mutual assistance, particularly towards astronauts[9].

Space tourists are referred to in common parlance as "astronauts", or more correctly "cosmonauts" when travelling on Russian spacecrafts. However, international space treaties afford certain privileges to "astronauts", this making it questionable whether space tourists are entitled to the same treatment[10]. Until 2001 manned space missions since Gagarin's flight[11] were state and/or agency operated and funded. The first space tourists have thus begged the question of direct regulation of space tourism by setting out on their space venture ahead of tailor-made tourist rules. At the same time, these voyages have thrown light on the potential of privately funded space tourism as a new source of subsidies for national human space programmes[12]

The interaction between rules of public international and national law complicates regulation of space tourism. The advent of a new era of space activities within the ISS framework has led to development of ideas for developing commercial use of the station which in turn have led to ideas for developing space tourism. The main framework for the ISS is regulated in the Intergovernmental Agreement (IGA)[13]. The IGA is a multilateral agreement between European partners (represented by ESA), NASA, Canada Japan and Russia on utilisation and the operation of the ISS[14]. It constitutes a source of obligations binding upon the state parties to it and is designed to encourage cooperation between partners on the ISS, while taking its evolutionary capabilities ISS into account[15].

The IGA specifically refers to the operation of the ISS within the primary law framework of international space treaties[16]. It is supplemented by four MOU's that contain rules relevant to cooperation, operational and commercial exploitation of the ISS[17]. In this context, space law relating to ISS operations contains rules of "soft law": the reliance on governmental agreements and codes or *modus operandi* in situations where peremptory rules neither apply nor exist. Space tourism is still in the process of developing and is governed by rules that are binding, cooperative and evolutionary in one.

It is precisely this evolutionary character of space law that should not be forgotten. The rules governing space activities are not yet comparable to those in the maritime or air transport sectors, where national statutes implementing international conventions have led to a unification of law between states.

National space legislation is still progressively developing in various countries, but there is not yet a harmonised or homogeneous body of effective, justiciable space rules at national level[18].

If commercial interests, including space tourism, are to flourish, continued thought will have to be given to the legal structure and enforcement mechanisms that surround commercial space law and dispute resolution. Dispute resolution systems for international trade conflicts between states[19] or between entities[20] are already in existence. The growth of commercial interests in space may lead to an increase in *acta iure gestionis* as seen from an international law perspective. At present, the IGA contains foresees consultation as the chosen method of communication between Cooperating Agencies. In the event of inability to reach agreement between the partners, the IGA contains provisions on dispute resolution[21]. This conciliatory approach reinforces the commercial character of the partners within the ISS framework. It marks a move away from classical dispute settlement between states under international law procedures under the jurisdiction of the International Court of Justice towards international commercial dispute settlement.

II. FROM STATE TO STATUS

The paradox of space tourism is one of status. The Outer Space Treaty defines astronauts as envoys of mankind and installs a code of mutual assistance in case of emergency[22]. The status of professional astronauts on mission is directly linked to that of their national or registering state[23]. The concept, and indeed status, of a space tourist is technically lacking, in that it was not the intention of the treaty makers to cater for this group. Unlike the astronaut, there is no immediate element of rights and duties in relation to a tourist. Space tourists are individuals, who do not represent their countries for research or scientific purposes. This has led to suggestions in support of the term *spaceflight participants*[24]. The private civilian status of space tourists is indisputable. However, space law has not yet installed a definitional model such as that contained in the Chicago Convention, where "crew" are linked to qualification and licensing requirements[25] and passengers are left to the realms of provisions on international carrier liability[26].

The need to adapt the current legal regime to accommodate private law elements that ensue with increasing private interests and activities in space is recognised and Article VI Outer

Space Treaty already foresees that activities be carried on by non-governmental entities. This process of adaptation must extend to procedures for commercial entities and space tourists alike. A distinct selection procedure relating to the qualification of a tourist permitted to travel in flight is needed[27]. Its equivalent already exists for professional expedition crew members[28]. The rules on qualification and suitability of ISS crew currently foresee nomination by the partner state and certification of general suitability towards the Multi-Crew Operation Panel (MCOP). Considerations such as health, compliance with the ISS Code of Conduct (CCOC) and further pre-requisites such as (foreign) language capabilities must be installed for the tourist.

An overview of space legislation reflects a relational imbalance between the public international and private law content of space law. Approximately one third of space law deals exclusively with public international law norms. The remaining two thirds deal with "earth-based principles" as extended to space activities, such as tort, contract, and property, as influenced by national and possibly international policy considerations[29]. This reinforces the increasing public / private interface of space law.

One of the most pervasive issues within this debate is whether national rules on specific earth-related matters[30] automatically extend to space. This has been addressed by the IGA in relation to the ISS where there is a co-existence of the five legal systems of its five partners. Art. 5 IGA repeats the jurisdiction of partners over their property in space, leading to this co-existence of national rules.

Today's objective is to interlink the private commercial sphere of space into the existing environment of public international law rules. These new market parameters demand the development of an optimal regulatory approach that will

- encourage commercial activity in space, including space tourism,
- adjust the public international law regime to allocate responsibility and supervision to the correct authorities (i.e. not just states),
- ensure parallel regulation as between states within the international community.

These points are taken up below.

III. NORMATIVE RULES FOR SPACE TOURISM

An optimal legal regime for commercial space tourism and utilisation of space must address the following issues:

- Rules of Liability in the event of accidents to private persons and property
- Rules for regulation of commercial vehicles and safety of missions
- Permissible interaction between operations and tourists

The UN space conventions, as previously indicated, do address some of these matters[31], but not from a commercially inspired perspective[32]. The provisions applicable in the event of liability and the permissible remit of tourist's activities must be clear. Licensing procedures for space vehicles must be established. It is perfectly conceivable and may be psychologically important that a space tourist be allowed to undertake useful tasks such as space life experiments while in flight. Shuttleworth, for example, performed experiments for three South African universities during his visit of the ISS. This raises potential issues of participation in intellectual property rights. The legal issues involved in space tourism are therefore addressed under the following five headings:

- registration, jurisdiction and control over space tourists (*Flight personnel*)
- regulatory framework for commercial space vehicles

- use of ISS for commercial services
- liability and insurance
- participation in intellectual and Industrial property rights (experiments).

Registration, jurisdiction and control over space personnel

Treaty rules as reiterated by the IGA cover registration and jurisdiction of objects in space. Both the IGA and Memorandum of Understanding (MOU) specify that the IGA should be operated in the spirit of these treaties. Art. II.1 Registration Convention imposes an obligation on member states to register their vehicles or objects launched into space[33]. Art. VIII Outer Space Treaty in conjunction with Art. II.2 Registration Convention, provides that launch partners retain jurisdiction and control over elements Registered and over personnel on the ISS who are its nationals. A state also retains jurisdiction over the "personnel" on the space object.

Space tourists may not fall within the meaning of *personnel* in terms of either the IGA or the Outer Space Treaty. "Personnel" is a specific term relating to official status of employees/ or persons with an official remit. The term is not neutral in the sense of "person". Nevertheless, within the ISS regime, a state extends the applicability of its national space legislation to nationals in outer space, whether crew, personnel or merely flight participants/passengers[34].

The mutual exercise of criminal jurisdiction on board is regulated under Art. 22 IGA, thereby ensuring partners' jurisdiction over their nationals in case of misconduct on board and in order to ensure the safety of the mission.[35]

The combined effect of these provisions in relation to space tourism is that the Russian state retains jurisdiction and control over the Soyuz rocket and personnel. It therefore has jurisdiction over the commercial astronaut/space tourist within the Russian-registered elements. The net result for orbital space tourism[36] is that criminal offences on the ISS can be sufficiently prosecuted, be it by the state of the perpetrator or by other ISS partner states. This may serve as a good model when devising a criminal liability scheme for space tourism.

Regulatory framework for commercial space vehicles

The importance of maintenance and safety regulation for space vehicles is self-evident[37]. Paradoxically, there are no legal provisions in the body of international space law governing safety of passenger launch vehicles. Nevertheless, international aviation rules could serve as a useful prototype when considering how to regulate this area.

An international aviation regulatory framework has operated under the auspices of the International Civil Aviation Organisation (ICAO) since 1945[38]. Any regulatory system for commercial space vehicles must be international in application to ensure global parity of standards. A parallel *modus operandi* to that of the ICAO for commercial space activities would seem a realistic and optimal goal for space tourist operations[39].

The US Federal Aviation Administration (FAA)[40] has already taken the lead by proposing the formation of an International Space Flight Organisation (ISFO) to mirror the ICAO. It is expected that other countries will respond to this initiative by creating a framework that will promote public safety. Certain states have already gone so far as to establish their own rules for introducing licensing procedures for commercially operated re-usable space vehicles. America[41] has gone down this road and Japan has established research committees to examine the question of commercial space transportation legislation[42]. Progress in this area will encourage other states to follow suit.

As mentioned at the outset, the Russian Soyuz spacecraft is the only carrier that meets the criteria for passenger transportation. ESA and the Russian Space Agency Rosaviakosmos had signed a framework agreement on terms for cooperating on the ISS in May 2001, thereby allowing European astronauts to access the ISS. Compliance with safety standards for space vehicles, qualifications of space specialists from pilot to mechanic, the regulation of space ports and navigational aids, air traffic control and operational rules such as refuelling facilities, storage, mining plant and equipment *etc.* are all contained in the specific agreements. Imposing regulation on the private sphere permits launching states to retain licensing control over commercial enterprises, and thereby tourists. Technical and safety rules, rules for redress alongside enforcement mechanisms are paramount to the success of commercial operations and private law relations.

Use of ISS for commercial services

The current phase of space philosophy looks towards regulating space life on a more permanent basis. Art. 1(1) IGA confirms the aim "... to establish long-term international cooperative framework ....for the design of a permanent inhabited civil International Space Station ...". Commercial use of the ISS is by no means prohibited and the partners[43] have reached agreement in principle on its commercial use for space tourists. Guidelines drafted by ISS Cooperating Agencies are already in existence[44]. The Multilateral Coordination Board (MCB) formulated rules for the road covering the long-term "expedition missions" to the ISS as well the short-term "taxi missions" which are required to replace the Russian escape vehicle.

These soft law rules are of primary significance in relation to space tourism. They regulate matters mentioned previously ranging from selection of space flight participants (including training pre-requisites), prescribe commercial use of ISS in the form of merchandising, advertising and entertainment, and latterly contain rules relating to conduct for the ISS crew.

For example, concerning the short-term tourist it is US and Russian space agencies that nominate tourists for a ride in the Space Shuttle and the Soyuz spacecraft, respectively. In contrast and with regard to long-term visitors, it is the Multilateral Crew Operation Panel (MCOP) that approves nominated tourists. It should also be recalled that in terms of the deal between ESA and Rosaviakosmos, the third seat on the Soyuz can theoretically be sold to non-professional (and thus fee-paying) passengers. Due to the Columbus disaster, however, it will be Soyuz that has to rotate the permanent ISS crews. Therefore, the agreement to fly European astronauts and tourists with the so-called taxi crews may not be fully implemented and tourist flights to the ISS may be suspended for the time being.

Further provisions deal with scientific research and development on the ISS. The guidelines offer at least an initial framework within which tourism can be operated. Generally, these rules demonstrate more negotiated frameworks rather than substantive legal rules. To acquire individual direct effect these provisions would necessitate implementation at national level[45].

Liability and insurance

Realisation of commercial ventures in space requires a pragmatic attitude to costs and mitigation of liability. There are two major rules that dominate the approach taken to liability:

- National law governs harm caused by space objects to those states co-operating in the space endeavour and to the nationals of those co-operating states, but
- International law (Liability Convention) governs harm caused by space objects to those states not engaged in a common endeavour.

In view of the mission costs and the corresponding level of liability when accidents occur, waivers of liability and insurance coverage go hand in hand with any space venture. Art. 16 IGA accordingly contains a cross-waiver of liability between the partners. Its purpose is to encourage participation in exploration, exploitation and use of outer space through the ISS, while achieving a reduction in insurance costs. Insurance is only required for commercial ventures in those fields where the cross-waiver does not apply. The cross-waiver applies to "partners involved in protected space operations" as against

- another partner state,
- a related entity of another partner state, and
- employees of any of the entities of another partner state and of a related entity of another partner state.

Effectively, each partner state can extend a cross-waiver of liability to its related entities by requiring subsequent waivers for all claims as against all persons, entities and related entities and persons.

Insurance is necessary for the areas excluded from cross-waiver. These are:

- claims between the partner state and its own entities or related entities
- claims by natural persons and their estates for death, damage or impairment of health
- claims for damage caused by wilful conduct[46]
- intellectual property claims
- claims for damage resulting from a failure of a partner state to extend the cross-waiver of liability to its related entities.

None of the foregoing affects the liability as provided in accordance with the Liability Convention (Art. 17 IGA with reference to Art. 16). Where a claim arises out of the Liability Convention, the partners and ESA will consult on apportionment or defence, as may be necessary.

To conclude: commercial enterprises are relieved of high insurance costs where cross-waivers are involved. Nevertheless the question of general liability for damage to persons and third parties remains an open issue to be addressed by national agencies/ NGOs[47]. There are certainly possibilities for developing insurance consortia with umbrella insurance provisions to cover such liabilities.

In the sphere of insurance, various practicalities come into play. Firstly, insurance policies, whether for life, medical care or accident insurance, loss of revenue *etc.* must cover the space activity in question. Secondly, insurance should cover not only individual damage or illness to the tourist, but also third party liability insurance of the mission/space flight.

This means that specific space insurance must be taken out to cover the individual activity, whether for the commercial operator or individual. The insurance market is already developing to cope with these demands. Certainly, life insurance policies were made available to both space tourists Tito and Shuttleworth via the Russian insurance companies, Avikos and Megaruss respectively[48].

Intellectual and industrial property rights

Of immediate interest for the space tourist is the right to undertake certain beneficial experiments while in space flight. Opportunities for space tourists to assist in flight experiments are certainly conceivable. Whether this takes on the form of any more than assisting in experiments or acquisition of intellectual or industrial rights deserves some attention.

Art. 21(2) IGA contains territorial rules whereby results of experiments are deemed to have occurred in the territory of the partner state that registered that element in which the experiments took place. If the activity takes place on ESA registered elements, a European partner may deem the activity to have occurred within its territory. There are provisions preventing recovery for infringement of intellectual property rights in more than one European partner state. This is to prevent duplicity of actions resulting from infringements relating to the same property right.

In effect, these provisions mean that results achieved by commercial astronauts and space tourists are protected within the IGA framework. Further details of attribution of ownership vis-à-vis a tourist who is merely carrying out experiments during flight on behalf of a commercial entity would require to be dealt with on a contractual basis.

Finally, it should be noted that, within the framework of the IGA, partners may sell or barter any of their allocations under the utilisation provisions of Art. 9(2) IGA[49]. This effectively entitles exchange of utilisation space in which additional experiments can be carried out.

IV. CONCLUSIONS AND OUTLOOK

There is a distinct need for further regulatory structure within the ISS era if space tourism is to become anything more than a gravitational adventure. The current regime governing human spaceflight reflects its historical origins that developed from the "envoy of mankind" vision of an astronaut. Regulation of space tourism is operated by analogy to the rules constituted, in particular, for ISS operations. They indeed mark a great degree of international cooperation between the partners involved. Their emphasis on multilateral regulation via the IGA, governmental understandings and guidelines, backed up by soft law agreements, such as the Code of Conduct for Crew (CCOC) are effective for such major international projects.

More specific regulation will be needed in the long term to ensure that commercial operations are under control. A *modus operandi*, detailing the finer terms and conditions under which tourists may join spaceflights, can only develop within a distinct framework. This pre-supposes national space legislation directly addressing specific aspects currently regulated in Codes. The next immediate level between the licensed commercial operators and individuals belongs to rules of contract law. Such contracts would have to comply with primary treaty law and include strict adherence to the codes of conduct and ISS operational structure.

Nevertheless, if commercial activities are to increase, it would appear reasonable to develop a structure that is similar to that achieved for air space activities over land. This current ISS era provides a perfect time for both the international space community and the partner states of the ISS to look towards the next regulatory phase. By that stage, the national legislator will have provided a suitable legal basis from which private space tourist contracts, even if not very common, are subject to legal control.

REFERENCES

[1] Market forecasts predict that, by 2021, commercial space travel could amount to an industry worth US$ 1 Billion. See Futron Corporation, *Space Tourism Market Study* (2002).

[2] *E.g.* centrifuge rides, training in the neutral buoyancy tank or mission simulations in a Soyuz simulator in Star City.

[3] The Economist, 30 August 2003 at 9. The cost to the tax payer has not been quantified here.

[4] See "Astrium Explores Challenge of Outer Space Tourism". See Space Daily, online: <www.spacedaily.com/news/tourism-00a.html> (date accessed: 27 September 2003).

[5] Even more developments are taking place in the US. For different concepts of commercial space transportation with relevance to space tourism in the US see especially FASS/AST, *2003 U.S. Commercial Space Transportation Developments and Concepts: Vehicles, Technologies, and Spaceports* (2003). See FAA, online: <http://ast.faa.gov/files/pdf/newtech03_final.pdf > (date accessed: 27 September 2003).

[6] NASA did not originally construct the Shuttle with a view to serving tourist purposes. It appears due for re-certification in 2010. See The Economist, *supra* note 3.

[7] It came as no surprise that the US space agency, NASA, initially opposed any tourist trips to International Space Station, arguing that the presence of amateur tourists would endanger the ISS astronauts.

[8] The first generation of treaties and conventions comprises the following conventions: *Treaty on Principles Governing the Activities of States in the Exploration and Use of Outer Space, Including the Moon and Other Celestial Bodies*, 27 January 1967, 610 U.N.T.S. 205, 18 U.S.T. 2410, T.I.A.S. No. 6347, 6 I.L.M. 386 [hereinafter *Outer Space Treaty*] (entered into force on 10 October 1967); *Agreement on the Rescue of Astronauts, the Return of Astronauts and the Return of Objects Launched Into Outer Space*, 22 April 1968, 672 U.N.T.S. 119, 19 U.S.T. 7570, T.I.A.S. No. 6599, 7 I.L.M. 151 [hereinafter *Rescue Agreement*] (entered into force 3 December 1968); *Convention on the International Liability for Damage Caused by Space Objects*, 29 March 1972, 961 U.N.T.S. 187, 24 U.S.T. 2389, T.I.A.S. No. 7762 [hereinafter *Liability Convention*] (entered into force on 1 September 1972); *Convention on Registration of Objects Launched Into Outer Space*, 14 January 1975, 1023 U.N.T.S. 15, 28 U.S.T. 695, T.I.A.S. No. 8480, 14 I.L.M. 43 [hereinafter *Registration Convention*] (entered into force on 15 September 1976); *Agreement Governing the Activities of States on the Moon and other Celestial Bodies*, 5 December 1979, 1363 U.N.T.S. 3, 18 I.L.M. 1434 [hereinafter *Moon Agreement*] (entered into force 11 July 1984).

[9] Art. V Outer Space Treaty.

[10] Astronauts are considered to be envoys of all mankind and entitled to all possible assistance in case of accidents, distress, or emergency landing. See *ibid.* However, the space treaties neither contain a definition of this term, nor of the terms "envoys of mankind" and "personnel". It could be argued that a "space tourist" should not be afforded the same rights because the space treaties were drafted without knowing the concept of space tourism. However, Article VI Outer Space Treaty expressly allows private activities so that, *de lege lata*, the scope of the international space treaties should also cover space tourists even if this may not be suitable for the future of space tourism. See *infra* note 23. Some authors maintain that tourists have some traits of astronauts, though not all, and as such they can be called "pseudo astronauts". See R. Jakhu & R. Bhattacharya, "Legal Aspects of Space Tourism", IAC-02-IISL.2.09 (2002).

[11] Juri Gagarin became the first man in space on 12.04.1961, travelling in the "Wostok 1".

[12] This paper does not assess or evaluate the economic aspects of space tourism. Space activities are not cost-effective, with the result that development of the private commercial sphere is inhibited by regulatory aspects that do not (necessarily) apply to public activities. This point has been addressed elsewhere. See The Economist, *supra* note 3. See also Futron Corporation, *supra* note 1.

[13] See *Agreement among the Government of Canada, Governments of Member States of the European Space Agency, the Government of Japan, the Government of the Russian Federation, and the Government of the United States of America concerning cooperation on the Civil International Space Station*, 29 January 1998 [hereinafter IGA] (entered into force 27 March 2001).

[14] The European partners are Belgium, Denmark, France, Germany, Italy, Netherlands, Norway, Spain, Sweden, Switzerland and UK.

[15] Art. 14 IGA.
[16] Art. 2(1) IGA.
[17] The Memoranda of Understanding serve to involve the national space agencies and describe their respective roles and responsibilities with regard to design, development and operations of the ISS.
[18] For full texts of national space legislation see Office for Outer Space Affairs, online: <www.oosa.unvienna.org/SpaceLaw/national> (date accessed: 29 September 2003).
[19] Arts. 34-36 *Statute of the International Court of Justice*, 26 June 1945, 59 Stat. 1055, T.S. No. 993, regulate the Court's competence and jurisdiction; the WTO has its own dispute settlement panel. See *Understanding on Rules and Procedures Governing the Settlement of Disputes*, which is annex 2 of the *Agreement Establishing the World Trade Organization*. See WTO, online: <www.wto.org/english/docs_e/legal_e/legal_e.htm#dispute> (date accessed: 29 September 2003).
[20] *E.g.* the International Chamber of Commerce.
[21] Art. 23(4) IGA
[22] Art. V Outer Space Treaty. The *Rescue Agreement*, *supra* note 8, develops on these principles and gives expression to the duties contained in the Outer Space Treaty.
[23] The classification of "astronauts as envoys of mankind in outer space" in Art. V Outer Space Treaty is inappropriate for commercial travellers.
[24] Spaceflight participants are individuals (e.g. commercial, scientific and other programs; crewmembers of non-partner space agencies, engineers, scientists, teachers, journalists, filmmakers or tourists) sponsored by one or more partner(s). See Art. III of the *Principles Regarding Processes and Criteria for Selection, Assignment, Training and Certification of ISS (Expedition and Visiting) Crewmembers*, (2001). See SpaceRef, online: <www.spaceref.com/news/viewsr.html?pid=4578> (date accessed: 29 September 2003).
[25] See Art. 32 of the *Convention on International Civil Aviation*, 7 December 1944, 15 U.N.T.S. 295, ICAO Doc. 7300/6 [hereinafter *Chicago Convention*].
[26] See C. Sgrosso, "Legal Status of the Crew in the International Space Station IAC-99-IISL.1.07 (1999).
[27] See Art. 11 IGA on selection of crew by each ISS partner and compliance with Code of Conduct.
[28] For ISS-Crew criteria, see ESA, online: <www.esa.int/export/esaHS/ESA9L2G18ZC_astronauts_0.html > (date accessed: 29 September 2003).
[29] See W. Kowal, "Legal Pre-requisites", Astrium/ EADS Working Paper (2002) at 25.
[30] *E.g.* copyright protection laws.
[31] In particular, registration under the Registration Convention and absolute and fault based liability under the Liability Convention and Outer Space Treaty.
[32] The allocation of state responsibility under Art. VI Outer Space Treaty for all national activities in space, whether governmental or non-governmental entities, beleaguers states in cases of vicarious liability for private undertakings.
[33] The obligation extends to notifying the UN Secretary General of the same.
[34] See Art. 5(2) IGA.
[35] Canada, the European partners, Japan, Russia and the US have mutual rights to exercise criminal jurisdiction over their respective nationals in relation to personnel or any flight element.
[36] Sub-orbital space tourism should be covered by existing air law instruments. See *Convention on Offences and Certain Other Acts Committed on Board Aircraft*, 14 September 1963, ICAO Doc. 8364; *Convention for the Suppression of Unlawful Seizure of Aircraft*, 16 December 1970, ICAO Doc. 8920; *Convention for the Suppression of Unlawful Acts Against the Safety of Civil Aviation; Protocol for the Suppression of Unlawful Acts of Violence at Airports Serving International Civil Aviation, Supplementary to the Convention for the Suppression of Unlawful Acts Against the Safety of Civil Aviation, Done at Montreal on 23 September 1971*, 24 February 1988, ICAO Doc. 9518; *Convention on the Marking of Plastic Explosives for the Purposes of Detection*, 1 March 1991, ICAO Doc. 9571.
[37] A detailed discussion of such technical matters goes beyond the ambit of this paper. See generally ISU, *Space Tourism – From Dream to Reality*, Final Report of the Summer Session Program 2000 (Illkirch-Graffenstaden: ISU, 2000).
[38] ICAO was founded in November 1944 during an International Civil Aviation Conference in Chicago. Fifty-four States attended the conference and 32 States signed the Convention setting up ICAO. See *Chicago Convention, supra* note 26. Because of delays in the ratification of the Convention, the conference had signed an

Interim Agreement, creating a Provisional International Organization of a technical and advisory nature for collaboration in the field of international civil aviation (PICAO). It operated from August 1945 to April 1947 when ICAO finally became operational.

[39] Given that even orbital space tourism will use airspace prior to entering outer space and given that there is no right to overflight over national airspace, ICAO has to play a coordinative role for the launch and re-entry phase. See also *supra* note 36.

[40] In the US, legal uncertainty is arising from the regulatory treatment of Reusable Launch Vehicles (RLV), a prerequisite for successful space tourism in the future. Currently both, the Aircraft Certification and Regulations Office, entrusted with regulating the commercial airline industry, and the Associated Administrator for Commercial Space Transportation, in charge of expendable launcher, compete for jurisdiction over commercial space flight. On regulatory issues for space tourism see also P. H Diamandis & P. Collins, "Creation of an Accredited Passenger Regulatory Category for Space Tourism Services", Conference on Space Tourism (1999).

[41] The Associate Administrator for Commercial Space Transportation regulates the commercial space transportation industry under 49 U.S.C., Subtitle IX, Chapter 701. In the US, repeated attempts are made to foster commercial space activities. Two bills are currently before the US congress that aim at creating space related tax incentives. See *Bill to amend the Internal Revenue Code of 1986 to encourage the timely development of a more cost effective United States commercial space transportation industry, and for other purposes*, H.R. 2358, sponsors: Rep. Calvert [CA-44] (introduced 6/5/2003) and *Bill to amend the Internal Revenue Code of 1986 to provide tax incentives for investing in companies involved in space-related activities*, H.R.914, sponsor: Rep Rohrabacher, Dana [CA-46] (introduced 2/25/2003).

[42] See generally N. Sugita, "Amendment to the Law Concerning the National Space Development Agency of Japan" (Proceedings of the Project 2001 – Workshop on Legal Issues of Privatising Space Activities, Vienna, Austria, 19 July 1999) 118-125. For an overview on Japanese space legislation see M. Sato, "The Japanese Legal Framework: Third Party Liability Resulting From NASDA Launch Activities?" (1998) 41 Proceed. of Colloq. on L. of Outer Sp. 128-129. See also Kowal, *supra* note 29 at 19.

[43] The cooperation exists between USA, eleven member states of ESA, Canada, Japan and Russia, defined as "partner states".

[44] See *Principles Regarding Processes and Criteria for Selection, Assignment, Training and Certification of ISS (Expedition and Visiting) Crewmembers*, *supra* note 24.

[45] *E.g.* in Canada by the *Civil International Space Station Agreement Implementation Act* (1999, c.35).

[46] Generally, wilful misconduct is an insurance exclusion and its coverage would drastically increase premiums.

[47] For other aspects of financial responsibility relevant to space tourism see Dennis J. Burnett "Space Tourism: A New Opportunity to Manage the Risks" IAC-03-IISL.1.08 (2003).

[48] See Avicos, online: <www.avicos.ru/Main> (date accessed: 27 September 2003). See also <www.space.com/missionlaunches/shuttleworth_isurance_020208.html> All risks have been reinsured on the western market.

[49] Where non-partner states are involved, all partners must consent.

IAC-03-IISL.1.13

THE UNIDROIT CONVENTION ON INTERNATIONAL INTERESTS IN MOBILE EQUIPMENT AND THE PRELIMINARY DRAFT PROTOCOL ON MATTERS SPECIFIC TO SPACE ASSETS
-
WHAT SHOULD BE THE POSITION OF GERMANY IN RESPECT OF THE PROTOCOL AND IN PARTICULAR THE VARIOUS OPT-IN/OPT-OUT ALTERNATIVES CONSIDERING THE COMMERCIAL NEEDS AND LEGAL IMPLICATIONS?

Ingo Förster
University of Applied Sciences Lüneburg, Germany

ABSTRACT:
The shift from a state/government dependant to a commercially oriented industry and the global context of the space business require new ways to finance space equipment. This is also supported by the immense amount of financial resources that are involved in the space industry. In response to this trend, the International Institute for the Unification of Private Law (UNIDROIT), has elaborated a Convention on Mobile Equipment. As regards space equipment a group of international experts formed the "Space Working Group" and commenced drafting a protocol specific to space assets, which shall provide the legal frame for modern asset based financing. This paper provides economic and legal background information for the raison d'être of the Convention/Protocol and identifies its merits. The main focus is the comparison of the current draft Space Protocol with German Law, in particular the different opt-ins and opt-outs. Due to these options a state is given the opportunity to choose between certain provisions by way of declaration. The paper examines different options and offers recommendations from a German industrial point of view. In conclusion, it points out the compatibility of the Convention/Protocol with German law and underlines its importance for the German Space Industry. The significance of the Convention/Protocol may even increase in the future, when production in space and permanent space transport through reusable launch vehicles will be technically achieved.

1. A NEW INTERNATIONAL LEGAL REGIMEN FOR SPACE ASSETS:

The development from a state/government dependant to a commercially oriented space industry and the global context of the space business require new ways to finance space equipment. This is also supported by the immense amount of financial resources that are involved in the space industry. In response to this trend, UNIDROIT[1] has elaborated the "Convention on International Interests in Mobile Equipment", hereinafter referred to as the "Convention".[2] As regards space equipment, a group of international experts formed the "Space Working Group" (SWG) in 1997 and commenced drafting the "Protocol on Matters specific to Space Assets, hereinafter referred to as the "Protocol"[3], which shall provide the legal frame for modern asset based financing.

This paper refers to the draft Protocol after the Rome meeting of the Space Working Group dated January 2002, UNIDROIT

[1] UNIDROIT is the acronym of the International Institute for the Unification of Private Law. It is an independent intergovernmental organisation with a history reaching back to the year 1926. Its purpose is to study needs and methods for modernising, harmonising and co-ordinating private and in

[2] The full text of the Convention is available for download under http://www.unidroit.org

[3] The text of the current preliminary draft Protocol can be accessed via: http://www.unidroit.org/english/internationalinterests/draftspaceprotocol/72j-10-e.pdf

Doc. No. 10. The development of the Protocol is still an ongoing process.

2. BACKGROUND, MERITS AND STRUCTURE OF THE CONVENTION/PROTOCOL:

Before analysing the implications with German law, it is required to extract the relevant rationales and merits of the Convention/Protocol.

2.1 Economic Background:

The evolution of the international space industry shows a shift from a formerly state/government dependent to a more and more privatised industry. To a great extent the satellite industry is the motor of this privatisation process. Whilst during the times of cold war many satellites were used for military purposes, more and more of today's satellites are utilized commercially. The spectrum of modern satellite applications ranges from telephony and mobile services over internet access to television and radio broadcasting. Growing revenues and profit margins of the majority of satellite operators show the economic success and profitability of the satellite operating business.[4] From 1965 until the end of 2001 531 geostationary satellites were sold with an estimated value of 47.9 billion USD plus another 227 satellites worth 2.8 billion USD for low earth orbit constellations.[5]

However, after the Globalstar and Iridium disasters and due to an overcapacity in the telecommunication market, it became more difficult to obtain financial resources and the commercialisation process experienced a slow-down. In particular new satellite operators suffer from financing difficulties since many of them do not have the financial standing to be attractive for lenders. A shift from debtor-based to asset-based financing, as provided by the UNIDROIT initiative, would enable these operators to obtain the required resources giving lenders the opportunity to sell the respective assets in case the borrower is in default.

2.2. Legal Background:

Apart from the aforementioned economic background the UNIDROIT initiative has also a legal dimension. Many legal systems as regards security rights follow the rule "lex rei sitae" and apply the rules of the State where the asset is situated. Due to the international context of the space industry where a space asset during its construction phase may move across various national borders and due to the fact that space assets, once they are launched, are located in outer space and then beyond the jurisdiction of any State[6], this approach seems inappropriate for space assets.

2.3. The Convention and its two-tier approach:

In order to overcome the problems connected with high value assets passing national frontiers, UNIDROIT has elaborated the Convention, which was originally intended to cover various categories of movable assets. However, this plan was later abandoned in favour of a two-tier approach where all the general rules are contained in the Convention and the asset-specific rules are provided by the 3 respective protocols for aircraft equipment, railway rolling stock and space assets. The driving force behind this decision was the aviation industry, which

---

4 For revenues of satellite operators see Euroconsult: "Operating revenue of satellite operators 1998-2000", page 24; for profit margins see Euroconsult: "Profit margins of satellite service providers 1997-2000", page 28

5 See Euroconsult page 81; for a complete overview see Euroconsult "Commercial geostationary communication satellites: Past deliveries and estimated backlog of prime contractors, 1965-2001", page 82.

6 See Article II of the Treaty on Principles Governing the Activities of States in the Exploration and Use of Outer Space, including the Moon and Other Celestial Bodies, 1967, UNTS 205, 208, hereinafter referred to as OST.

wanted to enjoy the benefits of the Convention as early as possible without having to wait until the asset-specific rules other than aircraft-equipment were drafted.[7] Due to the efforts of UNIDROIT and the International Civil Aviation Organization (ICAO), the Convention and the Protocol on Matters specific to Aircraft Equipment were adopted and opened to signature in November 2001. Since then the Convention and the respective Aircraft Protocol have been signed by 26 States and ratified by 1 State.[8]

In 1997 a group of international experts formed the Space Working Group (SWG) and began to elaborate a Protocol, which shall provide specific rules for space assets. For December 2003 a first session of a UNIDROIT Committee of governmental experts is scheduled for the initiation of the intergovernmental process.[9]

2.4 <u>The Merits of the Convention/ Protocol:</u>

The merits of the Convention/Protocol can be briefly divided into legal and commercial merits. Since the aim of this paper is an analysis of the Protocol under a German law perspective, they shall be briefly summarized at this stage.

2.4.1 *Legal Merits:*

One of the major legal merits of the Convention/Protocol is the introduction of standardised remedies[10] for creditors in order to overcome the aforementioned legal problems arising from the perfection of security rights in space assets. The Convention/Protocol ensures the enforcement of those remedies in cases of insolvent debtors through adequate insolvency rules.[11] A further novelty is the introduction of a worldwide register for international interests in space assets, which it is already common practice for ships and aircraft on a national level.[12]

2.4.2 *Commercial Merits/Circle of Beneficiaries:*

The commercial merits are those, which are expected to result indirectly from the provisions provided by the Convention/Protocol. Through the introduction of asset-based financing to the space sector, a large number of start-up companies with a lower financial standing will be enabled to access capital. Funds will also be available at lower interest rates resulting from a reduction in cost in the financial sector. This cost-reduction will be achieved through a lower risk for creditors as a result of the legal merits of the Convention/Protocol and through the standardisation of the sequences of operation, which the financial sector will establish once the Convention/Protocol will be ratified by a larger number of States. Lower interest rates will lead again to a higher demand of capital by operators, which will then be able to provide an increased amount of services to consumers. The increased number of operators, which are enabled to access capital as a result of the Convention/Protocol will demand more satellites and launch services. In conclusion, it can be said that the Convention/Protocol will be beneficial for all involved parties: manufacturers, financiers, insurers, consumers and even States, which will achieve macro-economic benefits from an increased tax income and less unemployment.

---

[7] See Stanford: "A broader or a narrower band of beneficiaries for the proposed new international regimen?: Some reflections on the merits of the Convention/Protocol structure in facilitating the former", in Uniform Law Review 1999-2, p. 244

[8] A status report can be accessed via http://www.unidroit.org/english/implement/i-2001-aircraftprotocol.htm

[9] See Panahy: "The Preliminary Draft Protocol on Matters specific to Space Assets: An Overview of its Objectives and Key Provisions, UNIDROIT 2003, C:G:E: Space Pr./1/W.P. 5, Rome, July 2003

[10] See Chapter III of the Convention, in particular Article 8

[11] See Article 30 of the Convention and Article XI and XII of the Protocol

[12] See Chapter IV and V of the Convention

3. THE UNIDROIT SPACE PROTOCOL AND GERMAN LAW

The following paragraphs will first focus on general issues of discussion, which have arisen during the recent years in Germany and will then analyse different opt-ins and opt-outs, which are contained in the Protocol enabling contracting States to choose by way of declaration to apply or to abstain from certain provisions. This paper will examine different options and offer recommendations from a German industrial point of view.

3.1 Space Assets:

The term "space asset" constitutes the heart of the space protocol since only those assets as defined by the protocol may be the basis for asset-based financing.

3.1.1. *Definition of Space Asset*

The Protocol defines the term space asset as "any separately identifiable asset that is in space or that is intended to be launched and placed in space or has been returned from space.".[13] It also comprises future developments such as space vehicles that are assembled on space stations or reusable space vehicles.[14] According to Art. I (f) (ii) of the Protocol the definition of space asset extends also to separately identifiable components that form a part of an asset, are attached to an asset or are contained within an asset. Such component may be located in space, intended to be launched or returned from space. It may also be assembled or manufactured in space.[15] The legal requirements for the identification of a space component are set forth in Article VII (v) of the Protocol.

3.1.2 *Article I (f) of the Protocol and § 93 of the German Civil Code*

The extension of the term space asset to components is contrary to § 93 of the German Civil Code, hereinafter referred to as "BGB", which provides that integral components of an object that cannot be separated without the physical destruction or alteration of its nature cannot be subject to separate rights.[16] Furthermore, as a result of § 93 in connection with § 947 BGB, a component manufacturer under retention of title looses his property rights the very moment when the component becomes an integral part of another object of higher value and he becomes unable to dispose over the supplied component. The same applies to secured creditors who cannot dispose over a component, which was subject of a security agreement and became an integral part of an object with a higher value. The argument behind the German rules is the prevention of objects from being dismantled by conditional sellers under reservation of title agreements and creditors under security agreements. Due to § 951 BGB the economic loss suffered may be compensated; a claim to restore the situation prior to the combination instead is denied. The original intention of these rules was to preserve the value of an object which was created through the assembly process and which is usually higher than the value of the components themselves.

3.1.3. *Problem: Satellite and Transponder*

The aforementioned conflict of law was originally identified by the German satellite industry and gave rise to further discussion in Germany.[17] Attention was drawn to the fact that § 93 BGB prevents the use of transponders as collateral. However, transponders play an essential role in the satellite and communication business. Each communication satellite carries a number of transponders, which are responsible for the transmission of

[13] See Article I (f) (i) of the Protocol

[14] See Article I (f) (iii) and (iv) of the Protocol

[15] See Article I (f) (ii) of the Protocol

[16] See Palandt Heinrichs: § 93 No. 4

[17] Mr. Arwed Hesse originally identified the issue in 1999. Mr. Hesse is a representative of the German satellite industry and a member of the Space Working Group. See also Hans-Georg Bollweg and Michael Gerhard: Sicherungsrechte an Luftfahrtausrüstung und Weltraumeigentum, in: Zeitschrift für Luft- und Raumfahrtrecht, 50. Jg. 3/2001, p. 388-389.

signals from earth to space and back. Commercial practice in the U.S.A. shows that transponders are subject of leasing agreements in order to maximise the capacity utilization. This development underlines the rising commercial importance of transponders for the satellite industry and the need for an adequate solution to secure financial interests in them.

3.1.4 *Possible Solutions/Workarounds*
The commercial need and the current practice of U.S. satellite manufacturers make the Protocol rules concerning components most welcome for the German space industry and financial institutions. Despite the fact that the German civil law property rules on components conflicts with the definition of space asset as provided by the Protocol, the German law system is nevertheless capable to accommodate the protocol component rules. Since the Convention and the Protocol constitute international (superior) and more specific legal rules on components, the UNDROIT rules would prevail in case of a German ratification and create an exception within the national law system which would merely apply to space components. An exception from the general principle of integral components e.g. represents the German "Wohnungseigtumsgesetz", which allows acquiring ownership in apartments (condominium), even though the apartments represent integral components of the entire building.

The component rule of the Protocol has not reached its full potential yet, once the technology will be achieved, it will also provide the legal basis for space or planetary stations consisting of several segments or apartments, which might then also serve as collateral and hence enable a larger circle of operators and manufacturers to benefit from asset based financing.

Another German concern was that a bank might sell a satellite in case an operator is not able to meet his contractual obligations under the loan agreement. It was argued that the new operator might move the satellite to another orbital position making it impossible for the owners or lessees of single transponders to continue with their business. This problem can be overcome since buyers or lessees of transponders may protect themselves through the use of specific clauses in the respective sale or leasing agreements. Such clauses could provide for compensation payments for the loss suffered by transponder operators in case a secured creditor moves the satellite to another orbital position.

3.2 Associated Rights
Another issue of discussion within the sessions of the Space Working Group was the transferability of licences or permits which are required for satellite operations. Licences for orbital positions and frequency bandwidths are granted e.g. by the International Telecommunication Union (ITU). Furthermore states are required to supervise the space activities of their nationals according to Article VIII OST. Such governmental supervision is carried out through national licensing procedures.

3.2.1 Definition of Associated Rights
The term "associated rights" as defined by the Convention comprises rights to payments, which are associated with the secured object. In contrast hereto the term associated rights as defined by the Protocol comprises all licences that are required to control, operate or use a space asset.[18] In order to distinguish the associated rights as defined by the Convention from the associated rights as defined by the Protocol a proposal was made during the Rome Meeting of the Space Working Group to establish a new term "linked" or "related

[18] Compare Article 1 (c) of the Convention with Article I 2. (a) of the Protocol

rights".[19] The creation of the new term "related rights" for licence rights was also recommended by Mr. Alfons Noll, member of the Space Working Group, during the UNIDROIT Colloquium on the Preliminary Draft Space Assets Protocol held at the Head Office of the European Space Agency (E.S.A.) in Paris on 5th September 2003.[20]

3.2.2 *Problem: Licences are not transferable in the majority of countries due to national licensing procedures*

The value of a space asset as collateral depends to a great extent on the transferability of licences. However, licences are mostly subject to national licensing procedures and limited to a specific operator. The Protocol recognises such national licensing procedures, which is indicted by the addition "to the extent permissible and assignable under the laws concerned". [21]

However, the non-transferability of licences diminishes the value of space objects as collateral. From a creditor's point of view transferability at least among "blue chip companies" that fulfil the standards of the national licensing procedures is most desirable.[22] In particular, a possibility of an unbureaucratic transfer would lead to further cost-reduction in the financial sector and hence to lower interest rates, which would be beneficial for operators and manufacturers.

3.2.3 *Possible Solutions*

A possible solution could be the regulation of licensing procedures through national space legislation. A German Space Act has been requested several times and a draft is currently under preparation. A national Space Act could provide procedures for the conditions under which a transfer of licences may be carried out.[23] Since the primary concern of governmental supervision is liability according to Article VI/VIII OST, the authorities will mainly focus on the reliability and creditability of potential licensees. If both prerequisites are given, it is most desirable that the transfer of licences may be permitted. Such practice may lead to transferability among a limited number of "forum" states, which provide the required environment for space related financing. Those states instead, which ignore the demands of the market and put an undue burden through increased bureaucracy upon commercial entities will be left out.

3.3 <u>Opt-ins and opt-outs: recommendations from a German perspective</u>

In response to the different law systems and attitudes of governments to allow alterations of their domestic legal system, the Protocol provides that states may choose or abstain from certain provisions by way of declaration. Prior example in international private law is e.g. the United Nations Convention on Contracts for the International Sale of Goods 1980 (CISG).[24] It is the intention of the following paragraphs to present some of the different opt-ins and opt-outs as contained in the Protocol, to compare them with German Law and to give recommendations from a German perspective considering the

[19] See Michael Gerhard in his comments on the occasion of the Rome Meeting of the Space Working Group., UNIDROIT, W.P.2, Rome, January 2002

[20] See Alfons Noll: "Contribution to UNIDROIT's Paris 2003 Colloquium on its Preliminary Draft Space Protocol", Geneva, August 2003, p. 3

[21] See Article I 2 (a) of the Protocol.

[22] See Hermann Ersfeld: "Industry Views on National Space Legislation" p. 46, in: "Project 2001 – Needs and Prospects for National Space Legislation", Munich, 5/6th December 2000

[23] See Michael Gerhard's proposal for a German Space Act: "Nationale Weltraumgesetzgebung – Völkerrechtliche Voraussetzungen und Handlungserfordernisse", in: Studies in Air and Space Law, founded by Karl-Heinz Böckstiegel, edited by Stephan Hobe, p.101/103

[24] See CISG e.g. Article 95, UNTS. 3, 19

commercial needs and legal implications. Due to the regulatory limitations for this paper as regards pages and time for presentation, the following examples do not represent the entirety of the opt-in and opt–outs contained in the Protocol.

3.3.1 Article VIII Protocol - Choice of Law:

Article VIII generally applies unless a contracting State declares at the time of ratification to the contrary and constitutes the only opt-out provision of the Protocol.[25] According to Article VIII the parties to an agreement may agree which law and to what extent it shall govern their contractual rights and obligations. However, certain jurisdictions, in particular Arabian countries, do not accept such clauses and generally apply the domestic law.[26] Since choice of law clauses are internationally widely used and the German law recognises such clauses, a German declaration as regards the non-applicability of Article VIII is not recommended.

3.3.2 Article XI Protocol - Remedies on Insolvency:

The value of the remedies as provided by the Convention depends to a great extent on the enforceability in the insolvency of the debtor. The importance of insolvency provisions has found its expression in Article XI of the Protocol. The applicability of Article XI requires a declaration pursuant to Article XXVI (4) (opt-in).[27] This is due to the sensitivity of states towards interventions into their legal insolvency systems. The declaration according to Article XXVI (4) shall also specify whether a State will apply alternative A or B of Article XI.

[25] See Article VIII (1) in connection with Article XXVI (1) (a) of the Protocol

[26] See Rosener in: Münchener Vertragshandbuch, Band 2, III.1 Nr. 85

[27] See Article XI (1) of the Protocol

3.3.2.1 Alternative A:

The text of alternative A is strongly influenced by title 11 of the United States of America Bankruptcy Code (U.S.C.). In particular section 1110 enables secured creditors, lessors and conditional sellers to take possession of secured aircraft equipment. The rule provided by alternative A introduces an equivalent right of possession for secured space assets in case of the debtor's default. In particular the strict periods of time[28] in combination with the inability of national courts to interfere with the creditor's right of possession, once a state has opted for alternative A, make this alternative a "hard" option.

From a German point of view the legal, lack of judicial control in combination with the fact that the creditor is not obliged to prove his "bona fidae" raise the question of whether such a self-help remedy is compatible with German constitutional law.[29] Self-help in German law is rarely seen; an example may be § 559 BGB where the owner of real estate may claim the tenant's interior as compensation for unpaid rent. In the present case of alternative A of the Protocol however, where highly valuable space assets are involved, the lack of judicial control seems incompatible with the German concept of the Constitutional State ("Rechts-staatsprinzip"), which grants the protection of property to its citizens and the right to take a case to the domestic courts in cases of disputes.[30] Bearing the aforementioned conflicts in mind, an opt-in for alternative A cannot be recommended from a German perspective.

[28] According to Article XI Alternative A (3) the waiting period has to be specified by the contracting State

[29] Article 14 of the German Constitution grants citizens property rights

[30] See Hans Prütting: "Verfassungsrechtlich garantierte Verfahrensgrundsätze, I. Rechtsstaats-prinzip, p. 224-226 and III. Der Anspruch auf rechtliches Gehör, p. 228-231", in: Kölner Schrift zur Insolvenzordnung

3.3.2.2 Alternative B:

During the sessions of the informal insolvency working group the "hard" self-help approach of Article XI of the Protocol was criticised for making it impossible for several governments to ratify the Convention/Protocol. As a result of this discussion Article XI, which to that time did not contain alternatives and was originally based on the text of the now existing Alternative A. Alternative B has been introduced on initiative of the French delegation. This initiative led to the split of the former uniform rule in two alternatives A and B, as contained in the present Protocol.

Alternative B, similar to Alternative A, provides that the debtor or insolvency administrator shall give possession or control and operation over the space asset.[31] This deviates in so far from German insolvency law as the domestic law strictly distinguishes between the case of a conditional seller under simple retention of title and a secured creditor.[32]

A conditional seller under a simple retention of title agreement may claim the separation of the space asset from the bankrupt's estate according to § 47 of the German Insolvency Code (Insolvenzordnung), hereinafter referred to as InsO, in connection with § 985 BGB. According to § 103 InsO the insolvency administrator may still be entitled to possession when he decides to perform all obligations under the sale contract. Only when the insolvency administrator decides to terminate the sale contract, the seller may take possession of the asset.[33] In so far the rule of alternative B to give possession to the creditor is consistent with § 47 InsO. The same applies to the choice of the insolvency administrator to opt either to cure the actual default with the result that he may keep the space asset or to give possession of the space asset. This approach is the equivalent of the aforementioned § 103 InsO.[34]

Under German law the precedent position of a conditional seller under simple retention of title has to be distinguished from a creditor under a security agreement. According to § 50 in connection with § 51 No. 1 InsO a creditor under a security agreement is not entitled to take possession of the secured asset, he is rather entitled to be satisfied out of the value of the asset. The realisation of the asset value however is effected through the insolvency administrator, provided he has possession of the asset, and not through the creditor.[35] In addition, the insolvency administrator is entitled to deduct 9 % of the realised value of the asset, which will be added to the bankrupt's estate.[36] In so far the rule provided by Alternative B (2) (b) of the Protocol, i.e. to give possession of the space asset, deviates from the German rule as regards secured creditors.

Nevertheless German law is capable to accommodate the Protocol's provisions on insolvency. The UNIDROIT rules on insolvency are generally not inconsistent with the German law system. Moreover, they would constitute merely an exception within the domestic insolvency law and grant conditional sellers under simple retention of title as much as lessors and creditors under security agreements a uniform right of separation of the secured space asset from the entirety of the insolvency estate. As a result of this, German Courts in case of a German opt-in would have to apply § 47 InsO also to

[31] See Article XI Alternative A (2) and Alternative B (2) (b) of the Protocol

[32] See Peter Gottwald/Jens Adolphsen: "Die Rechtsstellung dinglich gesicherter Gläubiger in der Insolvenzordnung, IV. Unterschiedliche Behandlung von Sicherungseigentum und Eigentumsvorbehalt" at p. 1053-1056, in: Kölner Schrift zur Insolvenzordnung

[33] See § 103 in connection with § 107 II InsO

[34] See Article XI Alternative B (2) (a) and (c) of the Protocol

[35] See § 166 InsO

[36] See § 170 in connection with 171 InsO

secured creditors and lessors conclusively.[37]

In contrast to Alternative A, no constitutional infringements can be identified within the text of Alternative B. Moreover, judicial control is granted by the formulation that possession of the space asset may be given "…in accordance with the applicable law."[38] Further judicial control is provided by Alternative B (3) and (5) which enable domestic courts to take additional steps as regards the transfer of possession. Another distinctive feature is the creditor's obligation to provide evidence of his "bona fidae".[39] The entirety of the aforementioned distinctive features characterizes Alternative B as a soft option in comparison to Alternative A.

Even though certain conflicts as regards secured creditors could be identified, German Law is perfectly able to accommodate the insolvency rules of Alternative B. The advantages of such strong creditor rights promise an increased financial involvement of banks at lower costs and subsequently better conditions for debtors in the space industry. Considering that Alternative B offers a balanced approach between strong creditor rights and judicial control, a German opt-in may be recommended.

4. CONCLUSION:

The Convention and the Protocol do not contain any substantial inconstancies with German law. The major points of deviation are the rules on components and on insolvency. However, the German law system is perfectly capable to accommodate the UNIDROIT rules as an exception to the general rules. The ratification of the UNIDROIT Convention and the Protocol is essential for an increased involvement of banks and sets the foundation for a further commercialisation of space activities. One of the major issues for the success of the Convention and the Protocol is a wide acceptance of the different provisions, which are subject to opt-in and opt-out declarations. States that will not accept interferences through international law may make use of the various opt-ins and outs to protect the integrity of their legal system. However, creditors will focus on those States where strong security rights are granted.[40] In the long run this may lead to a limited circle of nations "forum states", where the entirety of the Convention and the Protocol with all its "hard" opt-ins are accepted and the financing of space assets is undertaken.

Although the practical applicability of the Convention/Protocol today is limited to satellites and transponders as space assets, the Protocol will unfold its full potential with the technical evolution of the space industry when production in space and permanent space transport through reusable launch vehicles at reasonable costs can be technically achieved. Then, the Convention/Protocol may also provide the legal basis for commercial space stations and modules or components thereof.

---

[37] See Eva-Maria Kieninger: "Effects in Insolvency: a German perspective, in: Uniform Law Review 1999-2, p. 405.

[38] See Article XI Alternative B (2) (b) of the Protocol

[39] See Article XI Alternative B (3) of the Protocol

[40] This view was also expressed by Mr. Robert W. Gordon, representative of the Boeing Capital Corporation and member of the Space Working Group, in his speech "The Fundamentals of Asset-based Financing from the Perspective of the Lender" on the occasion of the UNIDROIT Colloquium on the Preliminary Draft Space Assets Protocol held at the Head Office of the European Space Agency (E.S.A.) in Paris on 5th September 2003.

Bibliography

Arbeitskreis für Insolvenz- und Schiedsgerichtswesen e.V., Köln (Editor)
Kölner Schrift zur Insolvenordung – Das neue Insolvenrecht in Praxis, 2. erweiteterte und aktualisierte Auflage, Verlag für die Rechts-und Anwaltspraxis, Herne/Berlin 2000

Bollweg, Hans-Georg/ Gerhard, Michael
Sicherungsrechte an Luftfahrtausrüstung und Weltraumeigentum – Die Entwürfe einer UNIDROIT/ICAO – Konvention über internationale Sicherungsrechte an beweglicher Ausrüstung und der Protokolle über Luftfahrtausrüstung und Weltraumeigentum, Zeitschrift für Luft- und Raumfahrtrecht, 50. Jg., 3/2001, p. 373-396

Ersfeld, Hermann
Industry Views on National Space Legislation, in: Project 2001 – Needs and Prospects for National Space Legislation, Munich, 5/6th December 2000, p. 39-51

Euroconsult
Satellite Communications & Broadcasting Markets Survey- Worldwide Prospects to 2010, A Euroconsult Research Report, Paris, January 2002

Gerhard, Michael
Comments on the Preliminary Draft Protocol on Matters Specific to Space Assets on the occasion of the Rome Meeting of the Space Working Group (30/31 January 2002), UNIDROIT W.P. 2, Rome, January 2002

Nationale Weltraumgesetzgebung – Völkerrechtliche Voraussetzungen und Handlungserfordernisse, Studies in Air and Space Law, founded by Karl-Heinz Böckstiegel, Edited by Stephan Hobe, Volume 19, Carl Heymanns Verlag, Cologne 2002

Gordon, Robert W.
The Fundamentals of Asset-based Financing from the Perspective of the Lender, on the occasion of the UNIDROIT Colloquium on the Preliminary Draft Space Assets Protocol held at the Head Office of the European Space Agency (E.S.A.) in Paris on 5th September 2003

Kieninger, Eva-Maria
Effects in Insolvency of the International Interest in Mobile Equipment: a German Perspective, Uniform Law Review 1999-2, p. 397-408

Noll, Alfons
Contribution to UNIDROIT's Paris 2003 Colloquium on its Preliminary Draft Space Protocol", Geneva, August 2003

Palandt, Otto (founded by)	Bürgerliches Gesetzbuch, Kommentar,Verlag C.H. Beck, 62. Auflage, München 2003
Panahy, Dara A.	The Preliminary Draft Protocol on Matters specific to Space Assets: An Overview of its Objectives and Key Provisions, UNIDROIT 2003, C.G.E. Space Pr./1/W.P.5 Rome, July 2003
	Prospective UNIDROIT Convention on International Interests in Mobile Equipment as Applied to Space Assets, International Business Lawyer, December 2001, p. 505-511
Panahy, Dara A./ Mittal, Raman	Prospective UNIDROIT Convention on International Interests in Mobile Equipment as Applied to Space Property, Uniform Law Review 1999-2, p. 303-312
Saunders, Anthony Walter, Ingo	Proposed UNIDROIT Convention on International Interests in Mobile Equipment as applicable to Aircraft Equipment through the Aircraft Equipment Protocol: Economic Impact Assessment, A Study Prepared Under the Auspices of INSEAD and the New York University Salomon Center, September 1998
Schütze, Rolf A (Editor).	Müchener Vertragshandbuch, 2. Band, Handels- und Wirtschaftsrecht, Beck Verlag, München 1997
Stanford, Martin J.	A broader or a narrower view band of beneficiaries for the proposed new international regimen?: Some reflections on the merits of the Convention / Protocol structure in facilitating the former, Uniform Law Review 1999-2, p. 242-251
UNIDROIT	Report of the Space Working Group Session held in Seal Beach, California, 23/24 April 2001 UNIDROIT 2001, Study LXXIII – Doc. 5
	Report of the Space Working Group Session held in Évry Coucouronnes, 3/4 September 2001 UNIDROIT 2001, Study LXXIII – Doc. 8
	Report of the Space Working Group Session held in Rome, 3/4 February 2002 UNIDROIT 2001, Study LXXIII – Doc. 10

IAC-03-IISL.1.15

LEGAL ASPECTS OF SOLAR POWER SATELLITES

Laurent Crapart*
Institute of Space and Telecommunications Law (IDEST)
Paris, France
laurent.crapart@idest-paris.org

Philippe Achilléas (IDEST), André Farand (ESA), Elisabeth Marescaux (IDEST),
Leopold Summerer (ESA Advanced Concepts Team)

This article is based on a Report made by the Institute of Space and Telecommunications Law for the ESA Advanced Concepts Team.

The present article tends to give a general overview of the legal principles applicable to solar power satellites – the so-called SPS. The idea to collect solar energy by Earth orbiting satellites, and then to beam this energy to Earth receiver stations in order to convert it to electricity, is not a new one. It has actually been studied since the late 1960's, and several space law eminent authors explored the legal aspects applicable to such possibility, mainly during the 70's and 80's, when first SPS projects arose. Recent technical advances have however conducted space agencies to reconsider SPS projects. The present paper will consequently attempt to come back on these legal aspects by taking the most recent law developments into account. For such purpose, first a general overview of the basic legal principles applicable to SPS will be given (I). Then, the paper will be divided according to the two main phases of a given SPS project – the construction (II), and the operational phase (III).

I. Issues relating to the basic legal principles applicable to SPS

Since SPS will be developed and operated in outer space, will require orbital positions, and use radio-frequencies, solar and eventually lunar materials, they will be subject to the relevant principles of space law, and firstly to the freedom of outer space principle, as stated by Article I of the Outer Space Treaty[1]. Secondly, and in the light of Article II of the Outer Space Treaty and Article 11 of the Moon Agreement[2], SPS shall not conduct to an appropriation of outer space. The legal notion of appropriation is generally described as constituted of three elements: *usus*, *abusus*, *fructus*. *Usus* refers to the ability to use a resource, *abusus*: the ability to destroy, to give and to sell it, and *fructus*: the ability to harvest its fruits. Applied to SPS, the consequence of the non-appropriation principle is that no use of the resources concerned (solar and/or lunar) shall conduct to its appropriation. This principle might constitute a problematic issue concerning the use of lunar resources by SPS, since such use tends to consume these resources, thus prohibiting any subsequent use by other entities – the conditions of *abusus*, as well as *usus* and *abusus* are met and such activity shall therefore be forbidden as an appropriation of lunar resources. SPS operators will therefore have to face such legal constraint in the eventuality of lunar-based SPS projects.

Thirdly, and since SPS involve a use of the radio frequency spectrum, both for telecommunications (the so-called space services) and for energy transmission, they will have to conform with the ITU regime, at least concerning space services. The issue of ITU rules applicability will however appear concerning energy transmission as such, since it does not enter the definition of "telecommunications" as defined by the Union. ITU regulation may nevertheless find application for such uses of the radio frequency spectrum, to the extent that they may cause harmful interference to other existing services. Legal requirements for getting frequencies will therefore also have to be met. On the contrary it must be underlined that ITU is not competent for regulating laser power transmission. Thus laser-based SPS concepts shall be regarded as free from any regulation in terms of frequency allocation.

II. Legal requirements for SPS construction

Three categories of legal requirements will subsequently be identified as applicable to SPS during their construction phase. The first category is linked to security issues (a), the second one to registration issues (b), and the third one to electromagnetic compatibility matters (c).

a) Security issues

Article IV of the Outer space treaty forbids the placement in outer space of any object carrying nuclear weapons or any other kind of weapon of mass destruction. Such weapons shall neither be installed on celestial bodies. Therefore, the construction of SPS shall be undertaken so as to avoid their qualification, once constructed, as weapons of mass destruction. Otherwise, their placement into orbit or on celestial bodies, such as the Moon, would be forbidden. Reference can therefore be made to international texts, according to which only three kinds of weapons are currently considered as entering the category of weapons of mass destruction – namely: nuclear, biological, and chemical weapons. While SPS projects here taken as reference are not intended to enter one of these three categories, some SPS concepts are based on laser power transmission. To that extend, and according to the Additional protocol on blinding laser weapons to the Convention on prohibitions or restrictions on the use of certain conventional weapons of 1995[3], SPS shall not be "*specially designed, as their sole combat function, or as one of their combat functions, to cause permanent blindness to unenhanced vision*".

b) Registration

According to Article VIII of the Outer space treaty, a State on whose registry an object launched into outer space is carried shall retain jurisdiction and control over such an object and over any personnel thereof while in outer space. Applied to SPS, this concretely means that the law of the State of registry will apply to the space object and to the activities of hypothetical personnel being in this object.

Particular attention shall therefore be given to registration issues before launching SPS. To that extend, the provisions of the Registration convention[4] shall be observed, which means that the launching State shall in particular furnish to the Secretary-General of the United Nations: the name of the State(s) launching SPS, the appropriate designator of the SPS or its registration number, the date and territory or location of SPS launch, as well as the basic SPS orbital parameters and general functions of SPS.

c) Electromagnetic compatibility

It has already been mentioned that SPS imply Earth-based stations in order to collect the solar energy transmitted by the satellites. Should they be territorially subject to European regulations, these ground stations will have to be constructed in accordance with the provisions of the EU Directive on electromagnetic compatibility[5]. This means that they will have to be constructed so that to insure that the electromagnetic disturbance they generate does not exceed a certain level allowing radio and telecommunications equipment to be operated as intended. If applicable to them, SPS constructors will have to design SPS ground stations electrical and electronic elements with due regard to the relevant provisions of the directive.

III. Legal requirements for the SPS operational phase

As far as the operational phase of SPS is concerned, four issues must be emphasised: jurisdiction and control issues (a), frequency issues (b), environmental issues (c) and liability issues (d).

a) Issues of Jurisdiction & control

While in outer space, jurisdiction and control over SPS and personnel thereof will be retained by the State of registry. The law applicable to SPS ground station(s) will be the law of the territory of the State where this (these) station(s) is (are) established. Should a SPS station be based in an extraterritorial zone, such as the high sea, the State retaining jurisdiction and control over this station will be the State of registry of the concerned maritime platform. In all cases, the State retaining jurisdiction on SPS will have to control them and insure, through national authorisations and licences, that SPS conform with the legal principles identified as relevant in this report.

b) Frequency issues

Frequencies will have to be allocated to SPS, for both space operation services and power transmission via radiofrequencies. Whereas the frequencies allocated to space operation services should not cause particular problems, due to the fact that it is already foreseen by the ITU Radio regulations, two different possibilities may be studied concerning the frequencies allocated for power transmission. The first solution is to use the bands dedicated by the ITU to the industrial, scientific and medical applications – the so-called ISM. This would present sound interest for SPS operators since according to the Radio regulations, radiocommunication services operating on ISM bands must accept harmful interference that may be caused by other ISM applications. SPS operators would therefore not face the risk of claims due to interference their services might cause. The second solution however foreseeable is to require new frequency bands before the ITU, specially dedicated to SPS, via competent national authorities.

c) Environmental issues

Environmental law, and in particular the prevention principle, must be regarded to be applicable to SPS operations as well. According to this principle, States have the responsibility to ensure that activities within their jurisdiction or control do not cause damage to the environment of other States or of areas beyond the limits of national jurisdiction. SPS operators will indirectly be submitted to this principle of international law, since they will, in particular, have to comply with national legislation stating radiation standards. In most cases, national measures in this field are based on the basis of the recommendations made by the International Commission on Non-Ionizing Radiation Protection (ICNIRP). In the European Union in particular, the Council Recommendation of 12 July 1999[6] strictly reproduces the standards formulated by the ICNIRP.

d) Liability issues

As far as liability issues are concerned, the main question relies in the applicability of the space law regime, as provided by the Outer space treaty and the 1972 Liability convention, to damage that could indirectly result from the beam projected on Earth by SPS. This issue, which has not found clear solutions yet, will be very important, since it will determine the regime applicable to SPS for such damage. The general international liability regime might be preferred by SPS operators, but it would be less advantageous for hypothetical victims than the space law regime. Even if this question has not been answered concerning other space applications, the potential damage that SPS could cause, notably on the environment, justify that this problem should be tackled with in a near future.

---

[1] Treaty on Principles Governing the Activities of States in the Exploration and Use of Outer Space, including the Moon and other Celestial Bodies, 27 January 1967, 610 *UNTS* 205.

[2] Agreement Governing the Activities of States on the Moon and Other Celestial Bodies, 18 December 1979, 1363 *UNTS* 3.

[3] Additional Protocol to the Convention on Prohibitions and Restrictions on the Use of certain Conventional Weapons which may be deemed to be excessively injurious or to have indiscriminate effects, Vienna, 12 October 1995, CCW/CONF.I/7.

[4] Convention on Registration of Objects Launched into Outer Space, 14 January 1975, 1023 *UNTS* 15.

[5] Council Directive 89/336/EEC of 3 May 1989 on the laws of the Member States relating to electromagnetic compatibility, as amended, *Official Journal* L 139, 23.05.89.

[6] Council Recommendation of 12 July 1999 on the limitation of exposure of the general public to electromagnetic fields (0 Hz to 300 GHz), 1999/519/EC, *Official Journal* L 199, 30/07/1999 p.0059-0070.

A REMOTE SENSING CONVENTION FOR THE ADVANCEMENT OF SPACE LAW

José Monserrat Filho *
Brazilian Society of Aerospace Law
Brazilian Society for the Progress of Science
monserrat@alternex.com.br

"Contemporary international law increasingly consists of lawlike treaties, aspiring to universal application and thus pulling towards greater equality. Its rules have become both more precise and better enforced, and it now poses greater limites on the powerful, too."

Nico Krisch, Max Planck Society for the Advancement of Science (1)

ABSTRACT

The space law debate on remote sensing of the Earth from Outer Space is not over, as well as the History after the Cold War has not came to an end. The remote sensing activities are underegulated in essential aspects. The 1986 Principles became a pale and impotent reference for such vital activities all over the world. They are distant from the technologically complex reality of current practice of remote sensing in fast evolution. This is a planetary lacuna in Space Law. This paper seeks to demonstrate the necessity of creating a comprehensive and effective convention on remote sensing. It has not only to be based on the 1986 Principles but also to shape a vigorous international regime of previsibility, regularity and equity for remote sensing activities. It is not enough to recognize the freedom of remote sensing from anywhere in the Earth, at any time, as well as the freedom of selling remote sensing data. It is necessary to guarantee reliable access to

freedom of remote sensing from

as the freedom of selling remote sensing data. It is necessary to guarantee reliable access to processed or analyzed data, specially by developing countries. It is also imperative to legally specify what it means, for instance, "not to conduct remote sensing activities in a manner detrimental to the legitimate rights and interests of the sensed State". What are the rights and obligations of sensing and sensed States? It is unavoidable to know. And to settle clearnees instead of vagueness in all rules. The commercialization and the privatization of remote sensing activities can and should be a way to stimulate as much as possible the spreading of their products, not to difficult the access to them. The business requirements are important but not the unique nor the main criteria to define the needed legislation. The appropriate State remains entirely responsible for the remote sensing activities carried out by private entities. The conclusion is that more than never the remote sensing activities have and deserve to be regulated in a detailed convention as an international public service of first necessity, a inestimable matter of international cooperation and an irreplaceable instrument of security and development for all States, without discrimination of any kind.

INTRODUCTION

As a starting position in the legal analysis of remote sensing activities today, it is fundamental to take a very clear rule of law approach.

Between minimum and maximum regulation, the later seems to be the better solution, as we are in an ample area of hazardous lacunas.

---

* Address: Av. Oswaldo Cruz, 73/701, Flamengo, Rio de Janeiro, RJ, CEP 22250-060, Brazil. Phones: 55 21 2552-9036 and 2552-6073. Fax: 55 21 2541-5342

"The rule of law in international affairs involves the existence of a comprehensive system of law, certainty as to what the rules are, predictability as to the legal consequences of conduct, equality before the law, the absence of arbitrary power, and effective and impartial application of the law", as wrote Sir Arthur Watts. (2)

The stronger the presence of these elements in the exploration and use of outer space, including remote sensing activities, the greater the security and the benefits of such highly risky and necessary activities to all states will be.

As nowadays there is a strong resistance to amend the space treaties or create new ones, it is worth to remind here a Manfred Lachs recommendation. According to him, the process of development of international space law "cannot be arrested", since "space technology and economic possibilities are continuously generating new questions to which law has to find adequate answers" and this vital process "has to grow at an ever greater speed to follow life in order to resolve the many problems for the benefit and in the interests of all men" (3). It is truth that remote sensing activities are today connected to "terrestrial" computer and Internet technologies, specially in the area of imagery dissemination. However, the imagery disseminated remains output of remote sensing, without which it could not exist. Therefore, the first responsible for the imagery is the State of the remote sensing operator, not the State of the computer or Internet one.

AN INACURATE RESOLUTION

The Principles Relating to Remote Sensing of the Earth from Outer Space is an annex to the United Nations General Assembly Resolution 41/65, adopted unanimously on December 9, 1986. (4) This document is today the only specific international reference in existence on the regulation of remote sensing (5).

The Legal Subcommittee of the United Nations Committee on the Peaceful Uses of Outer Space (COPUOS), discussed proposals on this issue more than 15 years ago and barely reached the modest terms of Resolution 41/65, where compromised solutions abound, subject to conflicting interpretations.

As highlighted by Professor Maureen Williams, the lengthy negotiations leading to the adoption of these Principles clearly reflect two main confrontations, as follows:

a) Between traditional principles of International Law, namely the freedom of exploration and use of outer space declared in Article I of the 1967 Outer Space Treaty (6) and the principle of sovereignty which, when applied to this field, may be seen as the principle of non-intervention in the internal affairs of States or principle of exclusive jurisdiction enshrined in Article 2.7 of the United Nations Charter, and

b) Between freedom of information (as applied to the distribution of the collected data) and the prior consent of the sensed State based on the principle of State sovereignty over natural resources, which has been repeatedly proclaimed by United Nations General Assembly Resolutions (7).

In the end, Resolution 41/65 formally incorporated both principles, without specifying in which cases and how each of them should be applied.

Symptomatically, Carl Q. Christol noted in 1988: "The Principles were the product of consensus, but there were numerous compromises along the way, This suggests that the consensus was, if not unsubstantial, at least so thin that some members of COPUOS have viewed the consensus as conditional and subject to review. It cannot be said that the agreement was a temporary one, but the commentary reviewed (...) suggests a grudging acceptance of some of the provisions, with the view on the part of developing countries in particular, that there is a need to reinforce the Principles beneficial to them in order to buttress existing assurances and commitments." (8)

As result, we have today an international satellite remote sensing order which is inacurrate and unbalanced in terms of benefits.

UNDEREGULATED ACTIVITIES

The 1986 Principles are surpassed by the skyrocketing technological advances in the sector that has occurred within these last 17 years.

It does not address the questions raised today by multiple satellite remote sensing programmes. A large part of them are operated by private companies with strictly commercial objectives. High resolution images (one meter and less) have been used exclusively by the Armed Forces until a short time ago , and are presently being sold worldwide.

Sridhara Murthi pointed out what he called the most important changes in the policy and technological environment affecting remote sensing activities around the globe, since 1986:

"- The emergence of commercial remote sensing systems in the late 1990's providing high-resolution remote sensing data globally as a sequel to several policy measures in the US.

- The spread of the Internet which facilitated global access to digital remote sensing data, triggering a new era of transparency and making some aspects of regulations on the flow of remote sensing data and information obsolete." (9)

The UNGA Resolution 41/65 says nothing about the role of the private sector in carrying out the Principles. It closed in on a certain governmental form of a certain civil segment of remote sensing from outer space as practiced till 1986, granting universal allowance for what was deemed generally permissible in that narrow band of remote sensing by the leading, space policy-setting space powers, as Wulf von Kries wrote. (10)

While remote sensing practices have rapidly evolved, and keep evolving, rule making has stopped. This, undoubtedly, should be a matter of great concern.

LEGAL VACUUM

Currently remote sensing by satellite is being operated by a number of States, *inter alia*, the USA, Russia, France, India, Chine, Israel, Japan, Brazil and Argentina. This number is expected to increase in the near future. At the same time, more and more commercial entities are capable of delivering complete remote sensing systems. More systems can provide more imagery to more users. Access to data collection from space is being benefited from technological software, cheaper computing power, and imagery data bases linked to the Internet, thus making on-line data access possible and opening an era of web-based Earth observation data availability. (11)

All this new reality is strange to the 1986 Principles, which do not cover the large spectrum of present remote sensing activities by satellite. Commercial remote sensing companies operate in a global marketplace devoid of international legal regulation. There are no limits.

Hence the timely proposal made by Shridhara Murthi: "The UN Principles could be further reviewed taking into account the new challenges of this era [of transparency] and with an aim to evolve legal principles for orderly development of commerce in this field, respecting the right of government to certain information from commercial entities when their territories are imaged." (12)

OUT OF THE TIME

Today, as the use of remote sensing satellite data for both civilian and military purposes is growing, it is also becoming increasingly difficult to distinguish between military and civilian technologies, including remote sensing ones. In this way, the dual-use technology notion is losing practical usefulness, as it is now depending more on the concrete employment of a specific technology than on its very nature as a typical space activity. Consequently, a clear dividing line between civilian and military remote sensing is becoming more and more difficult to draw. (13)

The 1986 Principles, which confine themselves to certain civilian, non-military and non-commercial applications, are inadequate to regulate the complex framework of 2003 remote sensing activities by satellite.

Meanwhile, the strictly military remote sensing activities are carried out without any specific international regulation. Is it sound?

TREATS TO PRIVACY

Sridhara Murthi observed: "The ready availability of one-meter resolution images in the market place and the promise of new better spectral characteristics are leading to an era of growing transparency. Apart from contributing to several beneficial uses, these images of one-meter resolution quality can also detect vehicles and identify aircraft. Tanks can be distinguished from trucks and road and bridge conditions can be seen."

According to this author, "governments are concerned about the widespread dissemination of such data in the public domain", as "present policies of dissemination and access make it extremely difficult for satellite operators to specify who the ultimate users of the data are and for what purpose they will use it". Moreover, they can be used "as support for terrorism, espionage by industrial competitors, intelligence on disadvantaged regions/populations and so on".

There are real threats to the rights of privacy due to possibilities of industrial espionage and the potential use of imagery by anti-social groups. Commercial corporations from one country could gather information on exploration of natural resources in another country without the knowledge of its government and could possibly gain strategic advantages in negotiations and in world market. (14)

The United States Department of Agriculture, for instance, used to take strategic world market decisions on the basis of about two thousand satellite images made each year on the most important plantations from 120 countries. And the Department of Citrus Fruits of the State of Florida has a special satellite remote sensing service monitoring the competitor's orange plantations in other countries, including Brazil. The Brazilian Association of Orange Export Companies considered this as a case of "industrial espionage". (15)

This is an open question, not yet handled by the international community of States, but which is surely worth a serious discussion.

FREEDOM WITHOUT COMPENSATION

In the absence of more precise international legislation on the matter, Kries contends that "three international remote sensing regimes have to be distinguished – proposal, "military remote sensing enjoys the unrestrained freedom of overflight, data collection and use as implicitly granted by the Outer Space Treaty"; the UNGA Resolution 41/65 is restricted "to common utility ends" ("Remote sensing for the common good, national or international, rests on the utilitarian and solidary nature of the UN Principles Resolution."); and "commercial observation from space is developing its own rules, steadily pushing back state intervention and control".

According to Kries "the three remote sensing regimes are evolving separately and differently". He foresees that "where military observation is concerned, sensing states will continue to be opposed to any intelligence gathering rules" and that "even global access to dual-use satellite imagery will, in all probability, not give rise to intergovernmental rule making."

He also foresees that "Commercial Earth observation will essentially be governed by internationally dimensioned private law, mainly relating to copyright and patent protection. Commercial remote sensing is becoming part of the global information business. More and more intimately linked to the web, commercial satellite imagery will fully evolve to become a freely traded commodity, individually owned and universally sold."

Kries's conclusion is that "There never was, and there never will be, one uniform remote sensing order covering Earth observation in all its aspects." (16)

This view is barely acceptable.

In the first place, there are no remote sensing regimes evolving separately and differently. What we have is some remote sensing activities (above all, military and commercial) not yet submitted to international regulation.

Secondly, in most legal systems there is a strong hierarchy based on the supremacy of public interests over any other regulation, thus giving public law, whether international or domestic, the highest place.

Thirdly, the Outer Space Treaty not only grants freedom of exploration and use of outer space (including freedom of overflight, data collection and use), but also – and in the first place – stipulates that the exploration and use of outer space be carried out for the benefit and in the interests of all countries". Thus, it follows that military remote sensing does not enjoy unrestrained freedom.

Fourthly, there is no any indication limiting the objectives and the scope of the UNGA Resolution 41/65 "to common utility ends", as it clearly affirms that the Copuos Legal Subcommittee was called "for a detailed consideration of the legal implications of remote sensing of the Earth from space, with the aim of formulating draft principles relating to remote sensing".

Fifthly, commercial remote sensing entities are not legally able to develop their own rules. To restrict state intervention and control is simply an illicit action. Regulating space activities is an exclusive competence of States. Not incidentally, the Outer Space Treaty establishes that only States bear international responsibility "for national activities in outer space (...), whether such activities are carried out by governmental agencies or by non-governmental entities, and for assuring that national activities are carried out in conformity with the provisions set forth in the present Treaty" (Article VI).

AGREEMENT IS MUCH BETTER

The UNGA Resolution 41/65, as all documents of the kind, is of an advisory character, and does not impose any obligations on the countries nor does it meet the need for a broad, secure and effective regulation of a strategic space activity for development by all countries. Remote sensing by satellites – which is an indispensable technology nowadays – must no doubt be regulated by a broad, compulsory and universally acknowledged instrument. In cases such as this, nothing can replace an international convention, negotiated and approved under the auspices of the United Nations, and open to the participation of all countries.

Carl Q. Christol suggested in 1988: "Perhaps the best long-term approach is to retain remote sensing on the agenda of Copuos so that efforts can be made to transmit the terms of the Principles into a treaty." In his view, "it is much better to have a formal international agreement, even interpretative considerations, than the more vague and uncertain constraints of customary international law." (17)

Joanne I. Gabrynowicz suggested that "Copuos ought to be encouraged to fulfill the intent of the Principles' drafters by transmitting their terms into a treaty". For this writer "the Principles must be defined to preserve and clarify these public good norms ["mutual cooperation of nations, equity, equality, and the use of outer space for the benefit and in the interests of all countries"] as well as to help define the rights, interests and obligations of public, private and hybrid entities". (18)

REMOTE SENSING IS MUCH MORE

Principle I limits "remote sensing" activities to the intention of "improving natural resources management, land use and the protection of the environment." The UNGA Resolution 41/65 does not include the use of remote sensing in observation, reconnaissance and monitoring activities of productive areas (agricultural, cattle, fishing, and industrial), transportation infrastructure (highways, railways, ports, airports) and services (meteorological, tourism), nor the verification of compliance with international treaties and activities strictly connected to military purposes which are growing by the day.

None of these activities, of clear economic and strategic relevance, have specific international regulations. This produces a legal *vacuum*, likely to cause serious harm to all countries, especially developing countries.

INTERNATIONAL PUBLIC SERVICE

Principle II states that "remote sensing activities shall be carried out for the benefit and in the interests of all countries, irrespective of their degree of economic, social or scientific and technological development, and taking into particular consideration the needs of the developing countries."

Principle III, in turn, reads that "remote sensing activities shall be conducted in accordance with international law, including the Charter of the United Nations, the

Activities of States in the Exploration and Use of Outer Space, including the Moon and Other Celestial Bodies, which, in particular, provides that the exploration and use of outer space shall be carried out for the benefit and in the interests of all countries, irrespective of their degree of economic and scientific development, and stipulates the principle of freedom of exploration and use of outer space on the basis of equality."

These indications extol the relevance of remote sensing activities for all countries. Thus, such activities are also "the province of all mankind," and should have a legal system worthy of such exalted consideration.

Therefore, it is necessary to regulate satellite remote sensing activities with the precautions required by an international public service that is essential to the global community.

UNILATERAL POINT OF VIEW

Some developed countries hold that the UNGA Resolution 41/65 continues to play a positive role, since it supports two principles that they consider to be priorities:

I) Unrestricted remote sensing by satellite of any point on Earth, at any time; and

II) Unrestricted sale of sensory data, with the sensed State being conceded merely the access to the data over its territory "on a non-discriminatory basis and on reasonable cost terms."

Indeed the guarantee of unrestricted sensing of any point on Earth is, without doubt, important, but it is far from exhausting the array of questions generated by an activity that is so essential to all countries. It is also necessary to garantee the access of sensed State to the data concerning its territory.

Not by chance, Shaida Johnston and Joseph Cordes observed: "It is in the national interest and general public good to ensure that data are collected, archived and disseminated on an open and non-discriminatory basis. But more and more, the pressure to privatize is drawing decision makers away from this public good argument towards that of commercial market viability." (19)

CONVENTION INSTEAD OF CUSTOM

It is not sufficient to admit, as international customs, the freedom of sensing the entire world and the freedom of selling the products of such sensing, which, in fact, were never disputed by any country since Resolution 41/65 was adopted.

These customs were recognized by the Workshop on Space Law in the Twenty-first Century, organized by the International Institute of Space Law and the UN Office for Outer Space Affairs on the occasion of the III UN Conference on the Exploration and Peaceful Uses of Outer Space (UNISPACE III, July 1999, Vienna).

However, this recognition did not prevent the Workshop from reaching the following enlightening conclusion, which provides a good idea of the size of the problem:

"The expanding growth in areas such as commercial remote sensing services, commercial complexity, the effects on international cooperation and scientific and industrial applications of services necessitates consideration of appropriate regulations. National restrictions on access to data are emerging." (20)

Joanne Irene Gabrynowicz, in a discussion paper submitted to the-above mentioned workshop held during UNISPACE III, observed that "the openness principle upon which most of remote sensing law is based is being weakened" and that "the restrictions are being implemented for commercial and military reasons." (21)

The commercial interest should be respected and even stimulated, but cannot supersede public interest. It should, to the contrary, adjust itself to the public function of remote sensing services.

A basic international legal system becomes necessary, in this case, in order to prevent national legislation from being imposed, in practice, on the international community, in an inevitable and unappealing form of extraterritoriality.

VAGUENESS

According to Principle XII, "as soon as the primary data and the processed data jurisdiction are produced, the sensed State shall have access to them on a non-discriminatory basis and on reasonable cost terms; the sensed State shall also have access to the available analysed information concerning the territory under its jurisdiction in the possession of any State participating in remote sensing activities on the same basis and terms, taking particularly into account the needs and the interests of the developing countries."

The expression "on a non-discriminatory basis and on reasonable cost terms" (Principle XII) is too vague and flexible. This does not formulate a secure and effective rule, nor does it guarantee the sensed States a minimum of essential predictability in the significant commercial transactions of our time and, above all, in light of the unfailingly rigorous and non-negotiable national security policies of the great world powers.

The regularity and predictability of remote sensing services by satellite must be guaranteed.

Winter Gerd rightly noted:

"There is no unlimited access to data concerning the sensed State. There is only access on a non-discriminatory basis. It follows that the observing State may retain data if it does this equally in relation to any other State. This possibility if of utmost importance with regard to data on mineral and other exploitable resources. In addition, free access is not much worth if the cost is high. Therefore, rules on costs are of crucial importance. Again, Principle XII is disappointing in this respect. "Reasonable cost" can well go beyond the cost of handling request (which is the formula of the USA Landsat Acts) and include an element of sharing the cost of obtaining and processing of the data. At this point it becomes clear postulating a customary principle of free remote sensing and of data ownership is very one-sided if one does not add, as a twin principle, that access of the sensed State must be provided unlimited and at incremental cost. Otherwise it would have been a bad trade-off for the sensed States to have, by agreeing to the UN Resolution, implicitly given up the strict sovereignty position on the one side and, on the other, to have gotten only half way to a full concept

TO PREVENT ACCESS RESTRICTIONS

"Appropriate regulations" are needed, guaranteeing not only the right of commerce but also the right to access. Precisely in view of this need, the above-mentioned Workshop recommended that "the Legal Subcommittee of the Committee on the Peaceful Uses of Outer Space initiate the drafting of a treaty covering remote sensing from outer space on the basis of the Principles Relating to Remote Sensing of the Earth from Outer Space (...), taking into particular account the expanding growth in commercial remote sensing services and preserving the principal of non-discriminatory access to data." (23)

Thus, a convention would be necessary for two principal reasons: the commercialization of remote sensing services; and the preservation of access to the data without discrimination.

These reasons become more powerful and convincing every day.

When Resolution 41/65 was passed, the commercialization of remote sensing services practically did not exist. It emerged afterwards, and underwent an accelerated process in the 1990's, with broad impact upon the entire world.

A highly complex business, it affects international cooperation, scientific collaboration and industrial development.

Thus, the regulation of such activities cannot be restricted to the freedom to sell data. This basic freedom must be detailed, so that it does not become an abuse of rights and a privilege to the detriment of legitimate interests of other countries and the international community as a whole.

At the same time, the principle of preserving access to the data without discrimination must be further regulated, moreover because, as was emphasized in the Unispace II Workshop, "national restrictions on access to data are emerging."

One may ask what type of discrimination are we talking about? This concept must be defined as concretely as possible, in order to be aware of the actual obstacles existing and to prevent anything that could hinder unrestricted access to data.

TO FIX RIGHTS AND DUTIES

According to Principle IV, "remote sensing activities (...) shall not be conducted in a manner detrimental to the legitimate rights and interests of the sensed State".

Such principle, for Bin Cheng, "sounds like an application of the principle of good neighbourliness," that is, merely as sign of good will with regard to countries subject to sensing. (24)

The demonstration of good will, it seems, appeared to be necessary, since as Bin Cheng himself observed, "the sensed State has been given no special treatment at all, except perhaps the very vague safeguard found in Principle IV." But even this safeguard, adds the jurist, "is subject to auto-interpretation."

"In sum," concludes Bin Cheng, "those who are apprehensive that data gathered from outer space by others might work to their detriment or that the data gathered from outer space might be misused by either the sensing State or by third parties to their detriment can probably find only scant comfort from the United Nations Principles." (25)

This actually concerns protection of something not yet duly defined – the rights and interests of sensed States. Fundamental concepts must be defined in a clear and detailed manner, filling in the significant gaps that exist today.

A convention on remote sensing would therefore be necessary for outlining, first of all, the rights and duties of sensed States, as well as the rights and duties of States carrying out remote sensing activities. Neither has been clearly outlined.

The international convention hereby suggested should further contain basic norms for the defence of intellectual property and patents, especially with regard to analyzed satellite sensed data, in order to protect legitimate rights, without, however, discontinuing or hindering access to data for countries that are in need of such information, especially sensed States. In this work, it would perhaps be useful to take into account the World Trade Organization (WTO) legal instruments.

Principle I (e) indicates that "the term 'remote sensing activities' means the operation of remote sensing space systems, primary data collection and storage stations, and activities in processing, interpreting and disseminating the processed data." This is a restricted definition.

It is imperative to define with precision the concept of "remote sensing activities" in order to ease verification of possible violations of the rights and interests of sensed States and, if so, for the perpetrators thereof to be held responsible.

Responsibilities must be established for the use of remote sensing data, particularly/concerning sensed States.

In fact, the use of the analyzed data is likely to cause more harm to sensed States than the operations involving collection, storage, processing and distribution of the processed data. It is precisely such use that is not included in the concept currently referred to of "remote sensing activities."

FOR BROAD RESPONSIBILITY

Principle XIV confirms this situation when it attributes international responsibility for remote sensing activities only to "States operating remote sensing satellites." As Nandasiri Jasentuliyana stressed, "there was no agreed interpretation of what it means to bear international responsibility for remote sensing activities, with developing countries arguing for rather broad responsibility and liability, and western countries arguing for narrow responsibility, not going beyond existing international law." (26)

This clash of interpretations, vis-à-vis a fundamental issue such as international responsibility, is another clear illustration of the need to elaborate a better and more effective international regulation for remote sensing satellite activities.

Moreover, Principle XIV, strangely enough, as noted by Bin Cheng, commits the imprudent error of limiting the application of Article 6 of the Outer Space Treaty of 1967, which establishes international responsibility for States for any and all national space activities – public and private to the "operations of remote

Thus, by means of Resolution 41/65, responsibility is established only for operations of remote sensing satellites and not for the use of the data obtained through such operations. Who is liable, then, for the use of remote sensing data that may cause harm to the sensed States? The question does not , so far, have a specific solution. And this is an issue which should not be delayed.

FOR BALANCE OF INTERESTS

Principle IV acknowledges both the freedom of remote sensing from space as well as the right and the interests of sensed States, without indicating how this conciliation may, in fact, be attained.

States carrying out remote sensing activities always stress the primacy of the freedom to carry out these activities. Sensed States seek to defend their rights and interests. Each group of countries has its own interpretation of the text.

Resolution 41/65, as drafted, allows for both interpretations. What actually prevails, in the end, is the view of the stronger side, namely the one which has the technological domain over remote sensing activities.

The Principles "often contain provisions which, according to their phraseology, can be interpreted in different ways," as stated in 1989 by Professor H.L. van Traa-Engelman, from the University of Utrecht, in the Netherlands. Therefore, in this writer's view, "it would be prudent to consider the established 'principle' as a universal code of conduct and as such a stage of development in a evolutionary process of international law-making." (27)

Balance, coherence, harmony and effectiveness should be given to the principles and rules governing remote sensing by satellite activities, in order to prevent contradictory interpretations.

FOR A JUST AND EQUITABLE LAW

According to Principle V, States carrying out remote sensing activities "shall promote international cooperation" in these activities and "make available to other States opportunities for participation therein," which includes sensed States.

However, the principle establishes, at the same time, that "such participation shall be based in each case on equitable and mutually acceptable terms."

If the conditions for participation of the sensed States are to be "mutually acceptable," this could mean that cooperation will always be subject to the will of the countries carrying out remote sensing activities. Thus, the application of the principle that establishes the obligation of the State carrying out remote sensing activities to cooperate with the sensed State would depend upon the acceptance of this obligation by the sensing State. In this way, the very rule that creates the duty is, at the same time, contributing in practice to its non-compliance.

Nico Krisch shrewdly pointed out that "every attempt by a state to weaken an existing rule or prevent a more stringent rule from developing can be regarded as a defense of freedom to act unilaterally." (28)

A just and equitable convention must ensure equilibrium between the technological and economical power of States carrying out remote sensing activities and the legitimate rights and interests of sensed States, which are the weaker party in this unbalanced relationship.

Gerson Fonseca, Jr. reminds us that "legitimate procudures offer the only way to ward off the crystallization of the principle of might makes right and to start building a solid basis for international relations in the twenty-first century". (29)

To discuss, elaborate and approuve such a convention is an almost impossible task. However, there does not seem to be any other method of attaining a higher level of justice and equality, which today does not exist yet. (30)

"I dont't fell optimistic, but I dont't think one should give in. One thing is to foresee, another one is to make ones's own choice", as I learned from the Italian philosopher Norberto Bobbio. (31)

FOR A REAL ADVANCEMENT

Conclusions and recommendations:

a) Satellite remote sensing activities must be regulated by a special and comprehensive

Subcommittee of Copuos on the basis of the Principles approved by the UNGA Resolution 41/65;

b) This convention should clarify, detail and develop the existing Principles and elaborate new ones, if necessary, in order to create a contemporary and effective legal instrument, ordering the international use of the most advanced remote sensing technology for the benefit of all nations and, in this way, harmonizing the legitimate rights and interests of sensing and sensed States.

c) The convention should stimulate an effective and sound cooperation among all countries and between public and commercial interests in remote sensing activities, recognizing the main function of these activities as a public service. "The international community prospers when law and power are in partnership, not when they are in conflict", as Sir Arthur Watts pointed out. (32)

d) The freedom of remote sensing must be preserved and the right of access by sensed States to data concerning its territory and natural resources must be guaranteed in concrete terms. It means – *inter alia* – to define the expression "access to data on a non-discriminatory basis and on reasonable costs".

Notes and references

1) Krisch, Nico, *Weak as Constraint, Strong as Tool: The Place of International Law in US Foreign Policy*, in *Unilateralism & US Foreign Policy – International Perspectives*, Edited by David M. Malone and Yuen Foong Khong, USA: Lynne Rienner Publishers, 2003, p.42

2) Watts, Sir Arthur, KCMG QC, *The Importance of International Law*, in The Role of Law in International Politics – Essays in International Relations and International Law, Edited by Michael Byers, USA, New York, Oxford University Press, 2001, p. 7.

3) Lachs, Manfred, *The Treaty on Principles of the Law of Outer Space, 1961-1992*, in Netherlands International Law Review, 1992, Vol. XXXIX, Issue 3, p. 302.

4) See <http://www.oosa.unvienna.org/SpaceLaw/rs.html>

5) There was a regional treaty on remote Transfer and Use of Data of Remote Sensing of the Earth from Outer Space, done on May 19, 1978, and signed by Bulgaria, former Czechoslovakia, Cuba, Germany (East), Hungary, Mongolia, Poland, Rumania and former URSS; and there is one sectorial text: the Resolution 40 of the World Meteorological Organization (WMO) on the exchange of meteorological data and products, including meteorological satellite data, adopted in 1995 (see Guidelines on Relationships in Commercial Meteorological Activities, 1996, in www.wmo,ch/index-en.html)

6) The Treaty on Principles Governing the Activities of States in the Exploration and Use of Outer Space, including the Moon and Other Celestial Bodies (the "Outer Space Treaty", adopted by the General Assembly in its resolution 2222 (XXI)), opened for signature on 27 January 1967, entered into force on 10 October 1967, 98 ratifications and 27 signatures (as of 1 January 2003). See <http://www.oosa.unvienna.org/SpaceLaw/treaties.html>

7) Williams, Maureen, *Observing the Earth from Space in Light of the Principle of Sovereignty*, Revista Brasileira de Direito Aeroespacial (Brazilian Review of Aerospace Law), Number 82, April 2001. Paper presented to the X Brazilian Symposium on Remote Sensing, Foz do Iguaçu, Parana, Brazil, April 21-26, 2001. See also, by the same author, *Reflections and Suggestions on Remote Sensing and International Law*, German Journal of Air and Space Law, 3-2001. See also Christol, Carl Q., *Remote Sensing and International Space Law*, Journal of Space Law, Number 16, 1988; Space Law, Past, Present and Future, Kluwer, 1991, pp. 73-95.

8) Christol, Carl Q., *Remote Sensing and International Space Law*, Journal of Space Law, Number 16, 1988; Space Law, Past, Present and Future, Kluwer, 1991, pp. 73-95.

9) Murthi, Sridhara, *Commercial Availability of High Quality Remote Sensing Imageries: Legal Issues*, Singapore of Journal of International and Comparative Law (2001) 5, p. 150.

10) Kries, Wulf von, *Towards a new remote sensing order?*, *Space Policy*, Volume 16, Number 3, August 2000, p. 163.

11) Kries, Wulf von, id ibid, p. 164.

12) Murthi, Sridhara, id ibid, p. 155.

13) Kries, Wulf von, id ibid, p. 164.

14) Murthi, Sridhara, id ibid, p. 152.

15) *O Globo*, Brazilian newspaper, from 24/09/2002.

16) Kries, Wulf von, id ibid, pp. 165-166.

17) Christol, Carl Q., *Remote Sensing and International Space Law*, Journal of Space Law, Number 16, 1988; Space Law, Past, Present and Future, Kluwer, 1991, pp. 93, 95.

18) Gabrynowicz, Joanne Irene, Expanding Global Remote Sensing Services: Three Fundamental Considerations discussion paper

first Century, organized by the International Institute of Space Law with the United Nations Office for Outer Space Affairs (OOSA), UNISPACE III, Vienna July 1999, A/Conf. 184/7, New York, 1999, pp. 100-101.

19) Johnston, Shaida, and Cordes, Joseph, *Public good or commercial opportunity? Case studies in remote sensing commercialization*, Space Policy, 19 (2003), pp. 23-31.

20) Proceedings on the Workshop on Space Law in the Twenty-first Century, United Nations, New York, 2000, p. 3.

21) Gabrynowicz, Joanne Irene, id ibid, p. 98.

22) Gerd, Winter, *Access of public to environmental data from remote sensing*, in *Droit, télédétection et environnment*, sous la direction de Simone Courteix, Paris: Sides, 1994, pp. 254-255.

23) Proceedings on the Workshop on Space Law, id ibid, p. 3.

24) Cheng, Bin, Studies in International Space Law, Clarendon Press Oxford, 1997, p. 590.

25) Cheng, Bin, id ibid, p. 596.

26) Jasentuliyana, Nandasiri, *International Space Law and the United Nations*, The Hague, The Netherlands: Kluwer Law International, 1999, p. 316.

27) Traa-Engelman, H. L. van, Commercial Utilization of Outer Space, The Netherlands: Martinus Nijhoff Publishers, 1993, p. 245.

28) Krisch, Nico, *id ibid,* p. 42.

29) Fonseca, Jr., Gelson, *The United States and Latin America: Multilateralism and International Legitimacy*, in *Unilateralism & US Foreign Policy*, Edited By David M. Malone and Yuen Foong Khong, United Kingdom: Lynne Rinner Publishers, 2003, 321-345.

30) *Why an International Convention on Remote Sensing of the Earth from Outer Space is necessary?*, Working Paper submitted by Brazilian Delegation to the Legal Subcommittee of the United Nations Committee on the Peaceful Uses of Outer Space (Copuos), Forty-second session, Vienna, 24 March – 4 April 2003 (A/AC.105/C.2/L.244).

31) Watts, Sir Arthur, KCMG QC, id ibid, p. 7.

32) Bobbio, Norberto, *O problema da guerra e as vidas da paz*, S. Paulo, Brasil: Editora Unesp, 2003, p. 115.

THE USE OF REMOTE SENSING TO SUPPORT THE APPLICATION OF ENVIRONMENTAL TREATIES

Nicolas Peter [(1) (2)]
[(1)] International Space University (ISU)
[(2)] Institut du Droit de l'Espace et des Télécommunications (IDEST). Université Paris Sud XI

Corresponding Author: Nicolas Peter (peter@isu.isunet.edu)
International Space University (ISU) Parc d'innovation, 67400 Illkirch, France
Phone + 33 3 88 65 50 19 Fax: +33 3 88 65 54 47

ABSTRACT

There is a growing realization of the increasingly varied and interesting possibilities for the use of earth observation data to ensure compliance with international obligations generally, and treaty obligations in particular. Most efforts at examining the application of earth observation data to monitoring states' compliance with international obligations focus on the environmental sector. This paper is contemplating the use of remote sensing satellites for the support of multilateral environmental agreements (MEAs) especially land monitoring MEAs such as the Convention on Wetlands of International Importance especially as Waterfowl Habitat (1971) [1]; the Convention on Biological Diversity (1992) [2] the United Nations Convention to Combat Desertification (1994) [3] and also the United Nations Framework Convention on Climate Change (1992) [4] and the Kyoto Protocol (1997) [5].

INTRODUCTION

In the last thirty years the rapid growth in the number of multilateral environmental agreements (MEAs) has been an encouraging sign of international commitment to protect the environment. The proliferation of treaties has resulted in an increasing need for spatial data on the Earth's biophysical systems. Although the existing satellites were not designed to meet the information requirements of environmental treaties, they can be used to generate key information necessary for developing and implementing international environmental treaties.

MULTILATERAL ENVIRONMENTAL AGREEMENTS

Recently, MEAs have proliferated as environmental protection has become a major issue worldwide. The 1992 Rio Conference, and the 1972 Stockholm Conference before it, reflected the rise of concern for the global environment and each was a catalyst for the creation of new accords. MEAs currently address a wide range of environmental phenomena, both regional and global in nature [6].

The proliferation of MEAs has resulted in an attendant need for spatial data on the health of the Earth. This information contributes to the design of improved policy instruments [7].

MEAS AND REMOTE SENSING

Earth Observation systems are tools, developed in recent decades, which have become essential for effectively conducting different types of environmental management and environmental research applications. However, although over 200 MEAs addressing a broad range of environmental issues and concerns have come into existence during the last few decades, but few explicitly incorporate or depend on data and information from space-based technology [7].

The International Convention for the Prevention of Pollution from Ships [8] is one of the only MEA explicitly referring to remote sensing in his articles as potential support in marine oil pollution monitoring.

At the World Summit on Sustainable Development, held in Johannesburg, South Africa, in 2002, state representatives adopted the Johannesburg Declaration, which identifies future environmental and development goals. The Johannesburg Declaration's supporting Plan of Implementation has identified earth observation as a crucial information source for a number of relevant disciplines to sustainable development. Earth observation is specifically mentioned as a key decision-making tool for better management of water resources, natural disasters monitoring, climate and desertification monitoring etc.

Despite the fact that Earth Observation systems are capable of assisting the MEA process, there are number of significant problems. These include lack of consistency and standardisation of data sets and fragmented and inadequate data archives. Remote Sensing technology may provide significant new types of data, as well as simply more or better quality data, but linking Remote Sensing data to policy is not straightforward.

The American Institute of Aeronautics and Astronautics highlighted that remotely sensed data can be used for various aspects of MEAs [9]. The application of Earth Observation systems to support MEAs can range from the identification of an new environmental problem (pre-negotiation phase) to the monitoring (negotiation phase) and assessment (implementation phase) of that problem, to the verification of compliance and subsequent enforcement (compliance and dispute resolution). However it is important to note that there is no binding international regime specifically addressing verification through remote sensing even though the concept of verification through remotely sensed data is not new (provisions in the 1970s' Strategic Arms Reduction Treaties) [10].

REMOTE SENSING DATA AND INTERNATIONAL JURISDICTION

Another issue is whether satellite data is accepted as legally binding proof when it comes to enforcement of treaties. In the past satellite images used for control purposes have been considered mainly as an indication tool that needed to be confirmed by ground verification rather than a complete system of proof by itself [10]. Remote sensing needs to be accepted by the court as legal evidence. This important aspect is not presented in this paper. Several cases exist were remote sensing has been used as proof :

One case when satellite imagery has been accepted as legal evidence in court is the Singapore "Song San" case. In 1996 oil pollution in the straight of Malacca was detected with satellite imagery together with laboratories analysis, the Singaporean tanker "Song San" was identified as the source of marine pollution. On the basis of the satellite data, legal proceedings in Singapore were initiated [11].

The International Court of Justice has accepted remote sensing imagery as proof in certain situation. In the Qatar/Bahrain Case, the Nigeria/Cameroon, Botswana/Namibia case the Court accepted satellite imagery as supportive tools for the chains of evidence to be created.

Satellite data has also considerably supported the work and judgements of the International Claims Tribunal for the Former Yugoslavia (ICTY) in The Hague.

The European Community Commission is using remote sensing in support of its agricultural, environmental and research policy through the Monitoring Agriculture with Remote Sensing (MARS) project, in order to calculate the compensations due. MARS project which aims among others to verify that the policy of fallow land is well implemented has established an operational agricultural monitoring system which monitors and predicts yields for the 10 most common crops across the European Union using field-sampling methods.

Remote sensing satellites for verification purposes is more and more recognized and utilized, even if it is not perfect. Despite the fact that Earth Observation systems are capable of assisting the MEA process, there are number of significant problems. These include lack of consistency and standardisation of data sets and fragmented and inadequate data archives.

APPLICATION OF A MEA FOR LAND MONITORING

This section provides examples of applications of remote sensing in four domains: The Ramsar Convention on Wetlands of International Importance Especially as Waterfowl habitat, The Convention on Biological Diversity (CBD) and The Convention to Combat Desertification in those Countries Experiencing Serious Drought and / or Desertification, particularly in Africa (CCD) and the Convention on Climate Change.

Convention on Wetlands of International Importance especially as Waterfowl Habitat

The Convention on Wetlands of International Importance especially as Waterfowl Habitat, signed in Ramsar, Iran, in 1971, is an intergovernmental treaty which provides the framework for national action and international cooperation for the conservation and wise use of wetlands and their resources. The Convention's mission is the conservation and wise use of wetlands by national action and international cooperation as a means to achieving sustainable development throughout the world.

Remotely sensed data could be useful to inform the Secretariat of the Convention, "at the earliest possible time if the ecological character of any wetland in its territory and included in the list has changes, is changing or likely to change as the result of technological developments, pollution or other human interference (Article 3.2). Remote sensing can help to do a survey of the actual wetlands repartition and extension (Article 8).

As key outcome of the United Nations Conference on Environment and Development or Earth Summit in Rio in 1992 several environmental issues such as : biodiversity, climate change and desertification were addressed. This resulted by the adoption of several international environmental agreements which defined specific government commitments to address these issues.

Convention on Biological Diversity

The overarching aim of the Convention on Biological Diversity (CBD) is the conservation and sustainable use of biological resources. This convention makes commitments to integrate the sustainable use and conservation of biodiversity into national and international decision-making, including:

- Scientific and technical cooperation: including access to and transfer of biotechnology
- Natural resource management: Establishment of protected areas and rehabilitation. Restoration of degraded ecosystems and threatened species. Prevention/control and eradication of alien species which threaten biodiversity.

According to the CBD remote sensing can help for habitat suitability mapping would help to "rehabilitate and restore degraded ecosystems and promote the recovery of threatened species, inter alia, through the development and implementation of plans or other management strategies" (Article 8, Paragraph f). This information would also help "develop, where necessary, guidelines for the selection, establishment and management of protected areas" (Article 8, Paragraph).

The Meso-American Biological Corridor is an excellent example of habitat suitability mapping. This biological corridor is a planned combination of protected areas and managed landscapes that forms a continuous wildlife migration route from Panama to the Mexican border. This project is a collaboration between the University of Maine, the Jet Propulsion Laboratory and the NASDA.

Convention to Combat Desertification

The Convention to Combat Desertification seeks to not only tackle the impacts of desertification but also to mitigate the effects of droughts in countries experiencing serious drought and/or desertification, particularly in Africa, through effective action at all levels, supported by international cooperation and partnership arrangements. Under the convention desertification refers to dryland areas vulnerable to over-exploitation and inappropriate land-use as a result of poverty, political instability, deforestation, overgrazing and bad irrigation. Implementation is defined at a regional level since the convention breaks down into five regions, as defined in the "Implementation Annex" of the convention. The regions are: Central and Eastern Europe, Africa, Asia, Latin America and Caribbean and the Northern Mediterranean.

The areas, which could directly benefit from use of spaceborne Earth Observation technology in the implementation framework of the Convention to Combat Desertification fall under three main headings:

- The collection and analysis of short-term and long-term data and information to identify causal factors, both natural and human, contributing to land degradation, desertification and/or drought;

increase knowledge of the processes leading to land degradation, desertification and drought;

- The systematic observation of the state of the environment to assess qualitative and quantitative trends in natural resources; evaluate the causes and consequences of desertification, notably ecological degradation; and monitor the effects of land degradation and desertification to improve the value of strategies to combat desertification; and
- The establishment and/or strengthening of early warning systems to evaluate the impacts of natural climate variability on regional drought and desertification and generate seasonal to inter-annual climate predictions to improve the efficiency of programs mitigating the effects of droughts on affected population.

PARTICULAR CASE OF THE CONVENTION ON CLIMATE CHANGE

Climate change, caused by the rapid and uncontrolled increase of greenhouse gases in the Earth's atmosphere during the past 150 years, is a major public, political and scientific concern worldwide.

Convention on Climate Change

Public concern resulted in the 1992 United Nations Framework Convention on Climate Change (UNFCCC) which is an official acknowledgement of the climate change phenomenon, as well as a recognition by international policy makers that immediate cross-border actions are required to halt and reverse the current destructive trend.

The convention sets an "ultimate objective" of stabilizing atmospheric concentrations of greenhouse gases at safe levels. Such levels, which the convention does not quantify, should be achieved within a time frame sufficient to allow ecosystems to adapt naturally to climate change. To achieve this objective, all countries have a general commitment to address climate change. The UNFCCC commits all parties to prepare "national inventories of anthropogenic emissions by sources and removals by sinks of all greenhouse gases not controlled by the Montreal Protocol, using comparable methodologies to be agreed upon by the Conference of the Parties".

The convention then divides countries into two groups: those listed in its Annex I (known as "Annex I Parties") and those that are not so listed (so-called "non-Annex I Parties"). The Annex I Parties are the industrialized countries who have historically contributed the most to climate change. They include both the countries that were members of the Organization for Economic Co-operation and Development (OECD) in 1992, and countries with "economies in transition". The principles of equity and "common but differentiated responsibilities" enshrined in the Convention therefore require these Parties to take the lead in modifying longer-term trends in emissions. All remaining countries have a time frame for the submission of their initial national communications, including their emission inventories, constraining than for Annex I Parties.

The Kyoto Protocol

The UNFCCC was in 1997 strengthened with the Kyoto Protocol which contains quantified, legally binding commitments to limit or reduce greenhouse gas emissions in the atmosphere that are related to human induced interference with the climate system to 1990 levels. The Kyoto Protocol commits Annex I Parties to limit or reduce their greenhouse gas emissions, adding up to a total cut of at least 5% from 1990 levels in the "commitment period" 2008-2012. The targets cover emissions of the six main greenhouse gases : carbon dioxide (CO_2); methane (CH_4); nitrous oxide (N_2O); hydrofluorocarbons (HFCs); perfluorocarbons (PFCs) and sulphur hexafluoride (SF_6).

Two of the main greenhouse gases under the scope of the Kyoto Protocol which can be addressed by the Remote Sensing community are the methane and the carbon dioxide [12]. While CO_2 released by burning of fossil fuels and methane by wetlands destruction constitute the most important emission source, the Kyoto Protocol allows emissions to be balanced by vegetation. Vegetation, which may sequester or release atmospheric carbon and methane depending on the land use, and this is where remote sensing potentially may come into relevance.

Earth observation can provide information about forest area, type, density and health. Satellite sensors can also be used to monitor agricultural activities and other important parameters include such as type, productivity of crops.... Taking several images during the growth cycle makes it possible to draw conclusions about field management practices, such as crop rotations, irrigation cycles and harvesting times.

The Kyoto Protocol sets specific resolution standards. Forest area must be determined using a spatial resolution no larger than 1 hectare, corresponding to a satellite sensor resolution of less than 100 metres. This limits data collection from earth observation sensors to two main types, available in 1990. These are the sensors on board the Landsat (US) and Spot (France) satellite series. Since 1990, a number of new sensors have become available for monitoring land inventories activities either so called passive (ADEOS series) and active systems (Radarsat series).

Earth observation is a very appropriate tool to provide the land-cover information required by the Kyoto Protocol [13]. However, a challenge remains in converting this information (land-cover information) into equivalent carbon stock figures. Some progress has been made since the establishment of the Kyoto Protocol, but more is needed in order to standardise methods.

Relevance of Earth Observation to the Kyoto Protocol

They are five specific areas where remote sensing may support the treaty:

- Provision of systematic observations of relevant land cover (Art. 5, Art. 10);
- Support to the establishment of a 1990 carbon stock baseline (Art. 3);
- Detection and spatial quantification of change in land cover (Art. 3, Art. 12);
- Quantification of above-ground vegetation biomass stocks and associated changes therein (Art. 3 Art 12);
- Mapping and monitoring of sources of anthropogenic CH_4 (Art. 3, Art. 5, Art. 10);

Within the context of the Kyoto Protocol, Article 10 can be recognised as a key driver, in which contributions can be made to provide systematic observations and data archives in order to reduce uncertainties in the global terrestrial carbon budget . [12]

For biomass retrieval as in the context of the Kyoto Protocol it is an absolute requirement that data acquisitions are performed in a consistent manner providing systematic, repetitive observations over large areas is potentially one of the strengths of remote sensing technology [14]. There is a general inadequacy of current data archives because high resolution satellites are not generally collecting data on a homogeneous way over large areas, but instead they are collected in a fragmented manner over several local sites that have been specifically requested by commercial or scientific users.

For regional scale applications, such as biomass retrieval over extensive ecological regions, it is an absolute requirement that data acquisitions are performed in both a spatially and temporally consistent manner. Gaps that inevitably do occur occasionally should be covered during the next cycle for minimal impact [14]. Timing is an important component of repetitive observations, as seasonality may introduce bias in time series of data. Annual acquisitions should therefore preferably be planned during the same season every year [14]. Most of the terrestrial parameters that need to be characterized and quantified within the Kyoto Protocol are in a state of constant change and in many cases, it is these changes that the scientific community are interested in, and so the temporal dynamics of the terrestrial parameters need to be taken into account. The temporal repetition frequency of the acquisitions have to be adapted with respect to the land use, and a land use based stratification of the Earth may thus be required in a global data acquisition plan [14].

World Summit on Sustainable Development

The World Summit on Sustainable Development, held in Johannesburg, South Africa, in 2002, was an important political reunion reinforcing the critical issues related to climate change and the potential support that can play remote sensing. Article 36 of the Plan of Implementation states that: "The United Framework Convention on Climate Change is the key instrument for addressing climate change, a global concern, and we reaffirm our commitment to achieving its ultimate objective of stabilisation of greenhouse gas concentrations in the atmosphere. Actions at all levels are required to: (g) Promote the systematic observation of the earth's atmosphere, land and oceans by improving monitoring stations, increasing the use of satellites, and appropriate integration of these observations".

CONCLUSIONS

In the last thirty years, international environmental agreements have proliferated as environmental protection has become a major issue worldwide.

The environmental protection of the Earth has given birth to a corpus juris specialized in environmental law. These international regulations have a general weakness due to the lack of mechanisms of control or constraints that would make them more effective.

Earth Observation systems have become essential for effectively conducting different types of environmental management and environmental research applications. They can prompt new agreements, influence behaviour under existing agreements, and evaluate past performance and effectiveness. Remote sensing imagery has already been accepted as legal evidence in court ("Song San" case) and in front of the International Court of Justice and is also used by the European Community Commission in support of its agricultural, environmental and research policy through the MARS projcct.

The use of remote sensing could be an important and effective support to MEAs. In order to fully achieve this goal the international community needs to move towards the legal recognition of the use of remote sensing imagery as proof, and as a decisive tool in the framework of the defense of the environment.

Remote sensing technology may provide significant new types of data, but linking remote sensing data to policy is not straight forward.

REFERENCES

[1] C.T.S. 9 as amended (1986) C.T.S. 46

[2] 31 *I.L.M.* 818

[3] *I.L.M.* 1328

[4] 31 *I.L.M.* 851

[5] 37 *I.L.M.* 22

[6] Kline, Raustiala. "International environmental agreements and remote sensing technologies". *Background paper prepared for the Workshop on Remote Sensing and Environmental Treaties: Building More Effective Linkages,* December 4-5, 2000:

[7] de Sherbinin, and Chandra "Remote Sensing in Support of Multilateral Environmental Agreements: What Have We Learned from Pilot Applications ?" *Paper prepared for presentation at the Open Meeting of the Human Dimensions of Global Environmental Change Research Community,* Rio de Janeiro. (6-8 October 2001).

[8] 12 *I.L.M.* 1319 (1973), as modified by the Protocol of 1978, 17 *I..L.M.* 546 (1978) (MARPOL 73/78) and Annexes

[9] American Institute of Aeronautics and Astronautics, *Sixth International Space Cooperation Workshop Report.* March 2001

[10] Hettling,: "The use of Remote Sensing Satellites for Verification in International Law", *Space Policy*, Volume 19 Number 1, February 2003, pp 33-41.

[11] Brehon, "Le Satellite au Service de l'Environnement", *Air & Cosmos*, 25-05-2001, p. 52.

[12] Rosenqvist, Imhoff, Milne, Dobson, "Remote Sensing and the Kyoto Protocol: A Review of Available and Future Technology for Monitoring Treaty Compliance". *Report.* Ann Arbor, MI, USA, October 20-22, 1999.

[13] Peter. "Supporting Environmental Treaties with Remote Sensing Data. An example of the application of a Multilateral Environmental Agreement : The Kyoto Protocol", *UNESCO / Eurisy Conference. Space Applications for Heritage Conservation.* Strasbourg, France 5-8 November 2002.

[14] Rosenqvist, "Systematic data acquisitions - a prerequisite for meaningful biophysical parameter retrieval ?" *3rd Symposium on Retrieval of Bio-and Geophysical Parameters from SAR Data for Land Applications,* Sheffield, U.K., Sept. 11-14, 2001

Acknowledgments

The author would like to thank Philippe Achilleas (IDEST) and Ake Rosenqvist (NASDA) who followed the work. The author would like also to thank Jill Ferrier (ISU) who played a major role with her valuable comments and suggestions.

THE IMPACT OF THE DECLARATION OF LEGAL PRINCIPLES ON THE DEVELOPMENT OF REMOTE SENSING'S INTERNATIONAL LEGAL SYSTEM: REVISITING THE CONCEPT OF STATE INTERNATIONAL RESPONSIBILITY

Author: Maria Helena Fonseca de Souza Rolim
Organization
Instituto Tecnológico de Aeronáutica - Brazil

Co-author:Fernanda Fernandez Jankov
Organization
São Marcos University - Brazil

Introduction

Mankind achieved unprecedented scientific breakthroughs in the 20th Century and stepped into the 21st Century with the necessary tools and expertise to access, via remote sensing, a slew of data on the atmosphere, land surface, oceans, polar regions, and the complex interrelations between the myriad environmental phenomena covering a wide spectrum of time and space coordinates. The importance of such data will be directly dependent on how effectively they are employed toward a sustainable development of the world's ecosystem.

From this developmental perspective, understanding the role that private concerns will play in the domestic and international legal system applying to remote sensing issues is of the essence. This paper aims to provide valuable insights into the legal aspects germane to remote sensing activities of non-governmental entities and a State's International Responsibility for these activities, with emphasis on those that are not in keeping with the precepts set out in Principle IV, *i.e.* the actions that do not abide by the principle of full and permanent sovereignty of all States and peoples over their wealth and natural resources, giving due consideration to the rights and interests of every State and all entities under its jurisdiction, in keeping with the dictates of international law.

To manage these natural resources, remote sensing by satellite stands out as the most effective means of collecting the data necessary for monitoring and studying environmental phenomena, the more so in nations stretching over a vast expanse of land, as in the case of Brazil. Remote sensing equipment may be mounted onto aircraft, rockets and balloons to obtain images from the Earth's surface, but these platforms are expensive and offer limited operational capabilities. States have resorted to man-made satellites as a platform for remote sensing equipment, and non-governmental entities have increasingly looked to this alternative as well. In fact, a satellite may gravitate around the Earth for quite a while, without the need for fuel and at such an altitude that allows it to capture images covering a large area, repeatedly and at a relatively low cost.

These aspects help explain the pressure that facts have brought to bear on the legal system.[1] After all, technology developments have a material impact on domestic and international law systems, and, in the specific case of remote sensing, several distinct legal systems may end up governing these activities, in that they may originate from a country's air space (subject to the principles of State sovereignty and, as such, governed by the pertinent domestic laws) or from outer space (subject to the prevailing principles and teleology of *corpus juris spatialis*).[2] This legal system, whose origin goes back to space-oriented operations during the Cold War period, assumes that there must be peaceful coexistence among the States, for which public international law serves as a common denominator primarily intended to govern space activities of the States worldwide.[3]

1. Remote Sensing and Outer Space Law

An analysis of the treatment accorded to remote sensing under current space law shows that the ground rules for this issue (*i.e.*, a detailed inventory of the rights and obligations attaching to sensing and sensed States, with focus on the permissibility of such activities, access to collected data, dissemination of data to third persons, or specific uses and legal framework for non-governmental remote sensing activities) are yet to be better defined in international treaties addressing these specific issues.

The Registration Convention and the Outer Space Treaty operate as the international space body of laws applying to remote sensing, with emphasis on the following major (hard law) principles: outer space activities must abide by international law precepts; sovereignty cannot be evoked in relation to outer space; exploration and use of the outer space must target the welfare and interests of all countries in whatever stage of development; all States must be allowed unrestricted access to outer space, on equitable and non-discriminatory conditions; a State's activities in this area must favour peace and international security; international co-operation must prevail; every State must advise the U.N. Secretary-General of the nature of outer space activities, as well as of the place where they will be performed and their ensuing effects; every State takes international responsibility for outer space activities carried out by its domestic governmental or non-governmental entities; every State where a space object is registered must advise the U.N. of such activities.

Nevertheless, in addition to this legal framework, the U.N. Declaration of Legal Principles has been particularly adopted as a guideline for remote sensing activities, prompting further consideration about the binding nature of such international law mechanisms. Legal writings are split over the legal nature of such international law dictates; some advocate that these principles should be construed as a rule of conduct to be followed by the States (soft law), while others contend that they are closer to a rule of usage and customs materialising into customary law (hard law), with binding force from an international positive law perspective.

In analysing the Principles Relating to Remote Sensing of the Earth from Space, adopted by the U.N. General Assembly in 1986, Gaudrat and Tuinder note that "these principles can now be considered as being a part of customary international space law."[4]

Within this international scenario, the U.N. acknowledged the need of devising new mechanisms for legal protection and regulation of outer space activities, and such task was incumbent on COPUOS.[5] And the time was ripe for international organisations to come to the fore as new players on the international law stage, with the leading role of conceiving and codifying space law in a way to accommodate new outer space technologies and uses. The Ancient Roman maxim also holds true in this case: *ex facto oritur jus*.

Understanding or coping with space law rules and their complexities, which have a universal reach and are of interest to the international community as a whole, calls for the participation of all States worldwide. In theory, this participation need not necessarily occur via international organisations, but it does materialise within the ambit of such organisations, especially the U.N., whose legitimacy in codifying universal principles derives from the authority bestowed on it by the member States towards the promotion of global peace and development. This legitimacy is also grounded on the U.N. General Assembly's mission of "promoting international co-operation in the political field and encouraging the progressive development of international law and its codification,"[6] as per Article 13, Paragraph 1(a) of the U.N. Charter.

The COPUOS actions toward the creation of outer space law have had a decisive impact on the progressive development of international law. The first landmark resolutions, containing some principles intended to guide the conduct of States with regard to use and exploration of outer space, served as a prelude to codification efforts in the outer space segment.

According to Prof. Lachs, "even though the U.N. General Assembly Resolutions, in principle, do not stand as law-creating instruments, they may have legal effects when adopted by unanimous decision. And, as such, the binding nature of these Resolutions is unquestionable. However, this fact alone does not release such Resolutions from taking a conventional format."[7]

For Faramiñan-Gilbert, "contemporary legal writings on public international law (drawing on the international experience originated from a massive number of Resolutions adopted by the U.N. General Assembly) tends to acknowledge that rules of conduct, whether adopted by unanimous decision or without valid objections from a legal perspective, should evolve into universal compulsory rules of international law, when developing and codifying certain incipient rules of usage and customs, in accordance with generally accepted principles of public international law and when they are confirmed by the general practice of States."[8]

These legal writings point to a complex interrelation between the formal sources of international law, but do not cast light on how legal mechanisms (of soft law) evolve into positive rules (of hard law), unless this move occurs through the mediation of customary rules or treaties.

In fact, these legal moves directly relate to the categories of international law, but indirectly reflect the economic/political/strategic interests of the myriad players in outer space activities. So far, the general legal framework and specific rule dealing with remote sensing issues is Resolution 41/65 adopted at the U.N. General Assembly, known as "Principles Relating to Remote Sensing of the Earth from Outer Space", which could be viewed as a legal system *in status nascendi* to govern these specific matters.

On 11 December 1986, the U.N. General Assembly approved Resolution 41/65 by unanimous decision. This Resolution consisted of fifteen "Principles on Remote Sensing", which had obtained consensus in the COPUOS.[9] A pragmatic and theoretical/prospective analysis of this legal instrument is worth consideration at two distinct levels.

Prima facie, our concerns would primarily relate to the legal nature of this international document. The validity of this Resolution rests on the consensus, which represents an intermediary stage in the development of international space law,[10] by laying down the major principles that will govern the deployment of remote sensing activities, and paving the way for the advent of international treaties over this specific issue. In this sense, this Resolution evolves from *de lege ferenda* into *lex lata* when it eventually takes the form of an international treaty. Bin Cheng highlights that "... this instrument took the form of a General Assembly Resolution and not, as was hoped by some States, a treaty, with the result that the principles, instead of being intended to constitute rules legally binding upon those that subscribe to them, are merely guidelines."[11]

This problem was also addressed at the Working Paper on Remote Sensing submitted by Brazil at the COPUOS Forty-Second Session in 2003. "Resolution 42/65, like all documents of the genre, is of a merely advisory nature and does not impose any obligations on States, nor does it meet the need for broad, secure and effective regulations of a strategic space activity for development by all countries. In cases such as this, nothing can replace an international convention, negotiated and approved under the auspices of the U.N. and open to all States."[12]

Nonetheless, it can be seen that the practice of States under the aegis of these principles builds up a rule of custom and, from this perspective, the principles nurtured in the Resolution become an integral part of customary law.

Secondly, one must look into the effectiveness of this legal mechanism, that is, whether this principiology would actually cater to factual needs and respond to this issue properly. The same Brazilian Working Paper submitted to COPUOS reads that "the only international text in existence on this issue is completely outdated: Principles Relating to Remote Sensing of the Earth from Outer Space (GA Resolution 41/65). This Resolution has been overtaken by the skyrocketing technological advances in the sector that have occurred over the last 16 years. It does not address the question raised today by the multiple satellite sensing programmes, a large number of which are operated by private companies with strictly commercial objectives."[13]

The Resolution has dubbed certain rules already present in international law. Examples: Principles III (abidance by the Outer Space Treaty); IX (Registration Convention); or XIV (Outer Space Treaty, Article VI on the State's International Responsibility). However, a closer look at the contents of Resolution 41/65 unveils the frailty of these principles vis-à-vis the wide spectrum of uses for remote sensing activities that are being developed, coupled with the sheer lack of a legal framework for remote sensing activities deployed by non-governmental entities. In defining 'remote sensing', Principle I limits the applicability of such mechanism to those activities intended to improve the management of natural resources, use of land, and environmental protection. Other uses are still devoid of legal protection.[14]

In implicitly admitting the extraterrestrial nature of outer space rules of law, Principle III notes that remote sensing activities must abide by the precepts of international law, including the U.N. Charter, the Outer Space Treaty, and documents pertaining to the International Telecommunications Union.

Principle IV, which refers to the rights and interests of sensed States, embodies the teleology of Article I of the Outer Space Treaty by furthering its legal structure when making express reference to the principle of full and permanent sovereignty of all States and peoples over their wealth and natural resources, clearly tipping the scales in favour of the rights and interests of all States and entities under their jurisdiction, for it is defended that remote sensing activities cannot be deployed in detriment to the rights and interests of sensed States. For Cheng, this principle "sounds like an application of the principle of good neighbourliness."[15]

For Christol, the reference to full and permanent sovereignty of the States over their natural resources shows that "... a major contest requiring resolution resulted from the views held on the one hand by States favouring international co-operation in the acquisition and dissemination of the product of remote sensing, and on the other by countries which emphasised the role of national sovereignty with is focus on the national privacy."[16] This approach sides with the principle of permanent sovereignty of States over their natural resources, a concept that made its debut in the U.N. General Assembly in 1952, and then ratified in a number of subsequent resolutions.[17] This concept is reaffirmed by the teleology applying to the new world order in the economic scenario, originally conceived in the 1970s[18] and materializing into Principle 2 of the Rio de Janeiro Declaration on the Environment and Development of 1992, when it was viewed as an essential element for the development of States.[19]

On the other hand, the Resolution acknowledges the freedom of remote sensing activities, as one particular manifestation of the freedom of space activities subject only to international law, as Principle IV expressly stipulates that remote sensing activities must be deployed in strict abidance with the precepts spelled out in Article 1 of the Outer Space Treaty. According to this international rule, outer space may be freely used and explored by all States, on an equitable and non-discriminatory basis pursuant to international law.

Principle IV has stirred up a great deal of controversies and paradoxes by establishing two antipodal concepts: freedom of remote sensing and the sovereignty and rights of the sensed State, on the one part, and the legitimate rights and interests of any State and its entities, on the other. Although adopting the concept of full and permanent sovereignty of the State over its natural resources, Principle IV does not change the fact that the sensed State has no veto rights to prevent it from being sensed, or even an exclusive or preferential right of access to ensuing data. Principle XII only provides the sensed State with a right of access to primary and processed data concerning the territory under its jurisdiction, on a non-discriminatory basis and at a reasonable cost.

Principle XIV (which is of fundamental importance, in that it directly relates to international responsibility of the State for outer space activities deployed by governmental or non-governmental entities) draws on a rule of conventional law when adopting the teleology of Article 6 of the Outer Space Treaty and highlighting the applicability of international law rules to the responsibility of States for remote sensing activities.[20]

2. International Responsibility of the State and Remote Sensing

International responsibility of States, originating from customary law principles, has come under scrutiny by the U.N. International Law Commission (ILC), which prepared the Draft Articles on Responsibility of States for Internationally Wrongful Acts.[21]

2.1. 'Responsibility' and 'Liability'

The term 'responsibility' means primary accountability. The obligation to answer for an act done and to repair or otherwise make restitution for any injury it may have caused.[22] In case of breach of a legal rule causing damage to another, legal responsibility entails a legal obligation incumbent on the author of the breach to make full reparation to the victim for the damage. 'Liability' represents merely one aspect of responsibility, and a consequence of responsibility in case the person responsible breaches an obligation that is incumbent upon it and, in doing so, causes damage to another. Under the Brazilian law system, 'responsibility' must apply to cover the two legal aspects discussed above.

The ILC has endeavoured to clarify the concept of responsibility: "...the term 'responsibility' should be used only in connection with internationally wrongful acts..."[23] This is central to the concept of State's responsibility. Article 1 of the ILC Draft Articles reads that "every international wrongful act of State entails the international responsibility of that State." Article 2, in turn, defines the elements of an internationally wrongful act: "there is an internationally wrongful act of State when conduct consisting of an action or omission is attributable to State under international law and constitutes a breach of an international obligation of State."

Therefore, a legal framework is necessary to characterise an act as 'wrongful' under international law. However, if this characterisation takes the form of a U.N. Resolution, the impact of a rule of this nature could produce a state of affairs in which the sensed State *per se* may be harmed.[24] Nonetheless, regulating this issue under current international customary law does not suffice.[25] The development of an international conventional on remote sensing is necessary for the updating of the Principles Relating to Remote Sensing and for the development of rules relating to new situations.

3. Legal aspects of the activities developed by non-governmental entities

States hold international responsibility for the outer space activities conducted by private individuals and entities within their jurisdiction, as well as by government entities.[26] The extent to which States should be held responsible for the remote sensing activities deployed by private players is an increasingly significant contemporary issue. Applicable rules are defined in ILC Draft Articles 4 through 11, through rules of "attribution" which indicate when an act should be regarded as an act of State. For Bodansky, "these rules are generally traditional and reflect a codification rather than any significant development of the law."[27]

Article 5, in turn, is thus worded: "the conduct of a person or entity which is not an organ of State under Article 4 but which is empowered by the law of that State to exercise elements of the governmental authority shall be considered an act of the State under international law, provided that the person or entity is acting in that capacity in the particular instance." Article 8 reads that "the conduct of a person or group of persons shall be considered an act of a State under international law if the person or group of persons is in fact acting on the instructions of, or under the direction or control of, that State in carrying out the conduct." These rules are the first, tentative steps toward the development of a legal system that will rest on States the responsibility for private conduct or for the composite governmental/non-governmental activities. However, doubts still remain over such major themes as the accurate meaning of being "under a state direction or control,"[28] or the system to be specifically adopted by the State for control and surveillance purposes.

In fact, no legal framework has been devised to govern remote sensing activities performed by non-government entities within the realm of conventional international law, whereupon the system envisioned in the Outer Space Treaty still applies. Within this perspective, private entities will be allowed to engage in remote sensing activities only under the authorisation and ongoing supervision by the State with jurisdiction over them. And the State will thus take direct responsibility for such activities. This state of affairs urges the development of domestic laws to govern this specific issue.

The interpretation on the extent of a State's responsibility for activities undertaken by non-governmental organisations based on the criteria of State's direction or control creates a paradoxical situation in which political and strategic influences may come into play, thus interfering in the characterization of the activity as being or not under the State's control.

According to Pamela Meredith, "the few States that have authorised private space activities to date have tended to consider it an internal matter for sovereign nations to determine what form the authorisation and supervision should take… Licensing regimes for private space activities that are much more rudimentary and general in nature exist in a few other countries."[29]

This international legal context gives us a glimpse of the complexities underlying this issue, and of the pressing urgency to prepare a multilateral international treaty whose effects on domestic laws may trigger the harmonisation of licensing standards, control and supervision patterns, security and safety measures, and other criteria germane to limitation of compensation and the legal status of private enterprise.

4. The Brazil Experience

In Brazil, the legal framework for remote sensing issues is at the *de lege ferenda* stage, meaning that the concerted efforts of the Ministry of Defence, Ministry of Science and Technology, and Brazilian Space Agency culminated in a Bill on air and space sensing regulations, already submitted for congressional review by the Executive Branch, as per Message No. 1248 of 8 September 2000.[30] Nevertheless, this bill is under discussion, and its original intent might still undergo substantial changes.

Article 4 of the Bill reads as follows: "Space sensing means the set of operations involving the reception, registration, processing, interpretation, treatment or distribution of data in any way on the land, air or maritime areas of the Brazilian territory, as well as on Brazilian jurisdictional waters, based on sensors or equipment mounted onto space platforms." This concept of remote sensing is all-too-general, making it difficult to bring it into practice or monitor the activities covered by it.

Under article 13 of this Bill, it will be incumbent on the Brazilian Space Agency: (1) to control and supervise space sensing throughout the Brazilian territory; (2) to lay down rules and to issue authorisations for remote sensing equipment made in Brazil or acquired abroad, when it enters the country; (3) to review and approve protocols involving remote sensing-related activities, to be entered into between Brazilian governmental or non-governmental entities and foreign governmental bodies or entities.

Such incumbencies are intended, among other factors, to protect certain strategic or defence interests within the Brazilian territory; to define title to and responsibility for safekeeping, maintenance of technical quality, and control of products originated from remote sensing activities; to keep domestic entities up-to-date with remote sensing know-how and expertise; and to prepare the National Remote Sensing Record.

In terms of international relations, it is worth mentioning the Working Paper submitted to COPUOS, at the 42nd Session of the Legal Subcommittee,[31] by Argentina, Brazil, Chile, Colombia, Cuba, Ecuador, Greece, Mexico and Peru, concerning the proposal for a new agenda item on the regulation of remote sensing by satellite. The core of this proposal is to include a discussion on the development of an international convention on remote sensing, taking the following key factors into consideration:[32](1) satellite remote sensing activities are currently insufficiently regulated from the international point of view; (2) satellite remote sensing activities are now indispensable and must be regulated by a broad, compulsory and universally acknowledged instrument; (3) many satellite remote sensing activities are not yet subject to international regulation; (4) it is necessary to regulate satellite remote sensing activities with the precautions required by an international public service that is essential to the global community; (5) the regularity and predictability of the remote sensing services by satellite must be guaranteed; (6) a basic international legal system must be formulated for the growing commercialisation of satellite remote sensing activities; (7) appropriate regulations are needed, guaranteeing not only the right of commerce, but also the right to access; (8) fundamental concepts must be defined in a clear and detailed manner, filling in the significant gaps that exist today; (9) responsibilities must be established for the use of remote sensing data, especially in relation to sensed States; and (10) coherence, harmony and effectiveness should be lent to the principles and norms regarding satellite remote sensing activities, in order to prevent contradictory interpretations.

Within the realm of bilateral international relations and co-operation in space activities, particularly concerning the exploitation of Earth observation techniques, Brazil and China established the China-Brazil Earth Satellite Programme (CBERS),[33] creating a true *corpus iuris spatialis specialis* comprising 14 bilateral agreements to govern remote sensing activities, adopting the principiology and teleology of international legal instruments prepared under the umbrella of COPUOS, and also drawing on contemporary international law.

Conclusions:

(1) The contemporary State takes upon itself the responsibility for preserving its environmental resources and ensuring an effective and sustainable development of such environment, observing the following principles, among others: (1) full and permanent sovereignty of all States and peoples over their wealth and natural resources, giving due consideration to the rights and interests of every State and entities under its jurisdiction, in keeping with international law precepts; (2) good neighbourliness; (3) prohibition against cross-border pollution; (4) mutual assistance and co-operation; (5) reciprocal treatment; (6) transfer of technology; (7) information; (8) non-interference in a State's domestic affairs; (9) equal sovereignty of the States; and (10) international responsibility of the State, with the consequent obligation to redress any damage caused by it.

(2) The legal and regulatory framework currently dealing with remote sensing activities is U.N. Resolution 41/65, titled "Principles Relating to Remote Sensing of the Earth from Outer Space", which stands as a legal system *in statu nascendi* to govern this issue. Court precedents and legal writings on the binding nature of U.N. Resolutions point to a complex interrelation among formal sources of international law, making evident that it is still uncertain how legal mechanisms acting as soft law evolve into positive rules of hard law, unless this evolutionary movement is mediated through customary law or treaties. In fact, these legal moves are directly related to international law categories, but indirectly reflect the economic, political and strategic interests of the several players in the space segment.

(3) Remote sensing activities developed by non-governmental entities have not been accorded a specific treatment in the form of conventional international law, which has left them dependent upon the Outer Space Treaty and its precepts until today. In this sense, private entities will only be allowed to engage in remote sensing activities under an authorisation and ongoing supervision of the State with jurisdiction over them. As a result, the State takes direct responsibility for such activities. This state of affairs has lent urgency to the development of domestic rules to govern this specific matter.

(4) The interpretation of the extent of a State's responsibility for activities undertaken by non-governmental organisations based on the criteria of State's direction or control creates a paradoxical situation in which political and strategic influences may come into play, thus interfering in the characterisation of the activity as being or not under the State's control.

(5) Principle IV of the Declaration of Principles on Remote Sensing has aroused a great deal of debates and conflicts by bringing two antipodal concepts together, namely: the freedom of remote sensing activities, on one part, and the sovereignty and rights of the sensed State, on the other, as well as the legitimate rights and interests of any State and its entities. Albeit acknowledging the concept of a State's full and permanent sovereignty over its own natural resources, this principle does not change the fact that the sensed State has no veto rights to prevent it from being sensed or even an exclusive or preferential right of access to ensuing data. Principle XII only provides the sensed State with a right of access to primary and processed data relating to the territory under its jurisdiction, on a non-discriminatory basis and on reasonable cost terms.

(6) A matter of central importance, in that it directly relates to a State's international responsibility for activities performed by governmental or non-governmental entities in outer space, Principle XIV embodies a conventional positive law rule by adopting the teleology of Article 6 of the Outer Space Treaty and emphasising the applicability of international law rules to a State's responsibility for remote sensing activity. laws.

[7] The attached chart portrays the impact of remote sensing activities on the Earth's ecosystem and, consequently, on the international legal system, which is still at the early *status nascendi* stages. This reflects the pressure that facts bring to bear on the legal system. Bin Cheng properly questions: "Arrival of Space Age: Roof Ripped Off the Castle?" In fact, Pandora's box has been opened, and the international community must be ready to cope with surprises arising from remote sensing activities, as well as from domestic legal systems. Thus the drafting of an international treaty on remote sensing, which will take into account the interests of both developed and developing countries, has become urgent.

Remote Sensing and Space Law

"Arrival of the Space Age: Roof ripped off the castle?"
Bin Cheng

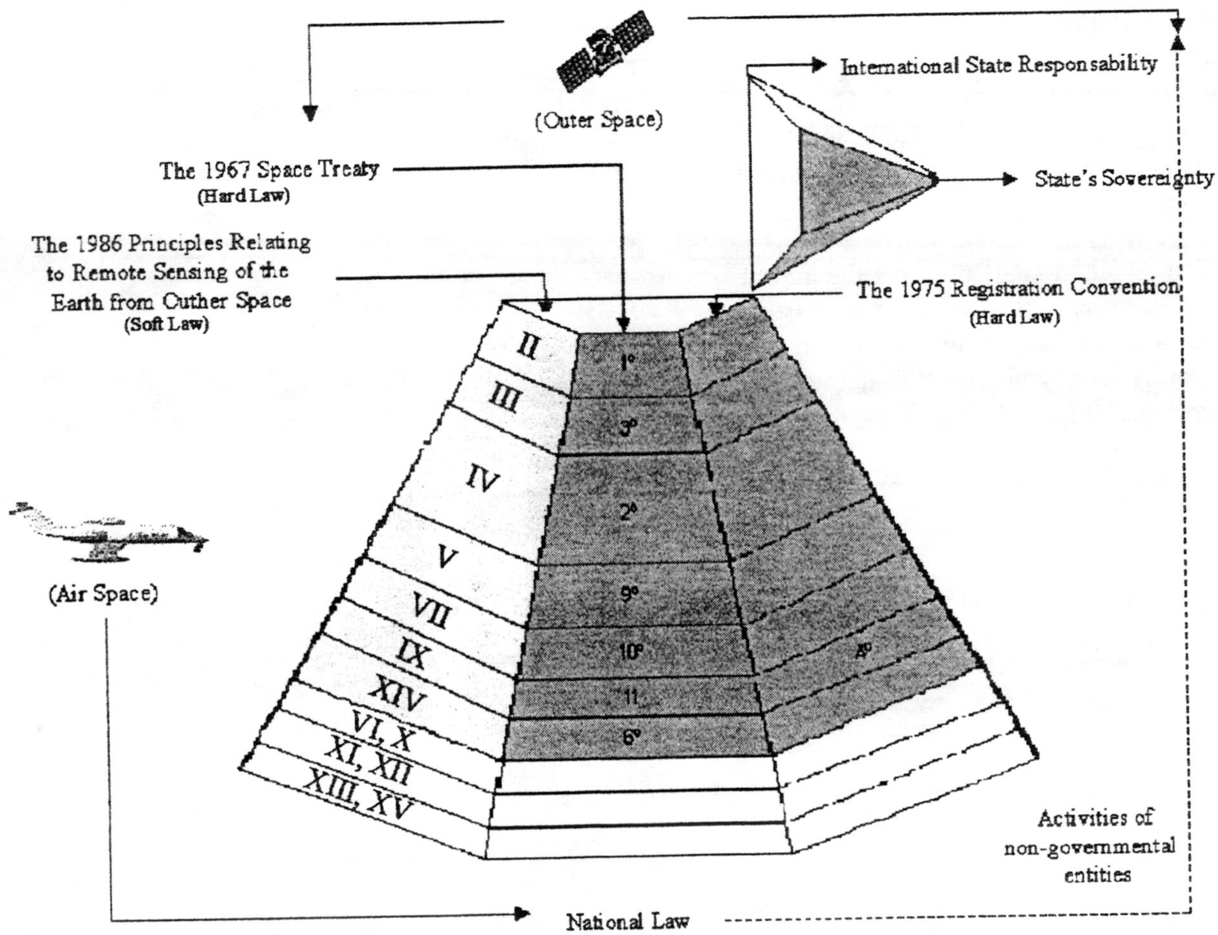

II - Special needs of developing countries
III - Respect of IL, UN Charter, Space Treaty, ITU
IV - Freedom of outer space. Respect to the other States' sovereignty over resources and their rights and interests
V - Opportunity for participation
VII - Technical assistance
IX - UN Secretary-General to be kept informed
XIV - International responsibility of the State
VI - Co-operation in data collection
X - Promote environmental protection
XI - Promote information regarding natural disaster
XII - Dissemination of primary data and analysed information to sensed State
XIII - Interests of sensed State
XV - Settlement of Disputes

Notes

[1] *See*, VISSCHER, Charles de. *Théories et Réalités en Droit International Public*, 4 ed., Pedone, Paris, 1970.
[2] *See* chart prepared by Christiano Sadock, engineering student at ITA, Brazil, p. 10 of this paper.
[3] According to Wassenberg, "present international outer space law is becoming obsolete, or at least totally inadequate, partially because it is based on the assumption that only states are to deploy space activities, or that space activities always have to come, in all respects, under the responsibility and liability of states, states being the only subjects of international outer space law. Only states enjoy the freedom of exploration and use of outer space (art. 1, second paragraph of the OST)." WASSSENBERG, Henri. *The Law of Commercial Space Activities*, in Outlook on Space Law over the Next 30 Years, Kluwer Law International, The Netherlands, 1997, p. 173.
[4] GAUDRAT, Philippe, and TUINDER, Paul H. *The legal status of remote sensing data*, in Outlook on Space Law over the Next 30 Years, Kluwer Law International, The Netherlands, 1997, p. 353.
[5] CHENG, Bin. *Studies in International Space Law*, Clarendon Press, Oxford, 1997, pp. 91 211; JASENTULIYANA, N. *The United Nations: Its Role in the Progressive Development on Space Law*, in Proceedings, 8th ECSL Summer Course on Space Law and Policy, University of Geneva, Switzerland, 1999, pp. 8/19; RANGEL, V. Marotta. *Codificação do Direito Espacial*, in Revista Brasileira de Direito Aeroespacial, 1995, pp. 2/7; UN Doc A/AC.105/358, in ECSL Space Law and Policy Summer Course, Martinus Nijhoff Publishers, 1993, pp. 12/26.
[6] RANGEL, op. cit., p. 3.
[7] *Apud* FARAMIÑAN-GILBERT, Juan Manuel. *Les Resolutions des Nations Unies sur le Droit de L'Espace*, in ECSL Space Law and Policy Summer Course, Martinus Nijhoff Publ., 19194, p. 15.
[8] FARAMIÑAN, op. cit., pp. 6/7.
[9] CHRISTOL, Carl. *Space Law - Past, Present, Future*, Kluwer Law and Taxation Pub., the Netherlands, 1991, pp. 73/95.
[10] CHENG, op. cit., p. 199.
[11] *Id.*, p. 590.
[12] Working Paper submitted by Brazil – *Why is an international convention on remote sensing of the Earth from outer space necessary?*, COPUOS, Legal Subcommittee, Forty-second session, Vienna, 24 March –4 April, agenda 9, Proposal to the COPUOS for new items to be considered by the LS, A/AC.105/C.2/L.244, p. 2.
[13] *Id.*, p. 1.
[14] "Resolution 41/65 does not mention the use of remote sensing for the observation, reconnaissance and monitoring of productive areas (relating to agriculture, cattle, fishing and industry), transportation infrastructure (such as highways, railways, ports and airports) or services (meteorological and tourism), nor for the verification of compliance with international treaties...None of those activities, of clear economic and strategic relevance, is governed by specific international regulations. This constitutes an unjustifiable legal vacuum which may cause serious harm to numerous countries, especially least developed countries." In Working Paper by Brazil, *op. cit.*, p. 2.
[15] CHENG, *op. cit.*, p. 500. This is also the stance taken at the Working Paper by Brazil at COPUOS, *op. cit.*, pp. 4/5.
[16] CHRISTOL, *op. cit.*, p. 75.
[17] Resolution 523 (VI) of 1952; Resolution 626 (VII) of 1952; Resolution 1803 (XVII) of 1962; Resolution 2158 (XXI) of 1966; Resolution 3201 (S-VI) of 1974; Resolution 3281 (XXXIX) of 1974; among others.
[18] In *Texaco v. Libya*, arbitrator Dupuy held that the principle of permanent sovereignty does not allow a State to strip itself or dispose of its sovereignty rights over natural resources, but gives no leeway to acceptance of an agreement that partially limits the exercise of such sovereignty over some resources within a certain area and for a determined period. *See* JO, Hee Moon. *O Investimento Estrangeiro e o Novo Papel do Direito Internacional*, Ph.D. dissertation, FADUSP, São Paulo, 1991, p. 104.
[19] ROLIM, Maria Helena Fonseca de Souza. *A Tutela Juridica dos Recursos Vivos do Mar na Zona Econômica Exclusiva*, Max Limonad, São Paulo, Brasil, 1st ed., p. 80.
[20] *See* CHENG, *op. cit.*, pp. 596/7. Christol, in turn, notes that ".. the double reference to condition of responsibility is based on historical differences. The term "State" responsibility antedates the space age. "International" responsibility is an important provision of art. 6 of the 1967 Principles Treaty. The former traditionally has protected an alien against the wrongful conduct of natural persons of the country in which he is situated, as well as against the wrongful conduct of natural and juridical persons in that country. The latter, while also dealing with the conduct of a foreign State and its natural and juridical persons, has been designed to secure protection against activities occurring in outer space, including the consequences of such activities in outer space, in air space, and on the surface of the Earth." *Op. cit.*, p. 235.
[21] Report of the ILC on the work of its Fifty-third session. Official Records of the General Assembly. Fifty-sixth session, Supplement N. 10 (A/56/10), chp. IV.E.I). November 2001.
[22] CHENG, *op. cit.*, p. 603. Black's Law Dictionary, 6th ed., West Publishing CO. 1990, p. 1312.
[23] CHRISTOL, *op. cit.*, p. 237.
[24] Christol notes that "it could be assumed that an alien purchase the end product of remote-sensing activity, known as 'analysed information'. If it could be assumed that the analysis of either the primary (raw) data or the processed data, which consist of the products resulting from the processing of the primary data, where conducted in a negligent manner (or where intentionally misrepresented), and if this were treated as an internationally wrongful act, and further, if the alien purchaser of the analysed information used it to its detriment, the international legal principle of State responsibility would become relevant", *op. cit.*, p. 241.
[25] "It is not sufficient to accept as international customary practice the freedom to sense the entire world and the freedom to sell the products of such sensing, which, in fact have never been disputes by any country since resolution 41/65 was approved. ....National restrictions on access to data are emerging... The commercial interest should be respected and even stimulated, but cannot supersede public interest...", in Brazilian Working Paper, cit., p.3.
[26] Outer Space Treaty, Art. VI. MEREDITH, Pamela et al. *Space Law: A Case Study for the Practitioner*, MNP, Netherlands, 1992, p.42.
[27] BODANSKY et al. *The ILC's State Responsibility Articles – Introduction and Overview*. The American Journal of International Law. Vol. 96:773, p. 783.
[28] "Important international tribunals have approached these question in quite different ways". *op. cit.*, p. 785.
[29] MEREDITH, *op. cit.*, p. 44.
[30] *See*, MUSSI, Raimundo. *O Sensoriamento Remoto e sua Regulamentação*, in Revista Brasileira de Direito Aeroespacial, n. 86, June 2003, pp. 8/11.
[31] Vienna, 24 March-4 April 2003, Agenda item 9, Proposals to the COPUOS for new items to be considered by the LS at its forty third session, A/AC.105/C.2/L.245.
[32] *Id.*
[33] *See* MONSERRAT FILHO, José. *Brazilian Chinese Space Co-operation*, in Revista Brasileira de Direito Aero-espacial, Brazil, n. 71, pp. 3/14, 1997. 39 ICLOS, Beijing, China, 1996.

Session 2:
SPACE TREATIES, LAW AND POLICIES AND TELECOMMUNICATION ISSUES

Chairmen: Lesley Jane Smith, Germany
H. Peter Van Fenema, Canada

Rapporteur: Martha Mejia-Kayser, Germany

IAC-03-IISL.2.01

Article I of the Outer Space Treaty and the International Telecommunication Union

FRANCIS LYALL

Faculty of Law, University of Aberdeen
Aberdeen, AB24 3UB, Scotland, U.K.

Abstract

The responsibilities and work of the International Telecommunication Union fit well within the requirement of Art. I of the Outer Space Treaty that space should be used for the betterment of all. This is true not only in relation to space, but more generally also through the terrestrial responsibilities and activities of the ITU. There remain problems of finance and the imbalance between financial contribution and voting power, and there is a danger that some ITU 'events' are without real impact on the needs of many countries, but in many ways there is hope for the future.

1. Introduction.

This is one of what has so far turned out to be a ten-year series. In 1993 at the Colloquium of this Institute held Graz, Austria, I discussed the reconstruction of the ITU by the 1992 Geneva Extra-ordinary Plenipotentiary Conference of the International Telecommunication Union.[1] But, before the Geneva documents came into force they were overtaken and revised in some details by the decisions of the 1994 Kyoto Plenipotentiary.[2] In 1997 in Turin I presented a paper which discussed Telecommunications and the Outer Space Treaty.[3] The Kyoto arrangements were further revised by the 1998 Plenipotentiary Conference, held in Minneapolis, USA,[4] which initiated a further reform process, so, in 2000 at the Rio de Janeiro Colloquium I took the opportunity to discuss some more possibilities.[5] This 'Bremen' paper takes into account the decisions of the Plenipotentiary Conference held in Marrakesh in 2002,[6] which to some extent implement some further reforms.[7] However, I must apologise that I have not cited as much discussion by others as I would have liked: sciatica has made impossible access to certain material which I do know exists. To those who may feel their work has been ignored – that is the explanation.

A major step at Geneva 1992 / Kyoto 1994 was the splitting of the previous basic single constitutional document of the Union, the Convention, into a Convention, intended to contain matters less likely to change at successive plenipotentiaries, and the Constitution containing other constitutional matters.[8] In this paper 'CV' indicates a reference to the Convention, while 'CS' refers to the Constitution. The numbers in brackets refer to the paragraph numbering in either document which it has become both customary, and given the complexity and length of some articles, convenient to use. The ITU has published a consolidated text of the Final Acts of the Geneva, Kyoto and Minneapolis Plenipotentiary Conferences, including the

ITU Constitution and Convention together with relevant Resolutions and Recommendations in force in 1999.[9] Technically an unofficial compilation, it (and its Index) are extraordinarily helpful. No doubt the ITU will publish a new consolidated text including the Marrakesh amendments and decisions.

As initially conceived this paper was to concentrate on whether and how the ITU meets the requirements of Art. I of the Outer Space Treaty, as to the betterment of all countries. As is well known, what constitutes 'betterment', and whether and how states have benefited, is a matter of dispute.[10] To my mind it is axiomatic that space telecommunications is the major example of benefit, as it has bettered the conditions of virtually all states. I do not propose to argue that point. The ITU and its procedures have been important in the accomplishment of the high aspirations of Art. I in the field of telecommunications. In the course of writing, however, my thoughts have broadened, and the paper strays into a wider field - the extent to which the ITU functions for the betterment of all, including its terrestrial as well as its space responsibilities.

2. Background.

The opening of the Space Age with the launch of Sputnik in 1957 took us by surprise, but may be it should not. In the twelve years after the end of the Second World War rocket technology had made great strides. Both the Russians and the Western Allies had scrambled to obtain custody of both the technical personnel responsible for that technology, and the materiel itself. Those twelve years had seen the Cold War develop, and the military interest in missiles already fostered by the exigencies of war, grow. Nonetheless, the technical leap from short-range missiles (even such as the V-2) to the intercontinental ballistic missile was great, and the ability to put a satellite into orbit, itself another leap. However, it is to be noted that putting a satellite into earth orbit was first done as part of the International Geo-physical Year, a major international co-operation in scientific endeavour. That itself indicated that the opening of space might be as important for peaceful as for military purposes. It also meant that much expenditure, formerly charged to military budgets, might be financed from civil and civilian sources. However, when the public purse, in the form of taxation revenues, (or later, private enterprise) is called on to shoulder such a burden, tax-payers (who are also electors of governments) look for an acceptable return for the expenditure they have financed.[11] In the case of finance for the exploration of space, scientific knowledge was a clear 'return', but the 'return' that was most obvious to the ordinary citizen/voter was a significant improvement in communications. There was there a 'benefit' to be obtained – a benefit that was readily understood, and one with the potential to benefit the entire world.

The United Nations early saw that space was something (if that is not too odd a way to refer to emptiness) that could be of benefit, and, in a series of Resolutions, expressed its views as to desirable developments in space, and as to how states using and exploiting space should conduct themselves. The preambular paragraphs of Resolutions 1603 (XV) of 1960, 1721 (XVI) of 1961 and 1803 (XVII) of 1962, move from expressing hope, to recommending and then, in Resolution 1962 (XVIII) of 1963 to 'solemnly' declaring 'principles' by which states 'should be guided' in their activities. The Preambles to these Resolutions also speak of the 'betterment of mankind' and of the 'benefit of States irrespective of their degree of economic or scientific development'. This is the language that appears in treaty form in Art. I, para. 1, of the Outer Space Treaty of 1967,[12] ratified by 97 members of the United Nations, and signed by 27 others.[13] This is a significant proportion of the states of the world,[14] and there is an argument that the idea that all states should 'benefit' and derive 'betterment' from Outer Space is a matter of customary international law.[15] Further, in this connection one should also now bear in mind the aspirations of the United Nations Millennium Declaration, adopted in 2000 as constraining at least some in their activities.[16]

3. The International Telecommunication Union.

The International Telecommunication Union did not need any spur to play an appropriate part in the international regulation of the use of outer space. Part D of General Assembly Resolution 1721 of 1961 noted that the ITU had already scheduled for 1963 an Extraordinary Administrative Radio Conference to start dealing with the requirements of space, and the allocation of appropriate radio frequencies for satellites. That function has continued, but there have been developments in the ITU structures and mechanisms. The ITU now consists of the Plenipotentiary Conference that meets every four years, a Council meeting annually, and the three Sectors through which most of the work of the ITU important for this paper is transacted - the Radiocommunication Sector (ITU-R), the Telecommunication Standardisation Sector (ITU-T) and the Development Sector (ITU-D).

3.1. Membership.

Membership of the ITU is open in two different forms, State Membership and Sector Membership, that is membership of one or more of the Sectors through which the ITU develops many of its rules and requirements. As at August 2003 there were 189 State Members of the Union. In other words virtually all countries in the world are members of the ITU. They are therefore capable, so far as they are willing and financially able, to influence developments important for all of us. Sector Members are all State Members as of right if they should so wish, together with non-state entities authorised by an appropriate State Member, which may generally authorise entities under its jurisdiction to apply for membership direct to the Secretary General.[17] Since Minneapolis there is also a category of Associate Member, which is available by permission of the Sector concerned to duly authorised entities which wish to take part in the work of only one Study Group within a Sector.[18] There are more than eighty of Associate Members. The numbers of Sector Members have grown over the years, and their work has been useful in the furtherance of the Union's work. As at August 2003 there were about six hundred and fifty Sector Members, most of them, understandably, in the Standardisation Sector, where there is a good representation of manufacturers, whose interest it is to have acceptable and reliable international standards.[19]

3.2. Finance.

It is good that membership of the ITU in all forms is wide, but whether the ITU is able to carry out its task to some extent depends on adequate financing. Regrettably, finance may become a problem.

The ITU has never used the usual UN method of assessing contributions for defraying its expenses. It uses a 'contributory unit', the value of which can be varied.[20] Marrakesh does not depart from this practice and with minor modification unimportant for this paper, the financial arrangements remain as provided for in CV Art. 28 (155-170) and CS Art. 33 (468-487). By CS Art. 33 1.1 (468) State Members of the Union choose a class of contribution from 22 possible classes, namely, 40, 35, 30, 28, 25, 23, 20, 18, 15, 13 10, 8, 5, 3, 2, 1 1/2, 1, 1/2, 1/4, 1/8, and

1/16. The last two classes are available only to Member States listed by the United Nations as being least developed or as allowed by the ITU Council (CV Art. 33 1.1*bis*). As I have often pointed out, from possible highest to lowest this represents a ratio of 460:1. Every Member State is required to choose its contribution for each new four-year cycle of the life of the Union. It is disappointing, and perhaps ominous, that the choice of classes for the current cycle, beginning 1 January 2004 and running to 31 December 2007, has resulted in a reduction of total Member States' contributions from 357 3/4 under the Minneapolis regime to 335 13/16, that is of 21 15/16 units or 6.13%. Sector Member contributions have also declined. These are also self-selected from the unit classes with a minimum of 1/2 unit, except for contributions to the Development Sector, where units 1/4, 1/8 and 1/16 are available. However, these last apply only to Sector Members from the least developed countries according to the UN Development Program list and approved by ITU Council. Sector Members choices reported to Council as at the Marrakesh Conference are all down from those of Minneapolis: Radiocommunication 122 (down 5), Standardisation 182 ½ (-9), and Development 29 ½ (3 1/8), a total reduction of 17 1/8 units or 4.88%. Overall the drop in units selected as at Marrakesh was 5.93%. However, the Secretary General reported to Council in March 2003 that taking into account new members and denunciations, the contribution of Sector Members had altered. The new figures were: Radiocommunication 122 ½ units (an increase of 1/2); Standardisation 175 ½ units (down a further 7); and Development 28 7/8 units (down a further 1 1/16).[21]

These are figures that should concern us. While we obviously would wish the ITU to run efficiently, and expend no more money than is required to do its tasks, there is a point where lack of finance could impede, not to say damage the ITU. The 2003 figures may indicate a level of dissatisfaction with the ITU on the part of some states,[22] although the same point can not be made in other cases.[23] That said, it is noticeable that no Member State has increased its contribution class. I would also note that as in the past that there remains a colossal imbalance between contributions. Seventy two per cent of the state membership contributes twelve per cent of the main income.[24] We should also note that for the developing countries the reduction for the Development Sector Members' units should be extremely worrying. That said, for the small contributors, which include the developing countries, the ITU must be good value for money,[25] and therefore to some extent classifiable as 'benefit' in terms of Art. I of the Outer Space Treaty, for they all make use of space telecommunications, and many gain from other space uses, all of which are dependent on the work of the ITU, particularly the Radiocommunication Sector. But an uncharitable question may now be whether the small contributors are not to some extent freeloading. It would be interesting to know what their contributions are to the UN Agencies which adopt the normal UN funding formula.

The result of the contribution unit selection as at Marrakesh is reflected in Decision COM/2 'Financial Plan of the Union for the period 2004 to 2007'. Broadly this provides for widespread cost reduction, including reduction in staff numbers (and hence costs) in the Union. The base budgets for the Sectors are reduced respectively: Radiocommunication – 2%, and Standardisation and Development both 1%; the General Secretariat reduces by 5%. Other reductions are also planned, e.g. in abandoning the production of many summary records, and reducing the length of plenipotentiary conferences to three weeks. Whether these reductions are without effect on the efficiency of the working of the Union remains to be seen.

3.3. Function, speed and presence.

One of the criticisms of the ITU has been the speed of its work and the need for a systematic programme of work. The Marrakesh Conference has introduced a formal requirement that the General Secretariat and the Bureau of each Sector each draw up a four year rolling operational plan for its work.[26] Previously the requirement was for an annual plan, although sensibly in practice each usually tried to work to a longer-term. That said, it is good that a more coherent approach is being required as a matter of constitutional duty. The efficient working of the ITU is clearly for the betterment of all.[27] The 'Strategic Plan of the Union 2004-2007' is Res. 71 of the Minneapolis Conference, as amended at Marrakesh, and in particular the Annex thereto.[28] Goals are set. We await their attainment. One longer term goal is the revision of the International Telecommunication Regulations and consideration of the place of their substance within the ITU documents, since telecommunications developments are rendering the Regulations and/or the process of their adoption and amendment obsolete.[29] Another point is that as part of its reforms of 1992/1994 the ITU became conscious of the need to have a strong regional presence, and not be seen by much of the world as a remote institution far away in Europe. Resolution 25 as further amended at Marrakesh continues to provide for the strengthening that presence.

3.4. The Sectors.

The reconstruction of the Union of 1992/94 and the creation of the three Sectors has been useful. Of these Radiocommunication and Development are of the most interest for this paper.

3.4.1. Standardisation.

Standardisation is of course important for us all, assisting in making telecommunications work properly, and affording bases on which manufacturers of equipment can rely and therefore make decisions to invest in particular products.[30] Steps are being taken to improve the role and effectiveness of ITU-T work.[31] There is also concern in the Sector as to a developing gap between developed and developing countries in the matter of standardisation, and steps are being taken to address the problem.[32]

3.4.2. Radiocommunication.

For space the Radiocommunication Sector is fundamental, but its work extends to all uses of radio. Without the Radio Regulations agreed uses of particular radio frequency bands negotiated through Radiocommunication Conferences and the work of Radiocommunication Sector Groups, and without the work of the Bureau in compiling and maintaining the Master International Frequency Register, there would be more harmful interference than there is. This is important for the attainment of the objectives of Art. I of the Outer Space Treaty, although not confined to space matters. As is well known, CS Arts. 44 and 45 (195-199) recognise the responsibility of states to ensure that radio frequencies are properly used. CS Art. 44.2 (196) states that radio frequencies and orbits (particularly the geostationary orbit) are limited natural resources, and as such to be used 'rationally, efficiently and economically'. Equitable access to orbits and frequencies and the special needs of the developing countries are specially noted.

By CV Art. 12.2.*c* (166) a function of the Director of the Radiocommunication Bureau is to provide assistance to the developing countries in their preparation for Radiocommunication Conferences. The needs of these countries are thereby more likely to be cogently expressed, and therefore are more likely to be met. Further when in terms of CV Art. 12.2.4.*a* (177) the Director carries out studies to help the maximal use of the radio spectrum in portions of the spectrum where interference is most likely to occur, the needs of member States requiring assistance and the developing countries are to be taken into account. Again this helps states which otherwise might lose out – benefit is therefore equalised.[33]

Of course there remains the argument as to the use of the radio spectrum. Should the spectrum be divided by agreement not only as to use, but also as to which states will use which frequency bands? Should the spectrum (or parts of it) be 'engineered' and states given rights to frequencies whether or not they use them, or should we stick with the existing position under which, with limited exception,[34] what is important is priority of entry on the International Master Frequency Register?[35] However, at present that argument does not seem to be live for space at least. The problem of 'paper satellites' caused by a rush to get a system on to the Register is still with us, but is being slowly resolved.[36]

Finally, by what may be a matter of general benefit, the Marrakesh amendments provide for an appeal process within the Sector. This is separate from negotiation between notifying administrations or the arbitral procedures available under CS Art. 56 (233-235) and CV Art. 41 507-518) and the (never yet used) Optional Protocol on the Compulsory Settlement of Disputes. By modification to CV Art. 10 (140), under a new Art. 10.2.2 (140), independent of the Sector the Radio Regulations Board will be able to consider appeals by interested administrations against determinations of the Bureau regarding frequency assignments. Previously all the Board could do was consider investigations made by the Director of the Bureau at the request of an interested administration, and make recommendations thereon. Whether this is good will have to await evidence as to use and practice. If the new appeal process results in the solution of disputes it will be useful. If it produces a 'litigious' frame of mind on the part of administrations, it will be regretted. The functioning of the ITU depends on practices of compromise and mutual accommodation on the part of administrations. I hope the new appeal process does not diminish or detract from these practices either in relation to space or terrestrial services. My fear is that the privatised providers of space telecommunications may bring pressure to bear on their governments to appeal Bureau decisions for commercial rather than procedural or similar reasons. The (ab)use of 'the law' to 'run interference' on competitors is a practice not unknown in rampant 'free markets'.

3.4.3. Development.

The 1992/1994 reforms introduced to the purposes of the ITU the promotion of technical developments to make telecommunication facilities 'so far as possible generally available to the public' (CS Art. 1 1. *d* (6)), the promotion of 'the extension of the benefits of the new telecommunications technologies to all the world's inhabitants' (CS Art. 1.1.*e* (7)), and, together with financial and development organisations, the promotion of 'preferential and favourable' lines of credit to develop social projects aimed 'inter alia at extending telecommunication services to the most isolated areas in countries' (CS Art. 1.2.*i* (19)). Also specified in various places in CS Art. 1 are duties to promote co-operation and collaboration. The Development Sector, operating under Ch. IV of the Constitution (Arts. 21-24 (118-145A)) and Sec. 6 of the Convention (Arts. 16-18 (208-226) together with the provisions common to all Sectors (CV Sec. 8, Arts. 19-22 (228-254)). is the main agent through which these purposes are sought to be effected.[37] That the Sector has suffered a cut of 1% in its general financing, coupled with a reduction of 4 3/16 contributory units in the sums from its Sector Members[38] is a matter for concern.

Major results have been the adoption of Declarations and an Action Plan at successive World Telecommunications Development Conferences (WTDC), the first at Buenos Aires in 1992, and subsequently at Valletta, Malta, in 1998 and most recently in Istanbul in 2002. The Valletta Plan, as amended, has particular chapters on the development of a global information infrastructure, and as to a special programme for developing countries.

A matter of major concern to the Sector, and to the ITU generally, is the possibility of an emergent 'digital divide'.[39] A gulf may indeed come into being between countries which are analogue-based in their telecommunications, and those (in the main the developed countries) whose telecommunications are increasingly moving over to digitally based technologies. The World Telecommunication Development Conference of Istanbul 2002 adopted its Res. 37 on the matter, and by its Res. PLEN/3 the Marrakesh Conference has instructed the Director of ITU-D to take measures to implement the Istanbul resolution and to take other related actions.[40] Of course, the ITU is not the sole organisation moving in this area, but its role is significant.[41]

4. Other Activities.

4.1. TELECOM.

For many years the ITU has organised world and regional TELECOM exhibitions and forums. Exhibitors attend to show their wares, which serves to inform both state officials and private entities as to technical and other developments to the benefit of us all. A TELECOM Board assists the Secretary-General in continuing to provide this method of fostering world telecommunications.[42]

4.2. The World Telecommunication Policy Forum.

A World Telecommunication Policy Forum to meet regularly was established by Res. 2 of the Kyoto Plenipotentiary Conference, and has met in 1996, 1998 and 2001. It provides a venue where 'high-level participants' can discuss global and cross-sectoral issues. How far the forum is of value has been questioned, and paras. 7 and 8 of Res. 2 as amended at Marrakesh interestingly provide that the agenda, themes and discussions should be based on a report by the Secretary-General, prepared with input from ITU conferences, assemblies, meetings and the views of State and Sector Members. Policy and strategy may now be discussed but the output of meetings as to any matter is not binding though reports and opinions may be submitted to relevant ITU bodies. Further there is now provision for Forums to be convened quickly on an ad hoc basis to respond to emerging policy issues.[43] This may indicate that previous forums have been less useful than expected, and we may hope that the tighter controls put in place by Marrakesh will be successful in improving matters.

4.3. The World Summit on the Information Society.

By its Res. 73 the Minneapolis Plenipotentiary Conference resolved that the holding of a World Summit on the Information Society (WSIS) should be put on the agenda of the UN Administrative Committee on Coordination. That action produced the desired effect and such a world conference is to be held in two sessions in 2003 and 2005.[44] Decision PLEN/1 of the Marrakesh Plenipotentiary Conference, with its Annexes sets out how the ITU input to the WSIS is to be dealt with. The development of information and communications technologies (ICTs), access to them and their use for sustainable as well as economic and social development, together with special actions for developing countries, least developed countries, underprivileged populations and isolated and remote communities, are to be fostered by the ITU participation in WSIS. A Working Group of the ITU Council (in which all Council Members may take part) has been established to provide a framework for the contribution of the ITU. Annex 2 to Decision PLEN/1 indicates also the relevance of the Strategic Plan of the Union for 2004-2007, and the roles which the Sectors of the ITU can be expected to play.

The question is whether the World Summit on the Information Society will be useful. I have myself, and I have heard amongst knowledgeable persons, fears that WSIS will be merely a talking shop. Over the years that I have watched international telecommunications the idea has been developed and then been ground into my mind that it is the engineers that do things. Engineers are interested in getting telecommunications systems that work, whether they are systems of governance or systems of technology. Let the businessmen in and their interest is in profits. Let the professional civil servants in and normally their lack of expertise in telecommunications, coupled with a major interest in the furtherance of their careers, diminishes the value of their contribution. Let the politicians in, and the aim seems also to be personal advancement through the enunciation of a fine sounding set of syllables, which lack real foundation. In short, I wonder whether WSIS is a good move. It just could provide an impression of action without the substance thereof (cf. 2 Timothy 3:5).

4.4. Disasters

Last in this section I simply point to Resolution 36, as amended at Marrakesh, which requires the ITU to play its part in disaster mitigation and relief and refers to the Tampere Convention of 2001.[45] This goes along with the more general duty under CS Art. 46 (200) imposed on all states to give absolute priority to, to reply to and to take action on distress messages.

5. A World Authority – Not yet.

Last is an observation that I have made many times before. It would be to the general good if the ITU were given more authority than it at present has. As we have it, it is an organisation which is the servant of its members, and which has problems in taking initiatives. While I would not discount the abilities of the officers of the Union to persuade Member States as to the wisdom of certain proposals and initiatives, and getting these introduced on the agenda of the Union through member States, the process is slow. I would like to see the officials of the Union able to make formal proposals. I would like to see the Radiocommunication Sector able to refuse to register notifications as to frequencies and orbits on the basis of the general world interest. I would like to see the ITU as a global FCC. I would like to see the ITU more able financially to bring betterment to areas where telecommunications technology is underdeveloped.

6. Conclusion.

But, even with Section 5 written, I do submit that the International Telecommunication Union, both in regard to the discharge of its responsibilities as to space matters, and more generally in its other and its terrestrial responsibilities, goes a good long way to meeting the requirements of Art I of the Outer Space Treaty as to the betterment of all countries without regard to their degree of social or economic development. There are still problems, but we must hope, and where we can, see that this betterment of all continues.

NOTES

[1] F. Lyall, 'The International Telecommunication Union Reconstructed', (1993) 36 *Proc. IISL* 78-88.

[2] Final Acts of the Plenipotentiary Conference of the International Telecommunication Union, Kyoto, 1992 (Geneva: ITU, 1992).

[3] F. Lyall, Telecommunications and the Outer Space Treaty' (1997) 40 *Proc. IISL* 385-92.

[4] Final Acts of the Plenipotentiary Conference of the International Telecommunication Union, Minneapolis, 1998 (Geneva: ITU, 1999). In the light of the Strategic Plan the 1999 Council established a Working Group on ITU Reform (WGR), and Reform Advisory Groups (RAG) have been established for the three ITU Sectors.

[5] F. Lyall, 'Re-thinking the ITU', (2000) 43 *Proc. IISL*, 309-19.

[6] Final Acts of the Plenipotentiary Conference of the International Telecommunication Union, Marrakesh, 2002 (Geneva: ITU, 2003)

[7] Cf. 'Strategic plan for the Union, 1999-2003', Res. 71, Minneapolis 1998. See Minneapolis *Final Acts* (preceding note) or *Collection* (n. 9 below).

[8] The process of simplification continues. The Marrakesh Plenipotentiary Conference moved a good deal as to the calling of conferences and their rules of procedure to the separate document that deals with such matters. CV Arts. 26-30 (299-323) are suppressed. See sentences following in main text for explanation of citation modes. The Rules are now matters for the conferences and assemblies concerned.

[9] *Collection of the basic texts of the International Telecommunication Union adopted by the Plenipotentiary Conference*, Edition 1999 (Geneva: ITU, 1999)

[10] The Declaration on International Co-operation in the Exploration and Peaceful Use of Outer Space for the Benefit and in the Interest of All States, Taking into Particular Account the Needs of Developing Countries' GA Res. 51/122, 4 February 1997; cf. M. Benko and K. Schrogl, 'The 1996 UN Declaration on "Space Benefits" Ending the North-South Debate on Space Co-operation' (1996) 39 *Proc. IISL* 183-6.

[11] The principle is the same as that motivating the private investor of modern times, although the private investor seems more likely to disregard 'return' in any form other than money.

[12] Treaty on Principles Governing the Activities of States in the Exploration and Use of Outer Space Including the Moon and Other Celestial Bodies, (1968) 610 UNTS 205; (1968) UKTS 10, Cmnd. 3519; 18 UST 2410, TIAS 6347; 6 ILM 386; 61 AJIL 644.

[13] See 2003 Report of the Standing Committee on the Status of international Agreements relating to Activities in Outer Space, A.D. Terekhov, Chairman, printed as an Annex to this volume, 2003 *Proc. IISL*.

[14] At August 2003 the United Nations has 191 Members.

[15] I intend to discuss this question and the role of UN Resolutions in the creation of custom elsewhere.

[16] UN A/RES/55/2 of 8 September 2000, the 'United Nations Millennium Declaration'.

[17] CS Art. 3 (24-28C), Art. 12.3 (86-66), Art. 21.4 (134-136), Art. 17.3 (110-112); CV Art. 19.1. (228-231) and Art. 19.3-4 (234-234C).

[18] CV Art. 19.12 (241A-241E.

[19] The ITU website (www.itu.int) provides list of State, Sector and Associate members.

[20] The Marrakesh Plenipotentiary conference set the maximum value of the budget deriving from contributory units in the period 2004-2007 at 330000 Swiss francs (approx. GB£ 150000; US$240900; Euro 214000), but instructed that in 2004-2005 the maximum should not exceed 315000 Swiss francs : See 2003 Council Doc. C03/E, 'Choice of Class of Contribution for Defraying the Union's Expenses'.

[21] All figures are taken from Council Doc. C03/E, 'Choice of Class of Contribution for Defraying the Union's Expenses' (2003).

[22] The Member States which have significantly reduced their choice of contributory unit are: Denmark and Finland, both down 1 from 5 to 4; Australia down 2 from 15 to 13. The Netherlands

and Sweden, both down 3 from 8 to 5; Italy down 5 from 20 to 15; and the United Kingdom also down 5 from 15 to 10. == 56

[23] Most Member States have left their choice of contributory units unchanged. Those unchanged and contributing 1 unit or more are: France, Germany, Japan, U.S.A. 30; Canada 18, Switzerland 15; China, Saudi Arabia 10; Spain 8; Belgium, India, Norway, Russia, South Korea 5; Brazil, Kuwait, South Africa 3; Ireland, New Zealand, Nigeria, Pakistan, Poland 2; Thailand 1 1/2, Algeria, Austria Cameroon, Chile, Colombia, Czech Republic, Greece, Hungary, Indonesia, Iran, Israel, Kenya, Libya, Lithuania, Malaysia, Morocco, Mexico, Poland, Senegal, Singapore, Turkey, United Arab Emirates, Venezuela 1. = 239 1/2

[24] As noted in the text, the Marrakesh figures show that the ITU States members contribute a total of 335 13/16 units (335.81). From the previous two footnotes that means that the four largest contributors produce one third of the State Member contributions – 120 units (35.7%). If we go down to 5 units, a total of 21 Member States (including the 4 maximum contributors) contribute 262 units (78%), and if we add the 32 which contribute 1 to 4 units, 53 Member States contribute 295 1/2 units (87.99%). The remaining 40 5/16 units are contributed by 136 Member States - 23 at the 1/2 unit level, 56 at 1/4 (the lowest permissible without special rules and permission) 20 at 1/8 and 37 at the 1/16 level.

[25] See immediately preceding note for a grouped breakdown of the units contributed by the 136 of the 189 Member States that contribute 40 5/16 units. To repeat what has been said in the text, 72% of the Member States contribute 12% of the main budget.

[26] Secretariat - CV Art. 5. *d. bis* (87A); Radiocommunication – CV Art. 12.4.*f* (181A); Standardisation - CV Art. 15.2.*g* (205A); Development - Art. 18.2.*g* (223A);

[27] But cf. above, Sec. 3.2 'Finance'.

[28] There is a Strategy and Policy Unit within the General Secretariat, whose work is accessible through the ITU Website. See also ITU Res. 72 as amended at Marrakesh, 'Linking strategic, financial and operational planning in ITU' which calls for a report to the 2006 Plenipotentiary Conference.

[29] The International Telecommunication Regulations were last revised in 1988 at Melbourne. See Marrakesh Res. COM5/7. 'Review of the International Telecommunication Regulations'. A report may go to the ITU Plenipotentiary Conference in 2006 with a view to a world conference on the matter in 2007 or 2008.

[30] At its World Telecommunication Standardisation Assembly, Montreal, 2000 an 'alternative approval' system providing a fast-track system by which informal approval of new 'standards ' can be obtained, was approved: WTSA Res. 37, 'Alternative approval process for ITU-D'. Such approvals are not binding as Recommendations are, but will considerably increase the speed at which ITU-D reacts to swiftly developing technologies.

[31] See Marrakesh Res. COM5/9, 'The evolving role of the World Telecommunication Standardisation Assembly'.

[32] See Marrakesh Res. COM5/8, Bridging the standardisation gap between developing and developed countries'.

[33] See also Marrakesh Res. COM5/8, Bridging the standardisation gap between developing and developed countries', which involves ITU-R as well as ITU-D and ITU-T.

[34] For Space, I refer to the outcome of WARC-ORB 1985-88 by which all states were assigned the right of a position within an orbital arc, together with uplink and downlink frequencies for broadcasting purposes, others being able to use these positions until required by the assignee state. The arrangement was modified by the Istanbul Radio Conference, Istanbul, 2002. In terrestrial radio there are such as the European Broadcasting Plan, which is shortly to be revised. This allocates frequencies and signal strength to particular countries for particular broadcasting services.

[35] CS Art. 1.2.*a* (11), Art. 6 (37-38), Art. 14.2.*a* (95), Art. 42 (193), Art. 45 (193-197); CV Art. 12.2.2.*e* (172): together with relevant Radio Regulations, particularly RRS4, RRS4.2-4, and RRS8, RRS8.1, RRS8.3 (international recognition of registered assignments) and RRS8.5 (duty to eliminate harmful interference caused to registered assignments).

[36] The backlog of unprocessed notifications of assignments is being reduced, and the newer requirements as to detail are having some effect.

[37] I should make it clear that before 1992/94 the ITU did undertake a certain amount of such work. For example, the former International Frequency Registration Board (IFRB) conducted training courses and the like.

[38] See above, Sec. 3.2 'Finance' at nn. 21-22.

[39] T. Kosuge, 'Bridging the Digital Divide in Asia' (2001) 5 *SJICL* 253-8.

[40] For the Istanbul Action Plan, see WTDC-02 Doc. 272, and for the Istanbul Declaration see WTDC-02 Doc. 270. Cf. the Operational Plan of the ITU Development Sector 2003, available from the Sector website. Cf. also Marrakesh Res. PLEN/4 as to 'Support for the New Partnership for Africa's Development'.

[41] See for example the Okinawa Charter on Global Information Society adopted by the G8 in 2000, and the follow-up actions, coordinated through the Digital Opportunity Task Force which it set up: available at www.dotforce.org. The G8 Meeting at Genoa in 2001 approved a plan of action, as to which see the dotforce website and www. eopl-net.org. On these questions see also R. S. Jakhu, 'Safeguarding the Concept of Public Service and the Global Public Interest in Telecommunications' (2001) 5 *SJICL* 71-110.

[42] See Marrakesh Res. 11 'World and regional telecommunications exhibitions and forums', which replaces previous versions of Res. 11.

[43] See the latter half of Marrakesh Res. 11 'World and regional telecommunications exhibitions and forums'.

[44] UN A/RES/56/183 of 21 December 2001, 'World Summit on the Information Society' which in its preamblular paragraph *Considering* indicates that the ITU has the leading managerial role in the preparation of the conference. The conference is to be held in sessions at Geneva in December 2003 and Tunis in November 2005. A 'Draft Declaration of Principles', of 13 July 2003, based on discussions at an intersessional meeting of WSIS has been issued: WSIS03/PCIP/DT/4(Rev.3).

[45] Convention on the Provision of Telecommunication Resources for Disaster Mitigation and Relief Operations, Tampere 1998 (not yet in force), available at www.reliefweb.int/telecoms/tampere/icet-98.pdf or through www.state.gov/www/issues/relief/tpere1.html.

The Concept of "Peaceful Purposes"/ "Peaceful Uses" in the Exploration and Use of Outer Space -- -- Some Practical Examples[1]

John B. Gantt, MIZRACK & GANTT, COUNSELLORS at LAW, Washington DC USA
johngantt@aol.com

Introduction

Much has been written about the concept of peaceful uses of outer space, including the Moon and other celestial bodies.[2] This paper will summarize the key aspects and show how the concept has been interpreted and dealt with in practice by the United States (U.S.) with respect to various multinational civil space activities.

In 1962, at the height of the Cold War, the U.S. Government made a unilateral declaration that it was not the desire or intention of the Government to orbit in space satellites which contained nuclear weapons or any other weapon of mass destruction. As a result of this declaration, the United States was able to get the agreement of the Soviet Union that this principle should be made a matter of common declaration by the UN General Assembly.[3] As a result, on October 17, 1963 the General Assembly unanimously adopted a resolution reciting this common commitment of the U.S. and the Soviet Union.[4] Prior to that, the General Assembly adopted the Nuclear Test Band Treaty (NTBT) to which each party agreed to "prohibit, to prevent, and not to carry out and nuclear weapon test explosion, or any other nuclear explosion" in "outer space". Later that year, the General Assembly unanimously adopted the Declaration of Legal Principles Governing the Activities of States in the Exploration and Use of Outer Space.[5] These principles, although not referring specifically to weapons of mass destruction, recognized in the preamble "the common interest of all mankind in the progress of the exploration and use of outer space for peaceful purposes."[6]

The U.S., not satisfied with the concept of "peaceful use" being expressed only in a set of non-binding principles, sought instead to have the principles expressed in the form of a binding treaty. Thus, after several years of negotiation, the General Assembly unanimously approved the text of the Outer Space Treaty of 1967 (OST).[7] In addition to the Preamble, articles IV, IX, and XI of the Treaty refer to "peaceful uses." It is Article IV that is particularly important in seeking to ascertain the scope of the terms "peaceful uses" and "peaceful purposes".

Relevant Provisions of International Law

1. UN Charter, Article 51[8]

Article 51 excludes from the Charter any obligation that would "impair the inherent right of individual or collective self-defense if an armed attack occurs against a Member..." Implicit here is the right of a Member to establish defensive measures prior to any such armed attack, such as a standing armed force and the necessary weapons to support such a force. This would include space-based defensive objects consistent with the provisions of the Outer Space Treaty (OST).

2. OST, Article III[9]:

This article requires that "in the interest of maintaining international peace" and promoting international cooperation and understanding, the States Parties to the Treaty carry on their activities in the exploration and use of outer space, including the Moon and other celestial bodies, in accordance with international law, including the UN Charter. Article 51 of the Charter[10] expressly recognizes the "inherent right of individual or collective self defense." Implicit in such a right is the right to be prepared to undertake such self defense should the need arise in the future, i.e., to establish and maintain a national or collective armed force.

3. OST, Article IV[11]:

The scope of the first paragraph of this article addresses the entire continuum of the universe, beginning with Earth orbit and extending throughout the void of space including the Moon and other celestial objects, and prohibits the placing, installing or stationing therein or thereon "any objects carrying nuclear *weapons* or any other kinds of weapons of *mass destruction*." (Emphasis added). Neither the term "peaceful purposes" nor "peaceful uses" appears in this paragraph, and the objects referred to are expressly confined to those carrying nuclear weapons or other weapons of mass destruction. Thus, space-based defensive objects in Earth orbit such as lasers and reconnaissance satellites are not foreclosed by this paragraph.

The second paragraph introduces the concept of use for *peaceful purposes,* but confines the requirement with respect to such use only to activities of the States Parties on the "Moon and other celestial bodies." Thus, with respect to activities conducted elsewhere by the Parties, i.e., in Earth orbit and elsewhere in the void of outer space, there appears no restriction to peaceful purposes, or at least in Article IV.

4. OST, Article IX:[12]

This article, *inter alia*, requires a party to the Treaty to consult with other Parties if it has reason to believe that activities or experiments planned by it (or its nationals) in outer space, including the Moon and other celestial bodies, "would cause potentially harmful interference" with the activities of other States in their peaceful exploration and use thereof. Likewise a Party to the Treaty may request consultations with another State if the former has reason to believe that an activity or experiment by the latter would cause such interference with activities in the peaceful exploration and use thereof.

5. OST, Article XI:[13]

This article sets forth elements of transparency as to activities conducted in outer space by States Parties to the Treaty so as to promote international cooperation in the peaceful exploration and use of outer space. This article formed the basis for the later Registration Convention.

Multinational Civil Space Activities

A review of four major multinational space activities of a commercial or quasi-commercial nature reveals that the approach adopted with respect to the concept of "peaceful purposes/ peaceful uses" has essentially been one of "non-aggressive" purposes/uses as opposed to non-military purposes/uses. The U.S., has taken the position that peaceful purposes/uses, in light of Article 51 (UN Charter), means "non-aggressive" uses/purposes. In the four multilateral undertakings discussed below, the U.S. was a major founding party in three of the organizations and successfully pursued this "non-aggressive" interpretation.

INTELSAT

The Preamble to the Intelsat definitive arrangements, which entered in to force in 1973, referred to a "single global commercial telecommunications satellite system [...] which will contribute to world peace and understanding." The Preamble also made reference to the Outer Space Treaty and the Principles set forth in Resolution 1721 (XVI) of the General Assembly. The terms peaceful purposes/uses weren't used into the definitive agreement.

Article II

It was a major precept of the definitive agreement that relations between an Intelsat Signatory and its government Party were to be governed by the domestic law of the Party. Therefore usage of the Intelsat system by a Signatory (i.e., owner/user of the Intelsat space segment) was to be governed by domestic law. Thus, the question of compliance with the provisions of the OST were in the first instance, an issue of domestic law of the Signatory's Party as to what type of telecommunications could be transmitted up to and received from an INTELSAT satellite by that Signatory.

Article III

Several priorities of telecommunication were established as to the type of telecommunications to be provided by signatories through the Intelsat space segment. The primary service was "international public telecommunications" which were defined in Article I (k) of the Agreement as

> *"fixed or mobile telecommunications services which can be provided by satellite and which are available for use by the public such as telephony, telegraphy, telex, facsimile, data transmission and transmission of radio and television between approved Earth stations having access to the Intelsat space segment for further transmission to the public and leased services for any of these purposes...;"*

The international public telecommunications service constituted the bulk of the telecommunications services provided by Intelsat under the definitive Agreement. It consisted of both private and government communications. For all practical purposes, one could not be distinguished from the other due to the technologies used to transmit these various services.

Article III (d) & (e)

An additional, albeit lower priority service, which INTELSAT was authorized in the Agreement to provide under certain conditions was "specialized telecommunications services" either international or domestic.

However, one of the conditions expressed in the Agreement was that the provision of these "specialized telecommunications services" could not be for "military purposes." Thus, while the international public telecommunications service could, and did include military communications, the express exclusion of "military purposes," mentioned only with respect to "specialized services," suggests that the parties didn't intend to exclude "non-aggressive" military uses from the international public telecommunications services.

Article XIV (a)

This was a general Article providing that the Parties and Signatories in exercising their rights and meeting their obligations had to do so in a manner fully consistent with and in furtherance of the principles stated in the Preamble and other provisions of the Agreement. Since, in practice, the international public telecommunications service of INTELSAT was used by Parties for government communications, including military, this use demonstrates a practice of these governments consistent with the "non-aggressive" interpretation "peaceful uses" / "peaceful purposes."

EUTELSAT

The European Telecommunication Satellite System (EUTELSAT) Agreement followed closely the provisions of the Intelsat Agreement. In this respect, Article III (f) (iii) concerning separate systems for telecommunications services, specifies that they must be for "other than military purposes." As in the Intelsat Agreement, this recognized that the Organization was established for peaceful purposes/uses of a "non-aggressive" nature since the public telecommunications contained no such express restriction as to "military purposes."

INMARSAT

INMARSAT was established initially for the provision of telecommunications services and safety of life at sea in support of maritime operations. During the course of negotiations of the INMARSAT Agreement, there was considerable focus on the use of the INMARSAT space segment for "peaceful purposes." As the result, Article III (3) states that, "the Organization shall act exclusively for peaceful purposes." Furthermore, Article IV (4), requires the Parties to ensure that their Signatories not act "in a manner which violates obligations" accepted by the Parties under the INMARSAT Convention or related international agreements. Therefore, to the extent that Navies have utilized the INMARSAT system could suggest a practice consistent with a "non-aggressive" interpretation of "peaceful purposes/uses as opposed to "non-military."

International Space Station (ISS)

The concept of "peaceful purposes" in the use of the ISS was raised and resolved near the end of the 1988 ISS IGA negotiations. As there was no consensus as to the scope of the term "peaceful purposes," the issue was resolved, consistent with the unique ownership, jurisdiction and control scheme of the partnership, Namely, each of the partner-furnished elements (e.g., modules), is owned and provided by and remains under the jurisdiction and control of the providing partner (i.e., no joint ownership). Thus, with respect to a given element, (e.g., the U.S. module), the owning partner (e.g. NASA) will determine whether activity and use of its element are under U.S. law for "peaceful purposes."

Conclusion

Of 3 key international satellite-telecommunications organizations initially established under international law, the drafters interpreted "non-aggressive" uses of the services and facilities as being consistent with the concept of "peaceful purposes"/"peaceful uses". In the case of the ISS, these issues weren't resolved in the IGA Agreement, but rather, due to the unique concept of jurisdiction and control of the various elements, was left to the individual partners as to their respective elements.

---

[22] See, e.g., Bin Cheng, *Studies in International Space Law,* Chapters 19 and 20, Clarendon Press Oxford (1997); Nandasiri Jasentuliyana, ed., *Maintaining Outer Space for Peaceful Uses*, United Nations University (1984).

[3] Statement of Hon. Arther Goldberg, U.S. Ambassador to the United Nations, at Hearings on the Treaty on Outer Spaace before the Committee on Foreign Relations, United States Senate. 90th Cong., 1st Sess. March 7, 1967, at 8.

[4] Resolution 1884 (XVIII).

[5] Resolution 1962 (XVIII) (December 13, 1963).

[6] Ibid.

[7] Treaty on Principles Governing the Activities of States in the Exploration and Use of Outer Space, including the Moon and other Celestial Bodies, entered into force, October 10, 1967.

[8] Article 51 reads:

> Nothing in the present Charter shall impair the inherent right of individual or collective self-defense if an armed attack occurs against a Member of the United Nations, until the Security Council has taken the measures necessary to maintain international peace and security. Measures taken by Members in the exercise of this right of self-defense shall be immediately reported to the Security Council and shall not in any way effect the authority and responsibility of the Security Council under the present Charter to take at any time such action as it deems necessary in order to maintain or restore international peace and security.

[9] Article III reads:

> States Parties to the Treaty shall carry on activities in the exploration and use of outer space, including the Moon and other celestial bodies, in accordance with international law, including the Charter of the United Nations, in the interest of maintaining international peace and security and promoting international cooperation and understanding.

[10] Article 51 of the UN Charter reads, in pertinent part:

> Nothing in the present Charter shall impair the inherent right of individual or collective self defense if an armed attack occurs against a Member of the United Nations, until the Security Council has taken the measures necessary to maintain international peace and security. ***

[11] Article IV reads:

> States Parties to the Treaty undertake not to place in orbit around the Earth any objects carrying nuclear weapons or any other kinds of weapons of mass destruction, install such weapons on celestial bodies, or station such weapons in outer space in any other manner.
>
> The Moon and other celestial bodies shall be used by all States Parties to the Treaty exclusively for peaceful purposes. The establishment of military bases, installations and fortifications, the testing of any type of weapons and the conduct military manoeuvres on celestial

bodies shall be forbidden. The use of military personnel for scientific research or for any other peaceful purposes shall not be prohibited. The use of any equipment or facility necessary for peaceful exploration of the Moon and other celestial bodies shall also not be prohibited.

[12] Article IX reads in pertinent part:

*** If a State Party to the Treaty has reason to believe that an activity or experiment planned by it or its nationals in outer space, including the Moon and other celestial bodies, would cause potentially harmful interference with activities of other States Parties in the peaceful exploration and use of outer space, including the Moon and other celestial bodies, it shall undertake appropriate international consultations before proceeding with any such activity or experiment. A State Party to the Treaty which has reason to believe that an activity or experiment planned by another State Party in outer space, including the Moon and other celestial bodies, would cause potentially harmful interference with activities in the peaceful exploration and use of outer space, including the Moon and other celestial bodies, may request consultation concerning the activity or experiment.

[13] Article XI reads:

In order to promote international cooperation in the peaceful exploration and use of outer space, States Parties to the Treaty conducting activities in outer space, including the Moon and other celestial bodies, agree to inform the Secretary-General of the United Nations as well as the public and the international scientific community, to the greatest extent feasible and practicable, of the nature, conduct, locations, and results of such activities. On receiving the said information, the Secretary-General of the United Nations should be prepared to disseminate it immediately and effectively.

IAC-03-IISL.2.03

BROADCASTING - SATELLITE SERVICES IN AIRSPACE OF THE HIGH SEAS: SOME LEGAL AND REGULATORY CONSIDERATIONS

Tare Brisibe, Regulatory Information Officer, Inmarast Limited, London, United Kingdom, E-mail: tare_brisibe@inmarsat.com

Abstract*

The United Nations Resolution 37/92 of 1982 on Principles Governing the Use by States of Artificial Earth Satellites for International Direct Television Broadcasting, represents the culmination of a yet to be resolved debate, attempting to balance the free flow of information against the right of States to exercise Sovereignty over territorial spaces. Contemplating this debate in the open spaces of the high seas also raises a number of legal and regulatory issues. This paper highlights the legal and regulatory issues arising from the reception of broadcast-satellite services, on-board aircraft traversing the airspace of the high seas (including relevant polar regions). In this regard, the prevailing international legal and regulatory regimes will be considered in the context of a worldwide direct broadcast satellite service offered to airborne passengers primarily on long range wide-body aircraft. Attention shall be given to the international rules governing international flight; peaceful uses of the superjacent airspace of the high seas; and broadcasting-satellite services, respectively.

* This paper is written in the author's personal capacity and does not represent, nor is it intended to represent, the views of Inmarsat Limited. Copyright

Introduction

To date, global mobile satellite systems have been successful in providing mobile satellite services to a number of niche markets including Maritime, Aeronautical and Land-based. When considering the next generation of aeronautical mobile satellite services* (AMSS) it becomes necessary to examine some of the international legal and regulatory issues which may influence service offerings for more mainstream markets, intended to deliver significant growth in numbers of satellite users. Whilst the AMSS market has traditionally offered services to three main sectors, including: passengers†, aircraft operations and airline administration; air traffic control, navigation and position reporting, the main thrust of this paper lies in the area of non-safety passenger services. In this respect, AMSS is comprised of digital voice and data services provided over satellite systems traditionally operating in the mobile satellite radio frequency L bands‡ at 1545 MHz - 1555 MHz and 1646.5 - 1656.5 MHz§ respectively.

There are also satellite systems currently providing live television (TV) services to both corporate and commercial aircraft overflying continental Landmasses**. These TV services are mainly provided over Direct Broadcast Satellites†† (DBS) that traditionally offer Direct To Home

(DTH) digital TV to land based users. The state of the art[‡‡] however is intended to deploy worldwide DBS services aimed at delivering live, multi-channel television video programming to airborne passengers primarily on long range wide-body aircraft.

One key observation concerning the geographic market or coverage area is the fact that a significant share of the addressable market is located at northern latitudes, especially within the long-haul intercontinental flight routes between European, North American and East Asian regions, overflying oceanic rather than continental landmasses. Assessing the legal and regulatory frameworks applicable to the provision of DBS services over the high seas would therefore require a re-examination of the rules applicable to the reception of TV signals in general[§§] albeit with an emphasis on the receipt of such signals by passengers over communications facilities for non-safety purposes, on-board aircraft relying upon satellites. These varied rules and, as will be revealed, non-complementary legal regimes are discussed hereinafter, thus providing a broad analysis of the international legal instruments that serve as the bedrock upon which non-safety aspects of aeronautical communications may be conducted in the airspace of the high seas.

Legal regime of the airspace over the high seas

A significant part of the geographical area over which the planned DBS services are intended to be provided to aircraft, construed as the high seas, by definition mean…"all parts of the sea that are not included in the exclusive economic zone, in the territorial sea or in the internal waters of a State, or in the archipelagic waters of an archipelagic State".[***] This definition it has been contended, infers that the exclusive economic zone[†††] (EEZ) is optional except where a coastal State includes such a zone, and that a significant proportion of the freedoms of the high seas (discussed hereinafter) are according to the UN Convention of the Law of Sea 1982, (UNCLOS), applicable in the EEZ[‡‡‡]. On the extent to which the regime set forth in the UNCLOS addressing the high seas is applicable, the Arctic region merits special attention, not only because it is comprised of sea-ice without any underlying landmass, but also because it is a region over which the conduct of civil aviation continues to take place and to which varying[§§§] claims of territorial sovereignty have been made. At the risk of oversimplification, suffice it to state that the current legal status of the arctic sea, and the existence[****] of polar routes thereto, would indicate that the use of polar airspace falls within the scope of arrangements involving individual States[††††], thus precluding the notion that the legal regime of the airspace over the arctic sea is similar to the regime applicable to the airspace of the high seas.

The UNCLOS pursuant to its Article 87, in addressing the legal regime of the high seas, has established the freedom of the high seas and provides that:

1. The high seas are open to all States, whether coastal or land-locked. Freedom of the high seas is exercised under the conditions laid down by this Convention and by other rules of international law. It

comprises, *inter alia*, both for coastal and land-locked States:

a. freedom of navigation;
b. freedom of overflight;
c. freedom to lay submarine cables and pipelines subject to Part VI;
d. freedom to construct artificial islands and other installations permitted under international law, subject to Part VI;
e. freedom of fishing, subject to the conditions laid down in Section 2;
f. freedom of scientific research, subject to Parts VI and XIII.

2.) These freedoms shall be exercised by all States with due regard for the interests of other States in their exercise of the freedom of the high seas, and also with due regard for the rights under this Convention with respect to activities in the area.

From the foregoing, it is evident that within the scope of the high seas also exists the superjacent airspace, to which the UNCLOS makes reference when establishing the freedoms mentioned hereinbefore, where States may exercise a freedom to fly over, individually or collectively. An area to which, it has been stated,[‡‡‡‡] relatively little attention has been paid, despite the extent of that airspace and it's commercial, strategic and environmental significance. This paper is not immediately concerned with the freedom to fly over the high seas, but rather considers the freedom to receive DBS signals on board aircraft exercising the right to fly over the high seas. An activity, which from the foregoing cannot be rightly stated as being comprehensively regulated by one the principal international instruments expected to regulate the use of the high seas and the superjacent airspace thereto. It is for this reason that the provisions of the 1944 Chicago Convention on International Civil Aviation[§§§§], as well as the Constitution, Convention[*****] and Radio Regulations[†††††] of the International Telecommunications Union, become pertinent, to which this paper now turns.

Civil aviation and non-safety aeronautical communications in the airspace of the high seas[‡‡‡‡‡]

Whilst the freedom of flight over the high seas is proclaimed in the UNCLOS, the regulation of flight in this geographical area is specifically dealt with under the provisions of Article 12, to the Chicago Convention, which provides that:

> Each contracting State undertakes to adopt measures to insure that every aircraft flying over or manoeuvring within its territory and that every aircraft carrying its nationality mark, wherever such aircraft may be, shall comply with the rules and regulations relating to flight and manoeuvre of aircraft there in force. Each Contracting State undertakes to keep its own regulations in these respects uniform, to the greatest possible extent, with those established from time to time under this Convention. Over the high seas, the rules in force shall be those established under this Convention. Each State undertakes to insure the

prosecution of all persons violating the regulations applicable.

The provisions of Annex 2 to the Convention implement the Rules of the Air referred to in Article 12 of the Chicago Convention. The foreword to this Annex provides *inter alia*..."the Annex constitutes the Rules relating to the flight and manoeuvre of aircraft within the meaning of Article 12. Therefore over the high seas these rules shall apply without exception". The applicability of Annex 2 without exception[§§§§§] is further re-iterated in the Annexes' Chapter 2.1.1, whilst its relevance to the high seas is confirmed in Chapter 2.1.2. The effect of Article 12 therefore is that the ICAO Rules of the Air stated in Annex 2, are mandatory for flights over the high seas and any discretion given in Article 37 of the Chicago Convention would not apply. A close examination of Annex 2 reveals that the regulation of communications set forth in Chapter 3.6.5, applies to controlled flights and deals with maintenance of listening watch, establishment of two-way communication and procedures on communication failure under the general heading of Air Traffic Control services. No mention is made of passenger non-safety communications such as would be conducted by providing DBS services directly to aircraft.

One other Annex to the Chicago Convention, which ought to contain detailed regulations addressing the receipt of non-safety related DBS signals by aircraft over the high seas, is Annex 10 (aeronautical communications). Annex 10 which is comprised of four volumes in essence implements specific provisions of the Chicago Convention, namely: Article 28 (Air navigation facilities and standard systems), Article 30[******] (Aircraft radio equipment), Article 69 (Improvement of air navigation facilities) and Article 83 *bis*, respectively. However, Annex 10 makes reference to the ITU Radio Regulations, which on a close examination, provide specific provisions relating to the conduct of aeronautical communications services for non-safety purposes. In this regard, and in order to ensure adequate protection for safety and regularity of flight messages, provisions are included in the Standards and Recommended Practices elaborated in the said Annex, thereby guaranteeing safety related messages, which have priority and pre-emption over other non-safety aeronautical users. Because these principles of priority and pre-emption guarantee the precedence of communications for safety purposes, non-safety communications must cease immediately if necessary, to permit transmissions of messages accorded a certain order of priority[††††††]. Considered within this framework, one can presume that non-safety communications, such as DBS services to passenger's on-board aircraft over the high seas, is by deduction permitted albeit on a non-interference[‡‡‡‡‡‡] basis.

At this juncture it is important to note that ..."the principle of the freedom of the high seas has been described as *multiforme et fugace*, and in truth it is a 'general principle of international law, or a policy concept, from which particular rules must be deduced. Its application to specific problems often fails to give precise results"[§§§§§§]. This statement explains the difficulty one faces in attempting to deduce the legitimacy of providing DBS services to passenger's on-board aircraft over the high seas. In this respect, the provisions of Articles 30(a) and (b) to the Chicago Convention which are intended to address the use of Aeronautical earth Stations for non-safety purposes over national territories (without any specific reference to the airspace over the high seas) have been interpreted[*******] on a literal basis and the said interpretation set forth in Resolution 36/1 adopted by the International Civil Aviation Organisation Assembly at its 29th Session in 1992[†††††††]. That Resolution provides:

> 1.) that nothing in article 30(b) of the Chicago Convention shall be taken to preclude the use by unlicensed persons of the radio transmitting apparatus installed upon an aircraft where the use is for non-safety related air-ground radio transmissions;
>
> 2.) that all Member States should ensure that use of such apparatus shall not be prohibited in their airspace; and
>
> 3.) that use of such apparatus shall be subject to the conditions set out in the Annex hereto.

The Annex referred to, reads as follows:

> Whenever a Member State is the State of Registry (or State of the operator under the terms of Article 83 bis of the Convention on International Civil Aviation… and is applied to a specific case) of an aircraft, the radio transmitting apparatus on board that aircraft may, while in or over the territory of another Member State, be used for non-safety air-ground radio transmissions subject to the following conditions;
>
> (i) compliance with the conditions of the licence for the installation and operation of that apparatus issued by the State of Registry (or State of the operator) of the aircraft;
>
> (ii) any person may use that apparatus for non-safety air-ground radio transmissions provided always that control of that apparatus shall be by an operator duly licensed by the State of Registry (or State of the operator) of the aircraft;
>
> (iii) compliance with the requirements of the International Telecommunication Convention and the Radio Regulations adopted thereunder as amended from time to time, including the applicable radio frequencies, the avoidance of harmful interference with other services and priority for aeronautical communications relating to distress, safety and regularity of flight; and compliance with any technical and operating conditions set forth in the applicable regulations of the Member State in or over whose territory the aircraft is operating.

An examination of this Resolution indicates that it's application is geared firstly, geared towards 'radio transmitting apparatus', secondly pertains to what is referred to as "air-ground communications", and thirdly is of relevance to the use of radio transmitting apparatus for non-safety air-ground communications in the airspace of sovereign States. DBS services to aircraft on the other hand will involve, antennae located on aircraft capable or "receiving" rather than "transmitting" signals, and for the purposes of this paper such activity will be conducted, predominantly in the airspace of the high seas.

Concluding Remarks

The analysis conducted hereinbefore, by deduction, leads one to believe that the provision of DBS services to aircraft overflying the high seas is permissible. The essence of the conclusion itself is premised *inter alia* upon the principle of the freedom of aviation, which underscores the fact that the airspace of the high seas "is an aerial highway open to all nations and not subject to the sovereignty of any State".[‡‡‡‡‡‡‡] This conclusion in turn gives rise to the question on whether the existing body of international laws and regulations are well suited to regulate such activity. It may be convenient to assume that in the absence of law and regulation, activity of this nature is legal if one believes that actions, which are not expressly forbidden, may be construed as permissible or even legitimate. Nonetheless, activity of this kind re-invent legal and regulatory issues within the on-going debate borne from the revolutionary development and simultaneously increasing involvement of private entities in space activities, within the framework of international law, principles and regulations, applicable to space as well as aeronautical activity. A persistent state of affairs that should not be ignored and hence the debate that causes one to enquire whether the existing family of international instruments adequately balances the various interests stemming from activities in outer space[§§§§§§§], though in this instance terminating in the airspace of the high seas.

On the maintenance of public order in the airspace of the high seas, the comment of the International Law Commission (ILC) to the effect that "[a]ny freedom that is to be exercised in the interests of all entitled to enjoy it *must* [emphasis mine] be regulated",[********] is pertinent. This author posits that the applicable and required regulations ought to be clear, consistent, predictable, enforceable and existent in the absence of conflicting positions either between Nation States and/or schools of thought, not because the transnational nature of DBS to aircraft over the high seas is capable of infringing upon territorial sovereignty, but specifically because..."introducing one technology into society may produce a seemingly predictable pattern of effects, at least on the surface. Another new technology will act entirely differently and raise unforeseen social and ethical issues. The nature of the technology, who has access to it, and the context into which it is introduced may greatly alter its impact upon society"[††††††††]. Therefore unless lawmakers, and governments keep pace with entrepreneurs and inventors, profits and commercialism will soon replace the international public order in the airspace of the high seas.

* *A service in which mobile earth stations ("MES") are located on board aircraft, without prejudice to "survival craft stations" and "emergency position-indicating radio-beacon stations"*. Article 1 paragraph 35 of the ITU Radio Regulations.

† Considered as being the most recent development in aeronautical communication, consists primarily of connections of onboard facilities with existing fixed networks e.g. domestic telephone networks, in addition to permitting the switching of connections to other aeronautical passenger facilities (via a ground station) thus enabling personal communications by/for passengers and crew.

‡ At present, Mobile-satellite spectrum at L-band (1.5-1.6 GHz) is fully assigned to operational geostationary MSS systems - in all, 10 mobile-satellite operators are assigned spectrum for 22 satellites within a 33 MHz block. The current mechanism utilised to assign spectrum to the mobile-satellite service on a global and regional basis is based on two Memoranda of Understanding between the administrations operating L-band GSO MSS systems. The MoU process, which is based on annual spectrum planning meetings between the L-band operators, is claimed to have been successful in that the spectrum congestion that was imminent a few years ago has been staved off, and the short-term spectrum requirements of the operators have so far been satisfied. However, there is little scope for networks to expand in the future, or for new networks to get access to L-band MSS spectrum. In contrast, the traffic in MSS systems continues to grow. New systems, some of which are planned for L-band, will therefore have to seek access to other bands, such as S-band (2.9-3.1 GHz). See: Radiocommunications Agency of the United Kingdom.: *Strategy for the future use of the Radio Spectrum*, 2002 at page 46

§ Frequency band allocations to the space services can be found in the ITU Radio Regulations.

** LiveTV, a Joint venture between Harris Corp and Sextant-In Flight System. LiveTV is the only system currently providing live TV to commercial aviation (narrow body aircraft and commuters). The system enables access to the programs delivered by the US DirectTV DBS platforms and therefore is available only over continental United States. Live TV is based on an on-board distribution system provided by Sextant-IFS enabling 1248 channels of audio or Video programming, In seat billing and collection is included as well as a back channel communication link for surveys and passengers responses. An Antenna system provided by Harris Corp is of dual polarization and installed on the aircraft through one single hole.

†† *A radiocomunication service in which signals transmitted or retransmitted by space stations are intended for direct reception by the general public. In the broadcasting satellite service, the term direct reception shall encompass both individual and community reception"*. Article 1 paragraph 38 of the ITU Radio Regulations.

‡‡ AirTV intends to deploy a worldwide DBS service to deliver *inter alia* live, multi-channel television video programming services to airborne passengers primarily on long range wide-body aircraft. The service will offer 40 TV channels customized to Airlines and route characteristics. The airborne equipment will include an S-band phased array receive antenna mounted on top of the fuselage and a Receiver/Decoder. Height - 12 cm, approximate length - 2.5 m. The Receiver/Decoder will interface with the In Flight Entertainment TV system. The system will operate within the S-band (about 2,6 GHz) and will include four geostationary satellites designed for and dedicated to this service. The AirTV satellite ground control station system consists of one primary satellite control center and three regional satellite control ground stations. The primary satellite control center will have all the necessary hardware and software to control the satellites in orbit via communications link to the regional satellite control ground stations. The design of the onboard aircraft antenna and receiver-decoder is optimized specifically for this application. It will utilize a phased-array approach for electronic steerability and includes the tracking system controller. It has the low profile required for mounting on aircraft, has relatively high gain and is customized to operate in the band segment transmitted by the AirTV satellites, while minimizing interference from other systems. Airbus has approved the antenna for installation aboard its A300, A310, A321, A330 and A340 aircraft models. A similar certification process is underway with Boeing. The major difference between AirTV and other announced systems for aeronautical communications is that it is the only satellite system dedicated exclusively to aeronautical services.

§§ Principles Governing the Use by States of Artificial Earth Satellites for International Direct Television Broadcasting (resolution 37/92 of 10 December 1982); N.M. Matte, *Aerospace Law: Telecommunications Satellites*, Butterworths, 1982 pp. 17 - 198; Nandasiri Jasetuliyana and Roy S.K. Lee, *Manual on Space Law*, 1979, pp. 283 – 302; John H. Chapman and Gabriel I. Warren, *Direct Broadcast satellites: The ITU, UN and the real world, AASL*, vol. IV, 1979, pp. 413 – 432; Simone Courteix, *International legal aspects of Television Broadcasting by Satellite*, pp. 102-112 in K. Tatsuzawa (ed) *Legal aspects of space commercialisation*, 1992.

*** Article 86 United Nations Convention on the Law of the Sea, Montego Bay, 10 December 1982.

††† "The exclusive economic zone is an area beyond and adjacent to the territorial sea, subject to the specific legal regime established in this part, under which the rights and jurisdiction of the coastal State and the rights and freedoms of other States are governed by the relevant provisions of this Convention". *Id* at Art. 55.

‡‡‡ Ian Brownlie, *Principles of public International Law*, (1998), p.229.

§§§ On the various schools of thought attempting to explain the legal status of the arctic sea, and the analysis of various writers on the "Sector Principle" see: Nicholas Grief, *Public International Law in the*

Airspace of the High seas, Utrecht studies in Air and Space Law, *vol. 14, 199*, pp. 24 - 28.

**** Although the new cross-polar routes take international flights over previously untraveled territory, commercial airlines have been flying in the polar region north of the Arctic Circle for more than 40 years. In 1954, Scandinavian Airlines System (SAS) inaugurated DC-6B service from Copenhagen to Los Angeles via Sondre Stromfjord. In 1957, SAS began polar service from Copenhagen to Tokyo via Anchorage. From that time through the mid-1980s, flights through the polar region increased as Anchorage became the primary stopping point for passenger traffic between Europe and East Asia. In 1983, Finnair inaugurated the first non-stop service from Europe to Japan by flying from Helsinki north through the polar region and down the Bering Strait to Tokyo. Today, hundreds of flights operate each week over the interior of Russia en route between Europe and Asia. Similarly, a large volume of traffic crosses the Atlantic north of Iceland and the Arctic Circle on flights between Europe and the West Coast of North America. Development of the new cross-polar routes began in 1994 when the Russian government initiated work with the airlines and the international community to establish a series of polar routes through its airspace. By mid-1998, the four cross-polar routes were defined and made available for demonstration flights. The first official polar route flight by a commercial airline was conducted in July 1998. U.S. and Asian airlines then conducted more than 650 demonstration flights under special arrangements with Russian authorities. Today, airlines operate non-stop 747 and 777 service to destinations in Asia via the polar routes.

†††† In 2001 NAV CANADA and the Federal Aviation Authority of Russia (FAAR) released a detailed feasibility concluding that polar routes are feasible and desirable for air travel. The end of the Cold War enabled aircraft to use a set of four polar routes, known to the aviation community as Polar 1,2,3 and 4. NAV CANADA intends to invest approximately $7 million (CDN), in this project, financed out of the normal budget for capital expenditures and subject to the FAAR securing the required financing for changes to its system. The Russian investment would be approximately $33 million (USD). The main cross-polar route, known as Polar 1, generally offers efficient routing from West Coast cities such as Vancouver and Los Angeles to destinations on the Indian subcontinent. The other main cross-polar routes, Polar 2, 3, and 4, generally are for flights connecting cities in eastern and central North America with destinations in China and East Asia. Several interlinking airways among the four major routes provide additional flexibility. The governments of Russia, China, Canada, and the United States are continuing to develop the polar route system through the ongoing activities of the Russian-American Coordinating Group for Air Traffic.

‡‡‡‡ P. Allot, *Mare Nostrum: A new international Law of the Sea*, AJIL, vol. 86 (1992), pp.764, 767; M. Nash Leich, *Contemporary Practices of the United States relating to International Law*, AJIL, vol. 84 (1990), pp.237, 241; Nicholas Grief *op cit*, p. 1

§§§§ Convention on International Civil Aviation, Chicago, 7 December 1944.

***** *ITU Constitution and Convention of the ITU, Decisions, Resolutions and Recommendations*, Final Acts of the Plenipotentiary Conference of the International Telecommunication Union (Kyoto, 1994), Instruments amending the Constitution and Convention of the International Telecommunication Union (Geneva, 1992) ITU, Geneva, 1995, ISBN 92-61005521-4.

††††† ITU *Radio Regulations*, Edition of 2001, adopted by the WRC-1995 (Geneva), revised and adopted by WRC-1997 (Geneva) and WRC-2000 (Istanbul).

‡‡‡‡‡ J.E. Carroz, *International Legislation on Air Navigation over the high Seas*, JALC, vol.26 (1959), pp. 158, 166-168.

§§§§§ On the right of States to deviate from the provisions of Annexes to the Chicago Convention, See: Bin Cheng, *Centrifugal Tendencies in Air Law*, (1957) *Current Legal Problems*, 200; *The law of International Air Transport* (1962); T. Buergenthal, *Law-making in the International Civil Aviation Organization* (1969) 76 *et. seq.*; C.H. Alexandrowicz, *The Convention on Facilitation of International Maritime Traffic and International Technical Regulation* (1966) 15 ICLQ 621. All cited in B.D.K. Henaku, *The Law on global Air Navigation by Satellite – A legal Analysis of the ICAO CNS/ATM System*, 1998, p. 33.

****** *"Aircraft of each contracting State may, in or over the territory of other contracting States, carry radio transmitting apparatus only if a license to install and operate such apparatus has been issued by the appropriate authorities of the State in which the Aircraft is registered. The use of radio transmitting apparatus in the territory of the Contracting State whose territory is flown over shall be in accordance with regulations prescribed by that State"*. Article 30(a) of the Chicago Convention, *"Radio transmitting apparatus may be used only by members of the flight crew who are provided with a special license for the purpose, issued by the appropriate authorities of the State in which the aircraft is registered"*. Article 30(b) of the Chicago Convention. The interpretation of these Articles to the Chicago Convention as far as their applicability to the use of Aeronautical earth Stations for non-safety purposes over national territory (without any reference to the high seas) is concerned, is set forth on the basis of a literal interpretation in Resolution 36/1 adopted by the ICAO assembly at its 29th Session in 1992.

†††††† The order of priority of communications include: Distress calls, distress messages and distress traffic; communications preceded by the urgency signal; communications relating to radio-direction finding; flight safety messages; meteorological messages; and flight regularity

messages. See Article 51 of the ITU Radio Regulations.

‡‡‡‡‡‡ Article 44 (2) of the ITU Constitution provides that: *In using frequency bands for radio services, Member States shall bear in mind that radio frequencies and any associated orbits, including the geostationary-satellite orbit, are limited natural resources and that they must be used rationally, efficiently and economically, in conformity with the provisions of the Radio Regulations, so that countries or groups of countries may have equitable access to those orbits and frequencies, taking into account the special needs of the developing countries and the geographical situation of particular countries.* Article 45 (1)(2)(3) provides that: *All stations whatever their purpose, must be established and operated in such a manner as not to cause harmful interference to the radio services or communications of other Member States or of recognized operating agencies, or of other duly authorized operating agencies which carry on a radio service, and which operate in accordance with the provisions of the Radio Regulations; Each member State undertakes to require the operating agencies which it recognizes and the operating agencies duly authorised for this purpose to observe the provisions in paragraph 1; Further, the Member States recognize the necessity of taking all practicable steps to prevent the operation of electrical apparatus and installations of all kinds from causing harmful interference to the radio services or communications mentioned in paragraph 1.*

§§§§§§ Brownlie *op cit* at page 231.

******* ICAO Doc. LC/28-WP/4-1 4/1 - Report of the Rapporteur on the Legal Aspects of the Global Air-Ground Communications; ICAO Doc 9588-lC/188 Legal Committee 28th Session Report, 1992, pp 4-1, 4-5. See also LC/28-WP/4-2 presented by the Delegate of Argentina; LC/28-WP/4-3 presented by the Observer of INMARSAT; LC/28-WP/4-4 presented by the Delegation of the United Kingdom. See also: Milde M.: Legal Aspects of Future Air Navigation Systems, *AASL*, Vol XII, 1987 at pp 87-98; Milde M.: Legal Aspects of Global Air-Ground Communication in G.R. Bacelli (Ed.), *Liber Amicorum Honouring Nicolas Mateesco Matte – Beyond Boundaries*, Paris 1989, pp 215 – 218; Guldimann & Kaiser, *loc cit*; Henaku, *loc cit*, pp 70-72; Stofel W.: Legal Aspects of Aeronautical Mobile Satellite Services – The ICAO FANS Concept, Proceedings *of the 36th Colloquium of the International Institute for Space Law*, 1993, pp 116-121.

††††††† ICAO Doc 9599, A29-LE Assembly, Legal Commission, 1992, Report and Minutes.

‡‡‡‡‡‡‡ K. Hailbronner, *Freedom of the Air and the Convention on the Law of the Sea*, AJIL, vol.77 (1983), p.490.

§§§§§§§ Frans G. Von der Dunk, *Public Space and Private Enterprise – The Fitness of International Space Law Instruments for Private Space Activities*, 1999 Proceedings of the Project 2001 – Workshop on Legal Issues of Privatising Space Activities 12.

******** YBILC, 1956, vol.2, p.253: para.5 of Commentary to Article 27 of the draft Articles concerning the law of the Sea (Doc.A/3159).

†††††††† T. Cooper, *Speed-Up and New Technology Ethics: An acceleration of Effects*, PTR, vol. 21/no.3 (2000), p.12

IAC-03-IISL.2.05

THE CRYSTALLISATION OF GENERAL ASSEMBLY SPACE DECLARATIONS INTO CUSTOMARY INTERNATIONAL LAW

Ricky J. Lee*
Ricky J. Lee & Associates
University of Western Sydney, Australia

Steven R. Freeland†
University of Western Sydney, Australia

ABSTRACT

The current instruments of international space law include the United Nations space treaties and the declarations made by the General Assembly on both general and specific issues of space law. Along with other General Assembly resolutions, the exact nature and effect of the space declarations in the context of general international law remain somewhat controversial. It is generally accepted, however, that a provision of a General Assembly resolution or declaration may be regarded as customary international law if it has codified an existing customary principle or has crystallised into customary law through state practice and *opinio juris*.

This paper analyses the provisions of the General Assembly declarations and assesses their current status in the context of customary international law. In particular, it discusses the specific provisions of the declarations concerning remote sensing, direct television broadcasting and nuclear power sources and their effect as customary principles.

INTRODUCTION

It is a commonly observed fact that, over the past fifty years, the United Nations has played a singularly important role in the development of international space law. In addition to the Outer Space Treaty, the Rescue Agreement, the Liability Convention, the Registration Convention and the Moon Agreement, the five sets of principles adopted by the General Assembly relating to both general and specific aspects of international space law have also had a significant impact. Scholars, commentators and practitioners can often be caught referring to the relevant principles as the "law" of remote sensing or nuclear power sources without actually determining whether the relevant provision(s) qualifies as "law" according to the tests enunciated by the courts.

This paper is an empirical study of the extent of the crystallisation into custom of the principles contained in these General Assembly resolutions. It first sets out the appropriate "custom test" to be applied, recognising some of the unique nature of international space law, and then seeks to apply such a "test" to each provision.

Custom Generally

Article 38 of the Statute of the International Court of Justice refers to "international custom, as evidenced by a general practice accepted as law". The elements in establishing a principle of custom, as detailed by Brownlie, are:

- uniformity and consistency of the practice of States;
- generality;
- duration; and
- *opinio juris et necessitatis.*[1]

While complete uniformity is not required to establish a principle of custom, there must be evidence of substantial uniformity in state practice and that this practice is the expression of a legal right of the State.[2] The International Law Commission has produced a non-exhaustive list of the forms that state practice may take, including treaties, decisions of domestic and international courts, domestic statutes, diplomatic correspondence, opinions of national legal advisers and the practice of international organisations.[3]

Similarly, universality is not required but it is necessary to determine the weight of abstention from objection by a number of States in the face of established practice by other States. This is because silence on the part of States may infer anything from tacit acquiescence to a mere lack of interest. The approach taken by the International Court of Justice was to establish a customary principle by evidence demonstrating an "increasing and widespread acceptance" of the practice.[4] Although Article 38(1)(b) of the Statute of the Court refers to a "general" practice, the law does allow for local or regional customs among a group of States.[5] Tunkin has suggested that socialist international law can be a considered a form of local customary law in the governance of legal relations between socialist States.[6] Clearly, if this proposition is generally accepted, then there is no reason why the space faring States cannot form a "local" or "regional" group in relation to the customary law for space activities.

In the case of *opinio juris*, the Court has suggested that there must be a distinction between a rule of international comity in contrast to a practice accompanied by a belief that it is in accordance with an international legal obligation.[7] As Judges Tanaka and Sørensen suggested, it is difficult to discover the necessary *opinio juris* as States rarely explain the motives behind a particular statement or practice.

The main issue with the determination of the existence of customary principles in the field of space law is the duration. Brownlie suggests that, provided the consistency and generality of a practice are proved then no particular duration is required.[8] In the case of space law, if this was not the case, it would indeed be very difficult to prescribe the principles of custom as a result of the relative youth of such principles.

In this regard, it is pertinent to recall the words of Judge Lachs in the *North Sea Continental Shelf Cases*:

> The first instruments that men sent into outer space traversed the air space of States and circled above them in outer space, yet the launching States sought no permission nor did the other States protest. This is how the freedom of movement into outer space, and in it, came to be established and recognised as law within a remarkably short period of time.[9]

Treaties, Declarations and Custom

In the *North Sea Continental Shelf Cases*, the Court was of the view that a treaty may relate to custom in one of three ways:

1. the treaty may be declaratory or a codification of existing custom;

2. the treaty may crystallise custom as agreed by the States during its negotiation process; or

3. the treaty provisions become accepted and followed by States as custom after its adoption.[10]

In the case of the United Nations space treaties, and in particular the Outer Space Treaty and the Liability Convention, the second and third alternatives may apply. In the various statements made during discussions in the Legal Sub-Committee of the United Nations Committee on the Peaceful Uses of Outer Space (COPUOS), the representatives often refer to binding legal principles in the context of specific space activities. Most of the provisions in the Outer Space Treaty and the Liability Convention, for example, are referred to by representatives as being the law regulating new fields of activities.

The same can clearly be said in the case of General Assembly declarations, in the sense that they may crystallise custom as agreed by States during discussions in COPUOS or became accepted and followed by the States as custom. For example, Brownlie suggests that adoption of a resolution by the General Assembly constitutes evidence of the legal opinions of States.[11] Unless the extreme position that only physical acts can constitute state practice is taken, there is no doubt that the adoption of such resolutions must in some way constitute practice. Akehurst, for example, defines state practice as "any act or statement by a State from which views about customary law can be inferred; it includes physical acts, claims, declarations *in abstrato* (such as General Assembly resolutions), national laws, national judgments and omissions".[12]

The effect of such declarations on the obligations of States can be considered in three ways. On the one hand, Schwebel, when he was Deputy Legal Advisor to the Department of State, wrote that:

> As a statement of U.S. policy in this regard, I think it is fair to state that General Assembly resolutions are regarded as recommendations to Member States of the United Nations. To the extent, which is exceptional, that such resolutions, [which] are *meant to be* declaratory of international law, are adopted with the support of *all* members and are observed by the practice of States, such resolutions are evidence of customary international law on a particular subject matter.[13]

Consequently, it appears that a General Assembly declaration must have the explicit intention of creating customary law and that it was accepted by a true consensus. This calls into question the effect of abstentions as well as challenging the accepted view that generality, rather than universality, is the requirement for the establishment of a customary principle.

As a middle view, in the *South West Africa Cases*, Judge Tanaka held that:

> What is required for customary international law is the repetition of the same practice; accordingly, in this case resolutions, declarations, etc. ... must take place repeatedly ... This collective, cumulative and organic process of custom-generation can be characterised as the middle way between legislation by convention and the traditional process of custom making, and can be seen to have an important role from the viewpoint of the development of international law.[14]

It can be seen from this that, while Judge Tanaka did not appear to be as strict as Schwebel in prescribing the requirements placed on custom-making resolutions, he did require for the resolutions or declarations to be repetitive in their statements of the custom.

At the other end of the continuum, Sohn wrote that:

> There is wide consensus that these declarations actually establish new rules of international law binding upon all States. This is not treaty-making but a new method of creating customary international law. ... Thus the United Nations has made possible the creation of "instant international law" ... In a rapidly changing world the United Nations has found a method, albeit restricted by the rule of unanimity or quasi-unanimity, to adapt the principles of its Charter and the rules of customary international law to the changing times with an efficiency which even its most optimistic founders did not anticipate.[15]

To some extent, the debate between the different viewpoints found in the three extracts above has been overtaken by the recent cases of the Court. In *Nicaragua*, the Court relied almost exclusively on General Assembly resolutions in stating the law on the use of force and external interventions.[16] A similar approach can be found in the advisory opinion given by the Court in the *Nuclear Weapons Case*.[17]

SPACE LAW DECLARATIONS

Overview

The five General Assembly declarations concerning space activities are:

- the Declaration of Legal Principles Governing the Activities of States in the Exploration and Use of Outer Space of 13 December 1963 (the "**Principles Declaration**");
- the Principles Governing the Use by States of Artificial Earth Satellites for International Direct Television Broadcasting of 10 December 1982 (the "**Broadcasting Principles**");
- the Principles Relating to Remote Sensing of the Earth from Outer Space of 3 December 1986 (the "**Remote Sensing Principles**");
- the Principles Relevant to the Use of Nuclear Power Sources in Outer Space of 14 December 1992 (the "**Nuclear Principles**"); and
- the Declaration on International Cooperation in the Exploration and Use of Outer Space for the Benefit and in the Interest of All States, Taking into Particular Account the Needs of Developing Countries of 13 December 1996 (the "**Cooperation Declaration**").

In these General Assembly declarations it may be prudent or at least convenient to separate their provisions into three groups:

- provisions that merely repeat existing treaty principles (the "**Repeating Provisions**");
- provisions that state, without more, the application of existing treaty provisions to specific situations (the "**Applying Provisions**"); and
- provisions that create new rights, duties or obligations of law that have not been previously stated in existing treaties or those that extend the applicability or content of the treaty provisions (the "**New Provisions**").

In the case of Repeating Provisions, the extent of the treaty provision's "migration" into custom must first be considered. For example, the fact that the Outer Space Treaty is considered by most States and commentators to have crystallised into customary international law means that any Repeating Provisions that repeat the provisions of the Outer Space Treaty would merely be restating existing custom.

Applying Provisions are, strictly speaking, not statements of legal principles but are instead "working examples" of specific applications of an existing treaty principle. Consequently, the only relevant consideration when determining the status of an Applying Provision in custom is whether the treaty provision being applied has crystallised into a principle of customary law.

In the case of New Provisions, it will be necessary to consider whether they crystallise custom as agreed during negotiations or if they have been subsequently accepted and followed as custom. As an empirical exercise, the *travaux préparatoire* and, as a secondary source, the writings of legal scholars and commentators are examined to determine whether a New Provision has been accepted by States to be a principle of customary international law.

Further, for the purposes of considering the Repeating Provisions and the Applying Provisions, the provisions of the Outer Space Treaty, the Rescue Agreement and the Liability Convention are considered to have crystallised into custom at the time that these treaties were adopted by the General Assembly.

Principles Declaration

The Principles Declaration, adopted by the General Assembly in 1963, is the only resolution considered to contain principles of space law that was declared before the adoption of the Outer Space Treaty and the Liability Convention. Consequently, the Principles Declaration is unique in that, at the time it was adopted, its provisions were all New Provisions. Since the adoption of the 1967 Outer Space Treaty, however, these provisions may be considered to have transformed into Repeating Provisions.

Between 1963 and 1967, the status of the provisions of the Principles Declaration would have required an evaluation of the *travaux préparatoire* to assess the level of their acceptance by States. Considering the positive statements made by almost all governmental representatives during the debates and negotiations, it is likely that the Principles Declaration is a codification of the customary principles accepted by States during the negotiations process. However, those provisions relating to the freedom of movement in outer space may well have already represented customary law by that time, as discussed above.

After 1967, the widespread acceptance of the Outer Space Treaty as customary law means that all that would be necessary is to compare the provisions of the Principles Declaration with those of the Outer Space Treaty. As the provisions of the Principles Declaration are virtually identical to their equivalents in the Outer Space Treaty, it is probable they can all be considered to have crystallised into customary law.

Table 1. Principles Declaration

Para.	Type	Treaty Provision
1	Repeating	Outer Space Treaty I
2	Repeating	Outer Space Treaty I
3	Repeating	Outer Space Treaty II
4	Repeating	Outer Space Treaty III
5	Repeating	Outer Space Treaty VI
6	Repeating	Outer Space Treaty IX
7	Repeating	Outer Space Treaty VIII
8	Repeating	Outer Space Treaty VII
9	Repeating	Outer Space Treaty V

Broadcasting Principles

The Broadcasting Principles may be considered to be the first of three General Assembly declarations that relate to specific space activities. The first three paragraphs provide for the purposes and objectives to be observed by States when conducting direct television broadcasting activities. Paragraph 6 requires States to make appropriate arrangements for international cooperation, taking into account the interests of developing States. Principle 11 requires States to cooperate on the protection of copyright and associated rights in the conduct of television broadcasting. A cursory glance over the *travaux préparatoire* of the Broadcasting Principles appears to show that there was substantial acceptance of the above provisions as being legal obligations, indicating their crystallisation into customary law.

Table 2. Broadcasting Principles

Para.	Type	Treaty Provision
1	New Provision — Custom	
2	New Provision — Custom	
3	New Provision — Custom	
4	Applying	Outer Space Treaty III
5	Applying	Outer Space Treaty I
6	New Provision — Custom	
7	Applying	Outer Space Treaty III
8	Applying	Outer Space Treaty VI
9	Applying	Outer Space Treaty VI
10	New Provision — Not Custom	
11	New Provision — Custom	
12	Repeating	Outer Space Treaty XI
13	New Provision — Not Custom	
14	New Provision — Not Custom	
15	Applying	ITU Instruments

Paragraph 10 provides that a broadcasting or receiving State has the right to request consultations with the other States on the satellite broadcasting service. Paragraphs 13 and 14 provide that a State establishing a new broadcasting service must notify the proposed receiving States and enter into consultations if requested. Paragraph 15 states that the instruments of the International Telecommunication Union (the "**ITU**") are exclusively applicable to the signal overspill from the service. There does not appear to be widespread acceptance on the part of States during the debates and negotiations. For example, Argentina considered the spill-over issue not to be subject to the ITU, while Czechoslovakia and India both considered prior consent to be necessary.[18] Accordingly, it is likely that these particular provisions may not have the sufficient acceptance by States to be considered customary principles of law.

Remote Sensing Principles

Observations concerning the Broadcasting Principles can similarly be made about the Remote Sensing Principles. While most of the provisions are applications of the Outer Space Treaty, there are a set of provisions relating to international cooperation and another set of provisions relating to the duty and the right to consult.

Principle II states that remote sensing activities are to be conducted for the benefit and in the interests of all States while "taking into particular consideration the needs of the developing countries". This is in effect a repetition of Article I of the Outer Space Treaty except that the treaty provision does not require the particular needs of developing States to be taken into consideration. The fact that this "change" is repeated through the subsequent treaties and declarations suggests that this is now an additional requirement that is supported by acceptance of most States.

Principles V to VIII, setting out the steps required of States in relation to mutual assistance and international cooperation, were not the subject of much controversy during the debates. Consequently, they may in all likelihood be considered to be custom created during the negotiations or soon thereafter. Principle XI requires States to transmit relevant data and information to States affected or likely to be affected by natural disasters. Similarly, this may be considered to be a small extension of the obligations under Article IX of the Outer Space Treaty and the absence of controversy suggests that this was widely accepted by most States.

Principle XIII requires "sensing States" to enter into consultations upon request with "sensed States" in order to make available opportunities for participation. This infers, as with the Broadcasting Principles, that the sensing States are required to notify sensed States of their sensing activities. This is in contrast to the prior consent requirement that a significant number of States advocated during the negotiations as part of their permanent sovereignty over natural resources. In the absence of uniformity, it would be appropriate to suggest that the provision is not custom.

Table 3. Remote Sensing Principles

Para.	Type	Treaty Provision
I	Definitional Clause	
II	Repeating	Outer Space Treaty I (except to take into account the needs of developing countries)
III	Applying	Outer Space Treaty III
IV	Repeating	Outer Space Treaty I, IX
V	New Provision — Custom	
VI	New Provision — Custom	
VII	New Provision — Custom	
VIII	New Provision — Custom	
IX	Repeating	Outer Space Treaty XI
X	Applying	Outer Space Treaty IX
XI	New Provision — Not Custom	
XII	New Provision — Not Custom	
XIII	New Provision — Not Custom	
XIV	Applying	Outer Space Treaty VI
XV	Applying	Outer Space Treaty III

Principle XII is a unique provision in that it requires sensed States to have access to primary and processed data relating to their territory on a non-discriminatory basis and on reasonable cost terms. This provision does not appear to be based on any existing principle of space law but is in fact a compromise reached between those States wanting free access and those that do not wish to provide any more rights to the sensed States beyond notification and consultation. In one of the later reports of the Legal Sub-Committee Working Group on Remote Sensing, it was evident that there were divergent views concerning the basis of those access rights, the type of data involved and the timing of the access and that the final wording was a compromise that did not satisfy a significant number of States.[19] Therefore, it would be difficult to support an argument that Principle XII is a legal obligation agreed to by all States.

NPS Principles

The NPS Principles contain eleven provisions of which Principles 1, 6, 7, 8, 9 and 10 are Applying Provisions in the sense that they merely restate the application of provisions of existing treaties to nuclear power sources. In particular, Principle 6 merits some attention as it requires States concerned with the re-entry of a nuclear power source will have a right to consultations. This may be considered to be a direct application of the right to consultations in the case of potential harmful interference as provided for in Article IX of the Outer Space Treaty. This is distinguished from the consultation provisions of the Broadcasting Principles and the Remote Sensing Principles in that their consultation rights are not dependent on the potential for harmful interference to the space activities of the affected States.

In the case of the New Provisions, namely Principles 3 to 5, it is pertinent to assess the legal basis of these provisions to ascertain their appropriate status in customary international law. Principles 3 and 4 are concerned with imposing a set of guidelines and criteria for the safe use of nuclear power sources, along with a requirement for a thorough safety assessment to be conducted prior to launch. This can be seen to be an elaboration of the obligations of States under Article IX of the Outer Space Treaty in that States are to have due regard to the interests of other States and to avoid harmful interference.

Principle 5 requires States to inform other States and the United Nations if an object containing a nuclear power source is malfunctioning. The notification must include the orbital parameters of the spacecraft and its radiological risk. The provision appears to have its origins from the following treaty provisions:

- Article IX of the Outer Space Treaty, requiring States to avoid harmful contamination and adverse changes to the Earth environment by introduction of "extraterrestrial" matter; and
- Article IV (3) of the Registration Convention, which imposes a duty on States to notify the United Nations if a registered spacecraft is no longer in Earth orbit.[20]

Table 4. NPS Principles

Para.	Type	Treaty Provision
1	Applying	Outer Space Treaty III
2	Definitional Clause	
3	New Provision — Custom	
4	New Provision — Custom	
5	New Provision — Custom	
6	Applying	Outer Space Treaty IX
7	Applying	Rescue Agreement
8	Applying	Outer Space Treaty VI
9	Applying	Outer Space Treaty VII Liability Convention XII
10	Applying	Outer Space Treaty III
11	Review Clause	

The widespread acceptance by States of the underlying provisions and the absence of significant dissensions during the debates suggest that Principle 5 may be considered, along with Principles 3 and 4, to have crystallised into international law either at the time of their declaration or soon after.

Cooperation Declaration

The Cooperation Declaration, adopted by the General Assembly without a vote in 1996, is special in that not all of its provisions contain mandatory obligations that would support a view that they are intended to have legal effect. For example, Paragraphs 7 and 8 merely suggests that States are to strengthen the role of COPUOS and to contribute to the United Nations space programs and initiatives. As such, they cannot reasonably be considered as legal obligations at all and certainly cannot be considered as part of customary law.

Paragraph 5 poses particular difficulties in its classification in that it requires States to keep in mind certain goals and objectives in framing activities involving international cooperation. It is unclear whether these goals are intended to be of a mandatory nature, as the words "promoting", "fostering" and "facilitating" are used. Even if the consideration of such issues is considered mandatory, the vagueness of the content of these goals makes it unlikely that States have intended for this to be a binding legal obligation.

Paragraphs 1 and 2 may be classified as Applying Provisions in that they are a specific application of existing treaty provisions in the context of international cooperation. Paragraph 2, for example, provides that States are free to determine all aspects of their participation in international space endeavours while ensuring compliance with legitimate interests of other States. This is in effect an application of Article IX of the Outer Space Treaty requiring States to undertake space activities with due regard to the *corresponding* interests of other States and Article I of the Outer Space Treaty in relation to freedom of exploration and use.

Table 5. Cooperation Declaration

Para.	Type	Treaty Provision
1	Applying	Outer Space Treaty III
2	Applying	Outer Space Treaty I Outer Space Treaty IX
3	No Mandatory Obligation	
4	Definitive Clause: Scope of "International Cooperation"	
5	No Mandatory Obligations	
6	No Mandatory Obligations	
7	No Mandatory Obligations	
8	No Mandatory Obligations	

CONCLUSIONS

This empirical exercise demonstrates that the provisions of the General Assembly declarations have, with the notable exception of the Cooperation Declaration, been substantially crystallised into custom. This has been done either through the application or extension of existing treaty provisions that have crystallised into customary law or through the codification of customary principles as agreed to by States during the negotiation processes.

Notwithstanding this conclusion, it should be noted that this analysis has been undertaken in the absence of a substantial body of state practice. In order for space law to provide a clear and certain basis for future human exploration and use, it may be necessary to consider the codification of these principles into separate treaties.

Notes

This paper is written in the personal capacity of the authors and does not necessarily represent the views of any organisations with which they are associated.

* Principal, Ricky J. Lee & Associates and Lecturer, School of Law, University of Western Sydney. Member IISL, IBA and ILA. Email: rjlee@rickylee.id.au.

† Lecturer, School of Law, University of Western Sydney. Member IISL, ILA and ANZSIL. Email: s.freeland@uws.edu.au.

[1] Brownlie, *Principles of Public International Law* (5th ed., 1998), at pp. 5-11.

[2] *Fisheries Case (United Kingdom v Norway)* [1951] ICJ Rep 116 at 131; and *Asylum Case (Columbia v Peru)* [1950] ICJ Rep 266 at 276-277.

[3] International Law Commission [1950] II Y.B.I.L.C. 368-372.

[4] *Fisheries Jurisdiction Case (United Kingdom v Iceland)* [1974] ICJ Rep 3 at 23-26.

[5] *Asylum Case, supra* note 2, at 266; and *Right of Passage over Indian Territory (Portugal v India)* [1960] ICJ Rep 6 at 257.

[6] Tunkin, *Theory of International Law* (trans. Butler, 1974), p. 444.

[7] *North Sea Continental Shelf Cases (Germany v Denmark; Germany v The Netherlands)* [1969] ICJ Rep 3, para. 77.

[8] Brownlie, *supra* note 1, at p. 5. This is supported by the *North Sea Continental Shelf Cases, ibid.* at para. 73.

[9] *North Sea Continental Shelf Cases, supra* note 7, at 230.

[10] *Ibid.*

[11] Brownlie, *supra* note 1, p. 14.

[12] Akehurst, "Custom as a Source of International Law" (1974-1975) 47 B.Y.I.L. 1 at 53.

[13] Schwebel [1975] U.S.D.I.L. 85.

[14] *South West Africa Case (Ethiopia and Liberia v South Africa)* [1966] ICJ Rep at 292.

[15] Sohn, in Bos (ed.), *The Present State of International Law and Other Essays* (1973) at 52-53.

[16] *Military and Paramilitary Activities in and against Nicaragua (Nicaragua v United States)* [1986] ICJ Rep 14.

[17] *Legality of the Threat or Use of Nuclear Weapons* [1996] ICJ Rep 226.

[18] See generally the *travaux préparatoire* of the Broadcasting Principles as reproduced in Jasentuliyana and Lee, *Manual on Space Law* (1979), vol. III.

[19] Report of the Chairman of the Working Group on Remote Sensing, U.N.Doc. A/Ac.105/271.

[20] Article IV (2) of the Registration Convention, although allow States to provide "additional" information concerning a space object, does not impose a mandatory obligation.

More Peaceful Use and International Cooperation in Activities in Outer Space

Toshio Kosuge
University of Electro-Communications
Tokyo, Japan

Abstract

In 1963"Declaration on Legal Principles Governing the Activities of States in the Exploration and Use of Outer Space" was adopted in the United Nations. Accordingly in 1969, the resolution on principles of exploration and exploitation of outer space was passed in the Japanese Diet. It clearly mentioned that any activity of launching space object into outer space and developing launching rocket should be exclusively for peaceful purpose. Japanese interpretations of 1963 Declaration and other related international space agreements have been qualified to more peaceful use and international cooperation.

Through more than forty years of development and experiences in space activities, technologies, and international cooperation among countries, it is important for us to analyze the present condition of implementing those principles and other related disciplines. Especially in close relation with international cooperation for developing countries, it would be very important matter for future development of space law to implement the principles adopted and agreed among states. In order to overcome the divide issues between the developed and the developing in the world, utilization of space resources and space technologies could bring and facilitate to bridge the divide among the states concerned.

It isvery important for us to review and evaluate the 1963 Declaration and other related international space agreements in relation with space activities in order to develop new space law and more international cooperation for peaceful use of outer space.

1. Since the Millennium Year of 2000, many international, regional and national declarations and policies have been elaborated in relation with alleviating the digital divide issues in the world. The digital divide issues are about differential access to information and communication technologies including satellite communication networks. Nowadays more than 600million people worldwide are using the Internet. As the Internet was rapidly popularized, the number of host computers increased by 15 times over the recent six years. Particularly the number of host computers in the US increased by 17times amounting more than 75% of the world. While Asia Pacific region including Japan shows the large growth by 20 odd times, which exceeds the world average, thc share in the world still ranks low. In Asia Pacific region more than 100million people are using the Internet. Even among Asia Pacific countries there is wide gap for accessing the Internet. In order to overcome digital divide issues from global perspectives, recently mentioned in ITU as "The New Missing Link", we must pay attention to the several issues; 1) In rural area of developing countries there exists no telecommunication infrastructure for even voice telephone service and other social infrastructure such as electricity and road. 2) Needs of large investment for infrastructure building to have telecommunication networks in rural area. 3) Even though information and communication technologies developed evolutionally and rapidly, in the process of privatization and competition after WTO Agreement on liberalization of telecommunication service, it is rather difficult and concerned issue for developing countries to change their

policies of telecommunication infrastructure development by the financial aids from developed countries and other international financial institutions into private telecom carriers to invest on rural network development, which might not be profitable.

2. International organizations made several proposals, action plans and hold international conferences for bridging digital divide issues between rural areas and urban areas in developing countries since the year of 2000.
   1) UN ICT high-level panel made report on digital divide and proposal to provide all the people in the world, not yet connected, the Internet access by 2004. UN also established DOT Force for implementation of action plans.
   2) G8 Okinawa Summit in its Okinawa Charter they agreed t alleviate the digital divide for every one to enjoy accessing to information and communication networks. Several projects have been implementing for bridging international information gap with Japanese government fund 15 billion US$ over five years.
   3) ITU has developed several action plans for rural information and communication network infrastructure. These plans include; (1) establishment of Multi-purpose Community Telecenter (MCT), (2) development of appropriate service and application for rural area, (3) establishment of Center of Excellence for human resource development of cyber space based on the Internet, (4) E-Commerce Initiative for developing countries for small scale industries and farmers, (5) support for NGO to achieve its development goals with utilization of telecommunications.
   4) In Asia Pacific Telecommunity Summit on the Information Society in 2000 also adopted the Declaration entitled "Asia Pacific Renaissance through ICT in the 21st Century and Action Plan". It includes common themes such as forming a shared vision for ICT, bridging digital divide, development information and communication infrastructure, essential applications for the information society, human resource development and enhancement of ICT literacy and regional cooperation and global coordination.
   5) The World Summit on Information Society Asia Pacific Region Conference in Tokyo, 2003 also adopted the proposal of alleviating digital divide issues and more initiatives to utilize ICT, to the WSIS Conference in Geneva in December this year. It also includes the proposal for Asia Broadband Plan to implement the proposal.

3. In order to bridging digital divide in Asia Pacific region, developing information and communication infrastructure should be most important and urgent for the improvement of universal service including the Internet. It is important for each country to introduce mobile and satellite systems and to adopt new technologies into access networks such as FTTH (fiber to the home), ADSL, as well as FWA (fixed wireless access), and the development of broadband networks. However the private sector finds little incentive for investment, the participation of the public sector is necessary in developing vital infrastructure in the field of public service telecommunications, such as telemedicine, e-learning, e-government, library, weather, crisis management, environment protection, agriculture, market information systems.
   In such cases, it is essential for governments to take the lead in promoting infrastructure development, with international support, if required. In the meantime, international cooperation is essential in such field as standardization or management of radio frequencies and satellite orbital slots that are needed for cost effective and efficient development of information and

communication infrastructure, including satellite communications. It is also necessary for developing countries to develop nation wide basic network, improvement of advanced infrastructure like broadband network in urban areas and of basic infrastructure in rural areas with support from developed countries and with international cooperation.

4. In relation with bridging digital divide, one of the very important and concerned issues will be how to implement universal service in the changing environment of technology and information and communication regime. In 1980s we still had a dream to realize that every one in the world could access to telephone by any means within walking distance. However there have been very rapid developments in analog technologies or information and communication, developing countries could catch up with analog technology. In 1990s it became clear that wishful suggestion in "the Missing Link" of the ITU could not be realized by the year of 2000. In the development of digital technologies, implications of information and communication technology have made digital divide wider than before. After liberalization and privatization of information and communication services in both domestic and international markets, operators could hardly implement universal service without any incentive or public policy, especially in the developing countries. Under these circumstances, ITU has elaborated new approach to over come the digital divide issues with concurrent international and regional conferences as "the New Missing Link". In order to alleviate emerging digital divide issues especially in the developing countries, it should be necessary for us to consider the role of government and international institutions to have more appropriate functions for solutions including more peaceful use and international cooperation of outer space, especially satellite communications.

5. As we have discussed about the importance of bridging digital divide issues, especially to improve information and communication network infrastructure in the developing countries, one of the effective and useful technologies could be satellite communication system recognized both developed and developing countries and regions. There are several successful cases in the developing countries to introduce the satellite communication systems for their improvement of digital divide issues including rural and urban gaps. One of the interesting cases utilizing satellite networks for rural area is the one in Thailand. There have been more than 3000 Vsat stations in the rural area connected via satellites. The satellite networks cover small villages and all the people could access to the phone within walking distance. In the case of Vietnam small village connected via satellite networks with Hanoi and village homes are connected by Wireless Local Loop from Vsat stations for voice, data and the Internet. In the case of the USPnet in the South Pacific Island Countries, they established their own satellite communication networks for their distance education systems among 12 countries via Intelsat. More than 10,000 young students enrolled in the higher education institutions scattered over thousand miles away in the Pacific Ocean, could follow many courses and get degree through distance education mode utilizing audio, video conference with intranet and Internet media. These cases are some of success stories, which showed good examples of solution for digital divides through more peaceful use and international cooperation in space activities. You could find these success stories in the ITU home page, which covers e-learning, e-health, e-commerce and e-government services in the developing countries.

6. Within a few years' information and communication networks could be

digitalized and IP based communication networks with broadband service in the developed countries. It could be also realized for the developing countries to be digitalized and IP based services within ten years utilizing wired and wireless communication networks including satellite.

7. As we discussed about the many proposals and action plans within the framework of "the New Missing Link" of ITU, Japanese government proposed Asia Broadband Plan during the WSIS Asia Pacific region conference in Tokyo this year. According to the Action Plan, they start the experiments for Asia Broadband network among Asian countries via satellite network. We have had more than ten years international cooperation among Asia Pacific countries for R/D and experiments of satellite communication through Partners and Post-Partners projects using Japanese communication satellites. Through this international cooperation among Asia Pacific countries including developing countries, we establish human networks, cooperation and collaboration schemes among us for more peaceful use and international cooperation in satellite communication. This kind of international cooperation in space activities shall be based on the principles and international agreements of space activities.

8. It would be very interesting for us to refer two Japanese experiment and demonstration satellites for future developments of satellite communication network systems. First one is Wideband InterNetworking engineering test and Demonstration Satellite (WINDS). Second one is Quasi-Zenith satellite system. WINDS is the research and development project to establish the world's most advanced information and telecommunication network. It is part of "e-Japan Priority Program" which was established by the Information Technology Strategy Headquarters. WINDS project aims at developing and verifying the main technology for future ultra high-speed satellite communications. It also aims to create and demonstrate new utilizations for satellite communications through various experiments such as Asia Broadband Project. WINDS project is open for international cooperation including both developed and developing countries in Asia Pacific for also implementing alleviation of digital divide issues. We are sure this kind of experiments and demonstrations among regional countries Partnership to be good example for peaceful use and international cooperation in space activities.

9. In order to gap the digital divide between the developed and the developing and between urban and rural area in the developing countries, it would be very important and useful to develop more peaceful use and international cooperation in space activities including especially satellite communications. In order to facilitate this kind of peaceful use and international/regional cooperation for bridging digital divide, the UN and ITU's role should be more functional to develop above mentioned projects with much more involvements with technology transfer and financial support. Environment of satellite communication technologies and business has changed into more private sectors and many more players involved. Particularly, ITU should have a new role of effective and practical management of limited resources, which could be regarded as common heritage of mankind according to the principles of space law. It would be appropriate for ITU to facilitate those functions for developing world to bridge the digital divide into digital opportunity and to give priority right of utilizations of those resources on the basis of international cooperation scheme.

10. Information and Communication Technology would be a powerful engine for development in 21st Century. We

should recognize that ICT, including satellite communications brings about enormous changes in every sector of the economy and society and also great benefits for us. However, there happens the digital divide between those who could access and utilize the Internet services and those not, and it brings us wider gap of income and quality of life, and also gaps between countries and between urban and rural areas and other sectors. It is very important for all to cooperate in finding solutions to ICT issues in both regional and international cooperation through international institutions with common goals of sharing benefits through more peaceful use and international cooperation in space activities within the framework of principles and international agreements.

References

1. Outer Space Treaty, Article IV
2. Cheng, *The Legal Status of Outer Space and Relevant Issues: Delimitation of Outer Space and Definition of Peaceful Use* (1983) 11 J.Space L
3. Cheng, Studies in International Space Law, Oxford, 1997
4. Christol, The Modern International Law of Outer Space, 1986
5. Morgan, *Military Use of Commercial Satellite*, (1994) 60 J. Air Law &Com.
6. 1982 Principles Governing the Use by States of Artificial Earth Satellites for International Direct Television Broadcasting, G.A. Res.27/92,U.N. GA.OR,(10 Dec.1982)
7. Matte, *A Treaty for Star Peace,* in Matte, Arms Control and Disarmament in Outer Space, 1987

SPACE LAW IN THE 21ST CENTURY: THE OUTER SPACE TREATIES REVISITED

P.M. Sterns*
L.I. Tennen**
Law Offices of Sterns and Tennen***
Phoenix, Arizona, U.S.A.

ABSTRACT

The 21st century will present new and unique challenges. The fundamental charter of space law, the Outer Space Treaty, entered into force more than 35 years ago, and was drafted under vastly different geopolitical and economic circumstances than exist today. Thus, it must be determined whether the Outer Space Treaty, as well as the additional international agreements derived therefrom, drafted in the last century, are adequate for the needs and requirements of the current era. Several organizations recently have sought to examine this issue, the results of which are compared and discussed in this article.

INTRODUCTION

The evolving commercial uses of space present both opportunities and challenges for the international legal community. The law of outer space was developed during the cold war, when the superpowers were the primary actors in outer space, and national security and international prestige often were included among the reasons for the conduct of scientific missions. It must be determined whether the existing space law régime is sufficient to effectively regulate present and foreseeable commercial uses of space, or whether modifications to the law are necessary to promote the orderly use of outer space by private enterprise.

The space treaties and other international instruments recently have been the subject of review by different organizations in the context of the emerging role of the private sector in space. Specifically, the International Law Association, the American Astronautical Society, and the Project 2001 - *Legal Framework for the Commercial Use of Outer Space*, have conducted studies of these questions and issued reports and recommendations.[1] This paper compares

* Director IISL, Member IAA, ASIL, ABA, IBA, ILA, Senior Member AIAA

** Former Commissioner, Arizona Space Commission, Member IISL, IAA, IEAS, ASIL, ILA, Senior Member AIAA

*** Member IAF

1. It is important to note that the conclusions of studies such as those under consideration herein often are developed by subcommittees or subgroups, utilizing a process which seeks consensus. However, given this division or fractionalization,

certain of the primary findings and conclusions of these studies.

Project 2001

Project 2001 was a joint research initiative by the Institute of Air and Space Law of the University of Cologne, and the German Aerospace Center (DLR). The purpose of the study was to examine the current status of space law, and to identify regulatory needs *vis-a-vis* the private sector. The Project was conducted through six working groups which focused on two questions: "firstly, the general impact of increased private activity with regard to the framework of existing international space law and, secondly, the actual process of privatization as well as development of trends and model structures used in privatization and commercialisation policies by governments."[2]

American Astronautical Society

In December, 2001, the American Astronautical Society (AAS) conducted a workshop entitled *International Legal Regimes Governing Space Activities.* The aim of the workshop was to examine the manner in which domestic laws of states reflect the international obligations set forth in the major space treaties. This workshop encompassed four working groups examining: "The Treaties," "Balancing Competing Interests," "Space Law Gaps and Barriers," and "The Role of the Private Sector." Due to the nature of the subject, commercial uses took center stage in the discussions.[3]

International Law Association

In 2002, the International Law Association(ILA) adopted a resolution which, *inter alia*, endorsed the Final Report of its Space Law Committee,[4] which, over a period of two years, had "elaborate[d] concrete proposals regarding possible amendments of, as well as possible supplements to, the UN space law instruments in view of commercial space activities." The work of the Space Law Committee was facilitated by four Special Rapporteurs, each examining a different treaty.[5] The Committee adopted the view that it was preferable to supplement the existing treaties with "principles and guidelines, codes of conduct or UNGA Resolutions" rather than to seek amendments to international

---

participants in one subgroup may or may not be acquainted fully with the deliberations and conclusions of another subgroup, even if the conclusions of all subgroups are included within a report or conference proceedings. Thus, notwithstanding a broad expression of consensus, specific findings and recommendations expressed by the studies may not necessarily reflect the opinions of all of the participants.

2. Reif, *'Project 2001': Conclusions and Recommendations of the "Working Group on Privatization" With Regard to Issues of International Space Law*, in PROCEEDINGS OF THE 44TH COLLOQUIUM ON THE LAW OF OUTER SPACE 3 - 4 (2002). The six working groups were divided into the following areas: Launch and Associated Services, Remote Sensing. Telecommunication, Space Stations, Privatisation, and National Space Legislation. *Id.* at 3.

3. AMERICAN ASTRONAUTICAL SOCIETY, FINAL REPORT WORKSHOP ON INTERNATIONAL LEGAL REGIMES GOVERNING SPACE ACTIVITIES (2001).

4. INTERNATIONAL LAW ASSOCIATION, REPORT OF THE 70TH CONFERENCE 13-16, 864 (2002).

5. The Special Rapporteurs were Stephan Hobe, Maureen Williams, Vladimir Kopal, and Frans von der Dunk.

agreements already in force.[6] Nevertheless, specific amendments to the Moon Agreement[7] were considered.

COMMERCIALIZATION AND THE OUTER SPACE TREATY

The absence of clear definitions of terms utilized in the space treaties long has been the subject of debate, and not surprisingly became a focus of the discussions in the context of commercialization. Specifically, issues arise concerning which state is the "appropriate state" for purposes of the authorization and continuing supervision obligations set forth in article VI of the Outer Space Treaty.[8] In addition, there is the lackof clarity as to what may constitute the "launching state" pursuant to article VII of the Outer Space Treaty, and article I(c) of the Liability Convention.[9]

With regard to the definition of the "launching state", the AAS noted that despite substantial uncertainty and differing interpretations of that term, among others, liability can be determined "through bilateral and multilateral agreements."[10] Project 2001 observed that the "launching state issue" was central, but that efforts toward clarification were unsuccessful. The ILA concluded that amendments to the definitions provided by the Liability Convention were not advisable at this time, but suggested that states consider making the dispute resolution procedures binding, and that it may be appropriate to consider a separate agreement concerning damages caused by space debris.[11] Thus, while general agreement exists that the term "launching state" is unclear, an acceptable definition has proven to be elusive.

Where a basis exists for more than one state to be considered as the "appropriate state" for purposes of authorization and continuing supervision of a commercial space mission, it is clear that there can be overlapping assertions of state control. The Project 2001 study concluded that "clarification should be provided on a case by case basis by agreement among the very states involved."[12] As a matter of fostering the role of the private sector in the commercial uses of space, Project 2001 strongly recommended that states enact national laws to implement the international obligations of authorization

---

6. ILA Report, *supra* note 4, at 193-94.

7. Agreement Governing the Activities of States on the Moon and Other Celestial Bodies, *entered into force* July 11, 1984, 1363 U.N.T.S. 3, *text reproduced in* UNITED NATIONS TREATIES AND PRINCIPLES ON OUTER SPACE 27 (2000), *and* 18 I.L.M. 1434 (1979) [hereinafter referred to as the "Moon Agreement"].

8. Treaty on Principles Governing the Activities of States in the Exploration and Use of Outer Space, Including the Moon and Other Celestial Bodies, *opened for signature* January 27, 1967, 18 U.S.T. 2410, T.I.A.S. No. 6347, 610 U.N.T.S. 205, *text reproduced in* UNITED NATIONS TREATIES AND PRINCIPLES ON OUTER SPACE 3 (2000) [hereinafter referred to as the "Outer Space Treaty"].

9. Convention on International Liability for Damage Caused by Space Objects, *opened for signature* March 29, 1972, 24 U.S.T. 2389, T.I.A.S. No. 7762, 961 U.N.T.S. 187, *text reproduced in* UNITED NATIONS TREATIES AND PRINCIPLES ON OUTER SPACE 13 (2000) [hereinafter referred to as the "Liability Convention"].

10. AAS Report, *supra* note 3, at 7.

11. ILA Report, *supra* note 4, at 13-14, 199.

12. Reif, *supra* note 2, at 5.

and continuing jurisdiction of non-governmental entities.[13]

Project 2001 noted that the enactment of national laws would impose certain regulatory burdens on the private sector in obtaining licenses to conduct activities in space, and that over-regulation should be avoided. It further was noted that especially within Europe, projects often are conducted on a multinational basis. It therefore was recommended that national laws should be harmonized with a "co-ordinated procedure" for the exercise of national laws regulating space activities,[14] which could extend to full reciprocity with a "one stop procedure" where a license granted by one state would be recognized by other states.[15]

Project 2001 also encouraged the "formulation of substantive international technical requirements and safety standards for space operations" to further streamline the regulatory licensing process.[16] It was noted that such international requirements and standards could be drafted under the auspices of the Scientific and Technical Subcommittee of UNCOPUOS, and could establish parameters for determining the existence of fault, where required, pursuant to the Liability Convention.[17]

The ILA Space Law Committee expressed its recommendation that states should "enact national legislation concerning authorization and continuing supervision of space activities carried out by non-governmental entities. . . ,"[18] but unlike Project 2001, the ILA did not call for harmonization of the regulatory regimes. The AAS adopted a different approach, and recognized that the Outer Space Treaty does not mandate any specific licensing regime, but rather lets states tailor their national systems consistent with the Treaty obligations.[19] The AAS recognized that a certain level of consistency between licensing regimes is desirable, and therefore endorsed as a best practice that "States should conclude, in appropriate circumstances, agreements concerning recognition and acceptance of the authorization granted for space activities by other launching States."[20]

The Outer Space Treaty does not obligate states parties to establish any specific licensing regime, but allows for each state to determine the level and extent of regulations.[21] The harmonization of regulatory regimes, beyond minimum standards and requirements, may be beneficial for regions, such as Europe, or other combinations of states which regularly have missions that transcend the borders of the members of the group. The

---

13. *Id.*

14. *Id.* at 6.

15. Makiol, *Project 2001: Final Results of the Working Group Launch and Associated Services*, in PROCEEDINGS OF THE 44TH COLLOQUIUM ON THE LAW OF OUTER SPACE 21, 23 (2002); *see also* Schmidt-Tedd, *Project 2001: Recommendations and Results Concerning the Process of Privatisation and Issues of Economic Law*, in PROCEEDINGS OF THE 44TH COLLOQUIUM ON THE LAW OF OUTER SPACE 14, 15 (2002).

16. Reif, *supra* note 2, at 8.

17. *Id.*

18. ILA Report, *supra* note 4, at 196.

19. AAS Report, *supra* note 3, at 6.

20. *Id.* at 14.

21. *See generally* F.G. VON DER DUNK, PRIVATE ENTERPRISE AND PUBLIC INTEREST IN THE EUROPEAN SPACESCAPE (1998).

implementation of such uniformity is a matter to be determined by the states involved on a case by case basis.

The creation of a uniform licensing regime on a global scale might avoid the potential problem of flags of convenience, but also would fail to take into account security or other specific concerns of states. In addition, the concern over flags of convenience may be overstated, as at present, all private launch service providers have a genuine link with one or more major space active countries, each of which could be expected to assert the right, and be held to the obligation, to license any launch activities. Moreover, the regulation of licenses ultimately is intertwined with the issue of international liability of states for damages caused by their non-governmental entities. As noted by the AAS, "primary state liability promotes responsible state legal regimes."[22] Therefore, states can be expected to be reluctant to agree to detailed harmonized standards in the first instance, or to continue to maintain such standards as part of the domestic licensing regime where it may conflict with a perceived national need. Nevertheless, there is widespread agreement that states should be encouraged to ratify the Outer Space Treaty, and to adopt an appropriate licensing regime in accordance with article VI.[23]

The development of uniform international technical requirements and safety standards would provide numerous benefits, both in terms of easing regulatory burdens and in facilitating a finding of fault for liability purposes, as noted by Project 2001. Additional benefits from such uniformity include the enhancement of safety in activities, as well as the promotion of more efficient and cost-effective techniques and procedures in designing and operating space missions. Nevertheless, these international standards and requirements should establish only minimum baseline requirements, and should not dictate commercial decisions which do not have a public policy component. That is, the potential exists for the establishment of preferences by means of regulations which extend beyond policy concerns and infringe on the exercise of free market forces. Such infringement can only be exasperated by the institutionalization of a harmonized regulatory regime. Moreover, whether imposed by one state or by a number of states by parallel regimes, the over-regulation of the private sector will have a debilitating effect on space commerce.[24]

The ILA Space Law Committee took the position that the Outer Space Treaty, while flexible in its provisions, should be updated as it was not drafted with commercial implications of space activities in mind. However, in view of the general perspective that the treaties should be supplemented but not formally amended, the Committee approved a Proposed Protocol to the Outer Space Treaty as set forth in **Figure 1**.[25]

The AAS noted that the "international regime recognizes the legitimacy of both governmental and non-governmental activities in space. . . ," but expressed doubt as to whether the right to conduct commercial activities was recognized.[26] The additions proposed to article 1, paragraph 3, by the ILA Space Law Committee, make it clear that the Outer Space Treaty is applicable to

22. AAS Report, *supra* note 3, at 7.

23. *See* Reif, *supra* note 2, at 5; Makiol, *supra* note 15, at 23; AAS Report, *supra* note 3, at 9; ILA Report, *supra* note 4, at 196.

24. *See* Schmidt-Tedd, *supra* note 15, at 15; Reif, *supra* note 2, at 8.

25. ILA Report, *supra* note 4, at 195-96

26. AAS Report, *supra* note 3, at 19.

commercial uses of space. The proposed revisions to paragraph 2 of article 1, are substantially similar to paragraph 1 of the *Declaration on International Cooperation in the Exploration and Use of Outer Space for the Benefit and in the Interest of all States, Taking into Particular Account the Needs of the Developing Countries*,[27] with the addition of the reference to "commercial" uses of outer space. The reference to commercial uses in paragraph 1 of the proposal implies that in its absence, commercial uses are not subject to the Outer Space Treaty. However, except for purely scientific ventures, it is difficult to envision the conduct of a space activity by a non-governmental entity which would not have some commercial component. Furthermore, ever since Telstar in the early 1960's, the practice of states has been to recognize, permit, authorize and supervise commercial uses of outer space.

The proposed ILA Space Law Committee addition to article VI urges states to adopt a national regime for authorization and continuing supervision of their private entities, as discussed above. The proposed addition to article VIII, however, appears merely to reiterate the obligations of states to register nationally and internationally objects launched into outer space as required by the Registration Convention.[28] The ILA Special Rapporteur discussed that the Registration Convention could be improved by requiring more detailed information, and the uniformity of national registries,[29] but neither of these matters are addressed by the proposed addition. Furthermore, it would appear that any protocol or supplemental instrument on this issue should be addressed also to the Registration Convention so as to prevent the possibility of overlapping but inconsistent obligations.[30] Of course, states should be encouraged to ratify both treaties.

The final ILA Space Law Committee proposed addition to the Outer Space Treaty similarly may be somewhat misplaced, as it encourages states to adopt binding dispute settlement mechanisms. Although this proposal may be specifically directed toward commercial uses of space, it is nevertheless a proper subject for consideration *vis-a-vis* the Liability Convention. Clearly, states have primary international liability pursuant to the Liability Convention, whether incurred as a result of the activities of governmental or non-governmental entities. In addition, states can and do adopt procedures to limit the risk of loss by regulatory requirements, such as cross-waivers of liability, or the mandating of insurance coverage. States could require licensees to accept binding dispute settlement procedures, including the Claims Commission or other means conducted pursuant to the Liability Convention. The difficulty with this approach, however, is that states have not yet themselves agreed that the mechanisms set forth in the Liability Convention shall be binding, which was noted by both Project 2001 and the ILA Space Law Committee as a

---

27. *Declaration on International Cooperation in the Exploration and Use of Outer Space for the Benefit and in the Interest of all States, Taking into Particular Account the Needs of the Developing Countries*, December 13, 1996, UNITED NATIONS TREATIES AND PRINCIPLES ON OUTER SPACE 56 (2000).

28. Convention on Registration of Objects Launched into Outer Space, *opened for signature* January 14, 1975, 28 U.S.T. 695, T.I.A.S. No. 8480, 1023 U.N.T.S. 15, *text reproduced in* UNITED NATIONS TREATIES AND PRINCIPLES ON OUTER SPACE 22 (2000) [hereinafter referred to as the "Registration Convention"].

29. ILA Report, *supra* note 4, at 200; *see also* AAS Report, *supra* note 3, at 8.

30. ILA Report, *supra* note 4, at 198.

major issue inhibiting commercial uses of space.[31]

COMMERCIALIZATION AND THE MOON AGREEMENT

By far the most controversial subject concerns the status of commercial uses of the Moon. Project 2001 observed that a cooperative discussion of the actual ways and means of exploitation, together with the actual benefits, may be of assistance. Accordingly, it was recommended that the parties to the Outer Space Treaty open negotiations to consider "the fact that such exploitation might be undertaken by private parties."[32] The ILA Space Law Committee Special Rapporteur, on the other hand, took the position that the Moon Agreement should either be "improved" or "discarded."[33] Accordingly, in an effort to improve the instrument, a series of amendments was proposed by the Special Rapporteur, as set forth in **Figure 2**.[34] This was a departure from the perspective that the space treaties should be supplemented rather than amended, but the Moon Agreement has received very limited acceptance since it was opened for signature in 1979.

The amendments proposed by the Special Rapporteur delete the reference to "natural resources in place" in article 11.3, and expressly declare that there is no moratorium on the commercial use of lunar resources by private entities, thus ending any uncertainty which otherwise may exist. In addition, the proposed amendments provide what are stated to be "more realistic rules" regarding the international regime of paragraph 11.5 The Special Rapporteur also recommended the deletion of paragraph 18 relating to the ten year review of the treaty, and the renumbering the subsequent provisions.

The proposed amendments are drafted from the perspective of promoting the commercial exploitation of the Moon, and are designed to blunt the major obstacles which have prevented widespread acceptance of the Moon Agreement. One of the most substantial obstacles has been the uncertainty surrounding the reference to the concept of the "common heritage of mankind." The proposed amendments delete the phrase and replace it with the "province of all mankind." This modification employs terminology which is consistent with and included in the Outer Space Treaty,[35] and presumably would not invite the same opposition that accompanied the common heritage of mankind. This proposed change, predictably, sparked considerable controversy, and a divergence of views emerged during the Space Law Committee discussions. Various alternatives to the terminology were suggested, including the "common concern of all mankind," "common concern of all lives," "common interests," and "for the universal benefit of all mankind."[36] A consensus of opinion failed to materialize, and a compromise resolution was adopted as follows:

4. Regarding the 1979 Moon Agreement:

---

31. *See* Reif, *supra* note 2, at 9; ILA Report, *supra* note 4, at 199.

32. Reif, *supra* note 2, at 8.

33. ILA Report, *supra* note 4, at 201.

34. *Id.* at 203-04 (bracketed material supplied by the Space Law Committee General Rapporteur).

35. *Id.* at 202, 226.

36. *Id.* at 224-27.

> **Considering further** that the common heritage of mankind concept has developed today as also allowing the commercial uses of outer space for the benefit of mankind, and that certain adjustments are suggested to article XI of this Agreement concerning the international régime to be set up for the exploitation of moon resources, which will make it more realistic in today's international scenario, ..."[37]

The amendments proposed by the ILA Space Law Committee Special Rapporteur are an ambitious attempt to resurrect the Moon Agreement. Many of the proposed revisions clearly are advantageous for the commercial exploitation of the Moon, but some of the revisions may encounter difficulties in obtaining the hoped-for widespread acceptance. For example, the proposed amendments introduce new terms which are of uncertain meaning. Included in this category are the concepts of commercial use causing "serious harm" or "substantial risk" to future exploitation and use. In the context of competing commercial ventures, serious harm and substantial risk can be fluid and expansive concepts.

The Moon Agreement is not the only international instrument to incorporate the concept of the common heritage of mankind, as the phrase is expressly set forth in the Law of the Sea Convention.[38] Just like the Moon Agreement, the LOS Convention initially was met with considerable opposition, and received only limited acceptance by the industrialized world. In an attempt to reinvigorate the LOS Convention, significant amendments were approved in 1994,[39] which introduced market forces into the regulation of ocean resources. As a result, both the industrialized and the developing nations reconsidered the objections to the LOS, and accepted the revised regime to govern the exploitation of deep seabed resources.[40] Thus, the inclusion of the principle of the concept of common heritage of mankind has been proven to not be fatal to the acceptance of an international instrument.

The governing authority under the 1994 Agreement is to be composed of representatives of the major consumers of minerals, the largest investors in deep seabed mining, the major land-based producers of minerals, the developing countries, and an overall equitable geographic distribution of states. This will help to ensure both broad based

---

37. *Id.* at 14 (quoting from resolution adopted by the ILA approving the Report of the Space Law Committee).

38. Convention on the Law of the Sea, part XI, art. 136, *opened for signature* December 10, 1982, U.N. Doc. A/CONF.62/122 (1982), *reprinted in* UNITED NATIONS, OFFICIAL TEXT OF THE UNITED NATIONS CONVENTION ON THE LAW OF THE SEA WITH ANNEXES AND INDEX, U.N. Sales No. E.83.V.5 (1983)[hereinafter referred to as the "LOS Convention"].

39. G.A. Res. 48/263 (July 28, 1994)[hereinafter referred to as the "1994 Agreement"].

40. *See generally*, Dept. of State, Council on Ocean Law, U.S. Commentary on the LOS Convention Including the 1994 Amendments, http://lcweb2.loc.gov/law/GLINV1/GLIN.html; Browne, *Congressional Research Service Issue Brief for Congress*, (June 6, 1997), *text available through* Committee for National Institute for the Environment, www.cnie.org/nle/leg-9.html.

representation, as well as to provide the industrialized nations with influence which is commensurate with their interests. Significantly, the 1994 LOS amendments provided for a small bureaucratic structure, and removed any requirement for mandatory transfer of technology in the development of ocean resources.

The Special Rapporteur's proposed amendments to the Moon Agreement articulate minimum attributes of the international regime that states parties undertake to establish pursuant to article 11. The first two attributes concern the establishment of national licensing procedures, and the creation of guidelines for such licensing. The next two attributes relate to the establishment of monitoring and registration procedures for licensed activities. However, the proposal also calls for the imposition of "reasonable registration fees," the definition of which is left for future determination.

The Special Rapporteur's proposed amendment requiring the creation of a procedure for both States Parties or their non-governmental entities to have "reasonable means to ascertain that their rights and interests are duly respected" is potentially expansive. In this regard, reference should be made to articles 2 and 15.1 of the Moon Agreement. Article 2 provides that activities on the Moon shall be conducted in accordance with international law, while article 15.1 stipulates that States Parties have a right of visitation to facilities, stations, and installations on the Moon to assure themselves "that the activities of other States Parties in the exploration and use of the Moon are compatible with the provisions of this Agreement."

The 1994 Agreement serves the common heritage of mankind principle by providing for equality of opportunity rather than the forced sharing of revenues or other form of tribute or taxation.[41] The emphasis on equality of opportunity is consistent with the view "that the common heritage principle fully comports with private economic activity in accordance with market principles."[42] The proposed ILA Space Law Committee amendments, however, do not appear to provide the same emphasis on market forces, and therefore may continue to encounter significant resistance, even if the phrase "common heritage of mankind" was to be deleted from the Moon Agreement.

CONCLUSION

The emergence of the commercial space age has engendered attention and discussion with respect to the adequacy *vel non* of the *corpus juris spatialis*. The recent studies of Project 2001, the AAS, and the ILA, have recognized that the outer space treaties were drafted to allow substantial flexibility. These studies differ, however, in their conclusions as to whether amendments or supplements to one or more of the treaties are desirable. Treaty amendments may present problems of conflicts between pre- and post- amendment regimes, as well as differences in ratifications. Thus, it must be determined whether the result is worth the

---

41. *See* Sterns and Tennen, *Institutional Approaches to Managing Space Resources*, in PROCEEDINGS OF THE 41ST COLLOQUIUM ON THE LAW OF OUTER SPACE 33 (1999).

42. U.S. Senate, 103rd Cong., 2nd Sess., UNITED NATIONS CONVENTION ON THE LAW OF THE SEA, WITH ANNEXES, AND THE AGREEMENT RELATING TO THE IMPLEMENTATION OF PART XI OF THE UNITED NATIONS CONVENTION ON THE LAW OF THE SEA, WITH ANNEX, Treaty Document 103-39, at 61 (1994).

effort, or whether the desired results can be achieved by a different means.[43]

Issues which will require continued study and debate relate to definitions of key treaty terminology; the adoption and possible harmonization or reciprocity arrangements of national licensing regimes; and the implications of the concept of the common heritage of mankind. In addition, issues concerning debris, the lack of binding international dispute resolution procedures, and the form of regulation to be imposed for the commercial use of lunar and other extraterrestrial resources, will impact on the pace of commercialization of space. The AAS recently announced plans for a follow-up workshop, and the ILA and Project 2001 continue to critically examine space law. Such proceedings, together with those of other organizations, including the IISL, and UNIDROIT, will continue to refine the rights and obligations of the private sector in space.

---

43. *See* ILA Report, *supra* note 4, at 198.

CONSIDERING the merits of the Outer Space Treaty in providing guidance for space activities since 1967,

NOTING the growth in recent years, of the commercial uses of outer space by states, international organizations and private enterprises,

NOTING FURTHER the change within the international economic order since the adoption of the WTO Agreement, and the GATS and TRIPS Agreements, as well as the entry into force of the Law of the Sea Convention and the 1994 Agreement on the Implementation of Part XI of that Convention,

HAVING IN MIND the 1996 UNGA Declaration on International Cooperation in the Exploration and Use of Outer Space for the Benefit and in the Interest of all States, Taking into Particular Account the Needs of the Developing Countries,

The Contracting Parties have adopted the following ***Protocol on Commercial Space Activities*** to give more precise meaning to the principle embodied in Articles I.3, VI and VII [sic] of the 1967 Outer Space Treaty.

Article 1 (Addition to Article I, para. 3 OST)

1. States Parties hereby agree that the use of outer space and celestial bodies is inclusive of all commercial uses.
2. States Parties are free to define the way in which they shall implement the principle of international cooperation. All commercial uses of outer space and celestial bodies shall be carried out for the benefit and in the interests of all states, irrespective of their degree of economic or scientific development and shall be the province of all mankind. Particular account shall be taken of the needs of developing countries.

Article 2 (Addition to Article VI OST)

States Parties undertake to enact national legislation concerning authorization and continuing supervision of space activities carried out by non-governmental entities.

Article 3 (Addition to Article VIII OST)

States Parties are under the obligation to register any object launched into outer space both on their national registries and on the international register maintained by the Secretary -General of the United Nations in accordance with the Convention on the Registration of Objects Launched into Outer Space.

Article 4 (New rules concerning the peaceful settlement of disputes)

States Parties undertake to adopt an international legal instrument on the peaceful settlement of disputes which should include provisions for binding mechanisms. In this sense, the 1998 ILA Convention on the Settlement of Disputes related to Space Activities is referred to as a model.

Figure 1

1. Amendment of Article 4.1

The exploration and use of the moon, *including commercial exploitation and use*, shall be the province of all mankind and shall be carried out for the benefit and interest of all countries, irrespective of their degree of economic or scientific development. *Commercial exploitation and use are, however, only allowable [permissible] in conformity with the provisions of Article 11.* Due regard shall be paid to the interests of present and future generations as well as the need to promote higher standards of living and conditions of economic and social progress and development in accordance with the Charter of the United Nations.

2. Amendments of Article 11.1

The moon and its natural resources are the *province of mankind [the common concern of all mankind]*, which finds its expression in the provision of this Agreement and in particular paragraph 5 of this Article.

3. Amendments to Article 11.2

The moon is not subject to national appropriation by any claim of sovereignty, by means of use or occupation, or by any other means. *This shall not preclude any commercial exploitation or use so long as in conformity with the provisions of this article, other articles of this Agreement or any legal régime regarding commercial exploitation and use to be established on the basis of this Agreement.*

4. Amendment to Article 11.3

Neither the surface nor the subsurface of the moon, nor any part thereof shall become the property of any State, international intergovernmental or non-governmental organisation, national organisation or non-governmental entity or of any natural person. The placement of personnel, space vehicles, equipment, facilities, stations and installations on or below the surface of the moon, including structures connected with its surface or subsurface, shall not create a right of ownership over the surface or subsurface of the moon or any areas thereof. The foregoing provisions are without prejudice to the international régime referred to in paragraph 5 of this Article.

5. Amendment to Article 11.5

States Parties to this Agreement hereby undertake to establish an international régime, including appropriate procedures, to govern the exploitation of the natural resources of the moon, *including commercial exploitation by non-governmental entities. Such international régime should include, as minimum*

– the duty of establishing a licensing obligation by means of national law [legislation] for every State Party whose non-governmental entities are interested in undertaking relevant activities;
– guidelines for the licensing requirements to be imposed;
– the duty of establishing a transparent, fair, and comprehensive monitoring system in respect of activities thus licensed;
– a procedure for international registration of activities on the moon licensed in accordance with this régime, including payment of a reasonable registration fee to the international authority charged with such registration; and
– a procedure for providing other States Parties involved, or their non-governmental entities involved, with reasonable means to ascertain that their rights and interests are duly respected.

In the absence of such a régime, commercial exploitation and use of the moon will be permitted on condition that no commercial exploitation or use of the moon should cause serious harm to the interests of other States Parties, including their economic interests, no substantial risk should affect future exploitation and use, and the moon's environment should not be put substantially at risk. *Likewise, such commercial exploitation and use will continue to be subject to the provisions of this Agreement, including the general principles of paragraph 7.*

6. Amendment to Article 11.7

The main purposes of the international régime to be established shall include:
(a) The orderly and safe development of the natural resources of the moon;
(b) The rational management of those resources;
(c) The expansion of opportunities in the use of those resources.
(d) *this provision is suppressed in Dr. von der Dunk's proposal* (emphasis supplied).

Figure 2

IAC-03-IISL.2.08

SNAPSHOT: THE PROCESS OF CHANGE IN INTERNATIONAL SPACE LAW POLITICS

E. E. Weeks, J.D.
Northern Arizona University
Political Science Department
Social and Behavioral Sciences, Box 15036
Flagstaff, Arizona 86001, USA
eew@dana.ucc.nau.edu

ABSTRACT

Space law is well developed in many areas. However, one area has generally been ignored by the established international space law community. This specific issue is: to what extent does international space law prohibit or permit private for-profit (commercial) space tourism. Specifically, does international space law, as is, prohibit for-profit space joyrides, short stays in orbital hotels, longer stays in orbital or celestial hotels, and/or for-profit outer space settlements. These appear to be the proposed stages of outer space tourism. Space tourism advocates are proposing to "take off", and initiate an industry within a few years. The proffered purpose of international law, in general, and international space law in particular, is to establish rules and norms around which actor expectations can converge. Yet, the very mention of this specific legal issue tends to border along the rim of unspeakable taboo, within the international space lawmaking machinery. This specific issue must be addressed today, between the various camps of space lawyers, to stave off future conflicts.

1. INTRODUCING: INTERNATIONAL SPACE LAW ON TOURISM

To understand where the law stands on the specific issue of outer space tourism, we must first distinguish it from related issues. Then it becomes easy to see that there is no current rule of international law regarding outer space tourism. Instead, there is a lot of legal discourse and interpretation on various related points of international space law. Space law is a very intense and difficult subject to grasp. There are many diverse, interrelated complex subject areas. In addition, issues concerning commercial outer space tourism, or commercial outer space settlement, arise in the space law literature as integral parts of other legal issues. It is very common to see an article, book or presentation start out with the subject of space tourism, and end by linking a main argument to being resolved through general debates on private property rights, space commercialization, or something else. This is problematic, since there are many areas falling within the broad umbrella of space commercialization, privatization and private property rights. For example, satellite industries, space transportation systems, launch services, remote sensing, space stations, solar energy and exploitation of resources and space minerals. To a great extent, these industries have prompted specific lawmaking activities from within the international space law community[1]. This has not happened with commercial space tourism or space settlement. Instead there is a body of discourse attempting to prove space tourism as a practical industry, along side a body of discourse arguing that international space law must be changed to encourage investment in these new industries. In unproved fields of outer space development, international space law is still vague. As such it is subject to varying interpretations, since no authoritative interpretation has been mandated by the

UNCOPUOS[2]. Regarding these proposed industries, there are no specific bodies of law. There are only piles of discourse. Yet, language tends to reflect political and legal situations and can indicate impending change. It also has the power to trigger change, or to maintain the status quo. This capacity to exercise power by the use of language depends on the actors, and on timing. We must view "action" as shaped by international structural eras. The current structural era might best be described as the Post Cold War era wherein the logic of capitalism is far less challenged. This structure shapes regimes, norms, and international lawmaking activity.

1.1 Is Tourism: An Emerging Regime?

Space tourism seems to have begun. It's hard to tell this by looking at the discourse on international space law. Although numerous scholars make note of the various gaps between international space law and commercial realities[3], the specific legal issue of to what extent does international space law prohibit or permit private commercial (for-profit) space tourism, has not been formally addressed by the mainstream international space law community[4]. In spite of this, the topic pops up more and more[5], and many are seriously determined to make space tourism a viable industry[6]. The space tourism advocates are proposing to "take off", and initiate an industry within a few years. Yet, the very mention of this specific legal issue tends to border along the rim of unspeakable taboo, within the international space lawmaking machinery. This specific issue must be addressed today to stave off future conflicts. Specifically, does international space law, as is, prohibit Phase I, Phase II and/or Phase III of space tourism. Travel in space used to be only for government astronauts. Some believe that stage one of space tourism has already started since others are beginning to go and to think about going into space - just to see it. Ideology has been deployed, creating new public perceptions of space access as now open to everyone. On the ground theme parks, space camps, and zero gravity flights already exist and are popular[7]. A space launch infrastructure and facilities exist and is constantly developing. The International Space Station has been a success. It has demonstrated that humans can live and work in a human space settlement. Spaces vehicles are in the process are being improved dramatically. Notwithstanding these accomplishments, many technological kinks will have to be worked before we can solely blame the law - or lack thereof - for inhibiting commercial space tourism. Still shouldn't the law precede any technological kickoff?[8]

2. INTERNATIONAL LAW'S PURPOSE

The above situation stands in direct contradiction to established perspectives on the very nature and purpose of international law[9]. Yet, a pattern has been established wherein international space law seems to be created after space industries take a foothold - not before. International space law, like international law, according to traditional theories, is supposed to create norms and rules so that international actors understand and comply with expectations and agreements. Herein, this is not the case. We see international space law playing catch-up to political moods. The result has been perpetual vagueness. The purpose of international space law, as Manfred Lachs informs, was to be classified as international law, "known to all of us as the system of law that has for centuries been regulating relations among States".[10] In addition, Lachs states "the law of outer space can and should, make a notable contribution: by becoming a staunch guide to man in his journey through time and space; by securing that the great achievements of science and technology serve the cause of international peace and security, the interest of men and nations". Similarly, Levi[11] explains the importance of predictability in the behavior of society's members.

3. PRIVATE PROPERTY RIGHTS

Within the international space law discourse, there is an issue that keeps creeping up - the issue of private property rights in outer space. There is an ongoing debate over whether international space law permits or prohibits private property or ownership rights to outer space resources[12]. Often quoted is Article II of the Outer space Treaty[13] which states: "outer space, including the Moon and other celestial bodies, is not subject to national appropriation [emphasis added] by claim of sovereignty, by means of use or occupation, or by any other means." Many space law interpreters will cite Article II in support of the argument that international space law permits private property rights because it does not explicitly prohibit them[14]. This argument is often intermingled with the contradictory argument that since the Outer Space Treaty does not explicitly mention private appropriation, there is legal uncertainty. This uncertainty is said to create disincentives to private commercial sector investment in space endeavors[15].

In taking this position, some argue that previous drafts distinguished between national and private appropriation and prohibited both, and that the final draft only contains explicit prohibition against national appropriation. Therefore, they assume that a decision must have been made to permit private appropriation[16]. This assumption overlooks the way in which politics can result in purposeful decisions not to decide on issues involving an ideological or philosophical impasse.

Other space law interpreters will argue that "appropriation" of outer space resources, by any entity or individual, strictly is prohibited[17]. They argue that the term "national appropriation" includes all forms of appropriation whether national, private or otherwise. Some taking this position, include the very concept of private property rights as "appropriation". However, this seems to depend on the current status of the activity or industry, in the public mind.

This issue of whether or not private property rights are permitted is a source of hot debate. So what! Debate is one thing, hard black letter law is quite another. And, there is no clear legal rule of law with respect to this particular issue. Addedly, there is further lack of consensus on how space law interpreters are to interpret various issues related to the extent to which private property rights are (or are not) permitted in accordance with international space law.

Stepping away from this tree and taking a birds' eye view of the forest, we can see that the field of policy studies offers tremendous insights. By viewing this legal situation through a policy studies lens, and borrowing concepts from this field of study, we can see that "discourse coalitions" and "rhetorical troupes"[18] are in place and at work selecting and using specific language linked to larger more established narratives. Space law authors, in criticizing and defending various perspectives, are writing for a purpose. This purpose is to persuade readers to subscribe to particular worldviews or discourse coalitions, where possible. For example, Fischer and Forester (1993: 1) argue that it is more realistic to see exercises in policy analysis and planning as actors engaged in "representing reality and being necessarily selective. As such they are tied to relationships of power, agenda setting, inclusion and exclusion, selective attention, and neglect". This framework enables us to understand the process described in this paper. The space law literature reflects a tendency to make arguments rely on metaphor, metonymy and irony in staking out certain sides of these ideological debates. This involves the process of argument, framing problems, constructing problems and constructing values. This literature contains footprints of the process of ignoring, oversimplifying, criticizing and pointing blame. Space law interpreters commonly use metaphor, metonymy and irony in attempting to make their points seem like the correct interpretation of international space law. As such, the process as described amounts to political exercises of power through discursive practices in an attempt to achieve partisan results[19]. If the space law community would view the activities resulting in the space law literature under this lens, perhaps we could get to a meaningful discussion on this issue.

3.1 The Common Heritage of Mankind[20]

The CHM principle is treated as an integral part of the private property rights debate. Although there is support for the Common Heritage of Mankind (hereinafter referred to as CHM) principle[21], there is a chorus of argument complaining that international space law inhibits commercial development of outer space[22]. Some space law interpreters argue that space law's flaw is its uncertainty on the issue of private property rights[23]. Within this discourse, some are placing blame the on the Outer Space Treaty[24]. Others are blaming the CHM principle[25]. Still others point the blame, for the CHM principle, on "developing countries"[26]. No matter the reason, this chorus chants the general complaint that defects in international space law create investor uncertainty, and therefore inhibits or prevents commercial space development.

This argument does not make sense for several reasons. First, the Outer Space Treaty (the backbone of international space law) (international politics is the brain of international space law) does not contain the CHM language. Instead it uses the term *Province of Mankind*, which, is open to varying interpretations. It is vague. Second, The Moon Treaty is not generally considered accepted international law, therefore, how can it be responsible for inhibiting commercial space development. While the Outer Space Treaty does not contain the CHM, The Moon Treaty does. Specifically, The Moon Treaty has only been signed and ratified by a handful of nations[27]. This lack of international acceptance was primarily due to the CHM concept. The Moon Treaty also contains specific language about what nations could not do. There is a steady stream of discourse launching an ideological attack on the CHM principle[28]. Many view The Moon Treaty as meaningless due to the general lack of international acceptance. In spite of this there is still much debate within the literature. The constant addressing of The Moon Treaty within the space law literature seems to contradict the perspective that The Moon Treaty is null and void. Thirdly, commercial development of outer space is not inhibited by international space law. There are many thriving commercial space industries operating within the confined of international and domestic space law. Many of the complaints against the CHM principle are fueled by an underbelly narrative implying that the issue is one of developing countries who are against private property, versus developed countries who of for private property[29]. This assumption is inaccurate. In reality, this is not a good description of the discourse conflict. For example, the US, as a state actor (as I understand it) has taken the policy position that the Outer Space Treaty should remain untouched. Then again, the CHM principle is not contained in the Outer Space Treaty. Still, the point is that not all developed countries feel that international space law is defective. In addition, various space law interpreters within the developed countries also take the positions ascribed to developing countries, and vice versa. Also a number of countries labeled as developing are participating in commercial outer space activities.

3.2 Space Tourism: An Issue Distinct from the General Issue of Commercialization

Many of the established space law authors will not address the topic of space tourism. Many have addressed the general issue of private property rights. Within this particular discourse, there is the tendency to treat private property rights as being synonymous with space commercialization. In order to highlight the issue of international space law, as it relates to for-profit space tourism or for-profit space settlement, it has to be examined as a specific legal issue - isolated from the issues of space commercialization and private property rights. Space commercialization has become generally accepted by the international community. There are several space industries which have officially gone through the process of becoming commercialized and privatized,[30] with the support and backing of the international law-making machinery. Strategic, targeted, specific agenda-setting activities occurred in order for these shifts to occur. Again, examples include communications satellites, direct television broadcasting industries, and remote sensing space transportation and private launch services[31]. Over time, more nations and more private companies became key players in the market. After 1980, there was an increase in domestic regulations governing space activities. The U.S. was the leader in this trend wherein domestic laws began to guide space ventures. Other nations have begun to do the same. Today, for example, the U.S. commercial space transportation industry is composed of a variety of private entities such as major aerospace firms and a multitude of other viable business entities and entrepreneurs engaged in space related businesses[32].

In order to understand the politics of international law, we must acknowledge that both processes and structures are at work, shaping interpretations and outcomes. For instance, the Post Cold War distribution of power seems to be shaping state behavior, and institutional response in many international treaty conventions. In international space law, we see a shift, after 1980, away from the international law-making arena to the reliance on domestic laws. What I see as the first era, was one where visionaries and dreamers wrote about what may happen one day if outer space was ever developed[33]. What I see as the second era, from 1957 to 1979, might be characterized as one wherein two superpowers dominated the shaping of international space law[34]. The process of creating international space law during this era involved the satisfying of two main state actors - the United States and the former Soviet Union. Space law actors during this era seemed to act out of sheer fear[35]. During this period, the United Nations was invited to act as the middleman between the two superpowers articulation of fears and aspirations, and the Committee of Peaceful Uses of Outer Space was established. In addition, other states were involved in providing input and suggestions regarding wording contained it what eventually became The Outer Space Treaty of 1967. This was the most fruitful period of international space law making. It was during this period that the five space treaties were negotiated and drafted. The United States and Soviet Union signed and ratified the first four.

The turning point for the third era came in 1979-1980. In 1979 the Moon

Treaty[36] was stillborn into the next new era of space law. The dominant international mood went from one of international cooperation (prompted by fears of what the superpowers might do) to a new mood of international apathy and lack of trust in international institutions by the dominant military and political superpowers. The new mood swing was the notion of self-reliance and a shift to domestic lawmaking abilities. This mood was intertwined with a global shift towards the spread of free market economics. Within the space arena, there was the development of the Space Shuttle, a massive shift from national space programs to commercial space development, and wider access to space by an ever-increasing number of other nations and private entities. Space development became more a matter of capitalist economics rather than the prior focus on accomplishments of science, military power and national prestige. Bills, laws and policies began to encourage commercial space development. We also sec during this era, unprecedented amounts of international cooperation even among former political adversaries in commercial space development projects. Commercial space endeavors were becoming big business.

The fourth era of space law began around the end of 1991, during a period that some refer to as the "fall of communism". I view this era as a part of a continuum related to eras described above as 1-3. During this Post Cold War era we see an escalation of the logic of capitalist economics becoming more of an influential factor in the re-shaping of international law. It is challenged less today than ever before. Within the context of this era, we can see a mounting of space law discourse arguing: international space law should be changed since it does not clearly establish private property rights in outer space. Those arguing this line of discourse tend to reason that international space law inhibits private investment and certainty, and therefore inhibits commercial outer space development.

The widespread acceptance of space commercialization does not apply to all imagined uses of space. Whether or not a specific space industry is viewed as acceptable by a critical mass is determined by, and in turn determines, whether or not it will benefit from a favorable interpretation of international space law. Even better, if a critical number of members of the space lawmaking machinery decide to make the determination that a specific industry has a mental green light, this tends to prompt specific international laws - tailored to suit the promotion of that industry. However, in order for an industry to warrant this type of treatment, it has to prove itself. It has to be seen as providing valuable material benefits to a significant number of relevant populations. In the current international structure there seems to be a pervasive acceptance of an ideology backed by the logic of capitalist economics. This seems to be the growing global norm. If an industry can be perceived as capable of providing the material bottom line (material sustenance, employment, income, valued goods and/or services, lucrative investments and so on), then it stands a chance of being placed on the international space law-making agenda. Policymakers understand that they are eventually accountable to various publics and that these people are primarily concerned with food, a home, paying bills, day-to-day necessities, comfort, education, medicine, entertainment, transportation and other aspects of maintaining themselves and their families. The Internet, cell phones and cable television have become key goods and services that many people value. The industries involved in providing these goods and services, also provide a multitude of jobs and have become a very real source of income for many people. In other words, they have proven themselves. Commercial Space tourism and Commercial space settlement have not. And, there are still enormous risk factors and a lack of technology involved with these industries. Perhaps, these are the real reasons that international space law, as it applies to these industries, is still covered with a cloak of vagueness and confusion.

4. INTERNATIONAL STRUCTURE

Many theorists have indicated that international law is shaped by and shapes international politics[37]. International space law certainly fits this description and has since its inception[38]. It was molded by the international political structure in place at the time of Sputnik's debut. Actual concrete lawmaking for space didn't manifest until after Russia had proven the technological hurdle of satellite circumnavigation. Analyzing the activity in the development and codification of international space law within the United Nations from 1957 to 1969, Hager[39] argues that the only way to understand the development of space law is to understand it as a function of international politics. The basic foundation of international space law exists in the five (arguably four)[40] international space treaties. The main one being The Outer Space Treaty of 1967 ("The Constitution"). These treaties were purposefully left vague, especially the Outer Space Treaty. Commercial development issues were thought best left up to each nation's ability to draft their own domestic laws governing such activity. So, here we are today. In the midst of space tourism without a clear understanding of what the rules, norms and laws are. The space law literature is full of conflicting interpretations and arguments. Other than established, proven space industries, there's no international consensus and no specific international legislation, on to what extent for-profit, commercial ventures are allowed. This makes sense in light of the vagueness of the core guiding principles of general international space law. Considering international treaties, declarations, resolutions and customary international law, it is generally understood that there are two ruling principles: "non-appropriation" and "freedom of use". Space law does specify whether non-appropriation is to be given more deference than freedom of use or vice versa. To complicate things further, both principles are to be interpreted under the umbrella of being for the "benefit all mankind"[41]. None of these three controlling principles are defined. Even worse, there are varying interpretations among the space law experts on how they should, be defined. Contrary to current criticism, this vagueness was not due to poor draftsmanship or lack of foresight into future space activities. Rather, vagueness was brilliantly and artistically built in, for acquiescence. In other words, it was the result of political compromise[42] influenced by the belief that the specifics of future commercial interests was thought to be best left to a future date when it would be more relevant so as not to risk the pressing concern of that time – preventing colonization of outer space and military installations on the Moon by the superpowers. The international community's primary focus, at that time was to get the US and Russia to sign, at the expense of vagueness.

Some space law interpreters when asked the question: "Does international space law allow private property rights?", might answer: "Yes. It certainly does". They may even point to examples of established industries wherein such rights have been routinely granted. For example, they may explain how the telecommunications, satellite or commercial launch industries provide private property rights. However, if you were to ask this same space law expert whether this legal interpretation extends over into the field of space tourism or commercial space settlement, they may answer sharply "no". Most will not extend this interpretation over into the realm of space tourism. This glitch in the law is problematic. While many space lawyers view the concept of space tourism as nonsense, hogwash, or worse, there are many serious space tourism actors gearing up and taking steps toward the formation of a new industry. To reiterate, space law actors who might answer in the affirmative to the general question of whether private property rights are permitted at all, may completely change their opinion after the point of reference is clarified to pertain to private for-profit space tourism or private for-profit space settlement.

CONCLUSION

Space entrepreneurs are thinking one way, depending on their link to particular industries, and space lawyers are thinking another way, depending on their link to the United Nations COPUOS, academia, industry, business and/or government. Academics are thinking, writing and speaking in other ways - legitimate professional interpretations of what is permitted or prohibited is subject to these varying interpretations. Socialization mechanisms and processes within various national boundaries produce differing views on what is equitable or sensible on how space law should be applied to commercial outer space activities and adventures. The problem addressed herein is something that the space law community knows about. Numerous scholars have commented on the way international space law and policy tend to lag behind "serious questions"[43], since the beginning. Taking a snapshot of international space law shows that the state of flux is really just a step in the *de lege ferenda* process. The time has come to take the next step - bridging the gap between the different epistemic communities of space lawyers. The various camps of space lawyers must begin systematically conferring with each, other instead of past each other. This is especially true on issues of ideological impasse. Ignoring that potential conflicts exist is sometimes politically necessary. However, this issue of commercial space tourism must be brought to the agenda table today.

REFERENCES

1 See generally A.S. Piradov, *International Space Law* (Honolulu, Hawaii: University Press of the Pacific, 2000); Bin Cheng, Studies in International Space Law (Oxford, New York: Clarendon Press, 1997); George V. d'Angelo, *Aerospace Business Law* (Westport, CT: Quorum Books, 1994); Peter D. Nesgos, (1991) "Commercial Space Transportation: A New Industry Emerges", XVI *Annals of Air and Space Law*, 393; Jonathan F. Galloway, *Politics and Technology of Satellite Communications* (Lexington, Massachusetts: Lexington Books, 1972).

2 At present, international space law-making is facilitated by COPUOS; it was established by UN General Assembly Resolution No. 1472 (XIV) in 1959. For a detailed analysis and explanation of the UN's role in international space law-making and on the UN's role as primary organ for the development and creation of international space law see Nandasiri Jasentuliyana *International Space Law and the United Nations* (The Hague, The Netherlands: Kluwer Law International, 1999).

3 Detailed discussions regarding space commercialization seem to apply only to fields such as remote sensing, direct broadcasting and telecommunications satellites, space transportation systems, launch services, space stations, and to some extent solar energy and exploitation of resources and space minerals. For further reading see Stephan Hobe and Jana Kristin Hettling (2002) "Challenges to Space Law in the 21st Century - Project 2001 Plus" in *Proceedings of the 45th Colloquium on the Law of Outer Space*; Karl-Heinz Böckstiegel (November, 1988) "Space Law-Changes and Expectations at the Turn to Commercial Space Activities" No. 8 *Forum Internationale*, 1-28; Susanne Reif (1999) "Project 2001: Shaping a Legal Framework for the Commercial Use of Outer Space" 15 *Space Policy*, 109-112; Bin Cheng, Studies in International Space Law (Oxford, New York: Clarendon Press, 1997); George V. d'Angelo, *Aerospace Business Law* (Westport, CT: Quorum Books, 1994); Dorinda G. Dallmeyer and Kosta Tsipis, *Heaven and Earth: Civilian Uses of Near-Earth Space* (The Hague: Kluwer Law International, 1997); Tanja L. Zwaan and Walter W.C. de Vries, Paul Henry

Tuinder, Ilias I. Kuskuvelis (eds.) *Space Law: Views of the Future: A Compilation of Articles by a New Generation of Space Law Scholars* (Deventer: The Netherlands: Kluwer Law and Taxation Publishers, 1988); Edward Ridley Finch, Jr. and Amanda Lee Moore, *Astrobusiness: A Guide to the Commerce and Law of Outer Space* (New York: Praeger, 1994).

[4] For example, Stephen Doyle (1992) "Legal Aspects of Space Commercialization" in Nandasiri Jasentuliyana's *Space Law: Development and Scope* (Westport, Connecticut: Praeger, 1992), Chapter 10; Carl Q. Christol, *Space Law: Past, Present, and Future* (Deventer, The Netherlands: Kluwer Law and Taxation Publishers, 1991).

[5] At numerous conferences, symposia and the like, around the globe, presenters are increasingly presenting on the topic of space tourism. For example, the following presented at the ISU symposium in 2002: Jim Benson, "The Role of the Private Sector/Entrepreneur in Future Human Space Exploration" p. 217-222; R.A. Goehlich "Economic and Technical Evaluation of Suborbital Spaceflight for Space Tourism" p. 223-230; A. P. Bukley and W. Mendell "Space Tourism - From Dream to Reality" p. 231-238; and I. Bouvet "Space for Entrepreneurs and Tourists: Some Legal Issues" p. 239-246, see the Proceedings of the International Space University's 7th Annual Symposium, 4-7 June, Strasbourg, France entitled "Beyond the International Space Station: The Future of Human Spaceflight" (Dordrecht: Kluwer Academic Publishers, 2002). Similarly many presentations on space tourism were made at the World Space Congress in 2002, in Houston Texas as well as many other conferences around the world.

[6] Paula Berinstein, *Making Space Happen: Private Space Ventures and the Visionaries Behind Them* (Medford, New Jersey: Plexus Publishing, Inc., 2002); U. Apel (1997, November) "Space Tourism - a Promising Future?" *Space Policy* 13:4, pp. 279-284; Tom Rogers (1998, May) "Space Tourism: A Response to Continuing Decay in U.S. Civil Space Financial Support" *Space Policy* 14:2, pp. 79-81.

[7] See *Ad Astra* (May/June, 2002) at 6.

[8] This is the sort of thing Andrew Haley (1958) warned about in "Space Law: Recent Practical Achievements", presented at the *American Rocket Society 13th Annual Meeting,* Hotel Statler, New York, N.Y. November 17-21.

[9] For an outline on existing theories and interpretations on the nature and purpose international law with implications for space law, Nandasiri Jasentuliyana, *Perspectives on International Law* (London, U.K.: Kluwer Law International, 1995).

[10] Manfred Lachs, Warsaw & The Hague, "The Law-Making Process of Outer Space" in Edward McWhinney and Martin A. Bradley (eds.) *New Frontiers in Space Law* (A.W. Sijthoffs, Leynden & Oceana Publications, New York, 1969), pg. 13.

[11] Werner Levi (1976) *Law and Politics in the International Society* (Sage Publications, Inc.: California & London) pg. 7.; See also Lasswell, H. (1963) *"Politics" Who Gets what, When, How* (Cleveland, Ohio: World Publishing); Lauterpacht, H. (ed.) *Annual International Law Reports* (London: Butterworth, 1970) *Private Law Sources and Analogies of International Law.* Hamden, Conn.: Archon Book, *The Development of International Law by the Permanent Court of International* Justice (London: Longmans, Press, 1934) and *The Function of Law in the International Community* (Oxford, England: Clarendon Press).

[12] Kelly M. Zullo (2002) "The Need to Clarify the Status of Property Rights in International Space Law" Volume 90 *The Georgetown Law Journal*, 2414 at 2424-2425; Virgiliu Pop (November 2000) "Appropriation in Outer Space: The Relationship Between Land Ownership and Sovereignty on the Celestial Bodies" Volume 16: Issue 4 *Space Policy*, 275-282; Nicolas Mateesco Matte (1984) "Space Activities and Emerging International Law" Report of a major research conducted by The Centre for Research of Air and Space Law, McGill University, p. 279-281.

[13] Treaty on Principles Governing the Activities of States in the Exploration and Use of Outer Space, including the Moon and Other Celestial Bodies, Jan. 27, 1967, 18 U.S.T. 2410, 610 U.N.T.S. 205 (The Outer Space Treaty of 1967).

[14] Pat Dasch, Michael Martin Smith, and Anne Pierce Director of Programs, National Space Society (1999) "Conference of Space Property Rights: Next Steps", p.174-178 and Wayne White, Jr. "Implications of a Proposal for Real Property Rights in Outer Space" p. 366-372, *Proceedings of the 42nd Colloquium on the Law of Outer Space.*

[15] Id.

[16] Wayne White, Jr. "Proposal for a Multilateral Treaty Regarding Jurisdiction and Real Property Rights in Outer Space" p. 245-253, *Proceedings of the 43rd Colloquium on the Law of Outer Space, 2000.*

[17] P.M. Sterns and L.I. Tennen (2002) Privateering and Profiteering on the Moon and Other Celestial Bodies: Debunking the Myth of Property Rights in Space" World Space Conference Paper No. COSPAR 02-A-01933, Houston Texas, October, 2002; Sylvia Ospina (2002) "The Concepts of Assets and Property: Similarities and Differences, and their Applicability to Undertakings in Outer Space", *Proceedings of the 45th Colloquium on the Law of Outer Space;* Armel Kerrest (2001) "Outer Space: Res Communis, Common Heritage or Common Province of Mankind" *Proceedings of the 10th ECSL Summer Course on Space Law and Policy,* University of Nice, France (August 27 - September 8, 2001).

[18] These terms are used respectively by Maarten A. Hajer in "Discourse Coalitions and the institutionalization of Practice: The Case of Acid Rain in Britain", pp. 43-76 and J.A. Throgmorton in "Survey Research as Rhetorical

Trope: Electric Power Planning Arguments in Chicago", pp. 117-144 in Frank Fischer and John Forester (eds.) (1993) *The Argumentative Turn in Policy Analysis and Planning* (Durham and London: Duke University Press, 1993).

[19] Id.; also see Deborah Stone, *Policy Paradox and Political Reason* (Glenview, Illinois: Scott Foresman, 1988).

[20] Unlike the indirect reference to the Common Heritage doctrine in the Outer Space Treaty, the Moon Treaty explicitly designates The Moon and its natural resources as part of the CHM. The CHM doctrine was derived from the Roman law concept, *res communis*, which states that certain property shall be treated as community property - it cannot be owned by any person(s), state, any other entity or combination of entities. See Heim at note 29.

[21] Maurice N. Andem (1999) "Twentieth Anniversary of the 1979 Moon Treaty: The Legal Status of the Moon and Other Celestial Bodies Revisited in the Light of the Commercialisation of Outer Space Activities", *Proceedings of the 42nd Colloquium on the Law of Outer Space*, 383-392; also see Rana, Harminderpal Singh (Fall, 1994) "The "CHM & The Final Frontier: A Revaluation of Values constituting the International Legal Regime for Outer Space Activities" Volume 26 *Rutgers Law Journal*, 225.

[22] Twibell, Ty S. "Space Law: Legal Restraints on Commercialization and Development of Outer Space." *University of Missouri at Kansas City Law Review. 65* Spring 1997, 589; Ty S. Twibell (1997) "Circumnavigating International Space Law" Volume 4 ILSA Journal of International and Comparative Law, 259.

[23] Kelly M. Zullo (2002) at note 12; Glenn H. Reynolds (1992) "International Space Law: Into the Twenty-First Century" Volume 25: No. 2 Vanderbilt Journal of Transnational Law, 225 and in (February, 1990) "Laying a Legal Foundation for Space Development", Ad Astra at 30 argues that international space law inhibits commercial development due to the uncertainty posed by the lack of clarity on the issue of private property rights. Some authors suggest that space law be changed to explicitly permit land grants to encourage outer space settlement. For example, Glenn H. Reynolds (Summer, 1992) "Environmental Rights and International Peace" Volume 59 Tennessee Law Review, 723. It is important to note that the land grant concept more probably would fall into the forbidden realm of "appropriation" as opposed to the permissible category of "use". However, this is just a guess.

[24] Robert Zimmerman (July-August, 2000) "Brave New World?: American Colonial History as a Guide to Building Space Societies", *Ad Astra* 32-34; Berkley, Richard. "Intellectual Property issues in East Asia Proceedings of the 1997 Symposium: Article and Comment: Space Law Versus Space Utilization: The Inhibition of Private Industry in Outer Space." *Wisconsin International Law Journal.* 15 Spring, 1997, 421; Risley, Lawrence L. (1998) "An Examination of the Need to Amend Space Law to Protect the Private Explorer in Outer Space." *Western State University Law Review 26:* 47.

[25] Cook, Kevin V. (Spring, 1999) "The Discovery of Lunar Water: An Opportunity to Develop a Workable Moon Treaty" Volume 11 Georgetown International Environmental Law Review, 647 provides over 70 pages of text detailing various reasons international space law is defective; Husby, Eric (1994) "Sovereignty and Property Rights in Outer Space" Volume 3 *Journal of International Law and Practice*, 359 also argues that space law is defective, for various reasons; Heidi Keefe (July, 1995) "Making the Final Frontier Feasible: A Critical Look at the Current Body of Outer Space Law" Volume 11 *Computer & High Technology Law Journal*, 345.

[26] Brian M. Hoffstadt (December, 1994) "Comment: Moving the Heavens: Lunar Mining and the "CHM" in the Moon Treaty", Volume 24 *UCLA Law Review*, 575.

[27] See note 40.

[28] For further reading see Edythe Weeks (May-August, 2001) "Continuing Pattern of Inequality Between North and South in Outer Space" Volume 79: No. 2 *Revue de Droit International De Sciences Diplomatiques et Politiques* 167.

[29] See Barbara Heim (1990) in "Exploring the Last Frontiers for Mineral Resources: A Comparison of International Law Regarding the Deep Seabed, Outer Space and Antarctica", Volume 23 *Vanderbilt Journal of Transnational* Law, 819.

[30] See note 1.

[31] George V. d'Angelo, *Aerospace Business Law* (Westport, CT: Quorum Books, 1994).

[32] For example, in the US, domestic laws and policy statements have encouraged privatization of the space transportation industry. The Commercial Space Launch Act of 1984 regulated private space transportation in the US. Prior to this, it was fragmentary and inconsistent. In 1984, the Department of Transportation was designated the lead agency for commercial launch activities. And other similar policy statements followed. For instance, the National Space Policy (1989), the Commercial Space Launch Policy (1990), the Commercial Space Policy Guidelines (1991), and the National Launch Strategy (1991) see Nathan C. Goldman *American Space Law: International and Domestic 2nd ed.* (San Diego, California: Univelt, 1996); Patrick Salin (June, 2002) "An Overview of US Commercial Space Legislation and Policies - Present and Future" *Air and Space Law*, Volume 27: 3.

[33] See Stephen E. Doyle (2002) *Origins of International Space Law and the International Institute of Space Law of the International Astronautical Federation* Univelt, Incorporated: San Diego, California); Howard E. McCurdy. *Space and the American Imagination* (The Smithsonian Institution Press, 1997).

[34] Von Bencke, M. J. (1997). The Politics of Space: A History of U.S. - Soviet/Russian Competition and Cooperation in Space. Boulder, Colorado: Westview Press.

[35] See Hager (1970) at note 39.

[36] The Agreement Governing the Activities of States on the Moon and Other Celestial Bodies (The Moon Treaty) 18 ILM 1434, GA Res. 34/68, GAOR, 34th Session., Supp. No. 46, at 77 (entered into force July 12, 1984).

[37] Much has been written on the relationship between international law and international politics. See Douglas M. Zang (1991) "Frozen in Time: The Antarctic Mineral Resource convention" Volume 76 *Cornell Law Review*, 722; Anne-Marie Slaughter Burley (1993) "International Law and International Relations Theory: A Dual Agenda" *The American Journal on International Law* Vol. 87 A.J.I.L. 205; Rosalyn Higgins "Integration of Authority and Control: Trends in the Literature of International Law and International Relations" in *Toward World Order*, Richard A. Falk (1968) "The Relevance of Political Context to the Nature and Functioning of International Law: An Intermediate View, in Karl W. Deutsch & Stanley Hoffmann's (eds.) *The Relevance of International Law* 133, 142; Louis Henkin (1979) *How Nations Behave: Law and Foreign Policy* 4 (2nd. Ed.); Hans J. Morgenthau (1967) *Politics Among Nations: The Struggle for Power and Peace* (4th ed.); Francis A. Boyle (1985) *World Politics and International Law*, Oran R. Young (1972) "International Law and Social Science: The Contributions of Myres S. McDougal", 66 *AJIL* 60; Harold Lasswell (1936) *Politics: Who Gets What, When, How*. Still, too few focus on the process of change within the context of political moods. For example, the US is often thought of as being against the CHM concept. This was not always the case. For example, prior to 1980, the US encouraged the "common heritage vocabulary in discussions of moon law and the Law of the Sea. This stopped with the election of Ronald Reagan" see Author Blaser (1990) Volume 5 *Journal of Law and Technology*, 79 at 89; see also Kim Alaine Rathman, (1996) *The Common Heritage Principle and the U.S. Commercialization of Outer Space,* Dissertation, Graduate Theological Union, Berkeley, California.

[38] C. Wilfred Jenks, Space Law (New York: Frederick A. Praeger, 1965).

[39] David Russell Hager (1970) in *Space Law: The United Nations, and the Superpowers: A Study of International legal Development and Codification, 1957-1969,* Dissertation, University of Virginia, Ph.D. Political Science, sets forth the central hypothesis that the development and codification of space law and the "nature, scope and pace" were significantly influenced by the variables of political competition and cooperation between the superpowers. Hager (1970: 8) asserts that international law is more accurately characterized as *de lege ferenda* (that which is developing to attain the objectives contemplated for it), rather that *de lege lata* (that which is established). Hager (1970: 8) explains that international law is shaped by all the elements that compose the international system and is "reflective of the structure of the world, transnational forces, the pattern of power and the political cultures of the main actors, and the relations among the units"; also see Tanja L. Masson-Zwaan and Pablo M. Mendes de Leon (eds.) *Air and Space Law de Lege Ferenda: Essays in Honour of Henri A. Wassenbergh* (Kluwer Academic Publishers, 1992).

[40] The Treaty on Principles Governing the Activities of States in the Exploration and Use of Outer Space, Including the Moon and Other Celestial Bodies (The Outer Space Treaty, 1967); The Agreement on the Rescue of Astronauts, the Return of Astronauts, and the Return of Objects Launched into Outer Space (The Rescue and Return Agreement, 1968); The Convention on International Liability for Damage Caused by Space Objects (The Liability Convention, 1971); and The Convention on the Registration of Objects Launched into Outer Space (The Registration Convention,1976). The questionable one is The Agreement Governing the Activities of States on the Moon and Other Celestial Bodies (The Moon Treaty,1984). Only nine states (Australia, Austria, Chile, Mexico, Morocco, The Netherlands, Pakistan, Philippines and Uruguay) have ratified it and five states (France, Guatemala, India, Peru and Romania) in addition have signed but not ratified. It only took five nations to enter it into force, however it opened for signature on December 18, 1979 and took five years to get the five requisite signatures. Conversely, The Outer Space Treaty was well received: it was ratified by ninety-six nations and signed by another twenty-seven states. See *Report of the Legal Subcommittee on Its Fortieth Session*, UN Committee on the Peaceful Uses of Outer Space, 40th Session, 22(a), United Nations' Document A/AC.105763 (2001) see http:www.oosa.unvienna.org/Reports/AC105_763E.pdf. Since the Moon Treaty has garnered such a low level of international support, some space law experts have reasoned it is "obviously unacceptable". Kelly M. Zullo (2002), note 12, citing Eilene Galloway, "Guidelines for the Review and Formulation of Outer Space Treaties", Presentation at the International Astronautical Federation *41st International Colloquium on the Law of Outer Space*, Melbourne, Australia, at 2, October 2, 1998.

[41] Katrin Nyman Metcalf, *Activities in Space Appropriation of Use?* (Uppsala: Lustus Forlag, 1999).

[42] Nandasiri Jasentuliyana, *Space Law: Development and Scope* (Westport, Connecticut: Praeger, 1992) at 37.

[43] See, for example, Carl Q. Christol (1965) "An Analysis of Certain Policy Approaches in the United States to the Emerging Law of Outer Space, *Proceedings of the 7th Colloquium on the Law of Outer Space*, pp. 4-9; Vladimir Kopal (1997) "Some Comments on the Significance of the 1967 Outer Space Treaty for the Establishment and Development of Space Law of Our Times"; and Frans G. von der Dunk (February 1996) "The Role of Law With Respect to Future Space Activities", *Space Policy*, 5-8.

IAC-03-IISL.2.10

LEGAL PRINCIPLES OF EXPLORATION AND USE OF OUTER SPACE: PAST ACHIEVEMENTS AND FUTURE CHALLENGES

A.A. Golrounia, Faculty Member
M. Bahrami, Director
Aerospace Research Institute
Ministry of Science, Research and Technology
Tehran, Iran
ali@ari.ac.ir

ABSTRCT

In the rivalry environment of years 1962 and 1963, right after Yuri Gagarin became the first ever man in earth orbit, Soviet Union and USA, the two space superpowers of the time conducted intensive negotiations regarding the course of activities in space. In coming up with an agreement, each side did its best to hinter the other sides' activities and to free its own hand in making use of outer space particularly keeping in mind its own military advantage in coming years. The end result was the presentation of Declaration of Legal Principles of States Activities in the Exploration and Use of Outer Space, presented to UN General Assembly and eventually its approval in December 1963. Even though the freedom of exploration and use of space by all states for the benefit of mankind were the main achievements of the Declaration, however there was no mention of "only peaceful use of outer space". This was a green light to the superpowers to start a cold war race in space.

The situation now, is different. Even though the Soviet Union is no longer in existence, however the Russian Federation does not seem to have given up the glories she has inherited, Europe is marching ahead, new comers like China, India, and to some degrees Brazil and Australia are going to become serious players in space activities.

The space exploration is advancing in different aspects with unprecedented rate. Space technology is getting into everyday usage, in particular communication and remote sensing. Commercialization of space activities and involvement of private sector in developing business from space technology achievements are new dimensions in space activities.

In this paper after presenting a brief review of the development leading to approval of the Declaration of the Legal Principles, and making some points on its shortcomings, the current situation in legal regime of space activities is studied, and some points to be noted in future developments are discussed.

INTRODUCTION

The development of the space law is closely related to evolution of space activities. Moreover, the growth of space exploration and its use has been dictated by a number of factors including technological capabilities, states policy and economic considerations. It is important to note that, in the past, whenever there have been new frontiers to explore, and the rule of law has been lacking, the evolution of legal principles has responded to the perceived interests of participating states. One needs only to recall the development of the rule of freedom of the high seas as a response, in part, to the commercial pursuits of states. Comparatively, in order to gain a clear understanding of future challenges of space law, it is necessary to analyze the evolution of space activities, and the future effect of these activities in space[1].

In 1967 when the Treaty on Principles Governing the Activities of States, Including the Moon and other Celestial Bodies was adapted in United Nations General Assembly, commonly referred to Outer Space. At the time, space activities were conducted mainly by two great space powers. During the cold-war era, the United States and the Soviet Union debated over which military activities in space should be allowed and which should be prohibited. Each side sought to legitimize a strategic military advantage through the formulation of a rule that favored its own military interests or hindered rival interests.

Until the beginning of 1970, space activities were conducted only by government entities and were restricted to governmental activities. The military potential of outer space had influenced the development of every aspect of satellite technology. Many space technologies possess a dual capacity: military and nonmilitary uses. Consequently, the policies of the two major space powers have always been characterized by the simultaneous desire to:

1) Encourage, under the auspices of the United Nations a legal regime for space to facilitate and promote international co-operation, and
2) Develop space technologies to advance military strategies and goals[2].

As space activities moved from the era of exploration by the two original space powers to commercial utilization by many nations, the U.S.S.R. and the U.S.A. found it more difficult to impose their views and policies on the world community in a changing international political system. While the period from 1963 to 1968 witnessed the predominance of the duo pole in the development of space law, such domination has since had to yield to the interests of the world community as a whole.

THE TECHNOLOGICAL TREND

Space technologies in terms of launching systems, transportation, telecommunications, remote sensing, environmental control, education, and health services have been improved sharply since the first space flight. Now much larger and more sophisticated stations can be built in orbit with possibility of living of men for years in orbit. Shuttles a reusable launch vehicle, as a mean of transportation can carry human and equipments to space and support them to carry out their mission.

Day to day life on earth, without telecommunication via satellites seems impossible and many people relay on the services, which somehow relate to space technology. Billions of data transmitted from one part of the world to another part with in few seconds.

Earth can be sensed from outer space for urban planning, mining, agriculture, environmental protection, meteorology and natural disaster control. Material can be made and laboratory tests can be performed, new and better medicine can be produced, taking advantage of microgravity. Even, energy can be generated in space and transmitted to earth.

CONVERSION OF MILITARY TECHNOLOGY

Due to the dual nature of space technology and related industrial infrastructure, which supports the outer space activities in both military and non military usage, many of these system such as satellites, launch vehicles and ground stations are used for both purposes.

After the end of cold war, many of these equipments for military purpose were redundant and had to be converted to non-military usage. On the base of disarmament agreements between two super powers many of ballistic missiles were useless and had to convert to civilian usage or to be destroyed. Infact safe keeping of these ballistic missiles or defusing them proved to be costly and very expensive. With some modification, these ballistic missiles are changed to civilian launcher which economic benefit of them specially for Russian Federation was significant. Development of private sector investment is crucial for success of this program[3].

ECONOMIC EVOLUTION

In 1957 when space race was started as a result of successful launch of sputnik by Soviet Union there were only two players, namely U.S.A and U.S.S.R., which in effect they were ready to pay virtually any price to succeed and hinder the rival side. In fact, space activities were the matter of prestige and national security. Economic factors were the secondary issues.

However, after the end of the cold war and reducing the tension between two super powers, public opinions were not in favor of spending the tax money in costly and ambitious space programs.

However the space activities have an enormous economic and social impact on the world. Telecommunications satellites, for example, provided a number of social services. Educational programs and health information, now concentrated in urban areas in both developed and developing countries.

A key element for space activities to succeed is to reduce the price of these activities in order to become more available and more affordable to the people of world in both developed and developing countries. Reduction in price means more investment and more research and development.

It is obvious that limited resources, which the Governments can allocate for Investment and R&D, cannot meet the necessary funds, which are required to meet new challenges.

Private sector investment is crucial for future development of space activities, which mean, the activities must be based on profit making, for invest. For many space-related services and products there are many possibilities of large-scale commercialization.

Annual revenues that are possible from space applicant can reach more than hundreds of billions of dollars from telecommunication, transportation, tourism, medical facilities, solar power, data transmission, and material processing.

THE EVOLUTION OF POLICY AND LAW

A prime function of law is to promote social order. The value of a rule in the social system should be measured by the degree to which it succeeds in maintaining and fostering social order.

Factors, which help to determine the value of a rule, include:

1) The reasons for its adoption;
2) The degree of community support for the rule
3) The degree to which the rule is respected
4) The degree to which the rule continues to be appropriate as circumstances change[4].

If we elaborate on the circumstances which have been changed since the adoption of the Outer Space Treaty of 1967 we will be in better position to know what need to be done in the future.

The military potential of outer space had a great influence on formation of the Outer Space Treaty of 1967. Although this role has not diminished, however its significant has much reduced.

Only two major players were active in outer space, therefore the outer space treaty of 1967 was tailored mainly to the interest of these two players. Since then, the circumstances have changed dramatically. Many new players are actively present in space arena.

As a result of ending the cold war the notion of prestige and national security have less importance and with the limited resources which are available, all activities must have economic justification, that means less role for government, and more active roles for entrepreneurs.

Growing concerns over environmental protection means more regulations and control specially when the number of players increase and private sectors get involved in space activities (International Regulatory Body).

Commercialization and privatization means more secrecy over the information, this means collecting the strategic information about natural resources and other valuable information from states and selling them according to their commercial interest, which is certainly not in the merit of the Outer Space Treaty.

The notion of intellectual and property rights can diminish the notion of the exploration and use of outer space should be carried out for the benefit of all peoples irrespective of the degree of their economic or scientific development.

With respect to developing countries and ensuring the equal access to the benefits of space technology for all countries. Taking into account that in the era of information we call the earth as "global village" which obviously means that information passes through the world in such speed that seems there is no distance between north to south and east to west. The same way as when anyone comes to a village, immediately everybody in the village knows about it.

But a village has its own definition and its own characteristics, which seems to have been forgotten or ignored in this global village of ours. The people in a village are used to know each other very well and call each other by first name. They care for each other, they are happy when their neighbors are happy and sad when they are sad. The life style and the standards of living of the people of a village more or less are the same.

However, in our global village not only we do not know each other, but also there are more than tow billions of us, who are hungry, with no education and no health services. In terms of space technology, more than one billion of us have never ever made even a single telephone call in their entire lifetime. Forget about mobile phone, computer and Internet. This is the reality of our global village

Someone may argue that these have noting to do with space law which in some degree I agree with. However, it should be noted that using the space technology is the quickest and cheapest mean to over come the pain that the people of the global village are suffering from the lack of education and health services.

Conclusions

During the first twenty years of Committee on Peaceful Uses of Outer Space, five space treaties and four sets of legal principles were negotiated and adopted. In recent years the process of space law making has become extremely slow and complex. With changing of space technology and as a result the benefits of new technology and its application, space faring nations are interested to address new subjects such as commercialization and privatization of space activities, intellectual and property rights, rather than issues in the general public international law principles, that were promulgated at the beginning of COPUOS.

Many of these new subjects such as outer space environmental control, debris, harmful contamination, safety of space operation, manned space flight, and space navigation need to be regulated.

It seems that the time is right for international community through COPUOS to establish an international organization such as ICAO, WMO or IMO for setting standards and recommended practices of more technical nature for space activities.

This international organization not only helps the safe and smooth operation of space activities but also by supplementing the existing space law treaties can fill gaps and weakness to accommodate new subjects and rapidly changing technology.

1
2
3
4

REFERENCES

1. Nicolas M. Matte," Space Activities and emerging International Law", Center for Research of Air and Space Law. McGill University, 1984, pp6.
2. Ibid, pp50.
3. UN Doc. A/48/221, Report of the Secretary General 1994, pp6
4. Nicolas M. Matte, "Space Activities and Emerging International Law", Center for Research of Air and Space Law, McGill University, 1984, pp50
5. Nandasiri Jasentuliyana, "Recent Development in United Nations Activities Relating to Outer Space" 38th International Colloquium on the Law of Outer Space, Oslo,1995, pp8

Some Remarks to General Clauses of Treaty Space Law

by Gyula Gál

Péter Pázmány Catholic University
Budapest

The progressive development of international space law after the Moon Agreement undeniably came to a standstill. To use an expression in style: it is on a parking orbit awaiting new, positive impulses. Obviously other grave cares of the international community prevail. New challenges concerning traditional institutions of the system of general international law come before the efforts to go on with building the structure of treaty space law.

The period of calm gives an opportunity to revive theoretical problems of positive treaty law. To reconsider certain questions of interpretation raised by the *jus conditum*. It may be perhaps useful to *jus condendum* for future law-making. With my modest observations I would like to contribute to the discussion on three characteristic general clauses of the Space Treaty and the Moon Agreement:

Province of all Mankind

The exploration and use of outer space shall be carried out for the benefit and interests of all countries, irrespective of their degree of economic or scientific development, and shall be the province of all mankind. (S.T. Article I.1)

Envoys of Mankind

States parties to the treaty shall regard astronauts as envoys of mankind in outer space and shall render them all possible assistance. (S.T. Article V.1)

Common heritage of Mankind

The Moon and its natural resources are the common heritage of mankind. (Moon Agreement Article XI.1)

I

The insertion of clauses containing certain general principles has been a generally accepted method of national and international law-making. Continental codifications of civil law one and all built into their system principles going back to Roman law. E.g. Treu und Glauben to *bona fides, aequitas, exceptio doli, boni mores* etc. (1) The theory of international law has been always ready to apply civil law analogies, principles and terms of Roman law to international legal relations. Our science of international space law does the same – e.g. *res communis omnium* for status of outer space.

The general clauses of domestic laws prescribe a certain behaviour for cases not regulated by specific provisions of the Act concerned. To bridge over shortcomings the legislator converts moral postulates into positive law rules. This is why the German Author *Justus W. Heidemann* wrote his book on general clauses (1933) under the title "Die Flucht in die General-klauseln" (Escape into general clauses). In his opinion the legislator using general clauses as means of technics of codification escapes from creating detailed rules for problematical legal relations. (2)

General clauses of space law treaties have a special common feature. Space age downed upon us when mankind is divided by fundamental antagonisms due to political, economic and moral differences, split by state sovereignties. In an international community comprising "high-tech" societies and groups of people living under rudimentary conditions. The exploration and use of outer space, however, is a global activity. Its efforts, advantageous or harmful, cannot be restricted to one nation or any group of nations. Today the structure of the international legal order lags behind technical achievements. The discrepancy fully could be solved only by the rather utopistic status of moral and political unity of mankind. It is not accidental, that the nucleus of all three general clauses of treaty space law is mankind itself. The first inevitable question for their analysis is therefore the legal meaning of mankind.

II

According to the Vienna Convention on the Law of Treaties (1969) a treaty shall be interpreted in good faith in accordance with the ordinary meaning to be given to the terms of the treaty in their context and in the light of its object an purpose. This provision of the Convention refers to the classic methods of interpretation.

The term **mankind** occurs in several international instruments. Among others in the Preamble of the U.N. Charter, Preamble of the North Atlantic Treaty (1959) the Treaty on the Non-Proliferation of Nuclear Weapons (1968) and especially in the, U.N. Convention on the Law of the Sea (1982). All without definition of mankind or any indirect information on the meaning of the term in the treaty.

What is the *ordinary* meaning of mankind?

According to various vocabularies and etymological works mankind is the human species (3), or human race (4). In Hungarian handbooks "emberiség" (=humankind) means the human genus (5), but also collectivity or "nation" of human beings. (6)

The common feature of definitions in the legal literature is that mankind comprises only human beings independently of politically motivated states. It is an abstract notion covering all humans wherever they are living. Moreover we find an opinion that mankind comprises all of our contemporaries, all the future generations to come, and men of the past also belong to it. (7)

By insertion into the Space Treaty and the Moon Agreement mankind became a conventional term, to be interpreted. The general clauses moved two outstanding pioneers of space law theory to attribute international personality to mankind.

Praising the Space Treaty *A. A. Cocca*, concluded that "the international community from now on has recognized the existence of a new subject of international law namely Mankind itself, and has created a *jus commune humanitatis.*" (COPUOS Legal Subcomittee June 19, 1967) (8) According to *M. G. Markoff* "for the first time in history mankind was recognized in positive law by the international legal order as a subject of this order" considering mankind as the main beneficiary of the results of the research, exploring and use of outer space. (9) In a more cautious formulation this opinion was accepted by some other authors. *M. I. Niciu* minded: "At present we are at the beginning of the process of the assertion of mankind as a subject of public international law, nevertheless mankind does not yet meet all the requirements for becoming a subject of international law." (10) In the Hungarian literature of international law we find similar views. "Mankind does not mean the totality of states assigning rights to it, but it may be user of certain rights granted by international law. It has therefore legal personality in a limited sphere." (*K. Nagy*) (11) "The passive legal personality of mankind has to be acknowledged." (*B. Nagy*) (12)

On the other hand the majority of authors does not accept the theory of legal personality of mankind. Main argument of the refusal is the unquestionable absence of any organization or institution representing it independently of and above the states.

S. Gorove puts the question: how could one state or group of states or an international organization be a spokesman or representative, of all mankind without some formal act of authorization or mandate involving such representation? (13) *N. M. Matte* accentuates the same doubt: one cannot avoid questioning the meaning of the word mankind and how it could be represented in a future international regime? (14) The negative answer to this question appears in the argumentation of the opponents almost unanimously. To quote some opinions: *A. Górbiel*: Every subject of international law must have an organ competent to represent it in the international relations. There does not exist any such organ representing the mankind as a whole, (15) *S. Courteix*: The human species named mankind (*ensemble du genre humain*) without an independent state-organization (*gouvernement supranational*) could act in outer space only by a "trustee" otherwise legal personality of mankind hardly would be accepted. (16) *K. Tatsuzawa*: A state or group of states can't represent the will of all mankind. Mankind is not yet institutionalized as such. It remains only a philosophical concept in the actual stage of human progress. (17) *R. Arzinger* The opinion that mankind would be a subject of international law which could act without representation as an entity do not have a base in contemporary international law. (18) *R. V. Dekanozov*: The term mankind speaking strictly legally is in fact conventional, since mankind is not an independent subject of international law with its rights and obligations. (19)

On my part I share the opinion of the opponents. A subject of international law is the bearer of rights *and duties*. (20) Definitions omitting the later element could hardly be found.

Sea law and space law making references to mankind as a whole granting certain rights to it and obliging states to a special behaviour towards it do not promote mankind to subject of international law. (21) If the alledged subject of international law does not have the ability to enforce rights (22) attributed to it, is no real subject of the international legal order. The *passive* legal personality is a typical *contradictio in adjecto* – self contradiction. (23) The presumption appearing also in the Hungarian literature that there exists an organ acting in the name of mankind, is erroneous. Mankind – totality of some 6 billion human beings – did not give an authority of representation to any organ or organization. Not excepted the United Nations which motivated by humanitarian objects repeatedly refers to it. (24) The interpretation of the term Mankind in the context of the three general clauses and in the system of the two treaties results in different conclusions.

III

Envoys of Mankind

From this viewpoint the "envoys of mankind" clause seems to be the least problematical. "States Parties to the Treaty shall regard astronauts as envoys of mankind in outer space" – nobody would conclude from this provision of Article V. of the Space Treaty that astronauts during their mission are envoys in sense of Article 14.1a of the Vienna Convention on Diplomatic Relations. The Space Treaty by this symbolical wording obviously confirms a moral obligation, namely to render to them all possible assistance in cases of accident, distress or emergency landing.

The Rescue Agreement in Articles I-III obliges the Parties (today 88 states) to measures which probably all states would undertake motivated by the moral consideration expressed in the general clause.

Province of all Mankind

"All space activities shall be carried out for the benefit and in the interests of *all countries* ...and shall be the province of *all mankind*." This provision of the Treaty occurs in the first Article of the Space Treaty and not in the Preamble where the States Parties to the Treaty only confirm the common interest of all mankind in space exploration. No doubt, it is to be recognized that the general interests principle of Article I.1 keeps its full binding force under present international law. (*M. Markoff*) (25)

The general clause clearly consists of two elements. Exploration and use of outer space shall be carried out in the interest of *all countries* i.e. not only of for today 97 states parties to the Treaty and will be the province of *all mankind*. (26) The difference is evident. This provision of the Treaty demonstrates the inherent ambiguity of general clauses. From the rather loose terminology one could follow, that the "province" relates to outer space including the Moon and other celestial bodies within the solar system. The grammatical interpretation of the first sentence of Article

I.1 makes clear that the "province" as a metaphorical expression is referred to *activities*: exploration and use of outer space.

Taking this clause literally: *a contrario* activities which are carried out not in the interest of all countries would constitute a breach of a treaty obligation. Some authors – I myself belonged to them (27) – in all good faith minded that e.g. the activity of military reconnaissance satellites which is carried out only in the interest of the launching state, is inconsistent with the principle of "interests of all countries." (28) The interstate practice long ago transgressed this interpretation. Moreover, the theory of space law is ready to attribute a peace-keeping role to this kind of space activity. Up to now no formal protest is known to have been made concerning the surveillance by satellites. The same can be stated for operational military space activities in armed conflicts. These are carried out clearly in the interest of a single state or group of states. The international community accepted it without referring to the general clause of Article I.1 of the Space Treaty. The silent consent seems to confirm that the clause felled victim to a continuous *desuetudo* by the interstate practice. (29) Similarly: is profit-oriented commercial space activity carried out for the benefit and in the interests of all countries? (30) The answer in certain cases may be positive. There are such activities indirectly contributing to general progress and development though literally not consistent with the "interests of all countries" clause.

Common heritage of mankind

The principle CHM with its symbolistical logic penetrated so quickly and deeply into the thinking of international lawyers that any critical approach to it seems to be a profanation. This opinion of *A. Bueckling* (31) is thought-provoking. It should be added, however, that nothing for the theory is a taboo, and nothing absolves it from the task of constructive criticism.

The CHM-clause differs essentially from the two others. It was formulated upon a civil law analogy to apply to the exploitable resources of the ocean protecting the interests of technologically less advanced states. The Convention on the Law of the Sea of 1982 (Part IX, Article 136) declares that the seabed and ocean-floor and the subsoil thereof... as well the resources of the area are Common heritage of Mankind. (32) In the same way the general clause of Article XI of the Moon Agreement lays down that the Moon and its natural resources are CHM. (33) This provision applies according to Article I to other celestial bodies within our solar system, and finds its expression in particular in par.5 of Article XI providing the establishment of an international regime to govern the exploitation of natural resources and par.6 on the equitable sharing in the benefits derived.

Analogy has a certain role in the development of drafting new rules of law. Law-makers are often ready to adopt existing legal institutions or concepts for changing needs. (34) It is relationship between two things which are similar in many though not in all respects. (35) In our case the analogy supposes the similarity of characteristic elements of two analogous legal relations.

Hereditas in Roman law – as contemporary heritage – was the succession to the whole right (*universum jus*) which the deceased had. It meant the complex of goods, rights and duties of the deceased i.e. the legal position of the heir who enters into the legal situation and legal relations of the deceased. (36)

Speaking on heritage of mankind delicate questions come up: From whom inherited the mankind the Moon and its natural resources? Who was the "*defunctus*" – the deceased? The former generation? But generations can not be separated in time. They are living together and the history of mankind is an unbroken chain of past, present and future. Who was the original proprietor? If nobody, the Moon and its natural resources could not become a heritage.

The Roman law analogy is also discernible in the theory of mankind comprising the future generations to come. (37) In this way as against the moderate wording of Article IV of the Moon Agreement (38) CHM would be extended to unborn generations, following the principle "*nasciturus pro jam nato habetur quotiens de commodia ejus agitur*". (An unborn child is considered born when his interests are taken into account.) The analogy, however, would be rather inappropriate. The rights of an unborn child in civil law systems can be enforced by an adequate representative. But who should represent our descendents – against us? All these questions demonstrate that the *per analogiam* application of the civil law concept of "heritage" to the Moon and other celestial bodies of the solar system unwillingly leads to a dead-end.

Concerning legal nature of the CHM-clause we find different views in the theory. Some authors regard it as a *real legal requirement* implying that any benefit from space activities should be for all mankind. Others consider it as an expression of socio-political ideas. (39) The extreme opinion is, that CHM is an imperative rule of general international law. "The principle is embodied in many legal instruments, treaties and resolutions and explicitly or tacitly recognized by state practice, which is evidence of the existence of a general consensus *together with the conviction of its nature as jus cogens.*" (40) This opinion leaves essential facts out of consideration: the Moon Agreement up to now has been ratified only by 10 states, moreover an interstate practice in this respect supposes the feasibility of the exploitation of Moon-resources. For the time being it is technically impossible.

The greater part of publicists accepted the view that CHM is not a legal but a philosophical and political concept, since the majority of states has not accepted it either explicitly or implicitly. (41) As expressed by Professor *A. A. Cocca*, most ardent follower of the idea of CHM from the very beginning: "it is an ethical norm and essential for survival *rather than a compulsory rule by force of law*... a symbol of harmony, progress, friendship, understanding and peace." (42) Coming back to my opinion of the special role of general clauses in the treaty space law,

Let me quote the statement of Professor *Christol*: the general clauses of treaty space law "can be understood only by taking into account the high expectation for humanity engendered by the enormous challenges presented to Earth-based humans as they have entered upon the exploration of the new dimension of the universe." (43)

* * *

General clauses are with all their contradictions elements of treaty space law – directly not enforceable as treaty provisions created or to be created in accordance with their rather moral guiding. In this sense they are legal norms. To take again an analogy from Roman Law: *leges imperfectae*. (44) Exceeding the limits of Parties to Treaties they relate to "mankind". *Leges perfectae* they will be only in a radically new structure of the international community based on confidence of state to state, men to fellow-men. I hope, the young generation of space lawyers will live to see it...

Footnotes

1.) See: German Civil Code (BGB) §.242, Hungarian Civil Code (PTK) §.4
2.) *A. Bueckling*, severely criticizing the role of general clauses in space law treaties wrote an interesting article "*Fluch* der Generalkauseln" – the play of words: instead of *Flucht* (fleeing), Fluch – "Curse of General Clauses". Zeitschrift für Rechtspolitik, Jg.16 (1983).
3.) *H. Watson–F. G. Fowler*: The Concise Oxford Dictionary of Current English. 1974, p.518
4.) *Webster's* Dictionary of English Language. New York 1991, p.607. *Black's* Law Dictionary. VII.Ed. 1999 St.Pal Min., p.971 *Oxford* Student's Dictionary II.Ed. pp.388-389
5.) Magyar Értelmező Kéziszótár (Hungarian Explaining Dictionary). Budapest 1977, p.316
6.) Magyar Szókincstár (Handbook of Hungarian Word-stock). Budapest 1999, p.217
7.) *B. Nagy*: Common Heritage of Mankind: the Status of Future Generations. IISL Coll. Proceedings 1988, p.319
8.) *A. A. Cocca*: The Common Heritage of Mankind Doctrine and Principle of Space Law – an Overview. IISL Coll. Proceedings 1986. The Polish authors *R. Hara–J. Stanczyk* criticize this "new Latinism" of *jus commune humanitatis* which as opposed to *jus gentium* has no roots in Roman Law. Space Law and Roman Law Concepts. – Postępy Astronautyki 1985, Nr. ¾, p.23
9.) *M. G. Markoff*: Traité de droit international public de l'espace. Fribourg 1973, p.272
10.) *M. I. Niciu*: Space Law and the Development of Public International Law. Revue Roumaine d'études international, XVIII. Année 6/74, p. 521. – Drept international public – Vol.I. Cluj-Napoca 1975, p. 89.
11.) *K. Nagy*: Nemzetközi jog (International Law). Budapest 1999, p.17
12.) *B. Nagy*: op.cit. Note 7. p.321
13.) *S. Gorove*: Studies in Space Law: the Challenges and Prospects. Leyden 1977, p.69
14.) *N. M. Matte*: Treaty Relating to the Moon. Manual of Space Law. Ed. by N. Jasentuliyana – Roy S. K. Lee, Vol.1. p.159
15.) *A. Górbiel*: International Regulation of the Use of the Lunar Natural Resources and the CHM Doctrine. Acta Universitatis Lodziensis 1983 Politiologia 9, p.12
16.) *S. Courteix*: L'accord régissant les activités des États sur la lune et les autres corps célestes. Annuaire Francais de Droit Public XXV. 1979, p.221
17.) *K. Tatsuzawa*: Political and Legal Meaning of the CHM. IISL Coll. Proceedings 1986, p.86
18.) *R. Arzinger*: On the Legal Contents and Significance of the CHM in Outer Space Law. IISL Coll. Proceedings 1985, p.210
19.) *R. V. Dekanozov*: The CHM in the 1979 Agreement Governing the Activities of the States on the Moon and Other Celestial Bodies. IISL Coll. Proceedings 1981, p.182
20.) E.g.: *F. Berber*: Lehrbuch des Völkerrechts. München-Berlin 1960, I.Bd. p.110. *O'Connell*: International Law. London–Dobbs Ferry N.Y. 1965. Vol.I. p.89. *G. Schwarzenberger*: A Manual of International Law (VI.ed.) London 1976, p.42. *J. G. Starke*: Introduction to International Law (VIII.ed.) London 1977, p.66. etc. In Hungarian Manuals: *H. Szegő*: Nemzetközi jog (International Law) Budapest 2000, p.19 ("rights and obligations laid down directly by the international law") *K. Nagy*: Nemzetközi jog (International Law) Budapest 1999, p.9 ("rights and obligations prescribed by the international law"). *J. Bruhács*: Nemzetközi jog (International Law) Budapest 1998, Vol.I. p.73. ("rights and obligations in case of disputes subjects of an international legal procedure")
21.) See: *M. I. Niciu* op. cit. Note 10. Space law and the Development... p.519
22.) Named "index of juristic personality" by *O'Connell*: International Law. London–Dobbs Ferry N.Y. 1965.Vol.I. p.89
23.) See: *B. Nagy* op. cit. Note 5, p. 321. ("The passive legal personality of mankind has to be acknowledged")

24.) The first sentence of the Charter declares as an aim of the UN "...to save succeeding generations from the scourge of war which twice in our lifetime has brought untold sorrow to *mankind...*"

25.) *M. G. Markoff* op.cit. Note 7, p.265

26.) From the grammatical interpretation of the provision it is obvious that the word *province* does not mean a space or territory, but the activities: exploration and use. See *B. Maiorsky*: A Few Reflections on the Meaning and the Interpretation of "Province of Mankind" and CHM Notions. IISL Coll. Proceedings 1988, p.60

27.) *G. Gál*: Space Law. Budapest–Leyden–Dobbs Ferry 1969, pp.170-171, 180

28.) *G. Gál:* The "Peaceful Uses of Outer Space" after the Space Treaty. Proceedings 1967

29.) *G. Gál*: Military Space Activity in the Light of General International Law. IISL Coll. Proceedings 2002, pp.164-165

30.) At the New Delhi Conference 2002 of the International Law Association the Space Law Committee proposed a separate protocol to the Space Treaty of 1967 giving a more precise meaning of the common benefit clause *in the light of present commercial space activities.* ILA Report 2002, p.196

31.) *A. Bueckling*: Zur juristischen Substanzlosigkeit des Begriffes: Gemeinsames Erbe der Menschheit. Deutsche Richterzeitung 1981 Aug. p.290

32.) *D. S. Myers*: Is there a CHM? IISL Coll. Proceedings 1990, p.335

33.) The origin of the idea to transfer the notion CHM into the system of space law is disputed in the literature Professor *A. A. Cocca*: suggested it to the COPUOS on June 19, 1967. Ambassador *Pardo* of Malta referred to CHM in a note-verbal on sea law August 17, 1967. *A. Bueckling* mentions a Resolution of the Institut de Droit International of 1937 on rights of sea fishery where it appeared in the form: "héritage commun de tous les hommes" in: Staatsgrenzen auf dem Mond. Juristenzeitung 1982 Nr.5-6, p.184

34.) *R. Hara–J. Stanczyk*: op.cit. Note 8, p.15.

35.) Webster's Dictionary. New York 1991 p.32

36.) *A. Berger*: Encyclopedic Dictionary of Roman Law. Philadelphia 1953. *Repr.* 1991, p.485

37.) *B. Nagy*: op.cit. Note 7, p.321

38.) "Due regard shall be paid to the interests of present and future generations..."

39.) *I. H. Ph. Diederiks-Verschoor*: An Introduction to Space Law. Deventer-Boston 1993, pp.91-92.

40.) Resolutions of VII (1969) and XII (1982) Kongresses of Instituto Hispano-Luso Americano de Derecho Internacional

41.) At the New Delhi Conference (2002) of ILA proposals were discussed for delation of the CHM formula replaced with "the province of all Mankind" (*Von der Dunk*) or "Common Concern of All Mankind" (*Maureen Williams*)

42.) *A. A. Cocca*: CHM a Basic Principle of the International Legal System. IISL Coll. Proceedings 1988, p.94

43.) *C. Q. Christol*: The Modern International Law of Outer Space. New York etc. 1982, p. 44

44.) This legal qualification of the general clauses has nothing to do with the obscure concept of "soft law" which by no means belongs to the treaty law, (See: *U. Fastenrath*: Lücken im Völkerrecht. Berlin 1991, p.178) and is more than "means of a semantic strategy" (See: *A. Bueckling*: Normative Erschöpfung im universellen Völkerrecht. (Ein Beitrag zur rechtlichen Archaik) Bayerische Verwaltungsblätter. 1984, Nr. 20, p.70)

IAC-03-IISL.2.12

INTERPRETING ARTICLE II OF THE OUTER SPACE TREATY

by

Wayne N. White, Jr.
Attorney at Law
1739 University Ave.
Oxford MS 38655
662-801-4515
wn_white@earthlink.net

Abstract

For many years, space lawyers have debated the meaning of Article II of the Outer Space Treaty. In particular, space lawyers have disagreed as to whether this provision prohibits "private appropriation" and private-entity ownership of real property rights. Various authors have also discussed the legality of *in situ* resource appropriation. In this article, the author analyzes these issues and offers his opinions on the legality of such activities under the terms of the Outer Space Treaty.

Introduction

98 nations are currently party to the 1967 Outer Space Treaty,[1] including the following spacefaring nations: Brazil, China, India, Japan, Russia, the United Kingdom, the United States, and the nations of western Europe.[2] Article I of the Outer Space Treaty says, among other things, that "Outer Space, including the moon and other celestial bodies, shall be free for exploration and *use* by all states without discrimination of any kind, on a basis of equality and in accordance with international law, and there shall be free access to all areas of celestial bodies" (emphasis added).[3] Article II of the Outer Space Treaty says that "Outer Space, including the moon and other celestial bodies, is not subject to *national appropriation* by claim of sovereignty, by means of use or occupation, or by any other means" (emphasis added). For many years, space lawyers have debated whether Article II prohibits "private appropriation" and private-entity ownership of real property rights. Taken together, Articles I and II have implications regarding the legality of use and appropriation of extracted resources.

In recent years several private organizations have been selling deeds to real property on the Moon and other celestial bodies,[4] while the Archimedes Institute has established a registry of claims to property in outer space on an internet web site.[5] Two other internet sites promote legal initiatives for the award of property rights or the recognition of property claims beyond the limits of national jurisdiction.[6] None of these commercial endeavors or legal initiatives require claimants to actually establish a permanent human presence or facility in the area claimed prior to the time when "title" is granted.

These real property endeavors and initiatives have generated controversy regarding the meaning of Article II. In this paper, the author interprets Articles I and II with respect to public and private-entity use and appropriation activities, including real property rights, and public and private use of *in situ* resources.

Real Property Rights

This author has written three previous articles concerning real property rights: *Real Property Rights in Outer Space,*[7] *Implications of a Proposal for Real Property Rights in Outer Space,*[8] and *Proposal for a Multilateral Treaty Regarding Jurisdiction and Real Property Rights in Outer Space.*[9] Other IISL members who have written about real property rights include Virgiliu Pop[10] and co-authors Patricia Sterns and Leslie I. Tennan.[11]

Clearing Up Some Misconceptions

The most prominent seller of real property deeds and titles is the Lunar Embassy, which was founded by Dennis Hope. The Lunar Embassy's web site states that "Well, in 1980, a very bright, young and handsome Mr. Dennis Hope, went to his local US Governmental Office for claim registries, the San Francisco County Seat, and made a claim for the entire lunar surface, as well as the surface of all the other eight planets of our solar system and their moons (except and the sun). Obviously, he was at first taken for a crackpot, until, 3 supervisors, 2 floors and 5 hours later, the main supervisor accepted, and registered his claim."[12]

Mr. Hope's narrative cannot be correct, however, because there is no such thing as a "US Governmental Office for claim registries." To the best of the author's knowledge, local government offices in the United States have no authority whatsoever to perform official services or render opinions on behalf of the United States federal government. The author believes that Mr. Hope probably prepared a written claim over the Moon and other celestial bodies in the solar system and then had the *County Recorder* for San Francisco County *record* that document. The discussions Mr. Hope had with various supervisors were undoubtedly because their office was not sure whether the claim document was the type of document that they could accept for recordation.

In the United States, the only purpose of recording a document at a county recorder's office is to prove that a document was prepared and executed on or before the recordation date, and to provide a permanent, public copy which the recorder can subsequently duplicate and certify as authentic upon payment of a fee. If the supervisor of the County Recorder's office agreed to record the document, it does not mean that either the US federal government or the San Francisco County government has decided that Mr. Hope's claim is valid. In the United States, only the courts can determine whether an interest in property is valid.

It follows from the preceding discussion that, to the best of the author's knowledge, United States federal, state and local governments have not taken any action which could be considered as an endorsement, approval or determination that Mr. Hope's claims have any legal validity or legitimacy under US law. Note also that the Lunar Embassy site does not cite any United States federal, state or local laws which would authorize sales of real estate in outer space or on celestial bodies, or which would establish a US registry of claims to areas of outer space. The author is not personally aware of any such laws in the United States or any other nation.

Does Article II Prohibit "Private Appropriation"?

In a private communication with the author, some space lawyers have asserted that many COPUOS delegates did not consider private participation in space activities to be feasible at the time when the Outer Space Treaty was drafted, and hence largely irrelevant to the drafting of the treaty. They say that the absence of any reference to private appropriation in Article II was just one manifestation of an absence of references to private parties, and not a specific exception to the general non-appropriation rule. They believe that private participation in outer space activities was not considered at all during Treaty negotiations.[13]

For several reasons, the author disagrees with these assertions. First, members of professional organizations clearly considered private space activities foreseeable at the time when the Outer Space Treaty was negotiated. In a draft treaty prepared in 1965-66, the International Institute of Space Law recommended that Article II specifically include a prohibition against "private appropriation": "Celestial bodies or regions on them shall not be subject to national *or private appropriation*, by claim of sovereignty, by means of use or occupation, or by any other means"(emphasis added)[14] One must assume that this draft treaty was transmitted to the COPUOS Legal Subcommittee, as the preamble says: "Intending to assist the general codification aims of the UN Charter and the efforts of the UN Committee on the Peaceful Uses of Outer Space concerning Celestial Bodies."[15] The Institute de Droit International also prepared a draft treaty which recommended prohibition of "any kind of appropriation."[16] This draft, along with two other draft treaties prepared by the International Law Association and the David Davies Memorial Institute of International Studies were apparently considered by the COPUOS Legal Subcommittee as well.[17]

Secondly, the Outer Space Treaty *does* specifically refer to private activities. The Soviet Union initially argued that space activities should "be carried out solely and exclusively by states,"[18] but the U.S. refused to accept that provision.[19] As a compromise, the United States proposed,[20] and the U.S.S.R. accepted,[21] the clause in Article VI which says that "[s]tates... shall bear international responsibility for national activities... whether such activities are carried on by governmental... or... *non-governmental entities*" (emphasis added).

Finally, the negotiating history of the Outer Space Treaty indicates that the United States, Great Britain, France, and Canada considered private activities both foreseeable and important, as reflected in their delegates' statements. In fact, private companies had already been formed to exploit the commercial facets of outer space when the treaty was negotiated. The best recitation of these facts is set forth in an article by J. F. McMahon, a fellow of Hertford College, Oxford, who, in

1963, wrote the following regarding the Soviet Union's Draft Declaration of the Basic Principles Governing the Activities of States Pertaining to the Exploration and use of Outer Space:

"Another basic and vital division of opinion concerned the question whether private corporations and international organizations, as well as States, might launch satellites and conduct activities in space. Paragraph 7 of the Soviet draft declaration of basic principles regulating outer space stipulated that: 'All activities of any kind pertaining to the exploration and use of outer space shall be carried out solely and exclusively by states . . . .'"[22]

"It is hardly surprising that Great Britain, France, Canada and America were vigorously opposed to such a provision. In Great Britain and America private companies have already been formed to exploit the commercial facets of outer space. The same countries, in order to facilitate a solution to the liability problem, would also seem to favour some system of licensing between States and private companies. International organizations, for example, the European Launcher and Development Organization and the European Space Research Organization, have already been established to achieve in a corporate manner what might be difficult for each State individually "[23]

Omitted footnotes in Dr. McMahon's article include specific quotes of the British, French and United States' delegates explaining their opposition to Paragraph 7 of the Soviet draft with citations to the United Nations documents in which they are recorded.[24]

On the basis of these facts, the author believes that the delegates that negotiated the Outer Space Treaty either deliberately chose to not include the phrase "private appropriation" in the language of Article II, or were unable to arrive at a consensus that such language should be included, perhaps because inclusion of the phrase might call into question the legality of private appropriation of extracted resources. This later interpretation is supported by the following quotes: "[i]n the discussions leading to the conclusion of the [Outer Space] treaty, France indicated more than once that she was not altogether satisfied with the wording of Article II . . . ." France's representative was "thinking in particular of the risks of ambiguity between the principle of non-sovereignty-- which falls under public law-- and that of non-appropriation, flowing from private law."[25]

In the original (long) version of the author's article *Real Property Rights in Outer Space*, he interpreted Article II as follows: "Outer space, including the moon and other celestial bodies is not subject to national [excluding private] appropriation, by claim of [territorial and not functional] sovereignty, by means of use or occupation or by any other means.[26] Twenty years later, his interpretation remains the same.

<u>Are Space Deeds Valid? Are Real Property Rights Prohibited by Article II?</u>

Because the language of Article II only refers to "national appropriation" and not private appropriation, this raises the question whether Article II prohibits private appropriation of territory and the more formal legal institution of real property rights. As the author explains in his article *Real Property Rights in Outer Space*, the Outer Space Treaty only permits states to exercise jurisdiction over their space objects, personnel, and arguably, zones of safety in the vicinity of their space objects and in areas where their citizens are conducting ongoing, significant activities. States have no jurisdiction or authority over any other areas of outer space or celestial bodies,[27] and therefore cannot grant or recognize permanent, immovable property rights in those areas. Granting or recognizing such rights beyond the limits of national jurisdiction, and thereby subjecting said areas to national jurisdiction, would violate Article II of the Outer Space Treaty because it would constitute "national appropriation . . . by any other means."[28] Depending on the size of the claimed area, granting or recognizing such property rights might also violate Article I, paragraph 2 of the Outer Space Treaty, which says that "Outer Space and celestial bodies shall be free for exploration and use by all states . . . ."

In the author's opinion, Treaty drafters intended that Article II would prohibit claims and exercise of territorial sovereignty by states party to the Treaty. Many prominent space lawyers who belong to the Institute have expressed the same opinion.[29] From a US perspective, one other authority on this point provides particular insight. Arthur J. Goldberg, then U.S. Representative to the General Assembly and principal U.S. negotiator of the Outer Space Treaty, made the following statements in United Nations Committee I (Political and Security) and in plenary session:

"[Outer Space Treaty Article I] goes on to make clear that the exploration and use of outer space shall be the right of all states without any discrimination and on a basis of equality. This and other provisions, *particularly that which prohibits claims of territorial sovereignty*, make clear the intent of the treaty that outer space and celestial bodies are open not just to the big powers or the first arrivals but shall be available to all, both now and in the future. This principle is a strong safeguard for the interests of those states which have, at the present time, little or no active space program of their own". (emphasis added).[30]

This quote enunciates what the author believes is the primary concern of those members of the Institute who insist that Article II of the Outer Space Treaty prohibits private appropriation as well as national appropriation: a concern that private appropriation of territory will result in *de facto* control of outer space by those nations that have the capability to develop and settle outer space first. The author believes that these fears are unfounded. He is not aware of any serious, informed lawyers from any nation who argue that states party to the Outer Space Treaty have a right to confer or recognize real property rights which involve any exercise of national jurisdiction over extraterrestrial territory. The only people who make such assertions are uninformed individuals who are neither trained in nor adequately knowledgeable about international space law.

In his article *Real Property Rights in Outer Space*, the author proposes a form of quasi property rights based upon the jurisdiction and control conferred by the Outer Space Treaty. The author further developed this proposal in *Implications of a Proposal for Real Property Rights in Outer Space* and *Proposal for a Multilateral Treaty Regarding Jurisdiction and Real Property Rights in Outer Space*. The author's principal purpose in developing this proposal was to bring the economic efficiency and benefits of real property rights to outer space while retaining the prohibition of territorial sovereignty in Article II of the Outer Space Treaty. The result is a new form of quasi property rights which are in reality a delegation of jurisdictional authority from Treaty parties to their national citizens. "Traditional" property rights, on the other hand, flow from and are based upon territorial sovereignty. Because they are based upon national jurisdiction over space objects and personnel, the author's proposed quasi property rights are moveable, as opposed to "traditional" property rights, which are immovable because they are tied to territory.

Some space lawyers believe that neither the US laws on private ownership of immovable property, nor any other national laws on such issues could ever apply to the moon or other celestial bodies.[31] However, many national property laws could be adapted to movable, non-permanent "property rights" such as those which the author has proposed, without requiring or providing a legal basis for permanent, immovable property rights. The author would therefore conclude that states party to the treaty cannot apply their laws on private ownership of real property, or any other national laws on such issues, to the moon and other celestial bodies, *to the extent that said laws would either explicitly or implicitly grant or recognize permanent rights in immovable property*. The terms of the Outer Space Treaty *do not* prohibit adaptation and extension of terrestrial property laws to *moveable* space objects, personnel and associated safety zones.

Does Sale of Space Deeds Constitute Fraud?

The fact that states party to the Outer Space Treaty cannot confer or recognize "traditional" real property rights leads one to question the validity of space property deeds. Do private entities that sell such deeds perpetrate a fraud upon purchasers? The author would submit that sales of such deeds may well constitute fraud, to the extent that the deeds convey title to territory beyond the limits of national jurisdiction, which the sellers represent as valid under national and international law.

The Lunar Embassy's main web site says that sale of Lunar Embassy deeds do not constitute fraud, and cites the silence of the United States and Russian governments, and the United Nations, as evidence that their deeds are valid. However, the web site, and possibly the deeds that the Lunar Embassy issues, state that the deeds are a "novelty gift." The web site says that their lawyers explained to them 23 years ago that labeling the property deeds as novelty gifts "can help avoid any frivolous lawsuits from a foreign country." However, the same section goes on to say that "this does not diminish the value of the property that you purchase in any way, as every deed is recorded and registered in the Lunar Embassy's registration database and every owners information is listed with that registration. *You own this property*" (emphasis added).[32]

Note that the main (US) Lunar Embassy web site does not prominently display an explanation that the deeds are only intended as novelty gifts. A person viewing the web site would have to search for and read the "General FAQ" (Frequently Asked Questions) to find that statement. The author questions whether a single statement that the deeds are novelty gifts, on a single web page, on a web site comprised of many web pages, constitutes adequate notice to purchasers of the true nature of their deeds. The adequacy of that notice is even more questionable given the statement *"You own this property."*

Because the Lunar Embassy deeds purportedly convey title to immovable real property, because states party to the Outer Space Treaty have no jurisdiction to confer or recognize such titles, because neither the United States nor any other nation has enacted laws regarding real property rights in outer space, and because private entities are not subjects of public international law, the Lunar Embassy has no authority to issue deeds or convey title to territory on celestial bodies or in outer space. The mere fact that Article II of the Outer Space Treaty does not prohibit "private appropriation" does not give private entities authority to confer or recognize titles to immovable real property. Furthermore, despite the Lunar Embassy's assertions, the silence of national governments and the United Nations cannot provide a legal basis for Dennis Hope's claim that he owns celestial bodies.[33]

Given the statement that its deeds are novelty gifts, and the differing definitions of fraud under various nations' legal systems, the author cannot conclusively say that the Lunar Embassy has perpetrated a fraud upon its customers. Other sellers of space deeds are more likely guilty of fraud, because several of those do not have "novelty" or other disclaimers.

What Action, If Any, Should Authorities Take?

Owners of space deeds, people who have registered claims on the Archimedes registry, and people asserting historical claims cause a certain amount of legal risk and uncertainty for prospective space entrepreneurs and their investors, and for prospective space settlers. Until such time as the law is clarified through national legislation and/or treaty law, there will always be a threat that deed owners and other claimants will file administrative claims and lawsuits against other entities that conduct activities or place space objects in outer space or on celestial bodies.

In fact, claimants have already sought administrative remedies and filed lawsuits. In 1997 three Yemeni gentlemen filed suit in a Yemen court alleging that Mars had belonged to their ancestors for 3000 years. They sought redress against NASA for trespassing on their property during the course of a Mars mission. The Yemeni men dismissed their suit when the prosecutor general threatened them with arrest. In another case, an Italian woman discovered that the Lunar Embassy had sold the same two plots that she purchased from a company called Celestial Gardens, and in September 2000 she reportedly sued for fraud and petitioned the White House and the United Nations.[34] The author does not know the outcome of that case.

In a more recent lawsuit, US citizen Gregory Nemitz sued NASA and the US State Department based upon a claim over the asteroid Eros, which Mr. Nemitz registered with the Archimedes Institute registry.[35] In the suit, Mr. Nemitz seeks a parking/storage fee from NASA for landing the NEAR spacecraft on the asteroid. He also seeks a declaratory judgment, alleging that NASA and the State Department unlawfully denied him property rights guaranteed by the United States Constitution.[36] The outcome of that case is still pending as this article is written, but the author would expect the US District Court to dismiss the case at an early stage of the proceedings.

Of particular interest in this case are the NASA and State Department responses to Mr. Nemitz' requests for administrative remedies prior to filing the lawsuit. In a letter dated April 9, 2001, then General Counsel of NASA Edward Frankle said the following:

"Your individual claim of appropriation of a celestial body (the asteroid 433 Eros) appears to have no foundation in law. It is unlike an individual's claim for seabed minerals, which was considered and debated by the U.S. Congress that subsequently enacted a statute, The Deep Seabed Hard Mineral Resource Act, P.L. 96-283, 94 Stat. 553 (1980), expressly authorizing such claims. There is no similar statute related in outer space.

Accordingly, your request for payment of a 'parking/storage fee' is denied. In taking this action NASA does not need to and does not take any position on whether the requirements of the Outer Space Treaty of 1967 apply to private individuals, or whether the Treaty should be amended for this purpose. Your claim depends on the establishment and validity of your ownership of asteroid 433. On the basis of the evidence provided, including your admission that the Archimedes Institute does not have legal authority to confer property rights, you have not established a legal right to any payment. Therefore, NASA has no authority to use its appropriated funds to pay your claim."[37]

In a letter dated August 15, 2003, Ralph L. Braibanti, the Director of Space and Advanced Technology in the Department of State's Bureau of Oceans and International Environmental and Scientific Affairs, wrote: "We have reviewed the 'Notice' dated February 13, 2003, that you sent to the U.S. Department of State. In the view of the Department, private ownership of an asteroid is precluded by Article II of the Treaty on Principles Governing the Activities of States in the Exploration and Use of Outer Space, including the Moon and Other Celestial Bodies (Outer Space Treaty of 1967). Accordingly, we have concluded that your claim is without legal basis."[38]

The preceding quotes seem to indicate that the views of NASA and the US State Department are consistent with the author's analysis. In light of what appears to be an international consensus regarding the illegality of "traditional" property rights, it seems unlikely that any informed national court would ever declare space deeds or other claims to immovable property valid. Nonetheless, administrative claims and lawsuits are a nuisance, entail defense costs, and may deter investment. What action should national authorities take in order to ameliorate or eliminate these impediments to space activity? Do the terms of the Outer Space Treaty obligate state parties to take action?

One course of action would be for state parties to file lawsuits against sellers of space deeds, educating the judiciary and establishing legal precedents in the process. Because space deeds and other property claims present the prospect of nuisance, defense costs and deterred investment, some may argue that state parties have an obligation to take legal action against purveyors of space deeds. That obligation would flow from Article VI of the Outer Space Treaty, which makes state parties internationally responsible for any activities of their citizens or other non-governmental entities in outer space and on celestial bodies, and requires state parties to authorise and continuously supervise those activities.

However, the author believes that nations which prosecute fraud suits will either be unsuccessful or find the cases not worth the cost of prosecution. Prospective fraud suits suffer from several possible infirmities. Because space deeds generally cost very little, the author suspects that most purchasers know that they are buying a mere novelty, and expect that the deeds will be nothing more than an interesting conversation item. The United States Lunar Embassy sells its space deeds for US \$19.99 ("Normal Deed") and US \$22.49 ("Deed with your name printed on it").[39] Other purveyors sell their deeds for small sums of money as well. Note that in the one instance where a citizen of the Netherlands sold space property for exorbitant amounts with no disclaimer, the perpetrator was promptly prosecuted for fraud.[40] The author does not know the outcome of that case or whether the court addressed issues of international space law.

Another weakness of prospective fraud suits is that victims of the allegedly fraudulent sales only suffer limited damages. The author would not expect courts to grant any remedy other than refund of the amounts that claimants spent on their deeds, and possibly, if requested, an injunction stating that the seller was prohibited from further sales of deeds until such time as their web site and other promotional materials prominently and unequivocally state that the deeds are sold as novelty gifts only. Because the prospects of succeeding in lawsuits against deed sellers are doubtful, and because the practical outcome of such suits might not produce any result other than limited monetary damages and a change of language on their web sites, the author does not believe that nations have been remiss in failing to take legal action. In the author's opinion, the best justification for such suits would be to clarify the law and establish a legal precedent. In the United States, Mr. Nemitz' suit may accomplish that purpose.

Aside from the issue of fraud, one might argue that deed owners and other claimants prospectively interfere with space activities such that Article IX of the Outer Space Treaty is invoked. Article IX says that "States Parties to the Treaty shall be guided by the principle of co-operation and mutual assistance . . . .," and also says "A State Party to the Treaty which has reason to believe that an activity or experiment planned by another State Party in outer space, including the moon and other celestial bodies, would cause potentially harmful interference with activities in the peaceful exploration and use of outer space, including the moon and other celestial bodies, may request consultation concerning the activity or experiment." In the author's opinion, consultations pursuant to Article IX, with the aim of amicably resolving mutual issues of concern, would be a productive way for states to proceed. Consultations might result in statutory language which states parties to the Treaty could enact uniformly, and possibly even a treaty which would expand upon Articles II and VIII of the Outer Space Treaty. This would be a very positive result for all concerned.

Resource Appropriation

If the terms of the Outer Space Treaty effectively prohibit immovable real property rights, what is the relevance of the term "private appropriation" with respect to Article II? Is it even necessary to determine whether Article II prohibits "private appropriation"?

First, the author believes that it is very wrong for academics to assert that the negotiators of the Outer Space Treaty intended to prohibit private appropriation, or did not even consider including the term, when the facts undeniably indicate otherwise. Academics should not attempt to rewrite history in order to support their views. Secondly, any conclusion regarding inclusion or exclusion of the term "private appropriation" in Article II has important implications with respect to resource appropriation. Analysis of those issues follows.

Is Private Resource Appropriation Prohibited by the Outer Space Treaty?

A broad interpretation of the term "private appropriation" would include both private appropriation of territory and private appropriation of extracted resources. However, the overwhelming majority of space lawyers regard private appropriation of extracted resources as permissible under the terms of the Outer Space Treaty. Ogunsola Ogunbanwo and Stephen Gorove are two prominent space lawyers that have expressed this opinion, in addition to other authors.[41] Another prominent space lawyer, D. Goedhuis, had the following to say in this regard:

"Art. II of the Treaty provides that outer space, including the moon and other celestial bodies, is not subject to national appropriation. Whereas this article has prohibited the appropriation of areas of outer space it is silent on the appropriation of resources. Although a number of commentators have contended that the appropriation of resources by a State would violate the 'benefit clause' contained in Art. I (1), the great majority of States, including the two Space Powers, consider the *de lege lata* appropriation of the natural resources of outer space, by analogy with the present rules underlying the freedom of the seas, merely forms part of the freedom of that space for exploration and use, a freedom which has been confirmed by the Treaty. Nothing has been said in the Treaty about the sharing or management of these resources.[42]

In his book THE MODERN INTERNATIONAL LAW OF OUTER SPACE, Professor Carl Christol sets forth the results of his detailed research regarding "the terms of Article 1, the meaning accorded to the words of the agreement at the time of its negotiation, the meaning assigned by publicists both contemporaneously with the negotiation of the agreement and recently, the practices of the space-resource States both prior to and following the entry into force of the Treaty, and the denials addressed to the claims put forward in 1976 by eight equatorial States. . ."[43] Because of the length of the analysis, that passage is not reproduced here. Fortunately, Professor Christol has provided us with a more succinct statement of his conclusions in another publication:

"In a larger context it is relevant to observe that international law does contain specific prohibitions against certain forms of conduct, but that in the absence of such prohibitions both States and other juridical and natural persons are entitled to engage in conduct without its being described as unlawful. Since Article 2 of the Principles Treaty did not prohibit the private use and exploitation of natural resources, and since one of the purposes of Article I was to allow for the sharing of benefits derived from the exploration and use of the space environment, it may be concluded that private persons were in effect encouraged to engage in private space activities. Such conduct would fit into the expectations fortified by the *res communis* concept in its joint application to the conduct of States, international organizations, and private natural and juridical persons. The absence of any prohibition on the private use and exploitation of the natural resources of the moon and other celestial bodies in the Principles Treaty must, therefore, allow such space activity to take place, unless such activity is prohibited under other norms of international law. None appear to exist.

The terms of Article 2 of the Principles Treaty restrict only national appropriation of spatial areas. Thus, to the extent that states, pursuant to Article 6 of that Treaty, authorize private legal persons to engage in exploitative activity regarding the natural resources of such spatial areas, such private activity would be permissible under both municipal laws and international law. If the drafters of the Principles Treaty had wished to bar the exploitation of the natural resources of the moon and other celestial bodies by private legal persons, or if they had wished to prevent the acquiring of private property rights in such materials, they could have done so. The fact that such rights to exploit and to establish property rights in such natural resources were not specifically granted to private persons cannot serve to deny such claims when they are put forward. Nonetheless, in the search for legal security it is always preferable to have reliance on specific grants of authority. This fact influenced the governments holding membership in COPUOS to begin the preparation of an international agreement on this subject in 1970."[44]

As most readers are well aware, the international agreement that Professor Christol refers to was eventually finalized as the 1979 Moon Treaty.[45] That agreement specifically prohibits real property rights, except perhaps under the auspices of the "international regime" established by the treaty, and mandates "an equitable sharing by all States Parties in the benefits derived from those resources, whereby the interests and needs of the devloping countries, as well as the efforts of those countries which have contributed either directly or indirectly to the exploration of the moon, shall be given special consideration."[46] The overwhelming majority of the world's nations decided not to become party to that treaty, including all of the spacefaring nations.[47] In light of the fact that there is no widely-accepted international agreement which governs resource appropriation any more specifically than the Outer Space Treaty, the author concludes that for all nations which are not party to the Moon Treaty, private and commercial appropriation of natural resources is permissible in outer space. The author bases this conclusion on the terms of the Outer Space Treaty, the previously-cited authorities, and in particular the detailed research and analysis performed by Professor Christol.

Is Public Resource Appropriation Prohibited by The Outer Space Treaty?

The analysis with respect to public appropriation of resources is slightly different. In this instance, there is a tension between the Article II prohibition of "national appropriation," and the Article I agreement that state parties may "use" outer space and celestial bodies. Does "use" of resources ever rise to the level of "national appropriation"? The language and terms of the Outer Space Treaty provide no real guidance.

The quotations from the work of Prof./Dr. Goedhuis and Professor Christol in the preceding section do assist us in this regard, however. Prof./Dr. Goedhuis says: "Whereas [Article II] has prohibited the appropriation of areas of outer space it is silent on the appropriation of resources."[48] Similarly, Professor Christol says: "The terms of Article 2 of the Principles Treaty restrict only national appropriation of spatial areas." These statements are consistent with the opinions of other prominent space lawyers,[49] including the author's opinion above that "Treaty drafters intended that Article II would prohibit claims and exercise of territorial sovereignty by states party to the Treaty."

Because Article II only prohibits national appropriation of spatial areas and the exercise of territorial sovereignty over such areas, one must conclude that public entities can appropriate natural resources in outer space and on celestial bodies, so long as their activities do not involve any permanent claims to, appropriation of, or exercise of authority over the areas in which resources are appropriated. Note that space objects and personnel occupy locations in outer space and on celestial bodies on a first-come, first-served basis,[50] and Article IX prohibits other nations and their private entities from interfering with activities at that location. Thus, public entities can appropriate resources without interference from other entities, but once a public entity ceases resource appropriation activities and removes facilities from the area, the entity loses all rights with respect to the area in question (*i.e.* it has no permanent rights). The same rules would apply to private resource appropriation.

Conclusion

In the author's opinion there are sufficient facts to support a conclusion that Article II of the Outer Space Treaty does not prohibit private appropriation. However, the Outer Space Treaty only permits states to exercise jurisdiction over their space objects, personnel, and zones of safety in the vicinity of their space objects and in areas where their citizens are conducting ongoing, significant activities. States have no jurisdiction or authority over any other areas of outer space or celestial bodies, and therefore cannot grant or recognize permanent, immovable property rights in those areas. Granting or recognizing real property rights beyond the limits of national jurisdiction, and thereby subjecting said areas to national jurisdiction, would violate Article II of the Outer Space Treaty because it would constitute "national appropriation . . . by any other means."

States party to the treaty cannot apply their laws on private ownership of real property, or any other national laws on such issues, to the moon and other celestial bodies, to the extent that those laws would either explicitly or implicitly grant or recognize permanent rights in immovable property. The terms of the

Outer Space Treaty do not prohibit adaptation and extension of terrestrial property laws to *moveable* space objects, personnel and associated safety zones.

To the best of the author's knowledge, United States federal, state and local governments have not taken any action which could be considered as an endorsement, approval or determination that space deeds or other claims to celestial bodies have any legal validity or legitimacy under US law. Sales of space deeds may well constitute fraud, to the extent that the deeds convey title to territory beyond the limits of national jurisdiction, which the sellers represent as valid under national and international law. Because the prospects of succeeding in lawsuits against deed sellers are doubtful, and because the practical outcome of such suits might not produce any result other than limited monetary damages and a change of language on their web sites, the author does not believe that nations have been remiss in failing to take legal action.

Consultations pursuant to Article IX of the Outer Space Treaty, with the aim of amicably resolving mutual issues of concern, would be a productive way for states to proceed with respect to real property rights. Consultations might result in statutory language which states party to the Treaty could enact uniformly, and possibly even a treaty which would expand upon Articles II and VIII of the Outer Space Treaty. This would be a very positive result for all concerned.

The overwhelming majority of space lawyers regard private appropriation of extracted resources as permissible under the terms of the Outer Space Treaty. There is no widely-accepted international agreement which governs resource appropriation any more specifically than the Outer Space Treaty, so the author concludes that for all nations which are not party to the Moon Treaty, private, commercial appropriation of natural resources is permissible in outer space.

Public entities can appropriate resources so long as their activities do not involve any permanent claims to, appropriation of, or exercise of authority over the areas in which resources are appropriated. Public and private entities can appropriate resources without interference from other entities, but once an entity ceases appropriation activities and removes facilities, the entity loses all rights with respect to the area in question. Although entities have no permanent rights with respect to any area of outer space or celestial bodies, quasi property rights based on jurisdiction could provide a market mechanism which would operate in a manner substantially identical to "traditional" property rights, with all the economic efficiencies of that institution.

The opinions expressed by the author herein do not constitute legal advice or representation. If any individuals or other private entities have any question about the legality of their business activities, they should consult an attorney or other properly licensed legal professional and obtain formal representation if necessary.

REFERENCES

1. Treaty on Principles Governing the Activities of States on the Exploration and Use of Outer Space Including the Moon and Other Celestial Bodies, *done* Jan. 27, 1967, 18 U.S.T. 2410, T.I.A.S. No. 6347, 610 U.N.T.S. 205 (*entered into force* Oct. 10, 1967).

2. The United Nations Office of Outer Space Affairs listed 98 nations as partes to the Outer Space Treaty as of November 12, 2003. http://registry.oosa.unvienna.org/oosa/treaty_status/index.stm (scroll down, "click here to search," Query: Name of Treaty: "Outer Space Treaty," State/Organization: "all states and organizations," Status: "party")(accessed Nov. 12, 2003).

3. *Id.*

4. IISL member Virgiliu Pop's article *The Men Who Sold the Moon: Science Fiction or Legal Nonsense?*, 17 SPACE POLICY 195, 195-197 (2001), contains an excellent, detailed discussion of the various organizations that are selling outer space deeds.

5. Archimedes Institute, Claims Registration, www.permanent.com/archimedes/PropertyRegistry.html (accessed Nov. 10, 2003). Note that the administrator of this registry has acted in a responsible and professional manner. The site's Disclaimer section says, among other things, "The Institute makes no warranties either express or implied regarding the validity of the claims filed with the registries by any and all claimants. . . . The Archimedes Institute makes no claims of ownership on space resources by virtue of this Registry."

6. *See* "The Lunar Settlement Initiative," www.lunarsettlement.org (accessed Nov. 10, 2003); "An Act to Promote Privately Funded Space Settlement," www.spacesettlement.org/law (accessed Nov. 10, 2003).

7. Wayne N. White, Jr., *Real Property Rights in Outer Space*, PROCEEDINGS, FORTIETH COLLOQUIUM ON THE LAW OF OUTER SPACE, at 370 (IISL, 1998).

8. Wayne N. White, Jr., *Implications of a Proposal for Real Property Rights in Outer Space*, PROCEEDINGS, FORTY-SECOND COLLOQUIUM ON THE LAW OF OUTER SPACE, at 366 (IISL, 2000).

9. Wayne N. White, Jr., *Proposal for a Multilateral Treaty Regarding Jurisdiction and Real Property Rights in Outer Space*, PROCEEDINGS, FORTY-THIRD COLLOQUIUM ON THE LAW OF OUTER SPACE, at 245 (IISL, 2001).

10. Virgiliu Pop, *Appropriation in Outer Space: the Relationship Between Land Ownership and Sovereignty on the Celestial Bodies*, 16 SPACE POLICY 275 (2000); Virgiliu Pop, *supra*, note 4.

11. Patricia Sterns and Les Tennan have written many articles on the subject of real property rights in outer space. The most recent is: Patricia M. Sterns & Leslie I. Tennan, *Privateering and Profiteering on the Moon and Other Celestial Bodies: Debunking the Myth of Property Rights in Outer Space*, PROCEEDINGS, FORTY FIFTH COLLOQUIUM ON THE LAW OF OUTER SPACE 56 (2003); published with same title at 31 ADVANCES IN SPACE RESEARCH 2433 (2003).

12. http://www.lunarembassy.com/ls/legeneralfaq_e.shtml (accessed Nov. 10, 2003).

13. Confidential written communication on file with the author. Not for public dissemination.

14. International Institute of Space Law, *Draft Resolution of the International Institute of Space Law Concerning the Legal Status of Celestial Bodies*, in PROC., SEVENTH COLLOQUIUM ON THE LAW OF OUTER SPACE 351, 353 (1965); *see also* PROC., EIGHTH COLLOQUIUM ON THE LAW OF OUTER SPACE 464-69 (1966); PROC., TENTH COLLOQUIUM ON THE LAW OF OUTER SPACE 13 (1968); Carl Christol, *The Common Heritage of Mankind Provision in the 1979 Agreement Governing the Activities of States on the Moon and Other Celestial Bodies*, 14 INT'L LAW 429, 439 (1980); Kiss, *General Principles for International Law of Celestial Bodies*, in PROC., SEVENTH COLLOQUIUM ON THE LAW OF OUTER SPACE 287,289 (1965).

15. *Circular No. 12, Annex I, Draft Resolution of the Working Group III of the International Institute of Space Law Concerning the Legal Status of Celestial Bodies with the Last Remarks Given at the VIIth Colloquium on the Law of Outer Space at Warsaw in September 1964*, PROC., EIGHTH COLLOQUIUM ON THE LAW OF OUTER SPACE 467 (1966).

16. Institute de Droit International, *Resolution on the Legal Regime of Outer Space (unanimously adopted Sept. 11, 1963)*, *reprinted in* C.W. Jenks, SPACE LAW 416 (1965).

17. O. Ogunbanwo, INTERNATIONAL LAW AND OUTER SPACE ACTIVITIES 21 (1975) ("The number of studies which were produced and which helped in the drafting of the various space treaties, were not limited to international jurists but included those studies prepared by professional international organizations. Among the most notable organizations were the Institut de Droit International, The International Law Association and the David Davies Memorial Institute of International Studies.").

18. Draft Declaration of the Basic Principles Governing the Activities of States Pertaining to the Exploration and Use of Outer Space, U.N. Doc. A/AC. 105/L.2 (1962); U.N. Doc. A/5181, Annex 3 (1962).

19. The United States maintained that a right had already been established for private firms to engage in space activities as reflected in the Communications Satellite Act of 1962. OFFICE OF TECHNOLOGY ASSESSMENT, U.S. CONGRESS, CIVILIAN SPACE POLICY AND APPLICATIONS 349 (1982); Carl Christol, *supra*, note 14, at 436.

20. U.S. Draft Declaration of Principles Relating to the Exploration and Use of Outer Space, U.N. Doc. A/C.l/881 at 23, art. 6 (1962).

21. U.N. Doc. A/AC.105/PV.22 at 37 (1962).

22. J. F. McMahon, *Legal Aspects of Outer Space*, 38 BRIT. Y.B. INT'L L. 339,351 (1963).

23. *Id.*

24. Great Britain: U.N. Doc. A/AC.105/C.2/S.R.10, Legal Sub-committee on Outer Space, 21 August 1962, p.3; France: U.N. Doc. A/AC.105/C.2/S.R.9, Legal Sub-committee on Outer Space, 21 August 1962, p.3; Canada: Ibid., p.6; America [United States]: A/AC.105/C.2/S.R.7, Legal Sub-committee on Outer Space, 21 August 1962, p.9.

25. U.N. Doc. A/AC.105/C.2/SR.70 at 14 (1966); U.N. Doc. A/AC.105/PV.44 at 41 (1966).

26. Wayne N. White, Jr., *Real Property Rights in Outer Space*, unpublished academic version, Copyright © 1985 by Wayne N. White, Jr., at p. 10 (copy on file with author); previously published in five installments, with same title and text but limited footnotes, in the monthly magazine L5 NEWS, Oct 1983 - July 1984.

27. *E.g.* Bin Cheng, *The Extra-Terrestrial Application of International Law*, 1965 CURRENT LEGAL PROBS. 132, 142 (1965). Therein Professor/Dr. Cheng said:

"Thus, until and unless territorial sovereignty has been established and recognised in outer space or on celestial bodies, no State will be entitled to exercise territorial jurisaction there. In the absence of territorial jurisaction, quasi-territorial jurisaction becomes supreme. None but the flag-State, however, is entitled to exercise quasi-territorial jurisaction over any spacecraft, or persons and things on board them, extra-terrestrially. If such persons are not subject to the quasi-territorial jurisaction of any State, then only the national State may normally exercise personal jurisaction over them. Any attempt to exercise jurisaction in outer space on celestial bodies in excess of these limits will be an infringement of the right of either the flag-State or the national State of the individual, as the case may be, and a violation of international law."

28. Virgiliu Pop agrees with the author in this respect. He says that "State endorsement of private appropriation [of spatial areas] would be a form of national appropriation." Virgiliu Pop, *supra*, note 4, at 199.

29. *E.g.* Manfred Lachs, THE LAW OF OUTER SPACE 42-43 (1972)(interpreting the language of Article II as referring to the various methods of perfecting a claim of territorial sovereignty); Cestmir Cepelka and Jamie H. C. Gilmour, *The Application of General International Law in Outer Space*, 36 J. AIR L. & COMMERCE 30, 35 (1970) ("Since article II of the Treaty clearly means nothing more than non-acquisition of territorial sovereignty, there can be no territorial

jurisdiction over any part of outer space, including celestial bodies."); Stephen Gorove, *Sovereignty and the Law of Outer Space Re-Examined*, 2 ANNALS OF AIR & SPACE L. 311, 321 (1977) ("As a final thought one would perhaps - with some caveat - draw the conclusion that the traditional aspects of territorial sovereignty are the ones that have been abolished in relation to outer space but the functional aspects of sovereignty, the exercise of sovereign rights and similar manifestations continue to be recognized. The one caveat to the preceding statement appears to be the state's exercise of its exclusive authority over a station (settlement, habitat) built in free space, particularly out of materials originating from the Earth."); *see* Martin Menter, *Commercial Participation in Space Activities*, 5 J. SPACE L. 53, 65 (1981) ("Disclaimer of sovereignty over the moon and other celestial land masses was intended to obviate possible conflicts over 'territorial claims' . . . .").

30. DEPT. OF STATE BULLETIN, January 9, 1967, p. 81.

31. *Supra*, note 13.

32. http://www.lunarembassy.com/ls/legeneralfaq_e.shtml (accessed Nov. 11, 2003).

33. Virgiliu Pop, *supra*, note 4, at 200 (and citations therein).

34. Virgiliu Pop, *supra*, note 4, at 197 (and citations therein).

35. Nemitz v. US Dept. of State, NASA, US Dist. Court for the Dist. of Nevada, Case No. CV-N-03-0599-HDM-RAM (filed with the Court Nov. 6, 2003).

36. http://www.erosproject.com/legal.html?source=ErosProject (and links therein) (accessed Nov. 11, 2003).

37. http://www.orbdev.com/010409.html (accessed Nov. 11, 2003).

38. http://www.erosproject.com/030824.html (accessed Nov. 11, 2003).

39. http://www.lunarembassy.com/ (select country, then click on "buy now" at top of page) (accessed Nov. 12, 2003).

40. The Netherlands ambassador of the Lunar Embassy was selling deeds for US $1,600.00 and failed to deliver deeds to purchasers. http://www.cbsnews.com/stories/2003/02/03/national/main539148.shtml (look for item entitled "Lunar Real Estate Agent Jailed")(accessed Nov. 11, 2003).

41. Stephen Gorove, *Implications of International Space Law for Private Enterprise*, 7 ANNALS AIR & SPACE L. 319, 323 (1982) ("Article II of the Outer Space Treaty places a ban on national appropriation of outer space, including the moon and other celestial bodies, by any means. While

the sweeping language of this article could have been interpreted to relate both to area as well resources, the United Nations Committee on the Peaceful Uses of Outer Space has not regarded Article II as a ban on appropriation or exploitation of natural resources. If it had, then the long debated issue whether the Moon Agreement would place a moratorium on the exploitation of natural resources would have been meaningless."); Alan Duane Webber, *Extraterrestrial Law on the Final Frontier: A Regime to Govern the Development of Celestial Body Resources*, 71 GEO. L. J. 1427, 1429, n. 22 (1983) ("Although the treaty refers only to free exploration and use, its legislative history demonstrates that article one applies also to exploitation of natural resources").

42. D. Goedhuis, *Some Recent Trends in the Interpretation and the Implementation of the Rules of International Space Law*, 19 COLUMBIA J. OF TRANSNATIONAL L. 213, 219 (1981).

43. Carl Q. Christol, THE MODERN INTERNATIONAL LAW OF OUTER SPACE 42 (1982).

44. Carl Q. Christol, *The Common Heritage of Mankind Provision in the 1979 Agreement Governing the Activities of States on the Moon and Other Celestial Bodies*, 14 INT'L LAW 429, 448 (1980).

45. Agreement Governing the Activities of States on the Moon and Other Celestial Bodies, U.N. Doc. A/AC.105-L.113/Add.4 (1979), *entered into force* Jul. 11, 1984.

46. *Id.*, at Article 11.

47. The United Nations Office of Outer Space Affairs listed ten nations as partes to the Outer Space Treaty as of November 12, 2003. http://registry.oosa.unvienna.org/oosa/treaty_status/index.stm (scroll down, "click here to search," Query: Name of Treaty: "Moon Treaty," State/Organization: "all states and organizations," Status: "party")(accessed Nov. 12, 2003).

48. D. Goedhuis, *supra*, note 42.

49. *Supra*, note 29.

50. Wayne N. White, Jr., *supra*, note 26, at 12 (and citations therein).

Transfer of satellites in orbit. An International Law Approach

Dr. Julian Hermida[(1)]

[(1)] *LL.M. and D.C.L (McGill), PDF (Ottawa), julianhermida@justice.com*

ABSTRACT

The legal literature has voiced concerns about the possibility of transferring satellite ownership in orbit, especially to a non launching state, as the Registration Convention does not expressly contemplate this situation. This assertion ignores the full array of possibilities permitted both by the Convention and general international law. The article intends to explore the legal feasibility of transferring satellites that are already in orbit both to launching and non launching states. The pivotal thesis is that an interplay between article II of the Registration Convention, which does not prohibit the transfer of all the jurisdictional and control rights, and the international –both conventional and customary- norms on stipulation of rights to a third State provides an adequate legal framework for the transfer of a satellite in orbit –even to a non launching state- without any amendment to the Registration Convention.

INTRODUCTION

The legal literature has voiced concerns about the possibility of transferring satellite ownership in orbit, especially to a non launching state, as the Registration Convention does not expressly contemplate this situation[1].

An analysis of International Law and conventional Space Law clearly shows that that these concerns are unfounded and that transfer of satellites in orbit is legally possible, even to non launching states.

CUSTOMARY INTERNATIONAL LAW

Since the State of registry has been defined in the Registration Convention as "a launching State on whose registry a space object is carried in accordance with article II", it follows from this definition that there may be only one State of registry.

Difficulties have arisen with respect to the transfer of satellites in orbit, especially in the case of sale of satellites. In this respect, two sets of facts have to be differentiated: the transfer of satellites between launching States and the transfer of satellites to a non launching State.[2] There have been some cases in practice, such as the transfer of satellites registered in the United Kingdom to China as a consequence of the hand over of Hong Kong or the sale of Canada's Anik CI and CII satellites to Argentina,[3] among some other ones. These isolated cases may not be considered to amount to a general and consistent practice of States followed from a sense of legal obligation, and thus there is no rule of customary international law governing the transfer of satellite ownership in orbit.[4] Since recourse to general principles does not either offer any solution to this problem the analysis must be done exclusively in light of the conventional sources.

TRANSFER TO LAUNCHING STATES

The legal literature agrees that transfers of satellites in orbit among launching States would be permitted under the Registration Convention and would not offer major difficulties, such as is evidenced by the Hong Kong precedent.[5]

This is so because according to the Registration Convention, in the event that there are several launching States these have to determine which one of them will register the object in its national registry. These States may further agree on the application of certain aspects of the legislation of the State which will not act as State of registry.[6]

TRANSFER TO NON LAUNCHING STATES

However, with respect to the transfer of ownership in orbit to a non launching State, the answer given in the literature is that the Registration Convention does not permit any modification in this case.[7] This is grounded on the premise that the according to the Registration Convention the State of registry has to be one of the launching States, i.e., a State which launches or procures the launching of a space object; a State from whose territory or facility a space object is launched[8].

This assertion ignores the full array of possibilities permitted both by the Convention and general international law[9]. In this respect, the Registration Convention allows the possibility of launching States to conclude agreements on jurisdiction and control over the space object and over any personnel thereof.[10] Thus, launching States can decide to transfer certain jurisdictional rights to others, such as in the case of criminal law under the Intergovernmental Agreement on the International Space Station.[11] As put forward by Aldo Cocca, this reflects the principle that special agreements override general ones and the unitary criteria of Art. II (1) of the Convention.[12]

Nothing in Art. II of the Registration Convention prohibits the transfer of all the jurisdictional and control rights. Therefore, it is legally possible for a State to register a space object and to enter into an agreement with another launching State to transfer part or all of the rights and obligations arising from the registration of a space object. Moreover, it is legally tenable to transfer rights to a non launching State, for the Registration Convention simply prescribes that any such agreement must be made among the launching States. In this respect, a launching State which intends to transfer rights to a non launching State will have to conclude with all the other launching States the transfer of jurisdiction and control rights and obligations to a third non launching State.[13] Under general public international law, the stipulation of rights to a third State is permitted both under customary and conventional law. In effect, in the Free Zones Case, the Permanent Court of International Justice held that "it cannot be lightly presumed that stipulations favorable to a third State have been adopted with the object of creating an actual right in its favor. There is however nothing to prevent the will of sovereign States from having this object and this effect. The question of the existence of a right acquired under an instrument drawn between other States is therefore one to be decided in each particular case: it must be ascertained whether the States which have stipulated in favor of a third State meant to create for that State an actual right which the latter has accepted as such."[14] Furthermore, Art. 34 of the Vienna Convention establishes that no rights and responsibilities may be created for third parties, except for with the consent of the third party. In such case, there must be acceptance of the third party. In case when the parties intended to create a benefit, the acceptance may be presumed. However, in cases when the States created an obligation acceptance must be in writing.[15]

Additionally, it must be borne in mind that the concept of launching state is not only acquired at the moment of the launch but may be acquired later as in the case of the state that procures the launch.

Thus, once a satellite is sold to a non launching state according to the provisions of international law that state becomes a launching state according to both the Registration Convention and the Liability Convention.

CONCLUSIONS

The transfer of satellite ownership in orbit is legally possible under international law. This, however, requires an agreement among the launching States to transfer all of the jurisdiction and control rights and obligations in favor of a third non launching State. In light of customary and conventional international rules on effects of treaties to third parties acceptance in writing of the non launching State is essential.

---

[1] Kerrest, "Remarks on the Notion of Launching State" (1999) 41 IISL at 309.

[2] J. Hermida, *Legal Basis for a National Space Legislation*, (DCL, Thesis, McGill University, 2003) [unpublished], at 65.

[3] In order to establish a temporary satellite system to comply with ITU timelines Argentina purchased the Anik CI and Anik CII satellites to Telesat Canada by the Argentine corporation Paracom S.A. Both companies -Paracom and Telesat- formed the Paracomsat joint venture, which was in charge of the operation of the Anik satellites. Both Canadian satellites had to be moved approximately 30° to the East from their original position, to be situated at 76° West (Anik CI) and 72° West (Anik CII). Paracomsat leased transponder capacity not only to Argentine corporations -ATC Cable, Crónica TV, Canal 8 de Mar del Plata-, but also to Uruguayan television channels -4, 10, and 12 of Montevideo-, which sets the basis for a potential regional system. The satellites remained registered in Canada. J. Hermida, "Argentine Space Law and Policy" (1996) XXI-II *Ann. Air & Sp. L.* at 177 [hereinafter "Argentine Space Law and Policy"].

[4] *Ibid.* at 178.

[5] R. J. Lee, "Effects of Satellite Ownership Transfers on the Liability of the Launching States" (2000) 43 IISL at 148. Kerrest, "Remarks on the Notion of Launching State" (1999) 41 IISL at 309.

[6] J. Hermida, *Commercial Space Law: International, National and Contractual Aspects* (Buenos Aires: Ediciones Depalma, 1997) at 63. It must be highlighted that in the International Governmental Agreement on the Space Station, States opted for the registration in a separate way of each element contributed by the States. European States delegated this responsibility to the European Space Agency. In effect, pursuant to Art. 5 of the Agreement each partner will register as space objects the flight elements which it provides, which are all listed in an annex to the Agreement. IGA, Art. 5.

[7] Kerrest, "Remarks on the Notion of Launching State" (1999) 41 IISL at 309.

[8] A. A. Cocca, "Registration of Space Objects", N. Jasentuliyana & R.S.K. Lee eds., *Manual on Space Law* (New York: Oceana, 1979) Vol. 1 at 180.

[9] J. Hermida, Legal Basis for a National Space Legislation (Dordrecht: Kluwer Academic Publishers, 2004) at 65.

[10] Registration Convention, Art. II.

[11] *Agreement among the Government of Canada, the Governments of Member States of the European Space Agency, the Government of Japan, the Government of the Russian Federation, and the Government of the United States of America concerning Cooperation on the Civil International Space Station, signed January 29, 1998*, Art. 22.

[12] A. A. Cocca, "Registration of Space Objects", in N. Jasentuliyana & R.S.K. Lee eds., *Manual on Space Law* (New York: Oceana, 1979) Vol. 1 at 180.

[13] Registration Convention, Art. II (2).

[14] Free Zones Case, France v. Switzerland, 1932, PCIJ at. 97.

[15] Vienna Convention, Art. 34.

SPACE POLICY PERSPECTIVES OF THE SPACE GENERATION

Isabel Pessoa-Lopes[1]
Space Generation Advisory Council
ipl@unsgac.org

ABSTRACT

Space Policy was a topic of discussion at the Space Generation Forum (SGF), UNISPACE III (1999) and its recommendations were further developed at the Space Generation Summit (SGS), an event held at World Space Congress (WSC) in 2002. This paper builds upon those findings and addresses key other emergent space policy issues.

The material in this paper, reports the work to date on consolidating the views of young space professionals regarding Space Policy issues, and strategic plans to help solving key questions currently facing the international space workforce. We also discuss the most relevant issues of SGAC's recent input to the United Nations Committee on the Peaceful Uses of Space (UN COPUOS) towards the implementation of the recommendations of UNISPACE III.

1. HISTORICAL BACKGROUND

Today, a new generation of inspired and driven people, that mutually share the passion and awe of exploring space, who wants to share the knowledge and experiences with all the people of the world, is gradually gathering together on a global scale independent of national borders, cultures and languages. The generations born and raised after Yuri Gagarin and the Apollo missions are now known as the '**Space Generation**'.

The Space Generation originally met at the **Space Generation Forum** (SGF), held during the Third United Nations Conference on the Exploration and Peaceful Uses of Outer Space (UNISPACE III), Vienna, Austria, in July 1999. The 200+ delegates and organisers of the Space Generation Forum were from 60 nations.
Their expertise covered all fields of space, including science, technology, law, ethics, art, literature, anthropology and architecture, and many other fields relevant to space.

These participants were encouraged from the beginning to think in terms of a broader perspective, encompassing all humanity, and to disregard national agendas. All participants spoke only as concerned individuals, guided by their conscience and a belief in the power of space to change humanity in positive ways.

The Space Generation Forum became an unprecedented opportunity for young space students and professionals from around the world to bring their vision and perspective on what should be the focus of space activities in the next century to the current leaders and decision makers in the space arena, as well as contribute to shaping humankind's future in outer space.

More than 40 fresh ideas, alternative scenarios and new insights from the viewpoint of highly skilled young people were generated and compiled into a report in an "extraordinary marathon against time".

[1] This paper is written in the Author's personal capacity and does not necessarily represent the views of the Space Generation Advisory Council (SGAC).

The discussions of the Space Generation Forum resulted in 49 recommendations[2] and the participants were then asked to choose their 10 best recommendations. Consensus was achieved concerning the selection of the 10 recommendations, and these were submitted[3] to the Secretariat of UNISPACE III. On approval at UNISPACE III final Plenary Session, these SGF recommendations were then included in the **UNISPACE III Report**[4] and detailed in **SGF Technical Report**[5] **to UNISPACE III.**

Last but not least, the **Vienna Declaration**[6] (prime summary of the whole UNISPACE III conference) consists of 10 recommendations of which half were directly incorporated from the work of SGF. This fact alone, if necessary, entitles the Space Generation to claim that SGF was indeed a remarkable youth success by any world standards!

The 10 SGF recommendations are the following (the ones in bold were included in the Vienna Declaration):

1: **Global Space Education Curriculum**
2: **Nobel Space Prize**
3: **Priority Access to Mobile Satcom Network for Disaster Emergency Management**
4: Action Plan for Meeting the World's Basic Needs through Technology
5: International Space Authority
6: International Space Chamber of Commerce
7: **Planetary Defence/Protection**
8: Establishment of an International Centre for Space Medicine
9: **UN Space Advisory Council**
10: SGF Follow-up

One of the main outcomes of SGF was the approval of its recommendation to ***"create, within the framework of the Committee on the Peaceful Uses of Outer Space (COPUOS), a consultative mechanism to facilitate the continued participation of young people from all over the world, especially young people from developing countries and young women, in co-operative space-related activities"***. (SGF Rec.9, incorporated into the Vienna Declaration as Rec. 22, and currently also known as UNI-3 Implementation Action Team 22).

[2] UNISPACE III docs: A/CONF.184/L.8, annex
[3] UNISPACE III docs: A/CONF.184/C.1/L.11
[4] UNISPACE III docs: A/CONF.184/6, Part 3, pgs 104-107 (http://www.oosa.unvienna.org/unisp-3/index.html)
[5] UNISPACE III docs: A/CONF.184/L.14
[6] http://www.oosa.unvienna.org/unisp-3/index.html

In order to create this consultative mechanism, the Youth Advisory Council (YAC) - the precursor of SGAC - was established in 2000 to serve as an *interim voluntary body* and to support its Advisors (ex-SGF Delegates) in assisting UN COPUOS and the Office for Outer Space Affairs (OOSA). At the end of this *interim period*, the **Space Generation Advisory Council in support of the United Nations Programme on Space Applications**[7] (SGAC) was formally created in June 2001, and registered in Vienna, Austria. Furthermore, SGAC was officially granted Permanent Observer Status to COPUOS at the UN General Assembly (fifty-sixth Session, NY)[8], in December 2001.

2. SPACE POLICY PERSPECTIVES OF THE SPACE GENERATION

Since its creation, the Space Generation Advisory Council has been consolidating the views of young space professionals regarding Space Policy issues, and strategic plans to help solving key questions currently facing the international space workforce. The key contributory element to its master performance, and portfolio of impressive results, has been the series of very successful events that SGAC has organised (or contributed to) which have always provided excellent international brainstorming sessions, and subsequent brilliant think-thanks and networks of contacts, on space policy issues. This section reports, in a chronological order, key contributions of the Space Generation to the Space Policy international debate.

2.1. GRAZ III (2002) UN/Austria/ESA Symposium on "Enhancing the Participation of Youth in Space Activities"[9]

This Symposium was the third and final meeting in a series of three dealing with the participation of young people in space activities. It was built upon the outcome of the first two symposia and served as a forum for the Space Generation Advisory Council (SGAC) to identify and strengthen avenues and mechanisms for pursuing its objectives in the future.

The main objective of the Symposium was to bring together young space experts from around the world as

[7] http://www.unsgac.org
[8] UN General Assembly Official Records (2001): http://www.oosa.unvienna.org/Reports/gadocs/pdf/A_56_20E.pdf (pg. 26, Section G, para. 211-219)
[9] Full Report may be found here: http://www.oosa.unvienna.org/Reports/AC105_793E.pdf

well as experts from major space education and outreach groups in order to discuss and define mechanisms to increase space education in various countries and to identify actions to involve young people in space-related activities. Their space policy perspectives also served as direct input to UNI-3 ATs[10].

Recommended Actions:

An Enduring Human Presence on Earth and in Space

- Developing a comprehensive, world-wide environmental monitoring strategy involves acquiring information on many parameters, some of which still need to be identified. Initial steps include finding ways to increase the use of remote sensing data in environmental monitoring and collecting addresses of web sites that provide useful information on one web page. The addresses could be included as part of the international space index proposed by SGAC in 2001.
- The main action that SGAC should take to minimise the harmful effects of space activities on the local and global environment is to increase awareness in order to promote the educated use of existing and future space transportation systems. Specifically, SGAC members should recommend the use of environmentally friendly fuels to designers of space launch systems; promote awareness of the danger that the use of weapons in space would represent; promote a greater understanding that the manufacture of space hardware (fuels, rocket systems etc.) can be harmful to the environment; and request States to discuss failures in public in order to promote mitigation measures.
- A space-based disaster mitigation system could be implemented using existing technology such as Earth observation data, satellite communications and global navigation satellite systems (GNSS) and ancillary technologies such as geographic information systems (GIS). Spin-offs that could support other development issues such as environmental protection and urban planning can result from the creation of such a system. In order to implement such a system, it is necessary to create an international organisation supported by the United Nations for disaster management and to create local organisations within countries. A number of legal and economic issues need to be studied.
- Possible actions that could be taken to improve the scientific knowledge of near and outer space include supporting existing co-operation projects as a basis for strengthened future co-operation; establishing a common infrastructure for sharing technical and non-technical information among agencies; and enhancing the opportunities for participation in missions on a global basis.
- The strategies that could be followed to improve the international co-ordination of activities related to near-Earth objects (NEOs) include the creation of a programme sponsored by the United Nations to co-ordinate NEO observations around the world, including a co-ordinating mechanism for data sharing. The programme could use existing optical and radio-astronomical systems linked by the Internet, co-ordinate with military systems to search for NEOs using detection systems already in place and plan a future space-based telescope network dedicated exclusively to NEOs.
- Nuclear power for systems operation or propulsion is needed for deep space missions where solar power is not available (or is available only at very low levels). Owing to the long-term character of nuclear power applications in space missions, young people should take a proactive role in defining international standards dealing with the launch and operation of nuclear-powered devices. It is proposed that SGAC establish a working group to discuss issues related to nuclear power sources and provide support to implementing recommendation 15 of UNISPACE III.
- Young people can increase awareness among decision makers and the general public of the importance of space by creating education programmes and materials that could be used in statistical reports on the applications of space technology and public communiqués that highlight the benefits that space technology can provide.

Another action would be to quantify the benefits obtained from space, that is, to
carry out a global space cost-benefit analysis.

Universal Space Education

- The participants in the working group dealing with universal space education indicated that space-related education was needed for all age levels, across all sectors of society, and that for that purpose it was necessary to develop a universal space education plan. Such a plan would contain central or core elements but would be adapted to the conditions of the country where it was to be implemented. The observations and recommendations of the working group are presented below.

---

[10] SGAC Progress Report to UNI-3 ATs (Jan 03) may be found here: http://www.oosa.unvienna.org/Reports/limited/pdf/AC105_C1_2003_CRP08E.pdf (pgs: 7-26)
Brief update to this Report (Jun 03) may be found here: http://www.unsgac.org/downloads/documents/AnnualReport/2002-2003Report.pdf (pgs 5-6)

- Space-related activities and materials need to be developed for children. Materials should be eye-catching, colourful and without much text, use simple language, be interactive and incorporate fundamental concepts of basic science and technology. Materials should be developed for use in non-conventional disciplines such as arts and social studies. Specific attention should be paid to encouraging girls to study science and technical disciplines.
- Written materials that focus on youth in rural communities need to be prepared in local languages taking into account specific local needs. Adults from local communities should participate in preparing such information.
- There is a need for more teacher training programmes aimed at motivating teachers to learn about space sciences and technology and providing them with supporting materials and examples of practical applications of space science and technology in the daily life of pupils.
- Governments should take an active role in promoting a better understanding of the importance of having a good national space science and technology education programme and in making possible and encouraging the participation of students in local, regional or international conferences and workshops to exchange information and experiences with other students.
- Literacy and rural education can be facilitated through tele-education. Some of the incentives that would appeal to user communities are the long-term benefits of education, equal education opportunities for girls and boys and the fact that the education programmes can be promoted within villages by local respected individuals. Programmes could be promoted by offering simple awards and scholarships and by schemes to pay graduates of programmes to teach younger people.
- Direct benefits of rural education that could help to convince Governments to use tele-education technology are improving farming through access to weather forecasts and information on better farming methods; addressing illnesses through tele-medicine and health education; and improving communication within the country.
- The use of redundant satellites or bands of telecommunications companies at discount rates and the use of electronic equipment that is being replaced in some countries could reduce the cost of infrastructure needed for tele-education.
- A universal space education programme would have dual benefits. The information on national space activities that would be gathered to develop the programme would also be a useful mechanism to co-ordinate space activities, and, because the programme would be based on a universal range of experience, it would be broad enough to be adapted to national circumstances. It is recommended that people and organisations in each country be involved in gathering such information, which can be used to celebrate events and educate people about space activities.
- One way to increase public awareness and promote space activities is by recognising outstanding contributions in the space sector. Such recognition could be through offering prizes for outstanding achievements. Options for space prizes that were identified included a Nobel space prize or a space prize created and promoted by SGAC and possibly sponsored by the United Nations. The latter could be linked to existing prizes.

Meeting basic needs ethically

- The working group proposed the creation of a network of health services, linked by satellites, that would include leading medical research centres. Such a network would serve to indicate available medical resources, distribute information on health issues and monitor the spread of diseases.
- Universal access to space communication services could be promoted through co-ordinated efforts by international organisations such as the United Nations Development Programme, the United Nations Educational, Scientific and Cultural Organisation, the World Health Organisation, the World Bank, and space agencies and local organisations that provide space communications and services. For that purpose, it would be necessary to create an international programme to pool the unused resources of existing satellite platforms and ground stations in order to provide developing countries with access to the Internet at low cost.
- SGAC could create a forum for an open discussion and identification of space research applications/products that could be used for achieving sustainable development. The results of those discussions could be shared with Committee on the Peaceful Uses of Outer Space and decision-makers to promote global awareness of the technologies that are available.
- Booklets containing ethical guidelines on the use of space technology should be prepared for the public and decision-makers. An international space ethics committee should be established to address issues such as meeting basic needs of a country while giving due consideration to neighbouring countries (e.g. in water or energy management). Space should be seen as a peaceful global endeavour unifying humankind.

- Space faring countries should improve the sharing of information on spin-offs from space activities with developing countries. A dedicated web site should be created that could serve as the focal point for the dissemination of information provided by Governments and relevant agencies.

Co-operation among nations

- The management of Earth's natural resources can be improved by educating youth about the importance of space technology for monitoring and preserving natural resources as well as for research on renewable energy resources.
- The education of the news media should be emphasised as a way to bridge the gap between society and the space community. A mechanism that is intergenerational, interdisciplinary, intercultural and international in nature could serve to provide feedback to the space community from industry, the public, decision makers and the academic community.
- Well-educated people are indispensable assets for space growth and development. Human resources can be developed by organising training courses and seminars and by setting up space infrastructure facilities. Capacity can also be built by establishing scholarships and fellowships for space enthusiasts. Budgetary resources needed to build capacity could be made available through grants by space agencies and donations by governmental and non-governmental entities. Some budgetary resources could also be included in proposals or requests for funding of space projects and, above all, by setting government and industry policies that foster education in space-related fields.

2.2. World Space Congress (2002)

2.2.1. Space Policy Summit[11] (Position Papers)

The SGAC, through the Space Generation Summit, was invited to contribute with a Position Paper[12] representing young space professionals' views to each of the four tracks of the Space Policy Summit. These were developed by gathering ideas and recommendations from precursor conferences to SGS and through an international consultation process of young space professionals. Recommendations were generated according to the principle that space exploration should be carried out for the benefit of humankind.

Cross Cutting Recommendations:
- Perform a Global Cost-Benefit Analysis of Space to justify space activities.
- Initiate a feasibility study into an International Body for the Long-Range Future.
- Establish an International Space Authority to co-ordinate exploration of space.
- Increase youth space education through a Global Space Curriculum.

SGAC Position Paper to SPS Track I – Pioneers
Key recommendations:
- Develop new launch systems through the creation of an International Centre for Advanced Propulsion and Launchers;
- Inspire excellence in research by establishing a global Space Prize.

SGAC Position Paper to SPS Track II – Prospectors
Key recommendation:
- Establish an International Space Chamber of Commerce.

SGAC Position Paper to SPS Track III – Peacekeepers
Key recommendations:
- Maintain space as a peaceful domain through a Treaty Banning Space Weapons;
- Use Space in Countering Asymmetric Threats;
- Undertake to Research into the Threat of Near Earth Objects;
- Undertake to Strengthen International Law in Space.

SGAC Position Paper to SPS Track IV - Protectors
Key recommendations:
- Implement the Recommendations of UNISPACE-III;
- Pursue a Permanent Settlement Beyond Earth within 15 years.
- Undertake Research into the Threat of Near Earth Objects
- Establish a norm that space agencies commit 1% of their funding to education

2.2.2. Space Generation Summit[13] (SGS) and SGS Space Policy Working Group

The Space Generation Summit (SGS) was a three-day meeting that gathered over 200 (18-35) international students and young professionals to develop a youth vision and strategy for the peaceful uses of space.

[11] The results of the Space Policy Summit can also be found at: http://www.aiaa.org/spacepolicy/report.html
[12] SGAC Position Papers to the Space Policy Summit: http://www.unsgac.org/sgs/papers/Breakdown/SPS.pdf

[13] Full SGS Report may be found: http://www.unsgac.org/sgs/papers

This conference, endorsed by OOSA/UN COPUOS, was held in conjunction with the World Space Congress (WSC) – the largest gathering of space entrepreneurs, scientists and policy-makers within the last decade - and took place in Houston/USA, October 11-13th, 2002. Delegates discussed ongoing youth space activities, particularly those stemming from the UNISPACE-III, SGF and also taken forward by the Space Generation Advisory Council (SGAC). Delegates addressed a variety of topics with the goal of devising new recommendations according to the theme, 'Accelerating Our Pace in Space'.

Vision:
To create a truly global community working towards a permanent international self-sustained human presence beyond Earth that simultaneously explores our origins and responsibly drives our future. We seek to ethically utilise the resources of space to minimise the risks posed to civilisation, provide a stabilising force for global security, and maximise the quality of life for all people by providing essential human rights.

Aims and Output:
The aim of the Space Generation Summit was to reinforce the vision of youth established at SGF, generate ideas to be implemented by senior space professionals and develop implementation plans for our own SGAC projects. SGS took advantage of the unique opportunities that WSC offered to present the global youth perspective on space issues to world leaders. The output of SGS and the projects of SGAC were presented at:

- The Space Policy Summit (4 position papers)
- WSC technical sessions (13 IAF papers)
- Within the SGS Final Report[12] (online)
- Within an invited WSC Plenary Statement from youth
- Through an Exhibition of SGAC and associated projects at an SGAC booth in the main exhibit hall of the WSC.

Fora and Working Groups:
Delegates were charged with the task of developing recommendations and implementation strategies according to the theme of 'Accelerating Our Pace in Space'. Delegates were divided into 4 forums, which were in turn sub-divided into working groups in order to facilitate discussion.

SGS FORUM I: SPACE EXPLORATION
Space Policy Perspectives of Young Space Professionals; Human Exploration of the Moon – a Youth Perspective; SETI and Astrobiology: Contact – a Youth Perspective; Establishing a Permanent International Human Presence in Space – a Youth Perspective; Human Mars Exploration and Development – a Youth Perspective; International Centre for Advanced Propulsion and Launchers.

SGS FORUM II: INTERNATIONAL COOPERATION
Youth Policy on Global Co-operation; Political Mechanisms for Space Development: Long-Term Committee on Survival; Innovative Ideas for Co-ordinating International Space Activities; Youth Initiatives and Projects on Human Rights and Ethics in Space Activities; Increasing Public Participation in Space Programmes.

SGS FORUM III: COMMERCE AND SPACE
Bridging the Worlds of Entertainment and Space to Increase Space Awareness; Space Tourism – A Youth Perspective; Global Space Prize – A Youth Initiative.

SGS FORUM IV: SPACE TO ENHANCE LIFE ON EARTH
Youth Policy on Space for Security; Planetary Protection – A Youth Initiative; Mobile Satellite Communications for Emergency Relief; Education and Sustainable Development.

SGS Space Policy Working Group Overview[14]:

Space Exploration

- Develop an international long-term plan for space exploration and science;
- Create a cohesive plan to avoid duplicate efforts;
- Use existing space agencies and organizations, or establishing an international space authority, to develop the plan;
- Incorporate national plans and resources;
- Set key milestones to achieve, in a stepwise manner, to reach larger goals.

Commerce and Space

- Establish an International Space Authority:
  Coordinate activities and enable countries to work together;
  Avoid duplication of efforts within such areas as space exploration, education and outreach, and standards and regulations.
- Establish an International Space Chamber of Commerce:
  Maximize the economic value of space activities by facilitating long-term investments to accelerate development within the space sector.

[14] SGS Space Policy WG Report: http://www.unsgac.org/sgs/papers/Breakdown/Exploration/Policy.pdf

- Establish a Global Space Prize
  - Inspire excellence in research and breakthroughs in the space sector.
- Encourage research of low cost launching systems
  - Define the 20 key obstacles of low cost space access;
  - Create prizes to be awarded for overcoming any of the listed obstacles.

Space Based Security

- Establish a Global Treaty to prohibit hostile interference or destruction of satellite systems by anti-satellite weapons;
- Include space based peacekeeping in the mandate of the UN Security Council;
- Use space assets to intensify monitoring of treaty compliance and verification provision;
- Undertake Research into the Threat of Near Earth Objects.

Space to Enhance Life on Earth

- Develop a process to identify and protect space assets/satellites that are beneficial to humankind;
- Integrate space technology to promote an effective interdisciplinary response to problems threatening the quality of life:
  - Agriculture and resource management;
  - Support of tele-medicine;
  - Advance research for cures of diseases.
- Use of space technology to allow for the widespread dissemination of information, particularly as required for relief in natural disasters

Highlighted Policy Issues:

Public Education

- Establish a Space Education Foundation with space agencies committing 1% of their funding
  - Educate youth and the general public via creation of a global space curriculum;
  - Space Camp for Politicians to demonstrate importance of space activities;
  - Advance the utilization of available space technology to support distance education in primary and secondary schools.
- Define methods to expose children from around the world to real space experiences such as rocket launches
  - Leverage SGAC's connections to the UN to identify funding;
  - Target students from developing countries;
  - Develop competitions to combine learning and selection process;
- Assist community service outreach organizations to include space education and outreach in their work, e.g., Raleigh International and Peace Corps;
- Establish a Junior SGAC that will help to establish cross-cultural friendships.

Continued Co-operation

- Foster a cooperative environment
  - Avoid nationally competitive efforts;
  - Reduce waste from duplicate endeavors;
  - Facilitate the efficient use of resources.
- Broaden horizons of space activities
  - Increase public awareness through nationalism;
  - Expansion of channels for space education;
  - Open doors for new ideas and technology.
- Invite additional space faring nations to participate in ISS:
  - Invite other countries as they become willing and able;
  - Identify roles for additional countries.

<u>2.3. National consultations with ESA/EU and contributions to the EU Green Paper: European Space Policy (2003)</u>

Young space professionals have been actively involved with European Space Policy and are attempting to set up a formal mechanism for representing the input of young people to EU/ESA. During 2003, the EU/ESA Space Policy team has submitted its input to the EU Green Paper on "European Space Policy". This team, and other SGAC European branches, have been meeting with prominent figures, including members of the European Commission and the Director General of ESA. A conference on European Space Policy is now scheduled to take place in Lisbon/Portugal.

2.3.1. EU/ESA Space Policy

Developing and Delivering Youth Vision on EU Space Policy

Key Recommendations[15]

The EU should:

- Substantially increase the scope of common EU space programmes, especially in light of the growing difference in scope from US programmes, by (a) increasing overall investment, (b) integrating national space / defence programmes, and (c) the continued efficient use of resources.
- Develop consolidate and expand capabilities in space security.
- Work to strengthen and enforce international space law, and in particular develop with its international partners an effective treaty prohibiting space weapons.
- Rescale programmes to develop a cheap launch capability for Europe by concentrating efforts on non-conventional technologies.
- Expand cutting edge programmes such as human spaceflight, outer solar system exploration, and advanced launchers – thereby inspiring students and reducing the drain of students away from the science and technology areas vital for a strong European future.
- Increase the public visibility of European space activities by establishing a norm that 1% of all space budgets be spent on education and outreach activities.
- Establish a centre for strategic interdisciplinary research – 'black sky thinking' – for long-term and innovative research into the space sector, to retain completive employment opportunities for education systems of highly capable, innovative and motivated people.
- Establish a "Youth Advisory Council" in support of the European Union Space Policy to represent the vision and ideas of young people from all over Europe on space, (analogous to the role of SGAC towards the UN).

2.3.2. International Space Policy

Developing Youth Vision on International Space Policy

This team has been invited to co-sponsor the follow up conference to the Space Policy Summit to be held in Strasbourg/France in May 2004. The Space Policy Summit gathered heads of space agencies and companies world-wide to discuss future space policy and which occurred in during the WSC. This team plans to develop further input for this meeting to build upon SGAC input to the SPS[16].

[15] Full Report submitted to the EU Green Paper: http://www.unsgac.org/downloads/documents/EU/EUSpacePolicy21.6.03.pdf

[16] SGAC Position Papers to the Space Policy Summit: http://www.unsgac.org/sgs/papers/Breakdown/SPS.pdf

FINAL CONSIDERATIONS

As a follow-up to the SGAC work on space policy issues, the tentative conference on "European Space Policy after the EU Green Paper" (to be held in Lisbon/Portugal) will incorporate, and voice, the continued views of young space professionals.

ACKNOWLEDGEMENTS

This paper was only possible, and justified, thanks to the ideas and continuos global network of individuals at SGAC. I hereby would like to acknowledge their contributions that took place at the following SGAC's space policy related events:

GRAZ III
UN/Austria/ESA Symposium on "Enhancing the Participation of Youth in Space Activities"

WG Implementation Action Teams co-Chairs:
M. Dejmeck (Canada), P. Figueiredo (USA), S. Kemper (USA) and I. Pessoa-Lopes (Portugal).

Delegates:
J. Aban (Japan), N. Abd-El Hamed (Egypt), M. Adjrad (Algeria), O. Arenales Vergara (Japan), F. Asante (Ghana), M. Attaba (Algeria), E. Babayef (Azerbaijan Rep.), N. Babcsan (Hungary), D. Balbueno Contreira (Brazil), D. Bizimana (Burundi), T. Brum Pretto (Brazil), F. Bwalya (Zambia), H. Camus Palacios (Chile), J. Canales Romero (Germany), D. Castagna Lunardi (Brazil), A. Chavarri Rodriguez (Mexico), E. Cristea (Austria), F. da Silveira Rodrigues (Brazil), P. De Leon (Argentina), M. Del Mundo (Philippines), A. Dia (Senegal), C. Dlamini (Swaziland), M. d'Ornellas (Brazil), G. Drayer (Venezuela), M. Ekiru (Kenya), S. El Kafrawy (Egypt), A. Elkhazmi (Libya), L. Escudero (Spain), W. Fan (China), M. Fatayer (Jordan), L. Fernando (Sri Lanka), F. Figueiredo (Brazil), L. Franco Padhila (Brazil), M. Franzon (Sweden), W. Gali (Tanzania), P. Gamboa Enciso (Peru), E. Garcia Romero (Peru), J. Garcia Villalobos (Peru), G. Gbodo (Benin), S. Gill (Australia), B. Gimenes (Brazil), R. Guarnieri (Brazil), A. Guidi (USA), L. Hidalgo (USA), L. Horst (Brazil), S. Ibrahim (Syria), S. Ibrahimova (Azerbeijan Rep.), N. Kasoma (Zambia), N. Kho (USA), G. Korankye (Ghana), A. Koru (Turkey), A. Kotarski (Poland), A. Kovacevic (Serbia), H. Lekamisy (Madagascar), R. Leon (USA), L. Lone (Brazil), T. Lone (Brazil), L. Lopes (Brazil), I. Majid (Pakistan), N. Medagangoda (Sri Lanka), D. Meister (USA), M. Menchaca-Brandan (Mexico), J. Mimouni (Algeria), H. Mirahmetoglu (Turkey), M. Moalusi (South Africa

Rep.), J. Morales (USA), S. Mugisha (Rwanda), V. Nunes (Portugal), B. Nyarko (Ghana), A. Nikolova (Bulgaria), F. Nzeyimana (Burundi), C. Nzioki Mbatha (Kenya), S. Oliveira Monteiro (Brazil), Z. Omarava (Kazakhstan), G. Omarava (Kazakhstan), Giuseppe Ottavianelli (Italy), B. Pecnik (Croatia), E. Pires (Brazil), N. Rawat (USA), M. Rockenbach Da Silva (Brazil), J. Rubira Chauca (Peru), R. Rustamos (Azerbaijan Rep.), J. Salazar Osorio (Peru), N. Savavessa Cardoso (Portugal), R. Schingler (USA), M. Sharav (Mongolia), T. Sinning (Germany), M. Sira Moran (Venezuela), Douglas Smith (UK), H. Spitzl (Austria), L. Szentpeteri (Hungary), Y. Takaya (Japan), A. Tan (Turkey), P. Tarikhi (Iran), F. Tawil (Syria), L. Ticona Salazar (Peru), J. Tizard (UK), I. Tunku (Malaysia), P. Vila Millones (Peru), Rui Vilhena (Portugal), L.Vo (Vietnam), A. Volp (Netherlands), L. Von Muhlen (Brazil), P. Wang (China), N. White (UK), G. Whitesides (USA), E. Xavier (Tanzania), F. Zougmore (Burkina Faso), M. Zoungrana (Burkina Faso).

WSC 2002

<u>Space Policy Summit (SGAC Position Papers)</u>

Conveener: *Iole De-Angelis (France)*
co-Authors:
Pioneers (Track I): *Stewart Gill (Australia)*
Prospectors (Track II): *Robert Schingler (USA) and Isabel Pessoa-Lopes (Portugal);*
Peacekeepers (Track III): *Iole De-Angelis (France)*
Protectors (Track IV): *William Marshall (UK) and Isabel Pessoa-Lopes (Portugal)*

<u>Space Generation Summit (SGS)</u>
<u>Space Policy Working Group</u>

Moderators: *Andrew Hoppin (USA) and Isabel Pessoa-Lopes (Portugal)*
WG Members:
Elizabeth Bloomer (USA), Kimberley Clayfield (Australia), Jenni Doonan (UK/Germany), Michela Munoz-Fernandez (Spain/USA), Jason Hair (USA), Matthew Lacey (USA), Aleksander Lyngui (Norway), Robert Peckyno (USA), Rui Ferreira-Pinto (Portugal), Deana Smith (Canada), Jose Lopez-Urdiales (Spain), Paul Reiley (Ireland), Brian Lund (USA), Michelle Lloyd (USA), Sing-Wei Chiou (USA), Bode Gbobaniyi, Sandra Sowah, Steve Kenny (USA), Rebecca Cutri-Kohart, Nchimunya Mwiinga (Zambia), Johanna Catena (UK), Jana Hettling (Germany), Maya Gluchmann, Reece Lumsden, C. Francis (Jamaica), G. Goh (USA), G. Mendeck (USA)

NATIONAL CONSULTATIONS WITH ESA/EU AND CONTRIBUTIONS TO THE EU GREEN PAPER: EUROPEAN SPACE POLICY

Athanasios Batagiannis, Mark Bentley (UK), Elizabeth Bloomer (USA), Jo Catena (UK), Iole De-Angelis (France), Sander Elvik, Gérardine Goh (USA), Jessica Hall, Jim Keravala (UK), Alex King (UK), Eric Laan (The Netherlands), Will Marshall (UK), Barbara Mollin, Sethu Nandakumar, André Nilsen, Chad Ohlandt (USA), Kevin Parkin, Bojan Pecnik (Croatia), Isabel Pessoa-Lopes (Portugal), Nicholas Peter, Alan Pritchard (UK), Robbie Schingler (USA), Julia Tizard (UK), Simone Zumbo.

Last but not least, a very personal word of thanks to Iole De-Angelis (France), William Marshall (UK) and Andrew Hoppin (USA) for all the memories of inspirational wisdom whilst editing this SGAC paper.

NATIONAL LIABILITY FOR DAMAGE OUTSIDE TERRITORY CAUSED BY SPACE OBJECTS AND SUGGESTION TO CHINA'S LEGISLATION

Xiaofeng Mo
Chinese Academy of Space Technology (CAST), Beijing, China
E-mail: muoxiaofeng@sohu.com

Abstract

This paper discusses on national liability for damage outside territory caused by space objects. Although precautionary measures are taken in order to reduce the high risk in outer space activities, sometimes damages do occur incidentally. Potential risk dangerousness caused by space objects should not be neglected. As signatory to the Outer Space Treaty and the Liability Treaty(both defined infra), China is now pressing on with enacting domestic law on space activity to acclimatize itself to the rapid growth in space field. Therefore, making a study of national liability for damage outside territory caused by space objects and similar regulations of States' domestic laws helps us to learn from others' strong points and offset our weakness and adjust measures to local condition. To start with, this paper analyses the dual responsibility frame of the two international treaties. Secondly, it discusses the difference and links between national liability for damage outside territory caused by space objects and national liability in traditional international law. Finally, it raises some constructive suggestions to China's legislation on space.

Great achievements had been made since the Sputnik 1, the world first satellite, was launched. Application of space technology, such as the development and utilization of observation satellite, telecommunication satellite, navigation satellite, have been infiltrated into various field of national economy and the people's daily livelihood, and also is closely linked with thousands of household. As these activities bring great benefits to mankind, the potential jeopardy, especially the possible risk made by use of nuclear force in outer space, should not be neglected, such as the crash of Cosmos 954, the Radar Ocean Reconnaissance Satellite which was powered by a nuclear reactor. [①] Although various precaution measures are taken to prevent the high risk of space activities, accident caused by space objects do occur and cause damage. This paper will review national liability for damage outside territory caused by space objects as well as national liability in international law, and raise some personal suggestions to China's legislation on space.

NATIONAL LIABILITY FOR DAMAGE OUTSIDE TERRITORY CAUSED BY SPACE OBJECTS

As is generally known, Treaty on Principles Governing the Activities of States in the Exploration and Use of Outer Space, including the Moon and Other Celestial Bodies (hereinafter referred to as "the Outer Space Treaty") came into force in October, 1967. According to the Outer Space Treaty, State Parties to the Treaty shall bear international responsibility for national activities in outer space, including the moon and other celestial bodies, whether such activities are carried on by governmental agencies or by non-governmental entities, and for assuring that national activities are carried out in conformity with the provisions set forth in the present Treaty. The activities of non-governmental entities in outer space, including the moon and other celestial bodies, shall require authorization and continuing supervision by the appropriate State Party to the Treaty.

Convention on International Liability for Damage Caused by Space Objects (hereinafter referred to as "the Liability Treaty") came into force in 1972. The Liability Trcaty provides that a launching State shall be absolutely liable to pay compensation for damage caused by its space object on the surface of the earth or elsewhere than on the surface of the earth or to aircraft flight, and in the event of damage being caused elsewhere than on the surface of the earth to a space object of one launching State or to persons or property on board such a space object by a space object of another launching State, the latter shall be liable only if the damage is due to its fault or the fault of persons for whom it is responsible.

As the Treaties mentioned above, no matter outer space activities are carried on by governmental agencies or by non-governmental entities, it shall be considered national acts of a launching State, which shall bear strict liability for compensation. In other words, all actual subjects engaged in space activity, no matter what status they are in domestic law, their activities in outer space are considered national act without exception. The liability for damage outside territory caused by space objects is all attributable to the State. Non-governmental entities, which carried out the outer space activities, shall not bear the liability for damage in international law. What it takes only is responsibility based on domestic law or on the launching contract.

COMPARISON BETWEEN NATIONAL LIABILITY FOR DAMAGE OUTSIDE TERRITORY CAUSED BY SPACE OBJECTS AND TRADITONAL NATIONAL LIABILITY IN INTERNATIONAL LAW

Differences between these two

Firstly, the two kinds of liability are different in nature. Traditional national liability is based on internationally wrongful act of a State. The wrongfulness of an act of a State usually means that the conduct of a State breached its valid international obligation assumed by it. All conducts of a State which breach rules and principles of international law will entail national liability of that State. For instance, the territorial water of a State is invaded by a warship of another State, or diplomat is immured by another State etc. These acts, which violate the principle of sovereignty over territorial water and the principle of diplomatic immunity, cannot but lead to national liability of the State. As supplementary to and development of traditional national liability, liability for damage outside territory caused by space objects does not depend on wrongfulness of an act, but on the damage fact which occurred outside territory. This is the main difference between these two.

Secondly, traditional national liability is based solely on subjective negligence or intent of a State, whereas national liability for damage outside territory caused by space objects applies to strict responsibility, and the State is not asked to have the fault in subjective aspect. Even if the occurrence of damage fact is predictable, it does not constitute violation to duty of the launching State.

Thirdly, for traditional national liability, if a State is able to prove it have taken all the reasonable measures to prevent the occurrence of event which breaching its duty. Then even if fails, it is still exempt from liability. But for national liability for damage outside territory caused by space objects, generally, as long as the damage outside territory occurred, the State shall bear the liability for compensation in addition to Article 7 of the Liability Treaty , the exoneration clause provided by the Liability Treaty.

Finally, for traditional national liability, it is enough reason for a State to take actions if another State breached its duty but did not cause actual damage. But for national liability for damage outside territory caused by space objects, as long as damage is actually caused by a State, the injured State has the right of claim. even if a State take remedial measures, such as giving compensation to the duty which is breached, it shall not continue this act freely. Because it is internationally wrongful act prohibited by international law. It might constitute an international crime if it is serious and that will no longer be solved only by taking remedial measures. On the other hand, for national liability for damage outside territory caused by space objects, the State is free in its conducts as long as the damage caused by the launching State are given just and reasonable compensation.

Links between these two

Firstly, the concept of national liability for damage outside territory caused by space objects can be regarded as derivation from the concept of traditional national liability. Both of these two aim at defining international liability which a State shall be liable for the consequence of conduct. In fact, traditional national liability itself contains certain element of national liability for damage outside territory caused by space objects. There is a rule in traditional national liability system that a State shall still make some compensation for the injured State after the wrongfulness of an act of a State was precluded. For instance, a State shall still make some possible compensation for an act, though it does not constitute internationally wrongful act in a situation of distress or due to force majeure, that is the occurrence of an irresistible force or of an unforeseen event, beyond the control of the State, if damage existed, a State should try its best to diminish damage consequence and be liable to pay for damage with the principles of justice and equity. If a State refuses to fulfill its duties, it would entail national liability of the State. In this sense, national liability for damage outside territory caused by space objects is an organic part of national liability, not the opposite side to it.

Secondly, national liability for damage outside territory caused by space objects supplements and improves traditional national liability. Although activities in outer space may cause damage consequence, the act itself is not prohibited by international law. It is hard to be solved satisfactorily for damage consequence caused by the act in accordance with traditional national liability. Considering the limitation of traditional national liability and the need of reality, the aim and effect of national liability for damage outside territory caused by space objects is not to weaken traditional national liability, but to further improve and complement traditional national liability theory.

SUGGESTIONS TO CHINA'S LEGISLATION

According to statistics of UN, more than 20 countries and regions promulgated domestic law or regulation on space and space activity. Along with the development of space technology on global scale, international cooperation of space activity is increasing gradually. As a subject of international space law, China shall ensure the fulfillment of all international obligations in the field of space activity and shall bear responsibility under generally recognized standards of international law and the provisions of international treaties to which it is party. China urgently needs legislation backup in support of her space technology development. Therefore speeding up the course of legislation on national liability for damage outside territory caused by space objects also is one of important embodiment to fulfill international conventions.

Establishing integrated national mechanism of risk guarantee

In order to prevent serious consequence caused by space objects, it can establish risk reserves system through legislation, i.e. enterprises engaged in outer space activity shall provide an insurance limitation for damage consequence occurred possibly. The exceeded part will be afforded by national finance. For instance, according to the statement [2] made by Arianespace, found by 11 European countries, Arianespace guarantee to pay maximum 400 million French francs for compensation, and the French government afford the exceeded part. Arianespace ask every client to pay a risk reserve, about 10% of launching fee, for any damage may caused by space objects in addition to launching fee. In fact, there is similar governmental document in China on civil nuclear activity. It provides that operator of nuclear activity shall be liable to pay compensation for damage caused by accident on principle, and if actual damage exceed the limit operator shall be liable for, Chinese government shall afford the exceeded part. The existing practice of Chinese government prescribes that the nuclear activist, such as operator of nuclear power station shall be liable to pay compensation, not extending Renminbi (RMB) 18 million Yuan (about US$2.18 million) for actual damage caused by a nuclear accident, and the operator could apply for national financial indemnification, maximum 300 million RMB Yuan (about US$34.1

million) if actual damage exceed the limit. It could be used for reference in the course of legislation on space in respect of national liability for damage outside territory caused by space objects. Chinese government could consult the practice in civil activity of nuclear field.

Implementing license system for outer space activities

To ensure space activities of non-governmental entities according with international space treaty, those countries which considered as the major space powers in the world have established strict supervision through space legislation, including license system. From a point view of legislation on space activity abroad, license system for space activities is one of important content in space law of these countries. It demands standard and perfect legal system to guarantee its implementation. With the trend that the subject of space activity is becoming more and more in China, China needs to consult the successful experience of those countries which are advance in space technology and legislation. It is one of effective measure to establish license system for space activities and canon commercial space activity in China.

Since 1990s, a trend of commercialization in space activity become more obvious. This tendency is growing more rapidly as we entered 21st century, believed as New Space Age. For space undertakings in a turning period, commercialization in space activity is a chance as well as a challenge. Although investor in space activity in China is still mainly state-owned enterprise, subject of investment is becoming more and more, and non-government-owned enterprises show strong interests to participant in civil space activity. It is fully necessary to establish license system for ensuring commercial space activity going on orderly; it is also useful to participant in international space technical application and market competition.

The basic frame for license system on space activities may include

The scope of acquiring a government license on space activities

It must be acquired a government license for engaging in the following space activities: space exploration and use of outer space, transnational space activities, development and manufacture of spacecraft and space launch vehicle, commercial launch, other space activities stipulated by authorities concerned.

The variety of license and condition for acquisition

Depending on the characteristic of different space activities, license will be issued accordingly, such as manufacture license, operational and management license, launch license etc., and condition for acquisition shall been set up. Meanwhile, China has began to draft "Interim provisions on the management of civil space launch".

The procedure for examination and approval

All engaged in space activity within license scope shall apply for license to authorities concerned and submit corresponding relevant qualifications materials. Authorities concerned shall examine applicant's qualification, therefore make a decision to whether to approve or disapprove the application.

Establishing compulsory third party insurance

Third party liability insurance provides insurance protection for physical injury and property loss caused during launch preparation and launching. The typical case is damage to third party caused by satellite launch failure, falling of satellite and launch vehicle debris, downfallen satellite from orbit, collision between satellites, such as experiment satellite of Japanese Institute of Aeronautics and Astronautics, did not entered normal orbit in Jan, 1995. It was confirmed that the satellite debris had dropped in Ghana, Africa. Proton, Russian launch vehicle failed and the debris of launch vehicle and satellite dropped in Kazakhstan in July, 1999. All these cases fall into the category of the third party insurance.

According to Amendment to Launch Act of Japanese Space Agency(NASDA), NASDA shall enforce the third party insurance of liability for compensation while launching.[③] According to the same law, NASDA also bear the third party insurance while offering commercial launching. Ukraine Ordinance on Space Activity stipulates that the list of types of compulsory insurance to be taken out in connection with the pursuit of space activity shall be established by the Ukrainian legislation currently in force.

Procedures for compulsory insurance shall be established by the Cabinet of Ministers of Ukraine. [④]

Space is no longer the domain of state-owned enterprises monopoly. It is imperative to establish compulsory third party liability insurance. A practicable way is to set up a provision in Act on compulsory insurance or to make compulsory insurance as a prerequisite for acquiring space activity license.

Improving and perfecting commercial insurance pattern of space activity

Chinese space insurance and compensation system develop gradually from nothing. During the early days, Chinese government provided solid back up to those space enterprises engaged in international commercial launching services. Started with liability for probable damage outside territory caused by commercial launching service is liable to Chinese government directly, later on, it switched to the mode that commercial underwriters provide insurance.

Growing commercial space activity on both international and domestic market demand Chinese government to set up strong guarantee frame as soon as possible and to make subject of liability, object of liability, third party of liability in space accident and the principle of compensation definitely, and to provide just and reasonable methods for compensation to coordinate and guarantee the right and duty of participant.

Common commercial space insurance are as follows. Some insurance businesses haven't been in operation yet in China.

Pre-launching insurance

Pre-launching insurance provides insurance protection for damage caused by accident due to fire, explosion, destroy etc. before manufacture, test and transportation as well as preparation period before launching. Period of responsibility usually begins from the manufacture of spacecraft and launch vehicle, ends with ignition or lift-off of launch vehicle.

Pre-launching insurance item includes manufacture fee, transportation supply fee and other additional expenses. The typical accident includes: water immersion accident caused by roof leaking of satellite manufactory, satellite damage accident caused by fire and so on.

Launching insurance

Launching insurance, beginning from ignition or lift-off of launch vehicle, ending wing entering the intended orbit, is the main part of space insurance. It embodies the main feature: high-tech, high-risk and high-value of space insurance and includes flight segment, the launch vehicle and the satellite separation, orbit transfer, excursion maneuver, antenna and solar panel deployment and on- orbit test and other stage.

The typical breakdown is that satellite fails to enter the intended orbit by the second stage due to launch vehicle explosion, engine premature ignition or lag burning and cause launching failure and other gross damage. Launching insurance covers all loses mentioned above.

In addition to total loss caused by satellite breakdown and loss, it also includes loss due to compatibility between launch vehicle and satellite which causing satellite can not achieve desired technical performance. For instance, all shall be paid for indemnity due to satellite performance degradation caused by abnormality of transponder, electrical power and attitude control system, or due to shortening of satellite life caused by insufficient fuel and power descent.

Life insurance

It also called on-orbit insurance, which provides insurance protection when satellite cannot be carry out scheduled work demanded and service life demanded caused by satellite abnormality after satellite entering intended orbit and starting normal operation. Typical cases include transponder failure, storage battery failure, solar array power descent and fuel leakage etc.

Life insurance normally counts manufacture fee, transportation fee and launching fee as insured objects. Applicant must present the report on satellite performance to the insurance company. The insurer will estimate the insurance condition and premium rate according to normal satellite work status provided by applicant's report.

Usually every satellite shall insure life insurance, however such as low and medium earth orbit communication system consisting of several satellites, including backup satellite on orbit, it can plan a blanket insurance.

Enacting national criterion and regulation on space debris mitigation

Of course, the most important thing is

still to put prevention first from technology perfection, in order to minimize the occurrence of accident, especially shall enact national criterion and regulation on space debris mitigation.

The proposed Chinese space debris monitoring and research program to minimize space debris was approved by the space specialists with the Commission of Science, Technology and Industry for National Defense. This is the first time that Chinese government organizes and plans a comprehensive national action plan on space debris research and monitoring to fulfill its international obligation in this area.

The proposed plan is to increase China's capability to observe, avoid and reduce space debris. China hopes that by 2005 the action plan not only gives its space program an independent ability to monitor orbital debris and issue warnings to protect space assets, but also offers technical support to the international exchange.

The action plan also determines the special goals in the related fields:

- establishing an initial observing capability through a dedicated fixed telescope and two mobile telescopes, with a capability of observing 30 cm objects in the geostationary orbit;
- developing a database on space debris environment and dynamics;
- developing and putting into service an international level risk assessment and emergency avoidance expert system;
- obtaining experimental data on active and passive protection through modeled experiments and computer simulations on materials and their structures, and fundamental theoretical research;
- mitigating space debris generation, particularly in resolving the issues of venting residual propellant in the launcher's upper stage and passivation of satellites at the end of their missions which includes meeting the requirements to exit the operational orbits.

---

① See Qizhi He & Huikang Huang Law of the outer space (Chinese) p.176

② Ibid p.89, p.271

③ See Bo Lu "Current situation of world space insurance" (Chinese)

④ See Song Li "Space insurance" (Chinese)

IAC-03-IISL.2.17

PROPOSAL FOR A STANDARD CURRICULUM AND A GENERAL COURSE ON SPACE LAW

Oscar Fernandez-Brital[*]
University Institute of the Argentine Federal Police

Ricky J. Lee[†]
Ricky J. Lee & Associates
University of Western Sydney, Australia

ABSTRACT

The authors have made suggestions during previous IISL colloquia and the recent United Nations Workshop on Capacity Building in Space Law in The Hague concerning the creation of a standard course for space law. This is necessary in order to ensure that the professionals of space law, especially those in developing countries, are equipped with the same basic knowledge and to promote awareness in space law.

The proposal paper also discusses the contents of such a program, along with ideas for a "general course of space law" to be given once every several years within the framework of the International Institute of Space Law that will promote research and scholarship in the field.

INTRODUCTION

During the United Nations / International Institute of Air and Space Law Workshop on Capacity Building in Space Law held in the Netherlands in November 2002, one of the issues addressed by the Workshop was the need for greater inclusion of space law in standard international legal studies in developing countries. It was with this objective in mind that the authors, independently of each other, came upon two separate but related proposals that they wish to bring to the attention of the International Institute of Space Law and its Colloquium on the Law of Outer Space.

STANDARD CURRICULUM

The first of these ideas is the formulation of a standard curriculum in space law that would set out in detail the topics and issues to be covered in the course. The intentions and objectives of this exercise were to provide some guidance to educators in countries with limited practice and experience in space law in planning a course in the discipline.

In doing so it is clear that a balance must be struck between three broad categories, or foci, of issues in space law. The first of these categories contain the fundamental principles of international law concerning space activities, including the status of astronauts, liability, non-appropriation and military uses of outer space. Although consideration of these broad principles may appear irrelevant to the priorities and goals of most developing countries as a result of their limited space capabilities in the short term, their roles as the protectors of space as the global commons and the enforcers of international obligations in space activities cannot be underestimated.

The second is the fluid and evolving practice of space law concerning private and commercial activities in outer space. The proliferation of such private and/or commercial activities, such as satellite telecommunications, remote sensing and direct television broadcasting have affected the ways of life in many developed and developing countries. Although a fine balancing act must be maintained, it should be recognised that most developing countries are likely to be consumers rather than providers of space-based services in the short to medium term and, accordingly, the focus of a standard curriculum on space law should be adjusted.

The third is the perceived increasing need for countries to adopt domestic legislation dealing with private space activities. Previously thought to be the exclusive province of spacefaring nations, it is a commonly observed trend that domestic laws dealing with private launches have found themselves placed on the legislative agenda of some developing countries. This is partly the result of the creation of a global and private launch industry in the previous decade as well as the use of "flags of convenience" for companies conducting launch activities or satellite operations, among other factors.

The proposed curriculum is as follows:

1. **Introduction to Space Law**
   - 1.1. Historical background
   - 1.2. Sources of Space Law: treaties, General Assembly resolutions and writings
   - 1.3. Definitional issues: definitions of outer space, celestial body and space objects
   - 1.4. Role of the United Nations and other regional and intergovernmental organisations

2. **Fundamental Principles**
   - 2.1. Delimitation between airspace and outer space
   - 2.2. Freedom of access, use and principle of non-appropriation
   - 2.3. Military uses
   - 2.4. Space debris

3. **Spacecrafts and Personnel**
   - 3.1. Definition of space objects
   - 3.2. Registration of space objects and difficulties with transfers
   - 3.3. Space stations
   - 3.4. Status of crew and tourists
   - 3.5. Control of space objects and jurisdiction onboard spacecrafts
   - 3.6. Search, rescue and return of spacecrafts and personnel

4. **Responsibility and Liability**
   - 4.1. Liability for space activities
   - 4.2. Extension to private launch activities and their supervision
   - 4.3. Procedure issues

5. **Domestic Regulation**
   - 5.1. Domestic licensing and regulation of launch activities
   - 5.2. Domestic licensing and regulation of satellite operations

5.3. Compulsory third party liability insurance for private operators

5.4. Liability between contractors and that of launch operators

6. Telecommunications

6.1. Role of the I.T.U. and associated legal instruments

6.2. Regulation of radio frequencies and orbital slots on the geostationary orbit

6.3. International commercial satellite organisations: Intelsat and Inmarsat

6.4. Privatisation of telecommunication services

7. Commercial Satellites

7.1. Conceptual legal issues with remote sensing

7.2. Collection and dissemination of remote sensing data

7.3. Conceptual legal issues with direct television broadcasting

7.4. Liability for errors in global navigation satellite systems

8. Commercial Legal Issues

8.1. International intellectual property rights for space-based inventions and discoveries

8.2. Legal issues in the sale and transfer of satellites

8.3. Export controls

8.4. Asset-based financing based on security interests in spacecrafts

9. Future Legal Issues

9.1. Passenger transportation and liability to passengers

9.2. Space tourism and permanent human settlement

9.3. Exploitation of natural resources on celestial bodies

General Course

During the Workshop, it was proposed that a general course in space law be conducted by the International Institute of Space Law to promote education and awareness in space law issues throughout the international community. There are two aspects to this proposal: the first is the selection of a distinguished teacher of space law to provide a short course on the fundamental principles of space law (which may be conducted in accordance with the standard curriculum as proposed above), to be done once every five years.

It is suggested, in relation to this part of the proposal, that:

- the distinguished teacher or host institution for the delivery of this short course be selected by the Board of Directors of the International Institute of Space Law;
- the selection of dates for the short course are to be at the discretion of the selected teacher or host institution;
- the structure of the short course to be agreed between the teacher or host institution and the Institute;
- the cost of attendance at the course should be kept at a minimum and, where resources permit, subsidisation of costs should be considered in case of attendees from developing countries;
- attendance of the course to be open to all students, academics, practitioners,

staff of international organisations and government officials; and

- the course should be videotaped and copies to be translated or subtitled and available to governmental agencies or institutions of developing countries.

The second part of this proposal is the introduction of a "special lecture" on space law, similar to the general course on international law as organised by the Hague Academy of International Law. The idea is that the International Institute of Space Law, either on an annual or biannual basis, would select a distinguished scholar to deliver a lecture of half a day or a day's duration on a specific topic or issue of space law, to be selected by the scholar with consultation of the Board of Directors of the Institute.

It is expected that such an exercise would allow for the detailed study of a special issue beyond the presentation of short papers at the Colloquium and, over time, provide future scholars of space law with an impressive collection of comprehensive treatises on space law principles and issues. This special lecture should be held in conjunction or adjacent to the annual Colloquium on the Law of Outer Space, with the lecture paper published as part of the proceedings of the Colloquium.

Notes

This paper is written in the personal capacity of the authors and does not necessarily represent the views of any organisations with which they are associated.

* Member IISL and ILA.
Email: fernandezbrital@movicombs.com.ar.
† Member IISL, IBA and ILA.
Email: rjlee@rickylee.id.au.

Planetary Protection - Legal Issues [1]

Philippe Achilleas
Director of the Institute of Space and Telecommunications Law
University Paris Sud – 11[2]
France
Philippe.achilleas@idest-paris.org

Abstract

The object of the present paper is to give an overview of the current international and national regulation applicable to planetary protection. As far as international space law is concerned, most of the obligations imposed on States are contained in the 1967 Treaty on Principles Governing the Activities of States in the Exploration and Use of Outer Space, including the Moon and Other Celestial Bodies. Among these obligations, the most relevant provision concerning planetary protection is Article IX according to which States shall pursue studies and conduct exploration of outer space so as to avoid its harmful contamination as well as adverse changes in the environment of the Earth resulting from the introduction of extraterrestrial matter. Consequently, COSPAR and NASA have adopted planetary protection standards for missions conducted in outer space. Environmental law may also have an impact on planetary protection regulations, since most of its applicable provisions focus on the potential effects that concerned activities may have, regardless of the nature of the activity. These provisions may therefore apply to space activities. The prevention principle may be regarded as one of the most important of them. According to this principle, States have the responsibility to ensure that activities within their jurisdiction or control do not cause damage to the environment of other States or of areas beyond the limits of national jurisdiction.

Introduction

In the Year 2003, the space community has shown a stronger interest in Planet Mars. The NASA Mars Exploration Rover Mission programme has lead to the launch of Spirit on 10 June 2003 and of Opportunity on 7 July 2003. The first rover is intended to land in January 2004. On 2 June 2003, the European Mars Express space probe was placed in a trajectory that will take it to Mars - getting there in late December 2003. While these missions will try to answer to some basic scientific questions such as the existence of life on Mars, presently or in the past, the issue of planetary protection has been raised again by space agencies, associations and universities. Planetary protection is a policy concerning the regulations against human contamination of celestial bodies - the so-called "forward contamination", and the contamination of the Earth by spacecrafts and space crews, possibly bearers of extraterrestrial micro-organisms returning from outer space, the so-called "back contamination". The rules that constitute a legal basis for imposing obligations on States in terms of planetary

[2] P. Achilleas is also Part-time resident faculty in Policy and Law at the International Space University central campus.

protection derive from two main branches of law: space law (Part I) and environmental law (Part II).

I. Space law principles

Some provisions of the Outer Space Treaty and of the Moon Agreement have a direct impact on planetary protection policies (A). However, the over-all effect of these treaties provisions is minimal since they provide no specific standards and no official method for clarifying issues and monitoring activities. That is why these obligations will need some detailed application policies, like the COSPAR guidelines or the NASA policy (B), to become really effective.

A. United Nations Treaties

Article IX - sentence two - of the 1967 Treaty on principles governing the activities of States in the exploration and use of outer space, including the Moon and other celestial bodies[1] (the Outer Space Treaty) constitutes the primary statement of international law, which has tended to protect and preserve the environmental integrity of Earth and space from the initial period of interplanetary exploration. According to the article: "States Parties shall pursue studies of outer space, including the Moon and other celestial bodies, and conduct exploration of them so as to avoid their harmful contamination and also adverse changes in the environment of the Earth resulting from the introduction of extraterrestrial matter and, when necessary, adopt appropriate measures for this purpose".

The rule only refers to activities for the investigation and exploration of outer space, but the scope of application of this sentence could be interpreted as a general principle of space law incorporating all space activities including commercial ones. For the purpose of avoiding negative effects to the environment, Article IX tends to limit the freedom of outer space principle, as stated in article I of the Outer Space Treaty. The question must however be asked immediately what the key expression "harmful contamination" is supposed to mean and how it has to be interpreted? There are many different interpretations of "contamination" in the space law literature but we should use the COSPAR guidelines that restrict the content of the expression to "biological contamination". The restrictive interpretation of the term "contamination" also results from the Preparatory Works of the Outer Space Treaty. We shall notice that Article XI of the Outer Space Treaty provides for greater protection for the Moon and other celestial bodies than for the Earth. Indeed, if "harmful contamination" should be avoided in outer space, including the Moon and other celestial bodies, the Earth is only protected against "adverse changes" in its environment. The issue of back contamination is less important in this article and will mainly be taken up by general international environmental conventions.

Article 7.1 of the 1979 Agreement concerning the activities of States on the Moon and other celestial bodies[2] (the Moon agreement) represents the second main rule dealing with planetary protection. According to the text: "In exploring and using the Moon, States Parties shall take measures to prevent the disruption of the existing balance of its environment, whether by introducing adverse changes in that environment, by its harmful contamination through the introduction of extra-environmental matter or otherwise. States parties shall also take measures to avoid harmfully affecting the environment of the Earth through the introduction of extraterrestrial matters or otherwise".

Under the Moon agreement, States shall also therefore take appropriate measures for all missions to prevent disruption of the natural environs. As Article IX of the Outer Space Treaty, this provision is extremely well intentioned but avoids the important definition of "harmful". However, even if this principle is extremely broad, like in Article IX of the Outer Space Treaty, Article 7.2 of the Moon Agreement establishes a follow-up mechanism since States have to inform the Secretary General of the United Nations of the measures adopted by States in order to respect planetary protection principle.

B. Detailed application policies

The 2002 COSPAR Planetary Protection Policy represents a statement on planetary protection for the reference of space faring nations, both as an international standard on procedures to avoid organic-constituent and biological contamination in space exploration, and providing accepted guidelines in this area to guide compliance with the wording of the Outer Space Treaty and other relevant international agreements. These principles do not constitute binding law. They may however be applied by States on a political voluntary basis, and shall therefore be regarded as so-called soft law, since COSPAR plays an important role as the standard-setting international organisation in the area of planetary protection. The COSPAR policy on planetary protection makes reference to Article IX of the Outer Space Treaty. Taking this provision into account, the COSPAR accepts that for certain space mission/target body combinations, controls on contamination shall be imposed in accordance with a specified range of requirements. The COSPAR policy makes distinction between five categories of target body/mission type combinations, with the corresponding protection regimes. These categories and regimes are reproduced in Annex of this document. COSPAR further recommends its members to provide information within a certain period about the procedures and computations used for planetary protection for each flight, in order to make reports available to the public and delivered to the Secretary-General of the United Nations. The required content of the reports is the following:

- The estimated biological burden at launch, the methods used to obtain the estimate (e.g., assay techniques applied to spacecraft or a proxy), and the statistical uncertainty in the estimate.
- The probable composition (identification) of the biological burden for Category IV missions, and for Category V "restricted Earth return" missions.
- Methods used to control the biological burden, decontaminate and/or sterilize the space flight hardware.
- The organic inventory of all impacting or landed spacecraft or spacecraft-components, for quantities exceeding 1 kg.
- Intended minimum distance from the surface of the target body for launched components, for those vehicles not intended to land on the body.

NASA has also adopted a Planetary Protection policy in order to implement the United Nations Treaties. In 1958 NASA adopted a resolution expressing the policy that planetary protection should be conducted so as to prevent contamination of celestial objects. In 1959, NASA adopted a stringent policy concerning planetary protection, to the effect of "payloads which might impact a celestial body must be sterilised before launching". This policy was strict, severe and inviolate. All payloads had to be sterilised. In 1964, the COSPAR published a recommendation called "Planetary Quarantine

Requirements" (PQR)[3]. NASA adopted the PQR and modified its original policy of sterilisation by implementing series of management instructions and policy directives. The new policy required that interplanetary missions had to be conducted in order to restrict the probability of contamination of the target body in prescribed limits. This probability was determined by a mathematical formula. The planetary protection policies were modified again in 1994, in anticipation of the exploratory missions to Mars. This revision to the policy was specifically about the utilisation of decontamination and cleanliness control everytime the mission objectives included life-detection experiments. The most recent revision by NASA to the planetary protection policy became effective in 1999 on the basis of the NASA Policy Directive on Biological Contamination Control for Outbound and Inbound Planetary Spacecraft[4]. The objective of this document is to implement the Outer Space Treaty as well COSPAR guidelines on planetary protection through national regulation. The policy directive applies to NASA Headquarters and NASA Centers, including Component Facilities, and to NASA contractors where specified by contract. The provisions of the directive cover all space flight missions which may intentionally or unintentionally carry Earth organisms and organic constituents to the planets or other solar system bodies, and any mission employing spacecraft which are intended to return to Earth and/or its biosphere from extraterrestrial targets of exploration. The policy directive enumerates the Associate Administrator for Space Science's responsibilities as far as planetary protection is concerned, namely: maintaining the required activities in support of the planetary protection policy at NASA Headquarters; assuring that the research and technology activities required to implement the planetary protection policy are conducted; monitoring space flight missions as necessary to meet the requirements for planetary protection certification. The Planetary Protection Officer is responsible for implementing NASA planetary protection policy, as stated in the directive. To that extent, the role notably involves prescribing standards applicable to all NASA missions, as detailed in the directive. In addition, it is foreseen that specific constraints imposed on spacecraft involved in solar system exploration will depend on the nature of the mission and the identity of the target body or bodies, in accordance with current scientific knowledge about the target bodies. The most likely constraints on missions of concern will be a requirement to reduce the biological contamination of the spacecraft, coupled with constraints on spacecraft operating procedures, an inventory of organic constituents of the spacecraft and organic samples, and restrictions on the handling and methods by which extraterrestrial samples are returned to Earth. In the majority of missions, there will also be a requirement to document spacecraft flyby operations, spacecraft impact potential, and the location of landings or impact points of spacecraft on planetary surfaces or other bodies.

II. Environmental Law Principles

Even though international environmental conventions do not specifically address space pollution and the contamination of celestial bodies, they may be applied to the issue of back contamination. Indeed, the hypothesis of pollution described in these conventions can in most cases apply to hypothesis of contamination due to matter imported from space or from a celestial body. General principles of environmental law, namely prevention and precautionary principles (A), also find application on the issue of planetary protection (B).

A. General principles of environmental law - Prevention and Precautionary principles

The International Court of Justice mentioned in 1997 the absolute need to prevent environmental damage, due to the possibility of irreversible effects[5]. The so-called "prevention principle" gives birth to a certain number of general obligations for States, that are notably implemented through the precautionary principle. Two international texts must be underlined as far as these principles are concerned: the 1972 Declaration of the United Nations Conference on the Human Environment[6] (the Stockholm Declaration) and the 1992 Declaration of the United Nations Conference on Environment and Development[7] (the Rio Declaration).

The prevention principle, as stated by the Stockholm declaration, applies to all activities within States jurisdiction that may cause damage to the environment. According to Principle 21: "States have [...] the responsibility to ensure that activities within their jurisdiction or control do not cause damage to the environment of other States or of areas beyond the limits of national jurisdiction". The so-called prevention principle makes no distinction between the activities concerned, as soon as these activities cause damage to the environment. It shall therefore be regarded as a sound legal basis for planetary protection policies. In addition, this principle may find application for both back and forward contamination, since not only damage to the environment of other States but also damage to areas beyond the limits of national jurisdiction is concerned.

Principle 2 of the Rio Declaration strictly reproduces in similar wording of the above mentioned Principle 21 of the Stockholm Declaration. In addition, and for the above-mentioned purpose of preventing damage caused to the environment of other States (...), Principle 15 of the Rio Declaration has for the first time explicitly recognised the Precautionary Principle: "In order to protect the environment, the precautionary approach should be widely applied by States according to their capabilities. Where there are threats of serious or irreversible damage, lack of full scientific certainty shall not be used as a reason for postponing cost-effective measures to prevent environmental degradation". Should it be regarded as binding on a customary basis, this principle could conduct States involved in space missions to take effective measures in order to prevent environmental degradation due to these missions.

The stated principles are contained in declarations, and shall therefore be regarded as soft law. The prevention principle, as stated by Principle 21 of the Stockholm Declaration and by Article 2 of the Rio Declaration, shall however be regarded as binding on a customary basis.

B. Specific environmental treaties applicable to planetary protection

Two specific environmental treaties may be specially relevant for planetary protection: the 1979 Convention on Long-range Transboundary Air Pollution[8] and the 1992 Convention on the Transboundary Effects of Industrial Accidents[9].

The 1979 Convention on Long-range Transboundary Air Pollution tends to tackle the possible adverse effects of transboundary air pollution. Article 1 of the convention defines "air pollution" as the introduction by man of substances into the air resulting in deleterious effects of such a nature as to endanger human health, harm living resources. As nothing in the convention is specified about the origin of the contaminating substance, it may have been imported from space or a celestial body. For the purpose stated by the convention, the parties have to improve their research and development in several fields such as instrumentation for measuring pollution, education and training programs or technologies for reducing the emissions of air pollutants. The most important obligation relies in the exchange of information between States parties: should a State party to the convention be affected by air pollution, consultations have to be held with other States. Moreover, States have to exchange data about their level of pollution and their way to improve it, as well as about their activities that might result in transboundary air pollution. Therefore, should a State party lead an activity in outer space or on a celestial body implying an unknown biological matter which might cause contamination on Earth, other States will have to be informed in accordance with the provisions of the convention. No specific responsibility regime is however provided by the convention concerning such activities. States parties responsibility may nevertheless be engaged on the basis of the general regime of international responsibility, as described above.

The 1992 Convention on the Transboundary Effects of the Industrial Accidents tends to tackle the harmful consequences of industrial accidents for the environment of the Earth. For the purpose of this convention, industrial accident means an event resulting from an uncontrolled development in the course of any activity involving hazardous substances. It does not apply to nuclear and radiological accidents, dam failures land based transport but may have an of space missions, if the latter involve hazardous substances that can possibly contaminate the environment. According to the convention, States have to take preventive measures to identify the risk of industrial accident and try to reduce pollution in this hypothesis. This obligation is a strong basis for a binding cleanliness and decontamination of spacecrafts containing hazardous extraterrestrial matters. States must give information to the public in case of industrial accident with contaminating consequences and inform other States that might be affected by this contamination. Moreover, States have an obligation to exchange their contamination prevention technologies, which could lead to an international cooperation program to improve spacecraft cleanliness technologies.

SELECTIVE BIBLIOGRAPHY

S. GOROVE, "Contamination and the outer space treaty", *IISL (14)*, 1971, pp. 63-66.

S. GOROVE, "Legal aspects of pollution and outer space", *IISL (14)*, 1971, pp. 67-71.

M. HINTZ, "Environmental aspects of settlements on the Moon and Mars - Planetary Protection-", *IISL (34),* 1991, pp. 59-63.

G.B. KRAUSS-ABLASS, "Protection of the terrestrial environment in outer space, a principle of international law", *IISL (14)*, 1970, pp. 72-74.

A.MCCLOUD, "Space pollution", *IISL (30)*, 1987, pp. 143-146.

D. POPESCU, "The draft convention on global environment protection and outer space conservation", *IISL (34),* 1991, pp. 298-303.

G.S. ROBINSON, "Earth exposures to martian matter: back contaminations and international quarantine regulations", *IISL (18)*, 1975, pp. 135-149.

G.S. ROBINSON, "Return of extraterrestrial biota: legal, ethical and moral participation by the public", *IISL (20)*, 1977, pp. 430-439.

P.H. SAND, "Space programs and international environment protection", *IISL (14)*, 1970, pp. 79-94.

P.M. STERNS, "The scientific/legal implications of planetary protection and exobilogy", *IISL (42)*, 1999, pp. 483-492.

P.M. STERNS, L.I. TENNEN, "Exobiology and the outer space treaty: from planetary protection to the search for extraterrestrial life", *IISL (40)*, 1997, pp. 141-149.

M. WILLIAMSON, "Protection of the space environment under the outer space treaty", *IISL (40)*, 1997, pp. 296-302.

Annex

Cospar Planetary Protection Policy (20 October 2002) – Extract

Category I includes any mission to a target body which is not of direct interest for understanding the process of chemical evolution or the origin of life. No protection of such bodies is warranted and no planetary protection requirements are imposed by this policy.

Category II missions comprise all types of missions to those target bodies where there is significant interest relative to the process of chemical evolution and the origin of life, but where there is only a remote chance that contamination carried by a spacecraft could jeopardize future exploration. The requirements are for simple documentation only. Preparation of a short planetary protection plan is required for these flight projects primarily to outline intended or potential impact targets, brief Pre- and Post-launch analyses detailing impact strategies, and a Post-encounter and End-of-Mission Report which will provide the location of impact if such an event occurs. Solar system bodies considered to be classified as Category II are listed in the Appendix to this document.

Category III missions comprise certain types of missions (mostly flyby and orbiter) to a target body of chemical evolution and/or origin of life interest or for which scientific opinion provides a significant chance of contamination which could jeopardize a future biological experiment. Requirements will consist of documentation (more involved than Category II) and some implementing procedures, including trajectory biasing, the use of cleanrooms during spacecraft assembly and testing, and possibly bioburden reduction. Although no impact is intended for Category III missions, an inventory of bulk constituent organics is required if the probability of impact is significant. Category III specifications for selected solar system bodies are set forth in the Appendix to this document. Solar system bodies considered to be classified as Category III also are listed in the Appendix.

Category IV missions comprise certain types of missions (mostly probe and lander) to a target body of chemical evolution and/or origin of life interest or for which scientific opinion provides a significant chance of contamination which could jeopardize future biological experiments. Requirements imposed include rather detailed documentation (more involved than Category III), including a bioassay to enumerate the bioburden, a probability of contamination analysis, an inventory of the bulk constituent organics and an increased number of implementing procedures. The implementing procedures required may include trajectory biasing, cleanrooms, bioload reduction, possible partial sterilization of the direct contact hardware and a bioshield for that hardware. Generally, the requirements and compliance are similar to Viking, with the exception of complete lander/probe sterilization. Category IV specifications for selected solar system bodies are set forth in the Appendix to this document. Solar system bodies considered to be classified as Category IV also are listed in the Appendix.

Category V missions comprise all Earth-return missions. The concern for these missions is the protection of the terrestrial system, the Earth and the Moon. (The Moon must be protected from back contamination to retain freedom from planetary protection requirements on Earth-Moon travel.) For solar system bodies deemed by scientific opinion to have no indigenous life forms, a subcategory "unrestricted Earth return" is defined. Missions in this subcategory have planetary protection requirements on the outbound phase only, corresponding to the category of that phase (typically Category I or II). For all other Category V missions, in a subcategory defined as "restricted Earth return," the highest degree of concern is expressed by the absolute prohibition of destructive impact upon return, the need for containment throughout the return phase of all returned hardware which directly contacted the target body or unsterilized material from the body, and the need for containment of any unsterilized sample collected and returned to Earth. Post-mission, there is a need to conduct timely analyses of the unsterilized sample collected and returned to Earth, under strict containment, and using the most sensitive techniques. If any sign of the existence of a nonterrestrial replicating entity is found, the returned sample must remain contained unless treated by an effective sterilizing procedure. Category V concerns are reflected in requirements that encompass those of Category IV plus a continuing monitoring of project activities, studies and research (i.e., in sterilization procedures and containment techniques).

---

[1] 610 *UNTS* 205.

[2] 1363 *UNTS* 3.

[3] COSPAR res. 26, COSPAR infor. bull. At annex 4 (1964), fifth international space science symposium, Florence Italy.

[4] 42 *U.S.C.* 2473(c)(1), Section 203(c)(1) of the National Aeronautics and Space Act of 1958, as amended - Expiration date : 19 February 2004.

[5] ICJ, 25 September 1997, *Gabcikovo-Nagimaros Project*, par. 140.

[6] 11 *ILM* 1416 (1972)

[7] A/CONF.151/26 Vol.I.

[8] 1302 *UNTS* 217.

[9] 31 *ILM* 1330.

Session 3:
SPACE LAW AND INTERNATIONAL SECURITY

Chairmen: John B. Gantt, USA
Yuri Kolossov, Russia

Rapporteur: Liara Covert, Canada

REMOTE SENSING AND NATIONAL SECURITY

By

Carl Q. Christol
Distinguished Professor Emeritus of International Law and Political Science
University of Southern California
Los Angeles, California 90089-0044

Abstract

Enemies in time of armed conflict have particular need for information relating to the disposition of opposing forces. Potential adversaries also benefit from the acquisition of information.

Remote sensing (RS) is carried out by States and by commercial firms. Countries impose constraints upon those who are subject to their jurisdiction so that sensitive data and analyzed information will not be available to their opponents. Constraints will also be imposed by States in order to provide protection to their political and military allies.

Sensitive policy issues exist when a space-resource State wishes to encourage the success of its commercial firms but at the same time considers it prudent to restrict sales. In forming policies a State will have to take into account the availability of data and information that can be supplied by non-national sources.

This analysis examines the policies and practices affecting the United States, its allies, and the enemies or potential adversaries of both.

1. Hybrid Capabilities

The data and analyzed information derived form RS contributes to commercial profitability and military efficiency. RS, with its hybrid uses, is a successful product of the space age. Its multi-faceted aspects have presented problems to all who share an interest in its use.

2. Commercial Aspects

Initially, because of the high cost of satellites and aircraft, only governments were able to engage effectively in RS. More recently the United States has fostered RS by private firms using satellites.

The Commercial Space Act of 1998 (P.L. 105-303) established policies whereby the U.S. government is to encourage commercial RS by not engaging in activities being pursued by the private sector and also to purchase data from commercial sources.

Until 1997 NASA was heavily engaged in commercial RS activities. Because the raw data and interpreted information derived from RS vitally affects national security, restrictions on private operations are substantial. Such activity must not, for example, jeopardize the "domestic national security, and foreign policy interests of the United States."

Within these limitations private firms whose clients are engaged in many commercial and scientific endeavors, have demonstrated their economic worth. Agriculture, fishing, mining, transportation, and weather forecasting are among the beneficiaries. The product of RS has contributed to the condition of globalization.

Consumers of the produce of RS can be either domestic or foreign. In each instance governments in imposing constraints on the sale of sensitive materials limit the consumer base of the product. In safeguarding national security by preventing sensitive materiel from being sold to potential adversaries, the private firms operate under economic handicaps. This can be stressful for a capital-intensive industry. One way this has been overcome is for the parent State to purchase both commercial and military products from its own private firms. To maintain national security against overly inquisitive foreign purchasers RS licensing procedures have been installed and regulatory bodies have been established. On occasion several agencies, viewing commercial and security needs from different perspectives, have promulgated opposing directives.

United States policy on RS has been heavily influenced by the Presidential decision Directive 23 (PDD-23) of March 10, 1994. As a classified document it defined national objectives for RS commercialization. It also identified the circumstances under which foreign access to RS space capabilities was to be permitted. The directive was accompanied by a Press Statement and a Fact Sheet. The latter identified commercial opportunities and the importance of environmental monitoring. The directive adopted the premise there would be a world-wide market for RS and its applications of $15 billion annually by 2000.

The Fact Sheet acknowledged the presence of competing considerations. While American policy posited support for and the enhancement of U.S. industrial competitiveness in RS it also noted the need to protect America's security and foreign policy interests. So that the latter would not suffer through foreign access to RS space systems, technology, products, and data the directive made reference to commercial and export licenses. The export of items on control lists was to be subject to existing laws and regulations. The restrictions under which American firms might engage in the international commercial aspect of RS were numerous and detailed. The Fact Sheet made it clear that when security considerations were present they would prevail over commercial interests. For particularly sensitive "know how" exportation was to be on a case-by-case basis and subject to "inter-governmental" agreements.

Failure to conform to existing governmental regulations has produced sanctions. In December 2002 in a case not involving RS two American exporters of satellites were charged with violations of the Arms Export Control Act and the International Traffic in Arms Regulations. In March 2003 the Boeing Company and Hughes Electronics Corporation entered into an agreement with the government to pay the Department of State $20 million in cash plus an additional $12 million to improve their international export compliance programs. These charges resulted from the failure of the two companies in the mid-

1990s to restrict their sale of sensitive space technology to China. This technology improved China's capability to develop ballistic missiles.

3. Military Aspects

At present the United States Department of Defense operates two agencies which engage in security-based RS activities. The National Reconnaissance Office (NRO) was created in 1960. It is charged with furthering unique and innovative technology, large-scale development and acquisition, and the operation of space reconnaissance systems. Its functions are based on the view that national security involves more than military data and information. Included in its mission are such areas as energy, the environment, and economic competition. Its military successes have included tracking the world-wide shipment of arms and implements of war, establishing proof that there was not a "missile gap" between the United States and the Soviet Union during the Cold War, and the recent provision of intelligence support to U.S. operations in Bosnia in 2001 and in Iraq in 2003. High on its agenda is the identification of nuclear capabilities by potential adversaries of the United States.

The second agency is the National Imagery and Mapping Agency (NIMA), which was established in 1996. It is a major intelligence and combat support instrumentality of the Department of Defense. It is charged with providing accurate geospatial intelligence derived from the exploitation and analysis of imagery and geospatial information describing and visually depicting physical feature geographically referenced activities on the Earth. This enables the United States to formulate security policy, and to engage in arms control and treaty monitoring activities, counterterrorism activities, nonproliferation, chemical and biological warfare activities, and operational activities.

NIMA following September 11, 2001 contracted with the American firm, Space Imaging Corporation, to provide data and information on Afghanistan. The agreement provided that the seller could not sell or share its imagery with anyone other than the U.S. government until January 5, 2002. This has been referred to as "checkbook shutter control." Shutter control exists when sensing devices are turned off thereby restricting the collection and dissemination of data.

NIMA subsequently entered into a similar agreement with Digital Globe Corporation for data and information. The combined cost was more than $100 million. NIMA also provided major support for the U.S. led war against Iraq in 2003.

4. Conclusion

A great stride was taken on December 3, 1986 when the U.N General Assembly adopted Resolution 41/65 entitled "Principles Relating to Remote Sensing of the Earth from Outer Space." Today it is recognized that foreign RC is an every day practice, and is not contrary to international law although some sensed States have complained that such activities are violative of their sovereign "right of privacy." At the same time a State is able to invoke its sovereign right of self-defense in order to forestall grave harms to it resulting from foreign activities. To alleviate concerns respecting the purpose or purposes for which a State engages in RS those countries which believe that they are either actually or prospectively experiencing detriment should insist on compliance with Article IV of the

1976 Convention on Objects Launched into Outer Space. It calls for launching countries to report on the "general function of the space object."

There are two basic threats to RS systems. The first is the possibility that governmentally acquired sensitive data and information will fall into the hands of an adversary or that competing private commercial systems will make such items available to an adversary. The second is the possibility of an incapacitating military attack on national space systems.

These concerns are reflected in the January 2001 report of the Commission to Assess United States National Security Space Management and Organization. This body known as the Space Commission was chaired by Donald Rumsfeld prior to his becoming Secretary of Defense. The Committee warned that adversaries could cause havoc by attacking satellites in space, communication links, and ground stations. It urged that steps be taken "to deter and to defend against hostile acts in and from space." The creation of superior space capabilities was recommended. Guerrilla warfare of the kind facing coalition forces in Iraq in 2003 has emphasized the need to protect communication facilities.

Both broad coverage and limited coverage space systems, with the former being dedicated to combat conditions and general violence, and the later designed to identify natural resources, can respond to the world-wide presence of militant terrorists and the ongoing development of weapons of mass destruction. Both aspects of RS, commercial and military, can assist in controlling such threats. In time of crisis the former can augment the capabilities of the latter.

The need by a country for ready and accurate access to the product of RS depends on its foreign policy commitments. The security aspects of RS have to be examined in a broader context than the availability of a foreign product to an American adversary or of an American product to such an opponent. It must also be seen in the light of availability of such data and information to a friend or ally of the United States.

For those States, which either by default or design, have been called upon to lead in the search for international peace and security, there is a manifest benefit to be obtained through the promotion of commercial and military efficiency in RS. A farseeing national space policy should encourage commercial RS not only for the benefits derived from it but also to supplement national military resources when national security is under challenge.

References

Carl Q. Christol, Remote Sensing and International Space Law, 16 *J. Space Law* 21, No. 1 (1988), reprinted in CARL Q. CHRISTOL, SPACE LAW PAST, PRESENT, AND FUTURE 73 (1991).

PETER L. HAYS, UNITED STATES MILITARY SPACE INTO THE TWENTY-FIRST CENTURY, Institute for National Security Studies Occasional Paper 42 (2002).

Sean Hitchings, Policy Assessment of the Impacts of Remote-Sensing Technology, 19 *Space Policy* 110, Number 2 (May 2003). Shaida Johnston and Joseph Cordes, Public Good or Commercial Opportunity? Case Studies in Remote Sensing Commercialization, 19 *Space Policy* 23, Number 1 (February 2003).

SPACE ASSET FINANCING AND TRADE ISSUES

By Paul B. Larsen, Georgetown University Law Center*)
(PBLspace@aol.com)

FIRST PART: UNIDROIT SPACE PROTOCOL

The International Institute for Unification of Private Law (UNIDROIT) is modernizing the law governing security interests in high value mobile property. The Convention on International Interests in Mobile Equipment was adopted in Cape Town, South Africa on 16 November, 2001. 1/ The Cape Town conference took the first step of extending the treaty to aviation assets by a special protocol. 2/ The next steps are to extend the Cape Town Convention to space assets and to railroad assets by special protocols. Adoption of a special protocol for space assets would facilitate international trade in space assets, expand financing opportunities and would lower the cost of financing. 3/

An industry working group on space asset financing has met several times. Represented on the working group are manufacturers, financers, insurers and operators as well as space lawyers. The intent is to involve people with practical experience in financing of space assets and space law. The group is chaired by Peter D. Nesgos. In several meetings the space industry working group drafted a protocol which was transmitted to UNIDROIT in January 2002. 4/ UNIDROIT in turn transmitted the protocol to Governments.

The space industry working group, joined by a number of invited government representatives, met again at the European Space Agency (ESA) in Paris on September 5, 2003. This Paris colloquium was chaired by Dr. Sergio Marchisio, vice chairman of the European Center for Space Law. The participants examined the draft space protocol, raising issues for the working group to consider in the short term. Some of these interesting issues include:

1. Are the Convention and the draft space protocols too open-ended? 5/ Blanket incorporation of existing space law may complicate financing under the space protocol because some space law is implemented and some is not.
2. Should satellite salvage rights to space assets be regulated ? 6/
3. Do national security restrictions on transfer of dual use space assets create uncertainty about the rights of the insurers and financiers to space assets? 7/
4. Are the creditors' remedies in cases of default by the debtor too vague? For example is the provision in the Convention's Art 8 (1) that the creditor shall exercise his rights for repossession, sale, or collection of income in a "commercially reasonable manner" too vague to be effective?
5. Is the space protocol project too ambitious? Should the scope of the space protocol be narrowed to simply establish an international registry enabling creditors and debtors to register and locate secured interests and nothing further?
6. Is there a need to redefine "associated rights" in the Space

Protocol's Art 1?
7. How should space assets be identified in the registry of secured assets? Should the registry permit multiple search criteria for identification of assets in the registry?

Conclusion to Part I:

The chairman stressed that the major purpose of the Space Protocol is to facilitate and expand financing of space assets rather than to harmonize the law governing secured interests in space assets. He encouraged COPUOS to continue its examination of the relationship between the space protocol and existing space law.

The space industry working group plans to remain active during the three years that the governmental experts are working on the Space Protocol. One reason for continued vigilance is that the government experts represent their sovereign governments and are not bound by the preparatory work of the industry working group. Individual members of the industry working group will assist the government experts or may even become such experts representing their governments. Furthermore, the working group will meet in between meetings of the government experts in order to assess the progress made. The chairman of the working group also plans to coordinate work on special topics (such as the topic discussed in Part II of this paper).

Another colloquium directed at Eastern Hemisphere communities is planned for Kuala Lumpur, Malaysia, in early 2004. The governmental experts' first meeting is in Rome, December 15 - 19 December 2003. That is to be followed by three more meetings at about eight months intervals. According to this schedule the diplomatic conference on the space protocol may take place in 2005 or 2006

SECOND PART: RESTRICTIONS ON TRADE IN SPACE ASSETS

The purpose of this Part is to list restrictions on trade in space assets. As parties to financing know, transfers of property rights to space assets are often restricted by national and international regulation. National and some international restrictions tend to be related either to trade competition or national security. Occasionally there are mixed motivations. Nevertheless an attempt is made below to sort out the restrictions according to their trade or security category. The list is compiled from U.S. law, but because so much of international trade in space assets touches on the United States, these restrictions affect many countries.

RESTRICTIONS WHICH ARE NOT RELATED TO NATIONAL SECURITY

<u>A. ITU International Laws and Regulations</u>: The ITU Constitution, Arts 33-44, 8/ gives ITU members the right to terminate illegal radio transmissions. Art 36 provides that ITU members may suspend international telecommunications service after due notice to ITU. Thus financial transactions are subject to ITU's international laws and regulations.

B. Unfair Trade Practices: U.S. Trade Act of 1974, section 301, 9/ prohibits unreasonable burdens and restrictions on U.S. Commerce. In 1985 a U.S. company, Transspace, 10/ filed a petition under Sec. 301 before the U. S. Trade Representative against ESA for subsidizing Arianespace and thus competing unfairly with Transspace alledging that:

1. Arianespace used a two tier pricing policy (a). a higher price to ESA members, (b) a lower price to others.
2. France subsidized range launch facilities
(3) France provided free technical experts.
(4) Arianespace provided free insurance

The ITR compared ESA practices to US practices. The ESA practice was found to be not sufficiently different from US practices to be considered unreasonable. Transspace lost the case thus indicating that Section 301 is perhaps not a very effective tool for regulation of unfair trade practices in space assets.

C. Nationality requirements for use of radio frequencies: Many States, including the United States, regulate transfer of radio frequencies for public policy reasons. The Federal Communication Commission (FCC) requires its permission to transfer use of radio frequencies and orbital slots.. Under Sec 301 of the Communications Act of 1934 11/ the FCC requires that no person shall use any radio frequencies except pursuant to license granted by the FCC. The FCC determines whether the public convenience and necessity would be served by the grant of an application for a license. In making its decision whether to grant a license The FCC considers several factors: availability of spectrum, effect on competition, technical characteristics, radio interference, eligibility requirements, as well as national security, law enforcement, foreign policy and trade. Prior to transfer of an existing license to another entity the FCC must find that the transfer will serve the public interest.

The US Communications Act limits foreign ownership of certain US radio licenses. These limitations involve ownership by foreign governments, corporations and individuals. 12/ Section 310(4) is of particular significance because it requires the FCC to address indirect ownership greater than 25% in broadcast common carrier licenses. In reviewing proposed foreign investment pursuant to Section 310, the FCC relies on principles set forth in the 1997 Foreign Participation Order which has a rebuttable presumption that foreign investment from WTO member countries is consistent with the public interest.

D. Rules on Competition: The Communications Act 13/ states that monopolies in radio communication are not permitted. The FCC is given the task of enforcement in the area of satellite communication. The U.S. Government may regulate monopolies and mergers under the anti trust laws (by the Department of Justice and the Federal Trade Commission). Application and enforcement of the European Union rules on competition are also possible.

NATIONAL SECURITY RESTRICTIONS ON TRADE

A. Wassenaar Agreement: 14/ The

Wassenaar Agreement requires export control of conventional arms and dual-use goods and technologies. Members of the Wassenaar agreement must inform its members when arms are transferred. Its purpose is to promote transparency; increase responsibility; and establish reporting requirements

B. The Missile Technology Control Regime (MTCR): 15/ The MTCR is a voluntary arrangement to stop missile proliferation. 29 member states agree to limit and restrict proliferation of missile technology. (The USA and many developed countries are members of the MTCR. China is not a member). "Missile" is defined as technology capable of carrying a 500 kg payload at least 300 km as well as delivery of weapons of mass destruction (WMD). (Included are ballistic missiles, space launch vehicles, unmanned air vehicles, cruise missiles including GPS satellites used to guide cruise missiles).

Enforcement is divided into two categories according to severity of the danger: Category I is most severe. It is subject to presumption of denial of permission to export. Category II covers a diversity of parts and components such as propellants, structural materials, test equipment, and flight instruments. These may be exported on a case by case basis.

C. U.S. Export Control Legislation of 1999: 16/
Particular problems with Chinese launch access of U.S. payload provoked US Congress concerns with satellite exports to China. Discussions in Congress were based on the Cox Report. The US legislation establishes the primary importance of national security over business interests.

1. Required export license plan must be approved by the Department of Defense (DOD).
2. Crash Investigation license is required for U.S. participants in the investigation. DOD will monitor such investigations. This requirement does not apply to NATO allies.
3. Annual report to Congress on export of US satellites for launch by China.
4. Registration and licensing requirements include all articles whether of US or foreign manufacture. Nothing may be exported or imported without a license. A $250 license fee payable to Department of State. Violation is a criminal offense.
5. Munitions transactions with countries that support terrorism are prohibited.
6. The President may waive trade restrictions if essential for the national security. 17/

D. ITARs and EARs: 18/ Control is maintained by the State Department under the International Traffic in Arms Regulations (ITARS) and by the Department of Commerce under the Export Administration Regulations (EARS).
Stricter US export control of space technology was established in 1999 when the US Congress moved responsibility for satellite export control from the Department of Commerce (DOC) to the Department of State (DOS). Satellites were placed in the same export category as military weapons systems. DOS regulation proved to be more extensive, restrictive and time consuming than DOC regulation. Added regulations resulted in added cost. Most of the impact on US business has been felt in the satellite

manufacturing side. US market share of satellite manufacturing has fallen from 75%to 45% in 2000. Export and import controls are also having adverse effect on the US launch vehicle market. 19/

<u>E. Iran Non-proliferation Act of 1999</u>: 20/ The Act bars the United States from buying space assets from Russia unless the President can certify that the Russian supplier is not supplying sensitive military technology to IRAN. For example this law restricts use of Russian spacecraft to supply the International Space Station.

Conclusion to Part II:

In the absence of the international regulation the parties to financing contracts are subject to existing national and international laws and regulations restricting trade in space assets.
The current draft space protocol provides the contracting states room to exercise existing national laws in the case of a creditor's insolvency. The draft protocol provides the parties to the treaty the following options: (1) They may opt to be subject to the insolvency laws provided under national law; (2) they may select space protocol article XI, Alternative A, which requires the debtor to hand over the space asset to the creditor at the end of a waiting period specified in a declaration filed by the contracting state which has primary jurisdiction over the insolvency, or (3) the contracting state may opt for space protocol, Alternative B, which requires the debtor to give notice to the creditor to cure the default or permit the creditor to take possession in accordance with applicable national law.

Footnotes

*) Copyright 2003 by Paul B. Larsen. Published by the American Institute of Aeronautics and Astronautics, Inc with permission. Released to AIAA to publish in all forms.

1. Convention on International Interests in Mobile Equipment, U.N. Doc. No. A/AC.105/C.2/2002/CRP.3 (Nov. 16, 2001).

2. Id.

3.Nesgos letter, New York, 31 August, 2003

4. Id. Larsen, Future Protocol on Security Interests in Space Assets, 67 J. Air L. & Com. 1071 at 1081 (2002)

5. Larsen supra n. 4 at 1085.

6. Salvage rights are extensively regulated in maritime law, Healy & Sweeney, Marine Collision, Ch. 15 (1998)

7. See Part II below.

8. ITU Convention, Project 2001, Legal Framework for Commercial Use of Outer Space (Satellite Communications), June 8-9, 2002 Berlin, Germany at 214 - 16.

9. 19 U.S.C. 2411(a)

10. 50 Fed. Reg. 29631 (1985).

11. 47 U.S.C. 301

12. 47 U.S.C. 310

13. 47 U.S.C. 314.

14. Wassenaar Agreement, see http://www.bis.doc.gov.Wassenaar/default.htm

15. Missile Technology Control Regime, see http://www.fas.org/nuke/control/mtcr/docs/mtcr96.htm

16. P.L. 105-261 (1998)

17. Boeing (Hughes) agreed to pay $32 million penalty and Loral agreed to pay $20 million penalty when the two American contractors provided sensitive rocket technology information to China during investigation into two separate failures of the Chinese Long March launch vehicle.

18. 22 CFR Part 120-130; 15 CFR 730 et seq.

19. Space industry has raised questions whether the U.S. Department of State has enough personnel to handle the large number of export license applications.

20. Iran Non-Proliferation Act of 1999

Remote Sensing Satellite and Promotion of Regional Security

HASHIMOTO, Yasuaki*
Associate Professor
National Institute for Defense Studies
2-2-1, Nakameguro, Meguro-ku
Tokyo 153-8648, JAPAN

Abstract

The ability of civil remote sensing satellites has improved remarkably in recent years, reaching a level at which they can contribute to regional/international peace and security. Space activities should be for the benefit of all mankind, for peaceful purposes and with international cooperation. This has been expressed in some United Nations resolutions. We have come to consider and examine the feasibility of an organization that will contribute to the regional security using existing space assets.

1. Background -New Threats to Contemporary World

Since the end of the Cold War, international society has faced new threats. The confrontation and feared all-out war between the east and the west has practically disappeared. However, the unforeseen new threats have become concerns around the entire world.

These include terrorism by fundamentalists, drug cultivation and illicit sale, large-scale and systematic pirating, domestic disputes and refugees caused by them, and cyber terrorisms. In addition, problems, such as environmental protection and natural resource conservation have become new security concerns, which were once considered to be separate from security concerns. These are not only threatening, but also seriously impact our safety, and affect the whole world. These new threats are now common challenges to global security.

Existing military power led by the superpowers has little effect on these new threats. They are being focused on areas that cannot be dealt by large-scale military power. It is therefore necessary to continue a constant small-scale response while leaving open the possibility of final, strong action using military power. In such cases, there can be little effect of a so-called top down type response led by superpowers. Careful bottom-up-type response actions types are more effective. The role that international and regional organizations such as the United Nations play is also important. Combination of such top-down and bottom-up responses so that they supplement each other is likely to be more effective in meeting the threats that present international society faces.

---

*Member of IISL, Mail:hashimoto@nids.go.jp

2. Possibility of Remote Sensing Satellites

The data obtained by remote sensing satellites as well as reconnaissance satellites cannot meet all of such new threats. For instance, reconnaissance satellites were designed to respond to threats perceived during the Cold War. They were used to survey large-scale military movements of potential enemies. Moreover, reconnaissance satellites were used for accurate location of targets in a military attack. In this sense, reconnaissance satellites were not designed for tomorrow's threats but for yesterday's threats.

Moreover, a satellite, for example, cannot detect cyber terrorism. Obviously, cyber space cannot be watched from outer space. However, old-fashioned methods such as satellites can be effective in meeting some new threats, such as pursuit of pirates and location of the drag cultivation regions. Survey of airfields for drug smuggling and pursuit of contraband ships may also be possible. In addition, views from outer space may be effective in detecting environmental pollution and locating its source. An advantage of using space assets is the elimination of risk and trouble on the ground in gathering information on refugees. There is also a possibility of locating terrorist training camps.

Of course, only remote sensing cannot make a complete investigation. Information gathering and proper analysis on the ground are necessary for that. The analysis includes signal interception and information gathering by humans. In a word, information becomes effective with multiangled analysis, and combining image information from signal information, human information, etc.

The threats that 21st century society faces aren't limited to one country, but can easily cross national borders. Terrorists act internationally, and come from a variety of races and nationalities. Refugees easily spread across national borders. Pirates are not only small-scale operators in the coastal area. They have sold stolen freight internationally, changed the name on a ship's hull, as well as her nationality, to resell. It is naturally insufficient to respond to such international crime by focusing on one specific country. Neighboring countries, regions, and global cooperative action will be needed. It is essential to share recognition and information on this threat. Information exchange can increase the effectiveness of responses to these crimes. Such a principle and necessity of international mutual understanding are similar to the principle of international space law, that is, the outer space shall be the province of all mankind and space activities shall be for the benefit of all countries[1]. How can we respond from outer space to 21st century's threats?

3. Promotion of Security Using Outer Space

After the end of the Cold War, the United Nations has advocated contributing to international peace and security with space activities via a series of Resolutions, which require that all space activities be for the common benefit of mankind, for peaceful purposes, and be promoted by international cooperation. We can see that international society wants to bear the responsibility for international peace and security, not only the superpowers but also other nations in some degree, since the Cold War period[2]. Of course, such Resolutions do not have legal binding force on member states. However, by adopting them repeatedly, they have some effect in making each country hesitate to take action in contradiction of them.

The intention of those Resolutions, especially in fact-findings and early warnings, might not be technically feasible, because the information gathered by civil remote sensing satellites may be insufficient for international security purpose at a given time.

But the technical situation is changing drastically. The technology of the civil remote sensing satellites has advanced rapidly during the past decade. The resolution has improved to about 60 centimeters. Investigations of pirates, the illicit drug trafficking, refugees, terrorist training camps, etc. become possible if combined with various related information on the ground. At this point, a series of United Nations Resolutions has changed in character from nominal, idealistic resolutions to feasible ones. We are now able to examine the concrete organization and its role in maintaining international/regional peace and security by fact-findings and early warnings using space assets.

Moreover, the entry of Asian countries into this field is also remarkable. Some countries such as China, India, South Korea, Japan, etc. have solely or jointly developed remote sensing technology and successfully launched satellites. In addition, some Asian countries have purchased satellite data and analyzed them themselves. Such nations have as much know-how for analyzing data and information as the actual users.

4. Promoting Regional Security in Asia –Regional Satellite Centre

If data from remote sensing satellites as well as reconnaissance satellites can be used to contribute to the solution of mutual concerns in the Asian region, it will promote the stabilization of the region. Each country's national interests, which are different, can be realized under a stable regional situation.

In this respect, there is a necessity for regional cooperation. To keep the region stable, the establishment of an international (regional) satellite center as a common use organization is being considered as follows.

1) Higher Organization

There is no appropriate higher organization in the Asian region. In other regions, there are several such regional organizations, such as WEU, EU, NATO, etc. These organizations mainly deal with security matters in and around their respective regions. In Asia, ASEAN Regional Forum (ARF) plays a certain role in security, but keeps no permanent secretariat office yet. However, ARF moves steadily from confidence-building to preventive diplomacy. It has established experts and eminent persons group for fact-finding missions, mediating disputes, and offering practical solutions to disputed issues. It is also thinking about establishing a system of self-reporting, through which member-states would report on their own perception of existing or potential security concerns; and developing an early warning system to identify danger points and emerging crises.

We might consider establishing a new organization to fill this gap until an appropriate higher organization appears. There are several variations in form, such as regionally independent organizations or regional enterprises in which Asian countries become stockholders. When a higher organization emerges, these entities will belong it. Actually, there is a precedent in Europe: the WEU Satellite Centre is now under the EU.

2) Establishment Form

a. Regional Organization

There may be a format for establishing a regional organization by international agreement in Asia. In this case, each country would allot the establishment and management cost according to a certain standard, and the engineers and the analysts would be sent from member countries. The dispatched personnel would have the same status as existing international organizations, and would collect and analyze information concerning regional security according to the requests of the member countries.

b. Regional Enterprise

In this case, each country would become a stockholder in this regional enterprise. This capital fund would be allotted to the establishment and management cost. Most members will be dispatched from stockholders. Each country would lodge requests about its own security concerns as a stockholder, and receive reports[3].

3) Roles to Play

In any such case, it would appropriate for member states/ stockholder states to be circulated requests from other members/stockholders and their answer reports. All countries in the same region would then learn the concerns of other countries and evaluate them as acceptable or not. By this procedure, the security concern of one country would be promoted to a common concern in the region. In this situation, regional states would hesitate to take any action that would exacerbate the problem by their own discretion, when all member countries easily find out what happened in the concerned area. In Asia, for example, information about military activities in the Spratly Islands; piracy in the Straits of Malacca, the Indian Ocean as well as the South China Sea; drug cultivation in Indochina; etc. would be useful for most regional members.

The EU Satellite Centre has already performed this function. The Satellite Centre in Spain functions as one organization of the European Union, and is used to settle on common diplomatic and security policy[4]. In Asia, there is no regional organization like the EU. Every country has its own individual security policy. However, needless to say, it is more significant to share security concerns between countries with different policies.

Conclusion

One decade has already passed since the end of the Cold War. Present society now faces new threats, which cannot be covered by past international security systems and laws. It is therefore necessary to construct a new system for response in order to supplement the present system. It may be expressed as "putting new wine into a new bottle." It is necessary to combine space assets newly and appropriately to contribute to peace and security on the earth. The theme of a concrete examination for such an effort is the feasibility study of a regional satellite center in Asia.

*Any opinion here is the personal opinion of the author, not the opinion of any organization, which the author belongs.

---

1 Outer Space Treaty, 1967, Article 1.

2 Y. Hashimoto "Legal Analysis of Military Observation from Outer Space," *Proceedings of the Fortieth Colloquium on The Law of Outer Space*, pp.229-233, AIAA, Washington, DC.

3 There is already a commercial company, which plays the same kind of roles. ImageSat International N.V. provides satellite data to the contracted countries through Satellite Operating Partner Program and Priority Acquisition Service Program. However, there is concern for continuity and reliability because of its style as a private sector. http://www.imagesatintl.com/#Scene_1

4 http://www.weusc.es/

Export controls and satellite launches: what's new?

by

Prof. Dr. H. Peter van Fenema

McGill University
Institute of Air and Space Law

c/o Jonker c.s. Advocaten
De Lairessestraat 73
1071 NV Amsterdam
The Netherlands
Tel. +31-20-676.5195
Fax +31-20-676.9886
pvanfenema@hotmail.com

Abstract *

Outer space activities have always been subject to export controls on the basis of both multilateral arrangements and national legislation. Considerations of national security and foreign policy play an important role in the way these controls are being applied in practice The launch business continues to be the specific focus of these controls because of its relation to the issue of missile (non-) proliferation. Heightened awareness of national and global security thus unavoidably produces tighter controls and ensuing uncertainties for the commercial launch industry. Some recent developments in this field will be reviewed.

Introduction

The September 11 terrorist attack and its aftermath have brought heightened awareness of the issue of proliferation of weapons of mass destruction (WMD), including the delivery systems, and of conventional weapons. Four multilateral arrangements in force today address various related threats through the creation of more or less harmonized national regulations which restrict the export of certain sensitive equipment and technologies. Two of these arrangements have a direct bearing on the launch business: the Missile Technology Control Regime of 1987 (MTCR) and the Wassenaar Arrangement of 1996 (Wassenaar).[1]

The MTCR seeks to limit the spread of delivery systems of WMD, *i.e.* missiles, missile technology and related equipment and know how, whereas the Wassenaar Arrangement focuses on trade in conventional weapons and in sensitive goods and technologies which (may) have both civilian and military applications or uses, the so-called 'dual-use' items. (Commercial) communications satellites are generally treated as dual use sensitive goods and are therefore subjected to national export controls. The U.S., for instance, treats these satellites as arms,

[1] The other two arrangements are the *Nuclear Suppliers Group* of 1975 which aims at preventing nuclear trade for peaceful purposes from contributing to the development of nuclear weapons, and the *Australia Group* of 1985 which addresses chemical and biological weapons proliferation. They will not be discussed in this article.

with correspondingly strict State Department export licensing procedures and sanctions.

These two regimes have a number of aspects in common:

(a) they are not treaties, but voluntary, non-binding arrangements and they have no enforcement mechanisms;
(b) the parties or members agree to restrict trade in the above goods and technologies through national export control and licensing systems;
(c) the parties share information about denials of export licenses to their own industries to prevent that foreign clients, rejected by one party, simply buy the sensitive technology from an other party;
(d) the 33 parties to both regimes are predominantly NATO members or NATO allies and – partly overlapping – European, mainly EU member state, countries;[2]
(e) the two regimes affect trade in launch services.

To begin with the latter aspect, it may be considered common knowledge by now that the technology applied to the development, manufacturing and operation of ballistic missiles is, in essence, virtually identical to that used for making (expendable) space launch vehicles. The MTCR therefore speaks of "rocket systems", "rocket stages" and "rocket engines", which encompass both of the above.

The MTCR strongly discourages the transfer of rocket equipment and technology. Technology in this connection means "specific information which is required for the development, production and use of a product", which includes instruction and training and technical data such as blueprints, diagrams and manuals.[3] In other words, an Arianespace engineer is not supposed to tell/show his colleague from Korea, the latest new MTCR member, how the rocket system of the Ariane 5 launch vehicle works.

Three remarks on this example:
(a) with the company Arianespace incorporated in France, French national export licensing regulations based on the MTCR guidelines will govern the interaction between the two engineers;
(b) the fact that both France and Korea are members of MTCR does not entitle the two countries to freely interchange this information. A U.S. Department of State Fact Sheet on MTCR puts it as follows:

"Membership in the MTCR does not involve an entitlement to obtain technology from another partner and no obligation to supply it. Partners have explicitly affirmed this principle. Partners are expected, just as in such trade between partners and non-partners, to exercise appropriate accountability and restraint in inter-partner trade."[4]

(c) the fact that Korea promises not to use the technology for the (further) development of home-grown missiles does not, as such, necessarily constitute sufficient guarantee for the French export control authorities to approve this exchange of information. True, the MTCR

---

[2] Present membership of MTCR: Argentina, Australia, Austria, Belgium, Brazil, Canada, the Czech Republic, Denmark, Finland, France, Germany, Greece, Hungary, Iceland, Ireland, Italy, Japan, The Republic of Korea, Luxembourg, Netherlands, New Zealand, Norway, Poland, Portugal, Russia, South Africa, Spain, Sweden, Switzerland, Turkey, Ukraine, the United Kingdom and the United States, see www.mtcr.info (accessed 24 September 2003). All these countries, except Brazil, South Africa and Iceland, are also members of Wassenaar. Bulgaria, Roumenia and Slovakia are parties to the latter arrangement only.

[3] See MTCR Equipment and Technology Annex – 11 June 1996, para 2 (Definitions)

[4] *Commonly asked questions on the Missile Technology Control Regime*, Fact Sheet, U.S. Department of State, Bureau of Nonproliferation, October 19, 2001, www.state.gov/t/np/rls/fs/2001/5481ph.htm (accessed 24 September 2003)

Guidelines "are not designed to impede national space programs or international cooperation in such programs..", but the Guidelines add to that declaration "..as long as such programs *could* not contribute to delivery systems for weapons of mass destruction."[5] This emphasis on 'could' means that France will have to make its own investigations into the capabilities and objectives of the missile and space programs of the recipient state and assess the end use of the transferred data. It also implies that, if such contribution to missile development cannot completely be ruled out, the French government will have to ask for assurances from the government of Korea that "the items [=the equipment and/or technology that will be transferred] will be used only for the [peaceful] purpose stated...[and that] neither the items nor replicas nor derivatives thereof will be re-transferred without the consent of the [French] government."[6]
Obviously, with a "strong presumption to deny such transfers" as guiding principle, both the international sale of missiles, but also legitimate cooperation between countries on the development of (commercial) space launch vehicles, have been affected.

A 2002 report of the U.S. General Accounting Office (GAO) concluded that the MTCR helped reduce the number of countries with ballistic missile programs: the MTCR "contributed to ending sensitive ballistic missile programs in a number of countries including Argentina, Brazil, South Africa and Taiwan and ...may have helped slow missile development in India, Iran, Israel, North Korea, and Pakistan.." [7]

And regime members have made it more difficult, more costly and more time consuming for 'proliferators' to obtain the expertise and material needed to advance their programs.
At the same time the regime and the way national governments applied the MTCR principles in practice may be 'credited' for slowing down the development of launch vehicles in India and Brazil and for discouraging exchange of post-launch failure investigation data or other cooperative activities between launch companies of different nationalities.[8]

The same GAO Report identified a number of weaknesses in regime activities, such as less than disciplined reporting on national export licensing decisions, disparities in national lists of controlled items and "significant differences in how regime members implement agreed-upon controls". The Report also identified obstacles which stand in the way of strengthening the effectiveness of the above multilateral export control regimes, such as the fact that decisions are consensus-based and can therefore be blocked by a single member and the voluntary and non-binding character of the regimes which make enforcement virtually impossible.
One could say, with an element of demagoguery, that these loopholes and weaknesses are bad news for non-proliferation efforts but good news for legitimate non-military space cooperation.

A specific problem mentioned by the Report deserves special attention because it was one of the reasons for a new multilateral non-proliferation initiative to supplement the MTCR: the growing

---

[5] *Guidelines for Sensitive Missile Relevant Transfers*, para. 1, MTCR, see www.mtcr.info/english/guidetext.htm (accessed 24 September 2003)
[6] *Id*, at paras 3 and 5
[7] *Nonproliferation – Strategy needed to strengthen multilateral export control regimes*, U.S. GAO Report to Congressional Committees, GAO-03-43, October 2002 (hereinafter referred to as GAO Report), at p.8

[8] On this aspect, *see The International Trade in Launch Services – The effects of U.S. laws, politics and practices on its development*, H. Peter van Fenema (1999); *Launch services and satellite export controls: recent developments in the U.S.*, by the same author, 'Project 2001' – Legal framework for the commercial use of outer space, Carl Heymanns Verlag, pp. 121-126 (2002).

capability of non-member countries to develop technologies used for weapons of mass destruction and trade them with other 'countries of concern' which undermines the regimes' ability to prevent proliferation. An example of this "secondary proliferation" quoted in the Report is North Korea's export of "significant ballistic missile-related equipment, components, materials, and technical expertise to countries of concern, including Iran."[9] And, one could add, any new customer willing to buy missile products or technology stimulates further production and sales thereof.

During its Presidency of MTCR in 1999, the Netherlands proposed to address, *inter alia*, this problem through a multilateral agreement which would be open to members and non-members of MTCR alike, thereby supplementing a Western-oriented, supply-side, sensitive trade-restricting regime addressing the 'haves' by a more global supply- ànd demand-side arrangement which says: 'don't sell, don't buy, don't develop and don't possess ballistic missile equipment or technology!'. As one expert explained: "this supplemental arrangement basically puts a warning on missiles and missile components, reading 'ballistic missiles are hazardous to your health!'"

The arrangement, which got strong support from the EU, and was the subject of a substantial number of meetings and consultations, in particular with non-MTCR members, was officially born on 26 November 2002 in The Hague, Netherlands, and was baptized as "*The International Code of Conduct against Ballistic Missile Proliferation*" (ICOC, or H[ague]COC).[10]

HCOC does not forbid ballistic missiles, but calls for greater restraint in the development, testing, use and spread of ballistic missiles. The Code also introduces a number of confidence building measures to increase transparency and reduce mistrust between member states. The most important one of these measures is the obligation to announce missile launches in advance (which will be reverted to later).

Echoing the spirit of the MTCR, the Code (through an express commitment to the U.N. Declaration on Space Cooperation of 1996) makes a distinction between, on the one hand, – permitted – peaceful international space (launch) cooperation and, on the other hand, space (launch) cooperation which may lead to missile proliferation. And, in order to separate one from the other, transparency is crucial.[11]

The Subscribing States commit themselves to the following transparency measures:

(a) with respect to ballistic missiles programmes, to make an annual declaration providing an outline of their ballistic missile policies (if possible including information on ballistic missile systems and land (test-) launch sites); and to provide annual information on the number and generic class of ballistic missiles launched during the preceding year.
(b) With respect to expendable space launch vehicle programs "and consistent with commercial and economic confidentiality

[9] GOA Report., supra note 7, at p.3

[10] For text and additional info, see www.minbuza.nl (search 'HCOC') (accessed 24 September 2003)

[11] See respective Principles 2 f, g and h, reading as follows: - "Recognition that states should not be excluded from utilising the benefits of space for peaceful purposes, but that, in reaping such benefits and in conducting related cooperation, they must not contribute to the proliferation of Ballistic Missiles capable of delivering weapons of mass destruction; - Recognition that Space Launch Vehicle Programmes should not be used to conceal Ballistic Missile programmes; - Recognition of the necessity of appropriate transparency measures on Ballistic Missile programmes and Space Launch Vehicle programmes in order to increase confidence and to promote non-proliferation of Ballistic Missiles and Ballistic Missile technology."

principles", to provide basically similar information as with respect to ballistic missiles, with the addition of a recommendation to invite international observers to their land (test-) launch sites.[12]

The HCOC contains another interesting confidence building measure which deserves full quoting:

"With respect to their ballistic missile and space launch vehicle programmes, to exchange pre-launch notifications on their ballistic missile and space launch vehicle launches and test flights. These notifications should include such information as the generic class of the ballistic missile or space launch vehicle, the planned launch notification window, the launch area and the planned direction;"[13]

This provision raises a number of issues, e.g. of a national security character. For instance, it is believed that the extent of transparency this clause would entail was the reason for China's decision not to subscribe to the Code of Conduct. There is no agreed pre-launch notification model as yet. This is a matter which will form the subject of talks to be held by the subscribing states. The U.S. government has indicated that it will base its notifications and annual declarations on the U.S. – Russian Pre-Launch Notification System under development and that it expects to multi-lateralize this system to – possibly – become the HCOC standard. The U.S. also observed that it will reserve the right to launch without notification in war-like situations (which gives a part – answer to the question of which launches are to be notified in the view of the U.S.[14]

This part of the Code has wider ramifications than the – already complicated - military and national security aspects which, understandably, are of primary concern tot the HCOC states. In particular, attention should be paid to the effect these pre-notification measures may have on the policies and practices of states with respect to the registration of space objects. The U.N. Registration Convention of 1976 requires the State of registry (which is a launching State which has registered a space object in its own national registry) to furnish information concerning that space object to the U.N. Secretariat Register "as soon as practicable". Although the purpose of the Convention, *i.e.* to assist in the identification of space objects primarily for the application of the Space Liability Convention, would justify availability of information on the launch of a space object *before* the launch, the predominant practice of the parties to the Convention has been to do so afterwards. (The Convention of course was not meant to be of a confidence-building nature).
The HCOC may have the unintended positive side-effect that Subscribing States, which are also parties to the Registration Convention, feel inclined to henceforth give their pre-launch notifications on launches of space objects with the *dual* purpose of HCOC confidence building and 'pre- registration' of the object for the purpose – and in the spirit - of the Registration Convention.[15]

---

[12] See subparas 4 (a) (i) and (ii) of the HCOC. The difference in approach lies in the fact that the information on ballistic missile systems and land (test-) launch sites is optional "as examples of openness", whereas the ELV programme declarations *should* contain information on both the policies and the launch sites.

[13] See subpara 4 (a) (iii) of the HCOC

[14] *Remarks at the Launching Conference for the International Code of Conduct Against Ballistic Missile Proliferation*, John R. Bolton, Under Secretary for Arms Control and International Security, The Hague, November 25, 2002, hereinafter referred to as ' Bolton remarks', see www.state.gov/t/us/rm/15488pf.htm (accessed on 24 September 2003). *The Agreement between the [USA] and the [USSR] on notifications of launches of intercontinental ballistic missiles and submarine-launched ballistic missiles* of May 31, 1988 may serve as a starting point for this new U.S. – Russia agreement.

[15] On 27 March 2003, Austria, the Immediate Central Contact of the HCOC, forwarded the first Pre-Launch Notification (PLN), that of Japan (*re* a planned H-IIA launch on 28 March), to the Subscribing States. As the date coincided with the

This is not too farfetched. After all, the first of the "General Measures" which the Subscribing States resolve to implement, is to ratify, accede to or otherwise abide by the Outer Space Treaty, the Liability Convention and the Registration Convention.[16] Where ratifying the space treaties may be seen as proof of responsible behaviour which will increase confidence, the other confidence building measures, such as pre-notification, may also increase the effectiveness of the space treaties, such as the Registration Convention and, as a result, also the Liability Convention. (In that respect the HCOC is supplemental not only to the MTCR but also, *de facto*, to the Registration Convention).
A matter which may therefore also be the subject of debate in the UNCOPUOS Legal Subcommittee is the relationship between the question of 'who will notify' under HCOC and the existing issue of 'who will register' under the Registration Convention, particularly in cases of private launches.

All U.N. member states, except Iraq, were invited to the Launching Conference in the Hague. Some 100 immediately became Subscribing States. The present count is 106, which includes all MTCR members except Brazil.[17] The latter country purportedly was not sure about the added value of the HCOC and has some hesitations as to the effect the Code may have on its (cooperative) space endeavours. Absent are, apart from China, referred to earlier, also Israel, India and Pakistan. The latter three are missile producing countries which have not signed the MTCR either. India is also active and successful in the space launch field, whereas Israel works hard on its goal to have independent access to space as well.

The HCOC is not a treaty but a voluntary arrangement; it is only 'politically binding'. Its effect on the trade in launch services is at this stage difficult to predict.

A positive point is the clear distinction which has been made between cooperation on Space Launch Vehicle programmes which is regarded as – in principle - covered by the U.N. Declaration on Space Cooperation (= 'good'), and cooperation on Ballistic Missile programmes (= 'bad').[18]

Whether this will indeed result in more cooperation in the field of civilian/commercial launch service operations is doubtful. This is not so much a question of the HCOC provisions, but much more of the spirit in which they will be interpreted and applied in practice by the Subscribing States. The 'post-9/11' national security focus has created a 'better safe than sorry' atmosphere which does not augur well for the launch trade. And the HCOC was not created to promote civilian/commercial space launch cooperation but to fight ballistic missile proliferation.

In that connection, the (tone of the) statement of the U.S. representative at the Hague Conference is illustrative:

"...we are not concerned about the states that have chosen not to subscribe to the Code. Far better to know who is actually prepared to live under its terms, and who is not. Far better to know who is

---

42nd Session of the UNCOPUOS Legal Subcommittee, the PLN was also distributed among the members of this Subcommittee (who, at the same session, had already been informed about the HCOC by the Netherlands delegation).

[16] HCOC para 3 (a)

[17] See www.minbuza.nl (search "HCOC", Annex – List of Subscribing States) (accessed 3 September 2003)

[18] See text of Principles in footnote 11. See also the "General Measures", para 3 (d): "To exercise the necessary vigilance in the consideration of assistance to Space Launch Vehicle programmes in any other country so as to prevent contributing to delivery systems for weapons of mass destruction, considering that such programmes may be used to conceal Ballistic Missile programmes."

truly serious about stopping the proliferation of ballistic missile technology and the risk that such technology could be used to carry weapons of mass destruction against innocent civilian populations."[19]

The above aspects of the HCOC do justify monitoring the practices of the subscribing states in the coming years.

- end -

[19] See Bolton remarks, *supra* note 14

THE IMPLEMENTATION OF EXPORT CONTROLS IN THE EUROPEAN COMMUNITY – MAKING BALANCE BETWEEN SECURITY AND COMMERCIAL CONSIDERATIONS

Laurent Crapart[1]
Institute of space and telecommunications law (IDEST)
Paris, France
laurent.crapart@idest-paris.org

The issue of export controls in European countries became a Communitarian one in 1994, when the first binding text dealing with the export controls of sensitive items were adopted at a Community level. These texts only constituted a first step in the harmonisation process that has characterised, at least partly, export controls in the European Community since this time. It however contributed to make the issue of dual-use exports passing from the competence of European States to the competence of the European Community. After having briefly examined the major phases of the historical process having conducted to the current Community regime (I), this regime will be concretely examined, concerning both dual-use exports (II) and arms exports (III). The impact of such regulations on the space industry will also be emphasised, trying to distinguish between security-oriented provisions, and commercial-oriented provisions of this regime.

I. Historical background

a) 1957 - 1994

The history of export controls in the European Community can be divided into the three following phases. In a first period, running from the European Community origin to 1994, export controls remained in the sphere of States' competence. For security reasons, States would quasi-systematically consider that export control matters were part of their national sovereignty. This security-oriented approach was based on article 296 of the EC Treaty, according to which States parties to the treaty can adopt every measures they consider being essential for their security, or every measures concerning the production or business of arms and war materials. A very extensive interpretation of article 296 at State level resulted in the persistence of important divergences in European export control procedures (licensing, etc.), to the detriment of the constitution of an effective common market in the field of sensitive items. The European Community was consequently weakened, both economically and industrially, notably compared to its two major industrial competitors: United States and Japan, which both enjoyed internal homogenous markets. In Europe, security considerations were still largely predominating over commercial ones until 1994.

b) 1994 - 1998

In a second phase, two major events contributed to disturb this situation largely based on security concerns. First event, the Council Regulation No 3381/94 of 31 December 1994[i] happened to be the first European Union legislation in the field of dual-use export controls in 1994. It is very relevant to notice here that this regulation was based on both article 113 (currently 133) of the EC Treaty and a Common Foreign Security Policy Joint Action 94/942/CFSP. Then, two major projections had been accomplished on the way of a Communitarian approach for export controls. First, dual-use export controls were partly based on article 113, which means on the Common commercial policy; second, the European authorities were consequently entitled to adopt a regulation concerning these dual-use export controls. That was done with the 1994 regulation.

The second event came from the European Court of Justice. On 17 October 1995, two judgements of the European jurisdiction[ii] confirmed that dual-use exports belonged to the sphere of the Common commercial policy (article 113 of the EC Treaty), and had therefore to be ruled at Community level. In both cases, German exporters had been confronted with national authorities in dual-use export processes. In the first case (*Leifer* case), they had exported items being considered as dual-use ones without having obtained the required licences. In the second case (*Werner* case), the exporters faced export licences delivery refusals from national authorities. Before national jurisdictions, they contested the right of these national authorities to rule dual-use exports, on the basis of article 113 of the EC Treaty. These jurisdictions consequently referenced to the European Court of Justice under article 177 of the treaty for preliminary rulings. The terms of ECJ judgements were exemplary. The Court firstly stated that the implementation of the common commercial policy, as foreseen by article 113: "*requires a non-restrictive interpretation of that concept, so as to avoid disturbances in intra-Community trade by reason of the disparities which would then exist in certain sectors of economic relations with non-member countries*". The consequences of this were secondly clearly stated: "*Article 113 of the EC Treaty is to be interpreted as meaning that rules restricting export of dual-use goods to non-member countries fall within the scope of that article and that in this matter the Community has exclusive competence, which therefore excludes the competence of the Member States save where the Community grants them specific authorisation*".

Then, the Court of Justice had made a major step forward, by ruling that dual-use exports were falling within the scope of the Common commercial policy, and as a direct consequence in the scope of the Community competence. The commercial approach was gaining ground over security concerns. However, one should not conclude that these concerns were blindly moved aside by the European jurisdiction. Its position was actually shaded in order to take them into account in the eventuality of a threat to public security. The Court indeed considered that in such eventuality, "*which is a matter for the national court to consider, an obligation on the applicant to prove that the goods will be used exclusively for civil purposes or a refusal to issue a licence if the goods can objectively be used for military purposes can be consistent with the principle of proportionality*". The Court added that Common commercial policy does not preclude national provisions instituting licences on the ground that this is necessary in order to avoid "*the risk of a serious disturbance to [...] foreign relations which may affect the public security of a Member State.*" The Court thus recommended a balanced approach, where the place to be given to security concerns was regulated and proportionate to market considerations.

c) Since 1998

The third phase of this historical process brought this evolution to a successful conclusion, with the adoption of the Council Regulation No 1334/2000 setting up a Community regime for the control of exports of dual-use items and technology of 22 June 2000[iii]. This regulation, which replaced the 1994 text, was indeed completely based on article 113 (previously 133) of the Treaty, relating to Common commercial policy. It is also very relevant that the preamble of this regulation expressly stated that: "*The existence of a common control system and harmonised policies for enforcement and monitoring in all Member States is a prerequisite for establishing the free movement of dual-use items in the Community*" (Point 3). The purpose of the regulation was therefore clearly presented as being the completion of the Internal Market, by creating an efficient common external "fence" for extra Community exports, recognising notably that some countries of destination may enjoy simplified controls. For such purpose, the Council Regulation established the following rules.

II. The Community regime for the control of exports of dual-use items and technology

The Regulation No 1334/2000 (as amended) tends to make balance between the legitimate security concerns of EC Member States and the need to avoid unnecessary burden on European exporters, to promote a competitive environment and the completion of the Internal Market. For such purpose, the main features of this text are briefly described hereafter.

a) A common list of dual-use items subject to control

The regulation of 2000 partly lends to the 1994 one, by establishing, in its Annex I, a list of dual-use items for the export of which an authorisation shall be required by EC Member States. This list is drawn up in conformity with the obligations and commitments that each of them has accepted as a member of the different existing international regimes - MTCR, Wassenaar Arrangement, Nuclear Suppliers' Group, Australia Group. It is periodically updated and amended on the Commission proposition, due to the Article 133 basis of the Regulation. Therefore, all EC Member States will control the same items, which tends to harmonise the European regime.

Nevertheless, and in order to take their security concerns into account, Article 4 of the Regulation provides for a "catch-all clause", which permits States to control the exports of more items than those listed in Annex I, when these items are exported to destinations under an arm embargo, and are or may be intended for use in connection with mass-destruction weapons or conventional arms. Therefore, EC Member States are able to keep a certain control over the exports involving security concerns.

b) A Community General Export Authorisation

On the contrary, a Community General Export Authorisation (CGEA) is instituted by the 2000 Regulation for numerous items (almost all figuring in Annex I), as soon as they are exported in one of the listed Community trading partners - namely: Australia, Canada, Czech Republic, Hungary, Japan, New Zealand, Norway, Poland, Switzerland, and the USA. This CGEA liberalises most of the trade of dual-use items with these countries, thus facilitating legitimate trade for the industry.

c) The enhanced mutual recognition of licences

For all other exports (than those falling under the CGEA) for which an authorisation is required, national authorities of the State where the exporter is established remain competent for granting export licences. The subsequent intra-community transfers necessary for the item to reach its final destination outside the Community are not subject to additional controls from the EC Member States concerned, unless expressly provided by the Regulation. The regulation indeed permits an enhanced mutual recognition of licences between Member States, by laying down rules for mutual information and consultation. A "Coordinating group", chaired by the Commission and at which every Member State is represented, is also set up in order to examine issues arising from the Regulation application. Nevertheless, an exception is made for most sensitive dual-use items of Annex I, the exports of which are submitted to an authorisation, even for intra-Community transfers.

While the Community regime thus tries to strike a balance between security and commercial concerns governing the export of dual-use items, the legal regime applicable to arms exports inside the European Community remains largely dominated by security considerations, as described hereafter.

III. The European Code of conduct for arms exports

a) Current regime

Every sensitive good/item which is not figuring on the lists annexed to the EC Regulation of 2000 may nevertheless be subject to control, as soon as European States qualify it as an "arm", according to its national regulation. Belonging to the security and defense sphere, this qualification is of the competence of Member States. Some disparities consequently remain in the European export control regime, as far as these goods are concerned.

In order to overcome these disparities, the European Union has adopted on 8 June 1998 a European Union Code of Conduct on Arms Exports. This text builds up common criteria for arms exports, denial notifications, as well as consultation mechanisms, and shall as such be regarded as a new stage in the development of a common approach for European export controls. It is however only indicative for EC Member States, which are not bound by this text which has no legal value.

b) Consequences for the space industry

The consequence of this for the European industry is that concerned companies are not able to benefit a common approach, notably for intra-Community transfers, as soon as the goods transferred are regarded as "arms" under national legislation. Practically speaking, this means that unless European States have concluded special arrangements for such matters, European exporters will have to obtain an export licence from every State territorially concerned by the export. To conclude with, the European export control regime has only partly become a Communitarian one, arms transfer still belonging to the competence of States under the current system.

---

[i] Council Regulation (EC) No 3381/94 of 19 December 1994 setting up a Community regime for the control of exports of dual-use goods, *Official Journal* L 367, 31/12/1994 p. 0001 – 0007 (no longer in force).

[ii] ECJ, 17 October 1995, C-83/94, *Leifer case*; C-70/94, *Werner case*.

[iii] Council Regulation (EC) No 1334/2000 of 22 June 2000 setting up a Community regime for the control of exports of dual-use items and technology, *Official Journal* L 159, 30/06/2000 P. 0001 – 0215, as amended.

IAC-03-IISL.3.08

The 40th Anniversary of the 1963 Treaty Banning Nuclear Weapon Tests in the Atmosphere, in Outer Space and Under Water (1963 NTB)

Maurice N. Andem
Professor of Private International Law and Comparative Law
Director, Institute of Air and Space Law
Faculty of Law, University of Lapland, Rovaniemi, Finland

ABSTRACT

The Treaty Banning Nuclear Weapon Tests in the Atmosphere, in Outer Space and Under Water was opened for signature on 5 August 1963 and entered into force on 10 October of that same year. It was a great achievement for the United Nations in its efforts to prevent the new domain of activities of states - outer space from becoming an arena for the arms race and military confrontation. This paper will examine and analyze the provisions of the Treaty in order to demonstrate its continuous importance and relevance to the maintenance of international peace and security in the 21st century.

Introduction

Before commencing with the subject-matter of my paper, it will be useful to make a reflection briefly on the events that led to the atomic/nuclear arms race.

The atomic/nuclear era began with the first nuclear explosive test, conducted by the United States at Alamogordo, New Mexico, on 16 July 1945. This was followed bythe explosion of two atomic bombs in August over Hiroshima and Nagasaki, Japan, as World War II neared an end. The Soviet Union conducted its first nuclear explosive test near Semipalatinsk, Kazakhstan, in 1949. In 1952, the United Kingdom conducted its first nuclear (explosive) test in the Monte Bello Islands off the Australian coast. France conducted its first nuclear (explosive) test near Reggane, in the Sahara, in 1960.

The United Nations (UN), prominent individuals and groups worldwide were very much concerned about radioactive fall-out from nuclear test explosions and the escalation of the arms race between the Superpowers. Albert Einstein, for example, was very sad when he learned of the destruction of Hiroshima and Nagasaki. Following World War II, he became an outspoken campaigner for a ban on nuclear weaponry.[1]

Furthermore, in April 1954, almost 10 years after the first nuclear weapon test, Indian Prime Minister Nehru proposed that nuclear weapon testing should be suspended. His proposal was the first initiative of its kind. Awareness of the harmful effects of atmospheric nuclear tests prompted increasing demands for testing to end.

It should also be borne in mind that the beginning of the space era coincided with the escalation of the arms race. Thus, in the Preamble of Resolution **1348 (XIII)** of 13 December 1958, the UN General Assembly recognized the common interest of mankind in outer space and that it was the common aim that outer space should be used for peaceful purposes only. A desire to avoid the extension of national rivalries into outer space was also expressed in the third paragraph of the Preamble.

In the Preamble of Resolution **1722 (XVI)** of 20 December 1961, the UN General Assembly noted with concern that the continuing arms race was a heavy burden for humanity and was fraught with dangers for the cause of world peace. It endorsed the composition of a Disarmament Committee comprising the following membership: Brazil, Bulgaria, Burma, Canada, Czechoslovakia, Ethiopia, France, India, Italy, Mexico, Nigeria, Poland, Romania, Sweden, the Union of Soviet Socialist Republics, the United Arab Republic, the United Kingdom of Great Britain and Northern Ireland and the United States of America.

Furthermore, in Resolution **1801 (XVII)** of 14 December 1962, the UN General Assembly requested the Secretary-General to consult further the Governments of the Member States to ascertain their views on the possibility of convening a special conference for signing a convention on the prohibition of the use of nuclear and thermo-nuclear weapons for war purposes, and to report on the the results of this consultation to the General Assembly at its eighteenth session.

The result of the indefatigable efforts of the United Nations in the field of nuclear weapons disarmament was the signing of the **Partial Test Ban Treaty (PTBT)** or the **Treaty Banning Nuclear Weapon Tests in the Atmosphere, in Outer Space and Under Water** in Moscow on 5 August 1963 by the United States, the United Kingdom and the Soviet Union. The entered into force on 10 October 1963.

At this juncture, it should be borne in mind that the PTBT was the first international nuclear arms limitation agreement. According to the information provided in a publication of the Comprehensive Nuclear Test Ban Treaty Organization (CTBTO PreCom), over 550 nuclear explosions were registered in the 18 years between the first nuclear explosive test on 16 July 1945 and the signing of the PTBT on 5 August 1963.

It is encouraging to note that, during the Cold War, two bilateral agreements on the limitation of nuclear explosions were signed by the

Soviet Union and the United States - the Treaty on the Limitation of Underground Weapons Tests (Threshold Test-Ban Treaty), limiting the yield of such tests to 150 kilotons of 3 July 1974[2] andthe Treaty on Underground Nuclear Explosions for Peaceful Purposes (Peaceful Nuclear Explosions Treaty), limiting the yield of individual nuclear explosions conducted outside nuclear weapon test sites to 150 kilotons.[3]

As we celebrate the 40th Anniversary of the PTBT of 1963, it is important to bear in mind that much has been achieved by the UN with the co-operation of its Member States, including Non-governmental organizations and prominent world leaders, to make all the environments of our Mother Earth nuclear weapons free. In this respect, four nuclear-weapon-free zone treaties have been signed during this period, namely, (i) the Treaty for the Prohibition of Nuclear Weapons in Latin America and the Caribbean (the Treaty of Tlatelolcol, Mexico) of 14 February 1967,[4] (ii) the South Pacific Nuclear Free Zone Treaty (the Treaty of Paratonga) of 1985,[5] (iii) the Treaty on the Southeast Asia Nuclear-Weapon-Free Zone (the Treaty of Bangkok) of 15 December 1995,[6] and (iv) the African Nuclear-Weapon-Free Zone Treaty (the Treaty of Pelindaba) of 11 April 1996.[7]

It should be pointed out, however, that the first nuclear-weapon-free zone was the Antarctic continent which was demilitarized and denuclearized under the Washington Antarctic Treaty of 1959. The five zones established in the treaties are considered as zones of peace, cooperation and friendship.

Furthermore, it is noteworthy to mention that the post Cold War years of the 1990s created the foundation for the building of more confidence, mutual trust, good faith and mutual understanding between the Parties to the PTBT to announce moratoria and cessations of nuclear testing. This paved the way for intensive negotiations between States and adoption of the final draft text of the Comprehensive Nuclear Test Ban Treaty (CTBT) on 10 September 1996 by 158 to 3 with 5 abstentions. The Treaty was opened for signature in New York on 24 September 1996 signed on that same day by 71 States, including the five States with nuclear weapons. As at 9 September 2003, 168 States have signed the CTBT, and a total of 104 States have ratified it.

This was a great achievement under aegis of the UN in the field of disarmament toward the end of the 20th century. It consolidated the provisions of the PTBT of 1963. Nevertheless, it is very disappointing to observe that among the Permanent Members of the UN Security Council, China and the United States have signed but have not ratified the CTBT.

The Treaty Banning Nuclear Weapon Tests in the Atmosphere, in Outer Space and under Water (PTBT)

In the foregoing paragraphs, I have tried to reflect on events which have had a substantial impact on the safety, peace and security of the human race. It should be recalled that the Partial Test Ban Treaty (PTBT) of 1963 was a great achievement in the midst of antagonism, bitterness, hatred and mistrust between the super powers. It was an important legal instrument, particularly during the early stage of the law-making process in the regulation of the activities of states in outer space. It declared outer space as a demilitarized and denuclearized zone. As at 29 August 2003, the PTBT had been signed by 108 States, ratified by 94 States and 23 have acceded to it. I would now like to briefly examine and analyse some of the provisions of the 1963 PTBT.

The PTBT consists of a Preamble and five articles. In the Preamble, the Governments of the United States, the United Kingdom and the Soviet Union proclaim as their principal aim "the speediest possible achievment of an agreement on general and complete disarmament under strict international control in accordance with the objectives of the United Nations which would put an end to the armament race and eliminate the incentive to the production and testing of all kinds of weapons, including nuclear weapons."

Similar wordings are also embodied in the Preambles of other instruments, for example, the 1974 US-Soviet Treaty on the Limitation of Underground Nuclear Weapon Tests. In the fourth paragraph of the Preamble, the Parties reaffirm their adherence to the objects of the 1963 PTBT. Furthermore, in the tenth paragraph of the Preamble of the 1996 CTBT, reference is also made to the 1963 PTBT as follows: "Noting the aspirations expressed by the Parties to the 1963 Treaty Banning Nuclear Weapon Tests in the Atmosphere, in Outer Space and Under Water to seek the discontinuance of all test explosions of nuclear weapons for all time."

It should be emphasized that the provisions of Article I are the main core of the PTBT of 1963. Pursuant to the provisions of paragraph 1 of Article I, "each of the Parties to the Treaty undertakes to prohibit, to prevent, and not to carry out any nuclear weapon test explosion, or any other nuclear explosion, at any place under its jurisdiction or control: (i) in the atmosphere; beyond its limits, including outer space; or under water, including territorial waters or high seas; or (ii) in any other environment if such explosion causes radioactive debris to be present outside the territorial limits of the state under whose jurisdiction or control such explosion is conducted. It is understood in this connection that the provisions of this subparagraph are without prejudice to the conclusion of a Treaty resulting in the permanent banning of all nuclear test explosions, including all such explosions underground, the conclusion which, as the Parties have stated in the Preamble to the Treaty, they seek to achieve."

Furthermore, according to the provisions of paragraph 2 of Article I, each of the Parties to the Treaty also undertakes furthermore to refrain from causing, encouraging, or in any other way participating in, the carrying out of any nuclear weapon test explosion, or any other nuclear explosion, anywhere which would take place in any of the environments described, or have the effect referred to, in paragraph 1 of Article I.

It is interesting to note that by extending these provisions of the PTBT to outer space, binding legal force is being given to the provisions of UN General Assembly Resolution **1884 (XVIII)** of 17 October 1963. In this resolution, the UN General Assembly welcomed the expressions of the Soviet Union and the United States of their intention not to station in outer space any objects carrying nuclear weapons or other kinds of weapons of mass destruction (WMD). All States are solemnly called upon: (a) To refrain from placing in orbit around the earth any objects carrying nuclear weapons or any other kinds of weapons of mass destruction, installing such weapons on celestial bodies, or stationing such weapons in outer space in any other manner;
(b) To refrain from causing, encouraging or in any way participating in the conduct of the foregoing activities. The provisions of this resolution were further consolidated in Article IV of the Outer Space Treaty of 1967 (OST 1967).

Although underground nuclear explosive tests are not mentioned in the provisions of Article I of the PTBT of 1963, it should be pointed out that the subterranean envirinment is part and parcel of the earth environment (biosphere). I believe that any underground nuclear explosions will surely have devastating effects on the people living on the surface of the earth sooner or later. Thus, it is submitted that underground nuclear explosions tests and the testing of weapons of mass destruction (WMD) fall within the legal prohibitions mentioned in these provisions.

However, it is encouraging to note that the obligations stipulated in the provisíons of Article I of the PTBT of 1963 have been more elaborated and consolidated in the provisions of Articles I and III of the Comprehensive Nuclear Test Ban Treaty of 1996 (CTBT 1996).

Let us take a brief overview of their provisions. Pursuant to the provisions of Article I of the CTBT, (i) Each State Party undertakes not to carry out any nuclear weapon test explosion or any other nuclear explosion, and to prohibit and prevent any such nuclear explosion at any place under its jurisdiction or control. (ii) Each State Party undertakes, furthermore, to refrain from causing, encouraging, or in any way participating in the carrying out of any nuclear test explosion or any nuclear explosion.

Article III stipulates the following national implementation measures:
1. Each State Party shall, in accordance with its constitutional processes, take any neccessary measures to implement its obligations under this Treaty, In particular, it shall take any necessary measures: (a) To prohibit natural and legal persons anywhere on its territory or in any other place under its jurisdiction as recognized by international law from undertaking any activity prohibited to a State Party under this Treaty; (b) To prohibit natural and legal persons from undertaking any such activity anywhere under its control; and (c) To prohibit, in conformity with international law, natural persons possessing its nationality from undertaking any such activity anywhere.

2.Each State Party shall cooperate with other State Parties and afford the appropriate form of of legal assistance to facilitate the implementation of the obligations under paragraph 1.

3. Each State Party shall inform the CTBT Organization of the measures taken pursuant to this Article.

4. In order to fulfil its obligations under the Treaty, each State Party shall designate or set up a national Authority and shall so inform the Organization upon entry into force of the Treaty for it. The National Authority shall serve as the national local liaison with the Organization and with other States Parties.

It could be seen from the provisions of Article III that the CTBT prohibits States to use their nationals (natural and juridicals persons) to carry out research studies on the development and use of nuclear energy and materials for military purposes.

This leads me once again to reflect on the legality of the on-going development of the various national defence systems by the United States, particularly under President George W. Bush. In previous sessions of the IISL Colloquia on the Law of Outer Space, I have pointed out that the US National Missile Defence Systems contravene contemporary international law, including the Charter of the United Nations, the Outer Space Treaty of 1967 and other SALT bilateral agreements.

Furthermore, an objective analysis of the **TIME Magazine Report** of May 14, 2001 with refernce to the provisions of the articles of the **PTBT** of 1963 and the **CTBT** of 1996 illustrates that the US Governments have not been fulfilling in good faith their international obligations under those treaties.[8]

It is also disheartening to read in one of the Finnish national newspapers that enriched uranium was used by the US and Britain during the wars in Iraq.[9]

Bearing in mind the foregoing, let us continue with our reflection on the **PTBT** of 1963.

Article II deals with amendments to the Treaty. Paragraph 2 provides that amendments to the Treaty must be approved by a majority of the votes of all Parties, including those of the all the Original Parties. The Treaty is open to all States (Art. III). It is of unlimited duration and each Party shall in exercising its national sovereignty have the right to withdraw from the Treaty (Art IV). Similar provisions are embodied in Article IX of the **CTBT** of 1996.

<u>Concluding Observations and Remarks</u>

In the foregoing pages I have tried to reflect on the events prior to the signing and and the entering into force of the Treaty Banning Nuclear Weapons Tests in the Atmosphere, in Outer Space and Under Water of 5 August 1963 (or Partial Test Ban Treaty (PTBT). Although there were some irregularities in the strict implementation of its provisions by the Original Parties, it has played and shall continue to play a major role in the general and complete disarmament process during the 21st century. As has been observed earlier, the Treaty provided the momentum for the conclusion of treaties for the establishment of Nuclear Weapon Free Zones in Africa, Asia/Pacific and Latin America. We hope that this momentum of establishing nuclear weapon free zones will be extended to the territories of states in the northern hemisphere during the 21st century.

It should also be noted that the provisions of the PTBT were supplemented by the Treaty on the Non-Proliferation of Nuclear Weapons of 1 July 1968 (NPT).[10] The latter has greatly contributed to the reduction of the nuclear arms race during the past 35 years.

Since the beginning of the new millennium, particularly after the sad events of 11 September 2001, peoples all over the world are now living in fear and anxiety about the future. This has been used as a pretext for the development and improvement in the manufacture of new nuclear weapons and other dangerous weapons of mass destruction. The events in Iraq in spring 2003 are a clear illustration of this. It should be pointed out that peace and security cannot be preserved or maintained through military might but instead require mutual trust, understanding, cooperation, mutual respect and transperency among States and peoples of the world, based on the strict observance of the "Golden Rule".

Furthermore, the strict observance and implementation of the purposes and principles, as embodied in the Charter of the United Nations, is a **must** for all the Member States. All states and peoples must comply with the spirit and letter of the UN Charter, as well as that of all international treaties and agreements. This also includes the subject-matter of the paper, together with those treaties referred to therein.

It should, moreover, be borne in mind that the Comprehensive Nuclear Test Ban Treaty of 1996 as an improved version of the PTBT of 1963 must be implemented by all States, because it provides a solid basis or foundation for making our mother Earth nuclear weapon free throughout the 21st century. Neverthess, they should remember that they have an international obligation to comply with all the provisions of UN Resolution **1884 (XVIII)** of 17 October 1963.[11]

Looking back at history, I am very convinced that nuclear weapons and other weapons of mass destruction are objects created through fear and hatred amongst peoples and nations, particularly by those who want to assert their superiority and domination over others. St. James in his Epistle in this respect correctly states: **"From whence come wars and fighting among you? come they not hence , even of your lusts that war in your members? (James 4:1).** And St. Paul advises us that: **"..God has not given us the spirit of fear; but of power, and of love, and of a sound mind." (II Tim. 1:7).** It should be pointed out that peace is one of the attributes of having those qualities in every human being. It is very essential for the progress of the human race in the 21st century. Everyone needs it at all time. Sri Chinmoy, commenting on the importance of peace in the human life states:

"Peace itself is strength. If you have inner peace, you will have joy and delight when you enter into the outer world. The outer world can be under your control when you have peace of mind. Wherever you go, you will make your own peace.

In great power there is quietude. One who is outwardly strong, like a great boxer or a sovereign, has great peace and confidence inside him. If a person is not very strong, he clenches his fists and gets ready to defend himself. He has to show that he can fight. But when someone has boundless inner strength, he does not have to display it outwardly. He is relaxed because his inner strength has given him inner confidence. He is like divine hero. At any moment, he can defeat the enemy or surmount any obstacle."[12]

I would like to conclude this paper with a quotation of Albert Einstein, the great German-born physicist and originator of the theory of relativity: "The unleashed power of the atom has changed everything save our modes of thinking and we thus drift toward unparalleled catastrophe".[13] This is true! It has been reported that over 2000 nuclear explosion were registered world wide in the

51 years between the first nuclear explosive test on 16 July 1945 and the adoption on CTBT on 24 September 1996.(Department of Disarmament Affairs, UN Secretariat and SIPRI).

Thus, it is the duty of the policy-makers and leaders of the world to start thinking of the coming generations by using this the power of the atom for peaceful purposes under the strict supervision of the International Atomic Energy Agency (IAEA). They should always remember that they have a duty to comply with the vision of the Founding Fathers of the United Nations as expressed in the Preamble of the Charter: **"We the peoples of the United Nations, determined to save succeeding generations from the scourge of war, which twice in our lifetime has brought untold sorrow to mankind....and for these ends..to practice tolerance and live together in peace with one another as good neighbours..."**

Thus, taking into consideration what has been reflected upon in this paper, it **is submitted that the human, financial and materials resources currently invested in developing new weapons, should be used in alleviating the sufferings and hardships facing billions of peoples all over the world.**

Finally, may I seize this opportunity to wish you all a Merry Christmas 2003 and a very Successful and Prosperous 2004. Thank you all for your kind attention.

NOTES

1. **TIME 100: Heroes & Inspirational Persons of the Century**, Time Books, New York (2000), p. 93.

2. For more details, see International Legal Materials, Vol. XV, Number 4 (July 1974), pp. 906-909.

3. For more details, see International Legal Materials, Vol. XV, Number 4 (July 1976), pp. 891-900.

4. For more details, see UNTS Vol. 634, No. 9068, p. 326 et seq.

5. For more details, see International Legal Material, Vol.XXIV Number 5 (September 1985), pp. 1442-1463.

6. For more details, see International Legal Materials, Vol. XXXV, Number 3 (May 1996), pp. 635-650.

7. For more details, see International Legal Materials, Vol. XXXV, Number 3 (May 1996), pp. 698-723.

8. See pp. 27-31.

9. For details, see, **Helsingin Sanomat** (**H.S**), 25. 5. 2003. Source used: **AP**. The article title in Finnish "**Irakin sodassa käytettin runsaasti köyhydytettya urania**". The main points were as follows:
- Enriched uranium was used in both Iraqi wars by the US and Britain
- A large amount was used
- 375 tons used in 1991
- between 1,100-2,200 tons used in 2003
- Only 11 tons used in Kosovo in 1999
- UNEP has encouraged a thorough scientific study of the possible effects of the use of depleted uranium in Iraq
- The sources of the depleted uranium are missiles fired from A-10 planes and Apache helicopters; if inhaled or ingested, the dust which results from the explosions of these missiles is believed to cause that harmful symptoms such as poisoning, tumors, fetal deformation and childhood cancer.
- Both Britain and the US deny the danger associated with the depleted uranium.

10. For more detail, see, **THE INTERNATIONAL LAW OF NUCLEAR ENERGY** Basic Documents, Part 2, Edited by ElBaradel. Mohamed M., Nwogugu, Edwin I. and Rames, John M., Martinus Nijhoff Publishers, Dordrecht, The Netherlands (1993), pp. 1479-1492. For a brief comments on the NPT, see, e.g., Andem, M.N., **International Legal Problems in the Peaceful Exploration and Use of Outer Space,** University of Lapland publications in Law, Series B20, Rovaniemi (1992), pp. 198-199.

11. For the legal status of that resolution, see, e.g., Jenks, C. Wilfred, **Space Law**, Stevens & Sons, London (1965), pp. 303-394; Andem, Maurice N., **op.cit.,** pp.53-62; Cheng, Bin, **Studies in International Space Law**, Clarendon Press, Oxford (1997), pp.125-149.

12. Chinmoy, Sri, **The Wings of Joy**, FIRESIDE, Rockefeller Centre, New York (1997), pp.171-172.

13. Telegram to prominent Americans, 24 May 1946, in **Nwe York Times**, 25 May 1945. Reproduced in **The Oxford Dictionary of Quotations**, 4th Edition OUP (1992), p. 268.

IAC-03-IISL.3.09

TINTALLË - KINDLING INTERNATIONAL SECURITY WITH SPACE LAW

Gérardine Meishan Goh*

Faculty of Laws, University College London, United Kingdom
vysionary@hotmail.com

The remarkable advancement of space-based technologies has led to an increasing reliance on space-based applications. This reliance is especially keen in the context of international security. Outer space is swiftly becoming a distinct theatre for military defence, initiatives and operations. This paper elaborates upon the intertwining of space law with the United Nations and the international law on the use of force. It highlights the significance of space law in the maintenance of international peace and security. This paper then proposes a legal framework in which space law operates as a nucleus for the achievement of international peace and security.

INTRODUCTION

Outer space is an area of growing economic and technological importance. It is also a developing theatre of military defence and warfare. Against this backdrop, this paper discusses the present *jus ad bellum spatialis* and the *jus in bello spatialis* as gleaned from the applicable law of armed conflict. This paper outlines a proposed enforcement mechanism for the law on the use of force in outer space. This proposed framework rests on a three-tiered system involving an International Tribunal for Outer Space, an International Space Surveillance Agency and an International Space Inspection Agency, co-ordinated through a Secretariat under the auspices of the United Nations Office of Outer Space Affairs.

This paper concludes that the maintenance of outer space for exclusively peaceful purposes is an essential component in the maintenance of international peace and security. Finally, this paper submits that international co-operation in the implementation of the proposed enforcement framework for outer space will form the nucleus for the maintenance of international peace and security.

JUS AD BELLUM SPATIALIS

The core of the *jus ad bellum spatialis* can be found in four multilateral treaties that provides a limited framework of international law governing the use of force in outer space.

The 1967 Outer Space Treaty[1]

The 1967 OST is considered the foundation for the international legal regime applicable to outer space.[2] The OST joined the 1959 Antarctic Treaty[3] and the later 1982 Convention on the Law of the Sea[4] in a unique class of "non-armament treaties".[5] These agreements have kept outer space, the Antarctic and the ocean floor free of weapons of mass destruction.

Peaceful Use & Exploration of Outer Space: Articles I & II

The first two Articles establish the framework for the peaceful exploration and use of outer space. Article I states that the exploration and use of outer space should be "carried out for the benefit and interests of all countries" and that "outer space shall be free for exploration and use by all States without discriminationon a basis of equality". These two principles are generally considered part of customary international law, binding on all States.[6] Linked with these two principles is the concept of non-appropriation enshrined in Article II. Articles I and II establish outer space as *res communis* under international law.

Maintaining International Peace & Security: Article III & the Preamble

The paramount provision with respect to the maintenance of international peace and security is

*LL.B. (Hons.) (NUS); LL.M. Graduand, University College London; Member, IISL. Grateful thanks are due to Mr. David Sagar, Lecturer in Space Law, Queen Mary & Westfield College, University of London, for his comments on an earlier draft of this paper. The views expressed and any errors contained herein are, however, entirely mine

Article III: States Parties to the Treaty shall carry on activities in the exploration and use of outer space, including the Moon and other celestial bodies, in accordance with *international law*, including the *Charter of the United Nations*, in the interest of *maintaining international peace and security* and *promoting international co-operation and understanding.*

Article III mandates that any activities carried out in outer space must be in the interest of "maintaining international peace and security". Paragraphs 2 and 4 of the Preamble reiterate the principle of the "peaceful purposes" of outer space. Paragraph 2 reads that the States Parties recognise The common interest of all mankind in the progress of the exploration and use of outer space for peaceful purposes

Seen in the light of the Preamble, Article III obliges State Parties to carry out activities "in the interest of maintaining international peace and security", in accordance with the UN Charter and international law. Thus, it evinces a prohibition on actions in outer space that threaten the peace.

Military Use of Outer Space: Article IV

The only specific limitation placed on the use of the outer void space (i.e. the empty space between celestial bodies beyond terrestrial national airspace) for military purposes in the OST is that found in Article IV(1).[7] Article IV(1) states: States Parties to the Treaty undertake not to place in orbit around the Earth any objects carrying *nuclear weapons or any other kinds of weapons of mass destruction*, install such weapons on celestial bodies, or station such weapons in outer space in any other manner.

The OST does not impose any other restriction on the military use of the outer void space.[8] Military activity not involving nuclear weapons or weapons of mass destruction may be permitted in outer void space, insofar as it does not contravene international law and the UN Charter.[9]

Subject to this limitation, States remain perfectly entitled to conduct any military activity, including research, experiments, exercises and manoeuvres in outer void space. This includes the testing, deployment and stationing there of satellites, ASAT weapons, ballistic missile defence systems, and any other kind of weaponry or devices, all either partly or exclusively for military purposes. Furthermore, Article IV(1) does not forbid States from sending any kind of weapon to their target through outer void space. The OST is certainly no obstacle to the passage through outer space of land-to-land, sea-to-land, or air-to-land ballistic nuclear missiles.

Article IV(2) restricts the use of the moon and other "celestial bodies" to peaceful purposes.[10] This points to a limited demilitarisation of outer space and a total demilitarisation of celestial bodies. Further, whilst the stationing of weapons of mass destruction in outer space is prohibited by the OST, nothing prevents the stationing of such weapons in a State's own territory, including its national airspace, provided they are not in earth orbit. Since there is no agreed delimitation of the boundary between national airspace and outer space, this can be an added source of conflict.[11]

State Responsibility: Articles VI & XIII

Article VI establishes that States bear "international responsibility for national activities in outer space . . . whether such activities are carried on by governmental agencies or by non-governmental entities." This extends State responsibility, making the State responsible for the space activities of its private citizens or organisations. Article XIII makes it clear that the OST applies to all activities in outer space whether States carry them out individually or jointly with other States.

International Co-operation: Articles IX & XII

One of the primary objectives of the UN is the pacific resolution of international disputes.[12] The Friendly *Relations Declaration* declares that the "obligation of co-operation" is an international obligation binding on all States.[13] Articles IX and XII expressly enshrine the principle of international co-operation in the exploration and use of outer space.

Article IX requires that the State be consulted if a hostile act could harmfully interfere with a third party State's assets. Article IX does not differentiate between military and civilian space activities. Thus, it applies to military space operations. Further, Article IX specifies a timeframe: consultations must occur "before proceeding with any such activity or experiment." Such consultations could notify the belligerent State of the expected offensive. Thus Article IX could create a disincentive to a use of force.

Article XII provides: All stations, installations, equipment and space vehicles on the Moon and other celestial bodies shall be open to representatives of other State Parties to the treaty on the basis of reciprocity. Part of the aim of Article XII was to help ensure that the demilitarisation provisions in Article IV were observed, by providing a mechanism for verification.[14]

The 1972 Liability Convention[15]

The Liability Convention unveils a tacit admittance that intentional destruction of space objects might occur under certain circumstances. Articles II and III establish liability for damage caused by space objects. However, Article VI provides exemption from absolute liability in cases where the damage was caused wholly or partially by gross negligence, or an act or omission done with intent to cause damage. The exemption for intentional damage in the Liability Convention clearly recognises the possibility of such intentional damage.

Article IV(2) however, states that no exoneration shall be granted in cases where the damage resulted from activities in violation of the UN Charter or the OST.[16] This acknowledges that violations of international law should not be exempt from liability.

The 1979 Moon Agreement[17]

Article 2 specifically applies the prohibition on the use of force in the UN Charter and the Friendly Relations Declaration to the Moon and other celestial bodies in the solar system excepting the Earth. Article 3 states that the Moon is to be used "exclusively for peaceful purposes". This provision specifically prohibits the use of force either on the Moon (and other celestial bodies within the solar system, except Earth) or from the Moon (and other bodies) in relation to Earth or man-made spacecraft. It is not forbidden to fire missiles from one point on Earth against another through outer space or from Earth against a military satellite in orbit or an incoming missile.[18]

Article 3(3) repeats Article IV(1) of the OST with special reference to the moon, adding a prohibition on the placing of nuclear weapons or other kinds of weapons of mass destruction in a trajectory to the moon. The Moon Agreement is in force. However, only a few States have so far accepted it.[19] The Moon Agreement shows how little a Treaty regime will accomplish if States consider its obligations to be outside their interests. States will simply refuse to accede to the Treaty, rendering it with little practical utility.

Limited Test Ban Treaty[20]

The Treaty forbids "nuclear weapon test explosion[s], or any other nuclear explosion[s](a) in the atmosphere; beyond its limits, *including outer space*".[21] The Treaty prohibits nuclear explosions for both testing and non-testing purposes. Thus, the Treaty prohibits an electromagnetic pulse in space via a nuclear detonation, particularly as an ASAT weapon. It however does not prohibit non-nuclear weapons such as conventional, biological, chemical, or high-energy laser weapons.

SUMMARY

The *corpus juris spatialis* partially demilitarises outer space by[22]

1. Banning the use of nuclear weapons anywhere in outer space;[23]

2. Prohibiting the stationing of weapons of mass destruction in the earth orbit, on the moon or other celestial body, or installing such weapons on the moon or other celestial body[24] ;

3. Restricting the use of the moon and other celestial bodies for "exclusively peaceful purposes"; and

4. Expressly forbidding military manoeuvres, the testing of weapons, or the establishment of military bases, installations or fortifications on the moon or other celestial bodies. This limited legal framework is, however, supplemented by the general prohibition on the use of force at international law.

THE GENERAL PROHIBITION ON THE USE OF FORCE

The Prohibition of the Use of Force in the UN Charter

The central rule on the prohibition of the threat or use of force is contained in Article 2(4) of the UN Charter: All Members shall refrain in their international relations from the *threat* or *use of force* against the *territorial integrity* or *political independence* of any State, or in any other manner *inconsistent with the Purposes of the United Nations.* States and commentators generally agree that the prohibition is not only treaty and customary law but is also *jus cogens*.[25]

What is particularly significant is that the prohibition in Article 2(4) includes forcible measures short of war. Further, Article 2(4) goes beyond the actual recourse to force and prohibits even the mere threat of the use of force.[26] Article 2(4) also includes the conjunctive phrase "or in any other manner inconsistent with the Purposes of the United Nations". It is submitted that these words create a "residual 'catch-all' provision".[27]

The foremost Purpose of the UN is enshrined in Article 1(1) of the Charter: To maintain international peace and security, and to that end: to take effective collective measures for the prevention and removal of threats to the peace, and for the suppression of acts of aggression or other breaches of the peace.[28] The Preamble of the Charter expounds the determination of the UN Members "to save succeeding generations from the scourge of war"[29]. Moreover, Article 2(3) prescribes: All Members shall settle their international disputes by peaceful means in such a manner that international peace and security, and justice, are not endangered.[30]

In this context, the correct interpretation of Article 2(4) is that the use of force by Member States for whatever reason is banned, unless explicitly allowed by the Charter.[31] In the *Nicaragua* case, the ICJ pronounced that Article 2(4) articulates the "principle of the prohibition of the use of force" in international relations.[32] Although the UN Charter preceded Humanity's entry into outer space, its provisions must be interpreted in the contemporary context of international law so as not to defeat the object and purpose of the Charter. Further, the GA has reiterated the importance of the maintenance of international peace and security in outer space through its peaceful uses in no less than forty resolutions between 1959 and 2002.[33]

The sweeping injunction against recourse to inter-State force is subject to only two exceptions: Collective security (Article 42) and self-defence (Article 51).

The Prohibition on the Use of Force in Outer Space as a Rule of Customary International Law

In the *Continental Shelf* case, the ICJ held that the substance of customary international law must be "looked for primarily in the actual practice and *opinio juris* of States".[34] There is ample *opinio juris* and State practice to support the existence of this prohibition on the use of force in outer space as a rule of customary international law.

It is recognised that GA resolutions can constitute evidence of State practice or *opinio juris*,[35] depending upon the contents and conditions of its adoption.[36] The question of whether the forty GA Resolutions concerning the *International Co-operation in the Peaceful Uses of Outer Space*[37] crystallised a rule of custom at the time of adoption depend on their wording and the circumstances of their adoption. The latter includes the intention of the drafters in the Committee on the Peaceful Uses of Outer Space (COPUOS) and the views expressed by the various member States of COPUOS.

The wording and language of these Resolutions demonstrate their binding force. They encompass the specific normative content necessary to create a binding legal document. The negotiations leading up to each of the forty resolutions were characterised by a series of similar and united views between the COPUOS members. States wanted an unequivocal and clear statement that outer space was to be preserved for peaceful uses and the benefit of all Mankind. The final texts of these forty GA Resolutions reflect an agreement between space powers and non-space States that the prohibition on the use of force applied equally to outer space. This consensus between States in what was almost an annual tradition of reaffirming the peaceful uses of outer space reflects the necessary *opinio juris* behind each Resolution.

Additionally, there is widespread, representative and virtually uniform State practice supporting the general prohibition on the use of force in outer space entering into customary international law.[38] States accept the prohibition on the use of force in outer space as a binding principle of international law. The domestic legislation of some States adopt language that makes specific reference to the prohibition on the use of force in outer space. Besides reaffirming the principles enshrined in the OST, the domestic legislations of these States explicitly require all national space activities to be carried out for exclusively peaceful purposes. Further, this requirement is passed on to commercial actors through each State's licensing agreements.[39]

Even where States have not adopted such legislation, the practice of these States shows that the prohibition on the use of force in outer space constitutes a rule of binding international law. The US legislation allows exceptions for the purpose of national security, in accordance with UN Security Council-sanctioned enforcement action. For example, auxiliary forces have requested use of INMARSAT assets for both tactical and armed military manoeuvres. This occurred in the Falklands War. After consultation with its member States, INMARSAT adopted a pragmatic approach. INMARSAT allows the use of its space assets by military forces only in three circumstances: UN-sanctioned peacekeeping operations and enforcement action, self-defence, and humanitarian purposes.[40]

States are thus bound by the prohibition on the

use of force in outer space because it has entered into customary international law. The ICJ has taken cognisance of international custom, as evidence of a general practice accepted as law, as a source of law under Article 38(1)(b) of its Statute.[41] The prohibition on the use of force in outer space satisfies both prerequisite elements of opinio juris and State practice to enter into customary law.[42]

EXCEPTIONS TO THE GENERAL PROHIBITION ON THE USE OF FORCE IN OUTER SPACE

There are only two exceptions to the prohibition on the use of force. These are

1. UN Security Council enforcement actions under Chapter VII of the UN Charter; and
2. Self-defence under Article 51 of the UN Charter

Chapter VII Measures of the UN Security Council

Under Article 24(1) of the Charter, the UN Security Council has primary responsibility for the maintenance of international peace and security. The UN system rests on an elaborate mechanism of enforcement measures against aggression in Chapter VII of the Charter.[43] The monopoly in enforcement power was made subject only to two exceptions: the unilateral or collective right to self-defence in Article 51, and enforcement measures by regional organisations authorised by the Security Council under Article 53.

Article 39 of the Charter provides The Security Council shall determine the existence of any threat to the peace, breach of the peace or act of aggression and shall make recommendations, or decide what measures shall be taken in accordance with Articles 41 and 42, to maintain or restore international peace and security.

Additionally, Article 42 of the Charter provides that the Security Council may take "such action by air, sea, or land forces as may be necessary to maintain or restore international peace and security". There is no mention of taking action in outer space in Article 42. However, it is submitted that Article 42 probably also encompasses the use of force in outer space. That outer space was not specifically mentioned was probably only due to the fact that Humanity had not entered outer space at the time of the Charter's drafting.

It has become clear from the subsequent practice of the Security Council and the UN Member States that the Security Council enjoys wide discretion in deciding when to take enforcement action under Chapter VII of the Charter. This does not mean however that the Security Council's authority is unlimited. The Charter and the principles of international law bind the Security Council. However, a threat to the peace in the sense of Article 39 seems to be whatever the Security Council deems a threat to the peace.[44] This is a political decision and is not easily subject to legal evaluation.[45]

Self-defence under Article 51 UN Charter

Self-defence is the other exception to the general prohibition on the use of force envisaged in the UN Charter. Article 51 provides: Nothing in the present Charter shall impair the *inherent right of individual or collective self-defence* if an *armed attack occurs* against a Member of the United Nations, *until* the Security Council has taken the measures necessary to maintain international peace and security. Measures taken by Members in the exercise of this right of self-defence shall be *immediately reported* to the Security Council and shall not in any way affect the authority and responsibility of the Security Council under the present Charter to take at any time such action as it deems necessary in order to maintain or restore international peace and security.

Article 51 allows the potential unilateral use of force, whether by an individual State or collectively through regional alliances. If a State deems that an armed attack has occurred against it, it is within its rights at international law to use force. There is much disagreement about the circumstances in which the "inherent right" of self-defence may be exercised.

Conditions for the Applicability of Self-defence

According to Article 51, there are two conditions for the applicability of self-defence. These are

1. The occurrence of an "armed attack"; and
2. The duty to report any action taken in self-defence to the UN Security Council.

"Armed Attack"

All States agree that if there is an armed attack the right to self-defence arises. However, there are disagreements as to what constitutes an armed attack.[46] Questions concerning the definition of the concept and the identification of the start of an armed attack arise out of the special characteristics of particular weapons.[47]

Article 51 limits the right of self-defence to situations "if an armed attack occurs". This means that the armed attack must have already occurred before force can be used in self-defence. The use of force before such an armed attack cannot be considered self-defence; it is more likely to be an act of aggression. In 1974 the GA adopted a resolution defining aggression.[48] This definition listed a series of acts that would amount to aggression. Under Article 5 "a war of aggression is a crime against international peace. Aggression gives rise to international responsibility". It follows that self-defence is permissible only after an armed attack has actually occurred. Confining self-defence to such cases has the advantage of objective precision. This is because the first armed aggression can usually be objectively verified. Further, this right of self-defence continues until the UN Security Council takes measures to maintain international peace and security.

The requirement that an armed attack must have actually occurred is particularly significant in the context of outer space. With satellite surveillance and communications systems, space-based assets often provide a State with early warning systems. These can alert a State of an imminent attack even before it actually occurs. With the precision and ease of space-based systems, it is tantalising for a State to pre-empt an enemy's attack by striking first and then claiming self-defence. Thus, it is submitted that this requirement of an actual occurrence of an armed attack serves to curb "trigger-happy" States from striking without cause. It also serves to maintain international peace and security by preventing a situation that could spiral out of control into mutual annihilation between the space-faring States. Hence, it is submitted that this requirement should be strictly enforced, especially in the context of outer space.

Duty to Report to the UN Security Council

The ICJ in the *Nicaragua* case held that "the absence of a report may be one of the factors indicating whether the State in question was itself convinced that it was acting in self-defence".[49] Since this judgement, States have taken seriously the Court's message that failure to do this will weaken any claims of self-defence.[50]

The Security Council also has a role in the control of the right of self-defence. This is through the stipulation in Article 51 that the right of self-defence continues "until the Security Council has taken measures necessary to maintain international peace and security". Given that the UN Charter aims not only to limit but also to centralise the use of force under UN control, it seems clear that the intention was to give to the Security Council the right to decide whether such measures terminating the right to self-defence had been taken.[51]

The use of outer space in particular warrants the strict enforcement of this requirement. The use of outer space is mandated to be for exclusively peaceful purposes, and the legal regime governing outer space requires international consultation and co-operation.[52] It is submitted that reporting to the Security Council of space-based use of force in self-defence is crucial to maintaining international peace and security. Transparency and open consultation of the use of outer space will serve not only as confidence-building measures, but also to ensure that the international community is aware and seized of the matter when States use force in outer space.

JUS IN BELLO SPATIALIS - CONDUCT OF THE USE OF FORCE IN OUTER SPACE

Through history, warring States have developed customary practices seeking to lessen the devastating effects of war. The principles distilled from customary international law amount to very few: discrimination, military advantage, necessity and proportionality. These principles are recognised in subsequent treaty law. They apply equally to all theatres, whether on land, sea, in the air or in outer space.

Discrimination & Military Advantage

The aim of any armed conflict is to achieve victory at the minimum of cost. Hence, the conflict must not involve means likely to cause unnecessary suffering or injury over and above that required to disable an enemy or secure the objective of an operation.

The principle of discrimination mandates that attacks must be directed only against military objects and objectives.[53] These are objects "which by their nature, location, purpose or use make an effective contribution to military action and whose total or partial destruction, capture or neutralisation, in the circumstances ruling at the time, offers a definite military advantage".[54] As a consequence, civilians are exempt from being made the object of attack, although it is not a breach of the law of armed conflict if civilians suffer injury incidental to an attack upon a lawful military objective. Attacks that fail to distinguish between military and civilian personnel or military and civilian objects are forbidden as indiscriminate.

Space military assets such as the Global Positioning System (GPS) facilitate the proper identification of targets. The distinction between military and civilian targets is made even more reliable by the usage of high-resolution remote-sensing satellites. Space technology allows for precise and surgical military actions. Although regrettably collateral damage cannot be completely ruled out, from a legal perspective space technology allows military officers a greater capacity to respect their legal obligations under the laws of armed conflict.

Further, the Registration Convention[55] obliges all States to register and indicate the function of their space objects.[56] A space object can therefore be clearly identified as being civilian in function. The converse however, may not apply, since military satellites and other assets may not necessarily be identified by their registration, since registration is mandated to occur only as soon as is practicable. Thus such assets may only be registered after their missions are complete. This situation is further complicated by the fact that space technology bears the burden of dual-use assets. However, it has been argued that the hiding of a military space object used to commit an act of force in outer space is akin to an act of perfidy.[57] The perfidious use of space assets endangers international peace and security.

Necessity & Proportionality

Self-defence must be necessary and proportionate.[58] The requirements of necessity and proportionality are often traced back to the 1837 *Caroline* incident. The *Nicaragua* case and the Advisory Opinion on the *Legality of the Threat or Use of Nuclear Weapons*[59]reaffirmed that necessity and proportionality are limits on all self-defence, individual and collective. These requirements are part of customary international law.

The rule of proportionality requires that the use of military force be proportional to the legitimate military objective. Analyses of the proportionality of military means will have to take a twofold form. First, any military means must be proportionate to a discrete, legitimate military end. Second, such military means must also be proportionate to the object of the war.

Although the decision as to proportionality tends to be subjective, it must be made in good faith. It involves weighing the success of the operation against the possible harmful effects upon protected persons or objects. There must be an acceptable relation between the legitimate destructive effect and undesirable collateral effects.

The general rule allows destruction of targets if it is proportionate to the military objective sought by the destruction. For example, infrastructure targets were lawfully destroyed during the 1991 Persian Gulf War that provided electricity both to the civilian populations and to the Iraqi military. The same rationale applies to dual-use satellites. To the extent a satellite is used for the support of a military purpose, it becomes a military objective and is lawfully subject to attack. This however assumes that the space asset is actually used for such a military purpose. It is insufficient that it merely has the potential to be so used.

SUMMARY OF THE PRESENT STATE OF THE LAW

From the foregoing analysis, seven conclusions can be drawn as to the present state of international law in this area.

Firstly, outer space presents a unique environment differing greatly from terrestrial environments. These characteristics transcend physical differences, involving unique commercial, technological and policy concerns. The legal framework must consider these concerns in order to be practically applicable and relevant to the realities of space activities.

Secondly, there is at present a limited treaty framework that governs the use of force in outer space. This framework centres on the principles enshrined in the OST.

Thirdly, general international principles and the UN Charter are applicable to outer space via Article III OST. This means that the prohibition on the use of force in Article 2(4) of the Charter applies to outer space, as do the customary and *jus cogens* prohibitions on the use of force.

Fourthly, the exceptions to the general prohibition on the use of force apply equally to outer space. Thus, force may be used in outer space in self-defence under Article 51 of the UN Charter and under Chapter VII enforcement action measures. However, it is submitted that these exceptions should be understood restrictively.

Fifthly, there are customary international law principles that govern the conduct of the use of force in outer space. These include the principles of discrimination, military advantage, necessity and proportionality. Any use of force in outer space must conform to these principles of the law of armed conflict.

Sixthly, the framework of international law in this regard is in flux. Given the rapid development of space-based technology, the burgeoning importance of the space industry, and changing geopolitical concerns, the present legal framework is fast becoming inadequate.

Lastly, it is desirable that a clear framework of international law be established in this area. There should be a strict prohibition on the use of force in outer space, with rigorously narrow exceptions in which the use of force in outer space may possibly be justified.

With these conclusions in mind, the next section will propose a framework for the development of the law.

A PROPOSED FRAMEWORK FOR THE DEVELOPMENT OF THE LAW

A Proposed Protocol to the OST

The development of the law governing the use of force in outer space is an urgent issue. This paper proposes that a Protocol to the OST should be drawn up under the auspices of the COPUOS. The involvement of COPUOS would also ensure a quicker process in the drawing up of international standards on essential issues.[60] This Protocol should reiterate the exclusively peaceful purposes of outer space, enshrining the strict prohibition on the use of force in outer space in accordance with international law. This Protocol should provide mechanisms for State responsibility through the establishment of a tribunal specialising in space-related disputes. It should also establish verification mechanisms. Further, it should establish a Secretariat, operating with the UN Office of Outer Space Affairs (UNOOSA), to co-ordinate the efforts of these three bodies.

A Proposed Role for the UN

The UN GA declared that "the United Nations should provide a focal point for international co-operation in the peaceful exploration and use of outer space."[61]

The UN can provide a platform to better harness the resources and synergies that these organisations can provide. Leadership is essential for analysing and proposing developments to the law. The COPUOS can undertake this task through a Joint Committee of its Scientific and Technical Subcommittee and its Legal Subcommittee. This Joint Committee should include experts from the IAF and its legal component, the International Institute of Space Law (IISL). Further, various non-governmental organisations and commercial space entities should be represented.

A PROPOSED ENFORCEMENT MECHANISM OF THE LAW ON THE USE OF FORCE IN OUTER SPACE

There is widespread scepticism as to the "effectiveness" of the enforcement and verification of the prohibition on the use of force at international law.[62] Like other branches of international law, the law of armed conflict in outer space has no permanent means to secure its observance.

Establishing a Mechanism for State Responsibility: A Proposed International Tribunal for Outer Space (ITOS)

Any breach of an obligation incumbent upon a State under international law, regardless of the subject matter of the obligation, entails international responsibility.[63] In conformity with this general rule, international responsibility is generated by recourse to inter-State force in violation of international law.

It was held in the *Chorzw Factory* case that "it is a principle of international law, and even a general conception of law, that any breach of an engagement involves an obligation to make reparation".[64] The Court went on to say that "reparation must, as far as possible, wipe out all the consequences of the illegal act and re-establish the situation which would, in all probability, have existed if that act had not been committed".[65] The aspiration to bring about a *restitutio in integrum* may be frustrated by the fact that restoring the *status quo ante* is not feasible in realistic terms. When restitution in kind is ruled out, the duty to make reparation becomes a duty to pay financial compensation "corresponding to the value which a restitution in kind would bear".[66]

Under the Liability Convention, States that cause damage to other States' space assets are also liable to pay compensation for such damage. It is submitted that a specialised International Tribunal for Outer Space (ITOS) for such space-based or space-originated damage should be set up under the auspices of the UN. This body would be tasked with allotting State responsibility for any space activity that causes damage, for resolution of space-related disputes, and for setting out the form of reparation necessary. This would allow a clear and unbiased account of the damage and reparation, and allow for an enforcement of the law on the use of force in outer space.

ESTABLISHING MECHANISMS FOR VERIFICATION & ENFORCEMENT

Verification of compliance with this proposed legal framework involves three distinct processes:

1. Monitoring the activities of States Parties to the Treaties and the proposed Protocol;
2. Interpretation of the information obtained by such monitoring; and
3. Appraisal of the risk posed by these activities to international peace and security.[67]

Monitoring Space Activities: A Proposed International Space Surveillance Agency (ISSA)

Verification of States' compliance can be done through an International Space Surveillance Agency (ISSA).[68] The numerous technical means for verification of outer space treaties would suitably be organised within one international agency. In order to ensure the quick and accurate verification of compliance, it would be advantageous to have global widespread observation stations. Since many States are both Parties of the OST and have space assets capable of such verification, it would be possible to organise such an ISSA.

Each participating State would aid in one or more parts of the verification mechanism. This would distribute the costs and responsibilities of the ISSA. Further, for States willing to aid in the verification but without space assets or technologies of their own, such equipment could be stationed within their territories. This would allow the ISSA to also act as an organisation that allows the transfer of technology for the benefit of all nations.

The ISSA should be affiliated with the UN, and with the ITOS outlined above. This would allow for the co-ordination of the observation stations with the international community and the compliance mechanisms that can invoke State responsibility and reparation in the case of default.

Interpreting Space Activities & Appraisal of Risk: A Proposed International Space Inspection Agency (ISIA)

The greatest innovation effected by Protocol I in relation to supervision of its execution is the establishment of a permanent International Fact-Finding Commission. It is competent to enquire into any allegation that a grave breach or other serious violation of the Conventions or Protocol has occurred, and to use its good offices to assist in helping to restore respect for those instruments. It can institute an enquiry with regard to the party's conduct either on a permanent or an *ad hoc* basis.[69] If the enquiry finds that a violation has occurred, the Party is obliged to end it.

Similarly, it is proposed that an International Space Inspection Agency (ISIA) should be set up under the auspices of the UN and pursuant to the proposed Protocol. Its powers and jurisdiction would be similar to the Commission as established under Protocol I to the Geneva Convention.[70]

It is proposed that this ISIA should work in conjunction with the proposed ITOS and ISIS under the co-ordination of the proposed Treaty Secretariat. This will allow a comprehensive means of verification and appraisal to ensure that space-faring States do not breach the prohibition on the use of force in outer space.

SPACE LAW AS THE NUCLEUS FOR THE MAINTENANCE OF INTERNATIONAL PEACE & SECURITY

The significance of international space law as a nucleus for the maintenance of international peace and security cannot be over-stated. The role of space law is supported by its historical emphasis and continuing aspirations for the building of international peace and security. This can be seen by the forty resolutions adopted by the GA between 1959 and 2002 on the *International Co-operation in the Peaceful Uses of Outer Space*.[71] Between 1994 and 2001, a further nine resolutions on the *Prevention of an Arms Race in Outer Space* were also adopted, without a single negative vote.[72] This places international space law in the unique position of historically and continually having supported steps for the maintenance of international peace and security, even as outer space itself developed into a distinct military theatre. However, it is submitted the continual reiteration and reaffirmation of the GA makes space law a suitable candidate for the development of an enforceable framework for the maintenance of international peace and security.

Secondly, space law provides a clean slate for the development of such comprehensive framework. Despite the presence of a developed corpus of treaty and customary international law, there is at present no framework for the enforcement and implementation of these laws. *Prima facie*, this fact seems to militate against the effectiveness of space law. However, it is submitted that this in fact now provides a clean slate for the comprehensive *de novo* development of a workable enforcement mechanism. Given the increasing military reliance on outer space, the space law community is presented with an unprecedented opportunity to create and implement a workable legal enforcement framework for the maintenance of international peace and security in outer space. This in turn can provide a stepping stone for the development of a general enforcement mechanism for international peace and security.

Thirdly, the space community is characterised by comprehensive international and interdisciplinary involvement and dialogue. This provides a lattice for the hybridisation of ideas and ensures that the dialogue is ongoing. Together with the close ties of the space community to the various international, national, academic, non-governmental and corporate entities, this enables space law to act as a crucible for the development of a practical, enforceable mechanism for the maintenance of international peace and security.

Thus, it is submitted that international space law should take the lead in the development of *lex specialis* for the *jus ad bellum* and the *jus in bello* for outer space. This *jus ad bellum spatialis* and *jus in bello spatialis* can in turn provide, by example and analogy, the building blocks for the development of public international law for the maintenance of international peace and security.

CONCLUSION

International space law grew up on the principles of public international law and the aspirations for the maintenance of international peace and security. It has matured and developed its own *corpus* of legal principles and frameworks, succeeding in keeping outer space thus far free from terrestrial conflict. Having come full circle, international space law now stands on the threshold of a crucial phase. How international space law will develop over the next decade will have great impact upon important aspects of the international prohibition on the use of force and its enforcement. It is submitted that international space law should grasp this opportunity to act as the kindling for international peace and security. For too long now, space law has resided in the shadow of terrestrial laws on the use of force and armed conflict. It is now befitting, indeed essential, that international space law takes on its role as *tintallë*[73] - kindler - in the development of a legal framework and enforcement mechanism for the maintenance of international peace and security. For only then can international space law really come into its own.

References

[1]Space Science Board, "Treaty on the Principles Governing the Activities of States in the Exploration and the Use of Outer Space Including the Moon and Other Celestial Bodies ," *610UNTS205 [hereinafter "OST"]*, 1976.

[2]Jasentuliyana, N., "A Survey of Space Law as Developed by the United Nations," *Jasentuliyana, N. (ed.)*, Perspectives of International Law *(1995) 349*, 1995.

[3]Antarctic Treaty, "," *402UNTS72*, 1959.

[4]United Nations Convention on the Law of the Sea, "A Survey of Space Law as Developed by the United Nations," *21 ILM 261 [hereinafter "UNCLOS"]*, 1982.

[5]Graham, T., "International Law and the Military Uses of Space," *(March 2003) 63 Disarmament Diplomacy, online at http://www.acronym.org.uk/dd/dd63/63op1.htm (Last accessed: 15 January 2003)*, 2002.

[6]Vlasic, I., "The Growth of Space Law 1957 - 65," *in Mankiewicz, RH., Yearbook of Air and Space Law 1965, 365 at 375*, 1957.

[7]Cheng, B., "The United Nations and Outer Space," *14 CLP 247*, 1961.

[8]GARes. , "," *1885 (17 October 1993)*, 1993.

[9]Cheng, B., "The Legal Status of Outer Space and Relevant Issues: Delimitation of Outer Space and Definition of Peaceful Use," *11 JSL 89*, 1983.

[10]Cheng, B., "Le Traité de 1967 sur l'espace," *95 JDI 532*, 1968.

[11]Cheng, B., "The Legal Régime of Airspace and Outer Space: The Boundary Problem -Functionalism versus Spatialism: The Major Premises," *5 AASL 323*, 1980.

[12]Article 1(3) UN Charter, Charter of the United Nations (1945), reproduced in Evans, "," *MD. (ed.)*, Blackstone's International Law Documents*, (1999, 4th ed.), at 8 [hereinafter "UN Charter"]*, 1980.

[13]Declaration on Principles of International Law Concerning Friendly Relations and Co-operation among States in accordance with the UN Charter, " ," *GARes 2625*, 1970.

[14]Petras, C., "Space Force Alpha: Military Uses of the International Space Station and the Concept of 'Peaceful Purposes'," *53AFLR 135 at 145*, 2002.

[15]Convention on International Liability for Damage Caused by Space Objects, " ," *961 UNTS 187 [hereinafter "Liability Convention"]*, 1972.

[16]Goh, G., "Elendilmir: Satellites - Threats or the Threatened?" *45th Proc. Coll. Law of Outer Space (forthcoming)*, 2002.

[17]Agreement on the Activities of States on the Moon and Other Celestial Bodies, " ," *UNDoc. A/34/664 (1979) [hereinafter "Moon Agreement"]*, 1979.

[18]Cheng, B., "The Moon Treaty," *33 DLP 213*, 1980.

[19] "As at 1 January 2001, only nine States have ratified the Moon Agreement: Australia, Austria, Chile, Mexico, Morocco, the Netherlands, Pakistan, the Philippines and Uruguay. Five States have signed the Agreement but not ratified it: France, Guatemala, India, Peru and Romania." .

[20] Treaty Banning Nuclear Weapon Tests in the Atmosphere, in Outer Space and Underwater, " ," *480 UNTS 43 [hereinafter "LTBT"]*, 1963.

[21] Article I, "LTBT," *supra note 20*.

[22] Petras, C., "Space Force Alpha: Military Uses of the International Space Station and the Concept of 'Peaceful Purposes'," *53 AFLR 135*, 2002.

[23] Article I, "LTBT," *supra note 20*.

[24] Article IV(1), "OST," *supra note 1*.

[25] *Military and Paramilitary Activities in and against Nicaragua, Nicaragua v. USA (Merits)*, " ," *14 ICJ Reports 97 [hereinafter 'the Nicaragua case'] para 190*, 1986.

[26] Sadurska, R., "Threats of Force," *82 AJIL 239*, 1988.

[27] Lachs, M., "The Development and General Trends of International Law in Our Time," *169 RCADI 9 at 162*, 1980.

[28] Article 1(1), "UN Charter," *supra note 12*.

[29] Preamble, "UN Charter," *supra note 12*.

[30] Article 2(3), "UN Charter," *supra note 12*.

[31] Mrazek, J., "Prohibition of the Use and Threat of Force: Self-defence and Self-Help in International Law," *27 CYIL 81 at 90*, 1989.

[32] *Nicaragua case*, " ," *supra note 25 at 100*.

[33] "Online at: http://www.oosa.unvienna.org /SpaceLaw/gares/index.html," *(Last accessed: 27 January 2003)*.

[34] *North Sea Continental Shelf Cases*, " ," *ICJ Rep. 3 at 35*, 1969.

[35] Shaw, M., "*International Law*," *4th ed. at 90*, 1997.

[36] *Legality of the Threat or Use of Nuclear Weapons*, " ," *ICJ Reports 226 at para 70*, 1996.

[37] "Online at: http://www.oosa.unvienna.org /SpaceLaw/gares/index.html," *(Last accessed: 27 January 2003)*.

[38] *North Sea Continental Shelf cases*, " ," *supra note 34 at para 73*.

[39] see the national space legislations, "Online at: http://www.oosa.unvienna.org/SpaceLaw/national/index.html," *(Last accessed: 27 January 2003)*.

[40] von Noorden, W., "INMARSAT Use By Armed Forces: A Question of Treaty Interpretation," *23(1) JSL 1*, 1995.

[41] *Asylum Case*, " ," *ICJ Rep. 276*, 1950.

[42] Akehurst, M., "Custom as a Source of International Law," *47 BYIL 1*, 1974.

[43] Schachter, O., "International Law in Theory and Practice," 1991.

[44] Akande, D., "The International Court of Justice and the Security Council: Is There Room for Judicial Control of the Decisions of the Political Organs of the United Nations?" *46 ICLQ 309*, 1997.

[45] Malanczuk, P., "*Akehurst's Modern Introduction to International Law*," *7th ed. at 426*, 1997.

[46] Grieg, D., "Self-defence and the Security Council: What does Article 51 Require?" *40 ICLQ 366*, 1991.

[47] Fulghum, D., "Network-Centric Warfare," *Aviation Week at 28*, 2002.

[48] " ," *GARes 3314 (XXIX)*, 1974.

[49] "*Nicaragua case*," *supra note 25 at para 200*.

[50] *Nicaragua case (Jurisdiction and Admissibility)*, "ICJ Reports 551 para 92 - 3," *The USA argued that the ICJ should not pronounce on claims of self-defence because Article 51 provides a role in such matters only for the Security Council. The Court rejected this argument, saying that the USA was attempting to transfer municipal law concepts of separation of powers to the international plane, whereas these concepts are not applicable to the relations among international dispute resolution institutions.*, 1984.

[51] Higgins, R., "*The Development of International Law through the Political Organs of the UN*," *at 198*, 1963.

[52] IX, A., "OST," *supra note 1*.

[53] 1(2), A., "Protocol I, Protocol Additional to the Geneva Conventions of Aug. 12, 1949, and Relating to the Protection of Victims of International Armed Conflicts, Dec. 12, 1977," *1125 UNTS 3 [hereinafter "Protocol I"]*, 1977.

[54] 52(2), A., "Protocol I," *ibid.*.

[55] "The Convention on the Registration of Objects Launched into Outer Space," *1023 UNTS 15 [hereinafter "The Registration Convention"]*, 1978.

[56] IV(1)(e), A., "Registration Convention," *ibid.*.

[57] Bourbonniere, M. and Haeck, L., "Jus in Bello Spatiale," *XXV AASL 1*, 2000.

[58] "Some writers have rejected these limits on self-defence as not established in customary international law: Kunz, "Individual and Collective Self-defence in Article 51 of the Charter of the UN" (1947) 41AJIL 872; Delivanis, La lgitime dfense en droit international public moderne (1971), Chapter 2," .

[59] "Nuclear Weapons Case," *supra note 36 at para 141*.

[60] Jasentuliyana, N., "A Survey of Space Law as Developed by the United Nations," *in Jasentuliyana, N. (ed.)*, Perspectives of International Law *349*, 1995.

[61] " ," *Resolution 1721B-XVI*.

[62] Cheng, B., "The Contribution of Air and Space Law to the Development of International Law," *39 CLP 181*, 1986.

[63] International Law Commission, "Report of the International Law Commission, 28th Session," *ILC YB 1 at 96*, 1976.

[64] "Case concerning the Factory at Chórzow (Claim for Indemnity) (Merits)," *(A/17 1928) 1 WCR 646 at 664*, 1928.

[65] " ," *ibid at 677 - 8*.

[66] " ," *ibid.*.

[67] Christol, C., "The Use of Outer Space for Peaceful Purposes," *28th Proc. Coll. Law of Outer Space 4*, 1985.

[68] Ekblad, U. and Orhaug, T., "Verification of Outer Space Treaties by an ISSA," *31st Proc. Coll. Law on Outer Space 22 at 24. The French Government made a similar proposal for the creation of an International Satellite Monitoring Agency (ISMA) in 1978, see Note Verbal (May 30, 1978), in Official Records of the General Assembly, A/S-10/AC.1/7. For a critical analysis of this proposal, see Doyle, SE., Civil Space Systems: Implications for International Security (1993) at 173*, 1988.

[69] 90(2)(e), A., "Protocol I," *supra note 53*.

[70] Doyle, S., "Confidence-Building Measures Using Space Resources," *40th Proc. Coll. Law of Outer Space 108*, 1998.

[71] The last of these was in 2002, G. A., "All 40 resolutions are online at," *http://www.oosa.unvienna.org/SpaceLaw/gares/index.html (Last accessed: 27 January 2003)*, 2003.

[72] "All 9 resolutions and their voting history are online at: http://www.oosa.unvienna.org/SpaceLaw/gares/index.html (Last accessed: 27 January 2003)," 2003.

[73] Tolkien, J., "Farewell to Lórien," *The Lord of the Rings: The Fellowship of the Ring (Book Two) at 368*, 1966, reprinted 1995.

SPACE WEAPONS

W. Marshall, G. Whitesides, R. Schingler, Andre Nilsen, N. Rawat
SGC Space Security Working Group, Bremen 2003, wsm@physics.ox.ac.uk

Abstract

The 'Peace in Space' initiative was conceived by students and young space professionals at the Space Generation Forum (SGF), at UNISPACE-III. The initiative was further developed at the Space Generation Summit (SGS), an event at the World Space Congress (WSC) which brought together 200 youth from over 50 countries to discuss and plan for future space activities and policy, and to revitalise the energy of young people in the space sector.

Most young space enthusiasts believe that humanity has a shared interest in a peaceful future in space. The recent demise of the ABM treaty, the lack of a comprehensive ban on weapons in existing space treaties, and American plans to deploy space weapons combine to create an urgent situation. International policy must be developed to regulate the peaceful use of space, prohibit the deployment of space weapons, and prevent an arms race in space. In this paper, we propose a comprehensive strategy to prevent the weaponisation of space. This strategy consists of three key steps: 1) creating a knowledge-base and increasing the profile of this issue, 2) convincing the US Congress to cut spending to a planned space weapons test bed, and 3) laying the groundwork for comprehensive international space security agreements.

This report is the result of a two-year youth working group with the end goal of ensuring the formation of regulatory mechanisms to prevent space weapons. After a brief history, we concentrate on the next steps required to help this situation. The working group has developed these ideas through discussions, meetings with military and United Nations diplomats, and discussions from the recent Pugwash conference dedicated to raising the profile of this international and inter-generational issue.

Why now?

This discussion is urgent because most developed nations possess the technology for developing and deploying weapon systems in space and the use of space weapons is relatively unrestricted. Moreover, political and military leaders in some developed nations have expressed support for the development and deployment of space weapons. Deployment may be imminent. It is critical that this dialogue takes place now, prior to the deployment of space weapons. Once deployed, it may be difficult to abolish space weapons, even if they prove useless or destabilizing before the onset of an arms race in space.

In this paper we seek to put the question of space weapons on the current international political agenda. To that end, and to encourage public debate on the subject, we first offer a brief introduction to the topic, including history, and relevant definitions. The short and long-term consequences of deployment are then discussed. Finally, we detail a comprehensive strategy to address this pressing issue.

A Brief History of Space and Defence

The military use of space is not new. The access to, and utilization of space is of national interest in terms of security, and economically. In addition to the economic potential of the exploitation of space and celestial bodies, space is the ultimate military high ground. Indeed, expenditure on space by the military has consistently outweighed civil spending. Even some scientific exploration missions have arguably been dominated by military objectives, such as the pursuit of technological supremacy during the Cold War which led both to the first satellite (Sputnik, 1957), and human (Yuri Gagarin, 1961) in space, and culminated with the manned lunar program (Apollo, 1963-72).

Historically, space military assets have been passive, concentrating on reconnaissance, communications, and navigation. No publicly acknowledged space weapon has been deployed to orbit, to date. The most serious related effort came during the parallel anti-satellite (ASAT) programmes developed by the US and Soviet Union during the 1960s. Specifically, these programs developed nuclear pumped X-ray lasers, space-based optical lasers, radiation belt weapons, ground-based reflected laser systems, and space-based interceptors. The testing of these systems was periodically prohibited or not funded by the US Congress during the 1980s and 1990s. The US military also expressed its disinclination to use kinetic kill ASATs because they tend to create large clouds of space debris. Even though these initiatives were not carried through, they created a technology base that would enable the near-term deployment of space weapons.

The potential components of future space weapon systems are already being used in current, passive, military space systems, and even in the civilian space sector. The telemetry, tracking, and control systems of a commercial communications satellite, for example, are very similar to analogous systems within a basic space weapon. Sensor and targeting technologies used in commercial remote sensing satellites have direct application to a space weapon system.

The broader international community has meanwhile repeatedly stated its support for space to be used solely for peaceful purposes. This position was codified early in the space age by the 1967 Outer Space Treaty (OST), in which 102 states to date, including the US and former USSR, have recognized the common interest of humankind in the peaceful exploration and use of outer space. In 2001, the UN General Assembly approved by a 156-0 vote the basis for a treaty establishing a permanent prohibition on space-based weapons (Resolution 56/535). The United States abstained. What remains at issue is the meaning of "peaceful." The United States and many other nations hold that peaceful does not mean non-military. The United

States and other nations, citing the United Nations Charter's acknowledgement of the inherent right of states to self-defense, reserve the right to use military force, including weapons for "defensive" purposes. They maintain that the use of defensive weapons in outer space is thus not prohibited by any international agreement, save the Outer Space Treaty prohibitions on weapons of mass destruction and military bases on the moon and other heavenly bodies.

Against this background of inactivity and caution, some have been advocating the development space weapons with strike capabilities. In April 2003, for example, the United States Congressman representing NASA's Florida base stated his support for weapons deployed in space, "We must adopt a doctrine that states that we as a nation will vigorously pursue the ability to project power to, through and from space against any aggressor." He also noted, "It would be inappropriate to deny ourselves this advantage simply because of romantic notions of some that space is some type of sacred place."

Perhaps more significantly, representatives of the United States military have advocated a strategy to include the deployment of space weapons within a matter of a few years. However, this position has not yet been adopted at the highest level. In fact, many military officers regard space-based weapons dubiously. The military focus on space, however, has been reaffirmed repeatedly in key documents such as Air Force Vision 2020, and other strategic planning documents.

Space Security Strategy

We present here a strategy to prevent the weaponisation of space. It was developed through the Pugwash Conferences on Science and World Affairs Workshop on the Weaponisation of Space. This strategy consists of the following three mechanisms: 1) creating a knowledge base and increasing the profile of this issue, 2) convincing the US Congress to cut spending to the planned space weapons test bed, and 3) laying the groundwork for comprehensive international space security agreements.

These three mechanisms are presented in greater detail below:

1. Increase the knowledge base

a. Space Security Index

A research-based trend analysis initiated by the Canadian Department of Foreign Affairs and International Trade (DFAIT) that provides a net assessment of the collective progress, or lack of progress, towards space security. The Canadian Space Security Index is envisaged to measure twelve indicators within three themes of space security; space environment (e.g. space debris, allocation of orbital slots), the intentions of space security actors (e.g. space military doctrine) and capabilities of space security actors (e.g. launch capabilities, ASAT, space weapon capabilities). This would facilitate a constructive international dialogue on the weaponisastion of space.

i. Coordinate a network of experts on space, especially from the scientific community, in order to facilitate the Space Security Index (SSI) and fulfill specified research and analysis needs

ii. Produce publication on space security to collate the knowledge base gathered in the SSI.

b. Increase Salience

i. Networking: reaching out to public, space scientists and space users

ii. Encourage the development of a Space Security Bulletin to inform the space community of recent news

iii. Convene a conference with Committee on Space Research (COSPAR) potentially on Space Weaponisation

iv. Reach out to commercial actors and industries using space assets and increase their awareness of the effects of the weaponisation of space

v. Increase public outreach through space NGOs

c. Further Research and Rigorous Analysis

i. Feasibility of threats to space-based assets from ASATs launched by non-traditional space powers

ii. Feasibility of a 'Space Pearl Harbor' scenario

iii. Space Security Index

iv. Costs and Benefits of space weapons

v. The impact of space weapons on the commercial space sector

2. Political Initiatives towards the prohibition of space weapons

a. Prevent the deployment of a US test-bed, planned for 2008

i. Engage the US Congress in dialogue to cut spending from space weapons development prior to a critical debate

ii. To convene a workshop to improve the understanding of the issue amongst politicians.

3. Laying the groundwork for a comprehensive space security approach

a. Initiate discussions with the US Military, Congress and the White House

b. Increase the visibility of existing as well as new research and reports

c. Use high-profile spokespeople to capture public attention

d. Organize an international space security summit

e. Consider the pros and cons of advocating a moratorium on no first testing, deployment or use of space weapons

g. Create a timeline for political/legal initiatives

i. On-going work on CBMs (debris management, compliance issues, etc.)

ii. Increase the number of parties supporting the Outer Space Treaty (OST), to move towards universalisation

iii. UNGA resolution to multilateralise agreement on non-interference with space assets, building on the provisions in the CFE and other treaties

iv. Negotiate the banning of ASAT, weapons in and from space, and create international rules of the road regulations, either as a protocol to the OST or as separate legal instruments.

Before Celestial Bodies Collide- Enhanced Dialogue and Coordination: Precursors to a Treaty for Effective Near Earth Object (NEO) Response

Author: Liara M. Covert,[1] Ph.D., Consultant, N.-B., Canada [liarac@yahoo.com]

Problems

Trans-border crises on Earth are increasingly serious and unpredictable.[2] Root causes are often socio-political, intercultural, natural and/or unexpected. Cooperation among actors is hindered by differing views about crises and viable solutions, from the State-level that drafts and grasps its own views of International Law (IL), to policy-level responses and operations practitioners who may know less about IL or interpret it as they will.

Another concern is that feedback loops seldom exist among policymakers, lawyers, tech. operations practitioners or other entities. Economic issues and power dynamics among actors in crisis prevention and response cause delays and determine who is given data or not.

Lack of information complicates IL applications. Legal practitioners base them on rules and principles that govern State relations. Yet, not all actors involved in trans-border crisis and response grasp the implications of State rights in Public International Law (PIL) or know how Private International Law (PrIL) addresses conflicts of private persons, natural or juridical, arising out of State situations. As lines between PIL and PrIL have been blurred, so has the clarity of relationships among international community members.[3]

Inevitably, at the fall 2003 opening of the UN General Assembly, Kofi Annan said, "we've come to a fork in the road no less decisive than 1945 itself, when the UN was founded."[4] He urged taking radical action to combat the global threats that cause global crises and reduce the value of cooperation, including views of terrorism and weapons of mass destruction, as well as situations where States may act unilaterally.

Chosen Case

The epitome of unexpected crisis would be a huge NEO collision with Earth. A NEO is a minor body of the solar system (e.g., a comet or asteroid) that enters Earth's vicinity. NEOs split into NECs (Near Earth Comets) and NEAs, (Near Earth Asteroids), the latter defined by orbits that never go further than 195 million km from the sun."[5]

Although the search for extra-terrestrial intelligence (SETI) group has proposed a global response model for SETI contact to the UN Committee on the Peaceful Uses of Outer Space (COPUOS),[6] the call for a parallel NEO defense model assumes a definite threat, and would benefit from clauses about the nature of NEO observations, more varied professional contributions, wider global promotion and intercultural debate. To help Earth better prepare for and respond to a large NEO collision, diverse actors need to better understand mutual data needs, share views of issues, coordination and responsibility.

The effectiveness of IL hinges on the evolution of interdisciplinary dialogue and striving for a clearer grasp of terms. This paper calls for a new mindset to help designate rotating coordinators and funding from varied nations for NEO sightings, to encourage the creation and upkeep of NEO observation programs in both hemispheres,[7] and guide cooperation among governments, and actors in crisis planning and response.

Outline

Recognizing that no global NEO program[8] yet exists,[9] the paper analyzes views of leaders and other actors.[10]

Firstly, the paper examines the impact of globalization on State sovereignty and international mindsets.

Secondly, the paper addresses why law and policy actors, as well as other practitioners, should clarify their understanding and use of terms, and how the nature of text may change in light of unique aspects of the NEO threat.[11]

Finally, the paper supposes an event like the destructive Tunguska meteor[12] of 1908 is foreseen in a populated area to discuss key precursors to a more cooperative, treaty mindset.

Impact of Globalization[13]

Before focusing on crises linked to a large NEO impact with Earth, one should note that forces of co-operation and conflict among cultures and civilizations influence who drafts or merely interprets IL,[14] as much as which nations and organizations influence wider State interpretation and execution of related laws and policies.[15]

Consider that State borders are now permeable in real space and cyber-space. Weaker borders intensify competition.[16] Global exchanges, economic transactions, and entities also dilute State sovereignty and weaken the enforceability of IL. Organizations (e.g., NGOs) even refer to IL to network internationally, in efforts to change State policies and laws.[17]

Major quarrels still continue among industrial States. These powers initiated both world wars and founded IL, "on hegemonic patterns of force monopoly."[18] Tensions continue among developing and industrial States about agriculture, trade, and other issues. IL has even been accused of reinforcing inequality.[19] It's arguable that smaller countries should derive greater benefits from IL protection against larger, economically powerful States. Yet, in non-security matters,[20] It's less likely claims will be made by weaker States to engage in pre-emptive or anticipatory conduct.

Not surprisingly, views of IL differ among law and policy actors and other practitioners. Terms can seem imprecise to people who deal with the practical sides of terrorism, disease, refugees, nuclear disasters, smuggling, environmental crises, electronic threats,[21] and drug trafficking.[22] For these people, treaties, conventions, and customary international law (CIL)[23] often appear too general or situation-specific.

Nonetheless, principles set forth in five Space Treaties[24] reflect the widespread State desire for international efforts to improve space cooperation and security. Diverging views on the role of national security helped justify space technology-related defense agreements and export control regimes emerging after the Cold War.[25] Military rationale also determines which States sign or opt out of the Nuclear Test-Ban Treaty.[26] Military defense is not the only interpretation of national security.

Civilian approaches to security are also used for trans-border disaster planning and response. Yet, when site imagery of an environmental disaster is needed, response teams must wait for images from commercial or scientific satellites, even if a military satellite is already nearby. Thus, military protocol obscures environmental defense strategy.

An effective NEO treaty would need a shared, interdisciplinary mindset among nations. The International Space Station (ISS) Program, its agreements and evolving interprofessional teams offer hope for new approaches to cooperation.[27] This mindset needs to expand so as to include more nations outside the ISS Program, and also to involve developing nations.

Definitions[28]

Interpretations of terms by different actors influence State compliance with IL.[29] The prospect of a large NEO impact with Earth[30] urges leaders and diverse actors to learn from small-scale crises in practice and scale-up possible future scenarios, but also to promote or provide input to regional, national and international fora.[31]

In essence, the pressing issues of security, sustainability[32] and planetary survival, urge actors from the State-level down[33] to review meanings of at least 7 key terms and recognize differences in interpretation and practice. Then, could the world be prepared to deal more effectively with unexpected asteroid events.

Term 1: 'Harm'

According to John Stuart Mill, power, "can only be rightfully exercised over any member of a civilized community [...] to prevent harm."[34]

Nonetheless, regarding security, diverse notions of *harm* exist at the State-level that drafts and interprets IL.[35] Documents such as the Hague Code of Conduct Against Ballistic Missile Proliferation[36] create a sharp distinction between what State action should and shouldn't be permitted. Yet, terms like *peaceful purposes* still have varied meanings in law and also in practice by non-lawyers.[37]

As it stands, lawyers mainly interpret harm after it's occurred, based on fault and evaluated damage,[38] and chiefly in liability and humanitarian law cases.[39]

Of special interest to technical practitioners is the U.S. Model State Defense Act. It requires States to mobilize and respond to "existing and increasing possibilit[ies] of unknown disasters of unprecedented size and destructiveness."[40] Yet, the measures to be taken are vague, and diverse actors' needs at local, regional and national levels aren't specified. This void is serious where the success of such policy is based on a changing execution during crisis.

Consider also the UNISPACE III Recommendations and Vienna Declaration on Space and Human Development.[41] These legal documents propose that space-based activity for telemedicine and controlling infectious diseases should be expanded and coordinated, that an integrated, global system should be implemented to manage natural disaster mitigation, and many other initiatives. Space technology applications are linked to human security, development and welfare, but issues of how, where, when, for whom and by whom are unspecified.

Term 2: 'Threat'

IL urges action should be taken to minimize a given *threat*. For example, the Biodiversity Convention states, "where there is a threat of significant reduction or loss of biological diversity, lack of full scientific certainty should not be used as a reason for postponing measures to avoid or minimize such a threat [...]."[42] Action required for planet survival should then be grasped in thought, word and deed. Yet, its unclear by when, whom or how.

Consider the historic ICJ declaration July 8, 1996, that the threat or use of nuclear weapons would be "contrary to the rules of [IL] applicable in armed conflict." The only exception was that, "the Court cannot conclude definitively whether the threat or use of nuclear weapons would be lawful or unlawful in an extreme circumstance of self-defense, in which the very survival of a State would be at stake."[43] Thus, an extreme threat could compel a new view of this ICJ verdict: any planetary defense strategy for asteroid deflection may call for nuclear technology applications.[44]

Term 3: 'Mitigate'

In the general NEO scientific community, *mitigate* implies actual deflection of the NEO away from Earth.

At the same time, disaster managers define mitigate as, "sustained actions to reduce or eliminate the long-term impacts and risks associated with natural and human-induced disasters."[45] In practice, this becomes response strategies more than prevention measures. Yet, action may still be taken before a disaster to reduce the event's risk of occurrence, to avert or diminish the eventual event impact.[46]

Engineers in debris communities see 'mitigate' as action taken to prevent additional space debris, especially in the centimeter and millimeter range. This term is defined in papers and technical studies.[47]

The legal community currently has no standard meaning for 'mitigate,' although legal groups have deliberated possibilities.

Academics have even proposed details to help define the term, including better construction, shielding, technical controls and safer ground management for satellites in Earth orbit.[48]

Term 4: 'Risk'

Definitions of *risk* are based on views and experience of different actors facing a potential threat. [49] Scientists, the public, governments, agencies and entities weigh risks based on interests and a grasp on a given situation. Actors in practice see risks 'at hand' differently.

Note that the U.S. Environmental Protection Agency (EPA), under the Comprehensive Environmental Response, Compensation and Liability Act (CERCLA), states a one in a million risk of getting cancer is the threshold for determining clean-up levels for sites contaminated with hazardous substances. Using statistics, CERCLA deals with risks much lower than those predicted from a major asteroid or comet disaster. The cost of cleaning up two sites (avg. cost 30$M each) is said to be comparable to the cost of a large asteroid detection program.[50] The complexity of reconciling national laws and policy can complicate efforts to avoid disasters.

Term 5: 'Self-Preservation'[51]

All life forms are seen to protect themselves against harm, which is the principle of inherent *self-preservation*.[52] This concept is found for instance, in the Rio Declaration[53] (art. II) and the 1992 Convention on Industrial Accidents. The latter stresses the need to identify risk of contamination (art. I), to convey information to States and the public (art. II), and to detail contamination protection (art. III). All people have "the right to life, liberty and security." [54] How such principles guide co-ordinated planetary defense is yet to be seen.

The need to prepare for unexpected crises requires that closer attention be paid to the precautionary principle.[55] This notion summarizes why governments must act to ward off potential harm, even when the likelihood of harm occurring is unclear.

Governments and other actors can also benefit from cooperative preservation. This implies that decision-makers at varied levels of authority can only meet a duty to protect citizens when they cooperate. Effective emergency planning and large disaster mitigation without cooperation are unlikely.[56]

Encouraging lessons can be learned from coherent IL applications in smaller disasters. See mechanisms used to deal with "international biological, chemical and nuclear threats, trans-boundary forest fires and the threat of infectious diseases across borders." [57]

Recall also the Chernobyl nuclear fallout. Art. 55 and 56 of the UN Charter set out the related human rights obligations of the UN member States.[58]

In respect of preservation, many governments give legal status to disaster preparedness reserve funds. The Canadian government used such a fund to help pay for unforeseen SARS, forest fire and flood-related expenses. The Ethiopia Disaster Prevention and Preparedness Commission (DPPC), formerly known as the Relief and Rehabilitation Commission (RRC), maintains a national famine relief fund.

Certain aspects of international human rights law remain in force in national emergencies. Some civil and political freedoms may be derogated, but only under highly- restricted conditions: derogation must be for a limited period, in a way that doesn't discriminate, and only to the extent required by a severe emergency that threatens the stability of a nation.[59] 'Rights' and 'protection' as terms are often left undefined. [60]

Ultimately, unresolved tension among actors about uncertainty of events and general disorganization[61] helps to explain why the self-preservation principle hasn't yet caused the emergence of more consensual views of IL applications in precautionary disaster planning and response. It could improve.

Term 6: 'Environmental Security'[62]

The views of *environmental security* embrace the military and non-military defense. Large NEO threats would compare to a theoretical post-global-nuclear war holocaust, or key bio-terrorism effects.[63] Security is also linked to environmental preservation.

Nonetheless, a Millennium Research Project reveals few States have official definitions of environmental security that unify thought and action. [64] Among the countries that have definitions are: The Russian Federation and the Commonwealth of Independent States. The U.S. has several working definitions and a Department of Defense (DoD) Directive that includes program-specific definitions. Embassy Representatives from Argentina and India noted their States have an official definition, but the text is not in writing. Respondents in China, Australia, and Hungary said their governments were creating a definition. Similar to the European Union (EU), China puts environmental security under the roof of "environmental protection."

Consider the UN Environment Program (UNEP) and World Heath Organization (WHO) don't define it. The UN Development Program (UNDP) refers to it in a 1994 report on human development (p.28): "Environmental threats countries face are a combination of the degradation of local ecosystems and that of the global system. These comprise threats to environmental security."

The label is addressed in four other instruments-The U.N. Secretary General's Bulletin (6 August 1999)-"Observance of UN Forces of International Humanitarian Law", the Geneva Convention's First Protocol (1977), International Criminal Court's Charter (Rome Statute), and Convention on the Prohibition of Military or Any other Hostile Use of Environmental Modification Techniques (ENMOD).[65]

A recent Rockefeller report on world security notes that a definition in the post-Cold War has "proven elusive despite massive efforts." Many irreconcilable views exist in statements, policies, and international agreements. [66]

'Duty'

IL imposes a certain *duty* upon States regarding States and individuals. Treaties are legally-binding by definition, unless parties withdraw or don't observe obligations.[67] Other legal duties exist to protect public welfare. This recognizes duties to research or simulate potential disasters like NEO collisions that aren't understood.[68] Moral obligations lead States to define and adhere to codes of conduct.[69]

Text Proposals: 'Harm'

Altruistic legal principles and declarations are drafted to prevent harm, but key terms seldom illustrate a grasp the phases of a disaster, or the diverse actors' needs for different data at different times. An eventual NEO treaty should note the degree of harm varies before and after awareness of a potential threat, and after harm occurs.[70] As well, roles of different practitioners, and the nature of the harm should be addressed and scaled from minor to severe. The timeframe for these activities to be completed and the distribution of responsibilities (hierarchies) among entities and actors also must be defined.

Text Proposals: 'Threat'

The term *threat* also needs to be understood on a time continuum and on a scale from minor to serious. Threats aren't linked equally with problematic socio-economic activities, or trans-border issues. Each threat has unique causes and processes with regard to which legal, scientific and policy issues need to be grasped and applied. Only by breaking down interdisciplinary elements can perceived rights, duties, obligations, and divisions of control be defined at each phase of awareness.

Text Proposals: 'Mitigate'

Technical, socio-political and other views need to be inter-related, on a timeline of awareness of the threat.

A big problem is that different professional groups have their own notions of 'mitigate' and the concepts aren't always understood by or useful to other groups.

Text Proposals: 'Risk'

This paper contends when States sign and accede to the proposed NEO treaty, they assume the risk as a political gesture, demonstrate a belief in a regime based on more than principle, and/or act as reciprocity strategy. The aim is to ensure observance of issues behind space law, humanitarian law, and other facets of IL. Risk need also be defined through time and other actors.

Text Proposals: 'Rights & Protection'

Terms need to be clarified with respect to existing IL and according to needs of actors before and after awareness of the threat, and also after harm has occurred.

Text Proposals: 'Self-Preservation'

New emphasis on the international scope, interdependence and practical urgency of terrestrial preservation could change the attitudes of authorities[71] and their views on intergovernmental responsibility for environmental security and NEOs.[72]

Text Proposals: 'Environmental Security'

This term requires both military and civilian contexts to be considered. Choosing one at the expense of the other for any NEO treaty would be inaccurate and unsatisfactory. Nature's involvement makes normal legal blame a problem. This term also needs to be defined at different points in a time continuum.[73]

Text Proposals: 'Duty'

The proposed NEO treaty requires consensual agreement about the existence of the NEO threat. If widespread agreement is not reached and no repercussions exist for non-observance of the treaty, States may undermine their shared moral duty to protect their citizens and global biodiversity.

The UN purposes are a helpful guide for the duties to be considered: to maintain peace and security, to develop friendly state relations, to achieve international cooperation in solving international problems, and to be a center for harmonizing national actions and attaining their common ends.[74]

If duties to prepare for and respond to large-scale threats such as NEOs are to be respected, people and entities[75] need to commit resources in anticipation of problems based on principle, rather than solely after attributing fault.[76]

Text Proposals: All Terms

Re-visiting notions of the above terms associated with natural and man-made disasters[77] could motivate domestic actors to learn more about or revisit the relevance of IL. All actors should reflect on three key reasons why their State joins treaties: (1) beliefs in treaty norms; (2) predictions about binding nature or binding other States for action; and (3) State interactions.

Key Problems with an NEO Treaty

At present, local policies and procedures are often defined after a local event, with plans to apply them in the future as a more effective means of prevention and crisis management[78]. Motives to enter into treaties vary and reveal how States may react to obligations during crises. Comparing political obstacles that complicate state commitment and compliance is helpful when considering different treaties.[79]

Reality is that the codification of key instruments and the accession to space treaties by a large majority of states, doesn't guarantee consistent or predictable State behavior in times of international crisis.[80] Problems with co-commitment and compliance at the state-level reveal the need to examine coordination and communication at decision-making levels and below that.[81]

Consider that large-scale disaster mitigation and management on Earth can mobilize multiple actors to co-ordinate a concerted intergovernmental response.[82] The will to cooperate thus already exists, even when emergency response systems tend to evolve within political jurisdictions. Although local, regional and national disasters may be partially controlled by existing procedures,[83] the impact of a major disaster has no limit, and repercussions aren't well understood at varied levels of awareness of a threat.[84]

Thus, the value of trans-national disaster mitigation and response relates to State motives to work together and learn from each other as much as State pressures to ignore historical patterns of compliance and commitment.[85]

Precursors to an NEO Treaty

In the event of a huge NEO collision in a populated area, acknowledgement of a single entity would best guide practical operations and applications of IL.[86] However, communication, co-ordination as well as interdisciplinary understanding of IL terms and implications must improve regionally and nationally before large-scale disaster management can be more effective and promote a the mindset for a NEO treaty.

For instance, OECD Workshop conclusions imply many industrial States have yet to acknowledge the outer space threat, enable a policy level response, promote State-level risk assessments, and support exploratory research and development (R&D) for mitigation.[87]

Further, decision-making about the development of an NEO treaty will need to breakdown the essential aspects of the surmised threat, including "long-time horizon, possible irreversibilities (physical and socio-economic), large uncertainties and impacts of future scientific progress."[88]

An effective NEO treaty could only evolve in interdisciplinary fora that exchange views on terms like *harm, threat, mitigate, rights & protection, and environmental security*, in ways applicable to policy and operations along a timeframe of awareness. The key may be to grasp the interdisciplinary nature of *mitigate*.[89]

Further, an NEO treaty could have no withdrawal clause or parties that would consider non-participation an option. This would differ from Geneva Conventions.[90] Views on self-preservation issues should evolve to motivate standard compliance.

Conclusion

Actual practice reveals that many factors determine whether legal terms offer an acceptable guide to lawyers, policymakers and other practitioners in emergency management. Problems arise where the intention of IL drafters is that the chosen terms will be read as only one community knows or understands them. Divergent, even conflicting, intentions may continue to underlie a given text unless proposed definitions integrate more practical elements in key concepts.

New approaches to dialogue and promoting IL applications could lead to more effective interactions among actors and the international, interdisciplinary, intercultural mindset needed to successfully execute an NEO treaty.[91]

If legal writings remain problematic to non-legal practitioners, and even lawyers fail to reach agreement about context of terms, perhaps interdisciplinary efforts to strengthen an evolving international mindset for global self-preservation can...

---

[2] See *Report on the Status of Multilateral Environmental Agreements in the European Region*, UNEP Regional Center, June (1998).

[3] See Brownlie, I.: *Principles of Public International Law*, 6th Ed., Oxford University; also see the Cornell University Law database.

[4] See Annan, K.A., "Speech for Opening of the UN General Assembly," Sept. 23, 2003.

[5] See *The Tumbling Stone*, Num. 1., Dictionary; "Origin & Evolution of NEOs," Morbidelli et al., (1998), p. 1-14; *Spaceguard* Asteroid Dictionary.

[6] Jasentulyiana, N., Kopal, V., Fasan, E., Sterns, P., Carrigan, D., SETI members

(Communications, 2003); COPUOS (2000) U.N. Doc. A/55/20; Official SETI Protocol www.seti-inst.edu (accessed Oct. 4, 2003).

[7] Coradini, M. Chapman, C., (Communications, 2003); Steel, D. (V.P. Spaceguard, comments).

[8] See Grabowski, M. and Roberts, K., "Risk Mitigation in Virtual Organizations," JCMC 3 (4) June 1998—interdisciplinary dialogue is key.

[9] See www.b612foundation.org (accessed Sept. 18, 2003); Komisar, L., "Avoiding the Impact," *Scientific American*, July 8, 2002, esp. former astronaut R. Schweickart's view; Kunich, J.C., "Planetary Defense: Legality of Global Survival," *AFLR*, Summer 1997; France, Lt.Col M.E., "Planetary Defense: Eliminating the Giggle Factor," *Air & Space Power Chronicles*, August 2000, p. 1-20; Bell, L. et al., "Planetary Asteroid Defense Study: Assessing and Responding to the Natural Space Debris Threat," April 1995; Nici, Lt.Col. R. and Kaupa, Lt.D., "Planetary Defense: DoD Cost for Detection, Exploration, and Rendezvous Mission of NEOs," *Airpower Journal*. Vol. 11, No. 2, 1997; Burnell, S., "U.S. Military Takes Asteroid Threat Seriously," www.rense.com/general29/threat.htm (accessed Sept. 10, 2003).

[10] Consider five decision-making levels analyzed in, "International Space Station Negotiations & Manned Space Strategy (MSS): Toward Consideration of a Multinational Astronaut Consortium (MAC)," Covert, L.M., (2002, Ph.D., Intro), Le Centre D'Études Diplomatiques & Stratégiques (C.E.D.S.), Paris, France.

[11] Michalowski, S., (Communications, March, 2002); OECD Global Science Forum, NEOs: Risks, Policies & Actions: Final Report, 13pgs, http://www.oecd.org/dataoecd/39/40/2503992.pdf (accessed Sept. 10, 2003).

[12] See Tunguska Catastrophe Event, www.orc.ru/~azorcord/page_sob.htm (accessed Sept. 10, 2003); Hartmann, W.K., "1908 Siberia Explosion: Re-constructing and Asteroid Impact from Eyewitness Accounts," http://www.psi.edu/projects/siberia/siberia.html (accessed Sept. 22, 2003).

[13] See Huntington, S.P., *Clash of Civilizations and the Remaking of World Order*, (1996).

[14] Recall the original ICJ Statute, June 26, 1945, art. 38(1)(a)-(d), 59 Stat. 1055,1060, 33 U.N.T.S. 993 (defines "international conventions", "international custom," and "general principles of law recognized by civilized nations").

[15] See for instance, Fidler, D.P., "American Society of International Law (ASIL) Insights: SARS and International Law," April 2003, http://www.asil.org/insights/insigh101.htm (accessed Sept. 16, 2003); also Ho, A., "Does the War on Terror Violate International Law?," *The Straits Times*, January 12, 2003, http://straitstimes.asia1.com.sg/columnist/0,1886,56-96106,00.html (accessed Sept. 10, 2003).

[16] See von der Dunk, F.G, *Private Enterprise and Public Interest in the European Seascape* (1998).

[17] Consider how Greenpeace lobbied European markets not to buy seal products in their efforts to fight the Newfoundland (Canada) seal hunts.

[18] See Baxi U, "Operation Enduring Freedom: Towards a New IL & Order?," *(LGD)*, 2001 (2).

[19] See Downey, J., "The Third World versus the West," *Open Democracy*, Global Policy Forum August 21, 2002 (1-4); also www.wto.int (last accessed Oct 4, 2003).

[20] National 'safety' can hinge on socio-economic, trade or defense issues, among others.

[21] Cyber-crime grew 400% to 83,000 cases--www.cert.org/stats/cert_stats.html#incidents (accessed Oct. 4, 2003)—(from 1999-2002).

[22] See Love, M.C., *Beyond Sovereignty: Issues for a Global Agenda*, 2nd Ed., 2003, 384 pgs.

[23] Codified in the Vienna Convention of Treaties, esp. Preamble ("*Believing* that the codification and progressive development of the law of treaties achieved in the present Convention will promote the purposes of the UN set forth in the Charter, namely, the maintenance of international peace and security, the development of friendly relations and the achievement of co-operation among nations, *Affirming* that the rules of [CIL] will continue to govern questions not regulated by the provisions of the present Convention [...]") and Art. VI; Sinclair, I., *Vienna Convention on Law of Treaties*, 1984, p. 22; Brownlie, I., *Principles of Public International Law*, 6th Ed., Ch. 27, "Law of Treaties," p.580, "nonetheless, a good number of articles are essentially declaratory of existing law and certainly those provisions which are not constitute emergent rules of general [IL]."

[24] See *The UN Treaties and Principles on Outer Space*, UN Publications, NY, 1999; Diedriks-Verschoor, I.H.P., *Intro. to Space Law* (1999).

[25] See the Missile Technology Control Regime (MTCR), and Anti-Ballistic Missile Treaty; Krepon, M. and Clary, C., "Space Assurance or Space Dominance? The Case Against Weaponizing Space," 2003, Henry L. Stimson Center, Washington, D.C., 131pgs.; van Fenema, P., "Export Controls & Satellite Launches: What's New?," IISL Paper (2003).

[26] See Chyba, C.F., van der Wink, G.E., and Hennet, C.B., "Monitoring the Comprehensive Test Ban Treaty: possible ambiguities due to meteorite impacts," *Geophysical Research Letters*. Volume 25, 1998; also "Preparing for planetary defense: detection and interception of asteroids on collision course with Earth," White Paper on NEO Planetary Defense, on-line at http://www.fas.org/ssp/military/dccops/usaf/2020/app-r.htm (accessed Sept. 20, 2003); also Preparatory Commission for the Comprehensive Nuclear Test Ban Treaty Organization, e.g., treaty signatories and follow-up programs, http://pws.ctbto.org/ (accessed Sept. 20, 2003).

[27] See Covert, L.M., "Multicultural Issues in Law & Ethics of International Space Station (ISS) Astronaut-related Medical Decision-making," IISL-00-IISL-1.08, p.1-15; also Covert Ph.D. Thesis (2002, 1-650), *supra.* note. 10.

[28] See Shue H. (1980). *Basic Rights: Subsistence, Affluence, and U.S. Foreign Policy*, 2nd Ed.; and Huntington, S.P., *supra.* note.13 (Intro).

[29] See Simmons, B.A., "Compliance with International Agreements", *Annual Review of Political Science*, June 1998, Vol. I. p. 75.

[30] See "Asteroid Threat in 2014": http://news.ninemsn.com.au/World/story_51450.asp (accessed Sept. 2, 2003); in contrast to "Asteroid Strike Ruled out for 2014": http://stacks.msnbc.com/news/960340.asp (accessed Sept. 3, 2003); "Report of the U.K. Task Force on Potentially Hazardous Near Earth Objects," 2000, 53 pgs; NASA "Study to Determine the Feasibility of Extending the Search for Near Earth Objects and to Smaller Limiting Diameters," August 22, 2003, 166pgs. http://neo.jpl.nasa.gov/neo/neoreport030825.pdf (accessed Sept. 5, 2003); Chapman C.R., "How a Near-Earth Object Impact Might Affect Society," (2003), p.1-25; also *supra.* note. 10.

[31] See selected national disaster management plans of the Red Cross Federation-- http://www.ifrc.org/what/dp/biblio/dpplans.asp (accessed Sept. 19, 2003); also *What Disaster Response Management Can Learn From Chaos Theory Conference Proceedings*, May 18-19, 1995, Koehler, G.A. Ph.D. (Ed.), http://www.library.ca.gov/CRB/96/05/; Canadian Office of Critical Infrastructure Protection and Emergency preparedness (OCIPEP) http://www.ocipep-bpiepc.gc.ca and Emergency Management Australia www.ema.gov.au (accessed Sept. 18, 2003); also UNCOPUOS Technical Committee Meeting Reports (various).

[32] See UNISPACE III Vienna Convention (space tech uses to enhance terrestrial sustainability and International Agreements on sustainability), http://www.sustreport.org/policy/international.html (accessed Sept. 22, 2003).

[33] See *supra.* note 10 generally, (1-650).

[34] See *The Oxford Dictionary of Quotations*, Fifth Edition, Knowles E. (Ed), p. 508 (18)—from *On Liberty* (1859) Ch. I.

[35] See Reijnen, Bess, C.M., *United Nations Space Treaties Analyzed*, 1992, p.163-170; COSMOS 954 incident where a nuclear-powered Russian satellite crash landed in Canada in 1978.

[36] http://projects.sipri.se/expcon/hcocfinal.htm (accessed Oct. 4, 2003).

[37] Consider the Outer Space Treaty (1967) and Principles Related to the Uses of Remote Sensing [resolution 3234 (XXIX); 1974]; Gantt, J.B., "The Concepts of 'Peaceful Purposes'/ 'Peaceful Uses' in the Exploration and Use of Outer Space... Practical Examples," IISL paper, 2003 where 'peaceful purposes' is interpreted as "non-aggressive" and/or "non-military."

[38] See e.g., Wetterstein, P.(Ed.), *Harm to the Environment: The Right to Compensation and the Assessment of Damages*. Oxford: Clarendon Press, (1997), esp. Jones, B. paper, "Deterring, Compensating, and Remedying Environmental Damage: The Contribution of Tort Liability."

[39] See International Disaster Response Law (IDRL) applied by the International Federation of the Red Cross and Red Crescent Societies.

[40] See Blanchard, W.B., *American Civil Defense 1945-1984: The Evolution of Programs & Policies* (1986) (describes Model Act history & development), cited in Seamone, E., "The Duty to Expect the Unexpected: Mitigating Extreme Natural Threats to the Global Commons Such as Asteroid & Comet Impacts with the Earth," *Columbia Journal Transnational Law* Vol.41 No. 3 (2003, 735-794).

[41] Note also Space Priorities for the 21st Century.

[42] See The Biodiversity Convention [Preamble].

[43] See ICJ Declaration on the Legality of the Threat or Use of Nuclear Weapons, (July 8, 1996). Note the U.S., U.K., France and Russia had all urged the ICJ not to consider the case.

[44] See Schweickart, R.L., "The Need for United Nations Asteroid Deflection Treaty to Establish a System for Trustworthy Mission Design and Execution," January 8, 2003, B612 Foundation, 7 pgs.; also B612 (*supra.* note 9) proposal to develop an asteroid deflection strategy by 2015.

[45] See OCIPEP, *supra.* note. 31; also Bartley, A., and Saucier, R. (Communications, Oct. 2003).

[46] Becking, I., Wilson, S., (Communications, 2003); also "Towards a National Mitigation Strategy," Discussion paper, OCIPEP, (2002).
[47] Kopal, V., Wiedemann, C. and Lips, T., (Communications, Oct., 2003); for other sample definitions, see UN Technical Reports on Space Debris; ESA Space Debris Mitigation Handbook.
[48] See *Special Project Report on MEO/LEO Constellations: U.S. Laws, Policies and Regulations on Orbital Debris Mitigation*, AIAA, May 1999; also UNCOPUOS Technical Committee Reports (various).
[49] See *Risk Analysis and Uncertainty in Flood Damage Reduction Studies* (2000), Commission on Geosciences, Environment & Resources (CGER); by the Commission on Geosciences, Environment and Resources (CGER).
[50] See Gerrard M., "Legal Issues in Defending Against Asteroids," NYLJ Vol 219, No. 58 (1998), p.5/12; contrasts smaller amounts of money requested by scientists and organizations.
[51] See Achilleas, P; Marchisio, S., IISL papers/03
[52] See Haley, A.G. "Space Law and Metalaw—A Synoptic View," *Proceedings of the VIIth International Astronautical Congress*, Rome, Italy, (1956) and "Survey of Legal Opinion on Extraterrestrial Jurisdiction," (1960); Fasan, E., "Asteroids and other celestial bodies - some legal differences," 26 *J. of Space Law* #1, (1998), p33.
[53] Also known as the 1992 Declaration of the UN Conference on Environment and Development.
[54] See Universal Declaration on Human Rights (UDHR) [Article 3].
[55] See Morris J., (Ed.), *Rethinking Risk & the Precautionary Principle*, Butterworth-Heinemann, 16 October 2000, esp. p.3-9 (from "defining the precautionary principle" and "the development of the precautionary principle" to applications of "the precautionary principle as a premise for international agreements."); also Seamone E., *supra*. note. 40 (1).
[56] Seamone, E., (Communications, Oct., 2003).
[57] Seamone, *supra*. note 40, (33- 41).
[58] www.chernobyl.info/en/Facts/Lessons/Lessons Security (accessed Sept. 19, 2003).
[59] See, "Legal Issues Arising from the War in Afghanistan and Anti-Terrorism Efforts," http://www.hrw.org/campaigns/september11/ihlqna.htm (accessed Sept. 21, 2003); UDHR, *supra*. note 54; also Human Rights resolution 1995/32.
[60] An exception can be found in, Battiste M., and Henderson, J.Y., "The International Intellectual and Cultural Property Regime," *Protecting Indigenous Knowledge and Heritage: A Global Challenge*, (2000), p. 171-200; Principles and Guidelines for Protection of the Heritage of Indigenous Peoples (Annex, UN document E/CN.4/Sub.2/1995/26).
[61] See Gollier, C. and Treich, N., "Decision-making under scientific uncertainty: economics of the precautionary principle," 2002 (7).
[62] Sample problematic definitions proposed by panelists of the Millennium Project- http://www.acunu.org/millennium/es-2def.html (accessed Sept. 20, 2003); also Gross O. and Alain F.N., "Emergency, War and International Law-Another Perspective," 70 *Nordic Journal of International Law* 29 (2001).
[63] See Spana, M.S., "Beyond Pacification and a Panicked Public: New Principles for Bio-terrorism Preparedness and Response," Interdisciplinary Committee to Catastrophic Events, Nov. 11, 2002, p. 1-2, commentary available at http://www.campbellinstitute.org (accessed Sept. 13, 2003); also Morone J.G. and Woodhouse E.J., *Averting Catastrophe: Strategies for Regulating Risky Technologies*, University of California Press (1986).
[64] See *supra*. note 62; Thomas, L., "A comparative analysis of international regimes on ozone and climate change with implications for regime design," 41 *Columbia Journal Transnational Law* 795-859 (2003).
[65] See "Environmental Security: UN Doctrine for Managing Environmental Issues in Military Actions," Exec. Summary, 2000, *supra*. note 62.
[66] Ibid.
[67] State reaction to treaty breaches have included UN sanctions and other international boycotts.
[68] Seamone, E., (Communications, Sept., 2003)—about the 2003 simulation in U.S. States.
[69] See e.g., the ISS Crew Code of Conduct, 14 CFR Sec. 1214.403-404 (1-1-03 Edition).
[70] For example, the Supreme Court of Canada has defined "serious bodily harm" vis-à-vis Terrorism in the Criminal Code as *any hurt or injury, whether physical or psychological, that interferes in a substantial way with a person's physical or psychological well-being, health or integrity*. Other meanings of the term "serious bodily harm" are more restrictive—see Parliamentary Bill C-36, (after Sept. 11, 2001).
[71] See "An Open Letter to the Australian Federal Government from International Scientists (Australia's contribution to Spaceguard)," at http://www4.tpg.com/au/users/tps-seti/pr_oz_sg.pdf (accessed Sept. 5, 2003); also Britt R.R. "Why We Fear Ourselves More than Asteroids," *Space News on-line*, 26 March, 2002, p.1-2; also "Letter to OECD Global Science

Forum Participants and Permanent Delegations about U.K. proposal for a follow-up Workshop on NEOs, Natural Hazard Assessment & Risk Methodologies," July 28, 2003.

[72] See Colonna, T.E. and Descencia, T.E., "Be Careful Saving the World from Near Earth Orbit Objects: You May be Breaking the Law," Mercury 28 No. 5., Sept./Oct., 1999: 36-40; also Crawford J., *The ILC's Articles on State Responsibility,* Cambridge, Jan. 2002, 422 pgs.

[73] Compare to U.S. Homeland Security (HSD) Personal Preparedness Guide available on-line at www.washingtonpost.ca (accessed Oct. 2003).

[74] See UN Charter, June 26, 1945, [Preamble].

[75] NATO military responses to large disasters may be partly translated into civilian responses.

[76] Theoretically, a self-binding pre-commitment to CIL applies before awareness of a threat on a timeline when responsibilities should be designated by a framework to apply in the event of potential harm- Seamone, E., (2003), *supra.* note 40; see also Davis E., press release entitled, "Legal Duty to Mitigate Asteroid or Comet Collisions with Earth involves Much More than Stargazing, says Policy Analyst," *Iowa Law Review*, April 14, 2002 or available on-line at http://www.prweb.com/releases/2002/4/prweb36870.php (accessed Feb. 17, 2003).

[77] For instance, floods, fire, droughts, landslides, earthquakes, avalanches, tidal waves, localized industrial pollution, and severe storms.

[78] See for instance, *supra.* note 31; also Bartley, A., Saucier, R., (Communications, Oct., 2003).

[79] The Antarctica Treaty, UN Convention on the Law of the Sea (UNCLOS)- *High Seas, Space Treaties comprise the *Global Commons*; Covert, L.M., and Gantt, J.B, "Autonomous Multilateral Teams & Their Impact on Customary Practice: New Contributions to Public International Space Law," (2001) IISL, 15pgs.

[80] See Covert, L.M., "Commitment and Compliance in the Evolution of the ISS Program," *Proc. of the 45th Colloquium on the Law of Outer Space*, p. 98-112 (2002); Covert L.M., *supra.* note 10 (1-650); supra. note 35; also Watson, G.R., "The Death of Treaty", 55 Ohio St. L.J. 781-2 (1994); McKinnon R.J., & Sullivan M.T., "Mir Emergency Management: National Arrangements for Managing Public Safety Aspects of the Re-Entry of the Russian Mir Space Station," 16 *Australian Journal of Emergency Management* (2001) p.36-37.

[81] "First and foremost, better coordination is needed between NASA and Air Force observation efforts. This is probably best accomplished by someone taking charge—that someone should be the Air Force (through the US Space Command-USSPACECOM and AFSPC)...," Kiziah, Lt. Col R.R., "Air Force and NASA Activities To Address the Threat of Asteroid/Comet-Earth Impacts," in *Air & Space Power Chronicles*, 2 May, 2000 (6).

[82] Consider the UN/ISDR World Disaster Reduction Campaign (2003) to raise awareness.

[83] See "Insurance: Unified Law for Disaster Management Favored," June 25, 2003 on-line at http://www.hinduonnet.com/thehindu/2003/06/26/stories/2003062602351800.htm (accessed Sept. 20, 2003).

[84] See UN Declaration of Preservation of the Human Environment (Stockholm, 1972); also Viikari, L.E., "Environmental Impact Assessment and Space Activities," *Proc. of the 45th Colloquium on the Law of Outer Space*, p.476-480 (2002); Seamone E., "When Wishing on a Star Just Won't Do: The Legal Basis for International Cooperation in the Mitigation of Asteroid Impacts and Similar Trans-boundary Disasters," *Iowa Law Review*, Vol. 87, No. 3, March 2002, 1093-1139, esp. Part V., "The Historically Entrenched Right to Global Survival," 1119-1139.

[85] Consider Pryke, I., former ESA representative to Washington, D.C., "ESA's future needs to be based on today's progress, not yesterday's achievements," (Pryke, Communications, 2002).

[86] Consider current uncertain State commitment and lack of interdisciplinary promotion of the *International Charter on Space Cooperation...for Natural or Tech. Disasters-* www.disastercharter.org/charter_e.html (accessed Sept. 10, 2003), related to U.N. Resolution 41/65 of 1986 on Remote-sensing; Gerrard M.B., Barber A.W., "Asteroids and Comets: U.S. and [IL] and the lowest probability, highest consequence risk," NYU ELJ (1997) p.1-45.

[87] See *supra.* note. 10.

[88] See *supra.* note 61, (6).

[89] See Schweickart, R.L., (Jan., 2003); *supra.* note. 35; Schweickart et al., "The Asteroid Tugboat," *Scientific American*, (Nov., 2003).

[90] See Geneva Conventions, Aug 12, 1949, art. 158, 75 UNTS 287 ; (and 1977 protocols).

[91] See Abbott K.W. and Snidal D., "Hard and Soft Law in International Governance," 54 *International Organizations* 421 (2000); Haug, H., "Neutrality as a Fundamental Principle of the Red Cross," 31-12-1996, *International Review of the Red Cross,* No. 315, (627-630).

Session 4:
SPACE TRAFFIC MANAGEMENT AND NAVIGATION

Chairmen: José Monserrat Filho, Brazil
Lubos Perek, Czech Republic

Rapporteur: Ulrike Bohlmann, ESA

IS THE PRESENT INTERNATIONAL SPACE LAW SUFFICIENTLY ARMED FOR THE PROTECTION OF ASTRONAUTS, FUNCTIONAL SPACE OBJECTS AND SPACE ENVIRONMENT AGAINST SPACE DEBRIS, OR SHOULD A LEGAL REGULATORY SYSTEM RELATING TO THIS ISSUE BE ESTABLISHED SOON ?

Dr. Vladimír Kopal [1]

Professor of Law, University of Pilsen, Czech Republik

Introduction

During the last decades, man-made orbital space debris has become one of the most discussed issues of the present and future development of space activities.From a growing number of papers published in recent years and discussions held at national and international levels, it is evident that an effective protection of astronauts, functional space objects and the space environment itself against the generation and proliferation of space debris has become one of the recognized objectives of the present space community.

I. United Nations and the issue of space debris

/a/ Consideration in the COPUOS Scientific and technical Subcommittee

For this reason, the United Nations Committee on the Peaceful Uses of Outer Space /COPUOS/,which has been serving as a focal point for international cooperation in the peaceful exploration and use of outer space,[2] included the item on space debris on the agenda of its Scientific and Technical Subcommittee /STSC/ already at its thirty-first session, in February 1994. [3] For a detailed consideration of space debris, the Subcommittee adopted a multiyear plan for the period 1996-1998 and established a special Working Group. It focused its attention on measurements of space debris, understanding of da ta and effects of that environment on space systems; furthemore, the Subcommittee drew its attention on the modelling of the space debris environment and risk assesment; and finally, the attention concentrated on space debris mitigation measures. As the result of that work, a Technical Report on Space Debris [4] emerged, which was assessed by the COPUOS as "an important achievement". This UN body also agreed that, "owing to the complexity of the space debris issue, discussions should continue in order to ensure further progress in developing an understanding of the issue." [5]

A new elementwas also introduced in further proceedings on space debris, when it was recomended that the Inter-Agency Space Debris Coordination Committee /IADC/, an international forum of governmental bodies for the coordination of activities related to the issues of man-made and natural debris in space, should be involved in these discussions. And at its 2001 session, the STSC "strongly endorsed the action undertaken by IADC to reach consensus on debris mitiga-

----

tion measures". The Subcommittee encouraged IADC to treat the topic with due priority, with a view to completing the task during 2002 so that the results could be reported to the Subcommittee at its fortieth session, in 2003. [6] At the same time, the Subcommittee, acting on the initiative of eight spacefaring nations, [7] agreed that starting from 2002, it should consider space debris according to another multiyear work plan. The IADC proposals on debris mitigation would become a centre-piece of that exercise and the Subcommittee would endorse the utilization of these proposals "as guidelines to be implemented on a voluntary basis through national mechanisms." [8]

The IADC fulfilled its task still before the end of 2002 and presented its proposals on debris mitigation guidelines based on consensus among the IADC members. [9] The STSC then began its review of these proposals, which should still continue in 2004, and discussed the means of endorsing their utilization. All member States of the COPUOS have been encouraged to study the IADC proposals and provide their comments before the 2004 session of the STSC.

Simultaneously with the discussions within the United Nations on space debris, or even before them, efforts tending to establish national policies on space debris and introduce debris mitigation standards, have been developed by the most active space-faring nations. For example, the United Sates of America, which started such efforts already in 1987, adopted in December 2000 the United States Government Orbital Debris Mitigation Standard Practices, which are implemented by each government agency according to its own set of policies and procedures.[10] In some other nations, too, /Germany, France, Japan, Russia/ or intermational organizations /ESA/, such standard making processes have or are being effected.[11] Of course, these initiatives and their results are unilateral. However, they help to create a basis for negotiations on standards and practices at international levels, particularly in the United Nations.

/b/ Initiatives to consider the legal aspects of space debris

The protection of space environment against pollution by space debris has also become a subject of concern of the world space law community. A number of monographs were published, many papers were presented and discussions on the issue of space debris were held at the meetings of international non-governmental organizations, such as the International Law Association /ILA/ and the International Institute of Space Law /IISL/ of the International Astronautical Federation. The legal experts participating in these discussions have mostly held the view that hand-by-hand with the consideration of the debris issue in the scientific and technical area, it is also necessary to ponder the availability and possible development of adequate legal measures for the protection against space debris.

A number of delegations to the COPUOS have been also well aware of this need and suggested two items relating to space debris for possible inclusion in the agenda of the Legal Subcommittee /LSC/ at its future sessions. The first one was entitled "Reviw of existing norms of international law applicable to space debris", the other was conceived wider and called simply "Legal aspects of space debris". [12] These items were also suggested during the informal consultations on future agenda at the following sessions of the LSC.

When the Technical Report on Space Debris was finalized at the

Scientific and Technical Subcommittee and adopted at the 1999 session of the COPUOS, a number of delegations expressed the view that there should be follow-up activity by the Legal Subcommittee on that report. A group of 13 countries led by France proposed to distribute the Technical Report widely and to request the COPUOS to instruct the LSC, inter alia, to review the applicability of the space treaties to space debris issues in the light of the report adopted by the STSC in 1999 and to assess whether the Subcommittee should consider additional matters with regard to its work.[13] On the other hand, some other delegations expressed the view "that it was still premature for the Legal Subcommittee to discuss the issue of space debris, and that the discussion of the issue by the Legal Subcommittee should be postponed at least until the technical report had been thoroughly analysed by member States and relevant space related organizations and industry."[14]

Since then, this division of opinions on legal aspects of space debris has remained in principle unchanged. It wasretained also during the discussions at the Third United Nations Conference on the Exploration and Peaceful Uses of Outer Space /UNISPACE III/ held in 1999[15] and the following sessions of the COPUOS, STSC and LSC.

A new impetus to discussing legal aspects of space debris in the LSC was given during the consideration of item "Information on the activities of international organizations relating to space law" at the forty-first session of the LSC in 2002 when the observer for the European Space Agency /ESA/, acting on behalf of member States of that organization and States cooperating with it, presented an analysis carried out by ESA on the legal aspects of space debris.[16] And some delegations from this group of States expressed the view that "while the work currently being carried out by the Scientific and Technical Subcommittee and the Inter-Agency Space Debris Coordination Committee /IADC/ should be fully supported, it would also be highly desirable for a declaration of principles relating to the prevention of space debris to be drafted and adopted as soon as possible." In some more specific terms, it was then proposed by this group of States to follow the example of the 1992 Principles Relevant to the Use of Nuclear Power Sources in Outer space /NPS/. Such a text "could proclaim and define as a matter of principle the obligation to limit the production of space debris. The text could also incorporate the rules endorsed by the COPUOS on the basis of proposals made by IADC."[17]

On the other hand, an opposing view also sounded during that session of the LSC, according to which "the scientific and technical aspects of space debris still required further examination and study". That delegation also expressed the view that the development of principles on space debris would require the consideration of numerous aspects of the existing United Nations treaties on outer space, as well as the Principles Relevant to the Use of NPS in Outer Space. Therefore, that delegation recommended to consider the development of such principles within the context of a universal comprehensive convention on outer space.[18]

The most recent initiative has been undertaken by the group of ESA member and cooperating States, led by France, at the last session of the LSC in 2003. Based on the assumption that the IADC guidelines presented to the foregoing session of the STSC would be adopted by the COPUOS in 2004, these States stressed the need for universal and prompt application of the guidelines. To this end the LSC should study all the legal implications of these guidelines /e.g. universal application, responsibility and control/. For this reason, a 4-year work plan was outlined, the essence of which would be the review of the existing legal regime applicable to space debris and of legal matters arising from the IADC mitigation guidelines. Its outcome should be inserted in a report setting out legal issues identified so that a legal instrument could be prepared for adoption by the COPUOS and the General Assembly. [19]

However, this initiative was again rejected by another group of delegations which continued to hold that "it was premature for the Legal Subcommittee to consider legal aspects of space debris in view of the multi-year work plan on space debris mitigation guidelines being carried out in the Scientific and Technical Subcommittee." 20

II. The question of applicability of the existing UN Space Treaties and Principles to space debris

The author of this report does not deny that he belongs to those proposing a close cooperation of scientists, engineers and lawyers in the elaboration of adequate legal tools for maintaining outer space clean and safe. [21] In this endeavour, the study of international law aspects of the space debris issue must be initiated, which should start by the question: Is the present international legal regime of outer space, which has been established during the last four decades by the United Nations, sufficiently armed to meet the needs of a satisfactory protection of astronauts, functional space objects and space environment against the generation and proliferation of space debris ?

The fundamental legal instrument of the international space law, the 1967 Outer Space Treaty /OST/, enshrined a number of general principles which as such are also relevant to the issue of space debris. According to its Article I, the exploration and use of outer space shall be the province of all mankind. In its Article VI, the principle of international responsibility for all national activities, be they carried by governmental agencies or non-governmental entities, i.e. by private persons, physical or juridical, and the groups thereof, has been declared. Moreover, in Article IX of the OST, which established the principle of cooperation and mutual assistance of the States Parties to the Treaty, a general principle of protection of the space environment was inserted: The States Parties to the Treaty shall pursue studies of outer space, including the Moon and other celestial bodies, and conduct exploration of them "so as to avoid their harmful contamination and also adverse changes in the environment of the Earth resulting from the introduction of extraterrestrial matter and, where necessary, shall adopt appropriate measures for this purpose." But can it be deduced that this language also covers the harmful effects caused by space debris ?

In its Article VII, the 1967 OST includes, as one of its essential principles, the international liability for damage caused by space objects or their component parts on the Earth, in air space or in outer space. This principle of the OST created the basis for the 1972 Convention on International Liability for Damage Caused by Space Objects. In Article I of this Convention, it is spelled out that the term "space object" includes "component parts of a space object as well as its launch vehicles and parts thereof." However, is it possible to qualify as component parts of a space object or parts of its launch vehicle the fragments of such objects which could threaten the life of astronauts during their extra-vehicular activities, damage a spacecraft and injure its crew, but which would be difficult to monitor and identify ?

The Liability Convention deals with two categories of damage, one caused by space objects on the surface of the Earth or to aircraft in flight, the other caused elsewhere than on the surface of the Earth to a space object of the launching State or to persons or property on board such a space object by a space object of another launching State. While in the first category of damage absolute liability is provided, the second one shall only be applied if the damage is due to the fault of the launching State or the fault of persons for whom it is responsible. However, the term "fault" has not been specified in the 1972 Convention. May it be assumed that not only "intent" but also "negligence" are to be considered as a basis of fault ? [22]

Furthermore, it should be observed that the term "damage", as defined in the 1972 Liability Convention, means only "loss of life, personal injury or other impairment of health; or loss of or damage to property of States and persons, natural or juridical, or property of international intergovernmental organizations". Therefore, it must be deduced from this definition that the Liability Convention does not cover a damage caused by space activities to the Earth or space environments.

Some provisions, which might be considered as applicable to space debris, can be found also in the 1975 Registration Convention, which established the duty of the launching State to register space objects both nationally and internationally /i.e. with the United Nations/. According to this Convention, each State of registry shall <u>inter alia</u> notify the UN Secretary-General "to the greatest extent feasible and as soon as practicable, of space objects concerning which it has previously transmitted information, and which have been but no longer are in Earth orbit." It is to be recalled that in the Registration Convention, the term "space object" is specified in the same way as in the Liability Convention, i.e. that it includes component parts of a space object as well as its launch vehicle and parts thereof.

Some attention should be also drawn to the 1979 Moon Agreement which, however, has collected only a limited number of adhesions thus far. It is worthwhile to observe that the States Parties to this Agreement, in exploring and using the Moon, are obliged to take measures to prevent the disruption of the existing balance of its environment, by its harmful contamination through the introduction of extraenvironmental matter or otherwise. This provision may also include the pollution of the Moon environment or the areas of the Moon by space debris, if it should be as big as to lead to a disruption of the balance of the Moon environment.

A certain step forward has been done only in the specific field of the Use of Nuclear Power Sources /NPS/ in Outer Space. The 1992 Principles implemented, <u>inter alia</u>, the idea of storing the nuclear reactors and radioisotope generators in a disposal orbit after the conclusion of the operational part of their missions. They also brought a certain specification of the general principle of liability for damage as far as the determination of compensation for damage is concerned. The relatively successful outcome of the efforts for the regulation of the use of NPS in outer space, effected by a set of principles adopted by the UN General Assembly on the basis of consensus reached in both Subcommittees of the COPUOS, offers an example for a similar approach to the solution of the problems of protection of the space environment against space debris.

III. Desirability of elaboration of a special legal regulation of space debris

As evident from the abovementioned examples, which might be completed by additional questions, the up-to-date international space legislation has been built on the concept "space object". This term has been used as a fundamental element for establishing the principles and rules governing space activities and has also become one of the basic notions in the space law doctrine. Accoding to Article VIII of the OST, a State Party to the Treaty on whose registry an object launched into outer space is carried shall retain jurisdiction and control over such object and over any personnel thereof, while in outer space or on a celestial body. Ownership of space objects, and of their component parts, is not affected by their presence in outer space or on a celestial body or by their return to the Earth. And they shall be returned to the State Party which furnished identifying data prior to their return.

In recent years, however, the growing number of remains of these objects, which,having ended their missions, became useless "space debris", raised completely new problems. They deserve a specific approach and require a sharp differentiation between the existing rules governing "space objects" and an appropriate regulation of "space debris". For this reason, the consideration of legal aspects of space debris is necessary and the elaboration of a special legal document on this subject in the United Nations is highly desirable. <u>Inter alia</u>, such legal document should clearly establish from which moment a space object or its parts become non-functional, useless and even harmful,and should be treated as space debris.

Such approach was also adopted by the Space Law Committee of the International Law Association /ILA/ when this non-governmental organization, which has been initiating the progressive development of international law and its codification, was preparing a Draft International Instrument on the Protection of the Environment from Damage Caused by Space Debris. This unofficial document, as adopted by ILA at its 66th Conference held in Buenos Aires, in August 1994, offers a model of a special document on space debris, which might be used as a basis for negotiations on the legal regulation of this issue in the United Nations.

When reading the ILA Draft Instrument, it is possible to ascertain that its legal definition of "space debris", which means"man-made objects in outer space, other than active or otherwise useful satellites, when no change can reasonably be expected in these conditions in the foreseeable future", is in harmony with the results of scientific and technological consideration of the issue. [24] Furthermore, the terms"environment" and "damage" are well defined. It is significant that the latter term means not only loss of life, impairment of health, and material damage, but also any adverse modification of the environment of areas within or beyond national jurisdiction or control, i.e. including the space environment.

The formulation of substantive principles of the ILA Draft instrument can also be used for consideration of the building blocks for the future official document to be negotiated. In particular, the principles of responsibility and liability for damage caused by space debris should be clearly stated in the official document. Finally, the dispute settlement system concerning the interpretation or application of such document should be also established. It is noteworthy that the ILA Instrument has remained flexible in this respect, trying to combine the method of amicable settlement with the compulsory methods of arbitration and adjudication.[25]

The progress reached in the studies of space debris and its results, particularly reflected in the 1999 Technical Report on Space Debris and the 2002 IADC space debris mitigation guidelines, enable to transform the main conclusions of these documents into condensed principles by which the Draft Instrument worked out in the ILA could be completed and innovated. The main duties concerning measures to be taken in the construction and operation phases of space objects might be included. The different methods of mitigation measures, such as limiting debris released during normal operations, minimizing the potential for on-orbit, post mission break-ups resulting from stored energy and break-ups during operational phases, could be transformed into legal principles and rules. Furthermore, the post mission disposal of space objects that have terminated their mission, particularly those in the geosynchronous region, should be made compulsory. And measures for prevention of on-orbit collisions should be also inacted.

Moreover, it could be also pondered whether the right of any State or international space organization to intervene larger pieces of space debris, particularly at the most exposed parts of space, should not be explicitly recognized. Of course, thisright would be applied rather exceptionally and should be subject to special conditions and procedures. In this respect, the space legislation might build on the experience from the field of the law of the sea, namely from the International Convention Relating to Intervention on the High Seas in Cases of Oil Pollution Casualities, which was concluded at Brussels on 29 November 1969.[26]

Another example from the area of the law of the sea,which might be used mutatis mutandis for establishing similar measures against space debris, is offered by the 1982 United Nations Convention on the Law of the Sea, which entered into force in 1994. Dealing with artificial islands, installations and structures in the exclusive economic zones /Article 60/ and also with those on the continental shelf /Article 80/, the 1982 Convention provides:"Any installations or structures which are abandoned or disused shall be removed to ensure safety of navigation, taking into account any generally accepted international standards established in this regard by the competent international organization."[27]

Conclusions

When dealing with the regulation of space debris, a close cooperation between experts studying scientific and technological aspects of this topic and those taking care of its legal problems is indispensable. Simultaneous considerations by both these communities and mutual exchange of information on the progress and results in both these areas are essential, well coordinated investigation programmes and joint discussions are desirable.

Without doubt, space debris is a very complex issue which requires pondering of different, some times even opposing, needs. The resolution of all problems involved cannot be expected to be fast. For this reason, and also due to the need for maintaining a continuity in the progressive development of space law, it is advisable to start with an analyses of the existing tools of international law that might be relevant to this issue and with the ascertainment of gaps in the up-to-date legal regime of outer space.

The main objective of the consideration of legal aspects of space debris should be the elaboration and adoption of a special legal document that would include principles relevant to all essential aspects of this issue. Such an instrument should clarify the interpretation of the relevant space agreements in force with regard to their possible application to space debris. Moreover, it should regulate those aspects of the issue, which are not yet governed by the present international space law.

As to the form of such instrument, an international convention, i.e. a legally binding treaty, would be the most exact solution. However, in the light of actual practice of the United Nations, a set of principles developed in the COPUOS with the participation of both its Subcommitteesand approved by a UN General Assembly resolution, would become the satisfactory form of an international regulatory instrument on space debris for the time being. In such principles, endorsed by the world organization, an agreement among its member States would be reflected and, at the same time, a certain degree of the rule of law would be ensured. A set of UN principles would establish a basis for a legally binding convention on the same subject to be concluded some time in the future. The compliance of States and international organizations with these principles, and the supervision of the activities of non-governmental entities by appropriate States, would lead to a unified practice in this field and to the creation of a conviction of all legal persons concerned on the desirability of such principles.

Simple guidelines for practice and policies, which should be implemented only on a voluntary basis through national mechanisms, though capable to improve to a certain extent the present practice, would not lead to internationally harmonized actions. Moreover, they would not give rise to the feeling of duty to comply with them, if the decision on their application should lie only with the addressee of the guidelines. And there would not be any international responsibility and sanctions applicable in cases of non-compliance with these guidelines. Such measures would not only lack any compulsory force, but also a sufficient recommendatory weight, thus remaining only a kind of advisory proposals for unilateral actions.

Conversely, the work on a set of UN principles relevant to space debris would have a potential to strengthen "broad international cooperation in the scientific as well as the legal aspects of the exploration and use of outer space for peaceful purposes", as aimed by the 1967 Outer Space Treaty, in this particular field. [28]

References

1. Chairman, UN COPUOS Legal Subcommittee; IAF General Counsel; IISL Vice-President. The views expressed in this paper are those of the author and do not necessarily reflect the positions of any of these organizations.

2. See the Report of UNISPACE III, Vienna, 19-30 July 1999, UN doc. A/CONF.184/6, para.15 at p.21.

3. This was done in accordance with the decision of the UN General Assembly inserted in its resolution 48/39 of 10 December 1993.

4. The so called Rex Report.See UN doc. A/AC.105/720, 1999.

5. See the Report of the COPUOS, GA Official Records, Fifty-fourth Session, Supplement No. 20/A/54/20, para.43 at p.6.

6. See Report of the STSC on its thirty-eighth session, UN doc. A/AC.105/761, para.128 at p.21.

7. Canada, China, France, Germany, India, Russia, United Kingdom and United States. See UN doc. A/AC.105/C.1/L.251/Rev.2.

8. See UN doc. A/AC.105/761, paras.129-130, at pp.21-22.

9. See UN doc. A/AC.105/C.1/L.260.

10. See National research on space debris, safety of space objects with nuclear power sources on board and problems relating to their collision with space debris, UN doc. A/AC.105/789/Add.1, p.8 et seq.

11. See e.g. the report of Germany on its coherent project entitled "Space debris end-to-end service" in the UN doc. A/AC.105/789/Add.1, p. 2 et seq.

12. See Report of the LSC on its thirty-fifth session, 1996, UN doc. A/AC.105/639, paras 54-56 at pp. 11 and 12. In an unofficial background note submitted by the delegation of the Czech Republic, which sponsored the first of these proposals, it was recommended to examine particularly the following questions: Does the definition of "space object" as contained in the 1972 Liability Convention and the 1975 Registration Convention cover space debris ? Do provisions of the 1967 Outer Space Treaty concerning the avoidance of harmful contamination of outer space and adverse changes in the environment of the Earth apply to the problem of space debris ? Should the protection of ownership of space objects, and of their component parts, also be extended to space debris ? Should liability for damage caused to a space object and/or its crew by space debris depend on the proof of fault as in the case of a collision of two space objects ?
In this proposal, it was emphasized that "these and other questions are of a legal nature and should be analysed and answered by legal experts" and that "the consideration of these questions would not amount to the drafting of new provisions but should serve to clarify the issues involved and help to improve the interpretation and application of the existing norms of international space law. See ibidem, Annexes, III/E, p.38.

13. See the Report of the COPUOS, GA Official Records, Fifty-fourth session, Supplement No. 20/A/54/20, Annex II at pp.18-19.

14. See the Report of the STSC on the work of its thirty-sixth sesseon, UN doc. A/AC.105/719, para. 40 at p.5.

15. Resolution 1 of the UNISPACE III, entitled "The Space Millenium: Vienna Declaration on Space and Human Development", mentioned in rather general terms "advancing scientific knowledge of space and protecting the space environment" in "the nucleus of a strategy to address global challenges in the future". And among the actions to be taken the action "To improve the protection of the near-Earth space and outer space environments through further research in and implementation of mitiga-

tion measures for space debris was listed.

16. See UN doc. A/AC.105/C.2/ 2002/CRP.5.

17. See the Report of the LSC on its forty-first session, 2002, UN doc. A/AC.105/787, paras 49-50 at p. 9.

18. See ibidem, para. 51 at p.9.

19. See Workplan on space debris, UN doc. A/AC.105/C.2/L.246 dated 1 April 2003.

20. See the Report of the LSC on its forty-second session, 2003, UN doc. A/AC.105/805, paras 147-149 at p. 23.

21. See e.g. V. Kopal,"Issues involved in defining outer space, space object and space debris" in Proceedings of the Thirty-fourth Colloquium on the Law of Outer Space, IISL, October 5-11, 1991, Montreal, Canada, AIAA, p. 38 et seq.; "Space debris: a review of the current regulatory structure" in Proceedings of the Thirty-ninth Colloquium on the Law of Outer Space, IISL, October 7-11, 1996, Beijing, China, AIAA, p.343 et seq.; "Present international law principles applicable to space debris and the need for their supplement" in Proceedings of the Second European Conference on Space Debris, ESOC, Darmstadt, Germany, 17-19 March 1997, p. 739 et seq..

22. In order to resolve this question, Professor Bing Cheng suggested to establish absolute liability or presumed fault for damage caused by undisowned space debris. See his article ""Space Objects", "Astronauts" and related expressions" in Proceedings of the Thirty-fourth Colloquium on the Law of Outer Space, IISL, October 5-11, 1991, Montreal, Canada, AIAA, p.25.

23. See K.-H. Böckstiegel, The Draft of the International Law Association for a Convention on Space Debris,"/including the text of Resolution Nr.5 on Space Law of the 1994 ILA Conference and the final text of the adopted Instrument/. For substantive and procedural aspects of the discussions on this document, see M. Williams,"The ILA finalizes its international instrument on Space Debris in Buenos Aires, August 1994", in Journal of Space Law, 1995, p.47 et seq..

24. See the UN Technical Report on Space Debris, 1999, UN doc. A/ AC.105/720, p.2; IAA Position Paper on Orbital Debris, Edition 2001, p.3; Inter-Agency Space Debris Coordination Committee space debris mitigation guidelines, UN doc. A/AC.105/C.1/L.260, p.5 and other documents.

25. For this purpose, the ILA Draft Convention on the Settlement of Space Law Disputes, as elaborated in 1984 and revised at the 68th ILA Conference in Taipei, 1998, shall be applied unless a Party to the Instrument on Space Debris has excluded such application. The text of the ILA Draft Convention on the Settlement of Disputes /as amended in 1998/ see in the Report of the Sixty-eighth ILA Conference, 1998, p.249 et seq..

26. See its text in United Nations Legislation Series, National Legislation and Treaties Relating to the Law of the Sea, UN doc. ST/LEG/SER. B/16, New York, 1974, p.439 et seq..

27. See The Law of the Sea, United Nations Convention on the Law of the Sea with Index and Final Act of the Third United Nations Conference on the Law of the Sea, United Nations, New York, 1983, pp.19-20 and 29.

28. See the preambular para. 4 of the 1967 Outer Space Treaty.

Status of the IAA Study Group on „Traffic Management Rules for Space Operations"

Corinne Contant, AIAA, Washington, USA (corinnec@aiaa.org)
Petr Lala, formerly UNOOSA, Vienna, Austria (petr@lala-web.cz)
Kai-Uwe Schrogl, DLR, Cologne, Germany (kai-uwe.schrogl@dlr.de)

Abstract

The investigation of space traffic and its management has only recently become a point of wider discussion. In particular the series of workshops organized by the American Institute of Aeronautics and Astronautics (AIAA) and other international organizations on international cooperation highlighted the issue. It was discussed thoroughly at the workshops, which took place in 1999 and 2001 respectively. It was at the 2001 workshop, when the suggestion was made that an International Academy of Astronautics (IAA) Study on the subject of space traffic management should be prepared. This suggestion was taken up and a proposal was presented to the Board of Trustees of IAA, which, in late 2001, accepted this proposal.

Following this, an interdisciplinary study group of around twenty persons was composed. One early milestone in the process of work was the conduct of an International Institute of Space Law (IISL)/European Center of Space Law (ECSL) Symposium alongside the 2002 session of the United Nations Committee on the Peaceful Uses of Outer Space (UNCOPUOS) Legal Subcommittee. This symposium consisted of presentations of members of the IAA study group. Also, close coordination with other study projects of IAA, in particular with the one on space debris, is sought.

This paper presents the status of work of the study group, in particular the approach and the scope of the study as well as its preliminary findings. The study group intends to finalize its work in early 2004, in order to be able to put the study before IAA and launch its review process before the 2004 International Astronautical Congress. Following this review, the study will be published and may be expected to make an impact in fora like the UNCOPUOS.

The authors of this paper act as the coordinators/the rapporteur to this study. The paper will be presented in the IAA- as well as the IISL-session dealing with space traffic, by that bridging the two areas and seeking input from various sources.

1. Scope of the Study

Space traffic already takes place. It seems, however, minuscle with regard to the dimension of near-Earth outer space. Around 10.000 man-made objects larger than 10 cm are currently tracked out of which only 650 are operational spacecraft. On the surface, it does not look, as if the management of space traffic was a pressing problem. Investigated further, this judgement has to be challenged. A high level or even growing number of launches from more and more launch sites and space ports, the entering of non-governmental entities, the positioning of satellite constellations, an increase in space debris and the advent of re-usable launch vehicles supports this judgement. Considering this scenario, conceptualizing space traffic management will turn out to become one of the most relevant tasks during the next two decades.

The dimension of this task can be assessed, when the following **definition of space traffic management** is taken into account:

> Space traffic management comprises technical and regulatory provisions for guaranteeing safe interference-free access into outer space, operations in outer space and return from outer space to Earth.

Since an authoritative definition of space traffic management does not yet exist, this definition has been set up for the purpose of this study. Through this definition, the purpose of space traffic management becomes clear: it is to provide appropriate means so that space activities can be conducted without harmful interference. By that it supports the universal freedom to use outer space as laid down in the Outer Space Treaty of 1967. It should also be clear that for this purpose of achieving a common good, actors have to follow specific rules, which is also in their self-interest.

The investigation of space traffic and its management has only recently become a point of wider discussion. In particular the series of workshops organized by the American Institute of Aeronautics and Astronautics (AIAA) and other international organizations on international cooperation highlighted the issue. It was discussed at its 5th and its 6th workshop, which took place in 1999 and 2001 respectively. The results of these deliberations including recommendations have been laid down in the proceedings of these two events.[1] But so far, these activities have not advanced considerably more the subject than it had been analysed with startling far-sightedness by Lubos Perek already in the early 80s[2] – a pioneering work, which has not been followed-up for more than a decade.

It was, however, at the 2001 workshop of AIAA, when the suggestion was made that an **International Academy of Astronautics (IAA) Study** on the subject of space traffic management should be prepared. This suggestion was taken up and a proposal was presented to the Board of Trustees of IAA, which, in late 2001, accepted the proposal. Following this, the study group was composed, which prepared the present study. One early milestone in the process of work was the conduct of an International Institute of Space Law (IISL)/European Center of Space Law (ECSL) Symposium alongside the 2002 session of the United Nations Committee on the Peaceful Uses of Outer Space (UNCOPUOS) Legal Subcommittee. This symposium consisted of presentations of members of the IAA study group.[3] Also, close coordination with other study projects of IAA, in particular with the one on space debris, is sought. At the International Astronautical Congress in Bremen in 2003, this outline of the study will be presented to a dedicated session for discussion.[4] It will also be presented during the IISL Colloquium.[5]

The approach and scope of the present study are as follows. The **approach of the study** is characterized by interdisciplinarity. The study group consists of experts from the technical as well as from the legal/regulatory fields. It is composed of a core team, which prepares the text. While these members initially draft sections in their particular field of expertise, the work is further done on the text as a whole so that no reference is made on contributors of specific sections but the study as a whole is to be regarded as a joint product of this core team. In addition to that, an independen team of advisors will contribute ideas and suggestions to the first complete draft of the study as a whole. This team will also consists of experts with different backgrounds broadening the input even further.

The **scope of the study** reflects the understanding of space traffic management as given through the definition laid out above and the interdisciplinary set-up by the study team. The study encompasses detailed analyses of the technical background for space traffic management and the regulatory spectrum. It starts with a report of the current status. This

[1] AIAA Workshop Proceedings "International Space Cooperation: Solving Global Problems" 1999, p.35-39 and "International Space Cooperation: Addressing Challenges of the New Millennium," 2001, p.7-14.

[2] Perek, Lubos, Traffic Rules for Outer Space, 82-IISL-09

[3] Proceedings of the IISL/ECSL Symposium on Prosepcts for Space Traffic Management, 2 April 2002, Vienna, UN Doc. A/AC.105/C.2/2002/CRP.7 of 4 April 2002.

[4] IAC-03-IAA.5.5.a. session on "Space Traffic Management" in the "Space Debris and Space Traffic Symposium".

[5] IAC-03-IISL.4. session on "Space Traffic Management and Navigation"

comprises the status of space activities as well as the status of the legal and regulatory environment and also comparable traffic regimes. This will provide the basis for identifying the needs for traffic management provisions in the two spheres of technology and regulation. The main part of the study lays out elements for a space traffic management regime for the year 2010. Subdivided into the three phases of space traffic, the launch phase, the in-orbit operation phase and the re-entry phase, needs for technology development and application as well as regulatory provisions are investigated. The result is a set of recommendations, how traffic management rules should look like in around one decade.

Through investigating these issues, the study does not only apply an interdisciplinary approach inside the realm of space. It also has to take into account and touches various other fields as air traffic management and telecommunications regulation and the work conducted by the relevant institutions, in particular the International Civil Aviation Organization (ICAO) and the International Telecommunication Union (ITU). It has to do so, since in these two areas there have already been prepared elements for space traffic management, i.a. for the use of the geostationary orbit. The present study brings these developments together and merges them into a coherent, encompassing approach. The recommendations are prepared in order to take action in the various relevant organisations, in particular in UNCOPUOS.

2. Dimensions and Phases of Space Traffic as a concept used in the study

Space traffic encompasses almost all space activities from their start to their end. Only planetary probes leaving the near-Earth environment fall under it for a shorter part of their lifetime. For the purpose of this study, activities on the Moon and other celestial bodies (except transfer thereto and therefrom) are also excluded.

Space traffic touches **two dimensions**. These are the **scientific and technical area** and the **regulatory field.** In chapter 2, the status in these two dimensions will be analysed. The relevant technical data for the use of outer space will be presented together with prospects for various space activities including the development of the space debris environment. On the other hand, the current legal and regulatory framework is analysed alongside the respective areas of space law, air law, telecommunications law as well as national space law, air law and licensing provisions. A comparison with comparable traffic regimes for air traffic and maritime traffic completes this chapter. So, this chapter will lay the groundwork for judging the prospects of space traffic, identify existing and lacking provisions for regulation and through this lead to the drafting of elements for a future space traffic regime.

In chapter 3, the two dimensions of space traffic will be applied to analysing the **three phases of space traffic**:

- the launch phase,
- the in-orbit operation phase,
- the re-entry phase.

They provide the structure for the in-depth analysis for elements of a space traffic regime for the year 2010. Each phase is subdivided into an analysis of the status and trends in technology developments on the one hand and the regulatory aspects on the other hand. A brief characterization of the three phases and the related problems could be summed up in the following way.

The **launch phase** does have to take into account expendable as well as re-usable launch vehicles, comprising operators from the governmental as well as the non-governmental field. Particular stress has to be put on aspects of debris mitigation. The regulatory aspects have to respond to a current lack of pre-launch notifications, a little harmonized system of national licensing provisions. In addition a close link has to be made with air law.

The **in-orbit operation phase** has to investigate the rules for the use of various orbits. Only the GSO so far can be seen as basically managed. Specifically movement of satellites on specific orbital plains or in altitude have to be covered by rules (who will have to give way?). This leads to the need of a comprehensive collision-warning system. It will turn out that the existence and access to on-time information about the status of space operations is essential for a functioning space traffic management system, as it is the case with the air traffic management. Another area of regulation in this context will be the mitigation of space debris including the use of disposal orbits. Additionally the question does arise, whether certain space activites should have priority before others (e.g. manned before unmanned?, science before applications?, "useless" activities like funerals in orbit before "usefull"?).

The **re-entry phase** is relevant for the operation of re-usable transportation systems as well as the intentional or un-intentional de-orbiting of other space objects including space debris. Again the link with air law provisions has to be drawn. New requirements for notification will be necessary in this context.

The division into these three phases seems useful with regard to their different technological characteristics and to the possibility to shape distinct blocks of regulatory provisions. In the following the three phases will be analysed in-depth and a synthesis of the findings and recommendations will be given as a model for space traffic management in the year 2010.

3. Preliminary findings

As pointed out, the study aims at an outline of a Comprehensive Space Traffic Management Regime. The preliminary findings can be summed up like this:

Framework:

- drafting of an international inter-governmental agreement building on and not replacing the existing treaties (includes provisions for liability and the basic principle that States are the primary actors but that provisions of the agreement are applicable for private activities as well through national licensing regimes; certain issues will be clarified in the agreement);
- comprises a legal text, which cannot be changed easily and technical annexes which can be adapted more easily
- three parts:

1. Securing the information needs

- definition of necessary data
- provision of the data (including financing)
- establishing a database and distribution mechanisms for data

[- establishing new installations for surveillance if needed]

2. Notification system

- pre-launch notification with better parameters than Registration Convention as well as other provisions (e.g. ITU and proposed UNIDROIT Protocoll)
- information on the end of active/operational lifetime of space objects
- pre-notification of orbital manoeuvres and active de-orbiting (communication rules and cooperation provisions)

3. Traffic management

- provides traffic management rules
    - clarification of "space objects"
    - for launch phase setting delimitation and clarifying the concept of the "launching State"
    - right of way rules for in-orbit phase
    - priorisation with regard to manoeuvres
    - specific provisions for GSO in harmonization with ITU rules
    - specific rules for LEO satellite constellations
    - zoning
- clarifying "fault" in case of damage caused in outer space
- gives framework and main features for national licensing regimes, which implement the provisions of the agreement)
- provides overarching debris mitigation mechnisms
- sets out an enforcement mechanism (e.g. renouncement of access to information)
- clarifies institutionalized interlinks with ICAO and ITU

4. Organisation

- the provisions of the three agreements are in a first step monitored by UNCOPUOS and handled by the UN Office for Outer Space Affairs (UNOOSA)
- in a second step (post 2020), the new Agreement may be (together with the existing space treaties) replaced by a comprehensive Outer Space Convention; ICAO's mandate may be enlarged to cover both the aviation and space traffic management legal frameworks; UNCOPUOS as well as UNOOSA functions could be integrated into new ICAO; space acivities by private actors will develop into the same legal status as in air traffic

It is planned that the study will also contain draft legal texts for these areas.

IAC-03-IISL.4.03

ON THE NEED TO REGULATE SPACE TRAFFIC MANAGEMENT

Professor Dr. Maureen Williams *
Chair of Public International Law, University of Buenos Aires
Chair of the ILA Space Law Committee
maureenw@fibertel.com.ar

Opening Remarks

This paper deals with the interaction between international law and the specific principles of space law as applied to space traffic management. The objective is to determine whether the time has come to lay down special rules on this question having in mind the sharp increase of commercial activities in outer space in the last decade. This, in turn, implies an analysis of the existing rules of international law with emphasis on the Space Treaties in force and, particularly, the 1975 Registration Convention. The relationship between space traffic management and the work of ICAO will be similarly addressed within this context, as also the issue of space debris.

The foregoing analysis will ease the way towards establishing whether it appears advisable, in the present international scenario, to engage in the drafting of detailed rules and regulations on this matter which, by their very nature, are unlikely to be long-lived. Likewise, the need to include the subject of space traffic management on the agenda of COPUOS will be evaluated from various standpoints and so will the possible role of the ITU in this field.

Should we conclude that the time is ripe for creating new law to govern this matter, the paper would then discuss -and possibly suggest- some general principles to serve as guidelines.

Introducing the problem

Nowadays it is not unfrequent for international space lawyers, both practitioners and academics, to engage in the analysis of the advantages and shortcomings of creating new law with the idea of giving a more precise legal meaning to the general principles stemming from the Outer Space Treaties presently in force.

Prompted by the advances of science and technology and the increasing commercial applications of space activities, certain specific areas have been the object of proposals. The general idea is to keep pace with such unprecedented advances in order to be consistent with the present reality. Within the evaluation of the possible laying down of new law to this end, the issues surrounding remote sensing and space debris take pride of place followed, somewhat closely in recent times, by the regulation of space traffic management. There is a growing feeling in this direction.

Thoughts are beginning to be voiced in many an international forum -private or intergovernmental- drawing attention to the need of proceeding without delay to the review of the existing law, in the case of remote sensing, and in the case of space debris and traffic management, to the creation of new law. At this stage the view that the existing law needs to be supplemented is gradually gaining ground.

Indeed, space debris and space traffic management are closely interwoven questions, particularly in today's world context and especially when it comes to considering a possible regulation of the latter.

Space debris, in accordance with the ILA International Instrument on this topic[1], means:

Man-made objects in outer space, other than active or otherwise useful satellites, when no change can reasonably be expected in these conditions in the foreseeable future.

Space debris may result, inter alia, from:

- ***Remote space operations including spent stages of rockets and space vehicles, and hardware released during normal manoeuvres.***
- ***Orbital explosions and satellite breakups, whether intentional or accidental.***
- ***Collision-generated debris.***
- ***Particles and other forms of pollution[2] ejected, for example, by solid rocket exhaust.***
- ***Abandoned satellites.***

In fact, in any down-to-earth attempt to suggest specific rules to govern space traffic management, the risk created by space debris is at the root of the problem. Professor Perek points out that today over 90% of all trackable objects in outer space come under that category, and so do almost 100% of objects that are so far too small to be tracked[3]. To this alarming statement we may add that, as technology advances day by day, it enables the tracking of very small particles of second generation debris. This technical possibility would have been unthinkable a few years back. Therefore, the figures would reach, in a short time, an even higher number.

Thus, a preliminary conclusion -to be confirmed or adjusted throughout this paper- is that space debris in the first place and, secondly, space traffic management, are topics to be included for discussion on the agenda of the Legal Subcommittee (LSC) of Copuos.

Terminology

The foregoing questions take us, in turn, to the problem of agreeing on definitions, particularly in the context of the 1975 Registration Convention. To ease the way for further regulation and to clear up outstanding doubts, the questions of terminology should be tackled from the outset.

Many of these terms -coined at the time of the drafting of the Space Treaties now in force- need more precision in today's world scenario. In the following paragraphs I shall address the terms which, in the general view, are considered directly linked to space traffic management and the need for regulation. At this stage, however, the importance of agreeing on a definition of outer space as *conditio sine qua non* for the enforcement of rules on space traffic management speaks for itself. It therefore seems redundant to discuss the issue within the scope of this presentation.

(a) The concept of space debris.

In the previous chapter mention was made of the ILA definition which, nowadays, is widely accepted by the doctrine[4]. Many of the members of the ILA who supported the adoption of this text in 1994 are equally members of the IISL and views generally coincide. The scientific consultants of the ILA Committee, namely Professors Rex (Germany), Perek (Czech Republic) and Ricciardi (Argentina), participated actively with the present writer in the different stages of the preparation of this text[5] and were, on general lines, in agreement with the Draft. To date, the Buenos Aires International Instrument on Space Debris continues under permanent review by the ILA Space Law Committee.

Professor Rex, in his comments to the Report submitted by the present writer to the 69th Conference of the ILA (London 2000), expressed his views in no uncertain terms. First, he stated that space debris was not covered by the 1972 Liability Convention and that it was urgent to agree on an international instrument to govern this issue to strictly limit the production of future debris, having in mind the huge economic importance of the issues involved, taking due care, at the same time, not to set obstacles in the way of beneficial space utilisation. Secondly, this expert strongly opposed the inclusion, by means of an amendment to the Liability Convention, of liability for damage caused by space debris. Thirdly, Professor Rex explained that the urgency to have a specific instrument on this matter was grounded on the rapidly expanding market in the field of telecommunications which would possibly include up to twenty satellite constellations with around one thousand satellites together in the low earth orbits [6].

If we have in mind the wide, non-exhaustive scope of the ILA definition one may easily conclude that it comes very close to the one advocated by Professor Perek in his presentation to this 46th Colloquium and embodied in the 1999 UN. [7] Let us take a closer look at this text.

Space debris are all man-made objects, including their fragments and parts, whether their owners can be identified or not, in Earth-orbit or re-entering the dense layers of the atmosphere, that are non-functional with no reasonable expectation of their being able to assume or resume their intended functions or any other functions for which they are or can de authorised [8].

It is therefore clear that in the present time we count with realistic definitions (and/or descriptions) of what should be understood by space debris. Consequently, it appears both timely and sensible to agree, at governmental level, on the meaning, scope and implications of this term. Such course of action seems a necessary previous step to enable the international community to embark in the development of space traffic management regulations.

This is the essence of the deeply-rooted conclusion of the doctrine holding that the legal aspects of space debris should be added to the agenda of the LSC of Copuos without further delay [9].

(b) The Registration Convention

Certain sections of this instrument are in strong need of amendment and clarification as a pre-requisite for the regulation of space traffic. We are light years ahead of 1975 when this Convention was adopted. Consequently, the definitions and requirements embodied therein are not enough to meet the needs and challenges of the present time.

The general view appears to be, however, that amendments to the Space Treaties in force be avoided[10]. As in the case of the Liability Convention, the prevailing idea is that any change or addition should be introduced by a separate instrument, such as a UNGA Resolution or Protocol, so that the original text of the Convention remains untouched.

The matter has been extensively discussed in recent years by the ILA, albeit not linked to space traffic management proper but, rather, to the growing role of private entities in space activities[11]. However so, as space traffic management is an illustrative example of a commercial activity, the conclusions are equally applicable thereto.

Professor Kopal, one of the Special Rapporteurs of the ILA Space Law Committee on this topic, championed the idea of unifying national registries kept by the launching states and supplementing Article IV of the Convention by making reference to the name and position of the subjects responsible for the launch and of the subjects owning and/or operating the space object in question. Moreover, this expert was very much aware of the obstacles which formal amendments to the Registration Convention were likely to bring about as a result of double standards. He stood clearly against the procedure of amendment to this Convention which could entail the withdrawal of some of its parties[12]. Both the national and international registrations, in the view of Prof. Kopal, should enable the identification of the launching state as well as other legal entities participating in launching activities[13].

Professor Bin Cheng has, likewise, provided useful thoughts on this question. He points out the need to update the requirements of Article I of the Convention (on definitions) observing that there is a problem regarding the "connecting factor" between private entities and the state, particularly with respect to the terms "a state which launches or procures the launching", a question to which a short reference will be made in the next chapter.

In his book *Studies in International Space Law* [14], Chapters 23 and 24, Prof. Cheng discusses a number of options to determine the referred link, such as nationality, domicile, residence, place of incorporation, place of business and so forth.

What follows is a glaring illustration of the problems likely to occur in connection with Article II (2) of the Registration Convention, as explained by Professor Cheng in his comments to the ILA Space Law Report adopted by the London Conference.

The above-mentioned provision deals with the case of two or more launching states in respect of one single space object, leaving it to them to establish which of them shall register the object in its national registry. This procedure may cause undue confusion and ought to be reviewed. To say the least, it eases the way for flags of convenience to proliferate in international space law[15].

I believe this situation would imply a serious obstacle to any attempt of laying down rules for space traffic. Moreover, as Prof. Cheng indicates, Article VII on the position of international intergovernmental organisations should be re-examined in view of their increasing role in space activities[16].

Presumably, in a not too distant future, these organisations will play an important part in the regulation of space traffic. In fact, the present writer believes that ICAO and the ITU would be the natural and most appropriate bodies to be entrusted with such challenging responsibilities.

These matters are no doubt of a highly sensitive nature which supports the conclusion that a cautious approach should be taken when considering amendments to the Space Treaties in force.[17] The political will for that purpose is lacking at the moment and the international community, as perceived in the different fora, does not see with favour any changes of the kind. Consequently, the idea of introducing clarifications, definitions or minor adjustments through separate instruments - binding or otherwise- appears the wisest solution today.

Along these lines the ILA New Delhi Conference considered, in connection with the 1975 Registration Convention, that

to ease identification a separate protocol or UNGA Resolution is suggested dealing, inter alia, with the unification of national registries and clarification of certain terms , such as "launching state", while maintaining its text intact[18].

(c) The term "launching State"

This topic was addressed by the present writer during the IISL Colloquium held in Houston in 2002 to which, *brevitatis causa*, reference is made hereby[19].

I shall simply recall now that on the occasion of the International Colloquium held in Cologne to mark the end of Project 2001, the Working Group on Launch and Associated Services expressed similar views, i.e. contrary to the amendment of the Space Treaties and, particularly, to changes in the terms "launching authority" and "launching State".[20] A consensus is therefore growing to the effect that the terms "launching state" and "launching authority" should not be changed in the space treaties as this would entail a very complex procedure of amendments at a time when the political scenario is not really prepared for it. Consequently, the role to be played by national space legislation in the present time becomes of major importance.

It is fair to say that the clarification of the terms "a State which launches or procures the launching" remains outstanding. This problem, common to the Liability and Registration Conventions, is today a matter of concern to space lawyers who have made their ideas abundantly clear in recent years at COPUOS, particularly Dr. Schrogl and members of his Working Group on the topic. On the private level the IISL and the ILA have dedicated considerable efforts to this issue.

Suffice it to say at the moment that, once these terminological controversies are sorted out and dissipated, all the other issues surrounding space traffic management will be easily resolved.

Conclusions

Just as the Space Law Treaties presently in force are considered sufficient to govern the commercial aspects of space activities in the present time, so are these Treaties and the existing customary law appropriate, so far, for the initial phases of space traffic management, an undoubted commercial activity.

Having said so, we cannot escape the fact that space activities, particularly those in the hands of private entities, are growing in geometrical progression. Hence, it does not seem unreasonable to start thinking of a more precise meaning for the existing law applicable to space traffic management. Similarly, the most appropriate ways of moving in this direction should be discussed.

With this objective in mind it is essential to move swiftly towards the clarification of certain concepts, *inter alia* those focused upon in this paper. We should have international rules on space debris, a topic to be included without delay on the agenda of the LSC of COPUOS, where the above-mentioned *ILA International Instrument on Space Debris* has been introduced and explained, and could serve as basis for discussion. The obscure definitions and requirements underlying the Registration Convention should be updated for more precision. And we should come to terms with the different interpretations of the concept of "launching state" embodied in the Liability and Registration Conventions, and agree on a definition common to all.

First and foremost, outer space must be defined.

The suggested steps would certainly ease the way of the institutions which, presumably, will be called upon to deal with space traffic management. As observed earlier, when the time comes, ICAO and the ITU appear the most appropriate.

In the private field, the work of study groups and think tanks would be more than welcome to provide the pillars and suggest the contents of what will -hopefully- become an international instrument to govern traffic in space.

Only then would we stand on safe grounds to move towards the LSC of COPUOS for discussion on effective regulations to govern space traffic management. Possibly, earlier than we think.

---

[1] *This text, known as the "Buenos Aires International Instrument for the Protection of the Environment from damage caused by Space Debris" was adopted by consensus at the 66th Conference of the International Law Association" in 1994. It was subsequently submitted to the Legal Subcommittee of COPUOS, with detailed explanations, and continues under permanent review by the Space Law Committee of the ILA. See Report to the 66th Conference of the ILA (Buenos Aires 1994) by the present writer (pp.305-325, also pp.9-13)*

[2] *In the context of the ILA International Instrument it was agreed that the words "pollution" and "contamination" would be considered synonyms. See op.cit. in note 1, pp.309-311.*

[3] *Cf. Lubos Perek, "Basic Problems in Space Traffic", paper submitted to t his 46th Colloquium on the Law of Outer Space, Bremen 2003.*

[4] *On 9 November 2001, on the occasion of a Conference on Space Debris held in London within the framework of the European Centre of Space Law (UK point of contact) it was recommended to use the ILA International Instrument on Space Debris as basis for international discussion for a convention on the subject.*

[5] *See Reports of the ILA Conferences, Space Law Committee (Queensland 1990, Cairo 1992 and Buenos Aires 1994). However, Professors Rex and Ricciardi did not recommend the inclusion of rules on international responsibility and liability. The ILA Space Law Committee, per contra, thought this was indispensable. The latter position was endorsed by the 66th ILA Conference. See Buenos Aires Report (66th Conference, pp.311-314).*

[6] *See Report of the 69th Conference of the ILA, London 2000, Report of the Space Law Committee by the present writer, pp.580-1.*

[7] *Technical Report on Space Debris adopted by the Scientific and Technical Subcommittee of Copuos in 1999 (A/AC. 105/720).*

[8] *Quoted by Prof.Perek in his presentation to the present Colloquium. See note 3, supra.*

[9] *Dr. Monserrat Filho, in his presentation to the IISL/ECSL Symposium on "Prospects for Space Traffic Management"(Vienna, 2 April 2002) stated that it was necessary to establish an international regime for all issues arising from space debris, such as its legal definition, procedures for the removal of space debris and its minimisation in the future. This, in this*

expert's view, would include the development of industrial standards and their implementation by States and private entities.

[10] *Such the conclusions of the ILA Space Law Committee submitted to the London (2000) and New Delhi (2002) Conferences, adopted without dissent. It should however be noted that this does nor apply to the 1979 Moon Agreement which, according to the ILA, is in need of dramatic changes and should be either "improved on or discarded".*

[11] *See ILA Space Law Committee Report to the 68th Conference (London 2000) pp. 585-6 (Prof. Kopal), op.cit. in note 6, and Report of the ILA Space Law Committee to the 70th Conference (New Delhi 2002), pp. 192-227, at pp. 200-201.*

[12] *See Kopal, Report of the 69th ILA Conference, pp. 575-6.*

[13] *Ibid.*

[14] *See Bin Cheng, STUDIES IN INTERNATIONAL SPACE LAW, Clarendon Press Oxford 1997, Chapters 23- 24, pp. 621-666.*

[15] *Op.cit in note 6, p.585.*

[16] *Ibid.*

[17] *Such the position of Professor Kopal in his Special Report to the 70th Conference of the ILA (2002), fully supported by the Space Law Committee and the Plenary Session of the Conference. See op.cit.in note 11, p. 201.*

[18] *Ibid., pp. 13-16. (Resolution 1 /2002 , English and French texts).*

[19] *See by the present writer, "Perceptions on the definition of a "launching State" and Space Debris Risks" , paper submitted to the 45th Colloquium onthe Law of Outer Space, Houston 2002.*

[20] *See Panel Working Group on Launch and Associated Services, in 'Project 2001' - Legal Framework for the Commercial Uses of Outer Space, Ed. Karl-Heinz Böckstiegel, Carl Heymanns Verlag, Köln, Berlin, Bonn, München (2002), pp.55-144.*

CREATING AN INTERNATIONAL REGIME FOR SPACE TRAFFIC MANAGEMENT - MOVING FROM GENERAL PRINCIPLES TOWARDS PRACTICABLE RULES

Lotta Viikari
Ph.D. Candidate
Faculty of Law, University of Lapland, Rovaniemi, FINLAND
Email: lotta.viikari@urova.fi

Abstract

This paper examines the possibilities of negotiating practicable rules for the management of space traffic. The findings should also apply more generally to the future development of space law because the analysis draws on experiences from a variety of multilateral treaty negotiations. A central starting point is an analysis of the framework convention-protocol approach commonly applied in current global environmental diplomacy. This basis for comparison is chosen because the UN space treaties from the 1960s and 1970s substantially resemble framework conventions in their non-specific nature, i.e., in providing only general principles and vague guidelines. Today, the needs of the space faring community are far more complex and the existing law of outer space is often unable to give sufficient guidance in the concrete situations that emerge in current space utilization. The world community has not been able to fill this legal vacuum other than by sets of principles adopted by the UN General Assembly and a few other recommendatory instruments. This is again a development resembling experiences from the application of the convention-protocol approach: although it has been relatively easy for countries to agree that something "should be done", disagreements flare up when it comes to drafting more specific and binding obligations.

INTRODUCTION

It is very difficult to achieve international agreement on anything, let alone issues regarding the use of outer space, which combine a high degree of scientific and technological complexity with politics, economics and the activism of various stakeholder groups. Additionally, the question how to manage a common resource and minimize the "free rider" problem intrinsically relates to all space activities, making problems related to the use of outer space even more complicated and difficult to resolve.

Traditionally, international legal standards, rules and regimes have been established through the adoption of treaties by states. Space issues are no exception. Consequently, the recent proposals for combating problems related to the management of space activities have most often envisaged the establishment of new treaties (or at least amendments improving the effectiveness of existing ones).

Unfortunately, the traditional approach to international norm-setting has severe weaknesses. In keeping with the doctrine of state sovereignty, international norms cannot, as a rule, be forced on states. Accordingly, conventional diplomacy is based on consensus or unanimity of all participants in treaty negotiations (excluding those who decide to opt out completely at some point, as a result of voting or otherwise). There may, however, be major differences in the needs and priorities of the negotiating parties, and in practice countries may be unwilling to make sufficient commitments to the intended objectives. In order to avoid voting and/or the withdrawal of important states, the measures adopted easily become limited to those acceptable to the least enthusiastic party, resulting in "halfway agreements" too poorly designed to achieve the objectives set (regardless of the number of ratifications the treaty gains). This problem is commonly referred to as the lowest-common-denominator approach.[1]

Such avoidance of conflicting positions through vagueness and ambiguity is by no means unfamiliar in space law either. Space activities are inherently international, which necessitates wide acceptance among the global community for any rules to be effective. However, broadening the scope of an international regime usually also means lowering its common denominator. It is obvious that the legal standards agreed upon for space activities to date have been based on the lowest common denominator and the compromise approach, resulting in no more than general principles. Indeed, traditional treaty-making techniques do not seem very suitable for the governance of space activities today. While these tools allow declaratory standards and suggestions to be adopted quite easily, they are likely to fail when it comes to creating effective rules that produce tangible positive results.

Effective solutions to current questions in the utilization of outer space would obviously necessitate new, innovative mechanisms for international standard-setting. Considering the fundamental status of the doctrine of state sovereignty and the institutionalized nature of international law and the international law-making system, the traditional treaty process can hardly be altered comprehensively; rather, it needs to be made receptive to modifications which help overcome some of its major shortcomings. Such modifications would include abatement measures such as those taken in other fields of international law that enable the negotiators of global treaties to overcome the lowest-common-denominator problem and better take into consideration the needs of all countries regardless of their state of technological development, for instance.

[1] Susskind 1994, p. 14.

THE FRAMEWORK - PROTOCOL APPROACH

Multilateral negotiations are typically initiated by international organizations (such as the United Nations, including its Committee on the Peaceful Uses of Outer Space). Procedural rules are usually formulated at the beginning of the treaty-making process. Global agreements are negotiated mainly in accordance with the formal rules and informal practices developed within the United Nations and its sister organizations, although these rules and practices do not necessarily always accommodate the particulars of multi-issue, multiparty negotiation as well as they might[2].[3]

Certain "trends" can be observed in the process of creating international legal arrangements. These include special area status, the convention-plus-annex, the protocol-plus-declaration and the convention-plus-protocol approaches.[4] In particular, the (framework) convention-protocol approach has been commonly applied in international environmental treaty negotiations lately. Most of these negotiations have been organized such that meetings are first held to review scientific evidence and draft a framework convention as a basis for the preparation of more detailed protocols by all or some States Parties [5], a procedure resembling that for the adoption of space agreements and subsequent sets of space principles, albeit not legally binding ones.

Although framework conventions may serve as reassuring proof that further action is required, this approach also allows countries to join conventions at a stage where there is not yet any agreement on the specific actions (timetables, procedures, etc.) which should eventually be taken. In some cases, such action may be carried out relatively easily (for instance, when scientific evidence is convincing enough to show that abatement measures are absolutely essential, or when world or domestic opinion necessitates such action). Most often, however, the convention -protocol process is very time-consuming and can easily lead to a situation where countries find it very difficult to reach agreement on the more specific follow-up protocols. In the meanwhile, the problems which the convention aims at curbing usually

[2] Susskind 1994, p. 6.

[3] Susskind 1994, p. 25. The Vienna Convention on the Law of Treaties (8 ILM 679) does not specify who should initiate treaty-making efforts, which countries should participate and how the process should proceed; it only says that adoption of the text of a treaty requires "a vote of two-thirds of the states present and voting, unless by the same majority they decide to apply a different rule" (Art. 9.2).

[4] Kütting 2000, p. 16.

[5] Such an approach has been applied, *inter alia*, in the Vienna Convention on Substances that Deplete the Ozone Layer 1985 [26 ILM 1529 (1987)], in the subsequent Montreal Protocol on Substances that Deplete the Ozone Layer (26 ILM 1550) and the four adjustments to the Protocol adopted in London (1990), Copenhagen (1992), Vienna (1995), Montreal (1997) and Beijing (1999).

only worsen.[6]

Clearly, the framework-protocol approach tends to yield only lowest-common-denominator agreements that incorporate (excessively) vague language and provide too little in substance. The great generality at the convention-writing level guarantees that the parties are at least able to agree that a problem exists and "something should be done", and makes it possible for even reluctant countries to sign. However, the vagueness in terminology and criteria undermines chances of successful implementation.[7]

Moreover, political considerations sometimes overshadow available scientific and technical information to the extent that the resulting instruments turn out to be infeasible, internally inconsistent or counterproductive. Countries tend to rely on scientific evidence which justifies the policies they prefer; this is particularly the case with the convention-protocol approach, where the implications of the policies adopted when drafting the framework convention need only be confronted later, in the subsequent protocol design phase. At worst, a framework convention may set terms which get in the way of producing technically appropriate agreements.

Furthermore, the ad hoc convention-protocol approach may encourage countries to resort to "hard-bargaining" strategies (including exaggerating or misrepresenting their real needs) and to focus on short-term interests. In practice, the convention-protocol process easily enables those negotiators that are most powerful (in terms of financial, military or research resources, for instance) to dominate the negotiation process, starting from setting the agenda, writing the rules of procedure and controlling the dissemination of technical information. Even less powerful states (developing countries, for instance) can play a significant role in treaty negotiations, provided that they are able to maintain sufficient coherence within their ranks. If not, the agreements that emerge may well be no more than a compromise among the few powerful parties. Moreover, the negotiators of these powerful few easily fail to explore the full range of possibilities, often locking into a battle over a small number of (not necessarily optimal) options instead. In such a setting, the results typically reflect rather little creative brain-storming and resolution of real differences.[8]

LESSONS FOR SPACE LAW

Given the similarities between the convention-protocol approach and developments within the law of outer space, an examination of the strategies applied in combating problems related to the convention-protocol approach may yield beneficial lessons for the future of space law negotiations. Of major interest is the question how to overcome the lowest-common-denominator problem and enable more nations to be involved in the negotiations and assume roles which are truly meaningful. This is vital since the generality of current space agreements and the failure of the international community to

[6] Susskind 1994, p. 31.

[7] Susskind 1994, p. 32.

[8] Susskind 1994, pp. 33-35.

produce more detailed legal obligations severely hamper current possibilities to manage space activities.

In general, reluctant negotiating parties can be persuaded to modify their positions through side-payments or political pressure. Negotiating experience has shown that, apart from outright political coercion, the most successful tools for making more demanding options attractive to parties include selective incentives, differential obligations, and the promotion of "over-achievement" by lead countries.[9]

"Selective incentives" refer to fringe benefits or special favors that may persuade a party to participate in collective action that it would otherwise find unattractive. Such clauses to accommodate special interests are common in international agreements, often allowing, for instance, technologically less developed countries to adhere to the instruments by postponing compliance with standards they otherwise find too stringent or providing them with benefits and aid from industrialized states. Such compromises may detract from the effectiveness of the instruments but are often essential in alluring important signatories. Moreover, without such clauses, agreement might have only been possible on a much lower level of collective commitment, whereby the selective incentives approach may even improve the overall standard of obligations (above the predictable lowest common denominator).[10]

Commonly used selective incentives relate to access to funding, resources, markets and technology [11]. In space activities, at least access to technical or financial assistance and clauses for the preferential acquisition of new technology might prove feasible. They could enable the construction of safer space objects (safer power supplies, for instance) and encourage more sustainable general patterns in space policies.

However, the Space Benefits Declaration of 1996 [12] affirmed in practice that no requirements of a legal nature can be derived from the fundamental Art. I of the Outer Space Treaty (OST)[13], according to which exploration and utilization of outer space is to be for the benefit and in the interests of all countries. In establishing that states are free to determine all aspects of their participation in international cooperation in space activities (para.2), the Declaration´s authoritative, current interpretation of the cooperation principle of OST Art. I eliminated hopes of obligatory transfer of financial and technological resources from the industrialized states to technologically

---

[9] See, e.g., Sand 1990, p. 6.

[10] Ibid.

[11] On the selective incentives used in international environmental instruments in particular, see Sand 1990, pp. 6-8.

[12] Declaration on International Cooperation in the Exploration and Use of Outer Space for the Benefit and in the Interests of All States, Taking Particular Account of the Needs of Developing Countries; UNGA Res. 51/122 (Dec 13, 1996).

[13] Treaty on Principles Governing the Activities of States in the Exploration and Use of Outer Space Including the Moon and Celestial Bodies (610 UNTS 205).

less developed countries.[14]

The selective incentives approach purports to treat states more or less equally and is based on a system of reciprocal rights and obligations: in practice it results in special treatment for selected parties. Such discrimination can seriously undermine the credibility (or acceptability) of an agreement. A more straightforward approach is to have an asymmetrical regime from the very outset with different treaty obligations being applied according to each party's special (economic, technological, etc.) circumstances. Such a **differential obligations** approach has been adopted in many environmental instruments, for instance, with these incorporating country-by-country time plans, differential assessment scales and weighted contributions; it is also found within the UN system, which includes various UN trust funds to finance joint programs.[15]

For space activities, a differential obligations approach might propose, for instance, a trust fund (based on weighted contributions) to compensate for the financial burden of the additional costs required to ensure safer operation of space objects. Also worth considering is some sort of an intergovernmental space management authority, the formation and operation of which could be financed through an international fund (with substantial economic responsibility on the major users of outer space). In light of the principle of equality and the idea of space being the province of all mankind (Outer Space Treaty Art. I, etc.), a suitable criterion for dividing countries into groups (in this case) could be their level of technological and economic development.

One additional strategy for avoiding the lowest-common-denominator problem is the **promotion of over-achievement**. Many environmental agreements, for instance, expressly confirm the right of parties to take (individually or collectively) measures more stringent than those required by the agreement itself. Even where treaties do not give explicit permission to over-achieve the goals set by them, they usually do not prevent additional action or stricter

[14] Viikari 2002, pp. 124-130. Moreover, it should be remembered that provisions to facilitate technology transfer were also adopted for the deep seabed mining regime established by the "original" 1982 United Nations Convention on the Law of the Sea [21 ILM 1245 (1982)]. This regime would have guaranteed substantial technology transfer benefits from industrialized world to less developed countries. In 1994, however, the system was altered dramatically by modifications introduced by the so-called New York Agreement [Agreement on the Implementation of Part XI of the 1982 Law of the Sea Convention; 33 ILM 1309 (1994)], which, i.a., abandoned all mandatory technology transfer obligations (Annex, Section 5). For a more detailed account, see, e.g., Viikari 2002. Considering this development and the 1996 Space Benefits Declaration together, it does not seem very likely that industrialized countries will acquire far-reaching technology transfer obligations in the very near future in the field of space activities either.

[15] Sand 1990, p. 8.

requirements, provided that these are non-discriminatory.[16]

The willingness of countries to take action unilaterally and adopt timetables and targets that affect only themselves is hardly enough to combat wide-scale adverse effects, but over-achievement provisions may, for instance, provide incentive and a starting point for subsequent negotiations in wider international arenas. Such initiative taken by only some countries within a larger group of nations has indeed often "played a pilot role" in more general target-setting and encouraged other states to do likewise, if possible.[17] At the same time, however, unilateral standards may give the countries who first apply them a dominating position in subsequent negotiations, where they might demand, for example, that those standards be made the norm.[18]

Framework conventions, which are originally meant as a framework for further action with additional but optional protocols then frequently concluded between (usually only some) parties, constitute a specific case in this respect.[19] Similarly, the sets of principles for the management of space activities adopted by the UN General Assembly can be seen as promoting over fulfilment of the vague obligations provided by the original space treaties and encouraging subsequent legally binding agreement on these issues. The same applies to the numerous non-binding instruments adopted by the International Telecommunication Union (ITU) in relation to both UN space treaties and the ITU Convention and Constitution [20], which aim at guaranteeing undisturbed space telecommunications.

Even declaratory instruments by prestigious non-governmental expert groups may gain influential status, such as the work of the International Law Association (ILA) on several legal issues [21], which includes the ILA Draft Convention on Space Debris from 1994. In compliance with this draft, many space actors have voluntarily taken such important steps as removing inactive satellites from the geostationary satellite

---

[16] Sand 1990, p. 12.

[17] Ibid.

[18] Susskind 1994, p. 31. In addition to a genuine will to alleviate harmful effects of their activities and to create a possibility to affect (to some extent) future developments in international target-setting, a distinct reason for states to "over-achieve" their goals (in cases where the price to be paid for that is relatively low) is also the simple fact that it often pays political dividends in terms of public attention and recognition. With many international accords, national achievements and pledges are recorded and compared annually; media coverage and international publicity should not be underestimated as influential incentives for states to act in a certain manner. Sand 1990, p. 13.

[19] Sand 1990, p. 12.

[20] These instruments can be found at http://www.itu.int/aboutitu/basic-texts/convention.html and http://www.itu.int/aboutitu/basic-texts/constitution.html [10AUG03].

[21] See Sand 1990, p. 16.

orbit [22]. On the other hand, some satellite operators had carried out such procedures even before the ILA Draft Convention and a recommendation issued by the ITU in the same year, both of which specifically recommended the removal of satellites at the end of their lifetime [23]. These unilateral measures can be considered as encouragement for the adoption of the later instruments urging such procedures.

CONCLUDING REMARKS

The entire field of space law seems to need improved approaches to the negotiation of international agreements if it is to create regimes that are effective both institutionally and in solving the problems they have been designed for. This is a demanding task, for international regimes typically emerge only after complex bargaining processes. Even when there exists a zone of agreement, it tends to be very difficult to identify common preferences, and efforts to reach agreement on a specific point within this zone easily give rise to hard bargaining and coercive diplomacy. Consequently, the negotiations often fail to result in agreements, or they yield less than optimal results, ones generally attributable to the problem of the lowest common denominator.

Due to the similarities between the convention-protocol approach commonly used in international environmental negotiations and the development of international law of outer space, an examination of the two-step approach can provide important lessons for the future of space law. This is particularly true as space activities most obviously are an arena where the same actors need to deal with each other on a continuing basis and in the context of various issues. Consequently, long-term working relationships, necessitating trust among the parties, are crucial, and it would serve all concerned better to avoid positional bargaining, such as that typically generated by the traditional treaty-making process.

One positive factor likely to promote coherent and widely acceptable agreements maximizing the common good in the utilization of outer space is that all spacefaring entities have many potential roles and are likely to be equally affected by the adversities related to space activitites. Even here, however, there remain numerous considerations that deserve special attention, particularly those connected to the status of outer space as the province of all mankind: how to guarantee efficient and reasonable management of this global common, how to preserve it as a legacy for future generations, how to secure access also for those parts of

---

[22] See, e.g., Jahku 1991, p. 208.

[23] The ITU Recommendation ITU-R S.1003 (on the environmental protection of the geostationary orbit) from 1994 requires that "a geostationary satellite at the end of its life should be transferred [- - -] to a supersynchronous graveyard orbit that does not intersect the GSO" (point 3). Similar recommendations have been given also i.a. by the Inter-Agency Space Debris Coordination Committee (Inter-Agency Space Debris Coordination Committee space debris mitigation guidelines, UN doc. A/AC.105/C.1/L.260 of 29 November 2002).The removal of inactive satellites is still far from being a standard procedure, however.

humankind which are not currently space faring nations, etc. "Traffic rules" for outer space are fundamental also for the very reason that as no one can (in principle, at least) be excluded from use, the burden of management and protection falls entirely on restrictions governing that use. The above examination of the traditional treaty process and the problem of the lowest common denominator in particular provides us with some ideas on how to develop these traffic rules and what they might contain.

One prospect, although rejected by recent instruments in the management of the resources of global commons, is that some sort of selective incentives approach could be developed on a more tempting basis for the industrialized countries. For instance, technology transfer could prove acceptable to industrialized states in exchange for some sort of extended access to space resources [24]. Such solutions obviously require a delicate balancing of interests and are likely to prove highly problematic also in light of the fundamental principles of space law. Nevertheless, they would seem to deserve thorough examination. Another interesting option is the idea of an international fund that could be harnessed to serve a variety of purposes in the management of space activities, including more sustainable space traffic management.

In order to enhance positive attitudes among space utilizers towards international regulation in general, it would also be of the utmost importance that, instead of applying the common approach in international treaty negotiations of focusing on allocating the losses or costs involved in new regulation, increasing attention would be paid to the gains resulting from wiser management of space activities. Otherwise, treaties are easily seen as merely new instruments of restriction and constraint rather than opportunities, and the economic losses such accords often entail (in the short run) provide excuses for many states to withdraw from the process even before negotiations have begun.

Finally, although legally binding international obligations might seem to provide the most secure basis for space activities, the role of recommendations and other non-binding instruments should not be underestimated. After all, in international law it is not the fear of sanctions but the genuine will of states to avoid outcomes that are rendered inauspicious which drives states to conduct their activities in a certain manner - also in outer space.

[24] Access to sustainable use of resources is a widely applied incentive in terrestrial surroundings in return for accepting environmental restrictions, for instance. See, e.g., Sand 1990, p. 7.

REFERENCES

Jahku, Ram S. Space Debris in the Geostationary Orbit - A Matter of Concern for the ITU-. Proceedings of the 34th Colloquium on the Law of Outer Space. October 5-11, **1991** (Montreal, Canada). AIAA. Pp. 205-214.

Kütting, Gabriela. Environment, Society and International Relations: towards more effective international environmental agreements. London, New York : Routledge. **2000**.

Sand, Peter H. Lessons learned in Global Environmental Governance. New York : World Resources Institute. **1990**.

Susskind, Lawrence E. Environmental Diplomacy: negotiating more effective global agreements. New York, Oxford : Oxford University Press. **1994**.

Viikari, Lotta. From Managanese Nodules to Lunar Regolith. A comparative legal study of the utilization of natural resources in the deep seabed and outer space. Publications of the Faculty of Law, University of Lapland. D Series : 1. Rovaniemi : Lapland University Press. **2002.**

IAC-03-IISL.4.06

BASIC PROBLEMS IN SPACE TRAFFIC

Luboš Perek*
Astronomical Institute of the Academy of Sciences
Prague, Czech Republic
perek@ig.cas.cz

ABSTRACT

Some of the tasks of the Management of Space Traffic can be addressed at present. When successfully accomplished, a necessary foundation for further discussions will be formed.

In the first place, the **meaning of technical terms** may depend on the context and on the field under consideration. Since Space Traffic covers many fields, a general understanding of technical terms has to be established in order to avoid confusion. Explanations, presented in the paper, could remove some of the frequent misunderstandings.

In the second place, the **existence of all classes of orbiting objects** has to be recognized by legal instruments because each class of objects participates in Space Traffic in its own way. The present situation, when the term *space debris* does not appear in instruments of space law, can hardly be defended. There is a basic difference, not recognized by space law, between valuable active spacecraft and valueless space debris. The fact is that over 90% of all trackable objects in space belong to the class of space debris and that fact cannot be ignored. The adoption of a legal definition of space debris would contribute to a good management of space traffic.

In the third place, an official up-to-date and complete **knowledge of the functional status** of spacecraft is essential for dealing with Space Traffic. At present, there may be doubts whether a particular spacecraft is active or not, or whether it is a valuable asset or a burdensome junk. The governmental announcements of objects launched into outer space made in compliance with the Registration Convention are incomplete, use different formats, are mostly published months or years after launch, and do not establish a link with ITU assignments of radio frequencies for telecommunications. An international agreement on completeness and a on a detailed content and format of the registration announcements of launchings would serve the purpose. In principle, the agreement could be voluntary but an obligatory arrangement would be more reliable and more durable when the number of launching entities increases in the future.

INTRODUCTION

Good management of Space Traffic is everything that improves safety, efficiency and economy of space activities for our own and future generations. It consists of several tasks or problems which have to be solved one after the other, starting with basic problems, laying thus the foundation for advancing to more complicated questions[1]. Among the basic stepping stones are:

- **the common understanding of important technical terms**
- **the legal recognition of the difference between active spacecraft and space debris,** and
- **a complete, timely and updated registration of the largest objects participating in space traffic.**

THE FIRST PROBLEM: TERMINOLOGY

Space Traffic requires a richer dictionary than we find in the instruments of space law. Existing space treaties do not contain terms, such as space debris, avoidance maneuvers, space station and many others. The geostationary orbit appears only in documents of the International Telecommunication Union, ITU, not in space treaties.

Technical terms are as a rule taken over from scientific and technical publications coming from numerous and different sources. The problem is that various sources use different terms for the same object, or the same term for different objects. An example of the first group is the *geostationary-satellite orbit*, used by the ITU, the *geostationary Earth orbit*, used by the Inter Agency Space Debris Coordinating Committee, IADC, and the simple term, *geostationary orbit,* used in the UN General Assembly Resolutions. An example of the second group is *space station*, used by the ITU for a radio receiver or transmitter carried on a satellite while for anybody else it is the biggest artificial object in the sky.

Most of the terms have been in use for a long time and a large number of authors and readers have become accustomed to them. To change the usage into a standard and logical terminology is a task for the future. At present we shall have to live with the prevailing multitude of terms. **The important thing is to understand which important concepts are meant by what terms in what context.**

Space objects

Space object is a term used in the treaties on space law. Consequently, it carries a connotation of a legal term. In case such a connotation is undesirable, the term "**object in space**" can be used.

Space system has been defined by the ITU (ITU Radio Regulations, term S1.110) as *any group of cooperating earth radio stations and/or space radio stations employing space radio communication for specific purposes.* The same term has been defined in the IADC Debris Mitigation Guidelines[2] as *spacecraft and orbital stages.*

Without any color is the term **spacecraft**, an analogy to aircraft. It has been defined by the ITU (term S1.178) as a *man-made vehicle that is intended to go beyond the major portion of the Earth's atmosphere.* The IADC guidelines define it in different wording, but in the same sense, as an *orbiting object designed to perform a specific function or mission.*

Active spacecraft and spacecraft in reserve or standby mode are considered **functional**, while spacecraft that can no longer fulfill their intended missions are considered **non-functional**. Possibly the concept of an **active** or **functional** object should be understood in a wide sense. Some spacecraft are valuable assets to their owners for other reasons than just activity.

A spacecraft may contain technical innovations which have to be protected, or it may carry classified information. In both cases the spacecraft are of value to their owners. Keeping information from undesired publication is a **function** of its kind.

Space debris.

According to the IAA Orbital Debris Position Paper[3] and the UN Technical Report on Space Debris (Rex Report)[4], **space debris** are *all man-made objects, including their fragments and parts, whether their owners can be identified or not, in Earth orbit or re-entering the dense layers of the atmosphere that are non-functional with no reasonable expectation of their being able to assume or resume their intended functions or any other functions for which they are or can be authorized.* Space debris may escape orbit around the Earth, reenter Earth's atmosphere or remain in Earth orbit. In the last case it is called also **orbital debris.**

Satellite Orbits

Sun Synchronous Orbits are synchronized with the Sun in such a way that they pass over the equator the same time each day. They are used for remote sensing because the ground is viewed under the same illumination in subsequent passes.

Widely used[5] are terms **Low Earth Orbit** (LEO) for orbits below about 2000 km above Earth's surface, with a period of 127 minutes or less, **Medium Earth Orbit** (MEO) for orbits between LEO and GSO, **Geosynchronous Orbit** (GSO) for orbits of a period equal to the period of rotation of the Earth (23h 56m 04s) about its axis. Geostationary Orbit (GEO), a special case of the GSO, is discussed in the following section.

According to usual practice and some encyclopedias[6], the simple **Earth orbit** refers to the orbit of the Earth around the Sun.

Geostationary orbit.

According to the IADC Debris Mitigation Guidelines **Geostationary Earth Orbit** (GEO) is an *Earth orbit having zero inclination and zero eccentricity, whose orbital period is equal to the Earth's sidereal period.* The altitude of this unique orbit is close to 35,786 km. According to the ITU Radio Regulations[7], the same concept is called the **geostationary-satellite orbit**. It is the *orbit of a geosynchronous satellite whose circular and* ***direct*** *orbit lies in the plane of the Earth's equator.* **Direct** means that the sense of orbiting is the same as the sense of rotation of the Earth, that is anticlockwise if viewed from the North.

The UN General Assembly resolutions and other documents[8] call the same orbit simply the **geostationary orbit.**

Orbital position.

A perfect geostationary orbit is a mathematical abstraction valid only for a spherically symmetrical Earth and in the presence of the gravitational attraction of the Earth only. In reality, the Earth deviates from a sphere. Moreover, spacecraft are also under the gravitational attraction of the Sun and of the Moon. These additional facts generate small forces called **perturbations.** These perturbations change the originally circular orbit into a slightly elliptical one. They also push the orbital plane out of the plane of the equator. Even a small eccentricity will cause an oscillation of the satellite around its nominal orbital position as seen from the rotating Earth.

The orbital position has to be maintained within a certain tolerance, as a rule 0.1° to the East or West and the same amount to the North or South. One tenth of a degree is, at the geostationary distance, equal to 74 km. Thus a spacecraft has to be kept within a square on the sky of 148x148 km extent. When the perturbations push the spacecraft close to the border of the ideal "parking box", an orbit maneuver has to be performed by activating thrusters on board the spacecraft. The process is called **station keeping**.

Orbital positions and radio communication frequencies are listed by the ITU in its Master International Frequency Register. An entry in the Register constitutes a statement that a radio station operated at the assigned location within the permitted tolerance and complying with other stated parameters, will neither generate, nor suffer from, harmful interference with other systems. The location of a radio station on a geostationary satellite is specified by projecting it from the geostationary orbit to the sub-satellite point on the equator of the Earth. The geographical longitude of the sub-satellite point determines the location unequivocally.

It has to be stressed that **the ITU registers space radio stations, not satellites.** One satellite may operate one or more space radio stations. Vice versa, one space radio station may be operated by radio transmitters on one or more satellite.

For obvious reasons, orbital positions in the above sense do not find application outside the geostationary orbit.

Phases of the lifetime of a spacecraft

The IADC Debris Mitigation Guidelines (see Note 2) introduced a very useful concept of operational phases of a spacecraft:

Launch phase*. the launch phase begins when the launch vehicle is no longer in physical contact with equipment and ground installations that made its preparation and ignition possible (or when the launch vehicle is dropped from the carrier aircraft, if any) and continues up to the end of the mission assigned to the launch vehicle.*

Mission phase*. The mission phase is the phase when the spacecraft fulfils its mission. It begins at the end of the launch phase and ends at the beginning of the disposal phase.*

Disposal phase*. The disposal phase begins at the end of the mission and ends when the spacecraft has performed actions to reduce the hazards it poses to other spacecraft or systems.*

It has to be noted that a spacecraft enters the disposal phase only if is capable to perform actions to reduce the hazards. In any case, after the operational phases have been terminated, the spacecraft, or its parts and fragments, continue orbiting and participating in space traffic as non-functional objects, i.e. space debris. Many space debris stay in orbit for a considerable time, from a few days at about 200 km altitude to millions of years at the GEO. From the point of view of space traffic, a post-operational phase should be added:

Space debris phase. The space debris phase begins when the spacecraft becomes non-functional and its operator lost any possibility to control it. That may happen at the end of either the mission phase or at the end of the disposal phase. The object may break up into smaller pieces, eventually decaying by evaporating in the atmosphere or impacting on the surface of the Earth

THE SECOND PROBLEM: SPACE DEBRIS

Each class of orbiting objects participates in Space Traffic in its own way. Active spacecraft is subject to other constraints than space debris. Consequently, all classes of objects have to be recognized in instruments regulating space traffic. Even natural objects, meteoroids, will have to find their place in space traffic regulation, possibly in automated warning practices of close encounters. Here we are concerned with artificial objects, i.e. with **space debris.** This term does not appear in any of treaties or agreements dealing with space law.

Definition

Over 90% of all trackable objects in space, and almost 100% of objects that are too small to be tracked, are space debris. This fact will have to be recognized by any future legal instrument dealing with space traffic.

Thanks to the IAA Position Paper (see Note 3), space debris is understood to mean all artificial objects in space that are non-functional, from burnt up rockets and stages, to satellites which have permanently terminated their activities, and down to fragments of various sizes and to flakes of paint. The lower limit of size of space debris has not been fixed. Dust particles or molecules of gases seem to be too small to be called space debris.

The question is when and by whom an object can be designated as space debris.

The Outer Space Treaty, in its Article VIII stated that *"A State Party to the Treaty on whose registry an object launched into outer space is carried shall retain jurisdiction and control over such object. Ownership of objects launched into outer space ... is not affected by their presence in outer space or on a celestial body or by their return to the Earth"*. Consequently, **only the launching state or a possible new owner can make a statement as to the functional status of its object with any authority**. This principle will most probably be preserved in the future at least for active satellites.

Participants in space traffic have to know the functional status of an object in particular in case of a close encounter. If they are likely to encounter an active object, communication with its owner may be of importance to decide which of the two objects can or should initiate an avoidance maneuver. In an encounter with a piece of space debris, the burden of an avoidance maneuver lies with the owner of the active satellite.

The necessity of providing information about a change of functional status from an active spacecraft to non-functional space debris has been felt by some owners of spacecraft. Indeed, some launching states or agencies provide information on the functional status of their objects but the practice is not uniform. Well known is the phrase *"Spent boosters, spent menoeuvring stages, shrouds and other non-functional objects*" used in the USA governmental announcements made in compliance with the Registration Convention[9]. That phrase is used when the object is non-functional at the time of detection or registration. When an object terminates its functions at a later time, no change of its functional status is, as a rule, announced. The decay of an object is announced as *no longer in orbit.* Contrary to the present practice of the USA, some states do not announce their non-functional objects at all.

As regards the termination of activities, we found announcements by Sweden concerning satellites Freja, Tele-X, and Astrid 2[10], and announcements by Italy concerning satellite BeppoSAX[11]. The Italian Space Agency announced in the UN document as well as in a diplomatic note verbale that "*the satellite is now space debris without attitude control and is only subject to the law of orbital* decay".

These examples show that a possibility of announcing changes of active objects into space debris exists but that it is used in some cases and not used in others. Space traffic law will have to make it an obligation to announce such changes in the interest of traffic safety.

Conclusion: space debris should be defined as permanently non-functional objects in space. The definition should call for announcements of changes of the functional status of spacecraft into space debris. The announcements should be obligatory for launching states or for those who became subsequently owners of the spacecraft.

The legal definition will have to be the result of an international agreement. Therefore we refrain from proposing a specific wording of the definition.

Regulation

Restricting the generation of new debris. The IADC Guidelines (see Note 2) should be adopted in their entirety.

The present wording of the recommendation determines only a wide interval of values of the solar radiation pressure coefficient, namely between 1 and 2, possibly leading to insufficient perigee distances of disposal orbits. Therefore, a specific recommended value of the solar radiation pressure coefficient should be stated in section 5.3.1 of the guidelines, in order to make the determination of the minimum perigee distance of the disposal orbit beyond the geostationary orbit unequivocal.

Small space debris. Shielding is a sufficient protection against impacts of debris up to about 1 cm. Such objects are as a rule fragments not requiring individual listing or tracking. They should neither be under the protection of the existing space treaties, nor carry the obligation of return to owner if found.

Larger debris requiring protection by evasive maneuvers of active spacecraft. If possible, these objects should be tracked, and warnings of close encounters with manned spacecraft should be issued. For this reason existing **space agencies should widely cooperate or agree on establishing a special international agency, as recommended by the AIAA Workshop in 1999**[12].

The obligation of return to owner if found should be limited to cases when the return is requested by the owner. The reason is that objects found have rarely any value at all.

Very large space debris. There are hundreds of space debris of one ton or more posing lethal danger to manned spacecraft in case of collision or close encounter. **International support should be given to scientific and technical efforts to devise methods for their de-orbiting before collisional breakups produce very large numbers of space debris.** These objects deserve individual tracking, listing and warning mechanisms.

Space Debris in the United Nations

A proposal of a Work Plan on Space Debris was put forward by France, supported by member and cooperating States of the ESA, at the 2003 session of the Legal Subcommittee[13]. The proposal, planned for the years 2005 – 2008, called for technical briefing on space debris and review of the existing legal regime applicable to space debris, for a review of the IADC mitigation guidelines and legal matters arising therefrom, and for the identification of the most appropriate legal instrument. No consensus, however, has been reached. Consequently, discussions on legal aspects of space debris, including its legal definition, will remain – for the time being – in the academic community.

THE THIRD PROBLEM: REGISTRATION OF SPACE OBJECTS

The Registration Convention is a legal instrument with a great potential. It could play an important role in the era of space traffic regulation. Unfortunately the launching registrations made in compliance with the Registration Convention are incomplete, there is no fixed deadline for submission of announcements, and the UN Register is an impenetrable jungle of hundreds of announcements, with widely differing formats and notations. Following a discussion in the UN Scientific and Technical Subcommittee, the UN Office of Outer Space Affairs prepared an Online Index of space objects listed in the governmental announcements. The index lists objects in the time sequence of launchings. It is frequently updated and supplemented by published data from other sources. It is accessible on the Internet[14]. It provides an easy access to all information contained in the UN Register.

Quite recently, the Legal Subcommittee of COPUOS recognized that the practice of States and international organizations in registering space objects on the register is widely divergent[15]. It reached consensus on adopting a four-year working plan (2004-2007) to examine the practice of registering with a view to identifying common elements[16].

In our opinion, the practice of registering space objects should go beyond identification of common elements. It should provide a compilation of authoritative information on space objects and establish links between

- **the registration of space objects in compliance with the Registration Convention,**
- **the ITU registration of space radio stations, and**
- **National Registers of space objects.**

To attain that aim, the registration should be guided by the following principles:

Completeness of registrations

The present UN Register, i.e. the set of governmental launching announcements, is rather incomplete[17]. There are many omissions to register by several launching entities. The problem could be removed by making the registration obligatory for all launching entities. Moreover, the **OOSA should be put in charge of following the completeness of registrations,** as part of their work on keeping the UN Register and on updating the Online Index. In case of a possible omission, the OOSA should be obliged to draw the attention of the respective launching entity to the obligation of registering.

Another problem is in the small number of States being parties to the Registration Convention. The yearly exhortation by the General Assembly to accede to the Registration Convention have not yet produced a massive response.

Some international organizations, such as Intelsat, do not register **by intention**. The reasons why prestigious organizations avoid registering their spacecraft should be examined and possible obstacles removed.

Any legal instrument dealing with the Management of Space Traffic would make sense only if all, or at least an overwhelming majority, of space users participated.

Fixed deadline for submitting registrations

Registrations have to be effected at a **fixed time** related to launch. The present wording in the Registration Convention, namely *registering as soon as practicable,* means that no deadline for registration has been set. Indeed, States have the information on a successful launch within hours, yet they submit their announcements within weeks, months or years after launch, as the case may be.

The preferable solution would be to submit announcements at a fixed time **before launch**. Launching into space has become a routine activity, in spite of highly complex technology. It should be known what is in space and what will go into space in the near future, whether from the ground, or from the middle of the ocean, or from an aircraft. The information is of particular importance to all operators of spacecraft.

Launching announcements are submitted in accordance with diplomatic protocol, of necessity requiring some delays. The possibility should be considered to make use of electronic submission of the basic information for insertion into the UN/OOSA Online Index, preceding the diplomatic note.

Obligatory content of announcements of registrations.

The following data and information should be obligatory:

International system of designations. Spacecraft can best be identified by the International System of Designations introduced by COSPAR in 1958. It is being systematically used by the scientific community and by some states in the launching announcements. It assigns a unique symbol to each man-made object in space. Its value would be increased if used by all launching entities.

National name or designation of spacecraft corresponding to the entries in National Registers.

Date and location of launch, as already required by the Registration Convention.

Shape, size and mass are not obligatory under the Registration Convention but should be included because they provide useful information on spacecraft, in particular for computation of lifetime.

Specific function. The "general function" required by the Registration Convention is sometimes given in very general terms, not providing any idea of the function of the spacecraft. The information should be at least as specific as it appears in the Aeronautics and Space Report of the President[18], e.g., GPS satellite, military satellite, solar science satellite, etc.

Approximate operational orbital data. Approximate **operational** altitudes of perigee and apogee, period and inclination, and nominal orbital position in case of geostationary satellites, would be more informative than the present practice of announcing initial orbital elements which are obsolete at the time of publication.

ITU names of space radio stations on board of the spacecraft and used frequency bands should appear in the announcements in order to provide a link between the ITU Master International Frequency Register and the UN Register or the OOSA Online Index. It would also provide information on active entries in the ITU Space Network List, thus partly alleviating the problem of the so called "paper satellites".

Manned spacecraft. Information should be provided on the crew, their functions, envisaged length of the mission and other relevant data.

Updating of information

All data should be **updated** after important changes, such as a change of function, a change of orbital position if the object is in the GEO, a change from an active satellite to space debris, and finally the decay.

National Registers

The Registration Convention requires in its Article II the establishment of **National Registers**. It would be helpful if National Registers were accessible on the Internet to provide an independent confirmation of data published in the UN Register and in the UN/OOSA Online Index.

The above steps would contribute to an orderly conduct of launchings and what is quite important, would make the governmental announcements of objects launched into outer space the most **authoritative** and **reliable** sources of information, as they deserve to be.

CONCLUSION

Traffic is regulated in detail on the road, on the sea, and in the air for obvious reasons of safety and efficiency. Outer space is an exception because of its wide expansion and a relatively small number of orbiting spacecraft. Things have changed with time, but regulation of traffic has not. It is still at the level of the 1960's. The only attempt at regulation was adopted in the GEO, not because of density of traffic but in order to avoid harmful interference of radio communications.

Time has come, however, to protect the valuable assets of some 500 to 600 active satellites from thousands of fast moving large debris and uncounted numbers of small but still dangerous fragments.

The task is enormous. Any meaningful regulation will require the use of extensive observations, and of instantaneous communications and computations.

Space debris should be legally defined as permanently non-functional objects in space and the role of owners to announce changes in functional status should be spelled out.

Registration of space objects should be complete and should be published at a fixed time. It should contain international designation, shape, size and mass of the object, specific function, approximate operational orbital data, ITU names and designations of space radio stations on board, and relevant data from National Registers.

Selected information has to be disseminated without delay to operators of spacecraft and to a certain degree to users of space applications.

Spacecraft will have to be designed with proper arrangements for disposal after termination of services.

A very difficult problem is posed by very large space debris already in orbit with no provision to shorten their lifetimes. Hopefully, methods for their removal will be found in the future. At present, **no legal barriers to the removal of unwanted objects should be created and those existing should be removed. Scientific studies of removal should be supported.**

The present paper has a modest aim to show that some traffic problems can be approached already now and that their solution will facilitate the systematic application of the principle of separation of traffic, of timely warning of close encounters and, in general, in keeping space fit for future uses.

NOTES

---

[1] L. Perek, Traffic Rules for Outer Space, Proc. 25th Coll. on the Law of Outer Space,AIAA, p.37, 1983,
L. Perek, Management of the Space Environment, Space Policy Vol. 10, No. 3, p. 189-198, 1994,
L. Perek, Maintaining the Space Environment, Liber Amicorum K.-H. Böckstiegel, Haymans, Köln, p.415-423, 2001,

L.Perek, Early concepts for Space Traffic, Proc. 45th Coll. on the Law of Outer Space, AIAA, p.496-503, 2002.

[2] Inter-Agency Space Debris Coordination Committee space debris mitigation guidelines, UN doc. A/AC.105/C.1/L.260 of 29 November 2002.

[3] Position Paper on Orbital Debris, International Academy of Astronautics, Updated edition, September 2001. First edition appeared in 1995

[4] Technical Report on Space Debris, adopted by the Scientific and Technical Subcommittee of the UN COPUOS, A/AC.105/720, New York, 1999.

[5] E.g., Orbiting Debris, A Space Environmental Problem, Background Paper, Congress of the United States, Office of Technology Assessment, OTA-BP-ISC-72, Washington, D.C., September 1990.

[6] E.g., McGraw-Hill Dictionary of Scientific and Technical Terms.

[7] ITU Radio Regulations, Technical Term S1.190.

[8] E.g. document A/57/20, Report of the COPUOS, UN, New York 2002.

[9] In the series of UN documents ST/SG/SER.E.

[10] Termination of activities of Freja was announced in document ST/SG/SER.E/318 of 21 January 1997, of Tele-X in ST/SG/SER.E/335 of 28 April 1998, and of Astrid 2 in ST/SG/SER.E/364 of 29 November 1999.

[11] UN document A/AC.105/803 of 23 December 2002 and Add.1 of 17 March 2003. BeppoSAX, 1996-027A, decayed on 30 April 2003.

[12] AIAA, UN/OOSA, CEAS, CASI Workshop on International Space Cooperation: Solving Global Problems, p. 37, recommendation 1, AIAA, Reston VA, 1999.

[13] UN document A/AC.105/C.2/L.246 of 1 April 2003 and A/AC.105/805 of 10 April 2003, para 147.

[14] Online Index of Objects Launched into Outer Space, at www.oosa.unvienna.org.

[15] UN document A/AC.105/C.2/L.241, of 26 March 2003.

[16] Report of the Legal Subcommittee, 42nd session, 2003, UN document A/AC.105/805, of 10 April 2003, para 136.

[17] L. Perek, The 1976 Registration Convention, Zeitschrift für Luft- und Weltraumrecht,47, p.351-360, 1998.

[18] Aeronautics and Space Report of the President, Fiscal Year 2000, NASA, NP-2000-10-259-HQ, p. 100-103, columns Mission Objectives and Remarks.

SOVEREIGNTY AND SPACE TRAFFIC MANAGEMENT

Álvaro Fabricio dos Santos
National Institute for Space Research (INPE)
São José dos Campos, SP, Brazil
alvaro@dir.inpe.br

ABSTRACT

The 1967 Outer Space Treaty states in its Article II that "*outer space including the Moon and other celestial bodies, is not subject to national appropriation by claim of sovereignty, by means of use or occupation, or by any other means*". However, nobody knows exactly the boundary between *air space,* in which States retain domain, and *outer space,* where the concept of sovereignty is not applicable. Discussions regarding delimitation of outer space occurred as early as the 1930's. Yet there are still no satisfactory legal definitions of boundaries. How is it possible to provide adequate and just space traffic management if the delimitation of outer space is unknown? This paper presents background data regarding the delimitation of outer space, summarizing the positions of some Latin American countries as presented before the COPUOS Legal Subcommittee to date, and shows the importance of establishing boundaries of national sovereignty to deal with future space shuttles and space planes already on the drawing board.

INTRODUCTION

According to the Brazilian *Veja* Magazine of May, 7th, 2003 (page 64), Jeffrey Bezos, the North American billionaire owner of the virtual bookstore "Amazon.com", has contracted former NASA physicists and scientists in order to design spacecrafts to take him to outer space. Three years ago he founded a space research company called "Blue Origin" to promote space tourism.

Another North American millionaire, Dennis Tito, who paid US$ 20 million to travel in a spacecraft, started this kind of tourism in 2001. Space tourism is already a reality. According to *Veja*, by 2021 many private companies will be able to take around 15,000 tourists per year to outer space.

"Space planes" are already on the drawing boards. One of them is the "Space Ship One" which is being developed by Scaled Composites Company. It was presented to the media in April, 2003. Another one is the "Space X" that has been financed by the South-African Elon Musk, owner of the Internet sales site "Ebay".

These projects show that there could be traffic congestion in space in the near future. In this context, space traffic management is necessary as soon as possible.

As it was pointed out by the author in another paper, "*while space exploration used to be the exclusive domain of individual governments, nowadays it generally involves large private companies, operating in different countries with different laws. Obviously, when the five international agreements were first issued, we could not predict such complexity involving governments and private business*"[1]. Hence, in space activities, the public interest has given way to commercial interests.

One of the pioneer thinkers in space traffic management is the Czech Professor Lubos Perek who states that "*traffic rules play an important role in three environments: on the road, on the sea and in the air. Although the conditions are quite specific for each of the environments, there are some general features. The main aim is to maintain safety of traffic by: a) establishing rules for avoidance of collisions; b) separating traffic in opposite directions; c) establishing specific rules on inactive vehicles; d) requiring specific rules on inactive vehicles; e) requiring proper identification of vehicles; f) requiring high technical equipment and qualification of personnel; and g) establishing rules on protection of environment*" [2].

These issues have been amply discussed in international forums, but none of these forums dealt with the question of exactly where these laws should apply. How is it possible to regulate space traffic if outer space boundaries are unknown? What is the boundary between air space and outer space?

BACKGROUND

The pioneers of space law were concerned about the need of establishing boundaries for outer space. In his book "Origins of International Space Law"[3], Dr. Stephen E. Doyle, Director of the International Institute of Space Law (IISL), provided some background in this regard. He observed "*at an air law conference held in Moscow in December 1926, a paper was presented by a senior official of the Soviet Aviation Ministry, V.A. Zarzar. The paper focused primarily on principles and pratices in the history of international air law but, Zarzar saw well the historical debates about the nature and the extent of national sovereignty in air space*". [4]

Dr. Doyle stated that the Czech Professor Vladimir Mandl wrote the world's first major work of substance on the entire field of space law in 1932. Doyle called attention to another Czech Professor, Vladimir Kopal, who wrote the Mandl's biography. Citing Mandl's monograph "The Law of Outer Space: a Problem of Space-Flight", Professor Kopal presented the concept of space law "*as an independent legal branch, based on specific instruments of space flight and governed by different principles than is the law of the sea or the law of the air (...) Mandl opposed the usual idea of sovereignty as applied to space without limits and asserted that sovereignty of States governs only the adjacent atmospheric space. Beyond the 'earth coastal spaces' a vast area begins which is 'free of the jurisdiction of any earthly State, coelum liberum*" [5]. This freedom may turn to chaos, however, if boundaries and space traffic laws are not established.

According to Dr. Doyle "*in Leningrad in 1933, at a conference dealing with air law, Y.A. Korovin presented a paper addressing issues arising from human penetration of the stratosphere and attendant legal problems*"[6]. In his paper, Korovin stated "*that there is an incontestable right in every nation to control its superjacent air space to take any action therein that is necessary to its preservation and at whatever altitude it may be necessary or useful"*[7].

The paper "The Challenge of the Space Ship" presented by Arthur C. Clarke to the British Interplanetary Society in London on October 5, 1946, is also mentioned in Doyle's book. At that time following the Second World War, soon-to-be world famous sci-fi writer Arthur Clarke stated that: "*I do not suggest that lawyers need start worrying immediately about the ownership of the Moon, but the ownership of space is already a matter of acute practical importance. If a country A fires experimental rockets across its neighbor B, what does B do? The air above B is admittedly its own property, but how far does that jurisdiction extend? There must be certainly some equivalent of the [maritime] three-mile limit, otherwise, in the course of a day, every country will lay claim to a large portion of the Universe"* [8].

Dr. Doyle cited many other authors each of whom stressed the importance of setting the limits for outer space. But the boundaries between air space and outer space have yet to be set. Lack of regulation makes it quite difficult to deal with space traffic.

DELIMITATION OF OUTER SPACE

The question of delimitation is a permanent item on the Legal Subcommittee of Committee on Peaceful Uses of Outer Space (COPUOS). In the 42nd Session of COPUOS Legal Subcommittee, held in April, 2003, the Delegate of the United States stated that this subject was nonsense because it had no practical application. In order to strengthen his position, he mentioned that the space shuttle was the only object which is able to fly both in outer and in air space. He said that the space shuttle did not fly over other States, but only over oceans and the North American territory during its re-entries into the Earth's atmosphere.

While this may be true at the moment, the former Soviet Union also had its space shuttle called "Buran" which was flown once in 1988. Buran de-orbited over the southern part of South Africa and flew over North Africa and re-entered Baikonur possibly over Turkey[9]. Although there was no formal complaint about this trajectory, there could have been serious legal diplomatic issues if it had crashed. Space traffic is increasing and the delimitation of outer space will be necessary sooner or later. China has already announced that its space shuttle will be able to travel in coming years.

There are several proposals to establish boundaries between air space and outer space. To start with, the boundary between air space might be considered the point at which Earth's atmosphere no longer exerts effects.

On March 28, 2003, during the 42nd Session of the COPUOS Legal Subcommittee, the Ukrainian Delegate Sergei A. Nekoda, stated "*substantial orbital space flight is possible only out of the dense atmospheric lays. Speeds of an atmospheric aircraft are dozens and hundreds of times less than of a spacecraft. These objective performance attributes lead us to the logical conclusion that definitely there is the border between air space and outer space, and this border has not only formal physical meaning.*[10]

In the sixties, the United States National Aeronautics and Space Administration (NASA) undertook the flight of the US Craft X-15 which performed flight at the altitude of 108 kilometers. NASA decided to qualify the pilots as astronauts when they reached 80 kilometers of altitude.

International practice adopts the altitude of 19,8 kilometers as the highest level for aviation activities. However, taking into account technological advancements, it would not be feasible to consider such an altitude as a parameter for the application of State sovereignty. Space planes will become a reality in the near future and they will probably fly in higher altitudes than 19,8 kilometers.

Some experts of the International Civil Aviation Organization (ICAO) consider that the upper limit of civil aviation interests is located at the altitude of 60 kilometers. According to them, activities undertaken above this altitude have space purposes.

The majority of space law experts consider that the lower boundaries to outer space are determined by the minimum perigee for artificial satellite movement, or 100 kilometers above sea level. Thus, States sovereignty might be extended up to this altitude.

Obviously, there are plenty of logical criteria that may be used to set the limits to outer space. What is missing is the will to do so.

AEROSPACE OBJECTS

Sovereignty is the strongest word to justify the delimitation of outer space. State has sovereignty over their air space and the objects traveling through it should be submitted to its national air law. The dual nature of modern air/space craft creates new legal questions. For instance, is a national air law applicable to a space shuttle during its re-entry into the Earth's atmosphere? If the answer is "no" it means that State sovereignty is not applicable to space objects even when they fly over foreign territories; it means that national speed patterns should not be followed; it means that a space object may do whatever it wants because there are no regulations for it when it is flying in air space; in short, it means that State sovereignty is not complete. On the other hand, if the answer is "yes", it means that a space shuttle may not fly over foreign territories without permission.

Currently, there is no clear definition for an aerospace object either in space law or in air law. The current distinction of crafts is no longer valid now that they navigate in both environments. They have dual status.

The first question of the questionnaire proposed by COPUOS Legal Subcommittee[11] is: "*Can an aerospace object be defined as an object which is capable both of traveling through outer space and of using its aerodynamic properties to remain in air space for a certain period of time?*" In this paper, for the sake of discussion, an aerospace object will be considered one that is able to fly either in outer space or in air space and to undertake activities in both environments[12]. Hence, space shuttles and space planes may be considered aerospace objects.

The existing legal framework needs to be improved to regulate activities undertaken by such objects. Otherwise there will not be an adequate international legal framework to deal with future legal issues.

If a space shuttle undertakes just an innocent passage through air space, it seems that it does not lose its characteristics as a spacecraft. In the same way, if a space plane undertakes just an innocent passage through outer space it need not be considered as a spacecraft.

Suppose that a space shuttle takes off from the Earth, taking dozens of tourists to the International Space Station. When the space shuttle is returning to the

Earth, it stops in different States in order to leave tourists in their respective countries. In this case, it seems that the space shuttle is functioning as an aircraft that is subject to air law.

Another hypothesis may be considered. If a space plane undertakes remote sensing activities during its flight in outer space it should be subject to the United Nations Space Treaties, because it is acting as a spacecraft.

Thus, the mission purpose is essential to establish what law will be applicable to an object. If an object undertakes just an innocent passage through an environment, it does not lose its status – spacecraft or aircraft; but if it undertakes activities in another environment, it should be subject to the laws of that environment.

This leads, once again, to the delicate question of space traffic management. The French Professor Armel Kerrest states that: "*The corner stone of the system misses: no State can exercise its sovereignty, there is no territorial State, no State able to exercise its territorial jurisdiction. Only personal jurisdiction applies. When there is only one territorial jurisdiction on a national territory, there is many personal jurisdictions applying on an international space if nationals or many States are using this space. When traffic management is concerned the problem is obvious. Who is going to make the rules, who is going to control their implementation, who is going to punish violations? As a matter of principle, if no special international regime is created, only personal jurisdiction applies. The State of nationality, registration, flag is the only competent State to set the rules, control and punish*"[13]. Since State sovereignty is not applicable in outer space, we must know, at least, the limits of air space, where national laws are valid.

SOME POSITIONS

Some Latin American countries have already sent their answers to the COPUOS Legal Subcommittee questionnaire. All of them are concerned about the lack of legal boundaries to deal with problems that aerospace objects may cause to States, properties, and people. The following countries are cited because their statements summarize the basic issues under debate.

Argentina's Position

In response to the questions as to whether there should be a new legal regime for aerospace objects, or merely special procedures within the existing regime, Argentina recommended further study. "*It would be necessary to conduct an in-depth study into the necessity of elaborating a new regime for such objects, since advances in aerospace technology may mean that in the future a specific regime will need to be established that takes account of situations not provided for under current international air and space law*" [14].

Chile's Position

Chile is concerned about the matter of innocent passage. This is one of the answers from Chile to the questionnaire: "*Although there are no provisions currently in effect which specifically regulate aerospace flights at the stage of entry into national air space, we feel that in the interests of the uniformity of the relevant legislation one should stay with the mission of the aerospace object and regulate the latter's innocent passage only*" [15]. In other words, Chile believes innocent passage through other countries' airspace needs regulation.

Colombia's Position

Colombia considers that the lack of regulation makes it difficult to deal with problems that may be caused by aerospace objects. "*The aerospace object should have a single legal designation, subject to special provisions determining the applicable regime, especially in view of the impossibility of specifying precisely where air space and outer space begin and end respectively, a problem which has made it difficult to reach a consensus on the criteria to be adopted in defining aerospace objects. Consequently, applying either air law or space law depending on the type of space crossed by the trajectory of the aerospace object would cause problems. Our preference is therefore for the second option of applying either one regime or the other throughout the entire flight, according to its destination*" [16].

Mexico's Position

Mexico states that the delimitation of outer space is necessary, especially to regulate activities undertaken by aerospace objects. In its answer to the questionnaire, Mexico emphasized that "*the particular aspects involved* [to define what law is applicable to aerospace objects] *should be worked out, but the relevant international legal regime should apply in air space, and the possibility should be considered of establishing a single law for aerospace objects in which the delimitation of air space is taken into account*" [17].

Peru's Position

Peru goes straight to the point of sovereignty. It stressed that "*because of ongoing advances in technology, situations could arise that are not provided for in the current air and space regimes. This should be taken into account by the creation of a special regime covering new situations and clarifying their legal status, with allowance for the territorial sovereignty of States*" [18].

Summary

According to the positions from the Latin American countries, delimitation of outer space, States sovereignty, and law regime applicable to aerospace objects are important issues to be solved.

Brazil has not yet sent its answers to the COPUOS Legal Subcommittee. Nevertheless, the Brazilian Society of Aerospace Law (SBDA)[19], a non-governmental entity, established a Work Group in 2002 to study the questions and to propose answers to the COPUOS questionnaire. SBDA's Work Group concluded that differences between air space law and outer space law are fundamental and that the existing legal framework should therefore be improved to deal with future problems. The Brazilian Ministry of Foreign Affairs is analyzing the answers proposed by SBDA in order to confirm if they are consistent with national interests. Brazil should send its answers to the COPUOS Legal Subcommittee before the end of 2003.

CONCLUSIONS

The Brazilian Professor José Monserrat Filho states that some measures are necessary to deal with space traffic management, such as: "*a) a new kind of international co-operation as deep and confident as we do not have yet; b) a complex and competent international system (network) with highly qualified international teams and state of the art hardware to fulfill all involved tasks; c) global space traffic management institutionally established*". He emphasizes, "*Without a permanent, efficient and self-sufficient institutional framework, true global space traffic management seems to be impracticable*"[20].

As it has been seen, beside the measures mentioned by Professor Monserrat, there is the need to delimitate outer space. Many legal aspects are closely related with such a definition, such as, applicable law, innocent flight, and speed patterns among others.

To deal with future legal matters one question has to be answered as soon as possible: what is the boundary of the State sovereignty? Without this answer we do not know what law is applicable: air law or space law.

Some countries consider that delimitation of outer space is not necessary because it has no current practical effects. However, it is important to note that a legislator has to think in advance; he should keep alert to the needs of mankind. If there is no law to regulate a situation it means that the legislator has not done his work well. Remember that at the time when the 1967 Outer Space Treaty was written, the presence of private companies in space activities was yet unknown; militarized space was not a threat. Nevertheless, legislators were sensible enough to foresee these and other aspects and to elaborate a Treaty that keeps working.

Space traffic has increased and absence of law definitely does not protect the interests of mankind. The COPUOS Legal Subcommittee, the International Institute of Space Law (IISL), and other specialized organizations should propose rules to delimitate outer space and to manage space traffic.

References

---

[1] See author's paper "Brazil and the Registration Convention", Proceedings of the Forty-Fourth Colloquium on the Law of Outer Space, published by AIAA, pages 78-86.

[2] In its article "Early Concepts for Space Traffic" presented in the IISL/ECSL Symposium on Prospects for Space Traffic Management on occasion of the 41st Session of the COPUOS Legal Subcommittee, in Vienna/Austria, on 2 April 2002.

[3] Published by Univelt, Incorporated, San Diego, California – first printing 2002.

[4] Op. cit., pages 1-2.

[5] Kopal, V. "Vladimir Mandl: Founding Writer on Space Law" quoted by Stephen E. Doyle (op. cit. page 8).

[6] Op. cit. page 10.

[7] Op. cit. page 13.

[8] Op. cit. page 16.

[9] Dudar, E.N., "Flight Dynamics Analysis of Aerospace System with Subsonic Carrier Plane", Russian/Ukrainian/ German Symposium on Space Transportation and Propulsion, DGLR Bericht, 26-28 May 1993.

[10] Negoda, Sergei A. "Proposals on Definition of the Border Between Air space and Outer Space".

[11] See document prepared by Office of Outer Space Affairs (OOSA) reference A/AC.105/635 (www.oosa.unvienna.org).

[12] The Space Law Work Group of the Brazilian Society of Aerospace Law (SBDA) proposed this definition.

[13] In its article "Space Traffic Management: Comparative Legal Aspects" presented in the IISL/ECSL Symposium on Prospects for Space Traffic Management on occasion of the 41st Session of the COPUOS Legal Subcommittee, in Vienna/Austria, on 2 April 2002.

[14] See document prepared by OOSA reference A/AC.105/635/Add.4. pages 5 and 6.

[15] See document prepared by OOSA reference A/AC.105/635/Add.3 page 5.

[16] See document prepared by OOSA reference A/AC.105/635/Add.5 page 5.

[17] See document prepared by OOSA reference A/AC.105/635 page 8.

[18] See document prepared by OOSA reference A/AC.105/635/Add.9 page 4.

[19] "www.sbda.org.br"

[20] In his paper "Space Traffic Management: Comparative Institutional Aspects" presented in the IISL/ECSL Symposium on Prospects for Space Traffic Management on occasion of the 41st Session of the COPUOS Legal Subcommittee, in Vienna/Austria, on 2 April 2002.

ASTROREGS – THE'RULES OF THE ROAD' IN OUTER SPACE

Jacob Zissu
Catholic University of America
Columbus School of Law
Washington, D.C.
jrzissu@hotmail.com

Abstract

Space travel has evolved greatly over the past five decades. From Sputnik to the Space Shuttle, from lunar landings to Mars, man's entry into space has come so far, and yet, in many respects, our use of space has just begun. One thing has proved constant - objects in space are becoming more numerous. As space travel comes of age, accident-free transportation will require the creation of common deconfliction measures. Will spacefarers of the future look to their Astronomical Collision Avoidance Regulations (ASTROREGS), for guidance?

This paper will provide a context for the creation of space navigation rules and will advance proposals for 'Rules of the Road' that deal specifically with anticipated encounters in space. Based on the precedents of transportation history, specifically road, maritime, and aviation modes, the existing norms and regulations have been expanded to accommodate the unique properties of outer space and the speed necessary for efficient inter-planetary travel.

Concurrently, in the fields of admiralty or insurance law, the existence of agreed-to navigational rules, and the deviation from those rules, have been used to determine fault. It stands to reason that with an increase in space transportation, the establishment of a standard method of determining fault will be a necessity for future space travelers as well.

Space's Unique Properties And The Dangers Of Collision

The unique properties of outer space and the speed necessary for efficient inter-planetary travel dramatically increase both the probability of, and the catastrophic consequences of, collisions.

Non-spacefarers frequently think of acceleration in terms of 'forward' or 'backward.' Acceleration along a single plane, without any outside forces, is regarded as one-dimensional travel. However, even one-dimensional travel has two-dimensional factors. The second dimension of travel, perpendicular to the first dimension, would be 'up' and 'down.' On Earth, this is normally associated with a force we take for granted, because it is, literally, right beneath our feet – gravity. We take gravity for granted because on the road and on the sea, gravity is relatively constant, keeping us at surface level. In collision avoidance on the land or sea, our most frequent concerns are with a third dimension of travel: direction. Thus, seafarers frequently avoid collisions by speeding up or slowing down, and by turning left or right. Similarly, in the air, a more true three-dimensional collision avoidance model, collisions are frequently avoided by increasing/decreasing altitude or turning left/right. (These maneuvers are preferred to speeding up/slowing down for reasons of aerodynamic stability.)

The three dimensions of travel described above are transformed in the context of space travel. To begin with, there is no absolute scientific line between the end of the Earth's atmosphere and the beginning of true space. Second, in true space there is virtually no friction – no air or water with which to react. Third, the further one travels from a given planet, the lower the immediate gravitational pull of that planet.

Gravity or, more correctly, *gravities* found in space take on a new significance. For example, at launch, the Space Shuttle will accelerate from 0-17,500 miles per hour in order to break free of the Earth's atmosphere.[1] Once in space, a craft may use a planet's gravity to further increase its own speed. The spacecraft Galileo first used the Earth as a 'slingshot' to reach a velocity of 20,250 mph. As Galileo encountered the gravitational pull of Io, one of Jupiter's moons, it was traveling at a velocity of 54,225 mph. Jupiter's enormous gravity force accelerated Galileo to its high speed.

It should be noted, however, that even at these incredibly hazardous speeds, interplanetary voyages currently take years to accomplish.[2] Current space flight operations, both manned and unmanned, often include trajectory changes or orbit maneuvers[3] to avoid the 2613 satellites, 90 space probes and 6079 debris objects currently estimated to be in orbit around Earth.[4]

The conduct of ordinary space transit must include procedures or 'Rules of the Road,' in order to avoid collisions with other spacecraft in transit, wherever such encounters may occur. Given the high speeds involved in interstellar travel, the expansion of commercial, scientific and military operations in space, and the acknowledged tendency for high-density traffic to clog certain space highways, the available distance and time within which a spacefarer may be able to react to a potential collision is significantly diminished. Standard evasion procedures are already needed to assist modern day spacefarers, and they will be increasingly necessary to avoid collisions in the coming years.

Current international law "provides no 'Rules of the Road' for outer space and does not determine which spacecraft has the right of way."[5] Furthermore, "because there are no rules as to who has the right of way, collisions may result in both parties 'being in the right.'"[6] "To create order in space activity, states must know what rules apply to them and where those rules apply ... In the future, more numerous and larger missions may affect each other and space planners must know what rules apply to them in order to avoid collisions and other possible harmful effects on the missions of other countries."[7]

Today the only traffic rules in space are those that govern the situating of satellites in geo-stationary orbit. These orbital "slots" are created and agreed to at the International Telecommunications Union.[8] There exist no specific international air traffic regulations especially tailored to space transportation systems. "In order to safeguard the re-entry of space transportation systems to Earth, air traffic lawyers and space lawyers will have to eliminate incompatibilities between their two regimes. Such efforts must take into account the legitimate rights and interests of States affected by any compromise, particularly as they pertain to security interests of international aviation."[9]

"The legal regimes used in regulating collisions of ships at sea and aircraft in flight provide the most relevant model allocating liability between spacecraft in flight. Differing degrees of conformity to an elaborate system of safety rules and regulations largely determine liability ... When rules of space navigation and traffic control are established through custom or explicit agreement, failure to comply with any such rules if such failure has caused or contributed to collision, will presumably be regarded as constituting actionable 'fault.'"[10]

The Law of the Sea

On the sea, frictional forces are different than those found on land. It takes longer to stop and greater force to change direction. Additionally, commercial sea-going craft tend to be more massive and thus even at slower speeds can create greater damage. A punctured hull and gradual loss of buoyancy can send even the most massive craft to the bottom of the sea. Thus, the dangers of collision at sea are catastrophic when compared to those on land.

Recognizing this, as early as 1910, the Convention for the Unification of Certain Rules of Law with respect to Collisions between Vessels was held in Brussels. By 1972, the nations of the world, recognizing the unique dangers of sea travel, signed the International Regulations for Prevention of Collisions at Sea (COLREGS). The COLREGS provide binding comprehensive regulations for the prevention of collisions on the water.[11]

Entered into force in 1977, the regulations were intended to standardize actions taken to avoid collision that had previously been established by custom and treaties:

Risk of Collision

(a) Every vessel shall use all available means appropriate to the prevailing circumstances and conditions to determine if risk of collision exists. If there is any doubt such risk shall be deemed to exist.

(b) Proper use shall be made of radar equipment if fitted and operational, including long-range scanning to obtain early warning of risk of collision and radar plotting or equivalent systematic observation of detected objects.

(c) Assumptions shall not be made on the basis of scanty information, especially scanty radar information.

(d) In determining if risk of collision exists the following considerations shall be among those taken into account:

- *(i) Such risk shall be deemed to exist if the compass bearing of an approaching vessel does not appreciably change;*
- *(ii) Such risk may sometimes exist even when an appreciable bearing change is evident, particularly when approaching a very large vessel or a tow or when approaching a vessel at close range.*

Action to Avoid Collision

(a)Any action taken to avoid collision shall, if the circumstances of the case admit, be positive, made in ample time and with due regard to the observance of good seamanship.

(b) Any alteration of course and/or speed to avoid collision shall, if the circumstances of the case admit be large enough to be readily apparent to another vessel observing visually or by radar;

a succession of small alterations of course and/or speed shall be avoided.

(c) If there is sufficient sea room, alteration of course alone may be the most effective action to avoid a close-quarters situation provided that it is made in good time, is substantial and does not result in another close-quarters situation.

(d) Action taken to avoid collision with another vessel shall be such as to result in passing at a safe distance. The effectiveness of the action shall be carefully checked until the other vessel is finally past and clear.

(e) If necessary to avoid collision or allow more time to assess the situation, a vessel may slacken her speed or take all way off by stopping or reversing her means of propulsion.

(f)

- *(i) A vessel which, by any of these rules, is required not to impede the passage or safe passage of another vessel shall when required by the circumstances of the case, take early action to allow sufficient sea room for the safe passage of the other vessel*
- *(ii) A vessel required not to impede the passage or safe passage of another vessel is not relieved of this obligation if approaching the other vessel so as to involve risk of collision and shall, when taking action, have full regard to the action which may be required by the rules of this part.*
- *(iii) A vessel the passage of which is not to be impeded remains fully obliged to comply with the rules of this part when the two vessels are approaching one another so as to involve risk of collision.*

Overtaking

(a) Notwithstanding anything contained in the Rules of Part B, Sections I and II, any vessel overtaking any other shall keep out of the way of the vessel being overtaken.

(b) A vessel shall be deemed to be overtaking when coming up with a another vessel from a direction more than 22.5 degrees abaft her beam, that is, in such a position with reference to the vessel she is overtaking, that at night she would be able to see only the stern light of that vessel but neither of her sidelights.

(c) When a vessel is in any doubt as to whether she is overtaking another, she shall assume that this is the case and act accordingly.

(d) Any subsequent alteration of the bearing between the two vessels shall not make the overtaking vessel a crossing vessel within the meaning of these Rules or relieve her of the duty of keeping clear of the overtaken vessel until she is finally past and clear.

Head-on Situation

(a) When two power-driven vessels are meeting on reciprocal or nearly reciprocal courses so as to involve risk of collision each shall alter her course to starboard so that each shall pass on the port side of the other.

(b) Such a situation shall be deemed to exist when a vessel sees the other ahead or nearly ahead and by night she could see the masthead lights in line or nearly in line and/or both sidelights and by day she observes the corresponding aspect of the other vessel.

(c) When a vessel is in any doubt as to whether such a situation exists she shall assume that it does exist and act accordingly.

Crossing Situation

When two power-driven vessels are crossing so as to involve risk of collision, the vessel which has the other on her own starboard side shall keep out of the way and shall, if the circumstances of the case admit, avoid crossing ahead of the other vessel.

Action by Give-way Vessel

Every vessel which is directed to keep out of the way of another vessel shall, so far as possible, take early and substantial action to keep well clear.

Action by Stand-on Vessel

(a)

- *(i) Where one of two vessels is to keep out of the way of the other shall keep her course and speed.*
- *(ii) The latter vessel may however take action to avoid collision by her maneuver alone, as soon as it becomes apparent to her that the vessel required to keep out of the way is not taking appropriate action in accordance with these Rules.*

(b) When, from any cause, the vessel required to keep her course and speed finds herself so close that collision cannot be avoided by the action of the give-way vessel alone, she shall take such action as will best aid to avoid collision.

(c) A power-driven vessel which takes action in a crossing situation in accordance with subparagraph (a)(ii) of this Rule to avoid collision with another power-driven vessel shall, if the circumstances of the case admit, not alter course to port for a vessel on her own port side.

(d) This Rule does not relieve the give-way vessel of her obligation to keep out of the way.[12]

The Law of the Air

The dangers of collision in the Earth's atmosphere are even more likely to result in fatality and complete destruction of the craft involved than those at sea. Aircraft are constructed of lighter and frequently more vulnerable materials than surface craft. This makes most aircraft very susceptible to damage. Additionally, because gravity is such a constant threat, an aircraft must always maintain the integrity of its lifting and control surfaces for aerodynamic purposes. Even the slightest damage can cause a loss of aerodynamic control.

"In 1943, the US initiated studies of ... civil aviation problems which, once more, confirmed the belief that they either were to be tackled on an international scale or it would not be possible to use [aviation] as one of the principal elements in the economic development of the world."[13] By 1944, a new organization, conceived in Chicago, had emerged. The International Civil Aviation Organization (ICAO)'s stated purpose is to develop the principles and techniques of international air navigation, and foster the planning and development of international air transport, to ensure the safe and orderly growth of international civil aviation throughout the world, to encourage the development of airways, airports, and air navigation facilities for international civil aviation, and to promote safety of flight in international air navigation.[14]

The ICAO has recognized that in order to ensure safety, regularity and efficiency of international civil aviation operations, international standardization is essential in all matters affecting them, that is, all matters in the operation of aircraft, aircraft airworthiness and the numerous facilities and services required in their support such as aerodromes, telecommunications, navigation aids, meteorology, air traffic services, search and rescue, aeronautical information services and aeronautical charts. A common understanding between the countries of the world on these matters is absolutely necessary.[15]

The ICAO Rules, also known as the "Chicago rules," appear below:

Operating near other aircraft

(a) No person may operate an aircraft so close to another aircraft as to create a collision hazard.
(b) No person may operate an aircraft in formation flight except by arrangement with the pilot in command of each aircraft in the formation.
(c) No person may operate an aircraft, carrying passengers for hire, in formation flight.

Right-of-way rules (Except water operations)

(a) Inapplicability. This section does not apply to the operation of an aircraft on water.
(b) General. When weather conditions permit, regardless of whether an operation is conducted under instrument flight rules or visual flight rules, vigilance shall be maintained by each person operating an aircraft so as to see and avoid other aircraft. When a rule of this section gives another aircraft the right-of-way, the pilot shall give way to that aircraft and may not pass over, under, or ahead of it unless well clear.
(c) In distress. An aircraft in distress has the right-of-way over all other air traffic.
(d) Converging. When aircraft of the same category are converging at approximately the same altitude (except head-on, or nearly so), the aircraft to the other's right has the right-of-way. If the aircraft are of different categories --
(1) A balloon has the right-of-way over any other category of aircraft;
(2) A glider has the right-of-way over an airship, airplane, or rotorcraft; and
(3) An airship has the right-of-way over an airplane or rotorcraft.
However, an aircraft towing or refueling other aircraft has the right-of-way over all other engine-driven aircraft.
(e) Approaching head-on. When aircraft are approaching each other head-on, or nearly so, each pilot of each aircraft shall alter course to the right.
(f) Overtaking. Each aircraft that is being overtaken has the right-of-way and each pilot of an overtaking aircraft shall alter course to the right to pass well clear.
(g) Landing. Aircraft, while on final approach to land or while landing, have the right-of-way over other aircraft in flight or operating on the surface, except that they shall not take advantage of this rule to force an aircraft off the runway surface which has already landed and is attempting to make way for an aircraft on final approach. When two or more aircraft are approaching an airport for the purpose of landing, the aircraft at the lower altitude has the right-of-way, but it shall not take advantage of this rule to cut in front of another which is on final approach to land or to overtake that aircraft.

In addition, altitude is the preferred method of separation, since aircraft maintaining different altitudes cannot collide no matter what their routes may be. The usual minimum is 1000 feet of vertical separation, though this is increased to as much as 5000 feet at very high altitudes.[16]

The Law of Space

With a legacy of codified collision avoidance regulations on the sea and in the air, it could be presumed that at the outset of the space age, a similar approach to standardized procedures should naturally follow. And yet, the progress of multinational agreement on space issues does not appear to have kept pace with the progress made in outer space.

It was not until 1967, a decade after the launch of Sputnik, that the United Nations Outer Space Committee announced the first agreement on a treaty governing Exploration And Use Of Outer Space, The Moon And Other Celestial Bodies.[17] The 1967 Space Treaty was followed in 1968 with an agreement on the rescue of astronauts in space, and in 1972, with a Convention on International Liability for Damage Caused by Space Objects.[18]

According to the 1972 Convention, a launching State is deemed liable for damage due to its faults in space. No means however, were provided to determine fault for an event occurring in space, (i.e., other than at the surface of the Earth or to aircraft in flight).[19]

The 1972 Convention states, in pertinent part:

Taking into consideration that, notwithstanding the precautionary measures to be taken by States and intergovernmental organizations involved in the launching of space objects, damage may on occasion be caused by such objects...

Recognizing the need to elaborate effective international rules and procedures concerning liability for damage caused by space objects and to ensure, in particular, the prompt payment under the terms of this Convention of a full and equitable measure of compensation to victims of such damage...

Have agreed on the following:

Article I

The term "damage" means loss of life, personal injury, or other impairment of health; or loss of or damage to property of States or of persons, natural or juridical, or property of international intergovernmental organizations.

Article II

A launching state shall be absolutely liable to pay compensation for damage caused by its space object on the surface of the Earth or to aircraft in flight.

Article III

In the event of damage being caused elsewhere than on the surface of the Earth to a space object of one launching State or to persons or property on board such a space object by a space object of another launching state, the latter shall be liable only if such damage is due to its fault or the fault of persons for whom it is responsible.

Article IV

1. *In the event of damage being caused elsewhere than on the surface of the Earth to a space object of one launching State or to persons or property on board such a space object by a space object of another launching state, and of damage thereby being caused to a third State or to its natural or juridical persons, the first two states shall be jointly and severably liable to the third State, to the extent indicated by the following:*
2. *... the burden of compensation for the damage shall be apportioned between the first two States in accordance with the extent to which they were at fault.*

Article VI

2. *No exoneration whatever shall be granted in cases where the damage has resulted from the activities conducted by a launching State which are not in conformity with international law including, in particular, the Charter of the United Nations and the Treaty on Principles Governing the Activities of States in the Exploration and Use of Outer Space, including the Moon and Other Celestial Bodies.*

Article IX

A claim for compensation for damage may be presented to a launching State not later than one year following the date of the occurrence of the damage or the identification of the launching State which is liable

Article X

2. *If however, a State does not know of the occurrence of the damage or has not been able to identify the launching State which is liable, it may present a claim within one year following the date on which it learned of the aforementioned facts; however, this period shall in no event exceed one year following the date on which the State could reasonably be expected to have learned of the facts through the exercise of due diligence.*

Article XI

2. *Nothing in this Convention shall prevent a state, or natural or juridical persons it might represent, from pursuing a claim in the courts or administrative tribunals or agencies of a launching state.*[20]

No subsequent multinational agreements have promulgated rules that would lead to determinations of fault for a collision in space.

"The legal regimes used in regulating collisions of ships at sea and aircraft in flight provide the most relevant model allocating liability between spacecraft in flight. Differing degrees of conformity to an elaborate system of safety rules and regulations largely determine liability ... When rules of space navigation and traffic control are established through custom or explicit agreement, failure to comply with any such rules if such failure has caused or contributed to collision, will presumably be regarded as constituting actionable 'fault.'"[21]

Through regulations, spacefarers can expect to have a reasonable degree of predictability in avoiding other spacecraft, and grounds for legal recourse should damage occur. Spacefarers should also have confidence that their own preventive decisions are in conformity with those of their fellow spacefarers, that there is a common understanding of the situation, and that they do not actually increase the danger or complicate situations further.

Dr. Lubos Perek, in his paper Early Concepts for Space Traffic, has discussed some of these ideals with regard to establishing rules for avoidance of collisions: "Knowledge of traffic rules enables drivers, helmsmen, or pilots to anticipate the actions of their counterparts and to choose the optimal action. Many rules exist in the 'Rules of the Road,' such as rules on right of way, priority at crossings, etc."[22]

As an initial proposition, "A State owes at all times a duty to protect other States against injurious acts by individuals from within its jurisdiction"[23] When one considers that launching states already have the duty to register and license spacecraft, it is only natural that a launching state should have a reasonable expectation of what capabilities and norms its spacecraft must have to avoid other states' craft. Thus, the U.S. Code delineates domestic responsibility to "regulate commercial space transportation industry, only to the extent to ensure compliance with international obligations of the United States and to protect the public and safety, safety of property."[24]

A New Dimension Of Collision Avoidance Thinking

Some "space traffic" rules are already in force, and what's more, are followed by all space users. The International Telecommunication Union has been applying traffic rules to geostationary satellites for a long time, almost since the beginning of the use of the orbital belt.[25] Limited avoidance maneuvers have been developed for use in particular in geostationary orbit. [26]

Collisions in space are unlike those at sea or within the Earth's atmosphere. They involve movement and positioning that is not oriented exclusively to the Earth. Thus, for example, it is recognized that due to the differences between the legal regimes of air and space law and the differences between the activities conducted in air and space, "the wholesale adoption of aviation law to the space environment is not a viable alternative."[27] However, modeling space traffic laws as closely as possible to existing ICAO regulations would make the transition to space travel easier in its formative years.

Looking at the COLREGS and ICAO as a foundation, we can propose a reasonable set of ASTROREGS, incorporating the special considerations of space travel. The "Chicago Rules," to a certain extent, resemble the COLREGS, and since both have been effective in regulating transportation, they set a strong precedent (just as the Antarctica Treaty concerning state claims of ownership was used to draft the Outer Space Treaty).[28] "Marine traffic is regulated by special International Regulations for Preventing Collisions at Sea. For the prevention of collisions in the air, sophisticated practices and technical elements have been introduced."[29] Space is the next venue for regulation.

Space law, however, must take into account an added 'dimension,' of travel that is unique to space itself. Currently all of our dimensional analysis is based on a common reference of "up"– that opposite the Earth's gravitational pull. We drive our cars sitting upright. We sail our ships standing with our feet towards the sea. Even in flight, we base our direction in reference to the Earth's horizon – presumed to be parallel, if not close to parallel, to our own perpendicular stance tangential to Earth.

Space is technically a 3-dimensional environment. But, while all of the current 'Rules of the Road' are based on gravity (perpendicular to the tangent of the Earth), in space there is either no gravity or multiple gravities, so that there exists no easy common reference for which dimension is which. In outer space, the lack of gravity or multiple forces of gravity will require a variation of these rules to establish commonality. This fourth-dimension - orientation - will be the principle change in adapting ICAO and COLREGS to ASTROREGS.

If a spacecraft is not facing the Earth it will turn 'right' the same way that a spacecraft facing the Earth will turn to its 'right.' Without a common gravity orientation, each may turn towards the other, even if intending to turn away. Additionally, some spacecraft may purposefully rotate by design (such as those using centripetal forces to simulate gravity or those who seek to avoid uneven radiation by a solar body), and thus 'right' is an ever-changing proposition with regards to other craft.

We currently orient our third dimension in terms of North and South, East and West. Earth's magnetic poles enabled early navigational tools based on magnetism to shape the nature of its common orientation. As primitive as these tools seem in the age of space travel, it is proposed that the concept of polar orientation can still serve a very significant purpose, as follows:

All planets rotate in one direction - using primitive terms: 'clockwise' or 'counter-clockwise.' Whichever way a planet is spinning, motion cannot be in more than one direction simultaneously. We can use this rotation as a basis to establish each planet's 'North' regardless of any intrinsic magnetic properties. Using Earth as the model, all planets will be judged to rotate counter clockwise. Based on a counter clockwise rotation, the top pole shall be north, and the bottom pole shall be south. This will be termed "polar orientation."

Concepts of "Meeting," "Crossing" and "Overtaking" have been refined to meet the added dimensions of space travel as well. Overtaking is currently defined by maritime regulations as being 22.5 degrees abaft of the beam. Since the beam of a craft in space would encompass 365 degrees in a plane perpendicular to the forward motion of travel, and because a space craft's direction of travel may not always be the same as its thrust orientation, the most logical determination of "Overtaking" would be the equivalent of 22.5 degrees abaft of that beam. In simpler terms, this would be a cone measuring 67 degrees opening opposite the direction of travel of the craft.

<u>Some Additional Adaptations from Air and Sea Laws:</u>

In addition to the 'Rules of the Road' proposals found at the end of this paper, it is submitted that additional matters found in air and sea regulations should be included in special rules complementing the ASTROGREGS:

1. <u>Jurisdiction</u>. Both the COLREGS and ICAO regulations define their jurisdiction. Although there is no current consensus, custom, or explicit agreement on where the border lies between atmosphere and space, proposed regulations delineate that a local space 'authority' be charged with defining such matters. The same local space authority, should also be charged with the governance of areas with increased traffic such as planetary, moon, space station, or spaceports. Since the local authority would most likely be in the best position to determine prevailing conditions of weather, density of traffic, gravitational forces, magnetic forces, and radiation influences, the local authority should also be charged with charting, defining, and maintaining navigational references, special transit lanes, and orbital separation schemes.

An example of such a local authority for our Earth and surrounding satellites might be an outcrop of the current United Nations organization. Outside the space-atmosphere border, the U.N. authority would promulgate the rules and regulations for near-Earth space travel. Inside the atmosphere, where travel requires different craft properties than used in space, the individual nations and spaceport authorities would promulgate their own regulations. Both inner and exo-atmospheric authorities would be expected to conform their rules as closely as possible to the ASTROREGS while fine-tuning the regulations to meet the circumstances of their varying areas.

2. Navigational Data Transmission. "More than any other environment, states that send objects into space require timely knowledge of positions and movements of other space objects ... Aircraft all over the world use relatively inexpensive equipment to serve the function of collision avoidance and traffic control. Given the advanced state of technology of space objects, the regime for outer space should also make use of electronic devices for these purposes."[30] Continuous automatic transmission of such positional and direction of travel data should be required. Authorities should promulgate reference points for effective interstellar transit. Additionally, prioritization of reference points within a set of special rules would assist computers in relaying their positions to other craft by automatic and continuous transmission.

3. Orbits Defined. On Earth, designated orbits are already in existence by virtue of efficiency and the peculiar gravitational forces of this planet. Geostationary satellites currently occupy a ring approximately 35,786 kilometers (19,323 nautical miles or 22,241 statute miles) above the Earth's surface.[31] To stay over the same spot on Earth, a geostationary satellite also has to be nearly directly above the equator. Other proposed orbits to be defined might be those of a Disposal Orbit – for space debris near a planet or a 'Space Anchorage,' where vessels too large to reenter a planet's atmosphere would position themselves while shuttlecraft carry goods or passengers to the surface.[32]

4. Pollution. Finally, with or without preemptive destruction, pollution abatement must be addressed.[33] In fulfilling its role of fostering all aspects of international civil aeronautics, the [ICAO] Organization is giving special attention to the impact that civil aviation has on the environment, with the aim of ensuring maximum compatibility between safe and orderly development of civil aviation and the preservation and enhancement of a wholesome human environment.[34] The Environmental Protection Agency regulates discharge of waste at sea. So, too, should a local space authority regulate the creation and disposal of space debris.

ASTROREGS
Astronomical Collision Avoidance Regulations

I. General

A. These rules shall apply to all craft in space and transiting atmospheres bordered by space.

B. Nothing in these rules shall interfere with the operation of special rules made by appropriate Galaxial, Planetary, and Satellite authorities for spaceports and space harbors. Such special rules shall conform as closely as possible to these rules.

C. Local authorities shall promulgate special rules to include, but not limited to:

(i) Explicit delineation of distance from a planet's surface at which the atmosphere/space border exists.

(ii) Charting, defining, and maintaining large objects, naturally occurring satellites, planets, and other navigational references.

(iii) Pollution abatement measures.

D. Traffic separation schemes may be adopted by the authority for the purposes of these rules.

E. Orbital separation schemes may be adopted by the authority for the purposes of these rules.

II. Responsibility

A. Nothing in these rules shall exonerate any craft, or the owner, master, crew or state of origin thereof, from the consequences of any neglect to comply with these rules or to the neglect of any precaution which may be required by the ordinary practice of space farers, or by the special circumstances of the case.

B. In construing and complying with these rules, due regard shall be had to all dangers of navigation and collision and to any special circumstances, including the limitations of the craft involved which may make a departure from these rules necessary to avoid immediate danger.

III. General Definitions

For the purposes of these rules, except where the context otherwise requires:

A. The term "Space" means not on the surface of a planet or traveling in the atmosphere of a planet.

B. The term "Craft" includes both those with propulsion and not under command. The term "Craft" encompasses all manned vessels, satellites, stations or transport. The term "Craft" also means all unmanned man-made vessels, satellites, stations or transport in active use.

C. The term "Propulsion-driven" means any craft propelled by machine, chemical, pulse, sonic, anti-gravity, or magnetic device.

D. The term "Solar-driven" means any craft propelled solely by solar power, solar sail or other means dependent on the radiation of a star.

E. The term "Not under command" means a craft which through some exceptional circumstance is unable to maneuver as required by these rules and is therefore unable to keep out of the way of another craft.

F. The term "Restricted in ability to maneuver" means a craft which from the nature of its employment is restricted in ability to maneuver as required by these rules and is therefore unable to keep out of the way of another craft.
G. The term "Restricted detection ability" means any condition in which the detection of other craft or objects is restricted or hampered by forces not normally encountered, to include, but not limited to visual, magnetic, and solar radiation interference.
H. The term "Meeting" means approaching head-on or nearly head-on angles.
I. The term "Crossing" means approaching at any angle other than head-on or from 0-67 degrees in any direction opposite from the direction of travel of another craft.
J. The term "Overtaking" means approaching from 0-67 degrees in any direction opposite from the direction of travel of another craft.
K. The term "Object" encompasses all naturally occurring debris, meteors, and asteroids.
The term "Object" also means all unmanned man-made debris or satellites not in active use.
L. The term "Orbit" means circumnavigating a planet in space.
M. The term "Pole" means the axis on which a planet rotates. Rotation in a counter-clockwise direction indicates a Northern aspect. Rotation in a clockwise direction indicates a Southern aspect.

IV. Situational Awareness

Every craft shall at all times maintain geographic awareness of their own positions and the positions and directions of travel of other craft and objects by all navigational means available, to include, but not limited to visual, computerized radar/sonar/laser and beacon oriented means.

V. Safe Speed

Every craft shall at all times proceed at a safe speed so that it can take proper and effective action to avoid collision within a distance appropriate to the prevailing circumstances and conditions. In determining a safe speed the following factors should be among those taken into account:

(i) The current capability of detection
(ii) Traffic density including concentrations of not under command craft and space objects
(iii) The maneuverability of the craft with regard to stopping distance and turning ability in the prevailing conditions
(iv) The presence of background conditions that might obfuscate navigational awareness and ability; and
(v) The possibility that detection capability may not be adequate to detect small objects at an adequate range.

VI. Risk of Collision

A. Every craft shall use all available means appropriate to the prevailing circumstances and conditions to determine if risk of collision exists.
B. Assumptions shall not be made on the basis of scanty information.
C. If there is any doubt, risk of collision shall be deemed to exist.

VII. Action to Avoid Collision

A. Any action taken to avoid collision shall, if the circumstances of the case admit, be positive, made in ample time and with due regard to the observance of good seamanship
B. Any alteration of course and/or sped to avoid collision shall, if the circumstances of the case admit, be large enough to be readily apparent to another craft observing visually or by other means of detection. A succession of small alterations of course and/or speed should be avoided.
C. Action taken to avoid collision with another craft shall be such as to result in passing at a safe distance. The effectiveness of the action shall be carefully checked until the other craft is passed and clear.
D. If there is sufficient distance and time, craft may communicate intentions to alter course or speed via radio, light or any other means available to other craft, provided that the receiving craft receives, understands, and agrees to those intentions. The sending craft must receive confirmation of agreement from the receiving craft.
E. A 'give-way' craft which, by these rules is required not to impede the passage of another craft shall, when required by the circumstances of the case, take early action to allow sufficient room for the safe passage of the other craft.
F. A 'give-way' craft, shall not be relieved of its obligation if approaching the other craft so as to involve risk of collision, and shall when taking action, have full regard to the action which may be required by the rules of this part.
G. A 'stand-on' craft which, by these rules is not to be impeded, remains fully obliged to comply with the rules of this part when two craft are approaching one another so as to involve risk of collision.

VIII. Traffic Separation Schemes

A. This rule applies to traffic separation schemes adopted by the organization and does not relieve any craft of its obligation under any other rule.
B. A craft utilizing a traffic separation scheme shall:

(i) Proceed in the appropriate traffic lane in the general direction of traffic flow for that lane.
(ii) So far as practicable keep clear of the traffic separation line or separation zone
(iii) Normally join or leave a traffic lane at the termination of the lane, but when joining or leaving from either side, shall do so at as small of an angle to the general direction of traffic flow as practicable.

C. A craft shall, so far as practicable, avoid crossing traffic lane, but if obliged to do so shall cross on a heading as nearly as practicable at right angles to the general direction of traffic flow.
D. A craft other than crossing or joining shall not normally enter a separation zone or separation line except n cases of emergency to avoid immediate danger
E. A craft not using traffic separation scheme shall avoid it by as wide a margin as is practicable.

F. A craft restricted in ability to maneuver when engaged in an operation for the maintenance of safety of navigation in a traffic separation scheme is exempted from complying with this rule to the extent necessary to carry out the operation.

IX. Conduct Of Craft In Awareness Of One Another
All craft cognizant of other craft and objects shall determine whether they are:
A. Meeting: typically referred to as 'head-on.'
B. Crossing: at any angle other than from 0-67 degrees in any direction opposite from the direction of travel of another craft.
C. Overtaking: 0-67 degrees in any direction opposite from the direction of travel of another craft.

X. Meeting Head-on Situation
A. When two craft are meeting on reciprocal or nearly reciprocal courses so as to involve risk of collision, the craft closest to the North Pole of the closest planet shall turn towards the North Pole of such planet. The craft furthest from the North Pole shall turn away from the North Pole. If both craft are equidistant from the North Pole, the craft closest the South Pole shall turn towards the South Pole and the craft furthest from the South Pole shall turn away from the South Pole. If both craft are equidistant from both the South Pole and the North Pole, the craft traveling in the direction of the planet's rotation has the right of way. If both craft are traveling in the direction of the planet's rotation, an overtaking situation will be presumed to exist despite craft orientation vis-à-vis each other. In any event craft shall pass clear of each other.
B. Such a situation shall be deemed to exist when a craft observes the corresponding course of the other craft. When a craft is in any doubt as to whether such a situation exists it shall assume that it does exist and act accordingly.

XI. Crossing Situation
When two propulsion-driven craft are crossing so as to involve risk of collision, the craft closest to the North Pole of the closest planet shall turn towards the North Pole of such planet. The craft furthest from the North Pole shall turn away from the North Pole. If both craft are equidistant from the North Pole, the craft closest the South Pole shall turn towards the South Pole and the craft furthest from the South Pole shall turn away from the South Pole. If both craft are equidistant from both the South Pole and the North Pole, the craft traveling in the direction of the planet's rotation has the right of way. If both craft are traveling in the direction of the planet's rotation, an overtaking situation will be presumed to exist despite craft orientation vis-à-vis each other. In any event, craft shall pass clear of each other and shall, if circumstances of the case admit, avoid crossing ahead of the other vessel.

XII. Overtaking
A. Notwithstanding anything contained in the Rules, any craft overtaking any other shall keep out of the way of the craft being overtaken.
B. A craft shall be deemed to be overtaking when coming up with another craft from a direction more than 67 degrees opposite the direction in which the stand-on vessel is traveling.
C. When a craft is in doubt as to whether it is overtaking another, it shall assume that this is the case and act accordingly.
D. Any subsequent alteration of the bearing between the two craft shall not make the overtaking craft a crossing craft within the meaning of these rules or relieve her of the duty of keeping clear of the overtaken craft until it is finally past and clear.

XIII. Action By Give-Way Craft
Every craft which by the function of these rules is to keep out of the way of another vessel shall, so far as possible, take early and substantial action to keep well clear.

XIV. Action By Stand-on Craft
A. Where one craft is to keep out of the way of another, the latter stand-on craft shall keep its course and speed. The stand-on craft may take action to avoid collision by its maneuver alone, as soon as it becomes apparent that the craft required to keep out of the way is not taking appropriate action in compliance with these rules.
B. When, from any cause, the stand-on craft required to keep its course and speed finds itself so close that collision cannot be avoided by the action of the give-way craft alone, the stand-on craft shall take such action as will best aid to avoid collision.
C. This rule does not relieve the give-way craft of its obligation to keep out of the way.

XV. Responsibilities Between Different Classes Of Craft
A. A propulsion-driven craft shall keep out of the way of:
  (i) A craft not under command
  (ii) A craft restricted in its ability to maneuver
  (iii) A solar-driven craft
B. A solar-driven craft shall keep out of the way of:
  (i) A craft not under command
  (ii) A craft restricted in its ability to maneuver
C. A craft restricted in its ability to maneuver
Shall keep out of the way of a craft not under command

XVI. Navigational Transponders And Lights
Computerized navigation shall be utilized to feed into constantly transmitting transponders, which will relay the charted position and direction of travel of the craft vis-à-vis the closest planet and other reference planets/sun/galaxy.

XVII. Navigational Beacons
A. Flashing White & Red – Outbound Traffic Separation Scheme
B. Flashing White & Green – Inbound Traffic Separation Scheme
C. Red – All Craft (direction opposite travel)
D. Yellow – Spinning Object/Craft
E. Green – Propulsion-driven craft

F. Blue/Flashing White & Blue– Craft not under command/Restricted in ability to maneuver

XVIII. Communications
May be made via Radio/Pulse/Light or any other means appropriate to a vessel's speed.

---

[1] http://seds.lpl.arizona.edu/ssa/docs/Space.Shuttle/general.shtml#four
[2] http://quest.arc.nasa.gov/galileo/Galileo-QA/Speed/Speed_of_the_spacecraft.1
[3] http://faculty.erau.edu/ericksol/courses/sp215/ch3/ch3_debris.htm
[4] Id.
[5] F. Kenneth Schwetje, Space Law: Considerations for Space Planners, reprinted in 12 Rutgers Computer and Technology Law Journal 245 (1987).
[6] Id.
[7] Lubos Perek, Delimitation of Air Space and Outer Space: Is It Necessary?, in Earth Oriented Space Activities & Their Legal Implications 275 (1981) in F. Kenneth Schwetje, Space Law: Considerations for Space Planners, reprinted in 12 Rutgers Computer and Technology Law Journal 245 (1987).
[8] http://www.spacefuture.com/habitat/law.shtml
[9] Germany's response to a U.N. Questionnaire at http://www.oosa.unvienna.org/aero/question04.html
[10] M.S. Mc Dougal, H.D. Lasswell & L.A. Vlasic, Law and Public Order in Space 569 (1963) in F. Kenneth Schwetje, Space Law: Considerations for Space Planners, reprinted in 12 Rutgers Computer and Technology Law Journal 245 (1987).
[11] http://www.csc.noaa.gov/opis/html/summary/irpcs.htm
[12] International Navigational Rules Act of 1977, October, 20, 1972, U.S.-U.K., T.I.A.S. No. 8587
[13] http://www.icao.int/cgi/goto.pl?icao/en/history.htm
[14] http://www.icao.int/cgi/goto.pl?icao/en/pub/memo.htm
[15] http://www.icao.int/cgi/goto.pl?icao/en/pub/memo.htm
[16] http://www.downport.com/bard/bard/gail/gail0005.html
[17] Codified by the United States in 18 U.S.T. 2410, T.I.A.S. 6347
[18] Codified by the United States in 24 U.S.T. 2389, T.I.A.S. 7762
[19] F. Kenneth Schwetje, Space Law: Considerations for Space Planners, reprinted in 12 Rutgers Computer and Technology Law Journal 245 (1987)
[20] Convention on International Liability for Damage Caused by Space Objects, Oct 9, 1973, United States-Great Britain-USSR, 24 U.S.T. 2389, T.I.A.S. No. 7762
[21] M.S. Mc Dougal, H.D. Lasswell & L.A. Vlasic, Law and Public Order in Space 569 (1963) in F. Kenneth Schwetje, Space Law: Considerations for Space Planners, reprinted in 12 Rutgers Computer and Technology Law Journal 245 (1987).
[22] Lubos Perek, Early Concepts for Space Traffic, IISL/ECSL Symposium on Prospects for Space Traffic Management (Apr. 2, 2002) reprinted in E-mail from Lubos Perek, Professor Emeritus, Astronomical Institute, Academy of Sciences, Prague, Czech Republic (Oct. 30, 2002, 13:33:21 –0500).
[23] Trail Smelter Case (United States v. Canada), III U.N.Rep. Int'l Arb. Awards 1905, 1907 (1949).
[24] 49 USC § 70101 (1998).
[25] Lubos Perek, Early Concepts for Space Traffic, IISL/ECSL Symposium on Prospects for Space Traffic Management (Apr. 2, 2002) reprinted in E-mail from Lubos Perek, Professor Emeritus, Astronomical Institute, Academy of Sciences, Prague, Czech Republic (Oct. 30, 2002, 13:33:21 –0500).
[26] Id.
[27] F. Kenneth Schwetje, Space Law: Considerations for Space Planners, reprinted in 12 Rutgers Computer and Technology Law Journal 245 (1987).
[28] Treaty on Principles Governing the Activities of States in the Exploration and Use of Outer Space, Including the Moon and Other Celestial Bodies, Jan 27 1967, 1967 ATS No 24; 610 UNTS 205 [1967 Space Treaty]
[29] Lubos Perek, Early Concepts for Space Traffic, IISL/ECSL Symposium on Prospects for Space Traffic Management (Apr. 2, 2002) reprinted in E-mail from Lubos Perek, Professor Emeritus, Astronomical Institute, Academy of Sciences, Prague, Czech Republic (Oct. 30, 2002, 13:33:21 –0500).
[30] Lubos Perek, Traffic Rules for Outer Space, Proc. 25th Colloq. On the L. Outer Space 37, 41 (1982) in F. Kenneth Schwetje, Space Law: Considerations for Space Planners, reprinted in 12 Rutgers Computer and Technology Law Journal 245 (1987).
[31] http://liftoff.msfc.nasa.gov/academy/rocket_sci/satellites/geo-high.html
[32] Lubos Perek, Early Concepts for Space Traffic, IISL/ECSL Symposium on Prospects for Space Traffic Management (Apr. 2, 2002) reprinted in E-mail from Lubos Perek, Professor Emeritus, Astronomical Institute, Academy of Sciences, Prague, Czech Republic (Oct. 30, 2002, 13:33:21 –0500).
[33] "States shall avoid harmful contamination of space and celestial bodies" reprinted in the Treaty on Principles Governing the Activities of States in the Exploration and Use of Outer Space including the Moon and Other Celestial Bodies, Oct 10, 1967, United States-Great Britain-USSR, 18 U.S.T. 2410, T.I.A.S. No. 6347
[34] http://www.icao.int/cgi/goto.pl?icao/en/pub/memo.htm

RULES OF THE ROAD FOR SPACE TRAFFIC*

Author: Stefan Kaiser**
Heinsberg, Germany

0. ABSTRACT

After almost 50 years of space flight, time has come to think about standards for navigation of space vehicles in outer space, „rules of the road“. But since space navigation is not the first means of navigation, such rules exist already. Rather than re-inventing the wheel, this paper examines, in a comparative approach, air law principles for their suitability to traffic in Outer Space. While considering the absence of national airspace and the characteristics of orbital dynamics, the attempt is made to establish prototype standards for space traffic and navigation including the use of Global Navigation Satellite Systems (GNSS) for space vehicles.

1. SPACE TRAFFIC RULES

In this first part selected standards and recommended practices of the General Rules of Annex 2 (Rules of the Air) to the Convention on International Civil Aviation (Chicago Convention) are analyzed for their suitability for space traffic. The more specific Visual and Instrument Flight Rules[1] and the airspace structure do not make sense for navigation in Outer Space.

1.1 Responsibility and Authority

A cardinal principle of air law is the responsibility and authority of the pilot-in-command of an aircraft. He shall "whether manipulating the controls or not, be responsible for the operation of the aircraft in accordance with the rules of the air, except that he may depart from these rules in circumstances that render such departure absolutely necessary in the interest of safety"[2]. "The pilot-in-command of an aircraft shall have final authority as to thc disposition of the aircraft while he is in command"[3]. Historically, this principle has evolved because the pilot-in-command was the person at the controls and the only one who could take responsibility of what he was doing. Even in today`s highly automated environments with on-board flight management systems, computerized

** This paper represents the personal views of the author and shall not to be attributed to any organization the author is affiliated with.

air traffic management and data links, this principle does not appear to change in the foreseeable future. However, the technological developments will make it increasingly unacceptable for the pilot-in-command to accept responsibility for automated and remotely linked processes that are not any longer in his hands alone.

As a matter of the technical evolution the command of a space vehicle is vested, de facto, in ground-based control centers. These control centers and thus the operator of the space vehicle bears the responsibility[4] and authority for the space vehicle. Unmanned space vehicles are the rule and no commander on board can potentially be vested with the responsibility and authority. On manned missions with more than one crew member, normally commanders designated. Yet, concerning the navigation of the spacecraft it is questionable if a crew member on board should take over the legal responsibility for compliance with future rules of the road in space, as long as ground control centers have a more comprehensive oversight of the navigational situation of the space vehicle.

1.2 Protection of Persons and Property

1.2.1 General Obligation to Act Diligently. Rules of the road typically contain a general principle stipulating that operations must be conducted diligently. Also standards for navigation in Outer Space should state that the operation of space vehicles is not to be exercised in negligent or reckless manner so as to endanger life or property[5]. In the existing legal instruments, general considerations of standard of care for space navigation have a significance only in connection with liability, i.e. Art. VII of the Outer Space Treaty (OST)[6] and the Liability Convention[7]. The more detailed rules of the road evolve, the clearer can violations of the same be determined. They will also provide a basis for determining liability, in case damage is caused by a violation of the standard.

1.2.3 Minimum Heights. Minimum heights, one of the regulatory elements for operation of aircraft[8], do not make sense for space vehicles operating in Outer Space.

1.2.4 Cruising Level System. More examination is required whether a system similar to aviation´s (semi-circular) cruising level scheme[9] could be applied to Outer space navigation. Under this scheme, the course of an aircraft determines its flight level and thus reduces the risk of head-on collisions. Theoretically such a system could be superimposed on a structure of orbits around the Earth. However, the numerous parameters of orbits, be it inclination or (non)centricity raise some doubts if such a system could reduce collision risks. In the end, it may be up to a scientific analysis, if the risk of collisions could be reduced by assigning bands of orbital altitudes to polar, eastbound and westbound orbits. In any case, trajectories of space vehicles transiting to regions farther away from Earth would cut through these assigned orbital bands – as do climbing and descending aircraft in ICAO´s cruising level scheme.

Another problem will be space debris, which, in case of explosions, will be scattered into a myriad of orbits beyond the assigned bands. Similarly, atmospheric friction in lower Earth orbits does not warrant a constant altitude without measures of station keeping that require fuel. As proposed for the avoidance of space debris, the designation of cemetery regions (beyond the geo-stationary orbit) appears a workable solution. This would need to be coupled with the obligation to actively remove a space vehicle at the end of its service lifetime either into the cemetery band or force it to decay in the atmosphere.

The existing regulation on the rational use of the geo-stationary orbit under Art. 33 of the Convention on International Telecommunication (ITU Convention) does not primarily aim at avoidance of collision risks. It is a tool for allocating a resource.

1.2.5 Prohibited and Restricted Areas. Given the nature of orbital dynamics, the designation of prohibited areas and restricted areas[10] is not directly applicable in Outer Space. From a practical viewpoint, they blur with the concept of assigning orbital bands to certain flight directions, because these areas would similarly need to be shaped as bands of orbits. From a legal viewpoint prohibited and restricted areas can only be established in territorial (air)space. In line with aviation and maritime practice, outside the sovereign territory, territorial waters and airspace, States may only notify other States about "danger areas".

1.3 Avoidance of Collisions

1.3.1 General Obligation to Avoid Collisions. In aviation regulations, avoidance of collisions is based, inter alia[11], on a general obligation to avoid collisions hazards[12] and rules on the right of way[13]. The general obligation for avoiding collisions is suitable for space navigation without change.

1.3.2 Right of Way and Priorities. The aviation rules on the right of way are not directly applicable to space traffic. However, some concepts could be adapted.

For Space traffic, concepts do not fit which require that two aircraft, approaching head-on, have to alter their heading to the right or that an aircraft, that has another on its right, shall give way.

More interesting is a priority listing of aircraft types according to their maneuverability[14]. Maneuverability is a factor in Outer Space, in case an uncontrolled space object is to collide with a controlled space vehicle. Then, indeed, as a matter of self protection the operator will attempt to prevent the collision. But this scenario should not be the basis for a right of way regulation, because no priority needs to be determined if one of the space vehicles is uncontrolled and cannot change its course anyhow.

In case of two controlled space vehicles on collision course, a potential collision between two controlled space vehicles will be foreseeable with longer lead time than in aviation. Advance contact of the operators of converging space vehicles is highly desirable. But it must be determined who has to burn up the limited fuel of its space vehicle in order to avoid the collision. Therefore it is recommended to establish an order of priority for the right of way in accordance with two factors: (a) the vulnerability of a space vehicle and (b) the damage potential. This could result in the following order of priority:

- manned space vehicles in an emergency,
- manned space vehicles,
- unmanned space vehicles
- unmanned space vehicles with a high damage potential, e.g. with nuclear powers source.

In addition, a controlled space vehicle violating other rules of the road, e.g. orbiting counter-wise to the direction designated for an orbital band cannot benefit from this order of priority.

1.4 Avoidance of harmful interference
Alternatively, collision avoidance in Outer Space could be covered by a new broadened concept on avoidance of harmful interference. If avoidance of interference were to include not only the radio spectrum, as in Art. 35 ITU Convention, but also physical impacts, i.e. collisions, and perhaps even the optical part and other scientifically important parts of the radio magnetic spectrum, a new concept beyond the roots of aviation and radio communication could be established.

2. GNSS FOR USE BY SPACE VEHICLES

This second part of the paper deals with the use of Global Navigation Satellite Systems (GNSS) for navigation of space vehicles. The International Civil Aviation Organization (ICAO) has studied extensively the use of GNSS for civil aviation. Aviation is a user group with very stringent requirements for terrestrial and atmospheric navigation within the territories of states and over the High Sea. Given the timely study in ICAO, the principles contained in the Charter on the Rights and Obligations of States Relating to GNSS services, adopted by ICAO Assembly Resolution A 32-19[15], can be considered as a useful regulatory basis also for other terrestrial user groups. But since GNSS will also be used for navigation of space vehicles[16], these principles require a review for uses in Outer Space by states other the providers of GNSS. The existing ICAO principles apply to terrestrial and atmospheric users, but not to users in Outer Space.

2.1 Paramount Principle of Safety
There is no doubt that safety is the paramount principle for the use of GNSS. But more broadly than in ICAO`s first principle[17], this safety aspect can be extended beyond international civil aviation and include safety of space vehicles and other human activities in Outer Space, in the Earth´s atmosphere and on the ground[18].

2.2 Non-Discriminatory Access
Likewise, non-discriminatory access under uniform conditions to GNSS services should be available not only for aircraft, but also for space vehicles of all states[19]. However, non-discriminatory access to GNSS need to be excluded for military space vehicles. Based on the concept of sovereignty in national airspace[20], where every state can (legally) control the military air traffic, this is not the case for military space vehicles in Outer Space. Also, ICAO principles do by definition not apply to state aircraft[21]; hence ICAO principles do not apply to military applications unless specifically agreed so by the member states. Also the "interest of maintaining international peace and security", as contained in Art. III OST, would become hollow if providers of GNSS were mandated to provide navigation services on a non-discriminatory basis to military space

vehicles of another state[22].

Non-discriminatory access does not mean that navigation services are provided for free. Indeed, it can be argued that making use of GNSS signals for the navigation of space vehicles justifies the levying of user charges, even when terrestrial and atmospheric users do not have to pay.

Regional augmentation systems also mentioned in this ICAO principle, e.g. the Wide Area Augmentation System (WAAS) in the United States of America and the European Geo-stationary Navigation Overlay System (EGNOS), do at the moment not seem to have a role for applications in space.

2.3 State Authority and Responsibility

Under Art. VI OST States bear the responsibility of the space activities of its nationals. As a consequence, some states adopted a licensing and supervision system. Any reference in ICAO´s GNSS principles relating to state authority and responsibility of safety and operations linked to national airspace[23] do not fit to the safety and operations of space vehicles. But within the framework of Art. VI OST every State definitely preserves its authority and responsibility to control operations of space vehicles to enforce safety and other regulations onboard.

Without any limitations, the GNSS principle on State sovereignty, authority and responsibility in the control of navigation and safety regulations[24] can be extended to space navigation. The fact that the GNSS of one State may be used for the space activities of another can definitely not result in any infringement or restriction of the user State´s sovereignty, authority or control. Likewise the user State's authority must also be preserved in the coordination and control of ground-based or space-based communications and augmentation segments for space navigation services.

But any such augmentation that is usable also in Outer Space, is subject to the non-discriminatory access and quality principles[25]. In this instance the user State will become a provider State for the given augmentation segment.

2.4 Quality of Services

The central principle on the technical and organizational quality of services applies to space navigation as it does to air navigation[26]. Every provider state is to ensure the continuity, availability, integrity, accuracy and reliability of space navigation services[27].

The *"effective arrangements to minimize the operational impact of system malfunctions or failure, and to achieve expeditious service recovery"*[28] should be interpreted as to maintain the *technical* means of minimizing failure impacts and providing for a recovery. These "effective arrangements" cannot mean to establish a new liability system. The liability regime for space activities is based on the fault-based principles and types of damages enshrined in Art. VII OST. At the moment, it appears too far-fetched to aim at non-fault based liability regimes in case of damages resulting from wrong navigation inputs of a provider.

References to *ICAO Standards* and *aeronautical information* in relation to the quality of services are not appropriate for space navigation. Also any reference to aviation related principles on navigation charges[29] have no footing for space traffic.

2.5 Co-operation, Interest of other States, Joint Provision of Service

The ICAO GNSS principles mention co-operation in different contexts. One relates to the (technical and institutional) uniformity in the provision of services[30], another to the global planning and implementation on a bilateral or multilateral basis[31]. Furthermore it provides that "*every State shall conduct its GNSS activities with due regard for the interests of other States*"[32] and "*nothing ... shall prevent two or more States from jointly providing GNSS services*"[33].

All this fits likewise to navigation services provided for and used by space traffic.

3. DRAFT STANDARDS

Based on the foregoing considerations, the following draft standards for space traffic and the use of GNSS by space vehicles are compiled. They are not a comprehensive and exhaustive set of "rules of the road", but a starting point for further elaboration.

3.1 Draft Standards on Space Traffic

1. The operator of a space vehicle shall be responsible for the operation of the space vehicle in accordance with these standards, except that he may depart from these standards in circumstances that render such departure absolutely necessary in the interest of safety.

2. The operator of a space vehicle shall have the final authority as to the disposition of the space vehicle.

[3. The operator may designate a person on board a space vehicle to exercise the authority for certain portions of the flight.]

4. A space vehicle shall not be operated in a negligent or reckless manner so as to endanger life or property of others.

[5. Assignment of orbital altitude bands to certain flight directions (e.g. polar, eastbound and westbound orbits)]

6. A space vehicle shall not be operated in such proximity to other space vehicles as to create a collision hazard.

7. When two space vehicles have converging trajectories, the right of way shall be in the order of priority as follows:

- manned space vehicles in an emergency,
- manned space vehicle,
- unmanned space vehicles,
- unmanned space vehicles with a high damage potential.

8. The operators of space vehicles shall inform each other, as soon as possible, when they detect that the trajectories of their space vehicles are converging as to create a collision hazard. The operators of the affected space vehicles shall co-operate in undertaking the necessary measures, in accordance with these standards, in order to prevent a collision.

[9. Space vehicles shall be operated in a manner as not to harmfully interfere, radio-magnetically, optically and physically with space vehicles operated in accordance with these standards (and operations on the Earth and other celestial bodies).]

3.2 Draft Standards on the use of GNSS by Space Vehicles

1. States recognize that in the provision and use of GNSS services, the safety of

international navigation shall be the paramount principle.

2. Every State and space vehicles of all states shall have access on a non-discriminatory basis under uniform conditions, to the use of GNSS services within the area of coverage of such systems.

3.a) Every State preserves its authority and responsibility to control operations of space vehicles and to enforce safety and other regulations for space vehicles under its jurisdiction .

b) The implementation and operation of GNSS shall neither infringe nor impose restrictions upon State's sovereignty, authority or responsibility in the control of navigation and the promulgation and enforcement of safety regulations. State's authority shall also be preserved in the coordination and control of communications and in the augmentation, as necessary, of satellite based navigation services.

4. Every state providing GNSS services, including signals, or under whose jurisdiction such services are provided, shall ensure the continuity, availability, integrity, accuracy and reliability of such services, including effective arrangements to minimize the operational impact of system malfunctions or failure, and to achieve expeditious service recovery. States shall provide in due time information on any modification of the GNSS services that may affect the provision of the services.

5. States shall co-operate to secure the highest practicable degree of uniformity in the provision and operation of GNSS services.
States shall ensure that multilateral arrangements are compatible with the principles and rules set out in this principles and with the global planning and implementation process for GNSS.

6. With a view to facilitating global planning and implementation of GNSS, States shall be guided by the principle of co-operation and mutual assistance whether on a bilateral or multilateral basis.

7. Every State shall conduct its GNSS activities with due regard for the interests of other States.

8. Nothing in this principles shall prevent two or more States from jointly providing GNSS services.

Endnotes:

[1] Chapters 4 and 5, Rules of the Air, Annex 2 to the Chicago Convention

[2] Standard 2.3.1, Rules of the Air, Annex 2 to the Chicago Convention

[3] Standard 2.4, Rules of the Air, Annex 2 to the Chicago Convention

[4] Of course, under Art. VI OST the state of the operator bears the responsibility under public international law.

[5] Standard 3.1.1 Rules of the Air, Annex 2 to the Chicago Convention "An aircraft shall not be operated in a negligent or reckless manner as to endanger life or property of others."

[6] Treaty on Principles Governing the Activities of States in the Exploration and Use of Outer Space, including the Moon and Other Celestial Bodies

[7] Convention on International Liability for Damage Caused by Space Objects

[8] Standard 3.1.2, Rules of the Air, Annex 2 to the Chicago Convention

[9] Standard 3.1.3, Rules of the Air, Annex 2 to the Chicago Convention and Procedures for Air Navigation Service - Aircraft Operations, ICAO Doc. 8168

[10] Standard 3.1.9 Rules of the Air, Annex 2 to the Chicago Convention

[11] Other standards relate to aviation specific areas which have no bearing for space navigation: landing, take-off, surface movement, lights, simulated instrument flights, operations in the vicinity of aerodromes and on the water, standards 3.2.2.4 to 3.2.6 Rules of the Air, Annex 2 to the Chicago Convention

[12] Standard 3.2.1.1 Rules of the Air, Annex 2 to the Chicago Convention "An aircraft shall not be operated in such proximity to other aircraft as to create a collision hazard."

[13] Standard 3.2.2 Rules of the Air, Annex 2 to the Chicago Convention

[14] Standard 3.2.2.2 Rules of the Air, Annex 2 to the Chicago Convention establishes the following order of priority: power driven heavier than air, airships gliders and balloons.

[15] Reprinted in Vol. XXIII AASL 325 (1998) and Vol. XXII Air & Space Law 219 (1997)

[16] See public announcement of the European Space Agency (ESA) of 9 May 2003 "Communication satellites telling us where they are". New onboard GNSS (Global Navigation Satellite System) receivers are being developed for communication satellites in low Earth and geo-stationary orbit in a project funded by ESA.

[17] Principle 1.: "States recognize that in the provisions and use of GNSS services, the safety of international civil aviation shall be the paramount principle."

[18] It is a political question, if this principle should expressly also mention protection of the Earth´s environment.

[19] Principle 2.: "Every State and aircraft of all states shall have access on a non-discriminatory basis under uniform

conditions, to the use of GNSS services, including regional augmentation systems for aeronautical use within the area of coverage of such systems."

[20] Art. 1 Chicago Convention

[21] Art. 3 (a) Chicago Convention

[22] Another issue will be the technical implementation of preventing a military space vehicle to receive GNSS signals while providing non-discriminatory access to civilian space vehicles.

[23] Principle 3.a): "Every State preserves its authority and responsibility to control operations of aircraft and to enforce safety and other regulations within its sovereign airspace."

[24] Principle 3.b): "The implementation and operation of GNSS shall neither infringe nor impose restrictions upon State's sovereignty, authority or responsibility in the control of air navigation and the promulgation and enforcement of safety regulations. State's authority shall also be preserved in the coordination and control of communications and in the augmentation, as necessary, of satellite-based air navigation services."

[25] See principles 2 and 4.

[26] Principle 4.: "Every state providing GNSS services, including signals, or under whose jurisdiction such services are provided, shall ensure the continuity, availability, integrity, accuracy and reliability of such services, including effective arrangements to minimize the operational impact of system malfunctions or failure, and to achieve expeditious service recovery. Such State shall ensure that the services are in accordance with ICAO Standards. States shall provide in due time aeronautical information on any modification of the GNSS services that may affect the provision of the services."

[27] For the definitions of these parameters see ICAO Guidelines for the Introduction and Operational Use of the Global Navigation Satellite System (GNSS) , 1996, Circular 267 AN/159 at 97 pp.

[28] See Principle 4 at endnote 26

[29] Principle 6.: "States recognize that any charges for GNSS services shall be made in accordance with Art. 15 of the Chicago Convention."

[30] Principle 5.: "States shall co-operate to secure the highest practicable degree of uniformity in the provision and operation of GNSS services.

[31] Principle 7.: "With a view to facilitating global planning and implementation of GNSS, States shall be guided by the principle of co-operation and mutual assistance whether on a bilateral or multilateral basis."

[32] Principle 8

[33] Principle 9

QUIS VADIT CUM VOBIS, GALILEO?

Institutional Aspects Of Europe's Own Satellite Navigation System

Frans G. von der Dunk
International Institute of Air and Space Law, Leiden - The Netherlands
F.G.vonderDunk@law.leidenuniv.nl

Abstract

With the decision early 2002 to develop Galileo, the second generation European GNSS-system, and to have it fully operational by 2008, the member states of the European Union (EU) and the European Space Agency (ESA) have taken a large step forward. The question "*Quo vadis, Galileo*?' has therefore, by and large, been answered – 'Into orbit!' However, many legal parameters for the future system have yet to be defined; amongst those one of the most important is the definition and establishment of the institutional structure which should bring Galileo there and make sure it remains there, in a safe, sensible and operational manner. In other words: '*Quis vadit cum vobis, Galileo?*' – 'Who goes (there) with you?'

The paper will present a brief overview of the issues involved in determining and developing the future institutional structure of Galileo, starting with the current Galileo Interim Support Structure (GISS) and the Joint Undertaking (JU) which will be its successor. This will lead into the issue of the prospective public supervisor and private operator which are supposed to be at the core of that institutional structure, tied together by a Concession Agreement-type of arrangement.

In reflecting upon the various issues, attention will be paid to an interesting precedent from the satellite sector, i.e. the privatisation of INMARSAT and its transformation into Inmarsat. Other issues to be touched upon in this light concern the possibilities for non-EU and non-ESA member states to join the Galileo core institutional structure, the need for co-ordination and interoperability with GPS and GLONASS (and possible other systems), issues of negotiation with non-European states, and dealing with liability issues.

1. Introduction

Early 2002, the member states of the European Union (EU) and the European Space Agency (ESA) gave the final green light for the development of Galileo.[1] According to the planned time schedule, by 2008 some 30 satellites in MEO will provide various timing, positioning and navigation signals, in a number of cases being vastly superior (in particular in terms of accuracy and integrity[2]) to signals emitted by the current GPS[3] and GLONASS[4] systems.

At ITU's WRC 2000 and the recent 2003 WRC the necessary frequencies for Galileo were secured. Then, last July also the contracts for the first two Galileo satellites were signed – one with Surrey Satellite Technologies, the other with Galileo Industries. In other words: all is set now for Galileo to prepare for Full Operational Capacity, due by 2008.

In further preparing the stage however, one of the major issues concerns the details of the institutional structure which is to run Galileo. Contrary to GPS and GLONASS, run by the military authorities of a single country with other governmental departments being merely involved through consultation boards and their likes, Galileo was envisaged from the beginning as a Public-Private Partnership (PPP). The private sector should be

fundamentally involved in financing, operating, maintaining and marketing the system – for in further contrast to GPS and GLONASS, Galileo will *inter alia* provide services against fees.
Whilst the question "*Quo vadis, Galileo?*' has thus by and large been answered, the question to be dealt with by this paper by contrast remains: '*Quis vadit cum vobis, Galileo?*' – 'Who goes (there) with you?'

2. The Galileo core services

Before going into further detail regarding this essentially institutional question, it is necessary to provide an overview of what the system will actually do, and why it was decided to develop it in the first place, in a little more detail.
Galileo will provide a number of signals, which through various combinations and the addition of data or other features will amount to five core types of services, considered as Galileo-only services:

- the Open Service (OS);
- the Commercial Services (CS);
- the Safety-Of-Life Services (SOL);
- the Public Regulated Services (PRS); and
- a contribution to existing Search-And-Rescue Services (SAR).

OS and CS might be classified as 'private services', in the sense that there are no direct public concerns – as opposed to general interests in economic and social benefits – calling for such services to be provided.
The Open Service essentially equates with the signals known as GPS SPS and GLONASS SPS (though it may offer somewhat enhanced accuracy and continuity), and will be provided without any integrity monitoring. As an open access signal it is available to anyone with the right receiver, without any user fee. Thus, there is no contract or quasi-contract involved. Such usage will as a consequence be individualised, and will focus on a number of personalised mass-market applications.
The Commercial Services by contrast will be provided against a fee, and hence be covered by a contract, to any value-added service provider or end-user willing to pay the price for the data added onto the signal proper, as well as for a service guarantee to be provided and other benefits (such as relating to liability). The positioning/navigation services provided as Commercial Services will likely be incorporated by value-added service providers in such areas as banking services, various telecommunications applications and Location-Based Services (LBS) – services with a certain commercial value, but not safety-sensitive and hence not specifically requiring high levels of continuity and integrity.
SOL, PRS and the contribution to SAR might in contrast with OS and CS be classified as 'public services', since their *raison d'etre* is a public need for safety- and/or security-enhancing services.
The Public Regulated Services in a sense also provide a second manifestation of a contractual Galileo service. Since their usage is envisaged in certain security-related and (other) governmental areas (police and emergency services, possibly also military usage), the signals will be encrypted and secured against unauthorised usage. Access to these services is principally available only to a closed user group of governmental (or closely government-aligned) entities, which will have to conclude a contract in some form to avail themselves of the necessary decryption keys required for access.
The Safety-Of-Life Services would then form the third manifestation of contractual core services to be provided by Galileo. They will also somehow – likely indirectly – be provided against fees, and will be fully augmented (including the level of integrity monitoring required by the aviation sector). Thus, somehow

contractual arrangements will underpin this service provision, though as of yet it is not certain how this would be structured, as a consequence of the current structure of navigation service provision in the aviation sector.

Additionally, Galileo will contribute to the existing global system of satellite-based Search-and-Rescue (SAR) services, notably as a European segment of the COSPAS-SARSAT system. In view of its special contributory character, however, this Galileo service will not further be taken into consideration here.

In addition to these five Galileo-only services as dealt with, from a broader perspective also Galileo local services are to be provided by Local Elements plus (optionally) Regional Elements; and Galileo combined services are to be provided by other systems together with any combination of Galileo, Regional Elements and various types of Local Elements.

The option of co-operating with Regional Elements is considered in order to allow those non-European regions interested in providing their own integrity monitoring to link up with Galileo. Local Elements are envisaged to be established wherever there would be a local need for even more enhanced accuracy and availability than the Galileo services themselves can offer.

3. Galileo: Towards a PPP

Galileo is a project initiated by the European Commission on behalf of the European Union and its member states and the European Space Agency and *its* member states.[5] The overarching political, economic and social mission of establishing Galileo has been summarised as "to develop and implement a competitive, leading edge Global Navigation Satellite system, which provides the best in choice and quality to the end user, attracting business investment and supporting ongoing social and economic growth in Europe".[6] In other words: Galileo is supposed to bring social, economic, safety- and security-related as well as political and strategic benefits especially to the European states and peoples involved, but in a wider sense to all states interested in such benefits.

It may be interesting to note in this respect that the People's Republic of China has declared its willingness early in 2003 to discuss a contribution in the range of 200 M€ to the development and deployment phase of Galileo in return for substantial and structural involvement in the system operations at the highest level – i.e. presumably either as member state of a relevant public supervisory body, or as partner thereof at a level of principled equality.

One key element of the Galileo project from the outset was the aim to include private participation, comprising from this perspective essentially both private investment and private operational and decisional involvement, in a fundamental and substantive fashion through some form of PPP. This aim is already reflected at the highest level in the choice to include both a public supervisor, taking care of the various public interests and concerns in Galileo, and a private operator reflecting the PPP at the core of the institutional structure.

The main reasons for involving a private operator as a key entity in the organisational structure for a system with obvious fundamental public aspects were the following:

- for flexible, non-bureaucratic and commercial modes of operation;
- for marketing purposes;
- for obtaining finances and investments from the capital markets in normal commercial modes;
- for dealing with IPR issues in a proper and more commercially-oriented fashion;

- for obtaining insurance against limited liability; and
- for making a sensible business partner.

A further envisaged beneficial aspect of a private operator is generally conceived to consist of the far better capabilities of, and opportunities available to, a private entity to develop new services and markets in a commercially assertive manner.

Vice versa, the reasons for involving a public oversight body as a key entity in the organisational structure for a system where private and commercial modes of operation have been deemed to be most beneficial were the following:

- for negotiating and concluding agreements with states 'external' to Galileo yet hosting Galileo-related assets/service providers;
- for licensing non-European augmentation and integrity providers (or negotiating and concluding agreements on such operations by the private operator);
- for serving the general public interests e.g. in regard of safety, security and search-and-rescue issues; and
- for (possibly) offering unlimited liability in the last resort to value-added service providers and end-users.

Further envisaged beneficial aspects of a public supervisor would generally be seen to consist of enhanced trust by the public at large in the system (with respect to such issues as certification and safety licenses), as well as by negotiating where necessary access for the private operator to the markets of states not belonging to the Galileo core group of states. Finally, also liaising with other relevant organisations (such as ICAO and IMO) would best be undertaken by such a public supervisor.

4. Galileo: the current status

Until recently, the task of preparing the ground for Galileo fell on the Galileo Interim Support Structure (GISS), essentially embodying the assignment of a number of expert ESA staff members to work under guidance from the European Commission. The GISS, established December 2001, *inter alia* took over supervision of the study projects going on in the EU framework, as well as setting the scene for a more permanent and institutionalised entity once the political hurdles at the highest level would have been overcome.

Once this was achieved, the overarching aim of combining the efforts, expertise and input of both the public and the private sector in Europe resulted in the final establishment of the Galileo Joint Undertaking (GJU) this summer following the relevant EU Council Resolution of May 2002.[7] Currently the GJU represents only the two key public partners in Galileo, the European Union through the Commission and the European Space Agency, whereas at a later stage it is envisaged that private partners would also participate (including through investments) in the GJU.

Legally speaking, the GJU is a unique animal: whilst it would, at least for the first period of its existence, essentially be the vehicle for co-operation of two intergovernmental organisations, the EU and ESA, it does not constitute an intergovernmental entity itself. To start with, it was not established by means of an international treaty, but through an EU Council Regulation. Furthermore, international legal personality was expressly excluded at various points in the texts. Whilst not a private entity properly speaking either, for the purposes of European law – or for that matter of the national laws of the state where the GJU is established, i.e. Belgium – it would nevertheless be subjected to the same regimes as private entities.

The present role of the GJU essentially consists of preparing the ground in general terms for the deployment and operational phases of the Galileo system, and more specifically of selecting the private consortium which would come to play the central role in the institutional structure as the private operator by that time. Though nothing specific has been decided or even indicated yet with respect to such a scenario, it may tentatively be assumed that the GJU (especially after the private operator has been chosen) will also prepare the ground for the public supervisor, or possibly evolve itself into taking such a role.

This last option would likely require the absence of private participation in the GJU other than in an advisory or contributory capacity, since the public supervisory character would fit ill with a (co-)decision-making role of private entities. It may be noted here that the GJU as such is established for an interim period, which indeed so far leaves all options open.

5. The public supervisor

So, on the one hand it has been decided to establish a public entity of the international variant – currently going by the name of Galileo Supervisory Authority (GSA)[8] – as a core element of the organisational structure for Galileo. This entity should at least take care of the evident public interests in Europe in building and maintaining the Galileo system in the first place (e.g. security, safety and general economic progress), as well as relevant international aspects (negotiations with third states), generally speaking by exercising some sort of control over the private operator.

In addition, the GSA may become the owner of the system as a preferred option; it should at a minimum be involved in maintenance, replenishment and further development thereof. However, this will be a matter yet to be determined by policy choices and concession negotiations.

More in detail the role of the GSA as public supervisor would have to focus on:

- providing the political credibility at the international level necessary to enhance, wherever necessary through international legal agreements, the business opportunities for the private operator, especially with regard to OS and CS;
- ensuring that the general public as well as specific European interests in Galileo are duly respected by the private operator's operations and activities, especially when it comes to SOL, PRS and the contribution to SAR;
- ensuring a proper and fair liability regime, possibly including a Compensation Fund, for relevant types of damage occurring in the course of Galileo activities and operations;
- ensuring a proper certification scheme as a specific means to enhance the overall trust of value-added service providers, end-users, consumers and the public at large in Galileo; and
- ensuring that any bankruptcy or other market failure of the private operator would not unduly prejudice the overall interests of the Galileo core states in Galileo, preferably through ownership of the system.

6. The private operator

On the other hand, the institutional structure shall at its core include a private company – currently named Galileo Operating Company (GOC)[9]: it should at least operate the system and market the services, as well as develop new markets, and in addition could possibly own the system or at least be closely involved in maintenance, replenishment and further development thereof. This, however, as indicated is in the last resort firstly a policy or political rather than a legal decision, and secondly, likely to be the subject of further negotiations as part of the bidding process for the Galileo concession.

The role of the GOC as private operator would consequently focus on:

- using its market know-how and other advantages of private modes of operation for turning the provision of Galileo services into a profitable business, in particular with respect to OS and CS;
- ensuring that the obligations imposed upon it by or through the GSA will be properly balanced with guaranteed long-term revenues, such as by availability payments or shadow tolls, and other relevant assurances with respect to SOL, PRS, and the contribution to SAR; and
- ensuring generally that the risks imposed on it through the PPP would be those it is capable of handling best, and this moreover in return for the proper incentives.

It would be the GOC's business for example to conclude contracts with value-added service providers interested in integrating CS into broader services to be offered to the latter's customers; e.g. by adding databases and communications facilities offering taxi companies a detailed and continuously updated traffic information system.

Under circumstances, the GOC might also come to act itself as value-added service provider; especially for the purpose of developing new markets by way of pilot projects this is an approach currently being contemplated. Also, whilst as such the concepts of Regional Elements and Local Elements have been developed envisaging those to be entities outside the Galileo institutional framework proper, nothing in principle would prevent the GOC from taking up such a role. At the same time, both possible extensions of the GOC's role would lead to considerable complications as a consequence of additional legal regimes and issues being involved.

By contrast to the above therefore, another option open to the future GOC would be to actually establish a daughter company for each of the Galileo core services which are to be delivered, in view of the fundamental differences between OS, CS, PRS and SOL (not to mention the contribution to SAR) also in terms of markets.

If commercially feasible, the private operator could also contract directly with individual users who are interested in Galileo timing or positioning information of a higher quality than the OS, and are willing to pay for it.

Finally, the GOC will serve the general public as well as the aim of opening up and developing new markets by the establishment of Service Centres of some kind, providing *inter alia* necessary information on standardisation and certification issues, liability arrangements and general opportunities for contracting with the GOC to obtain its services.

Again, as there are a number of serious alternative options available, in the end much will depend upon the bidding and negotiating process as well as upon who will finally win the concession.

7. The Galileo Legal/Functional Model

The above general analysis leads to a rather complex construction in terms of Galileo services and entities, which is best illustrated by the Galileo Legal/Functional Model developed in the context of various Galileo-related studies; a generic summary version of which, not including for example the special case of Galileo's contribution to SAR activities, is reproduced below as Table 1.

Table 1. The Galileo Legal/Functional Model (simplified generic version).

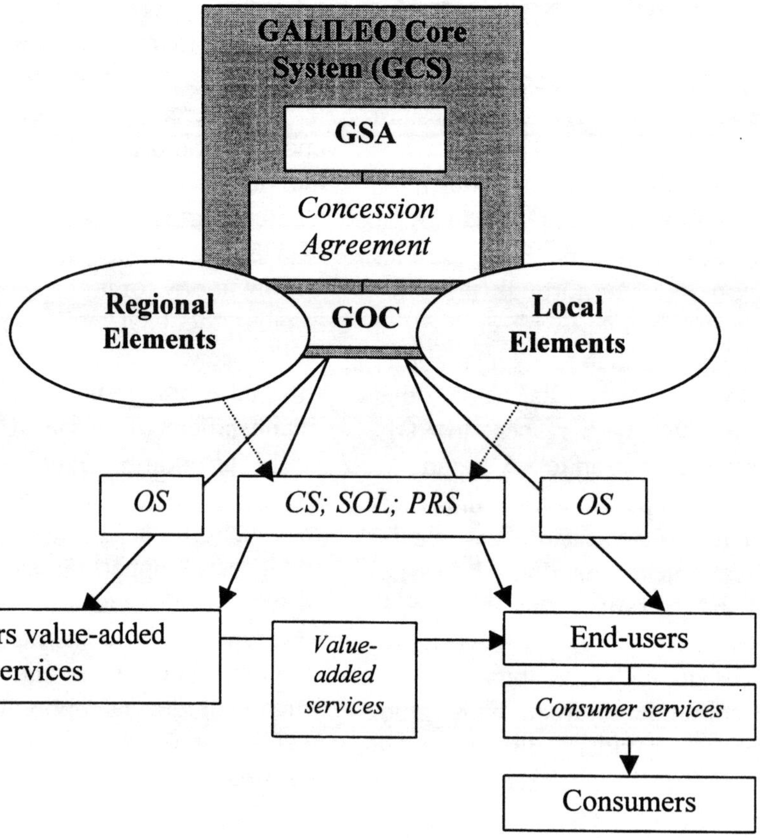

8. The Concession Agreement

The most important issue, in legal terms, of the PPP and the relationship between GSA and GCO at the heart of Galileo's envisaged institutional structure, is provided by a Concession Agreement, serving as an umbilical cord between the two entities.

From this perspective, such a Concession Agreement, including wherever relevant flanking arrangements, should first of all establish clarity on key issues such as the financing aspects which are at the heart of any PPP – read the respective shares and modes of financial contribution from public and private sectors. This, in close co-operation and consultation with the private sector which has to bid for the concession.

Such financing arrangements to be proposed should closely mirror the respective risks taken by public and private sectors under the concession PPP.

Generally speaking risks are to be borne by the respective PPP partner best equipped to handle them, and should thus distinguish between public and private risks. Public risks in this regard refer to such risks as policy, legal, regulatory and licensing risks, in particular as relevant for SOL, PRS and the contribution to SAR in view of the public characteristics of those services. Private risks would refer in particular to financing and commercial risks, such as revenue risks (especially for CS) and intellectual property rights-related risks (especially for OS). Finally, some hybrid risks should be dealt with jointly, such as most importantly liability risks.

The Concession Agreement either itself or through flanking arrangements should furthermore deal with the following important issues:

- the distribution of (contractual) liability;
- the possible need for denial of Galileo services in security-sensitive situations;
- potential bankruptcy or other fundamental failure of the GOC;
- how IPR should be distributed and dealt with;
- to what extent service guarantees would be imposed (in particular for SOL and PRS, whereas with respect to CS it should be left largely to the commercial freedom of decision-making of the GOC);
- certification;
- long-term planning issues, including re-competition issues and availability payments or other public sector contributions; and
- the applicable commercial law for any business disputes.

9. The Example of Inmarsat

For the future drafting of a Concession Agreement and any flanking arrangements, the case of INMARSAT-after-privatisation would serve as an interesting example. The residual intergovernmental organisation IMSO maintains, through a binding Public Service Agreement which can not be unilaterally altered or cancelled, control over the private operator Inmarsat with respect to those public services which the latter is obliged to continue to provide.[10] For Inmarsat, this mainly referred to the Global Maritime Distress and Safety System (GMDSS); in the case of Galileo, this should refer especially to the obligatory aspects of SOL, PRS and the contribution to SAR, as well as the more general obligations regarding security issues in particular.

The PSA is further 'flanked' by a set of arrangements, called Restructuring Arrangements, dealing with other specific aspects of the relationship IMSO-Inmarsat and the transitional period. These concerned:

- The Master Transition Agreement, the principal agreement between the old INMARSAT, the new Inmarsat companies established under the UK Companies Act of 1985, and the Signatories. The other agreements, with the exception of the LESO Agreements, were attached as schedules to the Master Transition Agreement.
- The Master Novation Agreements between the old INMARSAT, the Company and each Signatory relating to the novation of Signatory contracts. Under the Novation Agreements, INMARSAT ceased to be a party to any contract and was replaced by the Company.
- The Business Transfer Agreement between INMARSAT and Inmarsat Ltd. relating to the transfer of the business from INMARSAT to the Company.
- The Licence Agreement between INMARSAT and the Company relating to the use of the INMARSAT name and logo.
- The Shareholders Agreement between Holdings and the shareholders, by means of which the shareholders agreed to support the company to carry out an Initial Public Offering (IPO).
- The Land Earth Station Operators (LESO) Agreements between Inmarsat Ltd. and each of the LES operators. The LESO Agreement authorises the LES operators to provide services via Inmarsat.

Thus, a whole set of well-elaborated arrangements was necessary to ensure a proper transition from the old to the new situation, as well as a proper relationship between the new public and private partners.

10. Towards a Galileo Convention?

For a number of reasons, it might be desirable moreover to establish a dedicated Galileo Convention, i.e. an international treaty between the Galileo core group of states acting as an umbrella over the Concession Agreement. This Convention should *inter alia* provide for the proper establishment of the GSA including some measure of international legal personality and functional immunities; as well as deal with the residual responsibilities of the states behind it, security- and safety-interfaces with other relevant organisations and authorities, liability solutions in terms of a Compensation Fund, Galileo international relations, certification schemes and the role and competencies of any Galileo-dedicated regulatory body if such a body were to be established.

It should be noted here from an institutional perspective, that such concepts as 'GSA' and 'Galileo-dedicated regulatory body' in first instance would be referring to abstract roles, without prejudice as to which entity, new or existing, would eventually be entrusted with the relevant tasks, status and role.

Any Galileo-dedicated regulatory body however would for reasons of transparency and fairness obviously need to be clearly separate from a GSA, even as the latter will have some important public and semi-regulatory competencies as well. This means that if, for example, the European Union as represented by the European Commission would come to take up the role of regulatory body – which it seems excellently placed to do, in view of the extended regulatory machinery which the Commission can avail itself of – the role of GSA by contrast should not be played by any entity too closely aligned to, or even part of, the EU institutional machinery.

Whereas in the long run a Convention would provide the optimum solution, it is clear it might take a long time to become realised, and might even turn out not to be politically feasible. For both reasons, certainly in the short run EC law harmonisation measures, taking advantage of the well-weathered legislative machinery existing within the European Union, should in particular *complement* existing law and regulation not to be changed easily – in other words: in particular in those areas not yet structurally covered by legal regimes (mostly focusing on the multi-modal aspects of Galileo therefore, exceptions mainly arising in such areas as rail and road transport) and dedicated to the novel, overarching and comprehensive features of Galileo.

11. A special issue: liability and Galileo

Liability, as the most down-to-earth and financially quantifiable issue in GNSS, also presents a special issue from the institutional perspective. In principle, a number of existing relevant regimes would remain applicable also to cases of damage involving Galileo even if none of them are to any appreciable extent focused on GNSS or navigation-related issues. They would moreover, to the extent agreed upon at the international level, or conversely to the extent constituting a matter for national law of non-Galileo core states relevant as potential Galileo markets, not be easily changed by any regulatory effort within those core states and/or the European Union. This concerns in particular non-contractual (third party/tort) and product liability. Any Galileo-dedicated liability regime should therefore be essentially built 'on top of' such existing liability regimes, e.g. by efforts to harmonise relevant third party liability for Galileo-related cases at an EU level – as it was achieved to some extent in the area of product liability.

As to contractual liability, it would of course operate in first instance as between GOC and contracted service providers (and possibly end-users). The relevant contracts at the same time should deal most prominently with derogation of non-contractual liability claims addressed to the latter, to the extent erroneous or absent Galileo signals/services would be found to constitute the (ultimate) cause of the damage. This in turn requires the incorporation of monitoring equipment in the system, in order to distinguish such cases from those where other causes would be responsible for the damage, as well as a coherent certification system providing the GOC with a possible defence against undue claims.

Furthermore, in view of the Galileo business case, it would be desirable to establish a two-tier liability system in dealing both with direct non-contractual liability claims against the GOC, and with the contractual derogation of non-contractual liability claims against its contracted customers. The first tier would call for liability of the GOC up to a certain limit, for which the GOC would obtain obligatory insurance at reasonable cost. The second tier should be somehow taken care of by the GSA and/or the member states behind it, with the option of a Compensation Fund (similar to the cases of oil pollution[11] and the nuclear power industry[12]) presenting the preferable instrument.

Whilst these scenarios would obviously have to be integrated into the Concession Agreement or a flanking arrangement, preferably they would also be covered by the proposed Galileo Convention. In view of the distinct possibilities for such a Convention to be realised only at a later stage, or even not at all, it would be advisable in the meantime to use the contractual chain-concept developed for aviation-related liability in the context of Eurocontrol and to be embodied in the relevant Framework Agreement as much as feasible also in the wider context of Galileo, to ensure that a reasonably proper and coherent liability regime would be in place from the start.

Such liability 'guarantees' finally should be incorporated as a core element into the broader concept of service guarantees, as these would be foreseen for (in particular) CS (similar guarantees could also be envisaged *vis-à-vis* SOL and PRS, but would take on a different character for a number of reasons; in the first case it might be better to refer to 'integrity guarantees', in the second case to 'security guarantees') – but obviously subject to the commercial feasibility as perceived by the GOC-to-be. Such service guarantees would, beside guaranteeing a certain service level, also guarantee the continuous availability of that service level – in other words, effectively integrity.

12. Concluding remarks

It is clear that a highly complex, and in some respects quite revolutionary system such as Galileo is going to be, *inter alia* requires a sound institutional and legal framework within which to operate. Whilst the main contours of such a framework have by now gradually become clear, such as the PPP-structure encompassing a public supervisor and a private operator at the heart of the system and the need for a comprehensive Concession Agreement-structure preferably backed up with a proper Galileo Convention, these contours only raise further and more detailed legal and institutional issues. Some of them, e.g. how risks have to be allocated, how liability will have to be dealt with, and how to balance the respective competencies of the two entities thus involved, have briefly been touched upon in this paper. Some others, such as how to deal with IPR, standardisation and certification issue, still remain to be analysed in greater depth.

Yet, generally speaking, analysis would have to occur along the same lines; and the Galileo Legal/Functional Model also here may serve as an indicator as to how to proceed. In any event, there is still a lot of legal analysis and work to do, before Galileo will become operational in 2008.

Endnotes

[1]. See Conclusions of the Council, 2420th Council meeting, Transport/ Telecommunications, Brussels, 25/26 March 2002, SN 1790/02, pp. 19-21; Council Regulation (EC) No. 876/2002 of 21 May 2002 setting up the Galileo Joint Undertaking; OJ L 138, of 28 May 2002, pp. 1-8.

[2]. 'Integrity' refers to the trust a user can place in the correctness of the signals, and to his being warned if the signals are no longer within the bounds of such correctness as indicated by certain parameters. For the purpose of aviation, to allow for the use of any navigation aid in the course of precision operations, ICAO requirements call for monitoring such integrity in order to allow a Time-To-Alert (TTA) of 6 seconds maximum, i.e. within 6 seconds of a signal straying outside the relevant boundary values, the pilot should be informed to no longer trust those signals, allowing him to switch to other navigation aids and/or perform the necessary manoeuvres.

[3]. GPS stands for Global Positioning System, the US system providing signals to civil users since 1994.

[4]. GLONASS stands for Global Orbiting Navigation Satellite System, the Russian system providing signals to civil users since 1995.

[5]. It should be noted here that Norway and Switzerland as ESA member states are not member states of the European Union, yet shoulder their part of the financial burden at least when it comes to the development and deployment phases of Galileo. Conversely, EU-members Luxembourg and Greece are not members of ESA.

[6]. GALILEO Mission Requirements Document, Issue 5, Rev. 1.1, of 27 March 2003, p. 12. See further in more detail also GALILEO Mission High Level Definition, of 23 September 2002, pp. 12 ff.

[7]. Council Regulation (EC) No. 876/2002 of 21 May 2002 setting up the Galileo Joint Undertaking; OJ L 138, of 28 May 2002, pp. 1-8; Foundation Act of the Galileo Joint Undertaking by the European Community and the European Space Agency, ESA/LEG/274; 8 July 2003.

[8]. Alternative names have been coined, but the crucial issue is of course not the name chosen, but the legal character (in this case public), role, and competencies and responsibilities of such an entity.

[9]. Alternative names have been coined, but (again) the crucial issue is not the name chosen, but the legal character (in this case private) role, competencies and responsibilities of such an entity.

[10]. See Amended Convention on the International Mobile Satellite Organization of 1998, Artt. 3, 4(1); Public Services Agreement between the International Mobile Satellite Organization and Inmarsat One Limited and Inmarsat Two Company of 1998, Sec. 2.

[11]. As per the 1992 Civil Liability Convention and the 1992 Convention on the Establishment of an International Fund for Compensation for Oil Pollution Damage.

[12]. As per the 1960 Paris Convention on third-party liability in the field of nuclear energy and the 1963 Brussels Convention complementary thereto.

IAC-03-IISL.4.11

SECURITY ASPECTS OF THE GALILEO SERVICES

Mahulena Hofmann
Max Planck Institute for Comparative Public Law and International Law, Heidelberg, Germany*
mhofmann@mpil.de

ABSTRACT

In connection with the formulation of Galileo policies, many important legal questions occurred, one of them being the problem how to cope with the sensitive signals in a period of international crises. Unclear was the question whether a denial of certain emergency services within a zone of crisis would be legally possible and, if so, which would be the pertinent powers of the relevant security authorities. Under the provisions of the 1992 ITU Convention, it seems to be beyond any doubt that ITU-Member States are entitled to the suspension of their telecommunication services; the same conclusion applies, *a fortiori*, as concerns this right to suspend their telecommunication services in a situation of an international crisis, the only precondition being the notification to the Secretary-General. However: The structure proposed to deal with Galileo's security matters seems necessary to become more transparent in order to correspond more closely to the rule of law principles: Until now, it remains e.g. unclear which institution should according to which procedure decide about the mere fact whether or not an international crisis has in fact occurred.

I. INTRODUCTION

The high strategic importance of satellite navigation applications has been proved in several international crises. Both present systems – the US Global Positioning System (GPS) and the Russian Glonas network - are under military control. Since the Russian system has not generated any civil applications, GPS is used to a large extent for civil purposes but it can be cut off in the event of a crisis for civil users.

Thus, the autonomy of European countries in the sphere of distribution of satellite navigation signals in case of an international emergency and their independence from the existing system proved to be significant motives to develop an independent European network of navigation.

The European Commission presented an autonomous programme on satellite radio navigation, Galileo, in its communication of 10 February 1999 to be developed in four proposed phases: a definition phase in 2000, a development and validation phase up to 2005, a deployment phase up to 2007 and an operational phase thereafter[1]. The European Union Transport Ministers decided, on 26 March 2002, to launch this programme providing EU with satellite navigation and positioning system by 2008. It is aimed to create a civil systems managed by civil entities, interoperable with the existing Glonas and GPS systems, allowing users to combine different systems and giving them the benefit of optimised precision[2].

In connection with the formulation of Galileo policies, many important legal questions occurred, one of them being the problem how to cope with the sensitive signals in a period of international crises and emergencies, especially in relation to third States. Unclear was especially the question whether a denial of certain emergency services within a zone of crisis would be legally possible and, if so, which would be the pertinent powers of the relevant security authorities. Until now, the publicly available documents concerning the Galileo system have given only limited answers to these questions.

II. THE CATEGORIES OF GALILEO SERVICES

The Galileo system shall provide for international telecommunication services with various grades of sensibility:

The Open Service shall provide positioning, navigation and timing signals for the public that can be accessed free of charge; the Commercial Service shall provide encrypted data for commercial users.

The data of the Safety of Life Service and the Public Regulated Service belong without any doubt to the category of sensitive ones in the case of emergency. The Safety of Life Service is intended to provide a global warning of a loss integrity within a defined time-to-alarm limit; the coverage area of this service should be global. It is being defined in co-operation with COSPAS - SARSAT, and its characteristics and operations are regulated under the auspices of IMO and ICAO[3].

The Public Regulated Service should provide position and timing to specific users requiring a high continuity of service. It is expected to be used by groups such as police and customs. This form of service is required to be operational in all times and in all circumstances, notably during a period of crisis, when other services may be jammed. Technically, it will be separated from the other services, so it can be denied without affecting its operations[4]. The access to this encrypted ranging codes and data should be open to the European Union and its member states as well as other participating states authorised by the EU Member States who are supposed to maintain the control of distribution of receivers suggested for this form of Galileo Services.

III. THE SECURITY ISSUE IN THE GALILEO POLICY DOCUMENTS

The Galileo security policy seems to be defined by two basic documents: The *System Specific Security Requirements Statement Document* (SSRS) and the *Project Security Instructions* (PSI), both approved and maintained by the Galileo System Security Board (GBSS)[5]. These documents make clear that, together with the security of the infrastructure, the security of signals was of a central importance.

Concerning its security, the following measures are foreseen: To prevent the misuse of the system, a possibility of service denial under the control of the relevant security authorities within a zone of crisis is considered. This measure should be co-ordinated with other countries operating satellite navigation systems. In the case of Safety of Life Service, the need for formal notification prior to the denial is stressed.

Concerning the Public Regulated Services, the Galileo policy is based on the principle to consider the receivers developed for their signals as dual-use tools and as such submitted to the rules of the 1996 *Wassenaar* Arrangement[6].

The 2001 *Council Resolution on Galileo*[7] stressed that the security of Galileo network was an important element of the programme. It must guarantee not only the continuity of service required in certain application fields, such as affecting the safety of human life, but also those linked to access restriction or even access denials decided by civil authorities in crisis situations.

IV. LEGAL ASPECTS OF THE SECURITY ISSUE

IV. 1 Institutional Aspects

The general legal basis of the Galileo Security Policy are Articles 11 to 28 of the *Treaty on the European Union* devoted to the Common Foreign and Security Policy (CFSP). In accordance with these provisions the management of the security requirements of the Galileo system will be exclusively in the responsibility of EU institutions and EU member States:

Already in the development phase, the Galileo programme's management was shared between the EU Commission and the European Space Agency, each of whom has managed a certain number of contracts intended successfully to complete the programme's definition phase in accordance with their own administrative and budgetary rules. The Programme Management Board comprising a one representative of the Commission and one of the European Space Agency was attempting to compile the results of the activities and to draw up a co-ordinated plan for the future. Generally speaking, the political responsibility was in the hands of the Commission and the technical responsibility was held by the European Space Agency[8].

Until now, there are only a few references to a specific institution vested with the power to cope with security issues of the Galileo programme: In the literature[9], the System Security Board has been described as an institution which "approved and maintained" the basic Galileo security policy documents – the *System Specific Security Requirements Statement document* (SSRS) as well as the *Project Security Instructions* (PSI). The composition and powers of the Board remain unclear.

Despite of the existence of this body, the European Commission stressed in its 2001 *Communication to the European Parliament and the Council on Galileo*[10] that in the event of crisis, a European political body independent of Galileo management structures would be needed to be empowered to take the necessary measures. In addition, operational procedures have been suggested to be put in place between this designated body and the Galileo management structures in order to manage possible crisis situation.

This new institution has been introduced into the new structure of the Galileo programme following the present development phase: In order to prepare the conditions for the deployment phase, a new company structure, the Galileo Undertaking has been set up by the 2002 Council regulation (EC) No 876/2002 for a period of four years (Article 1 para 1)[11]. The aim of this structure based on Article 171 of the Treaty establishing the European Community is to guarantee a single management body for the programme and to enable a combination of public and private funding to be used. For reasons of legal certainty, this entity which is not designed to fulfil an economic purpose and is responsible for managing a public research programme of European interest, is considered as an international organisation within the meaning of the respective legal documents (Article 1 para 3)[12].

To deal with "security matters", a specific institution has been envisaged: According to Article 7 para 1 of the Regulation, a Security Board shall be established composed of one representative of each Member State of the European Union and of a representative of the Commission. Thus, the membership in this organ should remain limited to EU member states and not extended to other, with Galileo associated countries. According to Article 7 para 2 of the Council regulation, the Security Board shall adopt its rules of procedure. No more details on its functions have been made available yet.

After a four – years phase of the existence of the Joint Undertaking, a re-structuralisation of the Galileo system is envisaged: The *2003 Proposal for a Council Regulation on the establishment of structures for the management for the European satellite radio navigation programme*[13] foresees the dissolution of the Joint Undertaking and the transferral of its ownership to another institution – a Supervisory Authority. The main responsibilities of the Authority – again a Community body with legal personality (Article 4 para 1 of the Proposal) - should be to conclude the concession contract with a selected consortium on completion of the Galileo development as well as to ensure compliance by that consortium with the obligations arising from the concession contract. According to Article 19 of the Proposal the membership of countries which are not members of the European Union in this authority should be provided through bilateral agreements with the European Union to this effect.

Within the framework of the Authority, the security issues should be vested into the competence of a Centre of Security and Safety, a permanent and operational body under the auspices of the Secretary-General of the Council of the European Union (Article 20 of the Proposal). According to Article 22 of the Proposal the composition of the Centre should be determined by the Secretary–General of the Council, in liaison with the Commission. Also the operational procedures of this body should be "determined" by the Secretary–General.

The legal basis of the competencies of the Centre is Article 21 of the Proposal: According to this provision, the Centre should be given a general competence to fulfil any tasks in the area of security and safety which would be vested to it by the Council of the European Union. Second, it is expected – again very generally - to contribute to the actions relating to the safety of the European satellite radio navigation system. One of its most important tasks should be to give instructions to the operator of Galileo to "ensure the safety and reliability of the system".

Concerning its specific responsibilities defined by Article 21 of the Proposal, the Centre should be consulted on safety annexes to contracts, with a view of setting up the system, on the technical specifications of the government services (public regulated service) and the procedures and means of identifying the users. It should fulfil tasks in defining the cryptology that requires government approval and, when necessary, without prejudice to Article 300 of the EC Treaty provide the Commission with technical expertise within its ongoing negotiations with third States with regard to the safety of the navigation system.

The most sensitive feature of the Centre seems to be its role as an institution carrying the task of "giving instruction to the operator of Galileo to ensure the safety and reliability of the system" (Article 21 of the Proposal). The method of this "ensuring" should represent "in particular"..."compelling the operator to take such signals scrambling or interruption measures as may be required in the event of a crisis." From the legal point of view, the content of this "compelling" and the consequences of neglecting the instructions from the Centre by the operator require further elaboration.

In the practice, it is expected that the Centre should be capable of taking such measures as may be required in the event of crisis, especially by providing the operator with the necessary instructions (e.g. concerning jamming or cutting the signal). In addition, it should provide for an interface with the security authorities (European Member States, third countries and NATO) and with the operator[14].

IV.2 Material Aspects

All navigation services provided by the Galileo system belong to the category of "international telecommunication services" as formulated by the International Telecommunication Convention[15]. For the security aspects of the Galileo services, the rules of the ITU Constitution and Convention are applicable:

The right of Member States on suspension of services has been formulated in Article 35 of the 1992 ITU Constitution: According to this provision, each Member State reserves the right to suspend the international telecommunication service, either generally or only for certain relations and/or for certain kinds of correspondence, outgoing, incoming or in transit. The condition of the legality of this suspension has been an immediate notification of such action to each of the other Member States through the UN Secretary-General. No emergency situation is required[16]. This means, *a fortiori*, that, in an emergency situation, the Galileo Member States are entitled to suspend its signals under the condition that this suspension was notified in a prescribed formal procedure; this applies also to those data belonging to the group of Public Regulated Service.

One of the more complex questions connected with the activity of the Galileo is the problem whether a denial of Safety of Life services within a certain zone of crisis can be legally possible. Article 40 of the ITU Constitution gives those telecommunications which can be described as "Concerning Safety of Life" absolute priority if they relate to safety of life at sea, on land, in the air or in outer space[17]. The wording of Article 40 seems, however, not to exclude the safety of life services from the general scope of Article 35 of the 1992 ITU Constitution concerning the condition of suspension of telecommunication services giving these services priority in relation to other - not suspended - data. Applying a strict interpretation of Article 35 of the ITU Constitution, the suspension even of the Safety of Life Services seems to be legally possible under the condition of an immediate notification to the Member States through the Secretary-General.

This right of suspension under the ITU Constitution does not mean, however, that States cannot conclude arrangements exceeding such minimal standards and obliging themselves not to make use of their particular rights. This would be possible also under Article 42 of the ITU Constitution which gives the Member States the right to reserve for themselves, for the operating agencies recognised by them and for other agencies duly authorised to do so, the right to make special arrangements on telecommunication matters which do not concern Member States in general. Such arrangements, however, should not be in conflict with the terms of the Constitution, of the Convention or of the Administrative Regulations, so far as concerns harmful interference which their operation might cause to the radio services of other Member States, and in general so far as concerns the technical harm which their operation might cause to the operation of other telecommunication services of other Member States. This means that – theoretically - arrangements can be concluded by Galileo with third States excluding or minimising the possibility of suspending Galileo data both for the Public Regulated Services and for the Safety of Life Services.

Among non-EU countries, there is great interest in the Galileo signals. Generally, States which wish to be associated with the Galileo programme will be bound by specific agreements[18]:

In accordance with the mandate of the EU, the Commission started, in October 1999, formal negotiations with the countries having their own navigation systems – the United States and the Russian Federation – as well as with third countries having an interest in Galileo services: In Europe, the participation of Switzerland and the EFTA countries is assured, and discussions are under way with Central and East European countries and Ukraine. Also Canada is financially involved in Galileo studies, whereas Australia, Israel, as well as a number of Latin-American, African and Asian countries expressed a keen interest in the Galileo services. The contents of these arrangements including the possible provisions on signal denial in a crisis are not yet publicly available.

V. CONCLUSION

At the beginning of the paper, several questions were identified: the problem how to cope with the sensitive signals – the Public Relation Service data in a period of international crises and emergencies, especially in relation to third States. Unclear was especially the issue whether a denial of emergency services within a zone of crisis could be legally possible under the control of the relevant security authorities.

Under the provisions of the 1992 ITU Convention currently in force, it seems to be beyond any doubt that ITU-Member States are entitled to the suspension of their telecommunication services without there being any necessity of any special reason for that; the same conclusion applies, *a fortiori*, as concerns this right to suspend their telecommunication services in a situation of an international crisis, the only precondition being the notification to the Secretary-General. On the other hand, third countries interested in Galileo data will be wishing to have a guarantee as strong as possible that this situation will not occur in relation to their Public and Safety of Life Services. The presently applicable ITU rules allow - theoretically – for such arrangements in which the Galileo operator defines the continuity of the service precisely and obliges itself to refrain from using the right to suspend signals.

The proposed mechanism of the Galileo programme indicates, however, that a procedure would be introduced into its structures which would allow for a suspension of services in a period of crisis. However: Also in the interest of the potential customers of Galileo, it seems necessary to make this structure more transparent and as such corresponding more closely to the rule of law principles: Until now, it remains e.g. unclear which institution should according to which procedure decide about the mere – but essential - fact whether or not an international crisis has in fact occurred.

---

[1] COM(1999) 54 final, 10.2.1999.

2 WTDC-02, INF 25-E, 26 March 2002.

[3] Galileo. The European Programme for Global Navigation Services. ESA/European Commission, 2003, p.21.

[4] Ibidem, p. 21.

[5] Ibidem, p. 7.

[6] *L. Tytgat, R. Idiens*, GALILEO Status as of 5th April 2001-04-20, Galileo, Issue 3.5, April 2001, p. 8.

[7] Council resolution of 5 April 2001 on Galileo, Official Journal C 157, 30/05/2001 p. 0001-0003.

[8] Ibidem.

[9] Fn. 6, p. 8.

[10] Commission Communication to the European Parliament and the Council on Galileo, 16-17.

[11] Council resolution (EC) No 876/2002 of 21 May 2002 setting up the Galileo Joint Undertaking; entered into force on May 25, 2003.

[12] S. the second indent of Article 15(10) of the Sixth Council Directive 77/388/EEC of 17 May 1977 on harmonisation of the laws of the Member States relating to turnover taxes, OJ L 145, 13.6.1977 and the second indent of Article 23(1) of Council directive 92/12/EEC of 25 February 1992 on the general arrangements for products subject to excise duty and on the holding, movement and monitoring of such products, OJ L 76, 23.3.1992.

[13] 2003/0177 (CNS).

[14] Ibidem, p. 8.

[15] Signed on 22 December 1992 (Geneva), entered into force on 1 July 1994, as amended by the Plenipotentiary Conference (Kyoto, 1994) and the Plenipotentiary Conference (Minneapolis, 1998).

[16] Article 35 of the 1992 ITU Constitution reads as follows:

"Each Member State reserves the right to suspend the international telecommunication service, either generally or only for certain relations and for certain kinds of correspondence, outgoing, incoming or in transit, provided that it immediately notifies such action to each of the other Member States through the Secretary-General."

[17] Article 40 of the 1992 ITU Constitution reads as follows:

"International telecommunication services must give absolute priority to all telecommunications concerning safety of life at sea, on land, in the air or in outer space, as well as to epidemiological telecommunications of exceptional urgency of the World Health Organisation."

[18] Fn. 6, p.7.

QUASI-ZENITH SATELLITES SYSTEMS AND INTERNATIONAL COOPERATION UNDER SPACE LAW

Yuri Takaya
LL.M. of International Air and Space Law at Leiden University
e-mail: yuritakaya_japan@hotmail.com

ABSTRACT

Global Navigation Satellite Systems (GNSS) have been recognized in general as space military asset originally developed for military purpose (e.g. GPS, GLONASS). At present it offers multiple applications for commercial and military uses. Japan has been developing Quasi-Zenith Satellite Systems (QZSS) for purely commercial uses, since Article IX of the Constitution of Japan, namely 'renunciation of war', influences on space activities in Japan.

For QZSS project, the Advanced Satellite Business Corporation (ASBC), a private company, was established to promote business plans and to foster space industry. In the beginning of feasibility study, QZSS applications were to be for Asia-Pacific regional uses, however, at present it has changed service area only for domestic market in Japan without any international cooperation. It is worth suggesting ASBC to broaden QZSS service area to Asia-Pacific region under international cooperation.

1. BACKGROUND

Demand for satellite applications is increasing in both public and private sectors in Japan. For positioning and navigation systems in transportation, Japan has relied on the signal provision of Global Positioning Systems (GPS). Since GPS uses in Japan have been secured under the US-Japan Joint Statement of 1999[1], it is not necessary for Japan to build up new satellite systems as substitutes. However, due to geological reason that more than 70 % of Japanese land is mountainous, such areas need satellite systems that provides signals from the vertical point.

2. QUASI-XENITH SATELLITE SYSTEMS (QZSS)

The Quasi-Zenith Satellite Systems (QZSS) are complementary and augmentative to GPS signals. It would be deployed in Quasi-Zenith Orbit in 2008 with an inclination of 45 degree, using three orbit plane and three satellites in altitude of Geostationary Orbit. It offers (1) mobile communications (land-mobile services of data broadcasting and internet-access) (2) efficient use of frequencies (Quasi-zenith and geosynchronous satellites can share the same frequencies, as they are at different directions when viewed from ground stations) (3) navigation application (4) polar-region observations.

A government budget for R&B of QZSS was assigned to Communication Research Laboratory (CRL) in 1999, in the same year when European Commission announced Galileo project. The goal for QZSS project is not for independence from GPS reliance, but for fostering space industries and enhancing precision of signals in mountainous areas in Japan.

In July 2001, the Japan Business Federation proposed 'A grand strategy to expand the use of space frontier', and the Society of Japanese Aerospace Companies launched a feasibility study on QZSS in December 2001, resulting into establishment of a new working group for 'Advanced Satellite Business'. Such studies concluded that QZSS should be promoted under Public Private Partnership (PPP) for long-term benefits.

3. QZSS UNDER PPP

Under PPP, which is a key word to promote a long-term business plan, the roles of both public and private sectors were clarified separately in the Commission for the Development and Promotions of QZSS. In public sector, four ministries[2] cooperate for QZSS uses in the field of public services[3]. In private sector, several satellite companies established the Advanced Satellite Business Corporation (ASBC) in November 2002, with the aim of creating a new market in space industry[4], space communication and broadcasting[5], and related-equipment production industry[6]. In addition, feasibility study is conducted by a working group of the Association of the Development and Promotion of QZSS and ASBC.

In the phase of operation, ASBC would be the main actor for QZSS uses and Japan would support its activities as a launching state.

4. CURRENT IMPLICATION OF GPS USES

Since the US uses GPS for supporting military acts in several wars and for demonstrating National Missile Defense (NMD), such uses raise global debate against weaponization of outer space. In the case of QZSS, due to Article IX of the Constitution, which reflects historical background of Japan, the 'peaceful' uses of QZSS would be rather close to 'non-military', although this definition is changeable under the new Cabinet of Japan in September 2003.

4.1. GPS of US

In the US, originally GPS was designed and developed in the late 1960s and early 1970s as joint program of Navy and Air Force as the space-based sensors for communications and navigation for military purposes. Its scope was extended early in its development for complementary civilian uses as well.

Due to dual-use technology, the functions of GPS are not easily divided into civilian or military purposes since both sectors use it for communications, navigation, weather-forecasting, and remote sensing/reconnaissance.

Basically military space assets are categorized into 'non-aggressive' or 'aggressive'. Communication satellites, sensor satellites and navigation satellites which do not carry 'kinetic kill vehicles' are in the former, even though the military would use them for their interest of reconnaissance, surveillance and communications. And GPS is categorized into 'non-aggressive' satellites; however, it is deeply involved in NMD. Both NMD in space or on the ground requires GPS for early warning, communications and other support functions. The above testing relies on data from a GPS beacon for targeting ICBM to help detection of the intercept and assist mid-range tracking. Such military uses of outer space has started since the first 'space war', the 1990-1991 Persian Gulf War, when the U.S. army used GPS as space-based sensors to furnish communications at all levels in near real-time. In addition, military uses of GPS were conducted for the strikes on Yugoslavia in 1999, the Afghanistan War of 2001 and Iraq War of 2003.

In the definition of 'peaceful' of the Article IV of the 1967 OST, the US interpreted it into 'non-aggressive' that can read rather subjective in the above cases, although the 1959 Antarctic Treaty, which influenced on Article IV, uses 'peaceful' as 'non-military'.

Since the US withdrawal of the ABM Treaty, there is no arms control regime to prevent the US from deploying military asset in outer space. In 18 January 2002, the DOD of the US demonstrated the operational and live-fire testing of 161 military systems, which failed to prove the confident capability of the space-based interceptor for NMD[7]. Such military demonstration has continued for 1 year already even though it does not reach to the sufficient level yet.

4.2. QZSS of Japan

In Japan, the definition of 'peaceful' in the Article VI of the 1967 OST is based on Article IX of the Constitution of Japan which requires space activities to be conducted for purely scientific and technological progress under international cooperation.

Article IX of the Constitution of Japan (hereinafter the Constitution)[8] stipulates in Chapter II of Renunciation of War as follows;

> ***Article IX***
> *(1) Aspiring sincerely to an international peace based on justice and order, the Japanese people forever renounce war as a sovereign right of the nation and the threat*

or use of force as means of settling international disputes.

(2) In order to accomplish the aim of the preceding paragraph, land, sea, and air forces, as well as other war potential, will never be maintained. The right of aggression of the state will not be recognized.

Based on the Article IX, the utilization of QZSS is allowed only for peaceful purposes which irrelevant to NMD. It leads to security issues in public service for disaster management in Japan.

The author believes that Japan has fundamental background to enhance international cooperation for space benefit in conformity with space treaties and the Constitution.

ABSC

The Advanced Satellite Business Corporation (ASBC), established in 2002 would promote business and broaden business plan for QZSS service. Such business strategy is secured by the Joint Announcement[9] from the Second Japan-US GPS Plenary Meeting in 6 October 2002[10]. Both Governments decided to establish a technical working group to coordinate technical aspects related to QZSS and GPS.

5. LEGAL ASPECT OF LAUNCHING AND OPERATION OF QZSS

5.1. A Launching States of Japan

Since the first satellite of QZSS would be launched by Japanese government, the rest would be by ASBC from Japanese territory of Tanegashima island, it is clear that Japan is a launching state under Article II of the 1972 Liability Convention[11] (hereinafter the 1972 LC).

International Liability for QZSS Launching

In the phase of launching QZSS, in accordance with Article VII of the 1967 Outer Space Treaty[12] (hereinafter the 1967 OST), Japan would be liable for damage to another State Party to the Treaty, and to natural or juridical persons. In addition, in the case of damage on the surface of the Earth or aircraft flight, Japan would be absolutely liable under Article II of the 1972 LC.

International Liability for QZSS Operation

For QZSS operation, Japan is the only launching state responsible for the damage from collision with foreign satellites in outer space in accordance with. Article VII of the 1967 OST[13]. Since QZSS consists of three satellites being deployed in GEO[14] with 45 degree of inclination, it increases the possibility of collision with foreign satellites or space debris.

If the case of collision in outer space, Article II, III, IV, V, VI, and VII of the 1972 LC[15] would be applicable for compensation. In accordance with Article III of the 1972 LC, if damage caused elsewhere than on the surface of the Earth, Japan would be liable for damage only if the damage is due to its fault or the fault of persons for whom Japan is responsible.

5.2. QZSS Application under International Cooperation

In the beginning of QZSS project, service area of QZSS uses covers Asia-Pacific region including north part of Australia. However, the present feasibility studies for business promotion concluded that service area would be limited for domestic market, without international cooperation for space benefit. Regardless massive potential of QZSS applications, limitation of service are does not lead to a long-term benefit. The author examined possible reasons for limitation as follows;

(1) Geological Demand

Since more than 70 % of land is mountainous in Japan, it needs higher precision of positioning signals from the vertical point. If QZSS service area is broadened, the signal precision would not reach sufficient level inside of Japan.

(2) Fragile for Continuous Service

Since QZSS consists of three satellites and each provides signal for eight hours per day, in the case of service area focused in Japan, continuous service is not assured in technical study. In addition. if it covers the neighboring countries, the time of satellite operation would be longer than time for solar power charging, it is necessary for Japan to prove its technology before involving the neighboring countries into QZSS project.

(3) Liability Issues

Since QZSS would be operational by the private company, ASBC, it is lower risk if service area is limited for domestic market, especially in order to avoid liability issue under Article VII of the 1967 OST and Article II-CII of the 1972 LC.

However, since the neighboring countries have possibility to join QZSS business plan in future when technical and financial problem are solved, it is recommendable to involve them into PPP for a long-term space benefit.

6. INTERNATIONAL COOPERATION ON QZSS PROJECT

Under Article IX of the Constitution, satellite applications of Earth Observation and Communications have been conducted under international cooperation in Japan. However, for QZSS applications, the first priority is given to commercial interests by ABSC and its business plans seek for a short-term benefit by reducing service area. The author believes it is worth reminding PPP in Japan what principles and law are applicable to QZSS international cooperation.

6.1. Principle of International Cooperation

Besides the economical aspect, the political and legal issues have been increasingly focused on by the states concerned of Navigation Satellite System (NSS). The implementation of NSS for navigation and positioning needs international cooperation in order to realize seamless satellite navigation and positioning system. Especially for the world civilian aviation community, it is indispensable to implement it under cooperation with the space powers and developing countries with regard to the transport sector which several states are already dependent on the GNSS.

Principle of International Cooperation bases on the UN Charter and the 1970 Declaration of Principle of Friendship and Cooperation[16] to be regarded as international customary law. Under Article III of the 1967 OST, the Principle reflects in Article I, IX and X of the 1967 OST.

The above Declaration has the same purpose and principles of Article I and II of the UN Charter, and it obliges States Parties to cooperate each other to maintain international peace and security. In addition, such cooperation needs to be consistent with the UN Charter, even in outer space, to contribute to develop the mutual understanding, strengthen the friendly relations between States and peoples recalling the preamble of the 1967 OST.

Therefore, as long as QZSS applications are for peaceful purposes, it is recommendable to broaden QZSS service to Asia-Pacific region by involving neighboring countries into PPP of Japan.

6.2. Space Benefit Declaration[17]

NSS has potential application to create, maintain and share 'Space Benefit[18]' and Space Benefit Declaration provides an authoritative interpretation to Principle of International Cooperation. In 1988, Legal Sub-Committee of the Committee on the Peaceful Uses of Outer Space (COPUOS)[19] decided to add the 'space benefit' issue on the agenda of its 1989 session[20] and to establish a working group on that agenda item[21] in the same year. Such an attempt was realized during the 1991 session[22] resulting in 'Space Benefit Declaration', adopted by the General Assembly of the United Nations in 1996. Afterward, in 1999, this Declaration[23] contributed to the UNISPACEIII[24] resulting in the Vienna Declaration[25].

In the case of broadening QZSS service area, the following analysis of 'space benefit' would be recommendable to ASBC business plan.

> [Space Benefit Declaration] confirmed that the freedom of the exploration and utilization of outer space as well as reminds the space powers - in a productive and mutually fruitful manner - to fulfill their obligation to conduct their activities for the benefit of all countries, which means that the space powers should foster international cooperation -

on an equitable and mutually acceptable basis [26].

In accordance with Principle I, international cooperation should be taken into consideration in conformity with international law including the UN Charter and the 1967 OST. And Principle III encouraged space-faring countries to contribute to promoting and fostering international cooperation on an equitable and mutually acceptable basis. However, Principle III raises an issue for ABSC to consider the benefit and the interests of developing countries into business plans. Thus, this Declaration clarifies that space powers should involve developing countries into space activities 'on an equitable and mutually acceptable bases'.

6.3. Principle of Mutual Assistance

It is recommendable to consider marketing of QZSS applications to be based on mutual assistance with neighboring countries.

The definition of 'benefit' and 'interests' of Article I (1) of the 1967 OST clarified that Principle of Mutual Assistance prohibits space activities for the benefit and in the interests of 'specific' countries or region. However, those definitions should be interpreted in case of regional security as disaster management in Asia-Pacific region. In order to promote QZSS business plans, mutual assistance should be considered to involve the neighboring countries under international cooperation.

7. CONCLUSION

In 1999 Japan started a feasibility study on QZSS project for commercial benefit in Asia-Pacific regional uses. Since 70% of land is mountainous in Japan, it is necessary for positioning systems to obtain higher precision of signals from the vertical point. QZSS is complementary and augmentative to GPS signals, however, its goal is not independence from GPS reliance.

In order to promote business plans of QZSS for a long-term benefit, Japan has collaborated with four ministries and established one private company under PPP. When QZSS is be operational, the private company of ASBC would be responsible for all applications, therefore, QZSS is not for military uses but for commercial uses.

While the US GPS has been used for military purposes during several wars, and currently used for testing the capability of the ICBM interceptor for NMD after the withdrawal of the ABM Treaty. Japanese space activities are restricted for scientific and technological purposes under Article IX of the Constitution of Japan, namely 'renunciation of war'.

Feasibility studies on QZSS currently concluded into limitation of service area for domestic marcket. Regardless potential QZSS applications, ASBC does not promote business plan under international cooperation any more. However, the author believes Japan has fundamental background to promote international cooperation based on the Constitution.

It is worth reminding Japan as a State Party to space treaties that Principle of International Cooperation is applicable to QZSS which has potential application for Space Benefit in Asia-Pacific region. In order to promote QZSS business plans, it is possible to involve the neighboring countries into feasibility studies under international cooperation, which leads to a long-term benefit for Japanese space industries.

---

1 The US-Japan Joint Statement on GPS Uses, in 1999, made by US former president Clinton and Japanese former prime minister Obuchi.

2 Ministry of Public Management, Home Affairs, Posts and Telecommunications, Ministry of Education, Culture, Sports, Science, and Technology, Ministry of Economy, Trade and Industry, Ministry of Land, Infrastructure and Transport.

3 E.g. defense, national security, law enforcement, fire fighting, emergency, crisis management, next-generation ITS, transport administration, remote education, and warning system of global environment.

4 E.g. the industry of satellites, rockets, ground control stations, and satellite operators.

[5] E.g. platform industry, telecommunication service, broadcasters, positioning information service, internet service billing service, and advertising.

[6] E.g. mobile terminals, semi-conductor, information system integrator, contents creators, automobile, aerospace, shipbuilding, transport and logistics, construction, utilities (electricity and gas), insurance, medical services, education, surveying, agriculture, forestry and fisheries.

[7] Arms Control Association: Arms Control Today, Boese, W., "December Missile Defense Tests Yield One Success, One Failure", online at <http://www.armscontrol.org/act/2002_01-02/misdeftestjanfeb02.asp> (Last accessed: 02 Sept. 2002)

[8] Adopted on 3 November 1946, effective since: 3 May 1947, text is available at < http://www.oefre.unibe.ch/law/icl/ja00000_.html>

[9] Text is available at < http://www.soumu.go.jp/s-news/2002/021016_11_e.html>

[10] Both governments reconfirmed the US principle to continue to provide the GPS for peaceful, civil, commercial and scientific use, on a continuous and worldwide basis, and free of direct user fees.

[11] Convention on International Liability for Damage Caused by Space Object, UNGA resolution 2777 (XXVI), annex [24 UST 2389; TIAS 7762; 961 UNTS 187]

[12] Treaty on Principles Governing the Activities of States in the Exploration and Use of Outer Space, including the Moon and Other Celestial Bodies, UNGA resolution 2222 (XXI), annex [18 UST 2410; TIAS 6347; 610 UNTS 205]

[13] Treaty on Principles Governing the Activities of States in the Exploration and Use of Outer Space, including the Moon and Other Celestial Bodies, adopted on 19 Dec. 1966, opened for signature on 27 Jan. 1967, entered into force on 10 Oct. 1967. UNGA resolution 2222 (XXI) annex; 610 UNTS 205; UKTS No. 10 (1968), Comnd. 3519; 18 UST 2410, TIAS No. 6347.

[14] Geostationary Orbit, altitude: 36,000 km/

[15] Convention on International Liability for Damage Caused by Space Objects, adopted on 29 Nov. 1971, opened for signature on 29 Mar. 1972, entered into force on 1 Sept. 1972. UNGA resolution 2777 (XXVI) annex; 961 UNTS 187; UKTS No. 16 (1974), Cmnd. 5551, 24 UST 2389; TIAS 7762.

[16] Declaration on Principles of International Law Concerning Friendly Relations and Co-operation Among states in Accordance with the Charter of the United Nations, UNResolution2625 (XXV), 24 Oct. 1970

[17] Declaration on International Cooperation in the Exploration and Use of Outer Space for the Benefit and in the Interest of All States, Taking into Particular Account the Needs of Developing Countries, UNGA Resolution 51/122, 13 Dec. 1996

[18] On the early handling the subject, see, Jasentuliyana, N,. "Article I of the Outer Space treaty Revisited", Journal of Space Law 1989, (17,2), at 129-144, here at. 130-136

[19] COPUOS was established on 12 December 1959 by UNGA Resolution 1472 (XIV)

[20] See, the Report of the Legal Subcommittee on the Work of Its twenty-seventh session, UN Doc. A/AC. 105/411 of April 8, 1988, paras. 37-72.

[21] See, the Report of the Legal Subcommittee on the Work of Its Twenty-Eighth Session, UN Doc. A/AC. 105/430 of April 26, 1989, paras. 53 and 60.

[22] See, the Main Committee the Report of UNCOPUOS 1990, UN Doc. A/45/20, para. 120

[23] See, UN Doc. A/AC.105/385, 411 and 430

[24] Based on UNGA Resolution 52/56: International Cooperation in the Peaceful Uses of Outer Space, UN Doc. A/Res/52/56 (1997).

[25] See, The Space Millennium: Vienna Declaration on Space and Human Development, which was the final resolution to be adopted by UNISPACE III.

[26] See; Marietta Benko and Kai-uwe Schrogl, "The UN Committee on the Peaceful Uses of Outer Space Adoption of a Declaration on 'Space Benefits' and Other Recent Developments", in ZLW, Jg 2/1997 at 233.

IAC-03-IISL.4.14

CURRENT LEGAL ISSUES RELATING TO GNSS

Phillip R. Bower, Georgetown University Law Center, Washington, D.C., U.S.A.
philbower@hotmail.com*

ABSTRACT

Although GNSS has been active since 1970, there are still many legal issues surrounding its operation and applications that are unresolved. GNSS is engrained in the daily lives of millions of people, often without their knowledge. Its applications are numerous, spanning both military and civilian uses, from navigation of missiles and vehicles to recreation and safety. The economic market potential of GNSS is expected to reach $40 billion in the foreseeable future. These factors make the control of GNSS an important issue between countries. National and international policy making bodies should consider and understand the status of global GNSS systems – GPS, GLONASS, and Galileo – when making policy regarding GNSS.† Other legal issues, such as liability, control of GNSS, militarization of space, and coexistence of the several systems, surround GNSS and its potential applications. The international community must find solutions to these issues to ensure a seamless operation of GNSS for the common interest of mankind.

INTRODUCTION

Tomahawk cruise missiles, fired from hundreds of miles away, and guided by GPS, drop into a target with pinpoint accuracy. Hikers search for hidden caches in a popular recreational activity, geocaching, using GPS locators.[1] Drivers navigate through cities with GPS receivers in their cars.

These are only a fraction of the current worldwide uses of the Global Navigation Satellite System (GNSS). While GNSS has been active since 1970, with a decrease in the cost and size of receivers and an increase in accuracy, the use of GNSS has exploded. The yearly market for GNSS related services is expected to reach $40 billion in the foreseeable future.[2] The United States plans to begin phase down of several other radionavigation systems in 2010, increasing dependence on GNSS.[3] At the 2000 World Radiocommunication Conference, the International Telecommunication Union (ITU) allotted additional frequencies to GPS and GLONASS for upgrades to the systems, as well as providing spectrum to the proposed European system, Galileo.[4] The potential of GNSS has only begun to be tapped.

GNSS has become engrained in the daily lives of millions of people, whether they know it or not. The integrity of GNSS needs to be protected and maintained to ensure the safety of those dependent on the system. This paper will outline some of the outstanding questions and concerns that still face the GNSS industry. Section I will discuss the current status of the worldwide GNSS systems – GPS, GLONASS, and Galileo. Section II will explain some legal issues surrounding GNSS, such as liability, control of GNSS, militarization of space, and coexistence of the several systems. While many of these legal issues have surrounded GNSS from its conception, a continuing dialogue is necessary as GNSS applications affect more people and more nations.

* J.D. Georgetown University Law Center, May 2004 (expected). This paper was prepared as part of the Space Law Seminar, and the author would like to thank Professor Paul B. Larsen for his guidance and support. The author is solely responsible for the views represented in this paper.

† In this paper, GNSS will refer to the global navigation satellite system in general, while GPS will refer to the U.S. system specifically.

I. BACKGROUND: THE CURRENT STATUS OF WORLDWIDE GNSS SYSTEMS

Currently, the U.S. GPS is the only system that is fully operational. The Russian GLOSNASS system does not have the full number of operational satellites in orbit necessary to provide full worldwide service to users, and the Europeans are still developing their Galileo system.

A. United States – Global Positioning System (GPS)

In 1995, the United States GPS system achieved full operational capability.[5] The $12 billion[6] GPS constellation currently consists of 29 Block II satellites[7] that are in orbit 12,500 miles above the earth and situated in six 55-degree orbit planes.[8] GPS is managed jointly by the Department of Defense (DOD) and Department of Transportation (DOT) through the Interagency GPS Executive Board (IGEB).[9] Because the DOD is heavily involved in the management of GPS, the funding necessary to maintain the system is more easily obtained in military appropriations from Congress than if GPS only had civilian uses.

In the early days of GPS, the United States purposely degraded civilian GPS signals to 100-meter accuracy, while maintaining a much higher accuracy for the US military.[10] However, numerous reports in the 1990s argued that this restriction should be lifted.[11] On May 1, 2000, President Clinton lifted the restriction on GPS signals, allowing civilian users to gain accuracy within 20 meters of their actual position.[12] The move was part of a 1996 presidential directive to spur civil, commercial and scientific use of the GPS worldwide.[13] Interestingly, this change also allowed NASA to access to the improved signals, an access it did not previously have, and enabled spacecraft to navigate by GPS rather than by bouncing radar signals off earth-based tracking systems.[14] The U.S. is constantly upgrading the GPS constellation to improve signal strength and accuracy as well.

Around July 2004, the Air Force will begin launches for a series of eight new "modernized" satellites (GPS-2RM) that will feature additional military and civilian signals, as well as increased power for the military signal. When power is increased for the military, the civilian signal power will probably also increase, meaning less interference from natural or manmade sources. At least two more series of satellites are planned, the GPS-2F and the GPS-3. The launch of the upgraded GPS-3 system is currently scheduled to begin launching in 2012, but possibly as early as 2010.[15]

B. Russia – Global Navigation Satellite System (GLONASS)

The Russian GLONASS was developed in the 1980s and was fully deployed by 1996[16] under the control of the Russian military.[17] Currently the system is operating in a partial mode, with less than the operational quota of 21 satellites deployed.[18] The Russians did launch several satellites in late 2002 to gradually begin an upgrade of service.[19] Europe considers GLONASS to be more of an augmentation to GPS, rather than a stand-alone system, especially considering the economic situation of the country.[20] It does not appear that GLONASS will be a viable competitor or back up system to GPS in the foreseeable future.

C. European Union – Galileo

The European Union (EU) and European Space Agency (ESA) are now developing their own GNSS system, known as Galileo. Galileo is designed to be a stand-alone system that is also fully compatible with both GPS and GLONASS.[21] Specific plans for the service include: increased coverage over all of Europe, revenue generation through charging for high accuracy and/or data transmission over the navigation signal, Safety and Rescue uses, such as weather alerts or distress acknowledgments, and temporary map changes such as accident reports or tourist information.[22] However, the biggest unprecedented promise Galileo makes is to deliver real-time positioning accuracy down to the meter range to the civilian sector by using dual frequencies.[23] Galileo also will guarantee availability of the service under all but the most extreme circumstances and will inform users within seconds of a failure of any satellite, making the system more suitable for when safety is crucial, such as landing aircraft.[24]

The first experimental satellite is scheduled for launch in late 2004, with the full constellation of thirty satellites (twenty-seven operational plus three active spares) operational by 2008.[25] ESA estimates that it will have 1.8 million users of Galileo by 2010, doubling to 3.6 million users by 2020.[26] The total investment cost for the Galileo system is estimated to be 3.2 billion Euros, with an annual cost of 220 million Euros, including operations, maintenance and replenishment.[27]

Europe does not attempt to hide the fact that Galileo is an issue of European independence – it is developing Galileo because the military operators of GPS and GLONASS will not make any guarantees that they will maintain an uninterrupted service of GNSS.[28] Therefore, Galileo is planned as a civilian service, and will not be run by the military. ESA claims Galileo will be "guaranteed to operate at all times, bar the direst emergency."[29]

Europe gives several other reasons for Galileo as well.[30] After the constellation is in place, the number of GNSS satellites will more than double, allowing for more accurate readings globally, even in high-rise cities. Better coverage will be achieved at higher latitudes, such as in northern Europe, because the satellites will be at a greater inclination to the equatorial plane than GPS. Lastly, the increased civilian accuracy will allow for more commercial applications of GNSS. European manufacturers would like to get an increased share of the $40 billion GNSS market by developing equipment for these new applications.

Galileo may face several hurdles before it gets off the ground. For instance, in December of 2001, the transport ministers of the European countries involved with Galileo refused to endorse the project; some European officials voiced the opinion that this was due to the military applications of the proposed Public Restricted Service, an encrypted communications functionality for use by European security authorities.[31] As discussed in Section II.A. *infra*, there may be liability concerns if a fee is charged for Galileo's signal, and some experts question whether anyone will pay for GNSS access when GPS is free.

D. Augmentation

GNSS satellite signals are not currently accurate enough on their own to provide the precise location that some applications need. Additional ground-based stations or satellites provide a secondary signal to establish an additional reference point, which provides greater accuracy and integrity to the GNSS signal.[32] The U.S. Coast Guard maintains the Maritime Differential GPS (MDGPS) to provide coastal coverage around the United States and other navigable waters.[33] The Federal Aviation Administration (FAA) is developing two systems, the Wide Area Augmentation System (WAAS) and Local Area Augmentation System (LAAS), to aid air navigation as well as landing and maneuvering. The FAA has recently commissioned WAAS for instrument flight use, allowing pilots to navigate as low as 350 feet above the runway end using satellite navigation.[34] The MDGPS is also being expanded to provide coverage to all surface areas of the United States, forming the Nationwide Differential GPS (NDGPS) for surface users, providing an accuracy of 10 meters or better in all areas.[35]

Europe is developing an augmentation system known as the European Geostationary Navigation Overlay System (EGNOS).[36] This system uses additional satellites in geostationary orbit to provide supplemental signals and correction data, rather than ground-based stations like DGPS. Japan has coordinated its Multifunctional Transport Satellite-based augmentation system (MSAS) to operate with the U.S. WAAS, mainly for navigation purposes. More countries are sure to soon follow with their own augmentation systems as GNSS becomes cheaper, more common, and more powerful.

II. LEGAL ISSUES

A. Liability

Several possibilities for assigning liability for GNSS failure exist: The Convention on International Liability for Damage Caused by Space Objects, a new liability treaty, or existing national laws. The Convention on International Liability for Damage Caused by Space Objects provides that the launching state of a registered space object should be absolutely liable for damages caused by that object on the surface of the earth or to aircraft flight.[37] There is some suggestion that this should be extended to damages caused by the failure of GNSS, although causation, the fact that damage would be indirect, and the doubt that a GNSS signal is a "space object" under the Liability Convention, makes the Convention unlikely to cover GNSS liability.[38] For instance, GNSS failure could cause ships to wreck or run aground or cause an aircraft to crash on landing, but this damage was not created directly by a satellite hitting the ship; determining which system the GNSS signal actually came from would also be problematic.

With many navigation systems now dependent on GNSS, it is scary to imagine what could happen if GNSS was suddenly and globally knocked out. Understandably, the United States would not sign on to any convention that accepted liability for such a catastrophe. The United States argues that the cost of maintaining the GPS system, while at the same time providing it free of charge to the world, alleviates any liability responsibility.[39] As long as the United States refuses to join any liability convention, it will be a useless endeavor.

The U.S. is aware of potential weaknesses in the GPS system. A 2001 report for the DOT included the following recommendations: identify and develop appropriate low-cost back-up systems, implement systems to monitor, report, and locate unintentional interference, create awareness among GPS users about the vulnerability of GPS, and continue development of higher broadcast power and more civilian frequencies.[40] Liability aside, these are all common sense measures that the DOT and DOD are pursuing in most cases to ensure a stable GPS system for all users.

An interesting question arises with the possibility of Galileo charging user fees in order to pay for the GNSS signal. Without military funding behind it like what GPS receives, Galileo might be forced to charge the transportation industries a fee to maintain the highly accurate signals that are necessary for the industry.[41] If the service fails, liability might be more readily imposed than if the service was free. It is possible that insurance coverage could be included in the package if a subscription cost or annual fee is charged.[42] The U.S. Air Force conducted studies on the feasibility of user costs on GPS services and determined that a tax/trust fund method could be used to collect fees on DGPS.[43] The United States has decided not to pursue any revenue generation from GPS, partially because the military funding it receives has not made it a necessity and partially to avoid potential liability.

Liability arising under the provision of augmented GNSS signals is a serious concern. Generally, international governmental organizations that provide GNSS, such as EGNOS, would be immune, unless they submit to international or national liability laws.[44] Governmental organizations in the United States, such as the U.S. Coast Guard, are subject to the Federal Tort Claims Act (FTCA). Under the FTCA, federal agencies can be held liable for negligent acts except for discretionary acts. Air traffic control is not a discretionary act under case law, so it follows that the FAA or Coast Guard could be liable for any act that is "legally analogous to traffic control of airplanes and ships."[45] Private organizations that provide augmentation would be liable for negligence under the applicable Torts law.

Michael Jennison argues that liability should be kept separate from any international GNSS scheme for several reasons.[46] First, in most states surveyed, victims could recover for injury, death, and damages resulting from a negligent failure of a navaid under national laws, like under the FTCA. However, the FTCA does not cover claims arising in a foreign country or claims arising out of combatant activities of the military or naval forces, or Coast Guard, during time of war.[47] This substantially limits the type of liability claim arising from GPS failure that could be brought against the United States, and the United States is unlikely to expand the waiver of sovereign immunity for GPS. Second, Jennison says fact-finding liability systems can handle complex relationships and factual situations. But if the claims cannot even make it statutorily to the U.S. court system under the FTCA, this will be a moot point; there will be no way to recover or to enforce damages.

Third, Jennison argues linking liability reform with GNSS will weaken the prospects for both because the United States would be unlikely to sign on to such a convention, and the agreement would limit liability to one navaid. The United States would not sign onto such an agreement, unless it was an express waiver of liability, and such an agreement could cause the United States to limit service to the rest of the world. Fourth, Jennison says GNSS will be cheaper and safer than the current reliable systems, and it is rare for the negligent failure of a navaid to be the primary cause of an accident. Lastly, ICAO has previously spent years trying to develop a liability scheme for air traffic control, but removed the item from the agenda due to lack of interest. Therefore, there is not likely to be any change in the current liability scheme soon; users of GNSS seem to bear the risk of liability by using the system free of charge.

B. Control of the GNSS system

With GPS as the only fully operational GNSS system in use, many States are concerned about the control of GPS and that it could be shut down without notice. Concerns include who will control standards and quality. Despite the recent U.S. military conflicts and the availability of the free GPS signal to anyone with a receiver, U.S. officials have said there are no plans to restrict access to the civilian signal – a move that would require a presidential directive.[48] However, this assurance is not guaranteed or enforceable under international law.[49] Also, GNSS is vulnerable to interference from both intentional and unintentional sources, natural and manmade.[50] Simple, low cost jammers can disrupt the GNSS signal over large areas.[51] This rightfully has many users concerned.

The U.S. military is seeking money to provide higher power signals to the military, and therefore likely improve civilian signals as well.[52] The boosted signal "would make it easier for receivers to find other, low-power satellites, even in an environment full of electronic noise thrown up to drown out the GPS signal."[53] This would allow the U.S. military to jam an adversary's over-the-counter GNSS equipment on a battlefield, but still use its own. The Air Force has scheduled these power boosts to begin with the GPS-2F satellites that will be launched beginning in 2005, and continuing GPS-3 system in 2011.[54] DOD vehicles also carry secondary, non-GPS navigation system in case of GPS failure.[55] Civilians may benefit from increased GNSS power signals from upgraded satellites, but may not have access to secondary systems or cutting edge anti-jamming technology that would give greater assurances of seamless navigation.

As such, many people are skeptical about leaving GNSS in the hands of one country or one person – Europe cites this concern as one of its main reasons for building Galileo. Francis Lyall advocates an international public operational entity to ensure the public interest in GNSS is met.[56] Lyall would like to see an independent international organization charged with the operation of an international GNSS, possibly modeling itself after the pre-privatized Intelsat. Such an organization would not likely be joined by the United States, who would be reluctant to give up their military control, and it could lead to liability or anti-trust suits.

Langhorne Bond, former FAA Administrator, suggests that a multi-lateral treaty is the answer to the control problems.[57] Such a treaty would allow GNSS-provider states to maintain sovereignty over their systems, while stating the conditions under which they provide the signal to other nations. Bond believes a treaty should require the civilian signal to be provided continuously to all with the following exceptions: specific causes for signal withdraw or alteration, including terrorism and military causes at a minimum, and possibly economic sanctions. Turning off a signal as part of economic sanctions may create other problems, because the signals cannot be turned off along national boundaries, but rather over a region, potentially affecting other states as well. Bond argues that user charges should be decided outside of the treaty, no GNSS providers should assume liability for loss of signal, and the treaty should use ICAO SARPS to ensure interoperability. Bond believes the GNSS-providers will have the bargaining power to achieve the terms they want in the treaty and thus be held responsible under international law to the terms of the treaty.

However, the only real difference between the current scheme and the treaty proposed by Bond is that the United States would have to lay out all the possible scenarios in which it might turn off the signal and give notice of service disruption. Currently, the United States may turn off the GPS signal for any reason without notice, although it has promised ICAO that it will continue the signal.[58] It is unlikely that the U.S. would be willing to create such certain terms, especially in the interest of national security. Also, if liability is still assumed by the user, what is the penalty if service is disrupted outside of the terms of the treaty? The GNSS provider holds all the cards and may threaten to discontinue service altogether if penalized.

While Bond's argument for a multilateral treaty might not be feasible, his suggestion for ensuring interoperability in general is a good idea.[59] The bigger question is what international institutions, if any, should become the caretaker of GNSS. Several organizations, such as the International Civil Aviation Organization (ICAO) or the International Maritime Organization (IMO), are possibilities.

Of all the international groups, ICAO has been widely suggested because of its mandate under the 1944 Chicago Convention to create international Standards and Recommended Practices (SARPS) for aircraft navigation.[60] Article 37 of the Convention gives ICAO the authority to adopt SARPS for "air navigation aids,"Article 28 provides that each contracting state will provide facilities in accordance with the SARPS, and Article 44 charges ICAO to develop "the principles and techniques of international air navigation and to foster the planning and development of international air transport." These Articles appear to give ICAO the legal authority it needs to regulate air navigation by GNSS, and indeed, the United States has pledged to fully cooperate with ICAO in establishing those SARPS.[61]

In 1991, ICAO developed plans for a new navigation regime called Communications, Navigation, Surveillance/Air Traffic Management (CNT/ATM) that depends heavily on GPS and GLONASS.[62] ICAO created a panel of Legal and Technical Experts (LTEP) in 1995 in an attempt to create consensus on GNSS issues. The panel created a Charter of Rights and Obligations of States Relating to GNSS Services that was adopted by the ICAO Assembly in 1998 as a nonbinding charter. The Charter makes several pronouncements such as safety shall be the paramount principle, aircraft of all states shall have nondiscriminatory access to GNSS services, states retain responsibility and authority for air traffic control in their airspace, states providing GNSS services shall ensure their "continuity, availability, integrity, accuracy, and reliability," and will comply with ICAO standards.[63] These pronouncements are mostly policy restatements or implied by the Chicago Convention and existing policy guidance, suggesting that GNSS is simply another navaid for legal purposes.[64] Although ICAO has the authority to create SARPS for air navigation, it is unlikely that ICAO will gain regulatory control of the entire spectrum of GNSS applications.

C. Dual-Use: Militarization of Space?

GPS was developed by the DOD as the Defense Navigation Satellite System.[65] The satellites are designed with all the common military survivability measures, such as protection against electro-magnetic pulse effects of a nuclear blast.[66] Even with the current civilian uses overtaking the military uses, the DOD maintains responsibility for management and operations of the ground control and space-borne segments of the system.[67] If the military is so involved in the use and control of GPS, how can GPS be a "peaceful purpose" as aspired to under the Outer Space Treaty?[68]

Many satellites can have a military aspect, as well as a scientific or civilian purpose – weather, direct broadcasting, communication, remote sensing, etc.[69] The military uses GPS in personal, vehicle, marine and air navigation and for missile and bomb guidance. The U.S. military can locally jam or disrupt an enemy's GPS signal to yield a tactical advantage.[70] GPS satellites carry a secondary payload that can detect nuclear detonations (and therefore testing) anywhere on the earth's surface in near real time.[71] The background of GPS and many of its uses would seem to make it a military use in outer space, and not peaceful.

Several arguments exist to justify GNSS as a peaceful purpose. First, GNSS now has more civilian and peaceful uses than military uses, and the system is available for international use. Second, the specific language of the Outer Space Treaty does not appear to ban national security uses or defensive uses of space because it expressly forbids some activities in Article 4.

The theme of the peaceful use of outer space was established by the United Nations Committee on the Peaceful Uses of Outer Space (COPUOS) and was inserted in the preamble of the Outer Space Treaty in 1967. It was subsequently affirmed in later space treaties and UN resolutions relating to space, as well as in U.S. law.[72] The Outer Space Treaty first recognizes that the use of outer space for peaceful purposes is in the common interest of all mankind, and then continues that it is desirable "to contribute to broad international cooperation in the . . . use of outer space for peaceful purposes."[73]

Yasuaki Hashimoto suggested that a test for legality of an outer space use might be a triangle with common interest at the top and international cooperation and peaceful use at the bottom corners.[74] Using this test, it might seem clear that GPS is a legal use. GPS is free for all people in the world with a receiver. It is used for numerous peaceful applications and many are international in use, such as ship and aviation navigation.

However, on the other side of the puzzle, GPS is maintained exclusively by the United States, and is not a product of international cooperation. In fact, Europe is creating its Galileo system partially because of concerns that the United States has full control over GPS and could turn it off without notice.[75]

Another argument is that the peaceful applications are secondary to the military applications for which GPS was developed. The United States' position is that the Outer Space Treaty explicitly prohibits nuclear weapons or weapons of mass destruction in orbit, as well as military bases, installations, and fortifications, the testing of weapons, and military maneuvers on any celestial body.[76] By limiting Article IV to celestial bodies, the United States argues that the States did not desire to create a broad prohibition on military uses in outer space and that "peaceful" means "non-aggressive" rather than "non-military."[77]

This definition of "peaceful" is in conflict with other existing interpretations found in international law – the Antarctic Treaty defines "peaceful" as "non-military," and specific references to military installations are regarded as exemplificative rather than exhaustive in nature.[78] But the United States' interpretation is probably not in bad faith, and it is therefore a permissible interpretation under international law.[79] Even so, some authors still argue that allowing any military action in space is a wrongful literal interpretation of the treaty, rather than the proper interpretation in light of the objectives and purposes of the treaty.[80]

The Outer Space Treaty does allow for the use of space in the interest of maintaining international peace and security.[81] Harry Almond argues that Article III of the Outer Space Treaty is in fact a reservation by the States of their full rights to pursue measures for self-defense in outer space.[82] If a State believes outer space is a strategic and appropriate arena in which to deter or prevent aggression or other conduct contrary to a State's fundamental goals or policy, the State will use outer space to that means. Thus, the fact that outer space is a useful arena to the United States' military may mean that more beneficial commercial uses are created there are well, as demonstrated by the dual use satellite systems currently in place.

It does not appear that the dual use quality of GPS will change anytime soon in the United States, even after the introduction of Galileo. Domestic policy ensures funding for GPS maintenance, upgrade, and operation because of the military purposes. The United States has placed the DOT in control of civilian uses of GPS in order to make sure the military applications do not overrun civilian uses. GPS is probably too engrained in peaceful, civilian applications to be turned off any time soon, with the possible exception of a major military escalation.

D. Coexistence of the three systems (GPS, GLONASS, Galileo)

Because GPS is currently the only fully operational system, equipment design and standardization is fairly simple. However, the upcoming Galileo system and the potential for other future systems mean coexistence and interoperability could become a major issue for GNSS. To ensure the safety and usability of GNSS, all the systems should use the same language, receiving equipment should allow for seamless transition from system to system, access should be nondiscriminatory, true redundancy should be built into the system, and enough radio frequencies must be allotted to allow all the systems to operate.

The United States has recommended that GPS and augmentation standards be the standards for international use.[83] Japan has developed its augmentation system based on U.S. standards.[84] Because the U.S. is essentially the only GNSS provider in the world today, and all current equipment is based on that system, it makes sense for new systems to standardize to the GPS system.

Currently, a user can use GPS and GLONASS seamlessly.[85] It is anticipated that Galileo will be interoperable with GPS and GLONASS as well.[86] The European Commission states that one objective of cooperation with the United States is to ensure users will be able to GPS and Galileo with a single receiver, important for users who do want to have separate receivers for each system.[87] Users should also be able to access each system without discrimination, possibly not even knowing when a receiver has changed systems. However, in certain situations it might be important for a user to know which system he is currently receiving information from. One such situation could develop if the data received is wrong or the system stops transmitting and liability needs to be determined. A user might prefer to be on one system rather than on another, especially if Galileo provides the high accuracy signal it anticipates, charges for its signal, or admits liability. Receiver designs and the information they provide to users could alleviate most of these concerns, as well as signal disruption notification that GNSS providers plan to provide.

Another important consideration for GNSS providers is redundancy. If a natural electrical phenomenon or a jammer knocks out satellites or signals from one provider, there should be guarantees that the other system will not also be knocked offline. Future satellite designs increase the GNSS signal power, alleviating some jamming concerns. Also, it is possible that the U.S. military could be persuaded to release some of its older anti-jamming technology in a technology transfer program as it develops new equipment. However, it does not appear that Galileo would somehow be protected from electrical phenomena that would disrupt GPS, so true redundancy may still need to be pursued.

It is also important that the delegates at the 2003 World Radiocommunication

Conference recognize the importance of GNSS and allocate enough frequencies to the major GNSS providers so that they may continue to upgrade the quality of GNSS. The WRC 2000 did allot more frequencies to both GPS and GLONASS for upgrades and provided spectrum for Galileo.[88] This hopefully shows the international commitment to developing accurate and powerful GNSS worldwide.

CONCLUSION

With great power comes great responsibility. GNSS is a powerful tool that increasingly affects more of our everyday lives. Fortunately, so far the major players have recognized the importance of GNSS and have cooperated with each other. Many scholars have suggested that some type of legally binding international agreement ensuring the quality and availability of GNSS would be desirable that would put the force of international law behind the current assurances that the States active in GNSS have made. Liability, international control, dual use, and interoperability will all be major points of issue for any such agreement.

"The politics of GNSS is the politics of arrogance, veiled and competing national (and regional interests) in all its forms, frustration and coercion. It embodies all that is bad in international relations . . . [i]t involves finding a delicate balance. . ."[89] Therein lies the problem with an international agreement. The United States will not sign an agreement unless liability is waived for provider states and dual use is preserved. These concessions would make any agreement worthless.

Therefore the approach of ICAO seems more prudent: an internationally recognized body allows provider States to maintain their systems, but creates standards that are reasonable and based around safety. Once Galileo is operational, there will be less concern about what the United States *might* do with GPS. A more feasible agreement might then focus on ensuring global access to standardized GNSS, since it is in the provider states' interests to build and market standardized equipment and to use one navigation system worldwide. A predicted $40 billion market might alone be an assurance that those who provide GNSS will continue to do so to the best of their abilities. While GNSS might make for bad politics, it continues to open doors for innovative and creative applications and is here to stay.

REFERENCES

[1] *See, e.g.*, http://www.geocaching.com/.

[2] Paul B. Larsen, *Issues Relating to Civilian and Military Dual Uses of GNSS*, 17 SPACE POLICY 111, 111 (2001). By comparison, it costs the United States about $300-400 million a year to maintain and upgrade the system. *Id.*

[3] 2001 FEDERAL RADIONAVIGATION PLAN at 3-2 [hereinafter FRP], *available at* http://www.navcen.uscg.gov/pubs/frp2001/default.htm (Updated: October 10, 2002).

[4] Alfons AE Noll, *The ITU in the 21st Century*, 5 SING. J. INT'L & COMP. L. 63, 64-5 (2001).

[5] *Boeing: Global Positioning System General Information, at* http://www.boeing.com/defense-space/space/gps/m_gen.html (last visited May 12, 2003).

[6] Matthew L. Wald, *U.S. to Improve Satellite Navigation System*, N.Y. TIMES, Mar. 30, 1998, at 12.

[7] *Current GPS Constellation, at* http://tycho.usno.navy.mil/gpscurr.html (last visited May 12, 2003).

[8] David A. Turner and Marcia S. Smith, *GPS: Satellite Navigation and Positioning and the DOD's Navstar Global Positioning System*, Congressional Research Service, The Library of Congress, at 5 (February 15, 1994) [hereinafter CRS Report].

[9] FRP, *supra* note 3, at 2-2.

[10] CRS Report, *supra* note 8, at 8.

[11] *See, e.g.*, CRS Report, *supra* note 8, at 34-5.

[12] Alex Canizares, *U.S. Lifts Ban On Private Use of GPS at* http://www.space.com/ business technology/business/gps_ban_lifted_000501.html (01 May 2000).

[13] *Presidential Decision Document, Fact Sheet, U.S. Global Positioning System Policy*, Office of Science and Technology Policy and National Security Council (March 29, 1996), [hereinafter PDD], *available at* http://www.ostp.gov/NSTC/html/pdd6.html.

[14] Canizares, *supra* note 12.

[15] Jim Banke, Cape Canaveral Bureau, *Air Force Orbits GPS Satellite with Delta 2 Rocket, at*

http://www.space.com/missionlaunches/delta2_launch_030331.html (31 March 2003).
[16] *GLONASS – Summary, at* http:// www. spaceandtech.com/spacedata/constellations/glonass_consum.shtml (last visited May 12, 2003).
[17] CRS Report, *supra* note 8, at 28.
[18] *GLONASS*, *supra* note 16.
[19] *Id.*
[20] *EU Task Force on Public Private Partnership, Report to Commissioner Neil Kinnock*, at 5 (4 June 1999).
[21] J. Benedicto, et al., *Galileo: Satellite System Design and Technology Developments*, ESA, at 2 (November 2000), *available at* http://www.esa.int/export/esaSA/GGG0H750NDC_navigation_0.html (Last update: 11 March 2002).
[22] *Id.* at 2, 8.
[23] *What is Galileo?*, ESA, *at* http://www.esa.int/export/esaSA/GGGMX650NDC_navigation_0.html (Last update: 5 April 2002).
[24] *Id.*
[25] *Id.*
[26] *Market Prospects and Business Opportunities*, ESA, *at* http://www.esa.int/export/ esaSA/GGGMN850NDC_navigation_0.html (Last update 12 November 2002).
[27] *Id.* At time of writing, 3.2 billion Euros and 220 million Euros are approximately equal to 3.7 billion and 255 million U.S. Dollars respectively.
[28] *See, e.g.*, Peter B. de Selding, Space News Staff Writer, *Europeans Claim War Degrades GPS*, *at* http://www.space.com/spacenews/archive03/gpsarch_033103.html (31 March 2003). Another article reported: "U.S.-led coalition forces have destroyed six devices being used by Iraqis to try to jam signals from the GPS satellite navigation and weapon-guidance system. . . [I]n one instance, the jamming device was destroyed with a GPS-guided bomb." Jeremy Singer, *U.S.-Led Forces Destroy GPS Jamming Systems in Iraq, at* http://www.space.com/news/gps_iraq_030325.html (25 March 2003).
[29] *Why Europe Needs Galileo*, ESA, *at* http://www.esa.int/export/esaSA/GGG0H750NDC_navigation_0.html (Last update 11 March 2002).
[30] *Id.*
[31] Lisa J. Savitt, et al., *Aviation and Aerospace: Law and Policy Developments*, 36 INT'L LAW. 507, 522 (2002).
[32] Paul B. Larsen, *GNSS Augmentation: Legal Issues*, 40 PROC. COL. LAW OUTER SPACE 271, 273, IISL-97-IISL.3.17 (1997).
[33] FRP, *supra* note 3, at 2-3.
[34] *Satellite Navigation System Achieves Program Milestone*, FAA Press Release, *available at* http://www1.faa.gov/index.cfm/apa/1062?id=1756 (July 11, 2003).
[35] FRP, *supra* note 3, at 2-3, 3-4.
[36] Larsen, *supra* note 32, at 272.
[37] The Convention on International Liability for Damage Caused by Space Objects, March 29, 1972, 24 U.S.T. 2389, at Art. II.
[38] B.D.K. HENAKU, THE LAW ON GLOBAL AIR NAVIGATION BY SATELLITE, 224-28 (AST 1998).
[39] Larsen, *supra* note 2, at 111.
[40] FRP, *supra* note 3, at 1-7.
[41] Francis Lyall, *Legal Issues of Expanding Global Satellite Communications Services and Global Navigation Satellite Services, with Special Emphasis on the Development of Telecommunications and E-Commerce in Asia*, 5 SING. J. INT'L & COMP. L. 227, 232 (2001).
[42] *Id.* at 233.
[43] CRS Report, *supra* note 8, at 44.
[44] Larsen, *supra* note 32,at 273.
[45] *Id.*at 274.
[46] Michael Jennison, *Editorial: Satellite Navigation: The Dubious Quest for a Legal Framework*, 16 AIR & SPACE LAW 10, 11 (2002).
[47] 28 U.S.C. § 2680(j)-(k) (2003). *See also* Smith v. United States, 507 U.S. 197, 204 (1993) (holding that FTCA's waiver of sovereign immunity does not apply to tort claims arising in Antarctica, even though it has no government).
[48] Banke, *supra* note 15.
[49] Larsen, *supra* note 2, at 111.
[50] Report of the Commission to Assess United States National Security Space Management and Organization at 20, 23, 36 (January 11, 2001) [hereinafter Rumsfeld Report]. *See also* Langhorne Bond, *The GNSS Safety and Sovereignty Convention of 2000 AD*, 65 J. AIR L. & COM. 445, 446 (2000) (discussing the vulnerability of GPS to jamming).
[51] Bond, *supra* note 50, at 448.
[52] John J. Lumpkin, Associated Press, *Pentagon Proposes Power Boost in Future GPS Navigation Satellites, at* http://www.space.com/missionlaunches/gps_upgrade_020507.html (07 May 2002).
[53] *Id.*
[54] Jeremy Singer, Space News Staff Writer, *U.S. Air Force Scales Back GPS Upgrade Plans, at* http://www.space.com/spacenews/archive03/gpsarch_020303.html (03 February 2003).
[55] Bond, *supra* note 50, at 446.
[56] Lyall, *supra* note 41, at 232.
[57] Bond, *supra* note 50, 449.
[58] *Id.* at 447.
[59] *See* Section II.D., *infra*.

[60] The 1944 Convention on International Civil Aviation, December 7, 1944, 61 Stat. 1180 [hereinafter Chicago Convention].
[61] Letter of David Hinson, FAA Administrator, to the President of the ICAO Council, October 14, 1994.
[62] Jennison, *supra* note 46, at 10.
[63] ICAO, *Charter of Rights and Obligations of States Relating to GNSS Services*, Assembly Resolution 32-19 (1998) [hereinafter *ICAO Charter*].
[64] Jennison, *supra* note 46, at 11.
[65] CRS Report, *supra* note 8, at 4.
[66] *Id.* at 6.
[67] *Id.* at 11.
[68] Treaty on Principles Governing the Activities of States in the Exploration and Use of Outer Space, including the Moon and Other Celestial Bodies, Jan. 27, 1967, preamble, 18 U.S.T. 2410 [hereinafter the Outer Space Treaty].
[69] Subrata Roy Chowdhury, *Legal Aspects of Maintaining Outer Space For Peaceful Purposes*, 31PROC. COL. LAW OUTER SPACE 13, 13, IISL-88-004, (1988).
[70] de Selding, *supra* note 28.
[71] SCOTT PACE, ET AL., THE GLOBAL POSITIONING SYSTEM: ASSESSING NATIONAL POLICIES 269 (Rand 1995).
[72] Outer Space Treaty, *supra* note 69, at preamble. *See, e.g.,* Liability Convention, *supra* note 53, at preamble; Agreement on the Rescue of Astronauts, the Return of Astronauts and the Return of Space Objects launched into Outer Space, April 22, 1968, 19 U.S.T. 7570, at preamble; Convention on Registration of Objects Launched into Outer Space, Jan. 14, 1975, 28 U.S.T. 695, at preamble.
[73] Outer Space Treaty, *supra* note 69, at preamble.
[74] Yasuaki Hashimoto, *Legal Analysis of Military Observations from Outer Space*, 40 PROC. COL. LAW OUTER SPACE 229, 230, IISL-97-3.13 (1997).
[75] de Selding, *supra* note 28.
[76] Outer Space Treaty, *supra* note 69, at Article IV.
[77] Ricky J. Lee, Military Use of Commercial Remote Sensing Data, Proc. 49 PROC. COL. LAW OUTER SPACE 246, 247, IISL-01-IISL-3.05 (2001).
[78] *Id.*
[79] *Id.* at 248.
[80] Dr. Oscar Fernandez-Brital, *Legal Aspects of Maintaining Outer Space for Peaceful Uses*, 31 PROC. COL. LAW OUTER SPACE 27, 27-8, IISL-88-007 (1988).
[81] Outer Space Treaty, *supra* note 69, at Article III.
[82] Harry H. Almond, Jr., *Peaceful Purposes in Outer Space Precision, Ambiguity or Confusion?*, 31 PROC. COL. LAW OUTER SPACE 1, 4, IISL-88-001 (1988).
[83] PDD, *supra* note 13.
[84] Larsen, *supra* note 32, at 272.
[85] Paul B. Larsen, *Should GNSS Standards that are Uniform for All GNSS Users be Established, or are Unimodal Standards Satisfactory?*, 42 PROC. COL. LAW OUTER SPACE 109, 110, IISL-99-IISL.2.02 (1999).
[86] *Id.*
[87] *Galileo, European Satellite Navigation System, International Cooperation*, European Commission, *at* http://europa.eu.int/comm/dgs/energy_transport/galileo/international/cooperation_en.htm (last update: 03-04-2003).
[88] Noll, *supra* note 4, at 64-5.
[89] HENAKU, *supra* note 38, at 250.

Session 5:
NEW ISSUES RELATING TO NUCLEAR POWER SOURCES

Chairmen: Stephan Hobe, Germany
Marcia Smith, USA

Rapporteur: Gerardine Goh, U.K.

IAC-03-IISL.5.01

NUCLEAR AND RADIOISOTOPIC POWER IN SPACE: THE CUMULATIVE CONTENT AND EFFECT OF THE UNITED NATIONS SPACE TREATIES AND DECLARATIONS

Ricky J. Lee*
Ricky J. Lee & Associates
University of Western Sydney, Australia

ABSTRACT

The use of nuclear power in space has been a constant source of controversy ever since the early days of space development. The General Assembly declaration, for example, was intended partly to address the concerns of States concerning the use of nuclear power sources in space. Since the 1980s, however, the development of nuclear and radioisotopic means of power generation and propulsion has arguably gone beyond the scope of the General Assembly declaration.

This paper concerns itself with an analysis of the legal effect of the principles contained in the General Assembly declaration and their cumulative effect with the legal principles of the United Nations space treaties. These principles are then applied to the applications of nuclear power generation, radioisotopic power generation, nuclear propulsion and radioisotopic propulsion and the likely impact of any privatisation of such activities in space.

INTRODUCTION

The deployment and testing of nuclear weapons in space has long been the subject of significant legal focus. In 1963, the international community agreed to prohibit the testing of nuclear weapons in outer space.[1] The Outer Space Treaty of 1967 also prohibited the deployment of nuclear weapons in outer space and on celestial bodies.[2]

It was not until more recent times that concerns have been raised with the use of nuclear and radioisotopic power sources in space. In 1992, the General Assembly adopted the Principles Relevant to the Use of Nuclear Power Sources in Outer Space (the "**NPS Principles**"). The NPS Principles set out certain legal and regulatory requirements on the use of nuclear and radioisotopic power sources for non-propulsive purposes.

From the view of a launch operator or satellite operator, regardless of whether the venture is of a public or private nature, it is prudent to consider the cumulative effect of the United Nations treaties and declarations on the conduct of a space activity involving nuclear or radioisotopic power sources.

THE NEED FOR NUCLEAR AND RADIOISOTOPIC POWER SOURCES

Currently, around four hundred watts of electricity are needed for small satellites around Earth orbit. For short times and low power levels, chemical fuel cells and solar power cells may be used but at high power levels, for long durations and also for interplanetary probes, nuclear power is the only means of generating sufficient electricity known today. Further, solar power cells understandably require their exposure to the Sun while the spacecraft is in close proximity to it in order to generate sufficient power. The aggregate of these factors means that spacecrafts utilising solar or chemical cell

Historically, the former Soviet Union and the United States have taken a markedly different approach to the development of power sources in space. The United States has launched one nuclear reactor and forty-two radioisotopic fuel cells into space, while the Soviet Union had launched thirty-seven nuclear reactors and six radioisotopic fuel cells.[3] Nuclear reactors rely on the fission reaction, as in terrestrial nuclear reactors and nuclear weapons, to generate energy. On the other hand, radioisotopic fuel cells rely on the energy generated from the radioactive decay of unstable elements, such as plutonium-238.

In either case, the energy generated from a nuclear reaction is calculated by the following well-known formula:

$$E = \Delta m \times c^2$$

where E is the energy released (measured in electron-volts or eV), Δm is the loss in total mass and c is the speed of light in vacuum. In the case of a fuel cell using plutonium-238, the decay involves the creation of uranium-234 and an α particle (identical to a helium nucleus):

$$^{238}_{94}\text{Pu} \rightarrow {}^{234}_{92}\text{U} + {}^{4}_{2}\text{He}$$

For each atom of plutonium, the loss of mass between the plutonium nucleus and the sum of the daughter nuclei produces 5.59MeV of energy.

Plutonium-238 is often chosen for space missions because it has a reasonably long half-life of 87.4 years with each gram, which costs around US$300, producing forty-seven kilowatt-hours over a ten-year mission. This nevertheless dwarfs in comparison to the energy generated by nuclear fission reactors, as the same mass of uranium-235 can produce five hundred thousand times the energy produced by the decay of plutonium-238 over ten years. This is particularly crucial in the use of nuclear energy for the propulsion of spacecrafts.

Nuclear reactors rely on the fission reaction to generate energy. This involves the absorption of a neutron by a uranium-235 nucleus to form a highly-unstable uranium-236 nucleus, which almost spontaneously divides into two unstable nuclei. For example:

$$^{235}_{92}\text{U} + {}^{1}_{0}\text{n} \rightarrow {}^{236}_{92}\text{U}^{*} \rightarrow {}^{144}_{56}\text{Ba} + {}^{89}_{36}\text{Kr} + 3 \cdot {}^{1}_{0}\text{n}$$

$$^{235}_{92}\text{U} + {}^{1}_{0}\text{n} \rightarrow {}^{236}_{92}\text{U}^{*} \rightarrow {}^{140}_{54}\text{Xe} + {}^{94}_{38}\text{Sr} + 2 \cdot {}^{1}_{0}\text{n}$$

Chain reactions results from the neutrons produced in each fission reaction being absorbed by other uranium-235 nuclei. In a nuclear reactor, the chain reaction is controlled by water or graphite being used to slow down neutrons by collisions between them and the water molecules or carbon atoms in the graphite. While the risk of nuclear explosions is a common concern, what has been the focus of much academic attention is the potential spread of radioactive material in the atmosphere or on the ground. This is because the daughter nuclei of a fission reaction are unstable and are radioactive. In the second example given above, the xenon-140 nucleus undergoes a series of emissions of β^- particles, or electrons produced by the transformation of a neutron into a proton and an electron, as follows:

$$^{140}_{54}\mathrm{Xe} \xrightarrow{\beta^-} {}^{140}_{55}\mathrm{Cs} \xrightarrow{\beta^-} {}^{140}_{56}\mathrm{Ba}$$

$$\xrightarrow{\beta^-} {}^{140}_{57}\mathrm{La} \xrightarrow{\beta^-} {}^{140}_{58}\mathrm{Ce}$$

The cerium-140 nucleus is stable and will not undergo any further decay. In the process, however, it is apparent that a substantial amount of radioactivity would already have taken place before nuclear stability can be reached. Depending on the level of energy involved, a β^- particle have a stronger effect on biological matter than x-rays with two hundred thousand electron-volts of energy.

PATH TO THE NPS PRINCIPLES

One sad reality in the development of international law is that unfortunate events are often the catalysts and this is no exception in the case of the law concerning nuclear and radioisotopic power sources in outer space.

On 24 January 1978, the re-entry and disintegration of *Cosmos-954* left radioactive debris over six hundred square kilometres of Canadian territory, equivalent in area to the size of Austria. *Cosmos-954* was launched by the Soviet Union on 18 September 1977 carrying a nuclear reactor using enriched uranium, or uranium-235. Its mission, along with its sister satellite *Cosmos-952*, was ocean surveillance for three weeks, after which they were to be boosted into a higher "parking" orbit to allow for the natural radioactive decay to occur over 600 years. However, *Cosmos-954* could not be boosted into its proposed higher orbit as a result of a malfunction that took place near the end of its mission.

During the time between the malfunction and the eventual re-entry of *Cosmos-954*, there were worldwide fears of nuclear explosions and the introduction of deadly hazards into the atmosphere. These fears were further intensified by the re-entry of *Cosmos-1402* in 1983 and that of *Cosmos-1960* in 1988 as well as the Earth flyby of the interplanetary probe *Cassini* in 1999 on its journey to Saturn. These events partly prompted a multidisciplinary effort to study various means to improve the safety of nuclear and radioisotopic power sources in scientific and engineering circles as well as the legal means for the regulation of the use of such power sources in space. Both aspects of these efforts continue today, as can be seen in the attention regularly given to the issue by both the Scientific and Technical Sub-Committee and the Legal Sub-Committee of the Committee on the Peaceful Uses of Outer Space ("**COPUOS**").

It is not surprising that discussions took place in 1978 on this issue in both subcommittees of COPUOS. A Working Group was created in the Scientific and Technical Sub-Committee in the same year to study the technical feasibility of establishing standards for radiation levels, restrictions on nuclear power sources, safeguards, precautions, early notification of re-entry and appropriate emergency assistance for search, recovery and clean-up operations.[4] At about the same time, the Legal Sub-Committee was similarly instructed to analyse safety measures, notifications and other legal aspects of using nuclear and radioisotopic power sources in space.

After years of study and development, it was not until 1992, however, that the NPS Principles were adopted by the General Assembly. As discussed below, this has the effect of filling in some of the gaps in the regulation of nuclear and radioisotopic power sources in space.

THE NPS PRINCIPLES AS CUSTOM

As considered below, the NPS Principles contain eleven provisions of which Principles 1, 6, 7, 8, 9 and 10 merely restate the application of provisions of existing treaties to nuclear power sources.

In the case of the new provisions, namely Principles 3 to 5, one would suggest that they are merely extensions of existing principles, such as Article IX of the Outer Space Treaty. In any event, the widespread acceptance by States of the underlying provisions and the absence of significant dissensions during the debates suggest that the NPS Principles may be considered to have crystallised into international law either at the time of their declaration or soon after.

DESIGN

The Outer Space Treaty requires States to avoid harmful contamination and adverse changes to the environment of the Earth resulting from the introduction of "extraterrestrial" matter.[5] Even if the re-entry of nuclear or radioactive material is not considered to be "extraterrestrial" in character, the Outer Space Treaty nevertheless requires States to undertake "appropriate international consultations" before proceeding with an activity that has the potential of causing harmful interference with the space activities of other States.[6] Therefore, it is clear that, at the very least, States will be obliged to enter into consultations with potentially affected States concerning the potential effects of the nuclear or radioisotopic power source *before* its launch.

Even if the Outer Space Treaty does not impose an obligation to take necessary measures to avoid potential harm to other States through nuclear and radioisotopic power sources, the NPS Principles impose significant conditions on the design of nuclear and radioisotopic power sources onboard spacecrafts. Generally, Principle 3 requires the probability of accidents with potentially serious radiological consequences must be kept extremely small. Further, foreseeable safety-related failures or malfunctions must be capable of being corrected or counteracted by procedural or automatic means.

Specifically, Principle 3 requires the design of spacecrafts to ensure "with a high degree of confidence that the hazards, in foreseeable operational or accidental circumstances, are kept below acceptable levels as follows:

- observance and compliance of appropriate standards imposed by the International Commission on Radiological Protection; and
- take into account relevant and generally accepted international radiological protection guidelines to limit exposure in accidents.

Further, Principle 3 requires spacecraft design to, "with a high degree of confidence, restrict radiation exposure" geographically and to individuals to the limit of 1 millisievert per year.

In the case of spacecrafts containing nuclear reactors onboard, Principle 3 allows reactors utilising uranium-235 to be used on interplanetary missions or in Earth orbit. Those in Earth orbit are required to be inserted into a "sufficiently high orbit" or will eventually be "parked" in a sufficiently high orbit after its mission. A "sufficiently high orbit" is defined as one where the risk of collisions with existing or future spacecrafts are kept to a minimum and sufficient time is given for the radioactive material to decay. There is no recommended minimum altitude specified, though one may have thought that such a provision may be prudent. The design of the spacecraft must ensure that critical mass is not attained being reaching its operational orbit, including explosions, re-entries, impact or the submersion in or intrusion of water.

In the case of radioisotopic fuel cells, Principle 3 permits their use only in interplanetary missions or in Earth orbit provided that ultimate disposal is made. They must be designed with a system of containment that will withstand the heat and other conditions of re-entry and impact on the surface of the Earth or water to ensure that no radioactive material may be scattered into the atmosphere, the ocean or the soil. It appears from this that the international community considers radioisotopic power sources to be potentially more dangerous than nuclear reactors. This is likely to be the result of concerns over the long radioactive half-life and the potency of plutonium-238 and other radioisotopic materials.

Principle 4 requires the launching State which, for the purposes of the NPS Principles, is defined as the State exercising jurisdiction and control over a space object with a nuclear power source onboard, to conduct a safety assessment to ensure that the requirements of Principle 3 have been met.[7] Both Article XI of the Outer Space Treaty and Principle 4 of the NPS Principles require the results of the safety assessment to be publicised before the launch.

It has been highlighted that the NPS Principles do not provide for the appropriate measures to be taken where a third State disagree with the safety assessment of a nuclear power source to be launched.[8] This is partly because the concurrence of third States is not necessary for a space object containing a nuclear power sources to be launched. Presumably if a third State did indeed disagree with a safety assessment, Article IX of the Outer Space Treaty may be invoked to require relevant consultations to be held between the States concerned.

LAUNCH

In essence, the legal principles relating to the launch of a space object containing a nuclear power source is no different to those relevant to the launch of a solar or chemical powered spacecraft. For example, Article VI of the Outer Space Treaty applies to require States to bear international responsibility for "national" space activities and to authorise and continually supervise the space activities of non-governmental entities. Indeed, the application of Article VI has been affirmed by the NPS Principles.[9]

Similarly, the Registration Convention and General Assembly Resolution 1721B of 1961 require one of the States responsible for launching the space object to make an entry for it in its national register of space objects as well as that of the United Nations.[10] States are required to provide information relating to the orbital parameters and the launching State(s) of the space object.[11] The Registration Convention does not require the State of registry to submit details of the power source onboard.

OPERATION

Article IX of the Outer Space Treaty requires States to conduct all their activities in outer space with "due regard to the *corresponding* interests of all other State Parties to the Treaty". It may be argued, as often does by students in the Manfred Lachs Space Law Moot Court Competition of the International Institute of Space Law, that this provision imposes a general duty on the part of States to take all reasonable steps to avoid causing damage to the property of other States. However, the better proposition appears to be that the word "*corresponding*" is used in a limiting context with the effect of confining the duty to the rights of other States to conduct space activities.

Even within such contextual limits, however, it appears that States operating space objects containing nuclear or radioisotopic power sources is required to have due regard to the space activities conducted by other States. Although unclear, this may have the effect of requiring States to avoid collisions and radiation damage to other space objects.

Further, Article VIII requires the State of registry to retain jurisdiction and control over the space object.[12] As only one State can effectively exercise control and jurisdiction over a space object or a component thereof at any one time, where there are multiple launching States the Registration Convention requires them to agree among themselves which one was to be the State of registry.[13] This is particularly relevant in the context of the NPS Principles, which defines a "launching State" not as the States involved in the launch of the space object but rather the State exercising control and jurisdiction over the space object. Although the Registration Convention allows the State of registry to submit additional information to the United Nations concerning a space object, it is often suggested that an amendment requiring States to provide details of any nuclear and radioisotopic power source onboard may be appropriate.

ACCIDENT AND DISTRESS

Neither the Registration Convention nor the Rescue Agreement requires States to publicise information concerning space objects that have malfunctioned and have a risk of re-entry into the atmosphere. In recognition of this, the NPS Principles require a launching State (defined as the State with jurisdiction and control) to inform States concerned and the United Nations of a malfunctioning space object with a nuclear power source onboard that has a risk of re-entry to the Earth as soon as the malfunction is known.[14] The information must be updated "as frequently as practicable", especially when the anticipated time of re-entry approaches to enable States to have sufficient time to prepare responses.[15]

In addition to the information submitted pursuant to the Registration Convention, the NPS Principles require information about the type of nuclear power source and the "probable physical form, amount and general radiological characteristics of the nuclear material and the components that are likely to reach the surface of the Earth.[16] The launching States are further required to, as far as reasonable practicable, "respond promptly to requests for further information or consultations sought by other States".[17]

The NPS Principles require *all* States with space monitoring and tracking facilities to communicate any relevant information on the malfunctioning space object to the United States and the States concerned to enable assessments and the planning of precautionary measures.[18] Upon re-entry, States with returned components are required under the Rescue Agreement to take effective steps immediately to eliminate potential danger or harm.[19] To this end, there is an obligation to provide all necessary assistance to eliminate actual and potential harmful effects and to carry out recovery and clean-up operations.[20] This obligation is imposed under the Rescue Agreement on the States responsible for the launch and under the NPS Principles on the State having jurisdiction and control over the space object.

LIABILITY FOR DAMAGES

The Outer Space Treaty provides that the States responsible for the launch are liable for damage to another State.[21] This is supplemented by the provisions of the Liability Convention which provides for absolute liability for damage caused on the surface of the Earth and to aircraft in flight and fault liability for damage caused in outer space and on celestial bodies.[22] Where there is more than one State responsible for the launch, their liability under the Liability Convention is joint and several.[23] These requirements are repeated in the NPS Principles in the context of space objects with nuclear and radioisotopic power sources onboard.[24]

The Liability Convention provides that the compensation payable by the States responsible for the launch is to be determined in accordance with the principles of justice and equity to the extent necessary to restore the victims to their positions before the damage occurred, or *restitutio in integrum*.[25] This is the same formulation as prescribed by the Permanent Court of International Justice in the *Chórzow Factory Case*.[26] The same formulation can be found the NPS Principles.[27]

In relation to the costs of the recovery and the clean-up, the Rescue Agreement and the NPS Principles contain two substantially identical but procedurally different provisions. Under the Rescue Agreement, the expenses incurred for the recovery and return of the components of the space are to be reimbursed by the States responsible for the launch.[28] The costs of the clean-up and other steps taken to eliminate the hazardous nature of the returned components are excluded from this reimbursement provision. Presumably this is because the costs of the recovery and return are technically not "damage", while the clean-up costs of eliminating hazardous materials are necessarily "damage". Consequently, it is appropriate to establish a head of liability for recovery costs that is separate to that for damage.

The NPS Principles, on the other hand, provide that the compensation payable by the launching States in accordance with the Liability Convention and the Outer Space Treaty includes the reimbursement for "duly substantiated expenses for *search, recovery* and clean-up operations, including expenses for assistance received from third parties".[29] This means that, subject to the added requirement of "duly substantiating" the expenses, these costs are to be considered part of the "damage" to be compensated by the launching States. If the above analysis relating to the Rescue Agreement is correct, then the two provisions are clearly inconsistent. While this produces a procedural discrepancy, in practice it is doubtful that the relevant States concerned would make two separate claims relating to recovery costs and the damage arising from the return of a space object.

NUCLEAR PROPULSION

One issue of particular concern to space lawyers in this field is the utilisation of nuclear power sources for propulsion. The preamble to the NPS Principles specifies that:

> ... this set of Principles applies to nuclear power sources in outer space devoted to the generation of electric power on board space objects for non-propulsive purposes ... this set of Principles will require future revision in view of emerging nuclear-power applications and evolving international recommendations on radiological protection.

While it may be suggested that this has the effect of prohibiting nuclear or radioisotopic propulsion in space, this interpretation is not supported by the wording of the above paragraphs as well as the reference to the need for revision to cover "emerging" applications. In practice, this means that only the existing general principles in the treaties would apply to such a space object and the safety requirements of the NPS Principles would have no application.

CONCLUSIONS

It is clear from the above analysis that the space treaties, as supplemented by the NPS Principles, have created a body of law substantially adequate in addressing the safety concerns with the use of nuclear and radioisotopic power sources in space. At the same time, it should be recognised that this must be a continuing endeavour, especially in the context of the Registration Convention and nuclear propulsion, to ensure that the legal protection afforded the international community does not diminish over time as a result of technological developments.

Notes

This paper is written in the personal capacity of the author and does not necessarily represent the views of any organisations with which he is associated.

[*] Principal, Ricky J. Lee & Associates and Lecturer, School of Law, University of Western Sydney, Australia. Member IISL, IBA and ILA. Email: rjlee@rickylee.id.au.

[1] Treaty Banning Nuclear Weapon Tests in the Atmosphere, in Outer Space and Over Water (1963) 480 UNTS 45.
[2] Treaty on Principles Governing the Activities of States in the Exploration and Use of Outer Space, including the Moon and Other Celestial Bodies (1967) 610 UNTS 205.
[3] Bennett, "Space Applications" in Rowe (ed.), *CRC Handbook of Thermoelectrics* (1995) at p. 515.
[4] COPUOS, *Report on the Fifteenth Session of the Scientific and Technical Subcommittee* (1978) U.N.Doc. A/AC.105/216, at 28-32.
[5] Outer Space Treaty, Article IX.
[6] *Ibid.*
[7] NPS Principles, Principle 2.
[8] COPUOS, *Report of the Chairman of the Working Group on Agenda Item 3* (1993) U.N.Doc. A/AC.105/544.
[9] *Ibid.*, Principle 8.
[10] Registration Convention, Articles II and IV.
[11] *Ibid.*, Article IV.
[12] Outer Space Treaty, Article VIII.
[13] Registration Convention, Article II.
[14] NPS Principles, Principle 5(1).
[15] *Ibid.*, Principle 5(2).
[16] *Ibid.*, Principle 5(1).
[17] *Ibid.*, Principle 6.
[18] *Ibid.*, Principle 7(1).
[19] Rescue Agreement, Article 5(4).
[20] Rescue Agreement, Article 5(4) and the NPS Principles., Principle 7(2).
[21] Outer Space Treaty, Article VII.
[22] Liability Convention, Articles I and II.
[23] *Ibid.*, Article V.
[24] NPS Principles, Principle 9(1).
[25] Liability Convention, Article XII.
[26] *Case Concerning the Factory at Chórzow (Claim for Indemnity) (Merits)* (1928) PCIJ Ser. A, No. 17.
[27] NPS Principles, Principle 9(2).
[28] Rescue Agreement, Article 5(5).
[29] NPS Principles, Principle 9(3).

DISCUSSION ON EXTENDING/MODIFYING THE 1992 NUCLEAR POWER SOURCES PRINCIPLES TO BROADER SPACE OPERATIONS

By Yun ZHAO*

Abstract

After more than 10 years of existence, the 1992 Nuclear Power Source Principles stands now at the crossroads. Various parties have expressed the idea of extending NPS for broader space operations. While theoretical debates on the feasibility of such application do not help much in practice, pragmatic approach should be adopted: formulating new framework to accommodate the new demands. As a result, the revisit of the Principles is justified. This revisit shall be extensive, including the substantial aspects as well as the formality of the Principles. It is expected that the improved Principles shall well accommodate the renewed call for application of NPS in broader space operations and the well-being of modern society as a whole.

1. INTRODUCTION

Nuclear power sources (NPSs) have been used since 1961 for the purpose of generating energy for space objects[1] and have since then been recognized as particularly suited or essential to some space operations. The use of NPS in outer space aims at providing electric power for spacecraft sub-systems such as altitude control, communications, and command, as well as for the operations of various equipments on board. Two types of NPS are presently in outer space, namely, isotopic source and nuclear reactor.[2]

In the mid-1960s American government and industry looked to a cheaper and reliable alternative to chemical rocket engines. Other than Russian nuclear achievements in space at that time, no other entity had won at demonstrating the raw power of crafted nuclear rocket propulsion except Project Rover in the US.

However, the risks inherent in using NPS caused much concerns.[3] The risk and the disastrous consequence were well demonstrated by the incident in 1978 when the Russian nuclear-powered satellite Cosmos 954 crashed on Canada.[4] Discussions started since then on an international technical framework for the regulation of NPS in outer space.[5] Years of deliberation has finally led to the adoption of the United Nations (UN) Resolution on the safe use of NPS in 1992,[6] listing 11 principles for the safe application and assessment of NPS. While acknowledging the fact that national activities involve the use of NPS in outer space, it recognizes that certain restrictions are necessary to ensure the safe use of NPS. The Resolution aims to promote the protection of persons and 'the biosphere' against radiological hazards.[7]

According to Principle 11, these Principles shall be opened for revision no later than two years after their adoption. To date, however, revisions have not been made. After more than ten years' existence, it is time to take a serious look at the Principles again considering the rapid development of modern technology and the drastic change of the political atmosphere.

The present paper takes up the position in discussing the possible modification to the Resolution. Part 2 gives an overview of the Resolution and describes the necessity of making modification. Part 3 concentrates on the substantial areas for improvements and modification, which is followed by Part 4 dealing with the improvement on the formality of the Principles. A short conclusion in Part 5

---

* Lecturer, City University of Hong Kong; formerly researcher at Erasmus University Rotterdam, The Netherlands; LL.M., Leiden University, The Netherlands; LL.M., LL.B., China University of Political Science and Law, Beijing. The author may be contacted at <lwzhao@cityu.edu.hk>.

portrays a prospect for the Principles in the new century.

2. BRIEF REVIEW OF THE 1992 NPS PRINCIPLES

The 1992 Principles apply to NPS in outer space devoted to generation of electric power on board space objects for non-propulsive purposes. It considers only the use of nuclear fuel as it relates to NPS.[8] Principle 1 sets a broad framework for NPS: international treaties and customs shall be valid in the regulation of NPS. The present resolution is a further statement of these rules in the specific activity. Principle 2 defines the terms to be applied in this resolution. This shall help clarify the ambiguity concerning "launching State" and "State launching".

Principle 3 offers guidelines and criteria for safe use. It is the heart of the Resolution.[9] The use of NPS is strictly limited to space missions which cannot be operated by non-nuclear energy sources. Such use shall further be conducted in a reasonable way. The obligation of safety assessment is provided in Principle 4 in accordance with the criteria for safe use contained in Principle 3. Rules of the notification of re-entry, for consultation and requests for additional information between states are respectively provided in Principle 5 and 6. The issues concerning assistance to States, responsibility, liability and compensation, dispute settlement are ruled down in the next four Principles.[10]

The Principles provide the basic document guiding the use of NPS in limited situation. The necessity of the Principles is obvious: the high risks entailed in the use of NPS. This also justifies the limited use of NPS: not for propulsion purposes. The provisions satisfy the needs in the early 1990s with the existence of strong arms control advocates and environmentalists.[11] However, with the development of space technology and the enthusiasm for further exploration of outer space, the use of NPS again becomes the topic for heated discussion. The National Aeronautics and Space Administration (NASA) is now moving to revive its scheme to build nuclear-propelled rockets[12] and expand its use of atomic power to generate electricity on space probes and planetary rovers.[13] The program called Nuclear Systems Initiative is trying to develop safe and reliable nuclear power and propulsion systems.[14] The NASA announced its intention to revisit the issue of NPS in space early in 2002, shortly after the September 11th Event.[15] This announcement has on the one hand, advocated the use of NPS beyond non-propulsion purposes; on the other hand, closely referred to war against terrorism. The situation nowadays is no longer like that in 1994 or even later (two years or longer after the adoption of the Principles), the technical advancement and the reality has urged revision of the Principles and further accommodations.

3. IMPROVEMENT ON SUBSTANTIAL ASPECTS OF THE 1992 PRINCIPLES

Heated discussions had been in place before the adoption of the Principles. Various scholars recognized the necessity of rules guiding the legitimate use of NPS. After years of deliberation, the Principles were able to be successfully adopted. However, comments and evaluations continued to be presented on the merits and demerits of the Principles. In general, the Principles offer a platform for space activities involving the use of NPS. This set of Principles can be viewed as a great leap forward in the history. Considering the sensitive nature of NPS, it is appropriate to have a set of Principles in the first place: something is better than nothing. Nevertheless, it has been obvious to all even at the time of adoption that further revision is necessary. For various reasons, the speculated revision has not been made so far. But the necessity of revision is now at the forefront when the US put forward the plan of using NPS for propulsion purposes and other applications. Confronting the new challenge, it is, accordingly, the right time to study the Principles and make possible improvements.

3.1. Applicable Scope

The Principles have set clear applicable scope. As stated above, NPS shall be only allowed for non-propulsive purposes. According to the analysis of some scholars, the Principles do not refer to the use of NPS on celestial bodies including the Moon.[16] However, the reality is that NPS has been used[17] and can be further used for space operations, not only in outer space, but also at the stage before and after the space objects entering the outer space; not only as electric power, but also as propulsion power. Several NASA notables have mentioned publicly that nuclear power in space transportation deserves a closer look. The comments indicate that if public relation efforts can gain acceptance for the possibility, future interplanetary missions may include nuclear-power options.[18] The former "taboo" of not using NPS for propulsion purposes has been under severe challenge.

The efforts from the US's side serve as the powerful motive force. The justification presented is no doubt strong enough to stand against those sticking to the restrictive use of NPS. The European Space Agency (ESA), as a support for the restrictive use of NPS, is devoted to developing safer ways of propelling rockets and energizing space probes and planetary landers, which include solar electric propulsion and the use of "solar sails" and other solar technologies that stress the generation of electricity with new high-efficiency solar cells.[19] Nevertheless, such a position shall not prescribe the fact of using NPS for wider space operations. Outer planet exploration using advanced radioisotope electric propulsion has been evaluated by teams at the NASA Glenn Research Center in Cleveland, Ohio, as well as The Johns Hopkins University Applied Physics Laboratory in Laurel, Maryland.[20]

Some might quote the 1963 Treaty Banning Nuclear Weapons in the Atmosphere, in Outer Space and under Water (Limited Test Ban Treaty)[21] as proof against the use of nuclear fission as a means of space propulsion by referring to the provision that outlaws any nuclear weapon test explosion or any other nuclear explosion.[22] However, according to the provision, it directly refers to the prohibition of NPS application by means of explosion, the Treaty does not prohibit the use by means other than explosion. Moreover, this Treaty basically deals with nuclear weapons, not the use for normal space activities.

While witnessing the actual development, we should acknowledge that theoretical debates on feasibility of NPS's extensive use are meaningless, or at least diverging our regulatory direction. We have only two possible outcomes: either the Space will be colonized illegally, or the laws are to be changed.[23] Politically speaking, the right attitude should be to formulate an appropriate legal framework for their legitimate and safe application, offering a guideline for possible use of NPS in space operations (including heat, power or propulsion) in interplanetary traveling, in celestial bodies, in Earth orbit, beyond earth orbit, or even for launching spacecraft from the surface of the Earth. This is a pragmatic means to realize order in the use of NPS, which also represents the extension of positivism in the field of Space Law. The availability of legal framework for extensive use of NPS shall put a safe valve and provide preventive measures against future illegal use of NPS in all other cases.

Considering the ongoing discussions and technical development, it is time to justify the possible areas for extension. The application of NPS for propulsion purposes is one promising area. Nuclear propulsion can take many forms ranging from low thrust nuclear electric propulsion to higher thrust nuclear thermal propulsion and electrical or thermal "Pulsed nuclear" propulsion. Supporting arguments include the sufficient energy for space operation, which can largely shorten the necessary time for space operations. Actually, astronauts are among the most enthusiastic boosters of such a nuclear-powered mission.[24] The restrictive use of NPS will add to the cost, the length of the missions, which will levy burden on the pressure and anxiety of astronauts. Nuclear propulsion can be more efficient than any other traditional chemical propulsion, it has twice the propellant mileage of the chemical propulsion. The mere use of enriched uranium will reduce the efficiency of space operation and entail other disadvantages. Several other advantages have also been quoted: creating artificial gravity, the reuse potential of the nuclear thermal rocket.[25] Some space missions, though can be operated by non-nuclear energy sources, will not be able to enjoy the advantages of NPS. Confident assertion came from the Center for Space Science and Exploration, Los Alamos Laboratory that the future on nuclear activities in space will revolve around Nuclear Electrical Propulsion (NEP) at least in the immediate future involving light payload long duration missions.[26]

However, it is yet to be seen whether it is advisable to extend the use of NPS in the earth orbit or near earth regions. The nuclear powered rockets have been strongly argued not to be used to get off the ground, but only outside the Earth orbit. The nuclear system can be controlled to function only when the desired need to have them work and the distances involved would be far from any earthly influence in any event. Nevertheless, we cannot preclude this possibility with technological improvement. Thus, it is also necessary to bring this possible development into the legal framework: providing clear statement on whether its application in earth orbit is legal or not; if confirmed as legal, then higher standards should be provided.

Scholars have also been arguing whether the Principles apply to the use of NPS systems on planetary surfaces. [27] The Resolution itself does not contain clear guidance. It is thus necessary to clarify this ambiguity. To take the style of Space Treaty, outer space shall include Moon and other celestial bodies. The adoption of this conception shall ensure the consistency of the terms among international space law documents.

The extensive application of NPS shall no doubt add to the danger inherent in the NPS posed to the human beings, animals, plants and natural environments on the earth. Actually the cons over extensive use of NPS have been largely based on the concerns above. Thus, the vital point to substantiate the use of NPS is to provide a convincing mechanism to ensure the safety or lessen the risks entailed from legal and technical angles. Generally speaking, Principles 3 and 4 are appropriate in defining the safe use and assessment from a technical point of view; however, for the purpose of further extension, it is necessary to check the wordings and include the possible extension. This extension and revision shall include the higher level of safety standard, reconsideration of appropriate orbit position, etc. The duty to inform the use of NPS, duty to warn, international consultation, etc. have been defined in other Principles, but it is also necessary to review to keep up with the new development. Furthermore, when reviewing the Principles, we need to refer to the 1967 Space Treaty.[28]

3.2. <u>The "Reasonableness" Test in Principle 3</u>

With possible application of NPS closer to human being, high standards and preventive measures shall be adopted to procure against high risks. This shall have most relevance with the reasonableness test defined in Principle 3. With the availability and feasibility of solar energy well testified, a clear understanding of the term shall be needed. Failing the reasonableness test, relevant States causing the damage should bear higher level of liability accordingly.

The term "reasonableness" basically provides the idea of defining the applicable scope for NPS. The "chapeau" of Principle 3 provides that the use of NPS shall be restricted to space missions which cannot be operated by non-nuclear energy sources in a reasonable way. This chapeau has tried to rule out the use of NPS in other situations, however, the term "in a reasonable way" softens the assertion, which shall subject to an appropriate interpretation. Without defining "reasonable", the Resolution attempts to limit use of NPS while acknowledging that NPS is appropriate for some space operations. Nevertheless, the flexible use of the term has aroused much criticism after the adoption of the Resolution. It is now time to revisit this term.

While offering the chapeau, Principle 3 goes a step further by defining the situations when nuclear reactors and radioisotope generators can be operated. The principle further provides that the reliability of systems important for safety shall be ensured, *inter alia*, by redundancy, physical separation, functional isolation and adequate independence of their components. [29] It also lists several situations when nuclear reactors may be operated: on interplanetary missions; in sufficiently high orbits; and in low-Earth orbits if they are stored in sufficiently high orbits after the operational part of their mission. [30] According to the Resolution, "sufficiently high orbits" are those in which the orbital lifetime is long enough to allow for a sufficient decay of the fission products to approximate the activity of the actinides. Such orbits must be such that the risks to existing and future outer space missions and of collision with other space objects are kept to a minimum.[31]

However, the indeterminacy has been further exacerbated by the use of the terms like "sufficient", "long enough", and "minimum". While this Resolution provides the basic mechanism for securing the safe use of NPS, the crux is how to provide a safe valve for the application, not to preclude the use of NPS. We should take note of two relevant issues: applicable scope and the procurement of safe use within the applicable scope. The definition of "reasonableness" shall be directly related to the two issues above. The status confronting the new development should thus be the extension of NPS to broader space operations and provision of higher level of safety procurement from the technical part.

While the issue of extending applicable scope has been discussed earlier, we should now examine the formulation of appropriate standards for safety procurement. This proves to be a difficult one, having been evidenced by the tedious deliberations during the drafting of the Principle. The constant technological development has high possibility of making newly formulated technical standards outdated very soon. It is almost impossible to stabilize such rules in a legal document. As stated by some scholar, the inclusion of technical regulation in legal guidelines seems to be a resignation of law in the benefit of technology which could not solve its own difficulties and therefore decides to put law under its subordination. [32] One possible way out could thus be to differentiate technical issues from legal guidelines: while developing a treaty with broad and general guidance, the UN can leave to an international technical body to establish standards and recommended practices for States to follow. [33] The International Atomic Energy Agency (IAEA) and the International Commission on Radiological Protection (ICRP) can be appropriate bodies to undertake technical tasks. [34] While providing legal guidelines, the Principle can make express reference to the recommendations of these two organizations. This can resolve the heated debates concerning the adoption of technical standards in a legal document.

3.3. The Issue of Environmental Protection

Environmental protection or sustainable development has been an important issue considering the possible dangers posed to the earth. The issue of space debris has been deeply studied by various space law bodies.[35] We should note the Limited Test Ban Treaty,[36] one important consideration of which has been environmental protection: the prevention of global nuclear contamination, to put an end to the contamination of man's environment by radioactive substances. [37] It can even be viewed primarily as an environmental agreement rather than a military one.[38] The NASA conceded the serious dangers of a

Cassini accident in its Final Environmental Impact Statement for the Cassini Mission, the most recent nuclear space probe mission in 1997.[39] It is proposed that those space activities which might harm the local and global environment are carried out in a manner that limits such effects to the extent possible.[40] However, the discussions did not direct to NPS in space operations. This fact does not underestimate the highly dangerous nature of the pollution resulting from the use of NPS.

While providing the safety guidance for the use of NPS, the Resolution can be argued to have impliedly entailed the idea of environmental protection. Nevertheless, such an implied idea will not impose much strength on the actual performance. It is necessary to insert this principle into the main body of the Resolution, among those include the disposition of nuclear wastes. This shall promote the compliance from Members without further arguments. Moreover, international cooperation could thus be directed at addressing this issue.

By inserting environmental protection in the Preamble, we can have stronger stand and more justifiable commitment to support several measures in the main text, which include avoiding heavily populated parts of the Earth, safety measures, etc. As to state responsibility and liability arising out of the use of NPS, reference can be made to the existing Principle 8 and 9.[41] This is very important since we note that in resolutions relating to environmental questions, State responsibility and liability are not referred to and even in international agreements or conventions a trend can be observed to omit these questions.[42] Considering the magnificent work having been done on space debris, it is also necessary to refer to this achievement as far as the issue of environmental protection is concerned. Anyhow, the Conventions, Resolutions, Treaties, as long as they are related to space regulation, should be integrated and work effectively with the supplement of each other. Only through this way can space operations be carried out for the common interests of all mankind.

3.4. The Issue of War under the Guise of Research

While the high risks entailed in NPS applications were the main concerns for supporters of restrictive use of NPS, another topic can not be disregarded. This becomes even the truth after the September 11th Event with the severe challenge of terrorism. Besides the five original nuclear powers, several other States have claimed or been asserted to hold or have the ability to produce nuclear weapons. Nuclear power is not any more controlled by limited States, the spreading of nuclear power shall also add to the concerns over the legitimate use of NPS.

NASA's announcement, to a certain extent, has relevance to war against terrorism. How the Bush Blueprint on budget deficits and the war against terrorism will affect NASA is still under stressful study. However, states or relevant bodies may carry out space missions under the guise of research. The so-called "peaceful" use of NPS in space can be merely a cover to develop power systems to be used for space-based weapons. Once developed under the guise of space exploration, nuclear reactors could be used to drive dangerous space-based laser weapons. Such concerns are justified, however, such guise is difficult to identify. It is thus claimed that: the military's future testing and deployment of nuclear rocketry is necessary; security only works when people responsible for defense have access to advanced nuclear propulsion in space to perform the tasks.[43] Nevertheless, those concerns cannot hold back the earnest idea of using NPS for broader space missions.

Peaceful use of outer space has been widely advocated and ruled down in several international documents. The Space Treaty provides that States Parties undertake not to place in orbit around the Earth any objects carrying nuclear weapons..., install such weapons on celestial bodies, or station such weapons in outer space in any other manner.[44] The International Space Station (ISS) Agreement[45] also provides the application for the peaceful purpose.[46] However, the sensitive nature of NPS justifies the reiteration of this issue in the preamble of the Principles. The reiteration should, at least from the legal side, firmly rule out the possibility of war in outer space using NPS. Such a reiteration, while well accommodating concerns about war, shall provide a solid basis for claiming international liability in the possible use of NPS in outer space against terrorism.

3.5. Notification, Consultation and Miscellaneous

Naturally there are many other areas requiring improvements. First of all, several terms need to be clarified, including "launching State", "Procuring State".[47] Secondly, due to high risks to human beings and environment, it is necessary to notify and hold consultations with relevant parties well before, during and after the formal launching activities. Principles 5 and 6 have provided basic structure for notification and consultation. With further extension to broader space operations, notification and consultation appears even more essential. Various scholars have specified that Principle 5 is in conflict with the IAEA Convention on Early Notification of a Nuclear Accident,[48] it is necessary to elaborate this issue at this stage. One way out could be to make specific reference to this Convention, ensuring Principle 5 and the Convention are complementary in nature.[49]

Thirdly, to the extent space operations using NPS could harmfully interfere with other States, international consultations must be performed before proceeding with any such activity or experiment. This is also in accordance with the Space treaty.[50] Such an "obligatory" consultation could also provide a possible disincentive to carrying out space activities with military purposes.

4. THE 1992 PRINCIPLES: RESOLUTION VS. TREATY

The General Assembly adopted the Principles as a Resolution in 1992. Considering the pros and cons during the negotiations, it was sensible to adopt such a resolution to fix the guidelines and criteria for safe use as a first step. It is obvious from the nature of UN General Assembly and a Resolution that the Principles are addressed not only to the State Parties to the Space Treaty, but also to all the States.[51] The universal nature can to a certain extent strengthen the claim of the Principles as part of customary international law, which shall further give insight into the politically acceptable treatments of space. [52] However, the Resolution *per se* is not a formal legal instrument. [53] In view of the existing Conventions on space law, this Resolution can be at most regarded as supplement to the provisions of the Conventions with regard to the use of NPS by a set of recommendation. [54] The non-binding nature [55] has aroused some problems in further implementation, even though Members generally highly respect the Resolution. The Resolution only codifies the international perspective on the hazards presented by NPS in space, members have no obligation in strictly complying with the Resolution. Once disputes arise, Members can argue either way supporting their own position. The indeterminacy of the status of the Principles has thus allowed the implementation largely at the discretion of the Members.

Indeed, quite a lot of scholars have acknowledged that several Principles in the Resolution represent customary international law. More specifically this assertion refers to rules concerning notification and use of NPS in outer space that are of a fundamentally norm-creating character such as could be regarded as forming the basis of a general character of law. [56] The international practice has further evidenced this view. Ample examples showed that international society conforms to the Principles defined in the Resolution: sufficient notice, responsibility and liability, etc. The Russian reported to the UN Secretary General of its anticipated launch of the Mars 96 satellite powered by plutonium-238;[57] the US notified the UN of its launch of the Cassini space probe, containing about 35 kg of plutonium-238 dioxide.[58]

To the extent customary law exists for space law at all, it binds all States whether their consent be express or implied by silence in the face of emerging legal norms.[59] However, what little customary law for space there is has been derived from the activity of very few States. This is exact the truth in the use of NPS, only five States publicly claim to hold the nuclear power, and the rate of use has been comparatively low. Furthermore, with the increasingly role of treaties both in international law in general and space law in particular, customary law is of far less importance and its significance for outer space activities has, in many aspects, not been secured.[60] Except for the Principles widely regarded as part of customary international law, the status of other Principles is not settled. This drawback can largely weaken the effect of the Resolution on State practice.

After more than ten years of existence, it is now right time to consider concluding a treaty with regard to this issue. This is in accordance with the objective of the UN to the progressive development and codification of international law. The binding nature of a treaty can provide a strong impetus to the legal use of NPS, even more meaningful to the legitimate use of NPS in the proposed extensive arena. Such a binding treaty can also help provide a mechanism for international society in agreeing to the extended use of NPS and mitigating the anxiety.

5. CONCLUSION

The 1992 Principles provide a good framework for the use of NPS. Over the previous years, the international society has strictly complied with the Principles, creating an orderly regime for the use of NPS in outer space. Nevertheless, with rapid development of space technology, States have claimed that the use of NPS for other possible purpose is well justified. This trend is well led by the US in its NASA program, the ongoing review of the existing structure will no doubt exert heavy influence on the existing legal framework established by this Resolution. Acknowledging the advantages of using NPS in broader space operations, the technicians and space activists are leading the trend toward wider use of NPS. The theoretical debate on the appropriateness of such a wider use should no doubt give way to the pragmatic approach in formulating a proper legal framework in coping with the incoming severe challenge. The improvement of the legal framework shall include not only the substantial part, but also the formality of such a document. The initiative taken by the NASA can be the right incident that touches off the revision of the Resolution, provide an impetus to the realization of a formal treaty in this field, and push the development of space treaty after a blank period of space law legislation. Much cost can be saved or devoted to more promising projects if the result of the revision is known as early as possible. It is expected that the improved Principles shall well accommodate the renewed call for application of NPS in broader space activities and the well-being of modern society as a whole.

---

[1] The first nuclear satellite was Transit 4A, a navigational satellite launched on June 29, 1961. It was a time when space and nuclear power were seen by some as coupled.

[2] See further D. Tan, Towards a New Regime for the Protection of Outer Space as the "Province of All Mankind", 25 *Yale Journal of International Law*149 (Winter 2000).

[3] See generally R.I.R. Abeyratne, The Use of Nuclear Power Sources in Outer Space and Its Effect on Environmental Protection, 25 *Journal of Space Law* 17 (1997).

[4] The satellite was designed for ocean reconnaissance and was powered by a nuclear reactor working on uranium enriched with isotope of uranium-235. For discussion, see further B. Schwartz & M.L. Berlin, After the Fall: An Analysis of Canadian Legal Claims for Damage Caused by Cosmos 954, 27 *McGill Law Journal* 6767 (1982); A.F. Cohen, Cosmos 954 and the International Law of Satellite Accidents, 10 *Yale Journal of International Law* 80 (1984).

[5] M. Benko & K. Schrogl (eds.), *International Space Law in the Making: Current Issues in the UN Committee on the Peaceful Uses of Outer Space* 19-21 (1993).

[6] Principles Relevant to the Use of Nuclear Sources in Outer Space, UN G.A. Resolution A/Res/47/68 (December 14, 1992); GAOR, 47th Session, Supp. No. 20, UN Doc. A/47/20 (1992).

[7] Section 1.1 of Principle 3.

[8] R. Dusek, Lost in Space?: The Legal Feasibility of Nuclear Waste Disposal in Outer Space, 22 *William and Mary Environmental Law and Policy Review* 213 (Fall 1997).

[9] R.A. Ramey, Armed Conflict on the Final Frontier: The Law of War in Space, 48 *Air Force Law Review* 116 (2000).

[10] For further description of the Principles, see I.H.Ph. Diederiks-Verschoor, *An Introduction to Space Law*, 108-109 (Kluwer, 2nd Edition, 1999).

[11] In an attempt to square this circle, the Federation of American Scientists and Soviet colleagues in 1988 proposed a ban on the operation of nuclear reactors in earth orbit that would nevertheless permit their use for space exploration.

[12] P. Pae, NASA Seeks $1 Billion for Nuclear Propulsion Plan, *Los Angeles Times*, February 7, 2002, at 112.

[13] The Return of Space Nuclear Reactors, Secrecy News from the FAS Project on Government Secrecy, Volume 2002, Issue No. 11, January 31, 2002, available at <http://cndyorks.gn/apc.org>.

[14] NASA Administrator Honorable Sean OKeefe, NASA biography of OKeefe, available at <http://www.nasa.gov/bios/okeefe.html>.

[15] K. Grossman, Plutonium in Space (Again!), Global Network Against Weapons and Nuclear Power in Space, Covert Action Quarterly, No. 73, Summer 2002, available at <http://www.globenet.free-online.co.uk/articles/morenukesinspace.htm>.

[16] N. Jasentuliyana, An Assessment of the United Nations Principles on the Use of Nuclear Power Sources in Outer Space, *Proceedings 36th Colloquium on the Law of Outer Space* 316 (Graz, 1993).

[17] The US has launched some two-dozen spacecraft utilizing plutonium-powered electrical generators.

[18] G. Clark, Will Nuclear Power Put Humans on Mars?, available at <http://www.space.com>.

[19] New Solar Cells with Record Efficiency, ESA Press Information Note No. 0794, April 29, 1994.

[20] L. David, NASA to Seek Nuclear-Powered Spaceflight Alternatives, February 1, 2002, available at <http://cndyorks.gn.apc.org>.

[21] Done on August 5, 1963, 14 U.S.T. 1313, 480 U.N.T. 43 (entered into force on October 10, 1963).

[22] G.H. Reynolds & R.P. Mergers, *Outer Space: Problems of Law and Policy* 61 (2nd ed., 1997).

[23] S. de Cordoba, Changing Basic Space Laws: Popularity, Pragmatism and Historical Lessons, *Proceedings 36th Colloquium on the Law of Outer Space* 330 (1993).

[24] A fast mission using nuclear thermal rockets could get astronauts to Mars in as little as 4 months.

[25] For the discussion of the advantages, see further Clark, *supra* note 18.

[26] B. Behrhorst, Nuclear Rocket Power in Space: Generational Legacy, available at <http://www.nuclearspace.com>.

[27] See for example, M.S. Smith, Legal Aspects of Using Nuclear Reactors on the Moon, *Proceedings 35th Colloquium on the Law of Outer Space* 312 (1992).

[28] For example, Article XI of Space Treaty provides the commitment in providing the information to promote international co-operation in the peaceful exploration and use of outer space.

[29] Section 1.4 of Principle 3.

[30] Section 2.1 of Principle 3.

[31] Section 2.2 of Principle 3.

[32] A.A. Cocca, Are the Principles on the Use of Nuclear Power Sources in Outer Space a Progress in Space Law?, *Proceedings 36th Colloquium on the Law of Outer Space* 258 (1993).

[33] N. Jasentuliyana, A Survey of Space Law as Developed by the United Nations, in N. Jasentuliyana (ed.), *Perspectives in International Law* 349 (Kluwer, 1995).

[34] A.D. Terekhov, Review and Revision of the Principles Relevant to the Use of Nuclear Power Sources in Outer Space, *Proceedings 36th Colloquium on the Law of Outer Space* 340 (1993); see also Y. Lodico, Developing Legal Principles for the Safe Use of Nuclear Power Sources in Outer Space, *Proceedings 34th Colloquium on the Law of Outer Space* 134 (1991); E. Galloway, United Nations Consideration of Nuclear Power for Satellites, *Proceedings 22nd Colloquium on the Law of Outer Space* 135 (1979).

[35] J.M. Seymour, Containing the Cosmic Crisis: A Proposal for Curbing the Perils of Space Debris, 10 *Georgetown International Environmental Law Review* 907 (Spring 1998).

[36] Treaty Banning Nuclear Weapon Tests in the Atmosphere, in Outer Space and under Water, August 5, 1963, 14 U.S.T. 1313.

[37] Jankowitsch, Legal Aspects of Military Space Activities, in N. Jasentuliyana (ed.),

Space Law: Development and Scope 143 (1992).
[38] Reynolds & Merges, *supra* note 22, at 54.
[39] Final Environmental Impact Statement for the Cassini Mission, National Aeronautics and Space Administration, Solar System Exploration Division, Office of Space Science, June 1995, at 476. As stated, if an inadvertent reentry occurred and Cassini fell back into the Earths atmosphere, it would break up (it had no heat shield) and 5 billion of the world population could receive 99 percent or more of the radiation exposure.
[40] See further Vienna Declaration on Space and Human Development, Adopted by UNISPACE III, as it concludes two-week session, Third United Nations Conference on the Exploration and Peaceful Uses of Outer Space, UNISPACE III SPACE/V/9, Final Meeting (AM & PM) and Round-Up, July 30, 1999;.
[41] See generally A. Bianchi, Environmental Harm Resulting from the Use of Nuclear Power Sources in Outer Space: Some Remarks on State Responsibility and Liability, in F. Francioni & T. Scovazzi (eds.), *International Responsibility for Environmental Harm*, 231-272 (Graham & Trotman, 1991).
[42] M. Benko, G. Gruber & K. Schrogl, The UN Committee on the Peaceful Uses of Outer Space: Adoption of Principles Relevant to the Use of Nuclear Power Sources in Outer Space, *Proceedings 36th Colloquium on the Law of Outer Space* 238 (1993).
[43] See further Behrhorst, *supra* note 26.
[44] Article IV of Space Treaty (1967).
[45] Agreement Among the Government of Canada, Government of Member States of the European Space Agency, The Government of Japan, The Government of the Russian Federation, and The Government of the United States of America Concerning Cooperation on the Civil International Space Station, January 29, 1998, in S. Gorove (ed.), *United States Space Law: National & International Regulation (IV)*, 98-1 (1998).
[46] Article 1(1) of the Agreement requires that uses of the ISS be reserved for peaceful purposes.
[47] C.Q. Christol, Nuclear Power Sources (NPS) for Space Objects: A New Challenge for International Law, *Proceedings 36th Colloquium on the Law of Outer Space* 248-251 (1993); see also E. Molodtsova, Nuclear Accidents on Space Objects with Nuclear Power Sources: Applicable International Law, Proceedings 34th Colloquium on the Law of Outer Space 142-144 (1991).
[48] See for example, M. Hoskova, The Notification Principle in the 1992 NPS Resolution, *Proceedings 36th Colloquium on the Law of Outer Space* (Graz, 1993), at 304-311; A.D. Terekhov, The 1986 IAEA Conventions on Nuclear Accidents and the Consideration of the Use of Nuclear Power Sources in Outer Space in the Legal Subcommittee of COPUOS, *Proceedings 30th Colloquium on the Law of Outer Space* 403 (1987).
[49] Jasentuliyana, *supra* note 16, at 318.
[50] See further Article IX of Space Treaty.
[51] See A.D. Terekhov, International Responsibility for Using Nuclear Power Sources in Outer Space-Reflections on the text adopted by COPUOS, *Proceedings 34th Colloquium on the Law of Outer Space* 147-149 (1991).
[52] M.A. Gray, The International Crime of Ecocide, 26 *California Western International Law Journal* 247 (1996).
[53] S. Tai & T. Bissett, 2000 Manfred Lachs Space Law Moot Court Competition: Winning Briefs: Respondent Brief, 13 *Georgetown International Environmental Law Review* 328-329 (Fall 2000).
[54] V. Kopal, The Use of Nuclear Power Sources in Outer Space: A New Set of United Nations Principles?, *Proceedings 34th Colloquium on the Law of Outer Space* 128 (1991).
[55] M.B. Gerrard, Asteroids and Comets: U.S. and International Law and the Lowest Probability, Highest Consequence Risk, 6 *New York University Environmental Law Journal* 44 (1997).
[56] See *North Sea Continental Cases*, 1969 ICJ 3, at 71.
[57] A.D. Terekhov, U.N.G.A. Resolutions and Outer Space Law, *Proceedings of the 40th Colloquium on the Law of Outer Space* 101 (1998).
[58] Is Cassini Risky? Look to Facts, Not Emotion, 147 *Aviation Week & Space Technology*, No. 13, September 29, 1997, at 66.
[59] This is a reiteration of the Article 38 of the Statute of the International Court of Justice with regard to International custom. See further P. Malanczuk, *Akehurst's Modern Introduction to International Law*, 44 (Routledge, 7th edition, 1997).
[60] P. Malanczuk, Space Law as a Branch of International Law, 1994 *Netherlands Yearbook of International law* 147 (1995).

IAC-03-IISL.5.04

THE CONCEPT OF LAUNCHING STATE IN THE NPS PRINCIPLES

Viviana Iavicoli*
Researcher
Institute for International Legal Studies – National Research Council, Italy
Via dei Taurini, 19 – 00185 Rome (I) tel. 39 06 49937661 fax 06 44340025
e-mail: javicoli@isgi.cnr.it

ABSTRACT

The Principles Relevant to the Use of Nuclear Power Sources in Outer Space propose a wider concept of launching States since they provide different definitions of the term "launching State" contained in the Principle 2. This is because of the potentially insufficient *status* of the traditional launching State for the purposes of the Principles, which require that the launching State be able to exercise jurisdiction and control over the on board NPS. Furthermore, the Principles retain the classical notion of launching States, as stated in the Liability and Registration Convention, for the purposes of liability and compensation. This legal framework presents peculiarities of some relevance, especially regarding problem of transfer of jurisdiction and control over the NPS between launching States as could be deduced from the formulation of the Principle 2.

The Legal Regime of Nuclear Power Sources: Applicability of Rules of Different Branches of Law

The object of the presentation will be the legal regime concerning the use of Nuclear Power Sources (NPS) in outer space analysed from the point of view of the launching state. That is to say to relate the discipline dealing with NPS – with particular reference to the UN Resolution 47/68 adopted by the General Assembly on 14 December 1992 concerning Principles relevant to the Use of NPS in Outer Space[1] with the provisions of the launching State stated by the Liability and Registration Conventions.

The legal regime of NPS in outer space is characterised by the applicability of a complex interaction of norms pertaining not only to space law but also to nuclear law which includes international norms of conventional nature and numerous sources of soft law such as the procedures of IAEA and of the International Commission for the Radiological Protection (ICPR) for the development of technical standards, recommendations and other guide-lines[2]. The same Principles concerning the use of NPS which are directly applicable as *lex specialis* fall in the sphere of soft law and, therefore, among the normative sources non juridically binding for States. The Report of the Working Group of the Legal Sub-Committee charged with the "Review of international documents and national processes potentially relevant to the peaceful uses of NPS in outer space"[3] classifies a series of documents potentially relevant for the reconstruction of the legal regime governing the use of NPS in the outer space in different sets of norms, including, firstly, the relevant norms of the international conventions, particularly the IAEA Conventions, the recommendations of the International Commission for Radiological Protection, the IAEA relevant publications, the reports of the UN Scientific Committee on the Effects of Atomic Radiation (UNSCEAR) and various others technical documents issued by IMO.

It should also be considered that, in the organisation of these kind of mission equipped with NPS, the scientific community apply rules of Planetary Protection laid down by COSPAR, aimed at the protection of the space environment. Furthermore, the relevance of norms of national and international environmental law has been well established in the legal literature[4]. These provisions can be either Earth oriented or Space oriented. Even nuclear law fulfils these functions where it deals with protection of the habitat and of the human beings exposed to hazardous radiation.

It is in this context that issues concerning the launching States are included. The concept of launching State has given rise to numerous criticisms in their application, causing, as it is known, the intervention of the Working Group in the Legal Subcommittee, in order to clarify this concept. But Principles governing NPS only partially accept the traditional concept of launching State.

The double meaning of the term "launching State" in Res. 47/68 on the NPS

It is not common that in the same document we find a double meaning of the same term. But this is exactly what happened with the term 'launching State' in Resolution 47/68 concerning Principles relevant to the Use of NPS in Outer Space, in which Principle 2 determines the meaning of 'launching State' or 'State launching' on the bases of the aims of the States's actions.

Section 1 of Principle 2 states: "*For the purpose of these Principles, the terms of 'launching State' and 'State launching' mean the State which exercises jurisdiction and control over a space object with nuclear power sources on board at given point in time relevant to the principle concerned*".

The following paragraph, however, makes reference to the usual notion of 'launching State' as laid down in Article I of the Liability Convention and in Article I of the Registration Convention, applicable only to the interpretation of Principle 9 and therefore exclusively to questions of liability and compensation. Following this reasoning, it is possible to say that the definition in the Section 1 of Principle 2, is aimed at interpreting the whole set of Principles, with the exception of Principle 9, for which the usual notion of 'launching State' as expressed in the Liability Convention is applicable.

The reason for this dual use of the expression 'launching State' may be found in the fact that there might not necessarily be coincidence between the launching State according to the traditional definition and the launching State able to exercise jurisdiction and control over the nuclear device on board. In fact, the obligations as contained in the Principles can be reasonably fulfilled only by a State which has the capacity to exercise jurisdiction and control over the NPS.

Principle 3, e.g., states the obligation of the launching State to conform to the general objectives on safety measures; Principle 4 states that the safety assessment of the NPS, which is a highly technically complex procedure, can only be carried out by a State with wide knowledge of the nuclear device and of all phases concerning design, construction, manufacturing, operation and testing of the system. Again, Principle 5 attributes to the launching State the obligation of notification of any eventual malfunction of the NPS or of uncontrolled re-entry with the aim of obtaining technical information from the launching State in order to take the necessary measures[5].

The definition contained in Section 1 of Principle 2, furthermore establishes a temporal connection between a given moment in which obligations are fulfilled (*at given point in time*) and the prescribed activity to be carried out by the State involved (*relevant to the principle concerned*).

This definition, in fact, makes it possible that the State which exercises jurisdiction and control over the NPS might change in outer space. In this regard, I quote an example already hypothesised in the literature of the case of the launch of a US shuttle with an NPS on board which delivers the nuclear system to the Italian element of the Space Station, leaving the device at the disposition of an Italian astronaut. This situation necessarily implies the transfer of jurisdiction and control over the nuclear power source[6].

For the purposes of the Principles, it is important to identify the launching State which can materially fulfil the obligations as mentioned therein. This is the reason for which, in this context, the *status* of launching State as traditionally utilised is insufficient. However, this situation does not exclude, obviously, that there may be coincidence between the launching State described in Section 1 and that of Section 2; neither is it said that this situation will necessarily arise.

If the double meaning of the concept of launching State is a necessity for the sake of the Principles on NPS, the roots of a similar approach can be traced in nuclear law, where the distinction is known between the State possessing nuclear weapons on his territory and the State having jurisdiction and control over them, as in the case of the NATO Nuclear Sharing Arrangements[7].

Concerning space law, Principle 2 is based on the Article VIII of OST, according to which a State on whose registry an object launched into outer space is carried, retains jurisdiction and control over the object in outer space or on a celestial body[8]. This provision creates a link between the concepts of jurisdiction and control and that of registration, since registration is a pre-requisite for jurisdiction and control.

For the purposes of Article VIII of the OST, the case of NPS could constitute an exception according to the norms of registration, from which jurisdiction and control over the object arise for the State of registry while Section 1 of Principle 2, determines the attributions of such functions on the basis of the ability of a launching State to exercise them, thus creating a kind of 'functional jurisdiction'.

Through the double meaning of the concept of 'launching State' and the consequent distinction in the attribution of jurisdiction and control, the provision creates a sort of a 'concurrent jurisdiction' over the same space object, in the sense that one refers to the whole object, and the other limits itself to the device on board, which is part of the same object.

It is now important to verify to what extent there exists effective correspondence between the registration of the object and jurisdiction and control and what are their meanings under legal doctrine.

Registration, jurisdiction and control

Article VIII of the OST creates a perfect correspondence between the State of registry of the spacecraft and jurisdiction and control over it. However this provision has been subject to some criticism in legal doctrine both in itself and in its implications. For example, it has been noted that the article does not exclude *expressis verbis* that non-registered States cannot have jurisdiction and control[9] or that the same provision does not specify the consequences of non-registration[10].

Furthermore, while the same provision entails jurisdiction and control over spacecraft as a consequence of registration, it doesn't define the notion of jurisdiction and control, whose definitions cannot be found even in other UN general Treaties.

For these reasons, given the central role of the concepts of jurisdiction and control laid down in the Principles and lacking specific Treaty provisions on them, which might throw light on the problem, it seems useful to refer to some definitions provided by legal literature.

The concepts of jurisdiction and control are frequently used as synonyms, even if some authors deny the existence of a real distinction between the conceptual and functional aspects.

In Public International Law the concept of jurisdiction finds its origin in the notion of territory, within which the State exercises its authority over people and things[11]. Jurisdiction constitutes one of the attributes of State sovereignty but in the case of the exercise of sovereignty over things or persons beyond national borders, we make reference to the concept of jurisdiction rather than sovereignty.

Jurisdiction is based on the double capacity of the State to create and enforce legal norms, that is to say, prescriptive jurisdiction *(jurisfaction)* which consists in the right to make laws and in the right to guarantee the implementation of law (*jurisaction*).[12]

Furthermore, international law distinguishes three different kinds of jurisdiction, namely territorial, quasi-territorial and personal[13]. Through registration, the territorial sovereignty can extend itself over the spacecraft in the outer space, not in absolute terms but on quasi-territorial basis. Article VIII establishes a quasi-territorial jurisdiction on the spacecraft[14].

As regards the definition of the term control, it is frequently used as an aspect of jurisdiction, a kind of *genus* of jurisdiction itself[15], or as a consequence[16]. Control, however concerns the monitoring of technical conditions of the space object. This definition should not be interpreted only in the sense of passive observation but also as an obligation of the State of registry for the active guidance of the space object.

Some authors of the Soviet school point out that article VIII of the OST would imply a notion of control consisting in special activities for the State of registry aimed at monitoring the technical conditions of the space object during the launch, placing it in orbit and its functioning during landing.

This concept of control makes reference again to the art. VIII, that, in turn, constitutes the base of the Registration Convention and this provision has to be considered in relation with article II (2) of the Registration Convention[17], according to "*where there are two or more launching States in respect of any such space object, they shall jointly determine which of them shall register the object in accordance with paragraph 1 of this article, bearing in mind the provisions of article VIII of the OST and without prejudice to appropriate agreements concluded or to be concluded among the launching States on jurisdiction and control over the space object*". For our purposes, the second part of this Article is more relevant because it can create a disconnection between the launching State which registers the object and the State which assumes jurisdiction and control through the appropriate agreements. Through such accords, launching States can attribute jurisdiction and control to a State other than that of registry, even if, as has been noted by Gorove, "*it is not quite clear just how appropriate agreements would modify the jurisdiction and control granted to the State of registry*"[18]. This kind of agreements in fact have been rejected in maritime law.

Furthermore, it has to be highlighted that the formulation of the Article concerned, dealing with "*agreements...to be concluded*" seems to be perfectly applicable in the case of transfer of jurisdiction and control over a NPS device in outer space.

Finally, as such agreements are not subject to publication nor to notification to third parties, they could make difficult for the latter the identification of the State which exercises jurisdiction and control and the applicable law on board. Regarding this matter, Cheng wondered if following this provision *"in the light of Article VIII of the 1967 Space Treaty, once an object has been registered, States have any discretion to alter the link between registration and jurisdiction"*[19]. In the case of such agreements, in the lacking of the criterion of registration, it could be hard to found a link between the nuclear device and the State exercising jurisdiction and control over it[20].

The Principles on NPS, in the attribution of jurisdiction and control over the NPS to a simply launching State and not to the State of registry utilises a criterion of substance over form. It is evident that the ability of the launching State to exercise jurisdiction and control over the NPS determines the attribution of these competencies. Taking into account the criterion of effectiveness, which is well established in international law, the Principles provide a wider concept of a launching State, able to exercise jurisdiction and control over the nuclear device, independently from registration. And such a situation can happen in compliance with the space Treaty, in particular with the Registration Convention.

In this context, by virtue of the functional criterion adopted in the Declaration on Principles on NPS, the reference in Principle 9 to the traditional concept of a launching State being liable for the whole object assumes coherence with the rules of registration, in that it leaves liability to the State of registry, which follows than the formal criterion.

In the Principles governing NPS, the conceptual division of the two figures of launching States interrupts only a theoretical linearity of the relationship *launching State/registration/liability*, making it impossible to establish a connection between jurisdiction and control over NPS on the part of a determined launching State and the attribution of liability.

Conclusions

At this point, it is possible to highlight some elements of particular relevance:

1. First of all, the Principles on NPS, through the dual use of the term 'launching State' provide a wider concept of launching State than that generally used. The definition of 'launching State' able to exercise jurisdiction and control over NPS does not substitute the traditional concept but is added to it.
2. Another characteristic of the Principles with respect to the launching State governing NPS is that which foresees eventual transfer of jurisdiction and control from one State to another. In fact, the definition refers to a temporal criterion (*at a given point in time*) in relation to a given Principle (*relevant to the Principle concerned*). In this case, however, it should be obvious that we do not refer to a transfer of ownership of the space object but only to a transfer of jurisdiction and control over the NPS between launching States.
3. The definition of two different figures referring to the same term: 'launching State' should not leave doubt about the fact that jurisdiction and control might be attributed only to a launching States.
4. In addition to the requirement of the *status* of launching State, with the aim of attributing jurisdiction and control over the on board NPS, the Principles provide that the launching State has the capacity to exercise such functions over the nuclear device without the transfer of

jurisdiction and control implying registration. Since the attribution of jurisdiction and control over the NPS to a launching State is made using a substantive criterion (the capacity of the launching State to materially exercise those functions) and in absence of specific references to Article VIII of the OST and to the Registration Convention, the Principle does not require registration, even in the case of transfer of the mentioned competencies.

5. In fact, the hypothesis of registration would imply liability for the State of registry. The transfer of competencies concerning jurisdiction and control to a launching State having the technical capacity of exercising them might be considered as a *de facto* attribution.
6. From this framework however, the Principles do not foresee any further liability for the launching State having jurisdiction and control over the nuclear system, since that approach is in compliance with the rules of liability established in space law. Nethertheless, we cannot underestimate the situation where a launching State exercises some competencies of certain importance on a ultra-hazardous system, without assuming the correspondent liability, except for the liability arising from the *status* of being a launching State.
7. Finally, it may be said that the Principles do not provide any indication in order to clarify the relationship between the space object and the nuclear power sources on board. On one hand they seems to consider the nuclear device as an autonomous element with respect to the whole object (in fact the NPS and the object could have two different launching States exercising jurisdiction and control over them) and on the other hand, the nuclear system is not sufficiently autonomous to imply a separate registration.

In conclusion, it should not be forgotten that some of the characteristics of this Declaration derives from the ultra-hazardous nature of the use of nuclear energy whose risks cannot be underestimated.

---

1 On the background and negotiations of the UN Principles on NPS, see, in particular: FAUTEUX, *Sources d'énergie nucléaire dans l'espace: bilan réglamentaire et incertitude américaine* in *AASL* (1991), 267-305; KOPAL, *The Use of Nuclear Power Sources in Outer Space. A New Set of UN Principles?, IISL Proceedings*, 1991, 124-131; LODICO, *Developing Legal Principles for the Safe Use of NPS in Outer Space, IISL Proceedings*, 1991, 132-138; BIANCHI, *Il regime internazionale delle salvaguardie relative all'uso dell'energia nucleare nelle missioni spaziali* in FRANCIONI, POCAR, *Il regime internazionale dello spazio*, Milano, 1993, 113-167; BENKO, GRUBER, SCHROGL, *The UN Committee on the Peaceful Uses of Outer Space: Adoption of Principles Relevant to the Use of Nuclear Power Sources in Outer Space and Other Recent Developments* in ZLW (42,1), 1993, 35-49; BENKO, GEBHARD, *The Use of Nuclear Power Sources in Outer Space* in BENKO, SCHROGL *International Space Law in the Making*, Gif sur Yvette, 1993, 19-71; CHRISTOL, *Nuclear Power Sources (NPS) for Space Objects: A New Challenge for International Law, IISL Proceedings*, 1993, 244-254; COCCA, *Are the Principles on the Use of NPS a Progress in Space Law?, IISL Proceedings*, 1993, 255-262; HOSKAVA, *The Notification Principle in the 1992 NPS Resolution, IISL Proceedings*, 1993, 304-311; JASENTULIJANA, *An Assessment of the UN Negotiations on the Use of Nuclear Power Sources in Outer Space, IISL Proceedings*, 1993, 312-321; TEREKHOV, *Review and Revision of the Principles*

Relevant to the Use of NPS in Outer Space, IISL Proceedings, 1993, 336-348.

[2] See e.g. TEREKHOV, *The 1986 IAEA Conventions on Nuclear Accidents and the Considerations of the Use of NPS in the Legal Sub-Committee of Copuos, IISL Proceedings,* 1987, 403-410; COURTEIX, *The Legal Regime of Nuclear Power Satellite: A Problem at The Cross-Road of Nuclear Law and Space Law, IISL Procedings*, 1991, 117-123.

[3] "A Review of International Documents and National Processes Potentially Relevant to the Peaceful Uses of Nuclear Power Sources in Outer Space", UN Doc.. A/AC.105/781, 12 March 2002.

[4] See, among others: ANASTASSOV, *The Use of NPS of Energy in Outer Space and Certain Ecological Issues, IISL Proceedings*, 1988, 208-211; BOYLE, *Nuclear Energy and International Law: An Environmental Perspective*, BYIL, 1989, 257-313; ABEYRATNE, *The Use of NPS in Outer Space and Its Effect on Environmental Protection*, 24, JSL, 17, 1997, 17-28.

[5] CHRISTOL, *NPS for Space Objects,* cit,, 248; BENKO, GRUBER, SCHROGL, *The UN Committee on the Peaceful Uses of Outer Space*, cit, 40, 43-47.

[6] BENKO, GRUBER, SCHROGL, *The UN Committee on the Peaceful Uses of Outer Space*, cit., 38.

[7] Under the NATO Nuclear Sharing Arrangements, about US 150-200 nuclear weapons are deployed in Belgium, Germany, Greece, Italy, The Netherlands, Turkey and the United Kingdom but, during peacetime all of the weapons remain under custody and control of US forces. On this subject, see: http://www.basicint.org/pubs/Research/2000nuclearsharing2.htm.

[8] Article VIII of the Treaty on Principles Governing the Activities of States in the Exploration and Use of Outer Space, Including the Moon and Other Celelstial Bodies (hereafter OST): "A State Party to the Treaty on whose registry an object launched into outer space is carried shall retain jurisdiction and control over such object, and over any personnel thereof, while in outer space or on a celestial body" (Text in 610 UNTS 205,18 UST 2410).

[9] CSABAFI, *The Concept of State Jurisdiction in International Space Law,* The Hague, 1971.

[10] CHENG, *Nationality for Spacecraft?* In *Air & Space Law:* De Lege Ferenda, *Essays in Honour of Henry Wassemberg*, Masson Zwaan, Mendes de Leon (ed), 1992, 214.

[11] For a definition of jurisdiction in public international law, see, e.g. BOWETT, *Jurisdiction: Changing Patterns of Authority over Activities and Resousrces* in REISMAN, *Jurisdiction in International Law*, Dartmouth, Aldershot, Brookfield (USA), Singapore, Sydney, 1999, 237-262; CSABAFI, *The Concept of State Jurisdiction in International Space Law,* cit., 49 ss., 124-125; CHENG, *Studies in International Space Law,* Oxford, 1997, 72-80.

Gorove describes jurisdiction as a "legal concept used to describe a State's right to exercise legislative, executive and judicial powers with respect to a particular person, thing or event...State can still exercise jurisdiction and control over people and objects in outer space; however is not the launching State but the State of registry which is accorded this right" (*Developments in Space Law, Issues and Policy,* Dordrech, Boston, London, 1991, 330).

[12] CHENG, *Studies in International Space Law,* Oxford, 1997, 73-75.

[13] Definitions in CHENG, *Studies in Space Law,* cit, 72-73.

[14] "Quasi-territorial jurisdiction ...is the sum total of the powers of a State in respect of ships, aircraft and spacecraft having its nationality or registration....Quasi-territorial jurisdiction differs from personal jurisdiction in that it extends not only to the craft in question but also to all persons and things on board, including the activities od such persons, whether on board the craft or elsewhere" (CHENG, *Studies*, op. cit, 73).

[15] For the different definitions of control, see, e.g. REIJNEN, *The United Nations Treaties Analysed,* 1992, 118-119; CSABAFI, *The Concept of State Jurisdiction,* op. cit; 108 ss.

[16] "A kind of factual complement to or consequence of jurisdiction...The requirement of control is added to that of jurisdiction, to censure that the State of registration will also be able to enforce the legislation by exercise of its jurisdiction", VON DER DUNK, *Private Enterprises and Public Interests in the European Spacescape*, Leiden, 1988, 27.

[17] Convention on the registration of Objects Launched into Outer Space, 28 UST 695, TIAS 8480.

[18] GOROVE, *The U.S./International Space Station: Legal Aspects of "Space Objects" and "Jurisdiction and Control"* in *Developments in Space Law*, cit, 330.

[19] CHENG, *Studies*, op. cit, 473.

[20] CHENG, *Studies*, op. cit,, 415.

NASA'S PROJECT PROMETHEUS AND NUCLEAR PROPULSION SYSTEMS[1]

Robert M. Stephens, Esq.
Deputy General Counsel
National Aeronautics and Space Administration
Washington, DC

Steven A. Mirmina, Esq.
Senior Attorney
National Aeronautics and Space Administration
Washington, DC[2]

I. Introduction

The Mission Statement of the National Aeronautics and Space Administration (NASA), to understand and protect our home planet, to explore the universe and search for life, and to inspire the next generation of explorers, requires that NASA invest in technologies that will transform the Agency's capability to explore the universe. NASA's Space Science Enterprise is developing the tools, insights, and abilities necessary to answer some of humanity's most profound questions: How did the universe begin and evolve? How did we get here? Where are we going? Are we alone?

NASA began to answer such questions back in 1962, when it launched the Mariner 1 and 2 missions to Venus. These were the first missions to escape Earth's gravity and explore another planet in our solar system. At that time, NASA depended on chemical rockets to send spacecraft on their journeys. In order to escape Earth's gravity, a chemical rocket expends all of its thrust within the first few minutes after launch. Once the fuel is expended, the rocket is jettisoned, and the spacecraft begins its expedition by coasting along a fixed path to its final destination in space.

---

[2] The views expressed herein are those of the authors and may not reflect the views of the National Aeronautics and Space Administration or of the United States of America. E. Jason Steptoe, NASA Associate General Counsel for International and Commercial Law, and Reed E. Wilcox, Cross Program Launch Approval Engineering Manager at the NASA Jet Propulsion Laboratory, assisted in the preparation of this paper.

Occasionally, there is an opportunity for the spacecraft to swing around another planet to change the spacecraft's direction and velocity.[3]

While these launch scenarios have worked well and have allowed the Agency to explore many destinations in our solar system, the constraints they presented over 40 years ago are still present today. To overcome these limitations, NASA is pursuing alternatives to enhance its capability for launching missions to objects throughout the solar system and beyond. In the field of space exploration, this translates to finding more effective ways to safely power, propel, and maneuver spacecraft, while developing innovative scientific instruments to explore areas of the universe beyond our current reach.

Project Prometheus

In Greek mythology, Prometheus is attributed to be the wisest of the Titans, and he gave the gift of fire to humanity. The name Prometheus means "forethought." For NASA, the name "Prometheus" is indicative of NASA's hope to establish a new tool for understanding nature and for expanding exploration capabilities. Project Prometheus anticipates a tremendous advance in technology. Most noteworthy is its ability to provide orders of magnitude more power – thousands to hundreds of thousands of watts – to spacecraft. The amount of energy generated represents a true paradigm shift for mission planners, not only because of the amounts of power that could be made available to the scientific community, but also in the ability to provide continuous power to maneuver a spacecraft throughout its mission via nuclear electric propulsion.

[3] This maneuver – called a gravity assist – is highly dependent upon launching during a specific, and often very short, launch window. Once that window closes, the time and energy it takes to reach the target destination can change dramatically.

After NASA Administrator Sean O'Keefe took over the reins of NASA in December 2001, he instilled within NASA a comprehensive approach to space exploration that he called "building blocks" or "stepping stones." In his testimony to Congress, Mr. O'Keefe explained that human space flight capabilities should be enhanced to enable research and discovery. NASA ought to continue to expand human presence in space – "not as an end in itself, but as a means to further the goals of exploration, research, and discovery." [4] The same is true for technological developments. They should be crosscutting and emphasize technologies with broad applications, such as propulsion, power, computation, communications, and information technologies. This building-block approach ensures that NASA has a solid foundation from which to build its programs.

> But, our ability to fully achieve our Mission is constrained by the need for new technologies that can overcome our current limitations. We must provide ample power for our spacecraft as well as reliable and affordable transportation into space and throughout the solar system. We must deploy innovative sensors to probe Earth, other planets, and other solar systems. We must be able to communicate large volumes of data across vast distances, so that we can get the most from our robotic explorers.[5]

Achievement of this ambitious vision requires a bold approach to the next generation of spacecraft, including revolutionary improvements in energy production, conversion, and utilization. As Nobel Prize winning physicist and chemist Marie Curie stated: "... Never see what has been done . . . only see what remains to be done." NASA's

[4] Statement of Sean O'Keefe, NASA Administrator, Before the Subcommittee on VA-HUD Independent Agencies, House Committee on Appropriations, April 8, 2003.

[5] *Id.*

Project Prometheus proposes to develop the near- and long-term use of nuclear energy to power certain scientific missions that could not otherwise be accomplished.

In general, radioisotope power systems are limited to providing spacecraft with electrical power that would approximate the power needed for a few household light bulbs. However, the ingenuity of the science and engineering communities has adapted mission plans to this present reality and developed spacecraft and instruments capable of utilizing these small amounts of power. Since NASA's earliest days, this has been a constraint to the ability to gather and transmit data and, ultimately, to generate knowledge.

Today (chemical propulsion & radioisotope power)	**Future (nuclear electric propulsion)**
Launch, then coast	Much greater ability to change speed
Constricted ability to operate science instruments (power limits)	Much greater (practically unlimited) power for instruments
Constricted ability to transmit science data to Earth	Vastly greater ability to transmit science data to Earth
Constricted launch opportunities	Substantially fewer launch period constraints
Cannot orbit multiple moons of outer planets	Can orbit multiple objects or moons
Cannot change target mid-mission	Can change target mid-mission (to support change in priorities)

II. NASA's Experience with Nuclear Power Sources in Space

A. Brief History

On January 16, 1959, U.S. President Eisenhower unveiled what he called the world's first atomic battery -- the radioisotope thermoelectric generator (RTG). While not actually batteries, these amazing devices have become NASA's energy source for missions to the outer planets; they have proven to be rugged, compact, and capable of working in severe, sunless environments. Subject to environmental safety requirements, NASA is considering using radioisotope power systems to support the safe and peaceful exploration of outer space and the surfaces of planets and moons on potential missions.

The importance of the radioisotope power system's contribution to humankind's exploration beyond Earth orbit is often overlooked. To date, RTGs have flown on 17 NASA missions. They provided electricity, during lunar day and night, to five Apollo Lunar Surface Experimental Packages. They powered the two Viking Landers while they conducted research on the surface of Mars. They also powered the recently completed Galileo mission to Jupiter and the Pioneer and Voyager interplanetary missions as they explored the outer solar system. Amazingly, Voyagers 1 and 2 continue to operate today, after more than 25 years in space, exploring the outer frontiers of our solar system. An RTG currently powers the Ulysses spacecraft as it voyages around the Sun's poles, and the Cassini spacecraft relies on three RTGs for electrical power as it approaches the beginning of its multi-year orbital exploration mission of Saturn.

RTGs are lightweight, compact, extraordinarily reliable spacecraft power systems.[6] They are not nuclear reactors and have no moving parts. They use neither fission nor fusion processes to produce energy. Simply stated, they provide power through the natural radioactive decay of plutonium dioxide (mostly PU-238, a non-weapons-grade isotope). The heat generated by this natural process is changed into electricity by solid-state thermoelectric converters.

B. Europa and Jupiter's Icy Moons

Project Prometheus plans to utilize the extensive work done to date on space nuclear systems to embark on an ambitious science mission, the Jupiter Icy Moons Orbiter (JIMO), which would use nuclear fission for electric power and propulsion.[7] Nuclear fission would provide the high levels of sustained energy necessary to power larger payloads of more complex, "active" scientific instruments, power electric propulsion systems that would allow visits to multiple destinations per mission for close-range, long-term observations, and enable significantly larger amounts of data to be transmitted back to Earth.

In his testimony to Congress last June, Dr. Edward J. Weiler, Associate Administrator of NASA's Space Science Enterprise, explained that the initial activity for the fission power and propulsion program would focus on defining the near-term technology research goals, and on identifying planetary science missions uniquely enabled by nuclear fission electric power and propulsion. The JIMO would be an ambitious mission to orbit three planet-sized moons of Jupiter -- Callisto, Ganymede and Europa -- which may harbor vast oceans beneath their icy surfaces. The mission would orbit each of these moons for extensive investigations of their makeup, their history and their potential for sustaining life.[8]

JIMO's science instruments used to study these worlds would have far more power than those on Galileo and Voyager. More powerful cameras and spectrometers could document the entire globe looking for evidence of life, and lasers could measure the topography and characteristics of the surface. The huge amounts of data gathered by JIMO would be transmitted to Earth in torrents, using high-powered transmitters and optical communication links.[9]

Beyond JIMO, future missions making use of nuclear fission systems might visit destinations such as:

- Comets: to explore their surfaces and interiors and return samples to better

[6] Statement of Dr. Edward J. Weiler, NASA Associate Administrator for Space Science, Before The Senate Subcommittee on Science, Technology and Space, June 3, 2003 (Weiler Statement).

[7] At the same time, JIMO will respond to the National Academy of Sciences' ranking of a Europa orbiter mission as the number-one priority for a flagship solar system exploration mission: "The Europa mission has high scientific potential and would investigate the possibility that liquid water exists on that satellite of Jupiter." *New Frontiers in the solar system: An Integrated Exploration Strategy*, National Academy of Sciences, National Research Council (NRC), July 2002, at 3.

[8] Weiler Statement.

[9] *Id.*

understand the building blocks of the universe.

- Mars: to dramatically expand our capabilities for surface investigations, on-orbit exploration, and sample return.
- Various other destinations: interplanetary or interstellar probes to study Saturn, Uranus and Neptune, or investigate the interstellar matter beyond the Kuiper Belt region.

C. The Safety Review Process for NPS Missions

Use of nuclear and other advanced technologies involves certain risks and responsibilities. In all of NASA's missions, safety is the primary operating principle, and this has always been the case with nuclear activities in particular. Working with the U.S. Department of Energy (DOE), the Federal agency responsible for development and production of nuclear technologies for use by the government, NASA plans to extend that safety experience to the design, manufacture, and space flight of a fission reactor. NASA will continue to comply fully with environmental and nuclear safety launch approval processes applicable to the use of nuclear power systems in outer space. Safety must continue to be the predominant factor as humans explore the universe and attempt to unlock the many secrets it holds. NASA has an outstanding record of safety using nuclear power sources (NPS) in outer space.

Multiple agencies are involved in launching a U.S. nuclear-powered mission. Typically NASA builds the spacecraft and designs the mission, the DOE provides the power source and the nuclear safety analysis report (SAR), and the U.S. Department of Defense (DOD) provides the launch facilities. As a result, each Agency has a substantive nuclear safety responsibility for the mission. In addition, U.S. policy requires approval from the White House for the launch into space of systems involving nuclear power. This policy requires that an *ad hoc* Interagency Nuclear Safety Review Panel (INSRP) conduct, prior to launch, an independent review of the flight safety of a proposed mission with nuclear material on board.[10]

As part of the Space Nuclear Safety Review process for a mission using NPS, the detailed SAR prepared by DOE is reviewed by the INSRP established for the mission. This INSRP is comprised of four experts from NASA, DOE, DOD, and the Environmental Protection Agency (EPA), supported by subject-matter consultants from government, industry, and academia. With technical assistance from the U.S. Nuclear Regulatory Commission, the mission's INSRP evaluates the SAR and prepares a Safety Evaluation Report (SER). Based on a review of both the SAR and SER, and after seeking concurrence from DOE, DOD and EPA, NASA decides whether to request launch nuclear safety approval from the White House. NASA submits the request along with the SAR and SER to the White House -- precisely, to the Director of the Office of Science and Technology Policy (OSTP). The Director of OSTP may either grant approval or refer the request to the President for a decision.

III. The Legal Framework and Environmental Impact Assessments

Completely separate from the interagency process discussed above, as part of NASA's

[10] Presidential Directive/National Security Council Memorandum-25, Scientific or Technological Experiments With Possible Large-Scale Adverse Environmental Effects and Launch of Nuclear Systems Into Space, December 14, 1977. The mission's empanelled INSRP does not make a recommendation of nuclear safety launch approval or disapproval.

consideration of the environmental impacts of any mission using NPS, NASA complies with the National Environmental Policy Act (NEPA).[11] Congress enacted the NEPA, because it determined that the Federal Government has a "continuing responsibility ... to use all practicable means, consistent with other essential considerations of national policy, to improve and coordinate Federal plans, functions, programs, and resources" to protect the environment and the renewable resources. (42 U.S.C. § 4331) Among other things, NEPA requires that when a Federal agency anticipates taking major Federal actions significantly affecting the quality of the human environment, a detailed statement by the responsible official must be prepared, called the Environmental Impact Statement (EIS), concerning:

1. the environmental impact of the proposed action;
2. any adverse environmental effects which cannot be avoided should the proposal be implemented;
3. alternatives to the proposed action;
4. the relationship between local short-term uses of man's environment and the maintenance and enhancement of long-term productivity, and
5. any irreversible and irretrievable commitments of resources which would be involved in the proposed action should it be implemented.[12]

If an agency does not comply with NEPA requirements, judicial review under the Administrative Procedures Act (APA) can be sought. In the U.S., courts are allowed limited review of an agency decision. Pursuant to the APA, the court can hold an agency decision unlawful and set the agency decision aside only if the court finds the agency's conclusions are "arbitrary, capricious, an abuse of discretion, or otherwise not in accordance with law."[13] In certain instances, courts are deferential to the expertise of the agency.[14] For example, in the litigation concerning the Cassini spacecraft, the Court found that, in both the final EIS and the supplemental EIS, NASA noted that because of the vicinity of Saturn, where the Sun's intensity is only 1% of that experienced by the Earth, the use of "RTGs was identified as the only feasible power system."[15] The Court concluded therefore that NASA had demonstrated that solar power was not a feasible alternative to operate the Cassini spacecraft. The Court also concluded that NASA had adequately considered potential accident scenarios and potential health risks.[16]

The United States places the highest priority on assuring the safe use of nuclear materials on space exploration missions.

[11] 42 U.S.C. § 4332(2)(C) *et seq.*

[12] *Id.* NEPA also requires that copies of the environmental impact statements and any comments by other agencies shall be made available to the public, and NASA routinely provides copies to the State Department of its mission's EIS, and, for certain specific missions, such as launches with NPS on-board, NASA also requests that the State Department provide the EIS to concerned organs of the United Nations.

[13] 5 U.S.C. 706; *see also Marsh v. Oregon Natural Resources Council*, 490 U.S. 360, 376-77 (1989) (finding that an agency's EIS can be reversed only if it is arbitrary, capricious, or an abuse of discretion).

[14] *Natural Resources Defense Council, Inc. v. Hodel*, 819 F.2d 927, 929 (9th Cir. 1987).

[15] Final Environmental Impact Statement for the Cassini Mission dated June 1995 at 2-12.

[16] For a copy of the opinion, *see Hawaii County Green Party, and the Florida Coalition for Peace and Justice v. President Clinton, John Gibbons, Director, Office of Science and Technology Policy, and Daniel Goldin, Administrator, National Aeronautics and Space Administration*, CV. Nos. 97-01422DAE, 97-01423DAE, United States District Court, Hawaii, Oct. 11, 1997, and the *Order Denying Reconsideration*, Oct. 17, 1997, 980 F. Supp. 1160 (1997)

Accordingly, for the launch of a spacecraft containing nuclear materials (*e.g.*, Cassini), NASA, in cooperation with DOE, coordinates development of a multi-agency radiological contingency plan to address any potential mishap that could release radioactive materials into the environment.[17]

IV. Nuclear Power Sources and COPUOS

The international community remains interested in the use of NPS in outer space. The United Nations General Assembly (UNGA) adopted the Principles Relevant to the Use of Nuclear Power Sources In Outer Space, in 1992 ("NPS Principles"). The UNGA recognized that for some missions in outer space, the use of NPS in space is essential due to their compactness, long life, and other attributes, while it also recognized that the use of NPS should be based on a thorough safety assessment and risk analysis.[18]

The U.S. has long been interested in establishing a solid technical foundation for potential future deliberations within the Committee on the Peaceful Uses of Outer Space (COPUOS) on the use of NPS in outer space. The U.S. actively supported the multi-year work plan adopted by the Scientific and Technical Subcommittee (STSC) in 1998 that "focused on establishing a process and framework for developing information or data that would facilitate future discussions of safety processes and standards for nuclear power sources."[19]

Consistent with its commitment to further the work started in 1998, the United States supported intersessional Working Group discussions between the 39th and 40th meetings of the STSC. As a result of these discussions, the U.S. joined with Argentina, France, the Russian Federation, and the United Kingdom in proposing to the Subcommittee a new draft multi-year work plan for the Working Group on the Use of Nuclear Power in Outer Space (Working Group). This proposed work plan was adopted by the STSC in February 2003; it seeks to "establish the objectives, scope and attributes of an international technically-based framework of goals and recommendations for the safety of planned and currently foreseeable space nuclear power source applications."

NASA's experience demonstrates that development of safe and efficient spacecraft relying on NPS is a highly technical subject – and can be a controversial one. For this reason, it is essential to ensure that national and international discussions regarding the issue have a very solid technical foundation. COPUOS member states are highly aware of the necessity to forge common technical understandings among space faring and non-space faring nations concerning appropriate uses for NPS on spacecraft. Otherwise, without a technically sound basis what may appear to be effective but, in fact, are unrealistic standards, from a technical point

---

[17] This plan, developed in cooperation with U.S. Federal agencies with relevant responsibilities (e.g., Federal Emergency Management Agency, Department of Agriculture, and the Department of State), and other participants, including some state and local authorities, serves as NASA's implementation of the U.S. Federal Radiological Emergency Response Plan (FRERP), and the International Atomic Energy Agency's guidance described in Safety Practice Number 119 Emergency Planning and Preparedness for Re-entry of a Nuclear Powered Satellite (1996 Edition).

[18] *See* NPS Principles, U.N.G.A. Resolution 47/68 of 14 December 1992, Preamble.

[19] *A Review of International Documents and National Processes Potentially Relevant to the Peaceful Uses of Nuclear Power Sources in Outer Space: Report of the Working Group on the Use of Nuclear Power Sources in Outer Space*, A/AC.105/781, 12 March 2002, p.3.

of view, are unlikely to be implemented.[20] Accordingly, the STSC has been exploring ways and means of potentially developing common standards multilaterally, through direct discussions among national experts.

Several options regarding the development of effective NPS safety standards are under consideration. The first option would involve the International Atomic Energy Agency (IAEA) leading development of a non-binding space nuclear safety technical standard. The IAEA does have expertise in terrestrial nuclear power applications, but does not have significant expertise with space NPS. Also, such an initiative would likely require extra-budgetary funding resources. The second option is an STSC-led initiative. The limitation of this approach is that, while some advisers to the STSC delegation have access to technical expertise in NPS issues, the STSC itself does not function as the kind of technical standards-setting body needed to ensure development of suitable standards. This approach could also entail significant expense for the U.N., for example, for translator services to support extended meetings. The third option, a joint IAEA/STSC- led initiative, may suffer the combined limitations of the first two initiatives. Additionally, it is doubtful that such an approach could achieve consensus within a reasonable timeframe, given the demands of the coordination processes within and between the two organizations. The fourth option, and, in our opinion, the most advantageous approach, involves the generation of a model technical safety standard for NPS in space by a multilateral group of space NPS experts. This group would have substantial technical expertise in space NPS – a completely different environment than terrestrial use of nuclear power.

This approach of a multilateral group of space NPS experts holds the greatest promise of achieving consensus in the relatively near future. Such a group could include experts from the U.S., Russia, the European Space Agency (ESA), and the national agencies of European states, as well as the space agencies of China, India, Japan, Argentina, and others. Such a group would have the ability to peer review technical safety standards while ensuring their real world application, free from political or other influences unrelated to the actual technical safety standard. Space agencies would fund their own participation.

A. Proposal for a Multilateral Space NPS Expert Group

Such a multilateral group of space NPS Experts could operate similarly to the Interagency Space Debris Coordination Committee (IADC), which is composed of experts charged with developing technical guidelines for orbital debris mitigation. The IADC experts come from national space agencies with large, multifaceted programs, and they have recently developed recommended guidelines for spacecraft design and operation that would vastly diminish the potential for debris generation. COPUOS member states anticipate that the STSC will be in a position to endorse the IADC guidelines in the relatively near

[20] For example, although the U.S. did not block consensus at the UNGA on the NPS Principles, the U.S. issued an interpretive statement upon joining consensus. In a press release from the United States Mission to the United Nations, the U.S. repeated its concern that: "The principles related to safe use of nuclear power sources in outer space do not yet contain the clarity and technical validity appropriate to guide safe use of nuclear power sources in outer space." The U.S. stated that it "has an approach on these points which it considers to be technically clearer and more valid and has a history of demonstrated safe and successful application of nuclear power sources. We will continue to apply that approach." USUN Press Release #116-(92), October 28, 1992.

future, perhaps as early as February 2004. This approach of the STSC reviewing and endorsing the work of an independent body of technical experts like the IADC holds promise for yielding technically sound – and widely accepted—guidelines. The same approach could very well be effective for NPS. If a multilateral space NPS Expert Group were to formulate a technically accurate model safety standard for NPS, it could then present its findings to the STSC and/or the IAEA for independent review.

Indeed, the IAEA Statute specifically authorizes the Agency to collaborate with other competent UN bodies to establish or adopt safety standards.[21] If the STSC and/or the IAEA reviews the model safety standard recommended by the NPS Expert Group and judges it to be appropriate and technically sound, then either the COPUOS itself or the IAEA could endorse the standard and recommend that States voluntarily and expeditiously implement the standard in their national programs. Alternatively, the NPS Expert Group's standard could be presented to the UNGA for its endorsement of the group's results, perhaps leading to a UNGA resolution, encouraging states to voluntarily comply with this standard.[22] We hope that when the STSC discusses NPS next February, it will recognize the advantages of relying on such a multilateral group of space NPS experts for the initial work needed in this area. In our view, the actual procedural steps identified as the elements of a follow-on COPUOS work plan for NPS issues seem secondary to the central goal of fostering technical consensus on appropriate NPS standards or guidelines before attempting to forge political consensus.

Another important advantage of centering NPS discussions in a technical experts group, at least at this stage, is that it avoids burdening COPUOS with issues it may not be properly equipped to handle. COPUOS' charter makes clear that the Committee's primary focus is to "study practical and feasible means for giving effect to programs in the peaceful uses of outer space" which could appropriately be undertaken under U.N. auspices,[23] a responsibility it has discharged with considerable success and distinction. Reliance upon an outside group of NPS space experts could provide COPUOS the technical support it needs to fulfill its responsibilities to the UNGA.

B. Future Work of the STSC and LSC

The STSC will select one of the four options concerning development of effective NPS safety standards in 2006. If it agrees that formulation of a space NPS Expert Group is desirable, the STSC still has significant work to do. Future work might involve studying launch approval processes or

[21] *See* Article III, section A, paragraph 6, of the IAEA Statute. The IAEA is authorized to: "establish or adopt, in consultation and, where appropriate, in collaboration with the competent organs of the United Nations and with the specialized agencies concerned, standards of safety for protection of health and minimization of danger to life and property (including such standards for labor conditions), and to provide for the application of these standards to its own operation as well as to the operations making use of materials, services, equipment, facilities, and information made available by the Agency or at its request or under its control or supervision; and to provide for the application of these standards, at the request of the parties, to operations under any bilateral or multilateral arrangement, or, at the request of a State, to any of that State's activities in the field of atomic energy."

[22] The genesis for this idea comes from the U.K., which, in the context of the IADC orbital debris mitigation guidelines, suggested that the UNGA endorse the IADC's recommendations.

[23] UNGA Resolution 1472 (XIV), *International cooperation in the peaceful uses of outer space*, December 12, 1959 (establishing COPUOS).

exploring mechanisms for assuring that advances in space nuclear safety (including nuclear safety standards) become integrated into the infrastructure for potential future applications of the technology.

After the STSC completes its work, there is a possibility that the Legal Subcommittee (LSC) might become more involved in considering legal issues related to NPS. NPS has long been on the LSC's agenda, though the Subcommittee has suspended work on this item pending STSC consideration of technical issues. While it does not appear that the LSC would have a role in establishing NPS technical standards, it might be useful for the LSC to consider, at some future time, the potential applicability of existing international agreements to NPS safety in outer space. By way of example, the Working Group on the Use of NPS in Outer Space preliminarily examined the following international instruments for their potential applicability to NPS in outer space:

- The *Convention on Early Notification of a Nuclear Accident* (which entered into force in October 1986). All the countries that utilize NPS in outer space are Parties to this Convention. Any accident involving such a source that could lead to radioactive material re-entering the Earth's atmosphere could be potentially within the scope of this Convention;
- The *Convention on Assistance in the Case of a Nuclear Accident or Radiological Emergency* (which entered into force in February 1987). This Convention requires Parties to "cooperate between themselves and with the International Atomic Energy Agency ... to facilitate prompt assistance in the event of a nuclear accident or radiological emergency to minimize its consequences and to protect life, property and the environment from the effects of radioactive releases." It is likely that this Convention could apply in the case of an accident involving nuclear power sources reentering the Earth's atmosphere;
- The *Convention on Nuclear Safety* (which entered into force in October 1996). On one hand, the Convention does not apply to NPS in outer space, and contains no provision for reporting on or reviewing safety measures taken in relation to such sources. Nevertheless, the safety objectives and, where relevant, the specific safety obligations set out in the Convention may, to some extent, still be instructive or serve as a basis for guidance; and finally
- The *Convention on the Physical Protection of Nuclear Material* (which entered into force February 8, 1987). The potential relevance of this Convention relates to protecting or safeguarding nuclear material in international transport either prior to launch or subsequent to re-entry, as opposed to being directly related to launch nuclear safety.[24]

Although the Working Group preliminarily examined these instruments, it focused on those more specific to NPS.[25] Thus, after the STSC completes its work, it may be useful for COPUOS to ask the LSC to consider, from a strictly legal point of view, the potential applicability of these Conventions, or other instruments of international law, to NPS in outer space.[26]

---

24 Findings of the Working Group are provided in the *Review of International Documents and National Processes Potentially Relevant to the Peaceful Uses of Nuclear Power Sources in Outer Space* (A/AC.105/781, 12 March 2002).

25 *Id.* at 7.

26 The Working Group concluded that the Conventions' "direct application to the launch and

V. SUMMARY

Project Prometheus will enable the means for fundamentally improving humankind's capability for solar system exploration through increases in the power available to spacecraft. The program is managed by NASA and supported by teams from DOE, industry, and academia. The safety of using NPS in outer space is of the utmost importance to NASA, which will rely on rigorous, independent safety reviews throughout design, development, testing and use.

Once electricity has been generated by the NPS, it can be used to power the spacecraft's electric propulsion and communication systems and its scientific instruments. Moreover, with access to greater power, scientists could power most, if not all, of the science instruments simultaneously, if desirable, and could make use of the power to transmit all of the science data back to Earth in greater quantities and at faster rates than currently possible. Such an endeavor will realize the prediction of Werner von Braun, who stated back in 1947, "I wouldn't be a bit surprised if we flew to Mars electrically." New technologies often raise new issues that can require considerable creativity and resourcefulness to handle. However, technology should precede law – not the other way around. For this reason, it is our firm contention that support for the development of technically accurate safety standards for utilizing nuclear power in actual space operations must precede any initiative to consider drafting legal standards. While the COPUOS itself may not be the appropriate body for developing suitable NPS technical specifications effecting spacecraft design and operation, work by an independent, multilateral space NPS Expert Group may well provide a workable option for consideration by COPUOS. After the technical studies are completed, perhaps the UNGA, in due course, may consider endorsing the work of the NPS Expert Group and encouraging states to comply with the newly created technically accurate safety standards for NPS.

---

operational nuclear safety of space nuclear power sources is limited." *Id.* at 16. The four Conventions named above were originally drafted for terrestrial nuclear power applications.

SESSION REPORTS

SESSION REPORTS OF THE COLLOQUIUM IN BREMEN

Philippe Achilleas, Martha Mejia-Kaiser, Liara Covert, Ulrike Bohlmann, Gerardine Goh
(edited by Tanja Masson-Zwaan)

A) SESSION 1 - LEGAL ASPECTS OF APPLICATIONS AND PRIVATE SPACE ACTIVITIES

Chairmen: Prof. Maurice N. Andem (Finland) and Mr. Hermann Ersfeld (Germany)
Rapporteur: Prof. Philippe Achilleas (France)

(Due to unforeseen circumstances beyond our control, the report of session 1 could not be published in this volume – our apologies to all concerned).

B) SESSION 2 - SPACE TREATIES, LAW AND POLICIES AND TELECOMMUNICATIONS ISSUES

Chairmen: Dr. Peter van Fenema (Netherlands) and Mrs. Lesley Jane Smith (UK)
Rapporteur: Martha Mejia-Kaiser (Mexico)

Mr. Tare Brisibe (U.K.) presented the paper "Broadcasting-Satellite Services in Airspace of the High Seas: Some Legal and Regulatory Considerations". This paper addressed the legal issues arising from the direct broadcast satellite service (DBS) offered to airborne passengers, primarily on long range aircraft, while traversing the airspace of the high seas, including relevant polar regions. In the search of comprehensive regulation for this new service on board aircraft, Mr. Brisibe revised the UN Convention of the Law of the Sea (1982), the Chicago Convention on International Civil Aviation (1944) and the ITU Constitution, Convention and Radio Regulations. Mr. Brisibe concluded that there is no international regulation on this issue, and that it is necessary to establish clear, consistent, predictable and enforceable legislation, before the introduction of this technology may raise unforeseen social and ethical issues.

The paper "The Crystallization of General Assembly Space Declarations into Customary International Law" written by *Mr. Ricky Lee* (Australia) and *Mr. Steven Freeland* (Australia), addressed the results of an empirical exercise. They applied the "custom test" to specific provisions of the declarations concerning remote sensing, direct television broadcast, nuclear power sources and cooperation, in order to see if these General Assembly (GA) resolutions have crystallized into customary law. Taking into account the basic elements in establishing a principle of custom, as considered by important authors, *opinio juris* of the International Court of Justice and the International Law Commission, Lee and Freeland divided the General Assembly declaration provisions into three groups: repeating provisions, applying provisions and new provisions. They concluded that the GA provisions have, with exception of the Cooperation Declaration, substantially crystallized into custom.

In the paper "The Concept of 'Peaceful Purposes'/'Peaceful Uses' in the

Exploration and Use of Outer Space. Some Practical Examples" *Mr. John Gantt* (USA), examined the concepts "peaceful purposes" and "peaceful uses" of the space treaties under some relevant provisions of international law. He commented that United States pressed to have these concepts in the form of a binding treaty. Nevertheless, US later adopted the approach to consider them as "non aggressive", making them fit with Art. 51 of the United Nations Charter (right to self defense). He mentioned that Art. 51 gives implicitly the right to establish defensive measures prior to any armed attack, and this may include space-based defensive objects. He concluded that in the Intelsat, Eutelsat and Inmarsat agreements, the drafters interpreted "non-aggressive" uses as being consistent with the concepts of "peaceful purposes/uses".

In his presentation "More Peaceful Use and International Cooperation in Outer Space Activities" *Prof. Toshio Kosuge* (Japan) stressed the existence of a wide technological gap. Although the communications technology using satellite networks has increased in the recent years, in some countries there is a lack of basic infrastructure for accessing telecommunications means. He commented that the efforts of the ITU in respect to "The New Missing Link" should lead to a new role of effective and practical management of limited resources, which could be regarded as common heritage of mankind. Mr. Kosuge made reference to two Japanese satellite experiments to develop satellite communication networks systems.

Ms. P.M. Sterns & Mr. L.I. Tennen (USA) presented "Space Law in the 21st Century: The Outer Space Treaties Revisited". The paper focuses on commercial uses, and issues like:

(1) Which is "appropriate State" for continuing jurisdiction?
(2) What is "launching State"?
(3) Harmonisation of various national legislation
(4) Liability can be determined through bilateral and multilateral agreement.

A level of consistency between licensing practices important; these should be harmonised and implemented by States on a case-by-case basis. Existing Treaties should not be amended. The Registration Convention should be made more detailed, and uniform for various national registration legislations. Dispute resolution mechanisms should be established. States have not agreed that the dispute resolution mechanisms would be binding – this is a major issue inhibiting commercial use of outer space. A broad sweeping set of changes is proposed to the Moon Agreement. There is a proposed inference to leave moratorium out of the Agreement. More realistic rules would be necessary. The most controversial would be the "Common Heritage of Mankind" phrase. The proposal is to delete and replace with "Province of Mankind".

With the paper "Article I of the Outer Space Treaty and the International Telecommunications Union" *Prof. Francis Lyall* (U.K.) elaborated that the ITU has recently faced a reduction in the contributions of its members that may indicate a level of dissatisfaction with ITU. He noted that some events, like the "Wold Summit on the Information Society", may not have a impact on the needs of many countries. Prof. Lyall commented that the "digital divide" between countries which are analogue-based in their telecommunications and countries using digital technologies, is a major concern ITU needs to address. ITU has shortcomings, being slow for starting new initiatives or being timid when there is the need to refuse registration of certain frequencies and orbits in favor of general world interests. Nevertheless, Prof. Lyall concluded that the ITU has gone a good way of meeting the requirements of Art. I of the OST, in the sense that outer space should be used for the betterment of all.

The paper "Snapshot: the Process of Change in International Space Law Politics", by *Mrs. Edythe Weeks* (USA) focused on the question to what extent international space law prohibits or permits private for-profit space tourism. Mrs. Weeks pointed out that usually this question is linked to private property rights on outer space. She commented that many space lawyers state that international space law permits private property rights because there is no explicit prohibition, but at the same time consider space tourism to be prohibited. She proposes to separate the two issues. Mrs. Weeks concluded that there is an interpretation gap between space entrepreneurs linked to particular industries and space lawyers linked to industry, academia, government, etc. The time would have come to bridge this gap, in order to clarify what is permitted or prohibited in outer space.

Mr. Golrounia and *Mr. Bahrami* (Iran) presented the paper "Legal Principles of Exploration and Use of Outer Space: Past Achievements and Future Challenges". The authors outlined the change of the drivers for space activities, from prestige and security to economic reasons. The growing presence of the private sector in outer space triggered space legislation for protecting economic interests, instead of strengthening the benefit of all the countries referred to in the OST. The authors concluded that space technology can improve, among others, education and health services, making it necessary to develop space law into the direction of the common interest. They also commented that new problems, like environmental control, space debris, space navigation, etc., require the setting of standards and recommended practices for technical aspects.

Mr. Gyula Gál (Hungary) examined in his paper "Some Remarks to General Clauses of Treaty Space Law," three characteristic general clauses of Space Law: province of mankind, envoys of mankind and common heritage of mankind. "Mankind" being the nucleus of all three general clauses, Mr. Gál revised the meaning of this concept which commonly comprises only human beings, independently of politically motivated States. Although some authors assert that "Mankind" is a subject of international law, Mr. Gál is of the opinion that it does not yet meet all the requirements to fall under this label. In respect to the "Common Heritage of Mankind" concept, Mr. Gál considered this more a philosophical and political concept than a legal one.

In the paper "Interpreting Article II of the Outer Space Treaty" *Mr. Wayne White* (USA) discussed the interpretation of Art. II of the OST on the "prohibition of appropriation" of outer space, the Moon and other celestial bodies. Mr. White reported of the increasing sale of deeds to real property on the Moon and other celestial bodies by private organizations. Several private internet web sites are used to register claims of property in outer space or to promote legal initiatives for the award of property rights in outer space. He stressed that the absence of national laws to the public in general that clarify Art. II of the OST has resulted in the current confusion and controversy. He concluded that there is need to clarify the law and to implement national legislation and international consultations in this respect.

The paper of *Ms. Isabel Pessoa-Lopes* (Portugal*)*, "Space Policy Perspectives of the Space Generation" outlined the work of the Space Generation Forum (SGF), which is to consolidate the views of young space professionals regarding Space Policy issues and strategic plans and to help solving key questions of the international space workforce. As a response to the European Union Green Paper "European Space Policy", the SGF attempts to set up a formal mechanism for representing the input of young people in the European Union. A conference organized by the EU on European Space Policy will be held in Lisbon, Portugal, next year.

Mr. Xiaofeng Mo (China) presented the paper "National Liability for Damage Outside Territory Caused by Space Objects and Suggestion to China's Legislation". Mr. Xiaofeng mentioned that the Chinese government is working on national space legislation. One of the domestic legal instruments will be the "Interim provisions on the management of civil space launch". Mr. Xiaofeng suggested that issues like liability aspects, licensing systems, third party insurance should be taken into account. He underlined that the Chinese government is also working on a comprehensive national action plan on research and monitoring of space debris.

Mr. Philippe Achilleas (France) presented the paper "Planetary Protection-Legal Issues". He informed about the works done by COSPAR and NASA on planetary protection standards, for missions conducted in outer space. He expressed the need for certain clarifications, e.g. for the expression "harmful contamination". COSPAR restricts this term to biological contamination. He found desirable that States exchange their contamination prevention technologies, potentially leading to an international cooperation program. Mr. Achileas referred to a ruling of the International Court of Justice in 1977 calling for the absolute need to prevent environment damage, to avoid irreversible effects. In his opinion, this "prevention principle" gave birth to certain obligations of States and shall be regarded as the legal basis not only of our planet, but for planetary protection in general including the Moon and other celestial bodies.

Mr. Ricky Lee (Australia) and *Prof. Fernandez-Brital* (Argentina) presented the paper "Proposal for a Standard Curriculum and a General Course on Space Law". As a result of a proposal made during previous IISL colloquia and the "UN Workshop on Capacity Building in Space Law" (The Hague), the authors drafted the curriculum of a standard course of space law, that may provide guidance to educators in countries with limited practice and experience in space law. Taking into account other suggestions of the UN Workshop on a general course in space law to be conducted periodically by the IISL, they suggested some mechanisms for the selection of teachers, legal materials, related treatises, articles, and the possibility to archive courses on videotape.

Discussion:
In respect to Art. II of the OST related to the prohibition of national appropriation of outer space, including the Moon and other celestial bodies, *Mr. Gal* asked Mrs. Weeks about her opinion on the prohibition "...by means of use or occupation, *or by any other means"*.

Mrs. Weeks replied that Article II addresses "national" appropriation and thus binds States only, but not private persons. She commented that the absence of law in this respect, makes private property legal and permissible in this area. She also said that some concepts like "freedom of exploration" and "benefit of Mankind" are very diffuse and should be made clear. She stated that "space law" doe not exist as "law" but as "space policy".

Judge Vereshchetin disagreed and stated that the existing legal instruments on space law are the basis to be taken into account in a dispute settlement, and the International Court of Justice could not consider mere political reasons. Some scientists seem to consider that "space law" does not exist. But definitely the introduction of national space legislations provides proof that space law is existing law. Despite the lack of clarity of many space law provisions, he was of the opinion that the existing legal instruments, general statements and principles are to be applied and interpreted by lawyers in an adequate form.

C) SESSION 3 - SPACE LAW AND INTERNATIONAL SECURITY

Chairmen: Mr. John B. Gantt (USA) and Dr. Yuri Kolossov (Russia)
Rapporteur: Dr. Liara Covert, (Canada)

The first intervention was by *Prof. Paul Larsen* (USA). From the perspective of an international working group, he summarized the restrictions and legal obstacles to trade based on the activities of UNIDROIT. He noted that a number of UNIDROIT conferences took place in 2002 and 2003, and also how a number of revisions to the draft space protocols leave the state of negotiations with States rather open-ended. Prof. Larsen distinguished between restrictions which are /aren't related to national security, and concluded that the absence of a widely-accepted international regulation for parties financing space-related contracts means actors are subject to existing national and international laws and regulations restricting trade in space assets. The draft protocol under negotiation offers new options.

Prof. Yasuaki Hashimoto (Japan), addressed how remote-sensing satellites and non-binding resolutions are useful tools in the promotion of regional security in a post-Cold War environment. Mr. Hashimoto explained that China, India, South Korea, Japan and other Asian countries have solely or jointly developed remote-sensing technology to promote peace and help monitor environmental threats not covered by past international security systems and laws. He recognized the need for a regional satellite centre, but also questioned the feasibility of creating such a multilateral organization for the purpose of strengthening regional security that touches on national defense.

He referred to the functioning of entities like the WEU, EU, NATO, the Asian Regional Forum (ARF) to support consensus-building.

Prof. Peter Van Fenema, (Netherlands), drew from the U.S. Arms Export Control Act and its implementing International Traffic in Arms Regulations (ITARS) to outline serious political and legal obstacles to international cooperation in satellite launches. He noted the serious problems encountered by U.S. and non-U.S. companies that wish to participate in international satellite launches and related activities with regard to space assets, which are regulated by the Office of Defense Trade Controls in the U.S State Department. Since these assets are associated with national security, they're set forth in the Munitions List which complicates access to, movement of and specific use of any object for international trade.

Mr. Laurent Crapart (France) examined the history of export control laws from a European Community perspective. He emphasized the need to seek a balance between sovereignty and regional security, as well as to rethink the impact of export controls on commercial matters. Mr. Crapart recognized the existence of a European Code of Conduct in export control regimes for EC member states, as well as drawbacks to and lack of legal value of European export controls for non-EC states.

Prof. Maurice Andem (Finland) reflected on the 1963 Treaty Banning Nuclear Weapons Tests in the Atmosphere, Outer Space and Under Water. He summarized the highlights of 51 years of legal resolutions, treaties and events between the first nuclear test on 16 July 1945 to the adoption of the Comprehensive Test Ban Treaty (CTBT) on 24 September 1996. He stressed moral, ethical and humanitarian reasons for redirecting energy and resources from the weapon development to alleviating world suffering. He stressed that interpretation of legal duties should follow this idea.

Prof. Kolossov summarized the paper by *Dr. Gennady P. Zhukov* (Russia), "Russia-MTCR Participant". Russia has been participating fully in the MTCR from October 1995. The national approach of Russia to implementing MTCR provisions has attracted attention. It is expected to reduce the probability that missile technologies would be exported without the knowledge of the Russian government. There has been a development of a code of conduct with respect to ballistic missiles – there is also a suggestion that the June 26 2003 CD review should consider a ground control system. This suggestion is based on the existing bilateral agreements in the area of missile applications with a data exchange centre to be established in Moscow. So the MTCR participating states consider this code to be the more advanced and promising of the present initiatives. There is a long list of rules and regulations for international trade.

Prof. Galloway read *Prof. Christol's* (USA) paper about the hybrid (commercial and military) character of remote-sensing (RS) and legal agreements which have evolved in the United States to guide exchanges of information and images obtained from outer space. On the one hand, the Department of Defense (DOD) operates agencies that engage in security-based

RS activities and guide the development of security policy. On the other hand, commercial imagery is obtained and controlled based on market interest and State sovereign rights to privacy. The security aspects of RS should be understood alongside foreign policy commitments and the state of international relations between the U.S. and other countries.

Mr. Gantt read *Mr. Skip Smith's* paper (USA) about safety and liability issues regarding the 2003 Columbia Shuttle disaster. Overlapping legal considerations are addressed under the Liability Convention, substantive U.S. laws such as the Federal Tort Claims Act (FECA) and Federal Employees Compensation Act (FECA) The Columbia Accident Investigation Board Report, examples of civilian contracts to defense and reference to international space law instruments help to guide an analysis of remedies under U.S. law.

"Peace in Space", a paper by the *SGC Working Group* was summarized by Liara Covert. This paper is a summary of specific work group of the Space Generation Advisory Council. It is based on the demise of the ABM, the problems with the MTCR etc. The main proposal is to establish a network, and have conferences on peace in space, thereby promoting a campaign to unify support for a treaty for the non-militarisation of space. In turn, it is hoped that this will contribute to

(1) Prohibiting primary conventional weapons in space; and
(2) Reporting evaluation, public examination and the passing of appropriate recommendations to people in charge.

Dr. Liara Covert (Canada), examined precursors to a treaty concerning planetary defense from large Near Earth Object (NEO) collisions. Dr. Covert emphasized how trans-border crises are such that before individual countries and other actors can effectively act on both policy and technical levels, diverse actors need to define the nature of terms like threat, risk, harm, environmental security, self-preservation, right and duty along different points in time (before, during and after awareness of the threat) in relation to individual roles in mitigation and response strategy. Lawyers, engineers, policy-makers, disaster managers, technical and other practitioners interpret situations according to personal information needs and roles or functions in preparation for and ground-level disaster response. Lawyers need to develop an intra-professional mindset and contribute in different ways to facilitate information exchange, distribution and practical disaster response.

Prof. Kolossov read *Mr. Alexey Krasnov's* paper (Russia) which offered a history of the space activities undertaken by the Russian Federation in order to portray Russia's approaches to and promotion of international cooperation and non-proliferation at present day. Mr. Krasnov explained the role of Russian export controls and state security, and how they are interpreted in Russian national law. He acknowledged the challenges associated with continuing to promote international cooperation while strengthening protection of sensitive State technologies.

Ms. Gerardine Goh (Singapore) emphasized how the history and respect of outer space law provides a solid foundation for the development of multilateral frameworks and enforcement of global peace and security. Ms. Goh emphasized that the interdisciplinary dialogue and consensus-building which characterize space fora can lead to more effective mechanisms and enforcement of security using other forms of international law on Earth.

D) SESSION 4 - SPACE TRAFFIC MANAGEMENT AND NAVIGATION

Chairmen: Prof. José Monserrat Filho (Brazil) and Dr. Lubos Perek (Czech Rep.)

Rapporteur: Ms. Ulrike Bohlmann, ESA

The first presentation was given by *Prof. V. Kopal* (Czech Rep.) He concentrated on the question "Is the present international space law sufficiently armed for the protection of astronauts, functional space objects, and space environment against space debris, or should a legal regulatory system relating to this issue be established soon?" After giving a short overview of the current legal regime applicable to space debris, he underlined the desirability of a special legal document on this subject in the UN and cited the ILA Draft International Instrument on the Protection of the Environment from Damage caused by Space Debris as possible model.

Dr. Kai-Uwe Schrogl (Germany) presented a report on the "Status of the IAA Study Group on 'Traffic Management Rules for Space Operations'", written together with *Corinne Contant* and *Petr Lala*. The scope of the study reflects the definition of space traffic management as comprising technical and regulatory provisions for guaranteeing safe interference-free access to outer space, operations in outer space and return from outer space to Earth. He stressed the interdisciplinary approach of the study and prospected a synthesis of the findings and recommendations of the study group as a model for space traffic management in the year 2010.

Prof. Monserrat summarised the paper written by *Prof. Maureen Williams* (Argentina) "On the need to Regulate Space Traffic Management", in which she stressed the urgent need to delimit and define outer space.

In her presentation, entitled "Creating an International Regime for Space Traffic Management – Moving from General Principles towards Enforceable Rules", *Ms. Lotta Viikari* (Finland), after taking as a starting point the convention-protocol approach, detailed the traditional Treaty-making process and emphasized that also the gains connected to a Treaty should be borne in mind and not only the corresponding obligations. Furthermore, she advised not to underestimate non-binding regulations.

Subsequently, *Mr. Ken Hodgkins* (USA) gave a short overview of the current US practice with regard to the registration of space objects. He explained that the procedures had been sped up and that an on-line registry had been established. Since the practice of States in this context was uneven, he was of opinion that the Legal Subcommittee of COPUOS should have a close look at these practices.

Dr. Lubos Perek (Czech Rep.), in his paper entitled "Basic Problems in Space Traffic" first raised the issue of terminology, namely that the meaning of technical terms depending on the context and the field under consideration, for example, whether an expression is used in common language or with an ITU background. The next issue he highlighted was, that only a technical definition of "space debris" exists, but a legal definition still was missing. In this context, he was of opinion that an official up-to-date and complete knowledge of the functional status of spacecraft is essential for dealing with matters of space traffic. As a solution he proposed an international agreement on completeness, detailed content and format of the registration announcements of launchings.

Mr. Alvaro Fabricio Dos Santos (Brazil) concentrated his presentation on the subject "Sovereignty and the Space Traffic Management" mainly on the differences in the legal regimes applicable to airspace on the one hand and to outer space on the other hand. He stressed that – due to these structural differences – a delimitation of outer space was of utmost importance.

The presentation by *Mr. Jacob Zissu* (USA), entitled "ASTROREGS: The 'Rules of the Road' In Outer Space" offered some far-sighted views on the establishment of standard evasive manoeuvres in the case of collision courses between spacecrafts. In establishing his proposals he based himself mainly on the existing rules and regulations regarding maritime and air traffic.

Also the paper "Rules of the Road for Space Traffic" presented by *Mr. Stefan Kaiser* (Germany) concerned itself with the subject of traffic management with regard to spacecraft. Specifically, provisions of the Convention on International Civil Aviation and standards and recommended practices of ICAO Annex 2 were analysed. Furthermore, the use of GNSS for the navigation of space vehicles was addressed. By drawing analyses to the existing air law principles some prototype standards and recommended practices for space traffic and navigation were developed.

The paper by *Dr. Frans von der Dunk (*The Netherlands*),* "Quis vadit cum vobis, Galileo?" described in detail the institutional structure of the joint ESA/EU project Galileo, moving from the Galileo Interim Support Structure, GISS, to the Galileo Joint Undertaking, JU. He put special emphasis on the Private-Public-Partnership concept encompassing a public supervisor and a private operator tied together by a kind of Concession Agreement and drew parallels to the example of INMARSAT after privatisation.

Dr. Mahulena Hofmann (Germany) concentrated her presentation with the subject "GNSS and their International Legal Implications" mainly on the international telecommunication legal order and the need to guarantee the harmonisation of particular frequency requirements of the current systems and their potential successors.

Ms. Yuri Takaya (Japan) presented in her paper "Quasi-Zenith Satellites for Commercial Uses and State Responsibility" a Japanese project due to be launched in 2008. After explaining Article IX of the Constitution of Japan, which prohibits Japan from using outer space for aggressive purposes, she recommended the consideration of an enhanced international cooperation in the Asia-Pacific region with regard to the project.

The last speaker, *Mr. Phillip R. Bower* (USA) presented a paper co-authored with Prof. P. Larsen, on "Current legal issues relating to GNSS". He put special emphasis on the US point of view regarding liability for malfunction of signal, namely, that there could not be a liability as long as the service was provided free of charge. Furthermore, he underlined the necessity of interoperability of the co-existing systems and of a continuing dialogue between the different providers.

During the **discussion**, *Mr. Dos Santos* raised the question whether ICAO's mandate should be enlarged to include also regulations with regard to aerospace objects, which might carry out operations in airspace as well as in outer space.

Dr. Schrogl was of the opinion that in the long-term perspective, from 2020 onwards, ICAO could serve as a model for an international body that was to integrate also the activities of UNCOPUOS in the context of space traffic management.

Judge Vereshchetin put forward the idea to also consider the space-elevator-project in the IAA Study Group on "Traffic Management Rules for Space Operations".

Dr. Schrogl agreed that this project was of high relevance for the study, as well as the issue of aerospace objects and tethers. He underlined that additional input and ideas with regard to new technical features was very welcome.

Concerning the tethers project, *Dr. Perek* gave to consider that neither the material nor the techniques existed at present. In his opinion, the subject of space traffic management should content itself with dealing with the current problems.

E) SESSION 5 - NEW ISSUES RELATING TO NUCLEAR POWER SOURCES

Chairmen: Prof. Stephan Hobe (Germany) and Ms. Marcia Smith (USA)
Rapporteur: Gerardine Goh (Singapore)

In his paper "Nuclear and Radioisotopic Power in Space: the Cumulative Content and Effect of the United Nations Space Treaties and Declarations", *Dr. Ricky J. Lee* (Australia) deals with the legal issues concerning nuclear and radioisotopic power sources in outer space. This paper concerned the reasons as to the utilisation of nuclear and radioisotopic power sources in outer space and the legal principles applicable to such usage. It also enumerates the steps necessary to improve the existing legal regime with respect to nuclear and radioisotopic power sources in outer space. The paper notes that the Use of Nuclear and Radioisotopic Power Sources in Outer Space is restricted to earth orbit. In particular, it relates to high electric power applications. It notes also that it was recognised early on that there was a need to use such power sources in outer space. There is a perception that radioisotopic sources are more dangerous and risky than nuclear sources. The UN Declaration on Nuclear Power Sources is only a UN General Assembly Declaration. The question is whether the principles enshrined in that Declaration form customary international law. The controversy remains today as to whether they are binding international law.

In the paper "Discussion on Extending / Modifying the 1992 Nuclear Power Source Principles to Broader Space Operations", *Mr. Yun Zhao* (Hong Kong) states that Nuclear power sources provide electric power for spacecraft and operations of equipment on board. The 1978 disaster with Cosmos 954 served as an impetus for the 1992 UN General Assembly Resolution. It was to have been open for revision no later than 2 years after its adoption but no revisions have been made. This paper moots that it is time to think whether the NPS should be revised. It briefly reviews the 1992 Principles, gives its reasons for revision, and points out areas that would be suitable for revision.

Ms. *Viviana Iavicoli* (Italy) presented "The Concept of "Launching State" in the NPS Principles". This paper makes particular reference to the NPS Principles. It moots that the NPS is characterised by the applicability of norms pertaining not only to space law, but also that applicable to the nuclear power. Nuclear power sources and their use in outer space were the subject of a series of documents of the legal regime providing the use of nuclear powers in different sets of laws, including the Conventions. The scientific community also applies rules of environment. Thus international environmental law is also important. This can be earth- or space-oriented. However, there is a need to qualify the concepts, especially the traditional concept of launching State.

The paper "Nuclear Propulsion Systems" was written by Mr. *Robert M. Stephens & Mr. Steven A. Mirmina* (USA). The mission statement of NASA contains three premises. NASA is required to keep developing technology for the benefit of peoples. NASA depended on chemical propulsion for early launch capability. Although this has worked, it does present limitations. In order to overcome these, new evolution is required. Project Prometheus was developed to increase the capacity of these missions. This program is managed by NASA and supported by industry and academia. It will allow electricity to be generated by the NPS. This electricity is then used to power spacecraft's electric propulsion and communication systems. This paper argues for support for the development of technically accurate safety standards, and that this must precede any initiative to consider drafting legal standards. After technical studies are completed, the UN General Assembly could endorse these studies to create technically accurate safety standards for NPS.

IISL/ECSL Space Law Symposium 2003, held on the occasion of the 42nd Session of the Legal Subcommittee of UNCOPUOS

THE REGISTRATION CONVENTION: BACKGROUND AND HISTORICAL CONTEXT

Frans G. von der Dunk
International Institute of Air and Space Law,
Leiden – The Netherlands
F.G.vonderDunk@law.leidenuniv.nl

1. Introduction

The Convention on Registration of Objects Launched into Outer Space, usually going by the name of 'Registration Convention',[1] was the fourth treaty exclusively dedicated to outer space which was developed in the bosom of the United Nations Committee on the Peaceful Uses of Outer Space, after the 1967 Outer Space Treaty,[2] the 1968 Rescue Agreement[3] and the 1972 Liability Convention.[4] Only the 1979 Moon Agreement[5] was still to follow, which for general lack of success however heralded the end of a two-decade time-span in which COPUOS managed to develop the framework for international space law as far as binding legal instruments were concerned.

The text of the Registration Convention was, after some years of discussion and drafting, adopted in New York on 12 November 1974, and made public through a Resolution of the General Assembly – Resolution 3235(XXIX), which contained the text in the Annex and opened the Convention for signature as per 14 January 1975. It entered into force quite rapidly on 15 September 1976, after the fifth instrument of deposit had been received with the Secretary-General of the United Nations.[6]

2. The Registration Convention in the context of the other UN treaties on space

When evaluating the Registration Convention in the larger context of the *corpus juris spatialis internationalis* (in particular the other four treaties mentioned) and its development over time, the following further picture emerges. Compared to its three elder counterparts, the Registration Convention did not draw overly widespread ratification: only 44 states are parties to the Convention, with a further 4 states having signed but not (yet) ratified.[7] On the other hand, the Registration Convention distinguishes itself positively from the Moon Agreement not just by numbers but also by the importance of the states involved: in contrast to the latter treaty, most of the important space powers are party to the Registration Convention.

This 'middle position' is probably symptomatic for the Convention: a relatively simple and down-to-earth treaty consisting of just 12 Articles elaborating one rather straightforward concept: the registration of space objects. Whilst it would, on the one hand, from that perspective seem to provide few disincentives for states to ratify, ratification on the other hand would be directly relevant especially for those states actually launching space objects into outer space – which still constitute a minority amongst the states of this world.

From a slightly different perspective, the Registration Convention is closest to the Rescue Agreement and the Liability Convention, in that each of these are essentially elaborating one specific Article of the Outer Space Treaty which, as the framework treaty, provides for the fundamental principles.[8] For the Rescue Agreement this concerns Article V on astronauts as envoys of mankind, for the

Liability Convention Article VII on liability for damage caused by space activities, read space objects, whereas the Registration Convention elaborates Article VIII of the Outer Space Treaty which already posits both the concept of registration of space objects, and its major consequence, the possibility to exercise jurisdiction over the space objects so registered.

This very elementary similarity in approach and background also caused a considerable number of states, in considering their possible adherence to the space treaties, to treat these three as rather closely inter-related, and to ratify them together. In particular the Rescue Agreement and the Liability Convention were seen as almost constituting a package deal, balancing the interests of the space-faring nations in benign treatment of their astronauts and spacecraft with the interests of the non-space-faring nations in generous possibilities to see any damage caused by space activities compensated. The Registration Convention underpins this trade-off, as one major aim of the treaty is to enhance the chances of liable states being identified so that claims can actually be asserted.

3. The substance of the Registration Convention

Thus, upon second view, the relatively meagre ratification of the Registration Convention as compared to the other two probably indeed stems from the rather straightforward character of its subject-matter. Let me play a bit the role of the devil's advocate here: the benefits to the international community of ratification by the (still) select group of independently space-faring nations[9] are evident, but since the Convention only deals with the major parameters of the concept of registration and its major legal consequences, with one exception it does not contain any distinct rights or obligations for non-independently space-faring nations which would make it beneficial *for those states to ratify themselves.*[10]

The main rights such states could derive from ratification of the Registration Convention, as compared to simply being aware of its existence and the benefits if may offer in terms of identifying space objects having caused damage through a register accessible to everyone, amount to generic and rather basic ones. Only states party to the Convention are entitled to formally protest and bring forward legal claims in case another party to the Convention would fail to comply with its duties under it, since under general public international law only states parties to a treaty may consider their rights to be violated if another party does not fulfil the relevant obligations.

This is where the devil's advocate comes in. In the absence of substantive rights for non-registering states – with the one exception alluded to – this does not perhaps amount to much. In view moreover of the many loopholes and escape clauses and phrases which the Convention is saddled with (not to mention a general lack of sanctions and sanctioning mechanisms), as well as the fact that the UN Secretary General is supposed anyhow to represent the interests of such non-independently space-faring nations in adherence of the independently space-faring nations to the rules of the Convention, this perhaps provides a rather meagre incentive for such states to ratify.

The exception arises in Article VI of the Registration Convention, providing a state having become the victim of damage resulting from space activities with the right to be assisted by those states with relevant monitoring and tracking facilities for the purpose of trying to identify the launching state(s) of the space object at issue. This clause however, whilst most directly linking the Registration Convention to the Liability Convention as an effort to enhance the chances of identifying the liable state(s) and thus of considerable potential benefit to non-independently space-faring nations, upon closer view might not offer too much incentives for ratifying either.

On the one hand, it only provides for an obligation of effort (the duty to respond on the part of the state with monitoring and tracking facilities is qualified as "to the greatest extent feasible"), on the other hand it still requires "agreement between the parties concerned" – which anyway can also be arranged *without* referring to the Convention or being a party to it.

In other words: wrongly or rightly, non-independently space-faring nations might have considered (and might still do so) their interests in the Convention to be sufficiently served by comprehensive ratification *on the part of the independently space-faring nations*, without the need arising for their own ratification.

One should not be allowed to forego the benefits of Article VI of the Convention so easily, however; and this should probably be the main aim of reinforcing the Registration Convention.

4. Concluding remarks

So where does that leave us by way of introduction from a historical and background-perspective? Perhaps the Registration Convention should not be considered such an only-halfway successful treaty when it comes to its role and impact; in view of the partisanship of most relevant independently space-faring nations as well as the character of the substance of the treaty's rules, the mere number of ratifications does not provide us with the full picture.

At the same time and for that very reason attention is, or should be, largely redirected to reinforcing the Registration Convention in terms of substance, rather than simply exhorting non-parties to ratify. The treaty should, put plainly, be made of (even) more interest to (especially) non-independently space-faring states by indeed making it more effective – that also would be the best way to mount further political pressure upon those independently space-faring nations not yet having ratified.

Tightening and expanding the parameters to be registered respectively to be made available to the UN Secretary-General; including parameters necessary as a consequence of practical – read commercial – developments such as private ownership of satellites or leases-on-orbit and sales-on-orbit; ascertaining that another new and specific development – the UNIDROIT Convention and Protocol – will not dilute or interfere with the impact of the Registration Convention: those would be the focal points for near-term future legal development and codification.

This is therefore, what the current symposium has set out to contribute to. Since practical sense and reason tell us not to try and reinvent the wheel all over again, finally, presentations on the above issues are backed up by some examples of relevant practice *re* registration of space objects. All this, in order to set the tone for further beneficial development of the Registration Convention and its impact and relevance in practical terms.

[1]. Convention on Registration of Objects Launched into Outer Space (hereafter Registration Convention), New York, adopted 12 November 1974, opened for signature 14 January 1975, entered into force 15 September 1976; 14 ILM 43 (1975); 28 UST 695; TIAS 8480; 1023 UNTS 15.

[2]. Treaty on Principles Governing the Activities of States in the Exploration and Use of Outer Space, including the Moon and Other Celestial Bodies (hereafter Outer Space Treaty), London/Moscow/Washington, adopted 19 December 1966, opened for signature 27 January 1967, entered into force 10 October 1967; 6 ILM 386 (1967); 18 UST 2410; TIAS 6347; 610 UNTS 205.

[3]. Agreement on the Rescue of Astronauts, the Return of Astronauts and the Return of Objects Launched into Outer Space (hereafter Rescue Agreement), London/Moscow/Washington, adopted 19 December 1967, opened for signature 22 April 1968, entered into force 3 December 1968; 19 UST 7570; TIAS 6599; 672 UNTS 119.

[4]. Convention on International Liability for Damage Caused by Space Objects (hereafter Liability Convention), London/Moscow/Washington, adopted 29 November 1971, opened for signature 29 March 1972, entered into force 1 September 1972; 10 ILM 965 (1971); 24 UST 2389; TIAS 7762; 961 UNTS 187.

[5]. Agreement Governing the Activities of States on the Moon and Other Celestial Bodies (hereafter Moon Agreement), New York, adopted 5 December 1979, opened for signature 18 December 1979, entered into force 11 July 1984; 18 ILM 1434 (1979); 1363 UNTS 3.

[6]. See Art. VIII(3), Registration Convention.

[7]. As per 1 January 2003; see the web-site of the United Nations Office for Outer Space Affairs (UN OOSA), at http://www.oosa.unvienna.org/SpaceLaw/treaties.html. For the Outer Space Treaty, the Rescue Agreement and the Liability Convention the corresponding figures are, respectively, 98/27, 88/25, and 82/25; for the Moon Agreement by contrast 10/5. In addition, it may be mentioned that one intergovernmental organisations has deposited a relevant declaration accepting rights and duties under the Rescue Agreement, two have done so with respect to the Liability Convention, and two have done so with respect to the Registration Convention.

[8]. The Moon Agreement from this perspective represents an elaboration of roughly all of the Outer Space Treaty's substance with respect to specific *parts* of outer space, i.e. the moon and other celestial bodies.

[9]. The concept of 'independently space-faring' nations is meant to contrast with the majority of states which as of now undertake space activities, if at all, only within an international framework represented by intergovernmental organisations such as ESA, EUMETSAT, Intersputnik, Interkosmos and Arabsat, or under other, looser bilateral or multilateral arrangements.

[10]. This is in stark contrast with the Liability Convention, where partisanship is required for becoming a claimant under it (Art. VIII) and for enjoying all the rights of claimants (Artt. IX-XIII) up to and including the right to establish a Claims Commission (Artt. XIV-XX).

CHANGE OF OWNERSHIP, CHANGE OF REGISTRY? WHICH OBJECTS TO REGISTER, WHAT DATA TO BE FURNISHED, WHEN, AND UNTIL WHEN?

Kay-Uwe Hörl[(1)] & Julian Hermida[(2)]

[(1)]*LL.M. (McGill), Astrium GmbH, 81663 Munich, Germany, Kay.Uwe.Hoerl@astrium-space.com*
[(2)]*LL.M. (McGill), LL.D. (UCC), PDF (Ottawa), University of Cambridge, Lauterpacht Research Centre for International Law, Visiting Fellow, julianhermida@justice.com*

ABSTRACT

The Registration Convention has been a useful instrument to regulate the recording of space objects and to attribute jurisdiction and control. However, it has been criticized because of its several weaknesses and imbalances, such as in the case of the registration of newly created space debris or the transfer of satellites in orbit to non launching States.

Today, satellite operators rely on more detailed data than is provided by the Registration Convention. Nevertheless and contrary to the opinion of a wide sector of the legal literature, this article postulates that the Convention does not need amendment. It is argued that the alleged imbalances can be corrected by an interpretation of the Convention in light of general public international law and by the adoption of national laws to supplement the provisions of the Convention.

INTRODUCTION

The Registration Convention[1] was adopted by the United Nations General Assembly on 12 November 1974 (Resolution 3235 (XXIX)), opened for signature on 14 January 1975, and eventually entered into force on 15 September 1976. It supersedes the General Assembly resolution 1721 (XVI) B of 20 December 1961 and is one of the five international space treaties.

According to Art. III (1) of the Registration Convention, the Secretary General shall maintain a Register in which information furnished in accordance with Art. IV shall be recorded. This register is administered by the Office for Outer Space Affairs (OOSA) on behalf of the Secretary General. There is full and open access to the register and OOSA has set up a searchable index which can be accessed via the internet.[2] But how relevant is the information, which is contained in the register?

Soon after its adoption, scholars, academic institutions and international organizations have been proposing amendments to the Convention. This article will show that changes to the international instruments are not needed. Rather, it is predicated that the efforts should be concentrated on urging States to ratify the Convention. Also, all deficiencies in the Convention can be solved through the adoption of complementary norms at the national level.

WHICH OBJECTS TO BE REGISTERED?

The purpose of the Registration Convention is, *inter alia*, to furnish information which is called for by other, previous, space treaties.[3] Therefore the Registration Convention recalls Art. VI of the Outer Space Treaty and also refers to the State on whose registry an object launched into outer space is carried.[4] The Registration Convention also refers to the Rescue Agreement, which provides that a launching authority shall, upon request, furnish identifying data prior to the return of an object it has launched into outer space found beyond the territorial limits of the launching authority.[5] Eventually, reference to the Liability Convention is made because liability of a launching State attaches to damage caused by their space objects.

The registration obligation for a "launching State"[6] concerns its "space objects". As to the latter term, the Registration Convention provides that "[t]he term "space object" *includes* component parts of a space object as well as its launch vehicle and parts thereof"[7]. Therefore, launchers ought to be subject to the registration duty under the Convention. Concerning non-functional space objects, such as space debris, the situation is less clear. Because of the vague wording, the term "space objects" invites interpretation in this respect. The issue is whether "space objects" have to be functional or if non-functional space objects are also covered by the registration obligation of the Convention.

By way of an extensive interpretation, it is concluded that the definition of "space object" in the Registration Convention covers space debris since non-functional satellites were once functional. The same applies to "component parts" which once formed part of a functional space object. Because the Convention clarifies that space objects include component parts, it is argued that possible failures and separation of space objects are addressed. There is no apparent reason why a non-functional space object should not continue to be a space object.

The question, however, is whether newly created space debris requires an individual registration; *i.e.* in addition to the space object from which such debris results. It could be argued that newly created space debris does not have to be registered because the space object from which it originated is already subject to the registration obligation under the Convention. But even if the Registration Convention is silent on this specific issue, there may be other sources of international law. As to those sources, Art. 38 (1) of the International Court of Justice ICJ) Statute provides for the ICJ to apply "international conventions ... international customs ... and general principles of law recognized by civilized nations".[8]

General principles are of no direct relevance to the subject under study. The application of customary law, on the other hand, develops on the basis of general State practice. With regard to *opinio iuris*, a State must behave so that its conduct is "evidence of a belief that this practice is rendered obligatory by the existence of a rule of law requiring it".[9] When prolonged practice is usually required, "instant customary law"[10] has been suggested for international space law.

This would allow the period of time for a constantly confirmed and uniformly maintained behavior to be rather short.[11] Customary law exists next to treaty law[12] and its rules are binding *ex proprio vigore*, by their own force. Because of its nature as *ius nonscriptum*, but more importantly because of varying State practice,[13] no rule of customary law is apparent with regard to registration of space objects.

It can be concluded that the Registration Convention clearly covers functional space objects such as satellites and space stations. The situation with regard to launch vehicles and space debris is less clear. But the drafters of the Registration Convention believed that a registry would assist in identifying space objects. Therefore, it is argued that the registration obligation should be interpreted broadly to fulfill the purpose of the Convention.

WHAT DATA TO BE FURNISHED?

It should be noted that the States Parties to the Registration Convention believe that a mandatory registry for launched space objects would "*assist* in their identification".[14] In other words, it is recognized that the UN registry is not considered the sole mean for identifying objects in outer space. In any event, Art. IV in conjunction with Art. II of the Registration Convention requires that each State of Registry furnish, at a minimum, to the UN

(*a*) Name of launching State or States;
(*b*) An appropriate designator of the space object or its registration number;
(*c*) Date and territory or location of launch;
(*d*) Basic orbital parameters, including:
(i) Nodal period,
(ii) Inclination,
(iii) Apogee,
(iv) Perigee;
(*e*) General function of the space object[15]

for each space object carried on the national register. In addition to this obligation each State of registry may, from time to time, provide additional information concerning a space object carried on its registry.[16] Such voluntary registration information was provided by Brazil, Israel, Italy, Luxembourg and Malaysia and such appears in document series A/AC.105/INF.1-407.[17]

Naming the launching State or States does not constitute a problem. When it comes to the appropriate designator, the situation is different. Absent of a definition, it is left to the registering State to decide what is "appropriate". As a result, some States (*e.g.* US) provide only the international registration number whereas others (*e.g.* Russian Federation) officially provide only the name of the object.[18] The same inconsistency can be observed with regard to date and territory or location of launch as some launches outside the territory of the State of registry are not marked as such.[19]

Most unsatisfying is the requirement to provide basic orbital parameters. There various ways to chose a reference point for the required data (*e.g.* center of the Earth *vs.* Earth surface) but more importantly the required minimum information does not completely describe the position of a space object. According to Art. IV (1) it is not clear if this information is to be provided for initial or eventual orbits or even continuously. Therefore, the provided information is of little use in terms of collision avoidance or space debris observation and the registration obligation could be extended and/or detailed.[20]

Moreover, registering States are under an obligation to provide the general function of the space object. This information is often provided without real information content (*e.g.* "Experimental-technology mission" or "Space research and exploration" or "Development of heavier spacecraft"). Therefore, this information is of little value. So it comes as no surprise that States rarely use the chance to submit additional information in accordance with Art. IV (2) Registration Convention. The same applies to the obligation to take off the register space objects, once they are no longer in orbit. It becomes clear that the utility of the UN Register directly depends upon the timely, accurate and complete notification by the responsible launching State.[21]

WHEN AND UNTIL WHEN IS SUCH DATA TO BE FURNISED?

The Registration Convention also mandates States to communicate certain information regarding the space object recorded at the national level to the Secretary-General of the United Nations, who in turn must maintain a central registry where the information furnished by the States is recorded.[22] The Convention makes no specific reference to the time in which the information is to be given, *i.e.*, before or after the launch. Since the Convention is silent on this matter, States are free to decide on the time to make the notification to the Secretary-General of the United Nations. However, in light of the object and the purpose of the Convention, the notification, if possible, should be made prior to the launching or within a reasonably short time after it.

CHANGE OF OWNERSHIP, CHANGE OF REGISTRY?

The State of registry has been defined in the Registration Convention as "a launching State on whose registry a space object is carried in accordance with article II". From this definition, it follows that there may be only one State of registry and that the State of registry has to be one of the launching States, *i.e.* a State which launches or procures the launching of a space object; a State from whose territory or facility a space object is launched[23]. In the event that there are several launching States these have to determine which one of them will register the object in its national registry. These States may further agree on the application of certain aspects of the legislation of the State which will not act as State of registry.[24]

Difficulties have arisen with respect to the transfer of satellites in orbit, especially in the case of sale of satellites. In this respect, two sets of facts have to be differentiated: the transfer of satellites between launching States and the transfer of satellites to a non launching State.[25] There have been some cases in practice, such as the transfer of satellites registered in the United Kingdom to China as a consequence of the hand over of Hong Kong or the sale of Canada's Anik CI and CII satellites to Argentina,[26] among some other ones. These isolated cases may not be considered to amount to a general and consistent practice of States followed from a sense of legal obligation, and thus there is no rule of customary international law governing the transfer of satellite ownership in orbit.[27] Since recourse to general principles does not either offer any solution to this problem the analysis must be done exclusively in light of the conventional sources.

In this respect, the legal literature agrees that transfers of satellites in orbit among launching States would be permitted under the Registration Convention and would not offer major difficulties, such as is evidenced by the Hong Kong precedent.[28] However, with respect to the transfer of ownership in orbit to a non launching State, the answer given in the literature is that the Registration Convention does not permit any modification in this case.[29] This assertion ignores the full array of possibilities permitted both by the Convention and general international law. In this respect, the Registration Convention allows the possibility of launching States to conclude agreements on jurisdiction and control over the space object and over any personnel thereof.[30] Thus, launching States can decide to transfer certain jurisdictional rights to others, such as in the case of criminal law under the Intergovernmental Agreement on the International Space Station.[31] As put forward by Aldo Cocca, this reflects the principle that special agreements override general ones and the unitary criteria of Art. II (1) of the Convention.[32]

Nothing in Art. II of the Registration Convention prohibits the transfer of all the jurisdictional and control rights. Therefore, it is legally possible for a State to register a space object and to enter into an agreement with another launching State to transfer part or all of the rights and obligations arising from the registration of a space object. Moreover, it is legally tenable to transfer rights to a non launching State, for the Registration Convention simply prescribes that any such agreement must be made among the launching States. In this respect, a launching State which intends to transfer rights to a non launching State will have to conclude with all the other launching States the transfer of jurisdiction and control rights and obligations to a third non launching State.[33] Under general public international law, the stipulation of rights to a third State is permitted both under customary and conventional law. In effect, in the Free Zones Case, the Permanent Court of International Justice held that "it cannot be lightly presumed that stipulations favorable to a third State have been adopted with the object of creating an actual right in its favor. There is however nothing to prevent the will of sovereign States from having this object and this effect. The question of the existence of a right acquired under an instrument drawn between other States is therefore one to be decided in each particular case: it must be ascertained whether the States which have stipulated in favor of a third State meant to create for that State an actual right which the latter has accepted as such."[34] Furthermore, Art. 34 of the Vienna Convention establishes that no rights and responsibilities may be created for third parties, except with the consent of the third party. In such case, there must be acceptance of the third party. In case when the parties intended to create a benefit, the acceptance may be presumed. However, in cases when the States created an obligation acceptance must be in writing.[35]

Therefore, the transfer of satellite ownership in orbit is legally possible under international law. This, however, requires an agreement among the launching States to transfer all of the jurisdiction and control rights and obligations in favor of a third non launching State. In light of customary and conventional international rules on effects of treaties to third parties acceptance in writing of the non launching State is essential.

CONCLUSIONS AND RECOMENDATIONS

The Registration Convention has been a useful instrument. But there is room for improvement. This concerns both the adherence to the Convention but also details of the registered information. For practical purposes, today many satellite operators rely on more comprehensive data, such as the Two-Line-Elements,[36] for locating and tracking their satellites.

To make the Registration Convention even more attractive it would be desirable to have national laws with binding due dates for registration of objects. The recording of the requested data should be made in a reasonably short period after the launch, such as one month, for example. In addition to this, more precise information for the operational, and not the initial, orbit for spacecraft should be required.

Several prestigious international organizations have recently initiated studies aimed at creating new rules of international law or interpreting existing international norms to adapt them to the new scenario created by the increasing participation of private commercial entities in the pursuit of space activities.

Following the mandate of its 68th Conference, the Space Law Committee of the International Law Association conducted in depth studies geared toward reviewing the Space Treaties so as to establish the need for changes to keep pace with the present commercial context.[37] In connection with these studies, many scholars expressed their view in favor of adopting new substantive or interpretative rules of international law to accommodate the alleged needs of the space industry.[38]

COPUOS' Legal Subcommittee also indicated a certain trend to revise existing norms of international law to adapt them to a new private and commercial scenario. For example, it included the review of the status of all the outer space treaties and conventions as a response to the accumulation of recommendations for defining and extending concepts of space law,[39] and the study of the legal concept of launching State as contained in the Liability Convention and the Registration Convention.[40] Furthermore, many of its delegates voiced proposals for reviewing the international treaties.[41]

Several authors have also advocated for changing the international legal scenario alleging a need to provide the space industry with a clearer framework. For example, Aldo Cocca recommends the adoption of protocols to revitalize the Outer Space Treaty and the elaboration of new international instruments.[42] Karl-Heinz Böckstiegel struggled both within the International Law Association and other forums to develop a system of dispute settlement for space activities.[43] Based on the recommendations of international scholars, Eileen Galloway identified an extensive set of issues to reformulate the five legal instruments, which embraces the creation of new international institutions, including a world space agency, the adoption of insurance and liability provisions, and new norms clarifying the relation between national governments and the private sector.[44]

However, the review of the laws of the States which enacted national space legislation shows that any possible legal vacuum in the international space legal framework has been filled by domestic measures. Thus, for example, States have efficiently adopted a series of mechanisms to deal with the issue of the existence of multiple appropriate States both on a case by case basis[45] and through the enactment of specific provisions, such as the extraterritorial effects of the licensing requirements of the Commercial Space Launch Act[46] or the exemption mechanisms contemplated in the Australian Act when a space activity has been licensed by a foreign State[47], or the exemption certification of the UK Act on Outer Space Activities.[48]
Furthermore, the space industry has not advocated for any modifications in the international space legal scenario.[49] Therefore, new international rules or new interpretations of existing ones are clearly not needed, and they even risk imposing new and unnecessary burdens to the space launch industry and its customers.[50] Rather, national legislation should be to deal with those issues where the Registration Convention fails to provide an adequate solution. COPUOS' role, should thus be to urge States to adopt national legislation to implement the requirements arising from the Registration Convention and to deal with those aspects which were not the object of consensus at the time of the enactment of the Convention.

ANNEX 1

NORAD Two-Line Element Set Format

Data for each satellite consists of three lines in the following format:

AAAAAAAAAAAAAAAAAAAAAAAA

1 NNNNNU NNNNNAAA NNNNN.NNNNNNNN +.NNNNNNNN +NNNNN-N +NNNNN-N N NNNNN

2 NNNNN NNN.NNNN NNN.NNNN NNNNNNN NNN.NNNN NNN.NNNN NN.NNNNNNNNNNNNNN

Line 0 is a twenty-four character name (to be consistent with the name length in the NORAD SATCAT).

Lines 1 and 2 are the standard Two-Line Orbital Element Set Format identical to that used by NORAD and NASA. The format description is shown on the right.

Line 1	
Column	**Description**
01	Line Number of Element Data
03-07	Satellite Number
08	Classification (U=Unclassified)
10-11	International Designator (Last two digits of launch year)
12-14	International Designator (Launch number of the year)
15-17	International Designator (Piece of the launch)
19-20	Epoch Year (Last two digits of year)
21-32	Epoch (Day of the year and fractional portion of the day)
34-43	First Time Derivative of the Mean Motion
45-52	Second Time Derivative of Mean Motion (decimal point assumed)
54-61	BSTAR drag term (decimal point assumed)
63	Ephemeris type
65-68	Element number
69	Checksum (Modulo 10) (Letters, blanks, periods, plus signs = 0; minus signs = 1)

Line 2	
Column	**Description**
01	Line Number of Element Data
03-07	Satellite Number
09-16	Inclination [Degrees]
18-25	Right Ascension of the Ascending Node [Degrees]
27-33	Eccentricity (decimal point assumed)
35-42	Argument of Perigee [Degrees]
44-51	Mean Anomaly [Degrees]
53-63	Mean Motion [Revs per day]
64-68	Revolution number at epoch [Revs]
69	Checksum (Modulo 10)

Source: http://celestrak.com/NORAD/documentation/tle-fmt.shtml

REFERENCES

[1] As of 1 February 2001, 43 States have ratified, 4 have signed, and two international intergovernmental organizations (European Space Agency and European Organization for the Exploitation of Meteorological Satellites) have declared their acceptance of the rights and obligations provided for in the Registration Convention. See UN Office for Outer Space Affairs online http://www.oosa.unvienna.org/SORegister/regist.htm

[2] *Ibid.* at http://registry.oosa.unvienna.org/oosa/index/index.stm

[3] *I.e.* the *Treaty on Principles Governing the Activities of States in the Exploration and Use of Outer Space, including the Moon and Other Celestial Bodies* (the "Outer Space Treaty", adopted by the General Assembly in its Resolution 2222 (XXI), opened for signature on 27 January 1967, entered into force on 10 October 1967, 96 ratifications and 27 signatures (as of 1 February 2001); the *Agreement on the Rescue of Astronauts and the Return of Objects Launched into Outer Space* (the "Rescue Agreement", adopted by the General Assembly in its Resolution 2345 (XXII), opened for signature on 22 April 1968, entered into force on 3 December 1968, 87 ratifications and 26 signatures (as of 1 February 2001); *the Convention on International Liability for Damage Caused by Space Objects* (the "Liability Convention", adopted by the General Assembly in its Resolution 2777 (XXVI), opened for signature on 29 March 1972, entered into force on 1 September 1972, 81 ratifications and 26 signatures (as of 1 February 2001).

[4] See Preamble of the Registration Convention.

[5] *Ibid.*

[6] As defined by Art. I (a) Registration Convention.

[7] Art. I (b) Registration Convention. Emphasis added. The same definition is used by Art. I (d) Liability Convention.

[8] Statute of the International Court of Justice, see Charter of the United Nations, 26 June 1945, Can. T.S. 1945 No. 7 at 48.

[9] *North Sea Continental Shelf Case*, I.C.J. Reports 4 at 45 (1969).

[10] At first glance a *contradictio in terminis*, the concept has been suggested taking into account the rapid development in the space sector as "traditional" custom has been bypassed as a source of law. See *Studies in International Space Law* (Oxford: Clarendon Press, 1997) at 124-149 & 191-193.

[11] *North Sea Continental Shelf Case, supra* note 9 at 44: "Although the passage of only a short period of time is not necessarily, or of itself, a bar to the formation of a new rule of customary international law on the basis of what was originally a purely conventional rule,... ".

[12] Parties to a treaty can deviate from customary law with the limit of compulsory norms of *ius cogens*. See *Vienna Convention on the Law of Treaties*, 23 May 1969, 1155 U.N.T.S. 331, Art. 53 [hereinafter *Vienna Convention*]. The Convention, being an international treaty itself, is binding *inter partes* only but with many norms considered to be restatements of customary international law, it is an important instrument. On the role of *ius cogens* in international law see generally F. G. v. d. Dunk "Jus Cogens Sive Lex Ferenda: Jus Cogendum?" T. L. Masson-Zwaan & P. M. J. Mendes De Leon, eds., *Air and Space Law: De Lege Ferenda* (Dordrecht: Martinus Nijhoff Publishers, 1992) 219-239.

[13] The U.S. is announcing all objects, including newly discovered space debris. Providing information also about their decay in the atmosphere; the Russian Federation only announces launch and decay of functional objects; in addition to functional objects, information is sometimes provided on last stages of launchers, but never on space debris, by China, France and India. See P. Lála "The United Nations Register of Objects Launched into Outer Space"

Presentation to the United Nations/International Institute of Air and Space Law Workshop on Capacity Building in Space Law, The Hague, Netherlands, 18-21 November 2002.

[14] See Preamble of the Registration Convention. Emphasis added.

[15] Art. IV (1) Registration Convention.

[16] Art. IV (2) Registration Convention.

[17] P. Lála, *supra* note 13.

[18] This information is nevertheless collected by OOSA Such information is listed in square brackets and highlighted in green, which signifies that it has been obtained from other sources and has not been communicated to the United Nations in conformity with the Convention or Resolution 1721 B (XVI). See OOSA online Index of Objects Launched into Outer Space, Outer Space Affairs online http://registry.oosa.unvienna.org/oosa/index/index.stm.

[19] P. Lála, *supra* note 13.

[20] See *infra* Chapter Conclusions and Recommendations.

[21] For a listing of unregistered satellites see J. McDowell "Adherence to the 1976 Convention on Registration of Objects Launched into Outer Space" Somerville, MA., 1994 Dec 23, online http://hea-www.harvard.edu/~jcm/space/un/un_paper1.html and for the submission of incorrect data see J. McDowell " United States Military Spacecraft: Some Deductions From the United Nations Data" Somerville, MA., 1994 Dec 23, online http://hea-www.harvard.edu/~jcm/space/un/un_paper2.html.

[22] There is full and open access to the information of this central registry. The Convention is an improvement over the voluntary registration system not only because it makes registration mandatory but also in view of the fact that it provides for uniformity in relation to the data to be reported. See S. Gorove, "Convention on Registration of Objects Launched into Outer Space. Analysis and Commentary" (1976) 19 *IISL* at 292.

[23] A. A. Cocca, "Registration of Space Objects", N. Jasentuliyana & R.S.K. Lee eds., *Manual on Space Law* (New York: Oceana, 1979) Vol. 1 at 180.

[24] J. Hermida, *Commercial Space Law: International, National and Contractual Aspects* (Buenos Aires: Ediciones Depalma, 1997) at 63. It must be highlighted that in the International Governmental Agreement on the Space Station, States opted for the registration in a separate way of each element contributed by the States. European States delegated this responsibility to the European Space Agency. In effect, pursuant to Art. 5 of the Agreement each partner will register as space objects the flight elements which it provides, which are all listed in an annex to the Agreement. IGA, Art. 5.

[25] J. Hermida, *Legal Basis for a National Space Legislation*, (DCL, Thesis, McGill University, 2003) [unpublished], at 65.

[26] In order to establish a temporary satellite system to comply with ITU timelines Argentina purchased the Anik CI and Anik CII satellites to Telesat Canada by the Argentine corporation Paracom S.A. Both companies -Paracom and Telesat- formed the Paracomsat joint venture, which was in charge of the operation of the Anik satellites. Both Canadian satellites had to be moved approximately 30° to the East from their original position, to be situated at 76° West (Anik CI) and 72° West (Anik CII). Paracomsat leased transponder capacity not only to Argentine corporations -ATC Cable, Crónica TV, Canal 8 de Mar del Plata-, but also to Uruguayan television channels -4, 10, and 12 of Montevideo-, which sets the basis for a potential regional system. The satellites remained registered in Canada. J. Hermida, "Argentine Space Law and Policy" (1996) XXI-II *Ann. Air & Sp. L.* at 177 [hereinafter "Argentine Space Law and Policy"].

[27] *Ibid.* at 178.

[28] R. J. Lee, "Effects of Satellite Ownership Transfers on the Liability of the Launching States" (2000) 43 IISL at 148. Kerrest, "Remarks on the Notion of Launching State" (1999) 41 IISL at 309.

[29] Kerrest, "Remarks on the Notion of Launching State" (1999) 41 IISL at 309.
[30] Registration Convention, Art. II.
[31] *Agreement among the Government of Canada, the Governments of Member States of the European Space Agency, the Government of Japan, the Government of the Russian Federation, and the Government of the United States of America concerning Cooperation on the Civil International Space Station, signed January 29, 1998*, Art. 22.
[32] A. A. Cocca, "Registration of Space Objects", in N. Jasentuliyana & R.S.K. Lee eds., *Manual on Space Law* (New York: Oceana, 1979) Vol. 1 at 180.
[33] Registration Convention, Art. II (2).
[34] Free Zones Case, France v. Switzerland, 1932, PCIJ at. 97.
[35] Vienna Convention, Art. 34.
[36] *E.g.* the spacecraft NOAA 14 would be described as follows:
1. 23455U 94089A 97320.90946019 .00000140 00000-0 10191-3 0 2621
2. 23455 99.0090 272.6745 0008546 223.1686 136.8816 14.11711747148495
and the information could be de-coded according to the table shown in Annex 1. Each set consists of two 69-character lines of data which can be used together with NORAD's SGP4/SDP4 orbital model to determine the precise position and velocity of a spacecraft.
[37] M. Williams, Report: Review of Space Law Treaties in View of Commercial Space Activities (International Law Association: London, 2000) at 16.
[38] *Ibid.* at 2.
[39] E. Galloway, "Guidelines for the Review and Formulation of Outer Space Treaties", (1998) 41 *IISL* at 245.
[40] Official Records of the General Assembly, Fifty-second session, Supplement No. 20 (A/52/20).
[41] M. Williams, Report: Review of Space Law Treaties in View of Commercial Space Activities (International Law Association: London, 2000) at 14.
[42] A. A. Cocca, "A Way to Complement, Enforce and Improve the Space Treaty and Related International Instruments of Space Law", (1992) 35 *IISL* at 43.
[43] K. H. Böckstiegel, "Developing a System of Dispute Settlement Regarding Space Activities", (1992) 35 *IISL* at 27.
[44] E. Galloway, *supra* note 39 at 249.
[45] For example, under the British Act on Outer Space Activities, the Secretary of State may exempt persons or activities if satisfied that the requirement is not necessary to secure compliance with the international obligations of the United Kingdom. In these cases, an order must be made by statutory instrument, subject to annulment in pursuance of a resolution of either House of Parliament. United Kingdom Act on Outer Space Activities, 1986 Chapter 38, Art. 3 (3).
[46] J. Hermida, "Risk Management in Commercial Launches", (1997) *Space Policy* at 13.
[47] Australian Space Activities Act 1998: No. 123, 1998, Parts 11, 13 and 15.
[48] United Kingdom Act on Outer Space Activities, 1986 Chapter 38, Art. 3 (2) (b).
[49] E. A. Frankle & E. J. Steptoe, "Legal Considerations Affecting Commercial Space Launches From International Territory", (1999) 50 *IISL* at 10.
[50] *Ibid.* at 10. This study, however, endorses the encouragement to States for the approval of the option included in paragraph 3 of the General Assembly's Resolution 2777 (XXVI) for the decisions of the Claims Commission to be binding.

The UNIDROIT Registration of Security Interests and The Registration Convention: Compatible / Complementary, or Contradictory?

SYLVIA OSPINA, JD, LL.M
International Telecommunications / Space Law Consultant

ABSTRACT©
The development and launch of many new (privately owned) satellite systems has led to the need for greater compliance with the 1976 Registration Convention, whose main purpose is to assist in identification of space objects, in determining potential liability in the event of an incident involving a space object.

The investors in these new satellite systems have also sought to protect their massive investments, resulting in a proposal to register and secure their financial interests in space objects or assets. Thus, UNIDROIT has drafted a Protocol on Matters Specific to Space Assets, one of three Protocols to the Convention on International Interests in Mobile Equipment./[1]/

This paper will highlight the basic registration requirements set forth in these two documents, as well as in the International Telecommunication Union's Radio Regulations (ITU-RRS). It will also try to ascertain whether their purposes are compatible with and complementary to each other, or whether there are inconsistencies that should be resolved.

International Telecommunications / Space Law Consultant. Senior Member, AIAA., Full Member IAA, Member IISL Board of Directors.
Contact:sospina@bellsouth.net

Introduction
The increased mobility of objects, and of natural and legal persons, has led to a growing need to know what kind of object is being registered, where, and by whom. With the privatization and globalization of satellite systems, as well as of other economic activities, there is a growing need to know who owns and controls the assets, albeit for different reasons: insurance liability, collecting on a debt, cause of harmful interference, etc.

In regard to space objects, two systems of registration of spacecraft exist, each with its specific objectives and requirements as to the information needed. These are the 1976 Registration Convention (RC)/[2]/, and the International Telecommunication Union's Radio Regulations (ITU-RRS)/[3]/.

Under the terms of the RC, launching States are mandated to create a National Register, and to provide the information contained therein to the United Nations Secretary General (UNSG). Similarly, a National Administration forwards to the ITU the information submitted to it by the proponents of the satellite system, in accordance with national requirements./[4]/ A third system, to register security and financial interests, is being proposed by UNIDROIT. The ultimate goal of the three registers is to have information on objects launched to outer space, although the reasons for having this information differ among the entities maintaining or that would maintain the registers./5/

The following chart outlines the information sought by the three entities:

	REGISTRATION Convention	*UNIDROIT Protocol on Space Assets*	*ITU Constitution, Radio Regulations*
Legal "status"	Public Int'l law	Int'l Convention drafted by law private parties	Public Int'l law
Number of States Parties	Signed & Ratified by more than 40 States	Convention not ratified yet	180+ Member Administrations
Information required	Name of launching State(s)	Investor(s) creditor(s) seeking to secure financial interest	Notifying Administration (by country)
	Appropriate designator or its (national) registration number	File number would be issued electronically	Country and ITU number; identifying name of space system or number of space object
Notification/ Registration requirements	General technical parameters, including function of space object, nodal period, inclination, apogee, perigee. General function of the space object.	Any and all commercial transaction, existing and prospective sales and interests, rights, subrogation of any national and international interests may be registered	Very specific technical parameters, including coverage area, and function, satellite service (e.g., FSS, BSS, MSS, RNSS); frequency bands to be used, etc. (See App. 4, ITU-RRSI)
Notification/ Registration requirements	Registration with UN is mandatory for States that have ratified this Convention	Electronic filing/registration not mandatory	Advance notification mandatory; otherwise no protection against harmful interference
Time period for notification/registration	"As soon as practicable" (usually after launch)	Time of filing is considered the time of registration of the prospective international interest, prospective sale or prospective assignment.	Not more than 6, and not less than 2 years from when system will be brought into service.
Other notification requirements	Notification to UNSG of space objects no longer in Earth orbit	All transactions to be electronically recorded	Notification (and usually co-ordination) required for spacecraft, even if placed in same orbital position as one that is at end of useful life in orbit.
Definitions provided	"Launching State", "Space Object"; "State of Registry", as defined in RC and other outer-space related treaties and conventions	"Space Assets", "Associated Rights", as drafted by UNIDROIT	Cf ITU-RRS, Ch. RRS I, "Terminology and Technical Characteristics". (Precise definitions, used world-wide by ITU Member Administrations)

Obviously there are differences in the basic notification requirements of the entities with which space objects are registered. The ITU-RRS (and National Administrations) require very precise technical data for co-ordination, but these will not be elaborated upon here. Rather, the focus will be on the Registration Convention and certain aspects of the proposed UNIDROIT Convention and Space Assets Protocol./[6]/

The Registration Convention

Registration of mobile objects, ranging from automobiles, maritime ships, aircraft, and even space objects, is a basic requirement in most nations. One of the principal reasons for registering vehicles is to be able to determine ownership or control, for insurance and liability purposes. National requirements to register a mobile object differ from country to country and the conditions for granting licenses/[7]/ to use or operate mobile objects also vary in each jurisdiction.

The Registration Convention mandates that launching States establish a National Register of space objects launched, and that basic data on these objects be provided to the United Nations Secretary General (UNSG), which maintains an international Register thereof.

At the national level, several governmental entities are involved in obtaining the information required to register a space object: ministries regulating transportation, telecommunications, foreign relations, inter alia. Registration of a mobile object or vehicle, however, takes place with only one government authority. Similarly, the RC requires that there be only one State of Registry, although there may be more than one Launching State. The establishment of a *National Registry* of objects launched into outer space is at the core of the Registration Convention, and the State of Registry of the space object must have a National Register for that purpose.

The State of Registry of the space object notifies the UN that it has established its national Register, and submits its information to the United Nations Secretary-General (UNSG). This notification to the UNSG usually occurs *post launch,* "as soon as practicable," if at all.

While each State *may* provide additional information on space objects carried in its registry, it *shall* notify the UN Secretary General of space objects it *had* on its Registry, which are no longer in orbit./[8]/ The latter requirement reflects the States' on-going jurisdiction, control over, and liability for damage caused by its space objects, whether in outer space, in air or on Earth./[9]/

In brief, the information that the State of Registry is mandated to provide to the UNSG is readily available in the National Register. Consequently, registering the space object with the UN in a timely manner should take place at a time certain, rather than "as soon as practicable."/[10]/ Time of registration (of security interests) will become more important, if UNIDROIT's Space Protocol is adopted. First, a brief look at the ITU's notification requirements, which are similar to the RC's.

The International Telecommunication Union (ITU)

One of the principal activities of the ITU is aimed at making efficient use of the radio frequency spectrum (RFS) in the provision of telecommunications worldwide, to minimize harmful interference between satellite systems.

Like with the RC, that calls for only one State of Registry,/[11]/ one Administration/[12]/ only notifies the ITU of the space object(s) or satellite system that is planned or proposed. The notifying Administration compiles information from various sources, including the application(s) of proponents of the satellite system, and submits it to the ITU./[13]/ This information is published by the ITU, thus giving notice to other Administrations whose telecom systems may be affected, to facilitate co-ordination with them, and avoid harmful technical interference between the systems.

It should be noted, however, that the choice of orbits, as well as of the kind of service to be provided (telecom, broadcasting, navigation, etc.) is at the discretion of the satellite systems' proponents, with approval of the National Administration. While the ITU has no jurisdiction or control over the choice or use of orbits, use of the radio frequencies must follow the ITU allocations./[14]/ Further, the ITU keeps a master Register of the frequencies assigned by the National Administration(s), to ensure that these assignments fall within the ITU's appropriate allotments and allocations.

Despite the fact that both the Registration Convention and the ITU call for registering specific information on space objects (orbital location, apogee, perigee, general function or purpose)/[15]/ reliable information on the hundreds of satellites in orbit is not available, since not all of them have not been entered into the UNSG's Register.

In the last decade alone, hundreds of privately owned and operated satellite systems (subsumed under the designation of "Global Mobile Personal Communications Services", or GMPCS)/[16]/ have been launched to a variety of non-geostationary (NGSO) orbits, to provide personal communication services.

The GMPCS are owned and operated by multi-national consortia; frequently the financial operations are incorporated into a "holdings company" under the laws of a tax-friendly State, while the laws of another country govern "operations"./[17]/ Thus, the RC's "State of Registry" as well as the ITU "Notifying Administration" may not be one and the same.

This complex ownership situation, compounded by the bankruptcy filings, gives rise to a number of legal and financial issues. For example, the drafters of the UNIDROIT Space Protocol have commented on the legal uncertainty that is created by the fact that several agencies – and laws of different countries – are involved in licensing satellite systems. Together with this uncertainty is the lack of assurance that investors in satellite systems, such as GMPCS, can secure their investment, or protect themselves from default on loans./[18]/

Some of these issues, and others that are raised by UNIDROIT's Space Protocol and registration of security interests will be considered next.

UNIDROIT's Proposed Convention on International Interests in Mobile Equipment, International Registry, and Space Protocol

UNIDROIT's proposed Space Protocol is aimed at facilitating the privatization and commercialization of outer space/[19]/, by protecting private investments in that sector. In essence, the Convention would secure the financial interests of investors who have provided funds for outer space – related projects./[20]/

UNIDROIT also proposes the establishment of an International Registry, to secure the financial interests of investors in space systems and other mobile assets, thereby providing "...third parties with public notice of that interest."/[21]/ "Registration is also key to the international interest's validity against the trustee in bankruptcy and creditors in the obligor's insolvency..."/[22]/ Thus, a centralized recording system for the registration of interests in space property or assets is proposed.

Among the reasons given for creating an International Registry (to be managed by a Supervisory Agency), is that "several international agencies are involved in licensing satellite systems", but "...[n]one of them can offer a comprehensive registry of licensing of orbits, /[23]/ frequencies and other rights... nor of financiers' interests in them..."/[24]/ Thus, an international registration system is seen as an essential feature of the legal framework applicable to international interests in space property. Such a Register would provide the means of identifying some components of space property, even though they would not all have designator numbers./[25]/

Having a registry of financial interests in space hardware may allay some of the financiers' difficulties, but does not solve the problem of a lack of registration of some space objects, or of other "space assets" and "associated rights", as defined by UNIDROIT (licenses, orbits, frequencies), for several reasons, as will be explained below.

Definitions

Both the Registration Convention and the Space Protocol provide definitions of "space object" and "space assets", respectively. The RC's definition is: "The term "space object" includes component parts of a space object as well as its launch vehicle and parts thereof..."/[26]/

UNIDROIT's definition is more elaborate, and according to UNIDROIT's Report to COPUOS,/[27]/ definitions are very important to the Protocol, as is the applicability of UNIDROIT's regime to more than tangible space property.

UNIDROIT's definition of "space assets" needs to be read before, and in conjunction with what are postulated as "Associated Rights"/[28]/ in the Protocol. Article I (2) (f) of the Protocol provides the following meaning of "space asset":

(i) any separately identifiable asset that is in space or that is intended to be launched and placed in space or has been returned from space;

(ii) any separately identifiable component forming part of an asset referred to in the preceding clause or attached to or contained within such asset;

(iii) Any separately identifiable asset or component assembled or manufactured in space; and

(iv) any launch vehicle that is expendable or can be reused to transport persons or goods to and from space.

As used in this definition, the term "space" means outer space, including the Moon and other celestial bodies."/[29]/

The Protocol's definition of "space asset" is broader, yet clearer in some respects, than the one provided in both the Liability and Registration Conventions. One question arises, would the Moon and other celestial bodies fall under the meaning of "space assets", as defined by UNIDROIT? While they may be "space assets", celestial bodies, including the Moon and asteroids, are not "space property"; they are not subject to appropriation, nor subject to property rights./[30]/

Similarly, other "space assets", such as orbits, orbital positions, and the radio frequency spectrum (RFS) they *use*, may not be appropriated or converted into private property. *Use* of orbital locations or of parts of the RFS does not confer property rights on the *users* of these global commons, or global resources. In brief, a space object, may be a space asset, but a space asset is not necessarily a space object, let alone space property.

According to UNIDROIT, *"Associated rights" means:*
(i) any permit, license, authorization or equivalent instrument that is granted or issued by a national or intergovernmental or other international body or authority to control, use or operate a space asset, relating to the use of orbital positions and the transmission, emission or reception of radio signals to and from a space asset, which may be transferred or assigned, to the extent permissible and assignable under the laws concerned;
(ii) all rights to payment or other performance due to a debtor by any person with respect to space assets; and
(iii) all contractual rights held by the debtor that are secured by or associated with the space assets./[31]/

Art. I (2) (a) (ii) and (iii) refer to financial obligations and contractual rights in space assets; and thus, are not an issue. The first clause, (i) however, is problematic, for several reasons.

Having access to various rights [as defined above] would permit [inter alia] transfer of ownership rights in a spacecraft, of rights to operate the spacecraft, even the constructive repossession of a spacecraft./[32]/ It could also lead to private parties deeming that their contractual rights are superior to official authorizations.

The Protocol seems to view licenses/[33]/ as negotiable property, as commodities in which a financial interest can be secured; thus, licenses could begin acquiring characteristics or traits of tangible "property" that can be transferred or assigned, even attached, without official sanction.

Licenses, however, are not negotiable property, nor are they a "right"; they are essentially privileges and/or prerogatives, granted by an official governmental entity, to facilitate some activity, whether on earth or in outer space./[34]/ It is an official entity that decides, on the basis of certain criteria, whether or not to grant a license.

Deeming licenses or any other government authorization as a negotiable, transferable asset could lead to the gradual taking over of key government functions by the private sector. This, in turn, raises questions as to the value and usefulness of the official entities that issue licenses. The granting or withholding of licenses, however, still remains an important governmental function, one unlikely to be delegated to the private sector. As stated in one dictionary, "*a license is a mere personal permit; it is not property or a property right.*"/[35]/

Further, the licensing, launching and operation of an international satellite system is very complex, and requires the collaboration of many national administrations, each one with its own requirements and restrictions./[36]/ UNIDROIT is correct in stating that there is no international agency that issues licenses to [use] orbits, orbital positions or the requisite radio frequencies. The proponents of the satellite systems are the ones who decide how many spacecraft will be launched, to which orbital plane(s), for what function or purpose. Their National Administrations, in turn, assign the orbital positions and the radio frequencies/[37]/, and grant the appropriate licenses or permits for their use.

Consequently, it would be difficult to secure a financial interest in, or transfer a license for the use of a particular orbit or orbital position, since these are not subject to national or international regulations./[38]/ Hence, an international register of financial interests in components or operations of space assets, as proposed by UNIDROIT, would not necessarily solve the issue of trying to attach an orbital location or license to satisfy a debt.

Despite the globalization trend, every nation still has sovereign rights as to the issuance of licenses, to regulate the activities of its nationals, both on earth and in outer space. At the national level, regulatory agencies are the stewards (but not owners) of natural resources, such as the radio frequencies. At the international level entities such as the ITU, may be regarded as the "allocator" and custodian (not owner) of limited natural resources (such as the radio frequency spectrum and the geostationary orbit) that are considered "global commons"/[39]/.

If licenses (e.g., to use the spectrum or an orbital location) are considered negotiable "rights" (rather than privileges granted by an official national entity), the result will be the gradual appropriation by private parties of outer space resources. This outcome would be a clear violation of the spirit and the wording of the Outer Space Treaty, which states:

"Outer space, including the Moon and other celestial bodies, is not subject to national appropriation by claim of sovereignty, by means of use or occupation, or by any other means."/[40]/

One means of overcoming an impasse that could occur, due to UNIDROIT's current definition of "associated rights"/[41]/, as well as issues of national sovereignty over its licensing methods, would be to change some terminology.

Just as the term "space property" was changed to "space assets", to reflect differences in what constitutes "property" in different legal systems,/[42]/ it is submitted that "Associated rights" as stated in Art. I (2) (a) (i) of the Protocol should be re-named "Ancillary Privileges". The term "privilege" better represents the true nature of licenses, or authorizations or permits.

Perhaps this change in terminology would help overcome the reticence of some of the potential signatories of the Protocol. The governments would retain control of the licensing process, authorizing their nationals to *use* space resources, but neither licenses nor intangible space assets (such as the orbits and RFS) would be considered negotiable rights, let alone private property.

Conclusions and Recommendations

The Registration Convention, the ITU's

notification procedures and UNIDROIT's proposed Convention, have different objectives, since these institutions have different reasons for, and interests in ensuring compliance with their registration / notification requirements.

One lacuna in all these processes is the fact that at present no one single national or international entity seems to have a centralized registry of space objects or activities. Nor is any entity involved in planning the use of or allocation of non-geostationary orbits, where the vast majority of the privately owned and operated GMPCS satellite systems is or will be located.[43]

Other omissions becomes apparent when looking at the Registration Convention data base maintained by the UN's Office of Outer Space Affairs. States supply different data to the UNSG; some include information on space objects only if they have reached their orbit while others notify the UNSG of objects that have been de-orbited.[44] Still others do not provide data on many of their launches. "As a consequence, the UN Register…is incomplete, which restricts its usefulness".[45]

Improved compliance with the Registration Convention is becoming more urgent, due to the growing number of satellites in a variety of orbits, and the increasing number of countries with launch capabilities. Several benefits would inure from greater compliance: reliable information on the location of a space object facilitates the ITU co-ordination process, to avoid harmful interference; it reduces the possibility of collisions, and consequently, mitigates the creation of space debris.

A few actions could be taken to ensure better compliance with the Registration Convention. At the national level, the entities responsible for transmitting information to the ITU and to UNSG could improve co-ordination and sharing of data amongst themselves. The data required by the UN Registration Convention and the ITU is readily available from the States or Administrations, years prior to launch. Once the space object has been co-ordinated through the ITU, it could or should be entered into the National Register, and that information could and should be transmitted to the UNSG. The entry in the respective Registers should occur prior to launch, rather than *post facto*.

At the international level, some means of enforcing existing treaty provisions should be instituted, even though this would require amending the current treaties and Conventions. The new text(s) should reflect the private sector's growing role in space activities, including ownership, operations and responsibility or liability therefor. Additional information could be submitted when registering, which would be of benefit to those involved in space activities, from the design of a system, its financing, to its implementation.

Specific changes to the RC that could be made would include the following:

- Instituting a time certain for registration with the national authority, and subsequently with the UNSG, replacing the current "as soon as practicable".[46] This time frame could be contingent on when certain licenses[47] have been granted by the State of Registry.

In addition to the information required under present terms of Art. IV of the RC, other technical data could be requested, such as:

- Projected useful life in orbit of the space object;
- Plans for its de-orbiting at end of useful life.
- Date(s) of launch, and launch vehicle(s)./[48]/

"Contact" information:

- Administration notifying the ITU;
- Date of notification to the ITU;
- Date of entry into National Register.
- Launching State(s), for liability purposes.
- Insurance company or consortium providing insurance coverage;

Financial Data: (of a general nature)

- Primary owner(s) and operator(s) of the satellite system;
- Names and legal domiciles of major financing entities, especially those seeking to register or secure their interest in the space object or system.
- State (or city) of registration of financial interests in the space object(s), providing third parties with public notice of that interest./[49]/
- Insurance coverage: for launch, for components, including launch vehicle stages, and against malfunction of the satellite, its components, or its operation.

If the Registration Convention were amended to include additional information, such as general information on the ownership of the space object, possibly these changes would begin to meet one of UNIDROIT's objectives- of providing public notice as to the interests that have been secured or registered.

Information on financial matters, however, would not necessarily preclude the establishment of another International Registry, as proposed by UNIDROIT. One question that arises, however, is whether the UN's current Register is entirely compatible with the one envisioned by UNIDROIT.

In this respect, the main purposes of the three registration systems set forth in the chart, supra, should be taken into account:

- The Registration Convention is an international legal document, ratified by States, for politico-legal purposes. It is basically an "informational" document, but an important part of public international law and space law.
- The ITU is essentially a technical entity, concerned with technical issues. Its Constitution and Radio Regulations (also part of public international law) facilitate the technical co-ordination of satellite systems, but the ITU is not involved in granting licenses for the use of space resources or assets.
- UNIDROIT's proposed Protocol is an instrument drafted by a non-governmental group representing private interests of an economic / financial nature. Its main purpose is to secure these financial interests, and seemingly, to be able to collect on bad debts.

The basic technical data required both by the Registration Convention and the ITU are similar; they are relatively easy to compile, and transmit from the National Administration or State of Registry, to the appropriate entity (the UN or the ITU). Thus, a basic compatibility exists between these two organizations, and the data they require. Closer co-operation between the ITU and COPUOS/OOSA would enhance this compatibility.

In regard to consonance between the RC's Register and UNIDROIT's, an issue arises as to the compatibility of the functions (and goals) of these two entities: is the UN the most suitable "Supervising Agency" for the Space Protocol's implementation?

UNIDROIT seems to advocate a sort of "Global Securities and Exchange Commission", an entity that would register all transactions related to securing or transferring financial interests in space "assets" (or other mobile equipment).

If this is the case, the UN, an international political body, perhaps is not the best choice as the supervisory agency of the Space Protocol. Therefore, an alternative is suggested.

WTO as an Alternative venue for UNIDROIT's International Registry?

It is submitted that the World Trade Organization (WTO) may be a more appropriate venue for the Supervising Agency proposed in the UNIDROIT Convention on Mobile Equipment, and its associated Protocols. Several factors would seem to make the WTO a preferable alternative to the UN.

A principal factor is that the WTO is an institution geared to the economic and financial aspects of trade and commerce. Since 1997, when the Annex on Telecommunications was incorporated in the General Agreement on Trade in Services, it has been increasingly involved in satellite telecommunications as a trade issue. The Annex "recognizes the dual role of telecommunications services as a *distinct sector of economic activity* and as the underlying *transport means* for other economic activities."/[50]/ The Annex applies to all means of "telecommunications transport"/[51]/, including satellite communications, except for the distribution of broadcast of radio or TV programming. Thus, the WTO is already aware of many of the economic / financial aspects of satellite systems, of which countries and corporations are involved in them.

Further, it is more familiar with commercial terminology and transactions, such as filing of security interests, than any part of the UN dealing with outer space (COPUOS, or the OOSA).

Thus, it may be easier to set up and maintain an electronic international Registry of securities and other transactions related to all mobile equipment, not only of space assets, under the aegis of the WTO. While the Annex applies to means of telecom transport, perhaps it could also apply to other mobile equipment (aircraft, rolling stock) which is also used in transport, albeit of a different kind.

It should be noted, however, that neither the WTO nor any other international institution is mandated to license satellite systems, or the use of orbits or the radio frequency spectrum. These are still prerogatives of National Administrations, of States, which are the constituents of these international organizations.

Hence, having the WTO (instead of the UN) as the Supervising Agency of the International Register may allay some concerns regarding the privatization of outer space./[52]/ Does the international legal community really want the private sector to take over legal / political activities of official entities, supplanting the role of the State of Registry or the National Administrations?

Despite the trends toward globalization, national sovereignty issues and prerogatives still need to be taken into account, particularly in regard to granting licenses, and registering assets for use in outer space activities and operations. National sovereignty, however, does not extend to outer space, a global commons.

---

[1] UNIDROIT is the acronym for the International Organization for the Unification of Private Law, headquartered in Rome, Italy. UNIDROIT has drafted a "Convention on International Interests in Mobile Equipment, international interests in mobile equipment", and Protocols specific to the rolling stock of railroads, to aircraft, and to "space assets." Opened to signature in Cape Town, South Africa, November 2001. [Cited hereinafter as the Protocol.]

[2] Convention on Registration of Objects Launched into Outer Space, entered into force Sept. 1976. [Cited as the Registration Convention, or RC hereinafter.]

[3] The International Telecommunication Union, a UN agency, specializes in the technical aspects of telecommunications, in particular radio communications. Its Convention and Constitution, and Radio Regulations that govern the use of the radio frequency spectrum are amended periodically. [Cited as ITU-RRS hereinafter.]

[4] See, for example the USA's Federal Communications Commission (FCC) Main Form 601, Schedule K.

[5] See UNIDROIT Secretariat's Report to COPUOS, A/AC.105/C.2/L.225 (Jan. 2001) [Cited as UNIDROIT Report hereinafter.]

[6] UNIDROIT, note 1, supra.

[7] The term "license" is used generically, to include concessions, permissions, authorizations, permits, licenses; i.e., any authorization granted by a governmental entity.

[8] Art. IV (2), (3), Registration Convention. [Emphasis added].

[9] Art. VII, VIII, Outer Space Treaty. De-orbited satellites must be notified to the UN. (Should those that have been transferred to another owner / operator also be entered in the UN Register?)

[10] Art. IV (3), Registration Convention. It's debatable whether this notice applies only to de-orbited satellites, or to those that will be launched. If they are entered into the National Register, the information should be transmitted to the UNSG, as per Art. IV (1).

[11] Art. II (2), Registration Convention.

[12] The ITU Radio Regulations (ITU-RRS) define Administration as "any governmental department or service responsible for discharging the obligations undertaken in the [ITU] Convention and Regulations. Chapter SI, Sect. I, Art.. SI.2, ITU-RRS. (1997 version).

[13] See, for example, the FCC's Main Form 601, which requires very detailed information on the applicant and the technical characteristics of the proposed telecommunication system.

[14] See ITU-RRS, Appendix 4 (APS4), Annex 2A.

[15] Art. IV, RC; ITU-RRS, APS4.

[16] Among the GMPCS systems launched are IRIDIUM (66+ satellites; GLOBALSTAR (48+ satellites); ORBCOMM (36+ satellites); Worldspace (at least 3 radiobroadcasting satellites in GEO). Several other GMPCS systems have been proposed, but are unlikely to become reality.

[17] The majority of the GMPCS systems have had to seek protection from creditors under US Bankruptcy laws. While most of them reorganized and emerged from "Chapter 11", tracking down their new "owners" is rather complicated.

[18] Stanford, Martin: The Roles of International Organisations in Privatisation and Commercial Use of Outer Space: *UNIDROIT's project for the creation of a new regime governing the taking of security in high-value mobile assets: a window of opportunity in the context of* ***the privatisation and commercial use of outer space***. UNISPACE III: Workshop on Space Law in the 21st Century, Session 6.(Vienna, Austria, 20-23 July 1999).[Cited as Stanford hereafter.] [Emphasis added.]

[19] Ibid. Note emphasis, supra, note 18.

[20] UNIDROIT, note 1, supra.

[21] Stanford, note 18, supra.

[22] Idem; pp.3-4. UNIDROIT's proposed validity of the (registered) interest against a trustee in bankruptcy is worth noting, in view of the filing for bankruptcy protection ("Chapter 11") by most of the operational GMPCS systems (Globalstar, IRIDIUM, ICO, Orbcomm, inter alia.)

[23] It is the prerogative of national Administrations to issue the requisite licenses for satellite systems, for the use of certain frequencies, but no license is required for the use of particular orbits. While the systems are coordinated under the ITU-RRS, no international organization licenses [the use of] orbits, frequencies or other "rights".

[24] Stanford, note 18, supra.

[25] Par. 25, UNIDROIT Report, supra, note 5. But see the RC's requirement for such a number.

[26] Art. I(b), Registration Convention. This same definition is found in Art. I(d) of the 1972 Convention on International Liability for Damage

Caused by Space Objects. (Cited as the Liability Convention hereinafter.)

[27] Par. 20, UNIDROIT Report, note 5, supra.

[28] Protocol, Art. I (2) (a).

[29] Protocol, *supra*, note 1, Art. I (f). [Emphasis added.] It should be noted that the earlier draft of the Space Protocol spoke of "Space Property", which was replaced by "Space Assets", in response to concerns regarding the implications under civil law of the term "property". In this respect, see footnotes of the Draft Protocol discussions held at Evry, France, Sept. 2001. Also see UN documents A/AC.105/763; A/56/20, *inter alia, and* UNIDROIT, www.unidroit.org.

[30] Art. II, Outer Space Treaty. Art. 11 (2) of the Moon Treaty reiterates the non-appropriation doctrine, although Art. 6 allows States Parties to this Treaty to "collect on and remove from the Moon samples of its minerals and other substances". Agreement Governing the Activities of States on the Moon and Other Celestial Bodies. Entered into force 1984. [Cited as the Moon Treaty hereinafter.]

[31] Protocol, supra, note 1, Article I (2) (a). Revised in Rome, Italy, February 2002. [Emphasis added.]

[32] Par.20, UNIDROIT Report, note 5, supra.

[33] The term *"license"* will be used hereinafter, in reference to concessions, authorizations, permits, or licenses granted by a governmental authority, and only as they may relate to telecommunication satellite systems.

[34] The licensing system with which most people are familiar is the driver's license, which is issued by a governmental entity. A driver's license is highly personal, and cannot be assigned, transferred, or re-issued to a third party, with or without official authorization. Should licenses pertaining to space activities be more easily transferable than drivers' licenses, in view of the numerous national security (and financial security) issues involved?

[35] Black's Law Dictionary, St. Paul, Minn., West Publishing Co. [Emphasis added.]

[36] Many States have restrictions on foreign ownership of the media, of airlines, and other areas of strategic importance, such as the aerospace sector.

[37] The use of the RFS is done in accordance with the ITU's Radio Regulations and Plans that have been devised for certain satellite services

[38] An exception: use of geostationary orbital positions is subject to some regulation: the satellites must be located at 2 Deg. from each other, and there are only 360 Deg. in the geostationary orbital arc.

[39] In this respect, see V. Kopal, "Outer Space as a Global Common", Proceedings of the IISL, 1997.

[40] Art. II, Outer Space Treaty (OST). But see fn 2, Draft Protocol (Evry, France 2001), to the effect that there are no conflicts between the Protocol and the principles incorporated in the UN's Space treaties. Or could there be some potential conflict between the privatization of outer space and Art. II, OST?

[41] H. Kronke, Secretary-General of UNIDROIT noted that "the issues of how to define and how to deal with 'associated rights' pose a number of problems..." "The Draft UNIDROIT Convention..." Included in "Project 2001- Legal Framework for the Commercial Use of Outer Space", Karl-Heinz Bockstiegel, Ed. Carl Heymanns Verlag, Koeln, 2002, at p. 655.

[42] See note 27, supra.

[43] See note 16, supra, re: GMPCS systems.

[44] L. Perek, "Maintaining the Space Environment". Discussion Paper presented at Workshop on Space Law in the 21st Century. UNISPACE III, Vienna, Austria, 20-24 July 1999. Perek noted that only 40 States adhere to the Registration Convention, and that international organizations do not register their satellites. (The latter may be a moot point, since the International Satellite Organizations (ISOs) have been "privatized".)

[45] Perek, op.cit. One very complete database is available electronically, at www.harvard.edu/QEDT/, or www.jcm/space/un/un.html.

[46] Art. IV(1), (3); the latter section requires notification to the UNSG of space objects which are no longer in orbit.

[47] Several kinds of licenses may be required: a) to construct, build a satellite system; b) to operate said system; c) to provide certain services via that system; d) to use certain frequencies of the radio spectrum; e) license to export the satellite, both to the launch site and to outer space.

[48] This information is or should be known to the system owner(s), as well as to the insurance corporation(s) several months prior to launch.

[49] Stanford, note 18, supra.

[50] WTO, General Agreement on Trade In Services, Annex on Telecommunications, "1", Objectives. [Cited as the Annex hereinafter.] [Emphasis added.]

[51] Ibid. 3(a) provides the following definition: "Telecommunication means the transmission and reception of signals by any electromagnetic means."

[52] The privatization, not only the commercialization of outer space seems to be one of UNIDROIT's goals. Note the full title of Stanford, note 18, supra.

PRACTICE OF INTERNATIONAL ORGANISATIONS, E.G. THE EUROPEAN SPACE AGENCY

Gabriel Lafferranderie
ESA

IISL/ECSL SYMPOSIUM
REINFORCING THE REGISTRATION CONVENTION
On the occasion of the 42nd Session of the Legal Subcommittee of the United Nations Committee on the Peaceful Uses of Outer Space
Vienna, Austria, 24 March 2003

No scoop is to be revealed here. Firstly I would just like to underline the strong interest continuously brought up by ESA Member States to the Registration of space objects; included in ESA are the efforts displayed by its predecessors, ESRO and ELDO, which were granted the status of observers of the COPUOS. These efforts led to reduce a lacuna in the Outer Space Treaty, the fact that only States were granted the possibility to become parties to this Treaty. To reduce this lacuna, a remedy was found by European States in order to make it possible for international (intergovernmental) organisations, conducting space activities (IGO) to "declare" their acceptance of rights and obligations enunciated in the said Agreement/Convention, subject to the fact that a majority of Member States of the said organisation already are parties to the Outer Space Treaty and to appropriate Agreement/Convention, and subject to the acceptance of the above mentioned declaration of acceptance; this solution is a kind of "mini-status" vis-à-vis the other parties to the Convention, the Organisation being excluded from acquiring any rights attached to membership, like the right of amendment, of revision of the said convention. Nevertheless this procedure of declaration of acceptance constituted a progress towards the recognition of the role played by IGO. The European Space Agency (ESRO at the time) used this possibility for the Rescue Agreement, the Liability Convention and the Registration Convention; Eutelsat for the Liability Convention (but what is the situation now, Eutelsat having been privatised?); Eumetsat for the Registration Convention; neither Intelsat nor Inmarsat, etc. considered it appropriate to make such a declaration.

I. A specific legal scheme

The Declaration of Acceptance: ESA focuses its attention on the latter, either in studying and providing advice to its Member States, e.g. when the question of a possible revision of the Registration Convention came up, or by contributing to some working papers on, for instance, improving the Registration Convention. Here I am mentioning the initiative taken in 1988 by ESA Member States, members of the COPUOS and European States having concluded co-operation agreements with ESA (in total: 20 States out of the 61 Member States of the COPUOS at the time; doc A/AC.105/C.2/L.211/rev.1, March 30th 1998). This initiative, supported by a large majority of Member States, led to the study of the concept of "launching state", as a single-issue item. Chapter

III of this document held some proposals for improving the vitality of the Registration Convention, its adequacy. Some reflections are still valid, in my opinion, at least as "directions".

As you are aware of, ESA was the first IGO to deposit a declaration of acceptance (previously the ESRO information were transmitted through the French Government to the United Nations Secretary General on the basis of UNGA Resolution 1721); but accepting the Registration Convention raised some preliminary questions and required a clear understanding and agreement among the ESA Member States: obviously, the political, legal, ethical interest(s) of the Organisation itself to become a "quasi" party to the Convention, in addition to its Member States, already parties to the Registration Convention. Here the answer is contained in the ESA Convention: its mission (research and development in all fields of space activities, science, technology, applications, transportation systems), international co-operation (with non-member states, international organisations etc.) and of course its role in facilitating the coordination of national views; this mission does not exclude the expression of personal views by Member States. Programmes are decided and executed under the ESA Convention, as are the Agreements concluded with Partners (subject to the [unanimous] approval by the Council). However ESA, an organisation with specified and limited competences, cannot be assimilated to a state. For instance, reading the article VI of the Outer Space Treaty, ESA cannot exercise jurisdiction and control as a State can. Therefore the first interrogation we had was to correctly understand the legal implications of a declaration of acceptance. In relation with this, the ESA Legal Adviser raised some questions to the UNO legal adviser, for instance, on the possibility of keeping a "national" register. Having taken into account the United Nations Legal Adviser's answers, ESA set up its own registry, containing the elements enunciated in article IV of the Registration Convention and notified the information to the United Nations Secretary General, this information being published in OOSA's appropriate documents.

II. Implementation

ESA is entitled to maintain the register as provided for in the Registration Convention; therefore ESA is also, by construction, a launching State. Only launching States have the right to become registration States as well, for a particular space object.

The space object: Which space object? For a space object in the realisation, development, etc. and launching of which the "registration State" played an active role. Each space object registered by ESA is an item developed, built and financed by ESA, according to its mission, to its Convention. What happens in case of an international co-operation programme? Who is entitled to assert what a space object is? We have encountered this type of question in the first important manned space flight programme: the Spacelab Programme covered by an International Agreement (IGA) and a MoU between NASA and ESA part of the post Apollo shuttle programme. ESA's point of view was that the Spacelab was a space object to be registered by ESA (ESA having developed, built and funded the project and having been recognised as its "owner"). It was understood that the

Spacelab would be transferred to NASA. NASA took the opposite point of view, arguing that the Spacelab was not an autonomous object, receiving the resources needed from the shuttle; it was simply a payload in the shuttle cargo bay. NASA's opinion prevailed: the Spacelab was not registered and fell, like any other piece of the shuttle, under United States jurisdiction and control. When negotiating the International Space Station Agreement (1985-1988), we re-discussed the case in accordance with the status of the European contribution (having received strong guidance from the ESA Council at ministerial level – Rome and the Hague): the Columbus Laboratory attached to the Station. The discussion was intense on Article V of the IGA (Registration, Jurisdiction and Control). The 1988 solution also appears in the 1998 version. A space object is a contribution of a Partner State as listed in the Annex of the IGA. The Columbus Laboratory, this time, got the status of a space object, under jurisdiction and control of the European Partner, who entrusted ESA to register it (let's mention that the Canadian robotic arm also got the status of space object).

In conclusion on this point, all "space objects" developed and built under ESA authority and funding are entered in the ESA register, including space objects provided by ESA as part of a co-operation programme. Mentions of this policy are to be found in co-operation Agreements concluded by ESA - I have already mentioned the Intergovernmental Space Station Agreement) – with non-member States or with International Organisations, for instance:

- The Arrangement between ESA and the Russian Space Agency concerning their co-operation in the INTEGRAL Programme (signed in 1997); Article 13 "Registration of the Spacecraft" states that "ESA shall register the Integral Spacecraft as a space object in accordance with the Registration Convention on registration of objects launched into outer space of 14 January 1975".

- The Memorandum of Understanding between ESA and NASDA concerning the launch of Artemis by the H-IIA launch vehicle and its utilisation signed in April 1997. You are certainly aware that placing Artemis in the targeted orbit was a difficult task and that it was only very recently (end of January) that ESA engineers were able to put Artemis on its foreseen geostationary orbit (therefore we now have to register the spacecraft).

"ESA shall register Artemis as a space object in accordance with the Convention on Registration of objects launched into outer space".

What about the Ariane Launcher? On the Ariane launcher Registration (Convention ESA/Arianespace): the Ariane launcher has been developed and qualified under an ESA optional programme. Thereafter its commercial building and exploitation has been entrusted to the private French firm Arianespace. ESA has been entrusted with the registration of the upper stage of the launcher when the launch was an element of the Ariane development programme. In the case of commercial launching conducted by Arianespace, the French Ministry of Foreign Affairs is responsible for the registration of the commercial launcher operated by Arianespace from the Guyana Space Centre.

When ESA is the provider of the satellite and procure the launch, e.g. Agreements concluded between ESA and EUMETSAT concerning the

Meteosat second generation satellites (October 1996) and co-operation on the Metop satellites series (December 1999) state that:

MSG article 11: "Eumetsat shall notify the Secretary General of the United Nations of the Launch of the Satellites in accordance with the Convention on Registration of objects launched into outer space..."

Metop article 19: Registration: Eumetsat shall notify the Secretary General of the United Nations of the Launch of the Satellites in accordance with the Convention on the registration of space object launched in outer space..."

I can also refer to the contract concluded between ESA and the Eurockot company, which states: "the contractor (Eurockot) shall undertake to register the launch vehicle with the government of Russia as launching state... ESA shall be responsible to ensure the satellite is properly registered in accordance with the Convention on Registration of space objects launched in outer space..."

An interesting situation will now occur in Kourou with the launching of satellites via the Russian launcher Soyuz, from French Guyana, needing a separate launch pad but using ESA and CNES facilities. Launching Soyuz from Kourou will request several Agreements, including one between France and Russia and one between ESA and Rosaviacosmos etc.. The French Republic should arrange for the registration of the Soyuz launcher and the customer for the Registration of the satellite (these Agreements have not been yet concluded nor signed).

III. <u>Directions</u>

As Dr. Perek said "it seems the Registration Convention mostly provides obsolete orbital elements". The 1998 European initiative already indicated some directions to study. The Registration Convention invites the Parties to consider the updating of data and to add new information as appropriate (therefore there is no need to amend it).

ESA has updated data on the basis of events related to the registered space objects; e.g., its end of life, by putting the satellite on a "cemetery orbit", and so "liberating" orbital positions and frequencies on orbit (OTS, GEOS, Meteosat, and lastly ECS IV). This policy will, of course, continue.

More important are the additional information, provided on a voluntary basis. An internal proposal has been examined and endorsed but is not yet in force (it is based on practice and various recommendations and links like the COSPAR or ITU etc.), for instance:

The name of the space object;

- The name of the launching authority to indicate as appropriate in case of a co-operation programme, the name of the other launching state(s);

- Designator, to add the COSPAR numbering;

- The type of space object: sounding-rocket, launcher, platform etc.;

- The date of launch and the location of the launch site;
- All ground facilities used for the launching as well as for the telemetry, the control and the tracking of the launcher and the satellite;

- The total mass;

- If any, astronauts on board;

- If any, use of NPS (Principle 3 of the 1992 NPS Principles);

- The frequency plan: all types of frequencies used; information available from ITU;

- Expected date for the end of the mission and expected zone of re-entry;

- Measures taken for space debris mitigation;

- If any, transfer of ownership, user(s) of the space object in orbit.

The data should be, in principle, entered into the register within a delay of 10 days after the launch, and notified to the United Nations Secretary General within a fortnight of each launch.

ESA is hoping it will contribute to worldwide, needed effort, by granting more transparency and safety to the international community, thus leading to an increase of the number of Parties to the Registration Convention.

Annexes

I. Texts

- European Space Agency; Declaration of Acceptance of Rights and Obligations Provided in the UNO Registration Convention, January 1979. [Eumetsat has also adopted such a declaration of acceptance]

- Registration Convention; Articles II, III and IV

- Convention ESA/Arianespace; [Article 21]

II. Elements for a Bibliography

- G. Lafferranderie; L'application par l'Agence Spatiale Européenne de la Convention sur l'immatriculation des objets lancés dans l'espace extra-atmosphérique. Annales de droit aérien et spatiales, McGill, vol. XI, 1986, pp.229-236.

- Dr. Kaï-Uwe Schrogl (DLR) and Ch. Davis (OOSA); A New Look at the "Launching State"; IISL (Houston) 2002.

- L. Perek (Czech Republic); 1976 Registration Convention; Proceedings of the 1998 IISL/ECSL Symposium published in "Proceedings of the 41st Colloquium on the Law of Outer Space".

- Dr. Marietta Benkö and Dr. Kaï Uwe Schrogl; The 1998 European Initiative in the UNCOPUOS Legal Subcommittee to Improve the Registration Convention; IISL-98-IISL.1.07

- G. P. Sloup, A Guide for Space Lawyers to Understanding the NASA Space Shuttle and the ESA Spacelab, ZLW 196, 1977, p.204-205

- Dr. Von der Dunk; Possible Improvements to Space Object Registration and Other Possible Legal Tools; International Colloquium - Europe and Space Debris; Toulouse (France); 27-28 November 2002 (French Academy of Air and Space ANAE)

- M.G. Bourely, Legal Issues Relating to Flights of Spacelab, JSP 1980

IGA 1998

Article 5
Registration, Jurisdiction and Control

1. In accordance with Article II of the Registration Convention, each Partner shall register as space objects the flight elements listed in the Annex, which provides that the European Partner having delegated this responsibility to ESA acts in its name and on its behalf.
2. Pursuant to Article VIII of the Outer Space Treaty and Article II of the Registration Convention, each Partner shall retain jurisdiction and control over the elements it registers in accordance with paragraph 1 above and over personnel in or on the Space Station who are its nationals. The exercise of such jurisdiction and control shall be the subject to any relevant provisions of this Agreement, the MoUs and implementing arrangements, including relevant procedural mechanisms established therein.

Article 6
Ownership of Elements and Equipments

1.
2. The European Partner shall entrust ESA, acting in its name and on its behalf, with ownerships over the elements it provides, as well as over any other equipment developed and funded under ESA programmes as a contribution to the Space Station, its operation or utilisation.
3. -
4. ... Any transfer of ownership of any element listed in the Annex shall require prior notification of the other Partners.
5. .
6. The ownership or registration of elements or the ownership of elements shall in no way be deemed to be an indication of ownership of material or data resulting from the conduct of activities in or on the Space Station.

Columbus Development Programme Implementing Rules
(Approved by Council on 29 June 1989)

Article 7 §1
"It shall also register, acting on behalf of the Participating States, all Columbus flight elements, including those identified in the Annex to the IGA, and shall notify the Secretary General of the United Nations thereof."
[Based on the September 1988 IGA, Article 5.]

LIST OF SPACE OBJECTS ST/SG REGISTERED BY ESA

Document Symbol:	**ST/SG/SER.E/031**
Remarks:	Registration information for Ariane 3rd stage and technological capsule (CAT)

Document Symbol:	**ST/SG/SER.E/051**
Remarks:	Registration information for METEOSAT-2 (1981-057A), Ariane 3rd stage (1981-057B) and technological capsule (CAT) (1981-57C)

Document Symbol:	**ST/SG/SER.E/061**
Remarks:	Registration information for MARECS-A , Ariane L-04 3rd stage and Ariane L-04 technological capsule

Document Symbol:	**ST/SG/SER.E/073**
Remarks:	Update of geostationary position data of satellites METEOSAT-1, METEOSAT-2, GEOS-2, OTS-2 and MARECS-A

Document Symbol:	**ST/SG/SER.E/085**
Remarks:	Registration information for EXOSAT

Document Symbol:	**ST/SG/SER.E/093**
Remarks:	Registration information for Ariane 3rd stage

Document Symbol:	**ST/SG/SER.E/095**
Remarks:	Update of geostationary position data of satellites METEOSAT-1, METEOSAT-2, GEOS-2, OTS-2, MARECS-A and ECS

Document Symbol:	**ST/SG/SER.E/100**
Remarks:	Registration information for Ariane 3rd stage

Document Symbol:	**ST/SG/SER.E/112**
Remarks:	Registration information for EUTELSAT 2

Document Symbol:	**ST/SG/SER.E/115**
Remarks:	Registration information for MARECS PAC1

Document Symbol:	**ST/SG/SER.E/132**
Remarks:	Update of geostationary position data of satellites for May, June and July 1985

Document Symbol:	**ST/SG/SER.E/187**
Remarks:	Registration information for METEOSAT P2 & Ariane 3rd stage

Document Symbol:	**ST/SG/SER.E/266**
Remarks:	Registration information for EURECA, ERS-1, METEOSAT 4, METEOSAT 5, ULYSSES, HIPPARCOS, OLYMPUS-1, MARECS-A-EXP and MARECS-B-ATL

Document Symbol:	**ST/SG/SER.E/285**
Remarks:	Registration information for ERS-2

Document Symbol:	**ST/SG/SER.E/303**
Remarks:	Registration information for ISO and SOHO
Document Symbol:	**ST/SG/SER.E/375**
Remarks:	Registration information for XMM and Cluster satellites

IISL/ECSL Space Law Symposium 2003: Reinforcing the Registration Convention

The annual IISL/ECSL space law symposium was held on the occasion of the 42nd Session of the Legal Subcommittee of the United Nations Committee on the Peaceful Uses of Outer Space on Monday, 24 March 2003 in Vienna, Austria.

The symposium, held traditionally on the first day of the Legal Subcommittee's session, was well attended by delegates from many different countries. It was the first time that the symposium had not been organized by Dr Ernst Fasan (Austria), and in the opening words by the IISL Secretary on behalf of IISL President N. Jasentuliyana, he was warmly thanked for all his hard work to make the symposium into what it is today: an opportunity for delegates to hear about topical issues that might at some time require the attention of the Committee.

We were extremely pleased that Ambassador Peter Jankowitsch, Chairman of the Supervisory Board of the Austrian Space Agency and Past Chair of COPUOS, had agreed to chair the Symposium. His able leadership greatly contributed to the success of the event. Cicero dos Santos of the UN Office of Outer Space Affairs served as rapporteur, and IISL Secretary Tanja Masson-Zwaan had coordinated the programme.

The topic this year, "Reinforcing the Registration Convention", had been chosen in view of many recent developments, such as in-orbit sale of satellites, deployment of large satellite constellations by private consortia, etc, which may require us to rethink some of the provisions of, or gaps left by, the 1976 Registration Convention. The speakers came from a variety of countries and backgrounds, including Europe, the USA, South America, as well as industry, academia and international organizations.

A general introduction about the "Background and Historical Context" was given by Dr. Frans von der Dunk, Co-Director of the International Institute of Air and Space Law at Leiden University, The Netherlands.
Then Mr. Kay-Uwe Hörl, Team Leader of the Commercial & Contracts, Navigation & Constellations Business Unit of Astrium, Germany spoke on the complicated topic of "Change of Ownership, Change of Registry?, Which Objects to Register, What Data to be Furnished, When, and Until When?".
Next, Prof. Sylvia Ospina, a Consultant in international Telecoms/Space Law from Colombia discussed the "UNIDROIT Registration of Security Interests & The Registration Convention: Compatible / Complementary, or Contradictory?".
An example of the "Practice of National States", in particular the USA was presented by Prof. Joanne Gabrynowicz, Director of the National Remote Sensing and Space Law Center in Mississippi, USA, while the "Practice of International Organisations" and in particular the European Space Agency was discussed extensively by Dr. Gabriel Lafferranderie, the Chairman of ECSL.

Several delegates raised questions during the discussion, which focussed in large part on Ms Ospina's proposal to include the WTO instead of COPUOS or OOSA in Unidroit's plans for a new registry with the aim of protecting space assets.

Prof. Vladimir Kopal, Chairman of the UNCOPUOS Legal Subcommittee, thanked IISL and ECSL for organizing the symposium, and gave some concluding remarks. It was especially rewarding for the organizers to hear him say that some of the suggestions made by the speakers might well be taken up by the Committee during the remainder of the session!

After this, Ambassador Jankowitsch closed the symposium and invited all participants to a cocktail, sponsored by the IISL and ECSL.
We hope that next year will see yet another successful symposium!

Tanja Masson-Zwaan
IISL Secretary /former ECSL Board Member

ADDENDA

12th Manfred Lachs Space Law Moot Court Competition 2003

CASE CONCERNING THE MINERAL EXPLOITATION OF BOZNEMCOVA AND RELATED INCIDENTS

Vesta v. Ceres

PART A: INTRODUCTION

The 12th Manfred Lachs Space Law Moot Court Competition was held during the Bremen IISL Colloquium. The Case Concerning the Mineral Exploitation of Boznêmcová and Related Incidents (Vesta v. Ceres) was written by Michael Davis and Ricky Lee, both from Australia. Preliminaries were held at regional level in Europe (among 5 teams), the USA (among 7 teams) and in Asia Pacific region (among 13 teams).

The Finals were held at the Landgericht, and were as usual judged by three Judges of the International Court of Justice; i.e. H.E. Judge Guillaume, H.E. Judge Koroma and H.E. Judge Vereshchetin.

The German Aerospace Agency DLR and EADS Space Transportation sponsored the IISL dinner, and the University of Bremen has provided support. The IISL is most grateful to them. The famous Ratskeller restaurant in downtown Bremen was the location for the dinner, and the Landgericht kindly provided its beautiful courtroom for the finals.

RESULTS OF THE WORLD FINALS:

- Winner: University of Auckland, New Zealand (Jesse Wilson and Isaac Hikaka
- Runner up: Georgetown University Law Center, Washington DC USA (Amanda Shafer, Petra Vorwig, and Melissa Beiting)
- 2nd runner up: University of Bremen, Germany (Deirdre Ní Chearbhaill, Kamlesh Gungaphul, and Giorgi Kavtaradze)
- Eilene M. Galloway Award for Best Written Brief: University of Bremen, Germany
- Sterns and Tennen Award for Best Oralist: Petra Vorwig, Georgetown University Law Center

CONTACT DETAILS REGIONAL ROUNDS:
USA: SSMITH@sah.com
Europe: Alberto.Marchini@esa.int
Asia Pacific: ricky@myoffice.net.au

PARTICIPANTS IN REGIONAL ROUNDS

USA:
Georgetown University, Washington DC
University of North Carolina, North Carolina
Golden Gate University, California
University of St. Thomas, Miami
University of Virginia , Virginia
Vanderbilt University, Tennessee
Howard University, Washington DC

Europe:
University of Leiden, the Netherlands
University of Jaen, Spain
University of Milan, Italy
Univeristy of Warsaw, Poland
University of Bremen, Germany

Asia Pacific:
China University of Politics and Law
Chulalongkorn University ,Thailand
National University of Singapore
Sophia University,Japan
Tsinghua University, China
University of Auckland, New Zealand
University of Malaya, Malaysia
University of New South Wales, Australia
University of Queensland, Australia
University of Sydney, Australia
University of Technology Sydney, Australia
University of Tokyo, Japan
University of Western Sydney, Australia

JUDGES FOR WRITTEN BRIEFS:
Prof. Joanne Gabrynowicz, USA
Prof. Alexis Goh, Australia
Prof Francis Lyall, Scotland UK
Prof V.S. Mani, India
Ms. Martha Mejia-Kaiser, Mexico
Prof. Maureen Williams, Argentina

JUDGES FOR SEMI FINALS:
Prof. Stephan Hobe, Germany
Ms. Marcia Smith, USA
Dr. Olivier Ribbelink (The Netherlands)

12th Manfred Lachs Space Law Moot Court Competition 2003

CASE CONCERNING THE MINERAL EXPLOITATION OF BOZNEMCOVA AND RELATED INCIDENTS

Vesta v. Ceres

PART A: INTRODUCTION

The 12th Manfred Lachs Space Law Moot Court Competition was held during the Bremen IISL Colloquium. The Case Concerning the Mineral Exploitation of Boznêmcová and Related Incidents (Vesta v. Ceres) was written by Michael Davis and Ricky Lee, both from Australia. Preliminaries were held at regional level in Europe (among 5 teams), the USA (among 7 teams) and in Asia Pacific region (among 13 teams).

The Finals were held at the Landgericht, and were as usual judged by three Judges of the International Court of Justice; i.e. H.E. Judge Guillaume, H.E. Judge Koroma and H.E. Judge Vereshchetin.

The German Aerospace Agency DLR and EADS Space Transportation sponsored the IISL dinner, and the University of Bremen has provided support. The IISL is most grateful to them. The famous Ratskeller restaurant in downtown Bremen was the location for the dinner, and the Landgericht kindly provided its beautiful courtroom for the finals.

RESULTS OF THE WORLD FINALS:

- Winner: University of Auckland, New Zealand (Jesse Wilson and Isaac Hikaka
- Runner up: Georgetown University Law Center, Washington DC USA (Amanda Shafer, Petra Vorwig, and Melissa Beiting)
- 2nd runner up: University of Bremen, Germany (Deirdre Ní Chearbhaill, Kamlesh Gungaphul, and Giorgi Kavtaradze)
- Eilene M. Galloway Award for Best Written Brief: University of Bremen, Germany
- Sterns and Tennen Award for Best Oralist: Petra Vorwig, Georgetown University Law Center

CONTACT DETAILS REGIONAL ROUNDS:

USA: SSMITH@sah.com
Europe: Alberto.Marchini@esa.int
Asia Pacific: ricky@myoffice.net.au

PARTICIPANTS IN REGIONAL ROUNDS

USA:
Georgetown University, Washington DC
University of North Carolina, North Carolina
Golden Gate University, California
University of St. Thomas, Miami
University of Virginia , Virginia
Vanderbilt University, Tennessee
Howard University, Washington DC

Europe:
University of Leiden, the Netherlands
University of Jaen, Spain
University of Milan, Italy
Univeristy of Warsaw, Poland
University of Bremen, Germany

Asia Pacific:
China University of Politics and Law
Chulalongkorn University ,Thailand
National University of Singapore
Sophia University,Japan
Tsinghua University, China
University of Auckland, New Zealand
University of Malaya, Malaysia
University of New South Wales, Australia
University of Queensland, Australia
University of Sydney, Australia
University of Technology Sydney, Australia
University of Tokyo, Japan
University of Western Sydney, Australia

JUDGES FOR WRITTEN BRIEFS:
Prof. Joanne Gabrynowicz, USA
Prof. Alexis Goh, Australia
Prof Francis Lyall, Scotland UK
Prof V.S. Mani, India
Ms. Martha Mejia-Kaiser, Mexico
Prof. Maureen Williams, Argentina

JUDGES FOR SEMI FINALS:
Prof. Stephan Hobe, Germany
Ms. Marcia Smith, USA
Dr. Olivier Ribbelink (The Netherlands)

JUDGES FOR FINALS:
H.E. Judge Gilbert Guillaume, ICJ
H.E. Judge Abdul Koroma, ICJ
H.E. Judge Vladlen Vereshchetin, ICJ

PART B: THE PROBLEM

1. It is the year 2040.

2. The Principality of Ceres was an industrialised coastal State with a population of 25 million. The Republic of Vesta was a predominantly agricultural landlocked State with a population of 37 million that was originally part of neighbouring Ceres but seceded peacefully on 2 May 2014 after a plebiscite. The original Ceresan lunar colony located in the Sea of Tranquillity was divided between Ceres and Vesta on the same date, with the Ceresan half referred to as "Lunar Ceresia" and the Vestan half as "New Vesta". The Ceresan Government had been a strong supporter of the international campaign against terrorism, led by the United States since 2001, while Vesta had maintained its neutrality.

3. Astermine Aerospace Engineering, Inc. ("**Astermine**") was a company incorporated in 2017 in the Federal Islands of Boranatu, a Pacific island nation with a reputation as a tax haven. Since 2025, rising oceans resulting from global warming caused many Boranatuans to resettle as "environmental refugees" in a number of countries, including Ceres and Vesta. The Boranatuan Resettlement Agency, funded by the Ceresan Government, was based in the Ceresan capital of Salmonella. Its primary activity being to act as a coordination and welfare agency for the refugees in Ceres and its neighbouring countries, including Vesta. In Ceres, Boranatuans enjoy full citizenship and rights, but this was not the case in Vesta, where they are naturalised citizens but also subjected to social and economic discrimination. The treatment of Boranatuans in Vesta has been the subject of repeated reports of the Human Rights Commission and the Economic and Social Council of the United Nations.

4. Astermine operated as a registered foreign corporation in Ceres. Under Section 19A of the *Companies Ordinance 2017*, registered foreign corporations are subject to regulation by the Ceresan Corporate Commission as if they are local corporations incorporated in Ceres and are taxed for profits derived from activities in Ceres.

5. Astermine was the largest firm in the Ceresan space industry and was 100% owned by Vestan private interests (most of them Boranatuans who became naturalised Vestans). Astermine received research funding from the National Aeronautics and Space Research Agency ("**NASRA**") of Ceres that, over the past six years, contributed to 60% of its research and development costs.

6. In 2024, the flyby probe *Tombaugh*, a joint project of NASRA and Astermine that was launched from the space station *ISS Beta*, undertook spectral and mineralogical studies on four large asteroids: Atmos, Boznêmcová, Eros and Vesta. It was confirmed through this mission that Boznêmcová was rich in olivine, pyroxene, iron and nickel. It was revealed that Boznêmcová also contained rich deposits of palladium ores and helium-3 deposits, both precious resources that were previously not known to exist on Boznêmcová. The results of these studies were published in scientific e-journals and were available from both NASRA and Astermine's broadband web portals.

7. In 2026, prompted by a world shortage of palladium, Astermine began construction of a robotic mining facility spacecraft, the *Boznêmcová Miner*, in low Earth orbit with components launched from the Earth and assembled in space by Astermine engineers stationed on *ISS Gamma*. It was powered by solar panels and a rechargeable chemical battery (which was recharged only by the solar panels) but its propulsion system was a mixture of chemical thrusters and a newly-developed nuclear engine designed specifically for interplanetary systems.

8. The construction of the components of the *Boznêmcová Miner* was done in-house at Astermine facilities in Ceres. Upon completion they were there transported to Serratis, a developed country bordering Vesta. The ground control facility for these launches was located in Vesta. The launch vehicle was a Ceresan commercial reusable

launch vehicle. The launch facility used was owned by Astermine and located in territory leased by Serratis to Ceres for 99 years, which began in 2023. There were 71 launches scheduled for the construction of the *Miner*.

9. On 31 July 2028, one of the launches, designated with mission number BM-52, was unsuccessful. The reusable launch vehicle used by Astermine lost communications with the ground control facility and plummeted into Botulisia, the capital of Vesta, destroying the 31-storey headquarters of the Vestan Police and Justice Department as well as several surrounding buildings, causing over US$638 million damage and the loss of 231 lives.

10. Outraged by the tragedy, the Vestan Government ordered a full investigation, with which Astermine cooperated. It was soon discovered that the cause of the failure was human error and the two mission control engineers that were found negligent were both Boranatuans with ties to the Boranatuan Resettlement Agency in Ceres. The reason why the trajectory of the launch vehicle was over Botulisia was that the Vestan Airspace Command had provided Astermine with incorrect coordinates on its flight path clearance.

11. Convinced nevertheless that it was a deliberate act of terrorism on the part of Boranatuans, Vesta sent troops to occupy the launch facility used and detained the Boranatuan staff of Astermine at the facility and in Vesta. This forced Astermine to use its older secondary launch facility in Ceres and delayed the completion of the project by two years. Public outrage over the incident resulted in violence and property damage against Ceresans and Boranatuans in Vesta, especially in Botulisia.

12. As a result of the two-year delay in the construction of the *Miner*, the orbital motion of both the Earth and Boznêmcová had taken the asteroid away from its optimal location for capture. As a result, an additional $32 million was spent in redesigning the propulsion system and fuel to allow the *Miner* to reach its destination. The delay also coincided with the discovery of large and previously unknown palladium deposits in South America, causing world palladium prices to fall around 12% from the prices originally projected at the time of the return of the *Miner*.

13. Vesta demanded compensation from Ceres for the damage caused by BM-52. Negotiations between the two countries, mediated by the Secretary-General of the United Nations, resulted in Ceres paying US$860 million compensation to the Vestan Government on 14 November 2028. This payment was made by Ceres on an *ex gratia* basis while denying any liability to pay compensation under international law, and was expressed to be in full and final settlement of any claim by Vesta for damage to persons killed or injured by the incident as well as for damage to buildings and property. As part of the negotiated terms of settlement Vesta returned the recovered wreckage and components to Ceresan authorities, which returned them to Astermine.

14. In April 2030, the Vestan popular press noted that 211 workers and emergency services staff, or 77% of the total number who worked on the crash site of BM-52, had developed various forms of cancer. Eventually it was discovered in October 2030 that the payload of BM-52 was the nuclear propulsion engine to be used on the *Boznêmcová Miner*.

15. By April 2035, a further 534 people who worked in offices around the area of the crash were diagnosed with cancers which were probably linked to the radioactive fallout from BM-52. The radioactivity from the crash caused property prices in Botulisia to plummet by an average 60% in the four months from October 2030 to February 2031. The cost of cleaning up the radiation poisoning took four months and cost US$128 million. The devastation to the business sector as a result of the property crash and its inability to access a significant number of office buildings during the clean-up caused the Vestan economy to go into recession with economic growth at an average –1.9% per annum for the next three years instead of the +2.7% per annum originally forecast by the International Monetary Fund or the +3.4% per annum originally forecast by the Vestan Government.

16. Vesta proceeded to claim compensation from Ceres through diplomatic channels for the environmental damage, the fall in property prices, the subsequent economic recession and the creation of a trust fund for victims whose cancer may be linked to the incident. Ceres maintained that the settlement of 14 November 2028 was a full and final settlement of all existing and potential claims and that, in any event, Ceres was not liable to pay compensation for such heads of damages.

17. On 2 May 2036, a rocket-based missile hit and destroyed several buildings in the central business district of Salmonella and killed 1,016 people. Investigations undertaken by Ceresan authorities as well as investigators from the European Union indicated that the public activist group, Vestan Victims of Astermine ("**Astervic**"), was responsible for the attack. There was evidence (available to the Ceresan Government) that Vesta may have been indirectly financing the operations of the group, though it ceased funding the organisation after the attack and condemned it.

18. In response to what was seen by Ceres to be an act of state-sponsored terrorism, Ceres retaliated by attacking several Vestan watchtowers and forts along the border within the following two weeks. On 30 May 2036, the Vestan national communications satellite was destroyed in space by the use of space-based Ceresan laser technology, previously used as part of a Ceresan global navigational satellite system that Ceres claimed was being used by Vesta to plan an armed attack on Ceres. Both countries also began stationing defensive installations and batteries on the Moon along the border between Lunar Ceresia and New Vesta. The United Nations brokered a peace agreement between the two countries and Ceres subsequently removed their defensive installations on the Moon, but the Vestan facilities remained.

19. Despite the setback as a result of the launch failure of BM-52, the *Boznêmcová Miner* was completed in 2029 and arrived at Boznêmcová in 2032. The mining was in two stages: the first involved the extraction of ores and, after some preliminary processing, were collected in large canisters that were fired back to Earth orbit for collection from the space stations. Once Boznêmcová became small enough in mass, the *Boznêmcová Miner* fired its engines and moved the asteroid from its orbit and slowly migrated it to Earth orbit for a more extensive exploitation of its resources (an experimental process called "total capture mining"). The *Boznêmcová Miner* returned to Earth orbit with the asteroid in March 2035.

20. Most of the unused portions of the asteroid, containing mainly metallic compounds and various rocks, were used to produce concrete for the new Ceresan lunar colony to be located near Lake Armstrong. However, many fragments remained in orbit and occasionally caused interference to Vestan satellite transmissions, forcing their operations to move their satellites and install additional shielding to future satellites, significantly reducing their lifespan as well as the increased costs of constructing and launching new replacement satellites.

21. By Special Agreement, Vesta and Ceres bring their dispute before the International Court of Justice. Vesta seeks declarations that:

(i) Ceres is liable to Vesta for the payment of compensation for radiation damage and consequent economic losses caused by the failure of the BM-52 launch;

(ii) The destruction of the Vestan communications system by space-based lasers on 30 May 2036 was unlawful and entitles Vesta to compensation from Ceres for the damage sustained;

(iii) Ceres has violated international law by destroying an asteroid; and

(iv) All other relief sought by Vesta in its memorials and oral submissions should be granted and that all claims and relief sought by Ceres should be denied.

22. Ceres seeks declarations that:

(i) Ceres is not liable to Vesta in relation to the launch failure of BM-52;

(ii) If Ceres was liable to Vesta in relation to the launch failure of BM-52, that liability was fully extinguished by the payment of US$860 million to the government of Vesta and, in any event, the heads of damage claimed by Vesta are not recoverable;

(iii) The destruction of the Vestan communications satellite system did not cause Ceres to violate any applicable international legal principles;

(iv) The continuing presence of Vestan military facilities and installations in New Vesta is unlawful; and

(v) All other relief sought by Ceres in its memorials and oral submissions should be granted and claims and relief sought by Vesta should be denied.

23. The *Boznêmcová Miner* was registered in accordance with the 1968 Registration Convention and lists Ceres as the state of registry, except that the instrument of registration lodged did not indicate the launching States of the *Miner*.

24. Serratis has separately and peacefully settled any claims between Vesta and Serratis and between Ceres and Serratis on the basis that Serratis was not a launching State of the *Boznêmcová Miner*.

25. Ceres and Vesta are both parties to the 1967 Outer Space Treaty, the 1972 Liability Convention, the 1968 Rescue Agreement and the 1975 Registration Convention. Vesta became a member of the United Nations when it became independent from Ceres in 2014. Ceres was a founding member of the United Nations in 1945. Vesta has signed and ratified the 1979 Moon Agreement but Ceres has never signed it or recognised it as being part of international law.

26. Ceres and Vesta are both members of the International Monetary Fund, the International Bank for Reconstruction and Development (the World Bank), the International Telecommunication Union and the World Trade Organisation.

PART C: FINALISTS' BRIEFS

A. WRITTEN BRIEF FOR VESTA

AGENTS:

Amanda Shafer, Petra Vorwig, and Melissa Beiting, Georgetown University Law Center, Washington DC, USA

ARGUMENT

I. INTRODUCTION

The serious injury Vesta has suffered at the hand of Ceres requires that Ceres be made to compensate for such injury. International law must be brought to bear on Ceres, a nation that continues to show complete disregard for Vesta's interests and for its own international obligations. Therefore, Vesta requests this Court to find Ceres liable for the damages caused by the radiation leaked from the BM-52 crash and those caused by Ceres' destruction of Vesta's communications satellite. Furthermore, Vesta requests this Court find Ceres in breach of the Outer Space Treaty for appropriating a celestial body in the form of the Boznêmcová asteroid.

II. CERES IS LIABLE FOR THE PHYSICAL DAMAGE AND ECONOMIC LOSSES TO VESTA RESULTING FROM THE RADIATION LEAKED FROM THE BM-52 CRASH SITE.

Ceres breached international treaty law when the BM-52 launch vehicle, carrying the nuclear propulsion engine for the *Boznêmcová Miner* ("*Miner*"), crashed into Botulisia, resulting in the immediate death of 231 people and inducing cancer in another 745 people from radiation poisoning. Ceres should be held liable for all of the damages that resulted from the radiation contamination because Ceres was the launching State of the BM-52.[1] Furthermore, the health problems, loss in property value and economic recession suffered by Vesta directly resulted from the radiation contamination leaked from the nuclear engine on board the BM-52. Because these damages were discovered long after the initial crash and were the result of the radiation rather than the direct impact of the launch vehicle, the settlement of November 2028 did not extinguish Vesta's right to seek further compensation.

A. <u>Ceres is liable for the damage caused to Vesta by the BM-52 crash because it is the launching State under the Outer Space Treaty and the Liability Convention.</u>

Ceres is liable for the radiation damage and consequent economic loss under Article VII of the Outer Space Treaty and Article II of the Liability Convention because Ceres is the launching State for the BM-52. Both the Outer Space Treaty and the Liability Convention adopt the same four categories of launching State, under all of which a State may be held internationally liable for damage caused to another State by the launched space object.[2] These categories include States that (1) launch a space object, (2) procure the launch of a space object, (3) represent the territory from which the space object is launched or (4) own the facility from which it is launched. Ceres qualifies as the launching State for the BM-52 because the BM-52 was launched from Ceresan territory and because Ceres procured the launch of the BM-52. Ceres has recognized its status as the launching State by registering the BM-52 launch and the 70 other launches associated with the *Boznêmcová Miner*[3] under the Registration Convention.[4]

1. *Ceres is a launching State because the BM-52 launched from Ceresan territory.*

Ceres is a launching State liable for the crash of the BM-52 because the launch occurred on Ceresan territory that was leased from Serratis under a 99-year lease.[5] Though the Compromis does not state the terms of that lease, similar leases have provided the leasing State with "complete jurisdiction and control over and within said

---

[1] *See* Treaty on Principles Governing the Activities of States in the Exploration and Use of Outer Space, including the Moon and Other Celestial Bodies, Jan. 27, 1967, art. VII, T.I.A.S. No. 6347, 610 U.N.T.S. 205 [hereinafter Outer Space Treaty]; Convention on International Liability for Damage Caused by Space Objects, Oct. 9, 1973, art. I, T.I.A.S. No. 7762, 961 U.N.T.S. 2389 [hereinafter Liability Convention]; Convention on Registration of Objects Launched into Outer Space, Jan. 14, 1975, T.I.A.S. 8480, 1023 U.N.T.S. 15 [hereinafter Registration Convention]

[2] *See* Outer Space Treaty, *supra* note 1, art. VII; Liability Convention, *supra* note 1, art. I; BIN CHENG, STUDIES IN INTERNATIONAL SPACE LAW 637-38 (1997).

[3] Compromis, ¶ 23; Clarifications to the Compromis, ¶ 8.

[4] Registration Convention, *supra* note 1, art. II.

[5] Compromis, ¶ 8.

areas."[6] If a similar term was applied in Ceres' lease, Ceres had complete jurisdiction and control over the territory from which the BM-52 was launched. Though many commentators recognize that such a lease provision does not transfer sovereignty in the land,[7] the definition of a launching State in Article I of the Liability Convention does not clarify what level of control a State must have over the launching territory in order to qualify as a launching State.

Article 31 of the Vienna Convention on the Law of Treaties ("Vienna Convention on Treaties") instructs that "[a] treaty shall be interpreted in good faith in accordance with the ordinary meaning to be given to the terms of the treaty in their context and in the light of its object and purpose."[8] Under the Outer Space Treaty and the Liability Convention, "a State from whose territory or facility a space object is launched" is a launching State.[9] Ceres had control over the territory from which the BM-52 was launched and should not be allowed to skirt its responsibility based on a narrow interpretation of the word "territory." Such an interpretation would undermine the "victim-oriented concept of liability" established under the Liability Convention.[10] As the State in control of the territory from which the BM-52 was launched, Ceres qualifies as a launching State and therefore must be held liable for any damage caused by the BM-52.

2. *Ceres is a launching State because it procured the launch of the BM-52.*

Ceres also qualifies as a launching State because it procured the launch of the BM-52 by materially participating in the development of the *Boznêmcová Miner*, to which the BM-52 was carrying a component, and by supplying the launch vehicle to Astermine.[11] In order to procure a launch, a State must make an effort or take the initiative in bringing about such a launch.[12] Ceres has been deeply involved in the initiation, development and execution of the *Boznêmcová Miner* project. Ceres' National Aeronautical Space and Research Agency (NASRA) conducted jointly with Astermine the initial mineralogical studies of the Boznêmcová asteroid that ultimately led to the mining project and the need to launch the BM-52.[13] NASRA has also contributed funds to Astermine's research projects.[14] Finally, Ceres contributed the launch vehicle in which all of the components for the *Boznêmcová Miner* were to be carried into outer space, but instead crashed into Botulisia.[15] The launch vehicle was critical to the launch itself and evidences Ceres' participation in procuring the launch of the BM-52.[16]

3. *Ceres has recognized its status as a launching State by registering the BM-52 launch under the Registration Convention.*

Ceres has acknowledged its liability for each of the launches associated with the *Boznêmcová Miner* by registering each component of the *Miner* as well as the completed *Miner* in accordance with the Registration Convention.[17] Article II of the Registration Convention states, "when a space object is launched into Earth orbit or beyond, the *launching State* shall register the space object."[18] Article I of the Registration Convention adopts the same definition of a launching State established in the Outer Space Treaty and the Liability Convention, which includes States from whose territory a space object is launched and a

---

[6] Lease of Lands for Coaling and Naval Stations: Agreement between the United States of America and the Republic of Cuba for the Lease to the United States of Lands in Cuba for Coaling and Naval Stations, T.S. 418 (1903).

[7] SIR ROBERT JENNINGS & SIR ARTHUR WATTS, OPPENHEIM'S INTERNATIONAL LAW 563 (9th ed. 1992).

[8] Vienna Convention on the Law of Treaties between States and International Organizations or between International Organizations, May 23, 1969, art. 31(1), 115 U.N.T.S. 331, [hereinafter *Vienna Convention on Treaties*].

[9] Liability Convention, *supra* note 1, art. I.

[10] Susanne U. Reif, *'Project 2001': Conclusions and Recommendations of the 'Working Group on Privatization' with Regard to Issues of International Space Law*, PROCEEDINGS OF THE FORTY-FOURTH COLLOQUIUM ON THE LAW OF OUTER SPACE, 3, 7 (2001).

[11] Compromis, ¶ 5, 8.

[12] Motoko Uchitomi, *State Responsibility/Liability for "National" Space Activities: Towards Safe and Fair Competition in Private Space Activities*, PROCEEDINGS OF THE FORTY-FOURTH COLLOQUIUM ON THE LAW OF OUTER SPACE, 51, 52 (2001) [hereinafter *State Responsibility for National Activities*].

[13] Compromis, ¶ 6.

[14] Compromis, ¶ 5.

[15] Compromis, ¶ 8.

[16] Commentators disagree over what level of participation a State must exhibit to establish procurement, but even the most strict interpretation would consider provision of a major component of the launch as procuring the launch. *State Responsibility for National Activities*, *supra* note 12, at 52.

[17] Clarifications to the Compromis, ¶ 8.

[18] Registration Convention, *supra* note 1, art. II (emphasis added).

State which procures the launching of a space object.[19] Article I also defines a space object to include "component parts of a space object as well as its launch vehicle and parts thereof."[20] Ceres voluntarily registered each of the *Miner*'s component parts, including the nuclear engine and the launch vehicle for the BM-52. By deciding to become the registration State for the *Miner* and all of its component parts, Ceres acknowledged its status as the launching State as defined under the Registration Convention and its responsibilities as the launching State under Article II of that Convention. As the launching State for the BM-52 and the State responsible for the nuclear engine on board, Ceres must be held liable for the radiation damage caused by that engine.

B. <u>Ceres is absolutely liable for all damage caused in Botulisia under Article II of the Liability Convention.</u>

The Liability Convention creates two scenarios for liability: absolute liability for damage caused on the surface of the Earth and fault-based liability where damage occurs other than on the surface of the Earth.[21] Such damage may include "loss of life, personal injury or other impairment of health; or loss or damage to property of States or of persons."[22] All 745 instances of cancer, the lost property value, the cost of the clean-up and the economic recession fall under the definition of damages provided by the Liability Convention, and all occurred on the surface of the Earth. As a result, Ceres should be held absolutely liable for this damage.

1. *The 745 cases of cancer directly resulted from the radiation leaked from the BM-52 and Vesta must be compensated for the associated health costs.*

Though the damage to the health of hundreds of Vestans did not become apparent for several years, the unequivocal cause of the health problems was the nuclear engine in the hold of the BM-52 . A total of 745 people either working to clean up the crash site or working in the offices around the crash were diagnosed with cancer.[23] These injuries represent personal injuries that must be compensated under the Liability Convention.[24] The fact that the cancers developed several years after the crash does not reduce their compensability because the negotiating history of the Convention indicates that all negotiating States agreed nuclear damages were included in the Convention's definition of damage.[25] Such recognition would include the possibility of latent damage that would still be covered under the Convention.

2. *Vesta's loss in property value occurred solely as a result of the radiation contamination and must be compensated under the Liability Convention.*

The 60% loss in property value following discovery of the radioactive contamination also qualifies as "loss or damage to property of States or of persons" under Article I of the Convention. If the crash had not occurred, the value of the property surrounding the crash site would not have changed, and Vesta would not have suffered any loss attributable to radiation leaked from the nuclear engine.

3. *The economic recession also directly resulted from the radiation contamination and subsequent clean-up requiring Ceres to compensate Vesta for its loss.*

Ceres is also absolutely liable for the economic recession Vesta suffered as a result of the business disruption and clean-up because the economic decline was a direct loss of property under Article I of the Liability Convention. The International Court of Justice, (I.C.J.) recognized the need to protect a State's economic interests in the <u>Fisheries Jurisdiction Case</u>.[26] Like the value of the property surrounding the crash site, the Vestan recession represents a loss in the value of the economic assets held by Vesta. If the crash had not occurred or Vesta had been notified of the radiation at the time of the crash so that both could have been

[19] *Id.*, art. I.

[20] *Id.*

[21] "A launching State shall be absolutely liable to pay compensation for damage caused by its space object on the surface of the Earth or to aircraft in flight." Liability Convention, *supra* note 1, art. II. "In the event of damage being caused elsewhere than on the surface of the Earth to a space object of one launching State or to persons or property on board such a space object by a space object of another launching State, the latter shall be liable only if the damage is due to its fault or the fault of persons for whom it is responsible." *Id.*, art. III.

[22] *Id.*, art. I(d).

[23] Compromis, ¶ 14, 15.

[24] Liability Convention, *supra* note 1, art. I.

[25] BIN CHENG, STUDIES IN INTERNATIONAL SPACE LAW 323-24 (1997).

[26] *Fisheries Jurisdiction Case* (U.K. v. Ice.) 1974 I.C.J 1, 26-27.

cleaned up at the same time, business would not have suffered such a significant disruption and the contamination could have been limited. Had both the business disruption and the contamination been reduced, the economy would have grown by at least 2.7% each year over the three years under consideration.[27] Instead, the property value dropped dramatically due to the contamination and the Vestan economy experienced a three-year recession.

Though Ceres may attempt to characterize the damages sought as indirect, these damages directly resulted from the radiation that leaked from the nuclear engine on board the BM-52. Had the crash not occurred, 745 Vestans would not have suffered radiation poisoning. Had Botulisia not been contaminated with radiation, the property value would have remained the same. Finally, but for Vesta's need to clean up the radiation contamination, businesses could have continued to operate and the economy would not have entered into recession.

4. *Ceres should be made to pay for the health, property and economic damage Vesta suffered in order to return Vesta to the condition which would have existed had the radiation not leaked from the BM-52 crash.*

Ceres should also compensate Vesta for all health, property and economic damages in order to satisfy Article XII of the Liability Convention. Article XII requires the liable State "to provide such reparation in respect of the damage as will restore the person, . . . State or international organization on whose behalf the claim is presented to the condition which would have existed if the damage had not occurred."[28] Prior to the crash, Botulisia had a generally healthy population, a thriving business district and an expanding economy. Though the radiation contamination was not discovered for several years, the cost of the clean up and the disruption of business sent the Vestan economy plummeting. In the Chorzów Factory Case, the I.C.J. required Poland to pay reparations to Germany for seizing property that had been contracted to Germany in the Treaty of Versailles.[29] The Court required Poland to "wipe out all the consequences of the illegal act and re-establish the situation which would, in all probability, have existed if that act had not been committed" by making reparations.[30] If the radiation had not been released, the Vestan government and its citizens would not have suffered these losses. Ceres, like Poland, must compensate Vesta for these losses in order to return Vesta to the condition that would have existed if the BM-52 launcher, carrying a nuclear engine had not crashed into Botulisia.[31]

C. Ceres cannot be exonerated under Article VI of the Liability Convention because Vesta did not act with gross negligence.

Ceres cannot be exonerated from liability under Article VI(1) of the Liability Convention because Vesta's miscalculation of the flight path does not qualify as gross negligence, nor was the act "done with the intent to cause damage."[32] Gross negligence requires more than a calculation error; it requires a reckless disregard for the risk created by the action.[33] The incorrect coordinates provided by the Vestan Airspace Command do not, without affirmative evidence of recklessness, rise to the level of gross negligence. Therefore, Ceres should not be exonerated under Article VI of the Liability Convention

D. Ceres is also liable for all of the damages caused by the BM-52 crash under Article VI of the Outer Space Treaty.

Article VI of the Outer Space Treaty requires States to "bear international responsibility for national activities in outer space, including the Moon and other celestial bodies, whether such

---

[27] The International Monetary Fund ("IMF") IMF prediction has been used because it represents a more conservative prediction than that provided by the Vestan government and is internationally recognized as providing accurate predictions.

[28] Liability Convention, *supra* note 1, art. XII. *See also Case Concerning the Factory at Chorzów* (Ger. v. Pol.), P.C.I.J. No. 13.

[29] *Id.* at 31.

[30] *Id.* at 47.

[31] *Id. See also Corfu Channel Case*, (U.K. v. Alb.), 1949 I.C.J. 4, at 244 (providing compensation for the injuries and deaths of British naval personnel); *Trail Smelter Arbitration* (U.S. v. Can.), 3 R.I.A.A. 1905, 1907 (1941) (requiring Canada to compensate the United States for the reduction in value of land affected by pollution originating in Canada).

[32] Liability Convention, *supra* note 1, art. VI(1).

[33] The definition of gross negligence applied in the United States and several European countries emphasizes the need for much more than simple indifference to one's duty. *See* DAN B. DOBBS, THE LAW OF TORTS § 147 (2000); CHRISTIAN VON BAR, THE COMMON EUROPEAN LAW OF TORTS § 243 (1998).

activities are carried on by governmental agencies or by non-governmental entities."[34] In determining what is a national activity, noted space law scholar Bin Cheng explains that territorial jurisdiction over the launch activity and the launching entity overrides any other State's jurisdiction, including quasi-territorial jurisdiction and personal jurisdiction.[35] Ceres had territorial jurisdiction over Astermine's launch facility as the leaseholder for the territory and therefore must bear international responsibility for all of the launch activities, including the BM-52.[36]

Ceres also failed to fulfill its supervisory role mandated under Article VI of the Outer Space Treaty. Article VI requires "the appropriate State" to authorize and continually supervise the launch activities of non-governmental entities.[37] Many international scholars have recognized that the term "appropriate State" incorporates more than just the State of nationality.[38] Specifically, the State that exercises jurisdiction and control over the private enterprise would qualify[39] as would a State where the space object's components were produced.[40] Ceres had territorial jurisdiction over the nuclear engine that was launched by the BM-52 because all of the components for the *Boznêmcová Miner* were produced at Astermine's facilities in Ceres.[41] As the State with the strongest jurisdictional tie to the launch, Ceres must bear responsibility for all of the launch activities that occurred, including the crash of the BM-52.

As the launching State for the BM-52, Ceres must be held absolutely liable under the Liability Convention for all of the damages that resulted from the radiation leaked by the crash. Ceres must also be held liable for the damages as the State responsible for the launch activities of its nationals under the Outer Space Treaty.

III. THE INITIAL SETTLEMENT IS NOT FINAL WITH REGARD TO THE NEWLY DISCOVERED HEALTH AND ECONOMIC DAMAGE CAUSED BY THE BM-52 LAUNCH FAILURE.

The settlement reached immediately after the crash of the BM-52 does not bar Vesta's current request for damages under the Liability Convention or general principles of international law because Vesta was not aware of the nuclear engine on board the BM-52 at the time of the settlement. As a result, the settlement does not extinguish Ceres' liability for the radiation damages. Furthermore, Ceres failed to alert Vesta to the potential for nuclear contamination as required by the Principles Relevant to the Use of Nuclear Power Sources in Outer Space ("NPS Principles")[42] and customary international law.

A. Ceres can still be held liable for the radiation damage under the Liability Convention because Vesta did not agree to forego any future claims.

As required under Article IX of the Liability Convention,[43] Vesta sought compensation for the damage caused by the BM-52 disaster through diplomatic channels. Vesta and Ceres negotiated a settlement of US$860 million with the help of the Secretary-General of the United Nations (U.N.). In that settlement Ceres denied any liability for the damage, and payment was said to be "in full and final settlement of any claim by Vesta for

[34] Outer Space Treaty, *supra* note 1, art. VI.

[35] Bin Cheng, *Article VI of the 1967 Space Treaty Revised: "International Responsibility," "National Activities," and "The Appropriate State,"* 26 J. SPACE LAW 7, 23 (1998). *See also State Responsibility for National Activities*, *supra* note 12, at 52.

[36] Compromis, ¶ 8.

[37] Outer Space Treaty, *supra* note 1, art. VI.

[38] *See* Dr. Karl-Heinz Böckstiegel, *The Term "Appropriate State" and "Launching State" in Space Treaties – Indicators of State Responsibility and Liability for State and Private Space Activities*, PROCEEDINGS OF THE THIRTY-FOURTH COLLOQUIUM ON THE LAW OF OUTER SPACE, 13, 14 (1991) [hereinafter *The "Appropriate State" and "Launching State" in Space Treaties*]; Michel Bourély, PROCEEDINGS OF THE TWENTY-NINTH COLLOQUIUM ON THE LAW OF OUTER SPACE, 159 (1986).

[39] *The "Appropriate State" and "Launching State" in Space Treaties*, *supra* note 38, at 14.

[40] Eilene Galloway observed during a working group appointed to study the problems of interpreting the Outer Space Treaty, "The point would seem to be correct that there may be several 'appropriate states' with responsibilities under Article VI. Is it not doubtful, however, that the State Party whose only connection with the particular space activity was that some components or space instruments were produced on its territory would often be one of the 'appropriate states'?" Dr. Istvan Herczeg, *Problems of Interpretation of the Space Treaty of 27 January 1967: Introductory Report*, PROCEEDINGS OF THE TENTH COLLOQUIUM ON THE LAW OF OUTER SPACE, 108 (1967).

[41] *The "Appropriate State" and "Launching State" in Space Treaties*, *supra* note 38, at 14.

[42] G.A. Res. 47/68, U.N. GAOR, 47th Sess., U.N. Doc. A/RES/47/68 (1992) [hereinafter *NPS Principles*].

[43] "A claim for compensation for damage shall be presented to a launching State through diplomatic channels." Liability Convention, *supra* note 1, art. IX.

damage to persons killed or injured by the incident as well as for damage to buildings and property."[44] By denying liability, Ceres remains open to a claim under the Liability Convention, despite its original payment.[45] Furthermore, the condition placed on the payment only relates to the specific incident known to both parties at the time, namely the crash of the BM-52. Even though Ceres knew the crash would result in radiation contamination and significant future damage,[46] Vesta was unaware of this potential and therefore should not be assumed to have negotiated away all future claims arising from that contamination.

B. Even if the original settlement is found to be binding, Article X of the Liability Convention allows Vesta to amend its claim for damages having learned of the full extent of the radiation damage.

Article X allows a victim State to "revise its claim and submit additional documentation [after the initial claim] until one year after the full extent of the damage is known."[47] The full extent of the radiation damage did not become apparent until 2035 when all 745 instances of cancer and the full extent of the economic recession became apparent.[48] Upon learning of these damages, Vesta made several attempts to claim compensation[49] in accordance with the Liability Convention.[50] Though the damages did not reveal themselves for two years after the accident, Vesta made an initial claim for damages within one year of the accident as required under Article X(1).[51] Article X(3) allows Vesta to revise that claim up to one year after the full extent of the damage is known.[52] Upon learning of all of the damage in 2035, Vesta sought compensation well within the one-year limit imposed by Article X of the Liability Convention.

C. Ceres failed to notify Vesta of the highly dangerous nuclear payload that crashed into Botulisia and therefore should pay for the damages caused by this blatant omission.

Under principles of equity,[53] Ceres should not be allowed to skirt its responsibility to the Vestan citizens who suffered serious health and financial damage as a result of its failure to warn Vesta of the risk of radiation contamination. Ceres had a duty to warn Vesta that it faced serious harm from the nuclear engine on board the BM-52.[54] In the Corfu Channel Case, the I.C.J. held Albania responsible for damages caused to British war ships when Albania failed to warn Britain of mines located in the Corfu Strait. The Court determined that, based on their proximity to highly guarded territory, Albania should have known about the mines and therefore should have warned ships passing through the Strait.[55] Like Albania, Ceres should have known of the potential for radiation contamination because it knew the BM-52 carried a nuclear engine and should have warned Vesta of the danger.

The duty to warn of possible nuclear accidents resulting from space objects has become customary international law in the NPS Principles.[56] Customary international law develops from *opinio juris* and state practice.[57] *Opinio juris* with regard to a State's duty to warn of nuclear harm has been established by Principle 5 of the NPS Principles, which were adopted by consensus. Principle 5 states that "[a]ny State launching a space object with nuclear power sources on board shall in a timely fashion inform States concerned in the event this space object is malfunctioning with a risk of re-entry of radioactive materials to the Earth."[58] State

[44] Compromis, ¶ 13.
[45] *See* Cumulative Digest of United States Practice in International Law, 1981-88, at 237 (1989).
[46] Ceres had registered each component of the *Bo_nêmcová Miner* as well as the entire Miner. Clarifications to the Compromis, ¶ 8. Furthermore, Ceres was intimately involved in the BM-52 launch and, therefore, knew that the nuclear engine was on board when it crashed into Botulisia.
[47] Liability Convention, *supra* note 1, art X(3).
[48] Compromis, ¶ 15.
[49] Compromis, ¶ 16.
[50] Liability Convention, *supra* note 1, art. IX.
[51] The crash occurred on July 31, 2028 and Vesta sought compensation within three months after the accident. Compromis, ¶ 9, 13.
[52] *Id.*, art. X(3).

[53] Article 38 of the International Court of Justice Statutes allows the Court to decide cases based on principles of equity. Statute of the International Court of Justice, June 26, 1945, art. 38, T.S. No. 993, 3 Bevans 1179.
[54] *Corfu Channel Case*, (U.K. v. Alb.), 1949 I.C.J. 4, at 244.
[55] *Id.*
[56] *NPS Principles*, *supra* note 42.
[57] *See North Sea Continental Shelf Cases* (F.R.G. v. Den.; F.R.G. v. Neth.), 1969 I.C.J. 3; *Military and Paramilitary Activities in and Against Nicaragua* (Nicaragua v. United States of America), 1986 I.C.J. 14, 97. [hereinafter *Military Activities in Nicaragua*].
[58] *NPS Principles,*, *supra* note 42, principle 5.

practice has also developed since the NPS Principles were adopted. For example, Russian officials voluntarily warned Chile and Bolivia when the launch of the plutonium-powered Russian Mars 96 probe failed in 1996 sending the satellite's fuel into their territory.[59] Under this principle, Ceres had a responsibility to warn Vesta of the nuclear power source on board the BM-52 as soon as the mission control engineers knew the BM-52 was going to crash. Ceres at least had a duty to notify Vesta that a nuclear power source had landed in Botulisia.

Ceres must be held liable for the damages resulting from the radiation contamination, despite the original settlement, because Vesta did not agree to forego claims for future damages by accepting the settlement. Furthermore, Ceres should not be allowed to avoid the consequences of its failure to warn Vesta of the potential for radiation contamination as required under customary international law.

IV. THE DESTRUCTION OF THE VESTAN COMMUNICATIONS SYSTEM BY A SPACE-BASED LASER ON MAY 30, 2036 WAS UNLAWFUL AND ENTITLES VESTA TO COMPENSATION FROM CERES FOR THE DAMAGE SUSTAINED.

Ceres' use of a space-based laser against Vesta's communications system was a violation of both international treaty law, in the form of the United Nations Charter ("U.N. Charter") and the Outer Space Treaty, and customary international law. Such violations cannot be excused as a legitimate self-defense measure under Article 51 of the U.N. Charter or as a valid countermeasure under customary international law because the attack Ceres responded to was not perpetrated by Vesta. Ceres' actions were also unnecessary to alleviate any perceived threat presented by the communications satellite. Finally, destruction of valuable Vestan property, critical to Vestan communications systems was disproportionate to Ceres' perceived threat. Since the destruction was a direct action by the Ceresan government, Ceres is liable for the damage resulting from the satellite's destruction.

[59] *See* David L. Chandler, U.S. Said to Fumble Space Debris Alert, Boston Globe, Dec. 4, 1996, at A1. Russia also sent a note verbale to the United Nations to warn of the potential hazard. NANDASIRI JASENTULIYANA, INTERNATIONAL SPACE LAW AND THE UNITED NATIONS (1999).

A. Ceres' destruction of Vesta's communications satellite violates the U.N. Charter and the Outer Space Treaty.

Ceres' use of its space-based laser to destroy Vesta's communications satellite violates numerous obligations under international law. First, Ceres' use of force against Vestan property violates Article 2(4) of the U.N. Charter. Second, Ceres' action violated the basic principles of due regard and cooperation identified in the Outer Space Treaty as well as the Treaty's specific prohibition against stationing weapons of mass destruction in outer space.[60]

1. *Ceres violated Article 2(4) of the U.N. Charter when it used force against Vestan property without following the dispute settlement procedure established under Article 33 of the Charter.*

Ceres violated Article 2(4) of the U.N. Charter when it fired a space-based laser at Vesta's communications satellite. Article 2(4) forbids U.N. Members "from the threat or use of force against the territorial integrity or political independence of any State."[61] Ceres' attack on Vesta's satellite equates to an attack on Vesta's territorial integrity because the Vestan government owned and operated the satellite.[62] Though the satellite was located in space, Ceres' attack was equivalent to an attack on a Vestan government building or installation, and Ceres should be held responsible for violating one of the most fundamental principles in the U.N. Charter.

Article 2(4) also requires States to refrain from using force "in any other manner inconsistent with the Purposes of the United Nations."[63] Ceres engaged in a direct act of force against Vestan property in retaliation for activities over which Vesta had no control.[64] Ceres' attack directly contravenes the U.N.'s purpose established in Article 1(1) of the Charter to "bring about by peaceful means, and in conformity with the principles of justice and international law, adjustment or settlement of international disputes or situations which might lead to a breach of the

[60] Outer Space Treaty, *supra* note 1, art. IV.

[61] U.N. CHARTER art. 2, para. 4.

[62] Compromis, ¶ 18.

[63] U.N. CHARTER art. 2, para. 4.

[64] The missile that struck Salmonella was launched by an independent organization based in Vesta, but the Vestan government was unaware of the group's plans to attack Ceres, nor did the Vestan government participate in the attack. Compromis, ¶ 17.

peace."[65] By taking direct military action against Vesta's satellite without any consultation with Vesta, Ceres eliminated any opportunity to settle its dispute peacefully. Rather than directly attack Vesta's satellite, Ceres had an obligation to seek reconciliation with Vesta under Article 33 of the U.N. Charter.[66] Ceres failed to meet this obligation and, as a result, should be held liable for the destruction of the satellite.

2. *Ceres violated Article I of the Outer Space Treaty when it destroyed Vesta's communications satellite, interfering with Vesta's ability to use and explore outer space.*

Ceres violated Article I of the Outer Space Treaty when it destroyed Vesta's communications satellite. Article I of the Outer Space Treaty states that "outer space . . . shall be free for exploration and use by all States without discrimination of any kind, on a basis of equality and in accordance with international law."[67] Ceres' action against Vesta's satellite directly interfered with Vesta's ability to use and explore outer space. Communications satellites, such as the one Ceres destroyed, are integral to Vesta's developing industry. Article I is particularly applicable to the present case because it ensures that developing nations, such as Vesta, will have full opportunity to benefit from all that outer space has to offer. As indicated in the *travaux preparatoires* and the negotiating history of the Outer Space Treaty,[68] the negotiators intended to protect developing States from exactly the type of interference Ceres perpetrated on Vesta.

Such intentions were reiterated in the Declaration on International Cooperation in the Exploration and Use of Outer Space for the Benefit and in the Interest of all States, Taking into Particular Account the Needs of Developing Countries (Declaration on Use of Outer Space).[69] Article 3 of the Declaration on Use of Outer Space encourages States with developed space capabilities "to contribute to promoting and fostering international cooperation on an equitable and mutually acceptable basis" with particular attention given to the interests of developing countries.[70] As a developed nation, Ceres had a responsibility to consider the interests of Vesta, a developing nation. Instead, Ceres took advantage of its developed status to eliminate a valuable component of Vesta's industry. The goals of the Outer Space Treaty should not be undermined by a developed State's disregard for international law.

3. *Ceres violated Article IX of the Outer Space Treaty when it failed to give due regard to Vesta's interest in maintaining its communications satellite.*

Ceres' actions violated Article IX of the Space Treaty which requires Ceres to "conduct all [its] activities in outer space, including the Moon and other celestial bodies, with due regard to the corresponding interests of all other State Parties to the Treaty."[71] Vesta had an interest in maintaining its satellite in orbit for use in commercial and government endeavors. Ceres had a responsibility to respect that interest when acting in outer space, but failed to do so. As stated above, the I.C.J. recognized that a State must give consideration to the economic well being of another State,[72] which Ceres failed to do prior to destroying Vesta's satellite.

4. *Ceres' use of its space-based laser violated the strict prohibition against weapons of mass destruction in outer space established in Article IV of the Outer Space Treaty.*

Not only did Ceres ignore the general principles of respect and cooperation that are fundamental to the Outer Space Treaty, but Ceres also violated the specific prohibition against placing weapons of mass destruction into outer space established in Article IV of the Outer Space Treaty.[73] The laser Ceres used to destroy Vesta's satellite had sufficient power to exact massive amounts of damage, as shown by its ability to completely destroy a large communications satellite. Weapons of mass destruction have traditionally been defined by the amount of damage they are capable of inflicting rather than as specific categories of weapons, such as nuclear or chemical weapons.[74] Although the laser was not used against

[65] U.N. CHARTER art. 1(1).
[66] *Id.*, art. 33.
[67] Outer Space Treaty, *supra* note 1, art. I.
[68] BIN CHENG, STUDIES IN INTERNATIONAL SPACE LAW, at 234-36 (1997).
[69] G.A. Res. 122, U.N. GAOR, 51st Sess., U.N. Doc. A/RES/51/122.
[70] *Id.*

[71] Outer Space Treaty, *supra* note 1, art. IX.
[72] *Fisheries Jurisdiction Case* (U.K. v. Ice.) 1974 I.C.J 1, 26-27.
[73] Outer Space Treaty, *supra* note 1, art. IV.
[74] *See* Eilene Galloway, *International Institutions to Ensure Peaceful Uses of Outer Space*, INTERNATIONAL CO-OPERATION AND CONTROL: FROM ATOMS TO SPACE, 143, 156. The United Nations Commission for Conventional Armaments also defined weapons of mass

humans, its effect on the satellite evidences the laser's destructive capability. Ceres' decision to maintain and use a weapon capable of such power in outer space directly contravenes Article IV's prohibition against stationing weapons of mass destruction in outer space, as well as Article I and IX of the Outer Space Treaty.[75] As a result, Ceres should be held liable for such violations.

B. Ceres' action against Vesta's communications satellite cannot be excused under Article 51 of the U.N. Charter because it was not a valid form of self-defense.

Ceres' attack on Vesta's communications satellite fails to qualify as a valid self-defense measure because it did not meet the requirements established in Article 51 of the U.N. Charter, nor was it necessary and proportional to defend against the perceived threat posed by Vesta's satellite. Article 51 establishes each State's inherent right of self-defense if faced with an armed attack.[76] Upon exercise of this right, the State is required to immediately report the action to the U.N. Security Council. Ceres' actions failed to meet the definitional requirements of Article 51 when it acted without an armed attack launched by Vesta.

In addition to the requirements set out in Article 51 of the U.N. Charter, customary international law has developed to require actions in self-defense to be both necessary and proportional to the attack on the defending State.[77] Ceres' destruction of Vesta's satellite meets neither of these requirements because Ceres had a less destructive option of negotiations available and because there was no previous attack against which proportionality could be measured.

Even if Ceres had sufficient evidence to prove Vesta's satellite was being used to plan an attack, Ceres had no right to destroy it under a theory of anticipatory self-defense. Anticipatory self-defense has never been accepted as a tenet of international law and therefore cannot support Ceres' illegal actions against Vesta's property.

1. *Ceres' destruction of the communications satellite was not in response to an armed attack perpetrated by Vesta.*

In order for Ceres' attack to qualify as a legitimate self-defense measure, Ceres must have responded to an actual armed attack committed by Vesta.[78] Ceres justified its destruction of Vesta's satellite solely on its uncorroborated evidence that Vesta was using the satellite to plan an attack.[79] This justification does not establish a prior attack perpetrated by Vesta as Article 51 of the U.N. Charter requires. In Military and Paramilitary Activities in Nicaragua (Nicaragua), the United States attempted to justify financial and military support for the Nicaraguan "contras" as a collective self-defense measure authorized under Article 51 of the U.N. Charter. The I.C.J. rejected this argument, holding that the United States had not been the victim of an armed attack at the hands of Nicaragua.[80] Similarly, Ceres had not experienced an attack by the Vestan government prior to destroying Vesta's satellite, but rather relied on its own evidence that Vesta was planning an attack.

Even if Ceres had sufficient evidence that Vesta was using the satellite to plan an attack, a State cannot act against another until there is evidence of aggression against the potential victim State.[81] The purpose of the U.N. Charter as stated in Article 1 is "to take effective collective measures for the prevention and removal of threats to the peace."[82] Ceres' only evidence pointed to a *possible* attack. Ceres did not have evidence that troops were amassing or that Vesta was mobilizing weapons against Ceres.[83] Allowing States that perceive a threat to act on that evidence without consulting the U.N. or the other State would undermine the cooperative nature of the U.N. Charter. If a State were allowed to destroy another State's property based on uncorroborated evidence of a possible attack, the attacked State would never have an opportunity to prove their lack of ill intent nor would the international community have an

destruction to include "atomic explosive weapons, radioactive material weapons, lethal chemical and biological weapons, and any weapons developed in the future which have characteristics comparable in destructive effect to those of the atomic bomb or other weapons mentioned." BIN CHENG, STUDIES IN INTERNATIONAL SPACE LAW, at 530 n.23 (1997) (citing U.N. Doc. S/C.3/32/Rev.1).

[75] Outer Space Treaty, *supra* note 1, art. IV.

[76] U.N. CHARTER art. 51.

[77] *Air Services Agreement of March 1946* (U.S. v. Fr.), R.I.A.A. vol. XVIII, 417 (1979) [hereinafter *Air Services Agreement]; Military Activities in Nicaragua, supra* note 56, at 103.

[78] *Id.*

[79] Compromis, ¶ 18.

[80] *Military Activities in Nicaragua, supra* note 56, at 103.

[81] *Id.*

[82] U.N. CHARTER art. 1(1).

[83] Compromis, ¶ 18.

opportunity to pressure the offending State to change course peacefully.

The fact that Ceres had experienced a prior missile attack does not support its actions against Vesta's satellite because Vesta was not involved in the attack as the I.C.J. required in Nicaragua.[84] The I.C.J., relying on Article III of the Definition of Aggression set forth by the U.N. General Assembly,[85] held that self-defense measures can be taken only when the initial attack occurs through "the sending by or on behalf of a State of armed bands, groups, irregulars or mercenaries, which carry out acts of armed force against another State of such gravity as to amount to an actual armed attack conducted by regular forces."[86] Though Ceres claims to have evidence that Vesta provided funding to Vestan Victims of Astermine ("Astervic"), [87] the Compromis indicates that Vesta had no idea the money provided to the Better Vesta Foundation was being passed on to Astervic.[88] Ceres should not be allowed to justify an otherwise illegal attack on another State with information that cannot be corroborated. Furthermore, indirect funding provided without the knowledge of Vesta does not equate to sending armed bands on behalf of Vesta, as required in *Nicaragua*.

Ceres' destruction of the communications satellite should not be justified as self-defense because too much time had passed since the missile attack to be reasonably related to that missile attack. Ceres initially retaliated against Vesta's watchtowers and forts within two weeks after the missile struck Salmonella. It was not until four weeks after the missile attack that Ceres destroyed Vesta's communications satellite with its space-based laser.[89] A self-defense measure must be reasonably related to the original attack or States will have a license to attack a threatening State long after the original threat has dissipated. Ceres' attempt to justify its actions as self-defense is further weakened by the fact that it had already destroyed several of Vesta's watchtowers. Even if Ceres' initial attacks on the watchtowers are deemed to be legitimate self-defense measures, Ceres' attack on Vesta's communications satellite went beyond a valid self-defense measure, and Ceres should be held liable for the damage.

2. Ceres' destruction of Vesta's satellite was neither necessary nor proportional as required under customary international law.

Ceres' response to the perceived threat posed by the satellite was neither necessary nor proportional to the threat and is therefore an invalid self-defense measure. In the Air Services Agreement, the arbitration panel defined the element of necessity to include considerations of less destructive alternatives, such as negotiations. Proportionality, on the other hand, is to be determined based on any injury Ceres may have suffered as a result of Vesta's actions.[90] Vesta had not attacked Ceres prior to Ceres' destruction of the satellite nor did Ceres have any proof that any attack was imminent. Ceres should have consulted with Vesta rather than destroying Vesta's satellite. Such destruction was not necessary to protect Ceres' interests because a less harmful approach was available through diplomatic negotiations with Vesta.

Destruction of Vesta's communications satellite was also disproportionate to the perceived breach of international law. The concept of proportionality recognizes a State's need to restore equality in power between the parties in order to encourage negotiation toward a solution.[91] Ceres had yet to suffer actual harm as a result of any use of the satellite and had more than restored equality by attacking Vestan watchtowers and forts immediately after the missile attack on Salmonella.[92] By destroying the satellite without an attack by Vesta, Ceres gained a power advantage over Vesta in direct contravention of the purpose of valid self-defense. Furthermore, Ceres had not suffered any damage, yet proceeded to destroy a valuable satellite, representing an integral part of Vesta's communications infrastructure and developing industry. As a result, Ceres cannot be excused from liability for the damage caused to Vesta's communications infrastructure and economic well-being.

---

[84] *Military Activities in Nicaragua, supra* note 56, at 103. *See also Case Concerning the Gabcikovo-Nagymaros Project* (Hungary v. Slovakia), 1997 I.C.J. 7 (stating internationally illegal actions can be justified "if taken in response to a previous international wrongful act of another State and must be directed against that State.").

[85] *Military Activities in Nicaragua, supra* note 56, at 103 (citing G.A. Res. 3314).

[86] *Id.*

[87] The Compromis states, "There was evidence (*available to the Ceresan Government*) that Vesta may have been indirectly financing the operations of the group." Compromis, ¶ 17 (emphasis added).

[88] Clarifications to the Compromis, ¶ 13.

[89] *Id.*

[90] *Air Services Agreement, supra* note 76, at 443-36.

[91] *Id.*

[92] Compromis, ¶ 18.

3. *Ceres' actions cannot be justified under the invalid concept of anticipatory self-defense.*

Ceres' destruction of Vesta's satellite cannot be excused as anticipatory self-defense because such a concept is not an element of international law. Neither *opinio juris* nor State practice has developed to establish anticipatory self-defense as customary international law. *Opinio juris* cannot exist as acts of preemptive self-help have been summarily rejected by the I.C.J. In the Corfu Channel Case, the I.C.J. condemned Britain's attempt to sweep the mines laid in the Corfu Strait over Albania's objections, stating that respect for territorial sovereignty is an essential foundation of international relations.[93]

Similarly State practice has not developed sufficiently to establish customary international law. Although the United States and Israel[94] has launched attacks under the auspices of anticipatory self-defense, the acts of a few States does not create customary international law. As the I.C.J. stated in the Fisheries Case, when certain States adopt a practice while others disagree, such practice does not rise to the level of international law.[95] As a result, Ceres cannot claim that its attack on Vesta's communications satellite was lawful as a preemptive strike designed to ward off a future attack from Vesta. Such unprovoked acts of force directly contravenes the basic principles of the U.N. Charter and should not be sanctioned in this situation.

Ceres' failure to meet the requirements of a valid self-defense measure as established in Article 51 of the U.N. Charter and developed through customary international law, bars it from justifying destruction of Vesta's satellite. Ceres' actions were a direct use of aggression without Vesta's provocation, and as a result, Ceres should be held responsible for Vesta's losses.

C. Ceres' action against Vesta's communications satellite was not a legitimate countermeasure under customary international law.

Ceres' destruction of Vesta's communications satellite constitutes an invalid countermeasure because it represented an irreversible use of force[96] and was not preceded by an effort to negotiate.[97] Countermeasures are intended to restore equality between the parties to a dispute as a means of encouraging negotiation. In order to facilitate such use, countermeasures must be reversible and must be suspended as soon as the original violation has ended.[98] They are similarly limited by necessity and proportionality.[99] Ceres' use of its space-based laser created irreversible damage to Vesta and should not release Ceres from liability. Furthermore, Ceres failed to contact Vesta prior to use of the laser, thereby undermining the process of peaceful negotiations encouraged by the concept of countermeasures. Such failure, in combination with the disproportionate and unnecessary nature of Ceres' action, bars Ceres from justifying its destruction of Vesta's satellite as a legitimate countermeasure.

D. Ceres must compensate Vesta for the destroyed satellite under Article III of the Liability Convention.

Article III of the Liability Convention establishes a system of fault-based liability under which Ceres is required to compensate Vesta for the loss of its satellite.[100] Where damage is caused "elsewhere than on the surface of the Earth to a space object of one launching State . . . by a space object of another launching State, the latter shall be liable only if the damage is due to its fault."[101] Ceres, as the launching State for the space-based laser, is liable for the damage caused to Vesta's satellite. Ceres has admitted firing the laser at the satellite and is therefore directly at fault for the damage caused.[102]

V. CERES HAS VIOLATED THE OUTER SPACE TREATY BY MINING AND CAPTURING THE BOZNÊMCOVÁ ASTEROID.

[93] *Corfu Channel Case*, (U.K. v. Alb.), 1949 I.C.J. 4, at 244.

[94] In 1956, Israel invaded the Egyptian Sinai Peninsula claiming fear of an imminent Egyptian attack. The United States similarly argued the need to preempt a possible terrorist attack originating in Afghanistan as a reason for invading the country in 2001.

[95] *Fisheries Jurisdiction Case* (U.K. v. Nor.) 1974 I.C.J. 1.

[96] *See* Draft Articles on Responsibility of State for Internationally Wrongful Acts, G.A.O.R., 56th Sess., Supp. No. 10, U.N. Doc. A/56/10, art. 49 [hereinafter *Draft Articles*].

[97] *Gabcikovo-Nagymaros*, *supra* note 83, at 7

[98] *Draft Articles*, *supra* note 93, art. 49.

[99] *Gabcikovo-Nagymaros*, *supra* note 83, at 7.

[100] Liability Convention, *supra* note 1, art. III.

[101] *Id.*

[102] Compromis, ¶ 18.

Ceres, through the actions of Astermine, has violated Articles I, II and IX of the Outer Space Treaty by removing the Boznêmcová asteroid from available use to any other State. Such unilateral appropriation of a celestial body contravenes the fundamental tenet of cooperation upon which the Treaty is based. Ceres further threatened the safety of those occupying Earth by introducing extraterrestrial material into Earth's atmosphere without first determining the safety of such an endeavor. Such disregard for the economic and safety interests of other States must be discouraged, and therefore Ceres must be held responsible for its violations of international treaty law.

A. Ceres violated the express prohibition against appropriation outlined in Article II of the Outer Space Treaty by appropriating the Boznêmcová asteroid.

Ceres violated Article II of the Outer Space Treaty, first, by mining the asteroid and, second, by capturing the asteroid for complete exploitation. Article II states that "outer space, including the Moon and other celestial bodies, is not subject to national appropriation . . . by means of use or occupation."[103] The *Miner*'s initial mining of Boznêmcová qualifies as appropriation by use in violation of Article II.

The Boznêmcová asteroid is a celestial body that cannot legally be appropriated by use. The asteroid is a celestial body first because its size and fixed orbit through the solar system equate more to a body such as the Moon rather than specks of dust and rock floating in space.[104] Furthermore, this asteroid is not equivalent to easily controlled movable property as shown by Astermine's need to mine the asteroid down to a manageable size prior to moving it into Earth's atmosphere.[105] Astermine used the asteroid for its own benefit by extracting significant portions of the asteroid for use on Earth. By removing such large amounts of the asteroid, Astermine made the asteroid worthless to any other State.

Astermine further appropriated the asteroid by moving it into Earth orbit in order to more thoroughly exploit it.[106] Even if mining some material from a celestial body is found reasonable, the complete removal of such a celestial body from its orbit clearly violates Article II of the Outer Space Treaty. By moving the asteroid into Earth orbit, Astermine removed the celestial body from use by any other State. Such complete appropriation flouts the Outer Space Treaty's primary purpose to maintain outer space, including the Moon and other celestial bodies, "free for exploration and use by all States without discrimination of any kind, on a basis of equality."[107]

B. Ceres' appropriation ignored the principle of equal access to outer space expressed in Article I of the Outer Space Treaty.

By appropriating the Boznêmcová asteroid, Ceres also violated Article I of the Outer Space Treaty, which designates outer space, including the Moon and all celestial bodies as the "province of mankind." Article I requires that all exploration should be "carried out for the benefit and in the interests of all countries, irrespective of their degree of economic or scientific development."[108] This language creates an international obligation on the part of technologically advanced States, such as Ceres, to ensure that less developed States, such as Vesta, can partake of the wealth outer space has to offer. These obligations do not require States to share all material that is removed from outer space,[109] but the principle of equality expressed in the Outer Space Treaty implies that Ceres should have at least notified other States of Boznêmcová's valuable mining potential rather than destroying the asteroid after extracting all of the valuable minerals. Furthermore, Ceres had an obligation to preserve some portion of the asteroid for use by other States.

C. Ceres violated Article IX of the Outer Space Treaty by introducing extraterrestrial material into Earth's environment and by leaving asteroid fragments in orbit to interfere with Vesta's satellite capabilities.

The first stage of mining, during which canisters containing mined material were fired down to Earth,[110] violated Article IX of the Outer Space Treaty because Astermine performed only

---

[103] Outer Space Treaty, *supra* note 1, art. II.
[104] Virgiliu Pop, *A Celestial Body is a Celestial Body is a Celestial Body . . .*, PROCEEDINGS OF THE FORTY-FOURTH COLLOQUIUM ON THE LAW OF OUTER SPACE, 100, 105 (2001).
[105] Compromis, ¶ 19.
[106] Compromis, ¶ 19.
[107] Outer Space Treaty, *supra* note 1, art. I.
[108] *Id.*
[109] N. Jasentuliyana, *Article I of the* Outer Space Treaty *Revisited*, 17 J. SPACE LAW 129, 139-40 (1989).
[110] Compromis, ¶ 19.

preliminary processing on the extracted ore prior to introducing it into Earth's environment, and Ceres failed to apply appropriate measures to avoid contamination of the environment.[111] Such limited processing could not ensure that the canisters were free of materials that would contaminate the environment. Ceres' disregard for the integrity of Earth's environment was a violation of Article IX of the Outer Space Treaty.

Mining of the asteroid not only barred access to the asteroid but also left fragments of the asteroid in Earth orbit causing interference to Vestan satellite transmissions, increased costs of shielding future satellites and reduced satellite viability.[112] This aspect of the Ceresan mining effort violated Article IX in that the State responsible for space activities is required to undertake international consultations before proceeding with an activity the State knows will interfere with the outer space activities of another State.[113] Ceres, as the State responsible for authorizing and supervising the *Miner*'s activities, should have known that the project would result in debris that would ultimately interfere with Vesta's satellite transmissions.

Vesta could not have requested consultation under Article IX because Astermine, under the control of Ceres, did not publish its plans to mine Boznêmcová as required under Article XI of the Outer Space Treaty. Article XI requires States conducting activities in outer space to inform the Secretary-General of the United Nations, the public, and the scientific community of the nature, conduct, locations and results of such activities.[114] Although Astermine published the results of the *Tombaugh* probe in scientific e-journals and made them available on NASRA's and Astermine's web sites, Ceres failed to inform the U.N. of its plans to mine and ultimately capture the entire Boznêmcová asteroid.[115] Furthermore, greater effort should have been made to alert the public, particularly other States that might be affected, of the plan to destroy the asteroid. Astermine's destruction of the asteroid violated the basic principles of freedom to explore and access to the wealth outer space has to offer. Because Ceres was in the best position to control Astermine, Ceres should be held responsible for all of the treaty violations that resulted from Astermine's mining and ultimate destruction of the Boznêmcová asteroid.

VI. THE CONTINUING PRESENCE OF VESTAN DEFENSE FACILITIES IN NEW VESTA IS LEGAL.

Vesta's decision to maintain military facilities on the Moon does not violate international law because Vesta has a right to defend against Ceres' aggressive actions which continue to threaten Vesta. As a result, Vesta's facilities on the Moon do not violate international law.

A. Vesta had a right to defend itself against Ceres' aggression under Article 51 of the U.N. Charter.

Vesta's facilities on the Moon represent a valid self-defense measure in response to Ceres' repeated attacks. As described above, a valid self-defense measure must respond to an attack by another State; it must be necessary and proportional to the original attack and the defending State must alert the U.N. Security Council immediately after acting.[116] Vesta had been repeatedly attacked by Ceres prior to erecting its facilities on the Moon. The fact that a peace settlement was brokered did not reduce the potential threat arising from Ceres' space-based laser.[117] Furthermore, the facilities were necessary to protect New Vesta from possible attack as Ceres had shown its willingness to act aggressively in space.[118] The facilities also represent a proportionate response because they did not damage any Ceresan property unlike Ceres' actions against Vesta's watchtowers and communications satellite. Though the Compromis is silent on Vesta's notification, the fact that a peace deal was ultimately brokered indicates that the U.N. learned of the facilities soon after they were constructed.

B. Ceres cannot challenge any perceived violation of the Moon Treaty because Ceres is not a party to that agreement.

Article 34 of the Vienna Convention on Treaties specifically states that "[a] treaty does not

[111] Compromis, ¶ 19.
[112] Compromis, ¶ 20.
[113] Outer Space Treaty, *supra* note 1, art. IX.
[114] *Id.*, art. XI.
[115] Compromis, ¶ 6.

[116] U.N. CHARTER art. 51; *Military Activities in Nicaragua*, *supra* note 56, at 103.
[117] The Ceresan military maintained control over space-based laser. Clarifications to the Compromis, ¶ 5.
[118] Ceres had previously attacked Vesta's communications satellite with its space-based laser. Compromis, ¶ 18.

create either obligations or rights for a third State without its consent."[119] Ceres has never signed the Agreement Governing the Activities of States on the Moon and Other Celestial Bodies[120] and, under Article 34, has no right to challenge a perceived violation of that treaty.

VII. Conclusion

For the foregoing reasons, Vesta requests this Honorable Court to find Ceres liable for the medical costs associated with the 745 Vestans who developed cancer from radiation poisoning, the cost Vesta expended to clean up the radiation, the loss in property value caused by the radiation and the economic recession resulting from the business disruption caused by the radiation. Furthermore, Vesta requests Ceres be made to compensate Vesta for loss of its communications satellite and be held responsible for violating the Outer Space Treaty when it destroyed the Boznêmcová asteroid.

SUBMISSIONS TO THE COURT

For the foregoing reasons, the Government of Vesta, Applicant respectfully requests the Court to adjudge and declare that:

1. Ceres is liable to compensate Vesta for the health damage, clean up costs, lost property value and economic recession caused by the radiation leaked from the BM-52 crash.
2. Ceres violated international law when it destroyed Vesta's communications satellite with a space-based laser and must be made to compensate Vesta for that loss.
3. Ceres also violated international law when it mined and ultimately destroyed the Boznêmcová asteroid.
4. Vesta is not violating international law by maintaining defensive facilities on the Moon.

---

119 *Vienna Convention on Treaties*., art. 34.

120 Agreement Governing the Activities of States on the Moon and Other Celestial Bodies, G.A. Res. 34/68, U.N. Doc. A/RES/34/68; Compromis, ¶ 25.

B. WRITTEN BRIEF FOR CERES

AGENTS:

Jesse Wilson and Isaac Hikaka, University of Auckland, New Zealand

ARGUMENT:

I. INTRODUCTION

This case concerns a dispute between Ceres and Vesta with respect to five issues. First, there is a dispute as to whether Ceres is absolutely liable to Vesta in relation to the launch failure of the BM-52 in light of the twin facts that a Vestan facility was involved in the launch and that gross negligence by Vestan nationals caused the crash. Second, a dispute has arisen as to whether liability in relation to the crash has been extinguished by the settlement agreement of 14 November 2028. Third, this Court must determine whether consequent economic losses incurred throughout a national economy over a three-year period is a recoverable head of damage. Fourth, the question of whether the respondent properly exercised the inherent right to anticipatory self-defence in the face of a threat of attack must be addressed. Finally, this Court must determine whether the presence of military bases on the Moon is in violation of the clear words of the Outer Space Treaty. Ceres seeks a declaration ordering the removal of the lunar military installations and argues that all relief sought by the applicant must be denied. The Principality of Ceres respectfully submits to the Court's findings in this matter.

II. CERES IS NOT LIABLE TO VESTA FOR DAMAGE CAUSED BY THE LAUNCH FAILURE OF THE BM-52

Ceres submits that, given the absence of fault on its part, the only course of action by which Vesta might hold Ceres responsible is to argue that Ceres is absolutely liable for any damage caused by the launch failure of the BM-52. Ceres properly acknowledges that it is a launching state for the purposes of the Liability Convention. [1] However, Ceres submits that it is not liable to Vesta for damage caused by the launch failure of the BM-52. Liability is denied on two independent bases. First on the basis that Vesta was a joint launching state of the BM-52 and second, even if Vesta is not a launching state, Ceres is exonerated from liability because the damage resulted from gross negligence by Vestan nationals.

A. Vesta is also a launching state of the BM-52

Ceres submits that both itself and Vesta were launching states of the Boznemcova Miner. It further submits that one launching state in a joint launch cannot hold a fellow launching state in the same launch absolutely liable. Furthermore, since Vesta is a launching state it cannot make a claim for damages under the Liability Convention.

Vesta qualifies as a launching state of the BM-52 for two independent reasons. First, under Article 1(c)(2) of the Liability Convention it is a state from whose facility a space object is launched.[2] The ground control facility for the BM-52 launch was situated in Vesta. On the basis that this facility controlled all aspects of the launch of the BM-52, the facility was so fundamental that it was a launch facility for the purposes of the Liability Convention. The operation of the facility in Vesta caused the space object to take off in Ceres. Without it the launch would not have been able to be undertaken. The centrality of this facility to the launch process is evidenced by the impossibility of Astermine continuing its launch programme after occupation by Vestan troops of the facility until Astermine reopened an equivalent facility. It is indeed common that a launch facility and a ground control facility are geographically distant and on a proper construction of the Liability Convention both are launch facilities.[3] The facility is connected to Vesta by the fact that is situated within Vestan territory and Vesta exercises jurisdiction over the facility.

Second, Vesta procured the launching of a space object under article 1(c)(i) of the Liability Convention. Procure means to bring about, by paying for a launch or otherwise making it happen.[4] Ceres submits that the provision of the ground control facility was an act of procurement. The facility was situated in Vesta and staffed exclusively by Vestan nationals. The sole purpose

---

[1] Convention on International Liability for Damage Caused by Space Objects, *entered into force* Oct 9, 1973 24 U.S.T. 2389, T.I.A.S No.7762 (hereinafter the "Liability Convention").

[2] Liability Convention, *supra* note 1, Article 1(c)(2).

[3] See for example the US space programme, which has its launch facility in Florida but its ground control facility in Texas.

[4] K.H. Bockstiegel, "The Term "Launching State" in International Space Law" (1994) 37 Proc. Colloq. L. Outer Sp. 80. Stephen E. Doyle, "Legal Aspects of International Competition in Provision of Launch Services" (1987) 30 Proc. Colloq. L. Outer Sp. 203.

of the facility was to effect space launches. Ceres submits that as Vesta exercised control and jurisdiction over a facility that had the sole purpose of effecting space launches, Vesta brought about any launches controlled by this facility and thus has procured the launches.

Third, Vestan nationals procured the launch of the space object. Prior to the submergence of the Federal Islands of Boranatu, Astermine Aerospace Incorporated was a legal person by reason of its incorporation in that state.[5] A corporation exists by reason of the imprimatur of a state. As recognised by the US appellate decision in *Matimak Trading v Khalily*, "a stateless corporation is an oxymoron".[6] The non-existence of the state of incorporation means that Astermine no longer enjoys the protection of the corporate veil.[7] Accordingly it is proper for this Court to take account of the ownership interests of Vestan nationals and their responsibility for procuring the launch.

Under the Liability Convention Vesta is therefore a launching state.[8] Furthermore, Vesta is deemed by Article V(3) to be a participant in a joint launch, which states that:

> "3. A State from whose territory or facility whose space object is launched shall be regarded as a participant in a joint launching."[9]

The fact that the instrument of registration does not specify Vesta as a launching state is immaterial for two reasons. First, the instrument of registration is not the authoritative mechanism for assigning status as a launching state. The determination of which state or states were launching states must be made primarily in accordance with the relevant provisions of the Liability Convention. Second, Article II(2) of the Registration Convention[10] acknowledges that where there are two or more launching states only one launching state is required to register the space object.

Having established that Vesta and Ceres are both launching states of the BM-52, Vesta may not seek to hold Ceres absolutely liable for damage caused by the failure of the launch under Article II of the Convention. Article II contemplates absolutely liability in cases of damage by a launching state to an unconnected state. Article V and Article VII rebut any suggestion that one launching state can impose absolute liability on another launching state.[11] As a starting point, both participants in a joint launch are jointly and severally liable for any damage resulting from the launch.[12] They may conclude an agreement apportioning liability between themselves before the launch,[13] however no such agreement was concluded by Vesta and Ceres.

Moreover, compensation under the Liability Convention for damage caused to the nationals of a launching state is barred by Article VII. If Vesta is a launching state then it follows that Vesta cannot claim compensation on behalf of its nationals under the Liability Convention.[14] Citizens are expected to claim compensation through domestic mechanisms. This might involve either litigation in the domestic justice system or reliance on insurance arrangements as between the government and the commercial launch parties.[15]

B. Ceres is exonerated from absolute liability

If this Court were to hold that Vesta was not a launching state of the BM-52, Ceres would nevertheless be exonerated from absolute liability under Article VI of the Liability Convention. Article VI provides that a state may be exonerated from absolute liability where the damage was caused wholly or partly by the gross negligence or deliberate act of the claimant State or any persons it represents. Ceres argues that the provision of incorrect flight coordinates by Vestan Airspace Command was a causative factor leading to the crash and was the causative factor which led the BM-52 to crash into a highly populated city. This was an act of gross negligence.

Given that the term "gross negligence" is not defined in the Liability Convention, it is necessary to approach the issue by reference to principles of tort law as they have evolved in

[5] *Barcelona Traction, Light and Power Company Limited Case (Belgium v. Spain) (Second Phase)* (1970) I.C.J. Rep. 3.

[6] especially *Matimak Trading Co. v. Khalily* 118 F.3d 76 (2d Cir. 1997), *cert. denied* 118 S. Ct. 883 (1998).

[7] Mark Baker "Lost in the Judicial Wilderness: The Stateless Corporation After Matimak Trading" 19 Nw. J. Int'l L. & Bus. 130.

[8] Liability Convention, *supra* note 1, Article 1(c)(ii)

[9] Liability Convention, *supra* note 1, Article V(3).

[10] Convention on Registration of Objects Launched in Outer Space, Jan 14, 1975, 28 U.S.T. 695, T.I.A.S. 8480, 1023 U.N.T.S. 15 (hereinafter the "Registration Convention").

[11] Liability Convention, *supra* note 1, Articles V and VII.

[12] Liability Convention, *supra* note 1, ArticleV(1).

[13] Liability Convention, *supra* note 1, Article V(2).

[14] Liabilty Convention, *supra* note 1, Article VII(a).

[15] Background Paper for the United Nations Committee on the Peaceful Uses of Outer Space, *Review of the Concept of the 'Launching State'* A/AC 105/768, 21 January 2002.

various national jurisdictions.[16] In both common law and civil law[17] traditions, gross negligence or *culpa lata* (in the Roman Law tradition) is distinguished from negligence simpliciter by the element of outrageousness that is associated with gross negligence.

In *McLaren Transport v Somerville*, Tipping J framed the test as being whether 'the level of negligence is so high that it amounts to an outrageous and flagrant disregard for the plaintiff's safety.'[18] This test is an objective one, as explained by Salmon LJ in *Herrington's* case:

"In my opinion a construction [which defines gross negligence as] acts or omissions which the [person] either knows of but chooses to disregard or which ought to be so obvious to the ordinary man as to be inescapable is a proper one."[19]

The approach of Megaw J, considering the issue in the context of a shipping contract, rejected a subjective test of negligence, saying that:

> "Gross carelessness ... [is] is the doing of something which in fact involves a risk, *whether the doer realises it or not*; and the risk being such, having regard to all the circumstances, that the taking of that risk would be described in ordinary parlance as reckless.... If the risk is great, and the probable damage great, recklessness may readily be a fair description, however much the doer may regard the action as justified and reasonable.... The only test, in my view, is an objective one."[20] [Original emphasis]

Also, malicious intent is not properly a requirement for the test of gross negligence. Article VI(1) of the Liability Convention already covers acts done with malicious intent through the use of the words 'from an act or omission done with intent to cause damage.' Were the Court to hold that a malicious intent was required to satisfy the test of gross negligence under the Liability Convention then they would be causing a part of article VI to have no effect.

The amount of property at stake is a key factor in assessing the reasonableness or otherwise of a person's conduct, as has being acknowledged by Kirby P in *Legal & General Insurance Australia Ltd v Eather*:

"What is a 'reasonable precaution' ... will depend upon the circumstances. The greater the value of the property at risk of loss, the greater will be the obligation to take stringent precautions. The greater the foreseeable risk of a loss occurring in the circumstances, the greater will be the obligation to take precautions. The greater the possibility of precautions being take, the more readily will a court infer that they ought to have been taken."[21]

Applying these principles to the present case, there is a strong basis for holding that the damage resulted from gross negligence on the part of Vestan Airspace Command for three reasons. The function of an airspace command is to provide flight path coordinates that ensure aircraft are routed in such a manner that the potential for damage is minimised. The Vestan Airspace Command however, gave coordinates that in fact resulted in the greatest possible amount of damage being caused. But for these incorrect coordinates the BM-52 would not have plummeted into Botulisia. It is submitted that this negligence, fundamentally breaching the duty of the airspace command, is gross negligence and not mere negligence simpliciter. The extraordinary gravity of the risk is such that the Court can readily hold that it was reasonable to take stringent precautions. No such precautions were evident and no satisfactory explanation of the incident has been forthcoming form Vestan Airspace Command. It appears from the findings of the enquiry that had access to all the relevant evidence and the cooperation of Astermine the reason for the failure was human error. The absence of back-up measures in the event of human error suggests further systemic failures on the part of Vestan Airspace Command. In other words it was grossly negligent to design a command system for space launches which was so susceptible to human error and which provided no checks on such an eventuality. Despite the serious nature of space launches, the Vestan Airspace Command took an irresponsible approach towards ensuring the safe launch of the space object. Its failures are outrageous and as such constitute gross negligence. Therefore Ceres submits that it should be exonerated from absolute liability due to the fact that the damage resulted from the gross negligence of Vestan nationals.

III. THE SETTLEMENT OF 14 NOVEMBER 2028 FULLY EXTINGUISHED

[16] Marc Firestone, *Problems in the Relations of Disputes Concerning Damage Caused in Outer Space*, 59, TUL. L. REV. 747 (1985), p.761

[17] Daniel Howard "An Analysis of Gross Negligence" 37 Marq. L. Rev. 334, 337 (1953-1954).

[18] [1996] 3 NZLR 424

[19] [1971] 2 QB 107, 125; [1971] 1 All ER 897, 906

[20] *Shawinigan Ltd v Vokins & Co Ltd* [1961] 1 WLR 1206, 1214; [1961] 3 All ER 396, 403

[21] (1986) ANZ Insurance Cases, 60,749, 74,506

ANY CERESAN LIABILTY TO VESTA IN RELATION TO THE LAUNCH FAILURE OF THE BM-52

Ceres submits that even if it were liable to Vesta in relation to the failure of the BM-52, any such liability was fully extinguished by the settlement of 14 November 2028 (hereafter "the settlement"). Both Vesta and Ceres are bound to fulfil in good faith their obligations under this settlement therefore the Vestan claim is inadmissible.

A. The settlement is binding at international law

The "full and final settlement" is a treaty concluded between the two states. The requirement that the duly authorised agreement be in writing is satisfied on the facts before the Court.[22] The respective foreign ministries of both states negotiated the agreement.[23] The settlement is a treaty under Article 26 Vienna Convention on the Interpretation of Treaties.[24] The principle of *pacta sunt servanda* requires that agreements are to be observed.[25] Article 26 of the Vienna Convention provides that, 'every treaty in force is binding upon the parties to it and must be performed in good faith.'[26] The settlement was a bilateral treaty between Ceres and Vesta. In exchange for compromising its claim Vesta received a payment of monetary compensation which was fixed by negotiations between the parties. In exchange Ceres received the recovered wreckage and components of the BM-52 and an agreement in good faith that liability had been extinguished as between the parties. The treaty remains in force for the benefit and burden of both parties. Vesta cannot resile from the treaty and claim compensation in respect of the BM-52 crash.

In respect of the settlement's coverage of the damage, Ceres submits that the scope of the settlement and the scope of the Liability Convention are coextensive. The scope of the settlement relates to "any claim by Vesta for damage to persons killed or injured by the incident as well as for damage to buildings and property." Claims for the injuries suffered by its nationals as a result of radiation and damage to properties and buildings caused by the crash are covered by the clear terms of the settlement itself. Should Vesta attempt to bypass the terms of the settlement by reframing its claim, for instance as a claim for pure economic loss, then the heads of damage will fall outside the ambit of Article I as discussed below under submission III. All 'damage' allowed under the Liability Convention is provided for by the settlement. Accordingly, any damage which falls outside the terms of the settlement must be outside the Liability Convention.

B. The settlement is not invalidated by error or fraud

The settlement is not vitiated by reason of error. If Vesta were to assert that an error vitiated Vesta's consent to the settlement, Ceres submits that such an argument is misconceived for two reasons. First, Vesta assumed the risk that its assumptions as to the gravity of the damage might prove erroneous. Second, there is no mistake in the treaty. The treaty simply provides for a payment to extinguish claims that may arise from the incident. Third, during the four-month period between the date of the crash and the settlement, Vesta ought reasonably to have been expected to diligently investigate the crash in order to determine its nature, gravity and consequences. It is noteworthy that Vesta had exclusive possession of the recovered wreckage and components of the BM-52 during this period. Vestan troops were also in occupation of the launch facility. Furthermore, Ceres and Astermine provided full cooperation with Vestan government investigations. Vesta was therefore the best placed to make an estimate on the amount and type of damage and negotiate accordingly. It is not now open for Vesta to resile from the settlement by invoking its own lack of diligence as an invalidating factor.[27] Also, any claim put forward by Vesta that the settlement is vitiated by fraud is without merit. It is common ground between the parties that Ceres did not know that the BM-52 was carrying a nuclear payload.[28]

C. Any claim would be time-barred

Ceres rejects any suggestion that Vesta was entitled under Article X of the Liability Convention to revise its claim to take account of new

[22] Manfred Lachs Space Law Moot Court Competition 2003, Statement of Facts, p.2 §16.

[23] Manfred Lachs Space Law Moot Court Competition 2003, Additional Facts, p.1 §1.

[24] UN Charter Article 33, Vienna Convention on the Law of Treaties Between States and International Organisations or Between International Organisations, Article 26, *opened for signature* May 23 1969, U.N. Doc. A/Conf.39/27, 8 L.L.M.629.

[25] Vienna Convention, *supra* note 22, Article 26.

[26] *Id.*

[27] Temple of Preah Vihear 1961 ICJ.

[28] Manfred Lachs Space Law Moot Court Competition 2003, Additional Facts, p.1 §7.

information after the claim had been settled on 14 November 2028. Ceres submits, first, that Article X does not allow revision after a settlement has been finalised. Article X(2) states:

> "If, however, a State does not know of the occurrence of the damage or has not been able to identify the launching State which is liable, it may present a claim within one year following the date on which it learned of the aforementioned facts; however, this period shall in no event exceed one year following the date on which the State could reasonably be expected to have learned of the facts through the exercise of due diligence".[29]

This provision plainly envisages a situation in which a claim has not been submitted within the limitation period due to the fact that the damage or other essential facts were not reasonably discoverable by stipulating that the limitation period runs from the date of reasonable discoverability. It does not allow a final settlement to be reopened on the basis that one state has discovered information that has ratcheted up the amount of reparations. That would be contrary to the essential nature of a settlement agreement. Vesta assumed the risk of greater damage being discovered in exchange for a prompt payment of compensation and avoiding the risks associated with pursuing a contestable legal claim.

In any event, Article X(2) does not apply in this case because a diligent investigation on the part of Vesta would have discovered the radioactive contamination of the crash site. The applicable question is on what date did the damage become reasonably discoverable? Ceres submits that several factors suggest that a prudent state would have discovered the damage more than one year prior to 29 October 2035 when Vesta presented its fresh claim to Ceres. First, Astermine had fully cooperated with the Vestan government investigation. In the absence of any suggestion that Astermine mislead the Vestan authorities, it is proper to conclude that Vesta had the opportunity to discover the radiation damage. Second, Vesta was in the best position of the parties to determine the extent of the damage. Vesta retained possession of the recovered wreckage and components of the space object as well as occupying the launch facility. They had detained the staff of the facility who would have been able to assist the Vestan authorities in their inquiries. Third, in the event of such a major accident involving the launch failure of a space object, any reasonable state would have checked the crash site for traces of radioactivity. The failure to take such an obvious and presumably straightforward measure suggests that Vesta was not sufficiently diligent to entitle it to rely on Article X(2)

IV. THE HEADS OF DAMAGE CLAIMED BY VESTA ARE NOT RECOVERABLE

Vesta seeks to recover for consequent economic loss suffered as a result of the crash of the BM-52. Ceres submits that consequent economic loss is not recoverable under the Liability Convention.

Article I(a) of the Liability Convention provides that:

> "The term 'damage' means loss of life, personal injury or other impairment of health; or loss of or damage to property of States or of persons, natural or juridical, or property of international intergovernmental organisations;"[30]

Ceres submits that consequent economic loss is neither damage to persons nor damage to property. Rather, the damage that Vesta alleges, namely the fall in property prices and the subsequent economic recession, is damage that does not exist in any physical or moral sense but is damage only to an intangible economic position.[31] The Liability Convention is clear in that the damage must be suffered by either a person or property of a state or international intergovernmental organisation.[32] The consequent economic loss Vesta is seeking to claim for is more properly described as being 'pure economic loss' as the harm is caused to an economic interest well removed from the physical damage. Therefore it is a type of damage not recoverable under the Liability Convention.

Furthermore, the damage in the recession in the Vestan economy, whilst linked to the crash, was also influenced by a variety of other factors. Given the dynamism and unpredictability of an economy it is wholly speculative to attempt to assess what, if any, profits may have been made from the multitude of transactions and exchanges in the Vestan economy.[33] In order to claim compensation for damage, there "must be a causal link between

---

[29] Liability Convention, *supra* note 1, Article X(2).

[30] Liability Convention, *supra* note 1, Article I(a).

[31] David P. Lewis, "The Limits of Liability: Can Alaskan Oil Spill Victims Recover Pure Economic Loss" 10 Alaska L. Rev. 87 (1993).

[32] Liability Convention, *supra* note 1, Article I(a)

[33] *McCrae v Commonwealth Disposals Commission* (1951) 84 CLR 377.

the unlawful act and the damage for which compensation is claimed."[34] The Vestan government's counter-productive response to the crisis illustrates this point. The stigmatisation of ethnic Boranatuans and Ceresans by Vesta led to widespread violence and property damage against those groups.[35] Vesta also provocatively used military forces to occupy private facilities and irresponsibly alleged that the crash was the result of Boranatuan terrorism.[36] These actions must have exacerbated the recession by increasing economic instability and lowering investor confidence. Attribution of the consequent economic loss solely to the crash would be fallacious because it ignores the other factors that have played a part in leading to the loss. If the Court were to allow Vesta to recover for the consequent economic loss they would be inequitably burdening Ceres by forcing upon them to pay for indirect damage.

Finally, allowing recovery for consequent economic losses as to do so would floodgates to indeterminate liability.[37] The requirement that only physical or moral damage is recoverable is a valuable control device that ought to remain in place for policy reasons. The fact that the state parties did not specifically include economic loss as a category in Article I provides a sound reason to respect their policy decision.[38] Should the Court allow Vesta to recover for the consequent economic loss it has suffered, it would impose upon launching states a liability virtually unrestricted in scope. For instance, other states that suffered economic loss as a flow-on consequence of damage to the Vestan economy might also have a potential claim. In an inter-dependent global economy, the consequences would be extraordinary. At the least, indemnity insurance premiums would rise substantially and this would impose massive costs on private space actors and the market actors that utilise their services. Ceres submits that expanding liability beyond the limited categories in Article I would create indeterminacy.[39]

[34] *Lafico and Burundi* 96 ILR 279 (1994) 323.
[35] Manfred Lachs Space Law Moot Court Competition 2003, Statement of Facts, p.2 §11.
[36] *Id.*
[37] Lakshman Guruswamy, Sir Geoffrey Palmer et al, *International Environmental Law and World* Order, (St. Paul, Minnesota, West Group, 1999), p.651.
[38] *Travaux preparatoires* of the Liability Convention, A/AC.105/C.2/SR.118.
[39] *Ultramares Corp v Touche Niven & Company*, 255 N.Y. 17 (1931).

V. CERES DID NOT VIOLATE INTERNATIONAL LAW IN RELATION TO THE DESTRUC-TION OF BOZNEMCOVA

Ceres submits that the destruction of the Boznemcova was not contrary to international law. Ceres does not dispute that it had jurisdiction over and is internationally liable for the activities of the Boznemcova Miner.

A. The Respondent is not bound by the Moon Treaty or any principles therein

Ceres submits that this issue must be determined under the Outer Space Treaty and customary international law. Ceres cannot be bound by the terms of the Moon Treaty because it is not a state party due to the principle of *pacta tertiis nec nocent nec prosunt*.[40] The principles of the Moon Treaty, such as the Common Heritage of Mankind, could not be said to form part of customary international law because neither state practice nor *opinio juris* can be proven.[41] In particular the leading space powers have not accepted the principle of the Common Heritage of Mankind as being a binding customary norm.[42]

B. The mining activities were not contrary to the interests of mankind

The use of outer space and its resources is allowed under international law subject to certain requirements. Article I of the Outer Space Treaty[43] affirms that, 'outer space, including the moon and other celestial bodies, shall be free for exploration and use by all States.'[44] Certain limitations on the freedom to exploit outer space set out under Article I include that the exploitation must be in the interests of mankind, that usage must be on the basis of equality and without discrimination. [45] Article IX restricts the use of outer space to prevent

[40] Vienna Convention on the Law of Treaties, *supra* at n22, Art.34.
[41] North Sea Continental Shelf Case [969] ICJ Reports 4.
[42] Danilenko, "The Concept of the "Common Heritage of Mankind" in International Law", Annals of Air and Space Law Vol XIII (1988) 262, 263.
[43] Treaty on Principles Governing the Activities of States in the Exploration and Use of Outer Space, including the Moon and Other Celestial Bodies, Jan 27 1967 18 U.S.T. 2410 (hereinafter the "Outer Space Treaty").
[44] *Id.* Article I.
[45] Milton Smith,*The Commercial Exploitation of Mineral Resources in Outer Space*, Space Law: Views of the Future, 45 (1988) 47.

harmful interference with the activities of other states.[46]

Ceres submits that the mining operation carried out on the Boznemcova was not contrary to any of these constraints. A cost-benefit calculation is required to determine the legality of the activity.[47] Ceres submits that the mining of the Boznemcova was in the interests of all mankind for three reasons.

First, the mining project produced valuable palladium reserves with which to supply the world market. Palladium is a valuable and scarce commodity. As Milton Smith has observed, the requirement that states must use celestial bodies 'without discrimination of any kind, on a basis of equality'[48] is not a strict or narrowly prescribed requirement:

> "It imposes no requirement for direct sharing of benefits in any specific manner, but requires only that space activities be beneficial in a very general sense."[49]

One example is that scientific discoveries ought to be made public so that the knowledge may be disseminated.

The requirement of equality and non-discrimination is satisfied because there is no suggestion that these resources were sold in a discriminatory or non-free market manner. Astermine did not act unreasonably or purport to exclude particular nations from purchasing palladium. Whether or not every state received the same amount of palladium is immaterial to determining the legality of the mining operation. Each individual state was free to purchase palladium at prices that were determined by how much other states were prepared to bid for the same resource. States would have made varying choices based on their economic capabilities and needs.

Second, the mining project advanced the state of scientific knowledge by successfully applying the new technique of total capture mining. The advancement of scientific knowledge is an important interest of all mankind which is explicitly recognised in Article I of the Outer Space Treaty.[50] This knowledge was publicised through freely available e-journals and web portals.

Third, one of the applications of resources from Boznemcova was the manufacturing of concrete for use in the Ceresan lunar colony. This use of the Boznemcova advanced a legitimate interest of mankind in the exploration and development of human settlement on the moon. Human settlement is, from a long-term perspective, crucial to the consolidation of human achievements in space and will greatly improve the prospects for further achievements to take place.[51] This is recognised by the preamble of the Outer Space Treaty which states that the state parties to the Treaty are:

> *"Inspired by the great prospects opening up before mankind as a result of man's entry into outer space [and] recognizing the common interest of all mankind in the progress of the exploration and use of outer space for peaceful purposes."*[52]

The new Ceresan lunar colony is a peaceful installation that will increase the human presence on the moon. Accordingly, it is to be expected that the new colony will increase the productive capacity of the moon. Given the prohibitive costs of transporting large quantities of material from the Earth to the moon, which would be one possible alternative to using materials from Boznemcova, the mining of the asteroid provided a cost-effective benefit to mankind.

Ceres notes that costs were also associated with the mining of Boznemcova but nonetheless submits that such costs do not outweigh the benefits to other countries. Specifically, Ceres addresses three potential costs of the destruction of Boznemcova. First, it might be asserted that the destruction of the asteroid lessened the value of the 'province of mankind' by eliminating one constituent part of it.[53] Such an argument would rest on an unrealistic interpretation of the international legal framework on outer space. All productive activities incur opportunity costs in that a given resource is no longer available to be used for a different purpose or to remain untouched. If the

---

[46] *Id.* Article IX.

[47] Marietta Benko, and Kai-Uwe Schrogi, 'Article I of the Outer Space Treaty Reconsidered After 30 Years: "Free Use of Outer Space" vs. "Space Benefits"', in Gabriel Lafferranderie (ed.), *Outlook on Space Law Over the Next 30 Years: Essays Published for the 30th Anniversary of the Outer Space Treaty*, (Kluwer Law International, 1997) p.70.

[48] Outer Space Treaty, *supra* note 4o, Article I.

[49] Milton Smith, *supra* note 37, p.46.

[50] Article I: 'There shall be freedom of scientific investigation in outer space, including the moon and other celestial bodies, and States shall facilitate and encourage international co-operation in such investigation.'

[51] Marietta Benko and Kai-Uwe Schrogi, *Article 1 of the Outer Space Treaty Reconsidered after 30 Years: "Free Use of Outer Space*, Outlook on Space Law over the next 30 Years: Essays Published for the 30th Anniversary of the Outer Space Treaty 67 (1997) 71.

[52] Outer Space Treaty, *supra* note 43, Preamble.

labeling of outer space as the 'province of mankind' is taken to mean that any destruction of any part of outer space is prohibited, then that interpretation would place extraordinary restraints on human development. Indeed it would thwart objectives which are specifically endorsed by the relevant treaties and conventions, including the desirability of scientific advancement, human exploration and the peaceful use of outer space. It is more plausible and pragmatic to treat the destruction of an insignificant part of that province as not inherently objectionable. The legality or otherwise of such an action should be evaluated by taking into account all the circumstances rather than being unlawful *ab initio*.

Second, Vesta might point to the negative externalities of Astermine's destruction of the asteroid to assert that the costs outweigh the benefits that accrued to mankind from the mining of the asteroid. These negative externalities include damage to satellites from space debris and the increased costs of maintaining and constructing satellites due to the impact of space debris. Ceres however questions whether the creation of space debris as a byproduct of a space activity is sufficient in itself to make that activity unlawful. Such as result would unreasonably inhibit human activity in outer space, as the amount of space debris has continuously increased with man's exploitation of space.[54] Although this space debris is a significant problem, it would be too drastic for this honourable Court to effectively hold that the creation of space debris is contrary to international law. The unusual consequences of such a claim are readily apparent. On the basis that space debris is composed in part of mission-ended satellites, rocket bodies, and fragments resulting from break-up of operational components, Ceres asks whether any space launch is *prima facie* unlawful if such debris is foreseeable? Space debris is akin to pollution in terms of its deleterious effects. On this analogy, it is more prudent to explore methods of abatement or regulation rather than holding that pollution is illegal *per se*. Ceres does not at this point make any submissions on the question of whether space debris would give rise to a well-founded claim for reparations because no such claim has been presented. It does, however, reject the extraordinary contention that activities producing space debris are contrary to international law.

[54] Stephen Gorove, "Pollution and Outer Space: A Legal Analysis and Appraisal" 5 N.Y.U. J. Int'l L. & Pol. 54.

C. The asteroid was not subjected to national appropriation

Article II of the Outer Space Treaty prohibits the national appropriation of outer space and celestial bodies.[55] Ceres further submits that Astermine did not nationally appropriate Boznemcova by means of use, occupation or claim of sovereignty. It is submitted that private entities cannot make any recognised claims to territory in outer space and therefore no assertion of ownership by a private entity could amount to national appropriation within the meaning of Article II. The eminent jurist Stephen Gorove has argued that "national appropriation" has the limited meaning that naturally attaches to the plain words of Article II.[56] Article II prohibits appropriation by states. Ceres did not assert ownership or take any other action amounting to appropriation.

Even if the actions of private entities are covered by Article II, appropriation by occupation or claim of sovereignty may be reasonably ruled out on the basis that the facts disclose no basis for such an argument. This leaves the issue of whether the "total capture mining" of Boznemcova constituted appropriation by use.

The mining activities on Boznemcova constituted exploitation of resources which does not equate with appropriation. As a matter of law, mining celestial bodies does not constitute appropriation. There is a sound distinction between "acquisition of sovereignty and of resources."[57] Article II of the Outer Space Treaty prohibits the former but not the latter. The exploitation of resources in outer space is therefore a lawful activity subject to certain usage constraints, which have been previously discussed. The Outer Space Treaty does prevent the creation of proprietary rights *"in* situ by some form of occupancy."[58] In principle the availability of the resources of outer space and celestial bodies is comparable to the access by states to the resources of the high seas.[59] Astermine was therefore constrained only by the requirements of Article I and Article IX of the Outer Space Treaty.[60]

Ceres submits that economic and scientific development is a legitimate purpose for acquiring mineral resources, pursuant to the freedom of

[55] Outer Space Treaty, *supra* at n43, Article II.

[56] Stephen Gorove "Interpreting Article II of the Outer Space Treaty" 37 Fordham L. Rev. 349,352 (1968-1969).

[57] J.E.S. Fawcett, *Outer Space: New Challenges to Law and Policy*, 12 (1984)

[58] J.E.S. Fawcett, *supra* note 44, 13

[59] Outer Space Treaty, *supra* note 43, Article XI(7).

exploration and use provided under Article I of the Outer Space Treaty. The diminution of a body of resources as a result of use is properly described under law as extraction and exploitation, not appropriation. Therefore Ceres submits that national appropriation of Boznemcova did not occur and that the key question relates only to the usage constraints on exploitation. In other words, if the exploitation of Boznemcova was in the interests of mankind then Astermine did not act contrary to international law.

VI. CERES DID NOT VIOLATE INTERNATIONAL LAW BY DESTROYING THE VESTAN NATIONAL COMMUNICATIONS SYSTEM ON 30 MAY 2036

Ceres submits that its military action against the Vestan National Communications System was justified on the basis of self-defence under Article 51 of the United Nations Charter. If the Applicant were to argue that the action was inconsistent with Ceres' obligations under the International Telecommunications Union, Ceres submits that the telecommunications in question constituted a threat to Ceresan national security under Article 34 of the Constitution of the International Telecommunications Union. Ceres denies any claim that positioning laser weapons in Earth orbit is unlawful *per se*. The Outer Space Treaty prohibits only weapons of mass destruction from being deployed in orbit.[61]

A. Justification under Article 51 of the United Nations Charter

The use of force is prohibited by Article 2(4) of the Charter subject to two well-recognised exceptions. The first exception relates to authorisation by the United Nations Security Council acting pursuant to Chapter VII. The second exception is self-defence under Article 51. Article 51 provides that if an armed attack occurs nothing shall impair the inherent right to self-defence.[62] The use of the term "inherent" recognises that the right to self-defence existed at international law prior to the Charter and that the ambit of self-defence at customary international law is relevant to the interpretation of Article 51.

Ceres relies on two alternative grounds for justifying its actions. First, the destruction of the satellite was an act of anticipatory self-defence against a potential attack by the Vestan military. Second, the destruction of the satellite was in self-defence against an attack by the Vestan-based terrorist group, Astervic.

1. Anticipatory self defence against Vesta

Ceres submits, first, that there is a customary right to anticipatory or preemptive self-defence in certain limited circumstances based on the *Caroline Incident*.[63] Following the exchange of diplomatic notes between the United Kingdom and the United States, this was accepted as reflecting an existing norm of customary international law. The threat in the *Caroline Incident* was a vessel ferrying supplies and reinforcements to Canadian rebels.[64] This right survives under Article 51 notwithstanding the use of the words "if an attack occurs". These words are capable of meaning that the right to self-defence is triggered if an attack is an immediate probability. Any practical construction of Article 51 would necessarily entitle states to act preemptively in a situation similar to that in the *Caroline Incident*. The practicality of *Caroline* is of the utmost relevance in the present context of military technology. The stark reality for states in the age of ballistic missiles, weapons of mass destruction, information warfare and highly mobile military units is that the first strike might be the only strike. The time horizon between the mobilisation of military forces and the actual attack is more truncated than at any time in human history and the level of firepower capable of being applied has also increased exponentially.[65] The point in time when defeat can be averted and the survival of a state secured is before the missiles or bombs strike.

Having established the existence of the right to preemptive or anticipatory self defence, Ceres submits that the threat posed by Vesta and the Ceresan military response were within the ambit of the Caroline doctrine and Article 51 of the United Nations Charter. The criteria by which the action ought to be evaluated are whether there was an overwhelming necessity to act whether the state

---

[61] Outer Space Treaty, *supra* at n43, Article IV(1).

[62] Charter of the United Nations, June 26, 1945, Can TS 1945 No.7.

[63] John Moore. *A Digest of International Law*, 409, 412, vol.II (1986). The principles of the Caroline Incident are derived from an exchange of diplomatic documents between the United States and Great Britain in 1842.

[64] *Id.*

[65] Rex Zedalis, "Preliminary Thoughts on Some Unresolved Questions Involving the Law of Anticipatory Self-Defence" (1987) 19 Case W. Res. J. Int'l L. 129, 131. Zedalis offers the examples of the Cuban Missile Crisis of 1961 and the 1981 Israeli strike on the Tamuz I nuclear reactor as reflecting the danger of weapons of mass destruction.

purporting to rely on the right to self defence acted proportionately.[66]

The discovery by Ceres of evidence that Vesta was planning to use its communications satellite for an armed attack on Ceres created a military necessity to act. The likelihood of an armed attack by another state is a threat of the highest order for a state. Article 51 is not self-executing; it requires value judgement and action on behalf of states based on their good faith interpretation of their international legal obligations and the application of those obligations to the facts as they appear to them.

Second, the threat was immediate. It therefore required decisive and robust action on the part of Ceres. As discussed above, orbital weapons have fundamentally changed the time horizon in which military strikes can be made. An attack by Vesta could have been carried out soon after the political decision to do so. Given the heightened state of tensions as a result of the terrorist strike from Vesta and the open hostilities along the border, it appeared that full-scale war was imminent. In this context, with the Ceresan capital having been bombarded by a missile and Ceresan and Vestan troops engaging each other in combat, a Vestan attack would not have been subject to the delays that might ordinarily be expected when one state makes a decision to attack another. Vestan forces were already mobilised and the political atmosphere within appeared ready to sanction the use of force against Ceres. Moreover, a standard mobilisation of soldiers by Ceres would be too slow in comparison to the speed of an orbital attack and at any rate would be entirely ineffective as a means of defence. Ceres could not have been expected to compromise its military situation by leaving itself open to attack while it attempted to avert the attack by diplomacy.

The issue of proportionality can be dealt with relatively briefly. If Ceres' submissions in relation to the existence of a military necessity to act in response to an immediate threat are accepted, then it is difficult to deny that the Ceresan strike was proportionate. The destruction of a satellite system is not an excessive response to a threat of armed attack. The strike caused no human casualties and only moderate economic damage by comparison with convention warfare on the Earth's surface.[67] By severing the linkage on which Vestan command and control systems relied, the Ceresan attack might be properly characterised as a "surgical strike" in the sense that it involved the destruction of a specific target in order to disable a large number of military threats.

2. Self defence against Vestan-based terrorists

Ceres submits that the missile strike against Ceres on 2 May 2036 constituted an “armed attack” giving rise to a right of self defence. The terrorist attack is attributable to Vesta for several reasons. The decision of this Court in *Diplomatic and Consular Staff in Tehran* case is authority to the effect that a state can have conduct imputed to it as a result of having breached a relevant obligation at international law. In that case, the hostage taking was attributed to Iran not because the hostage takers were agents of the state but instead because Iran had breached its international obligations by not recognising the special protection to which diplomatic staff are entitled and by not bringing the crisis to an end. In the instant case, Vesta breached its obligations under United Nations Security Council Resolution 1373 and therefore can be held responsible by Ceres for the missile attack on 2 May 2036.[68] Specifically, Vesta acted inconsistently with SCR 1373 by failing to actively suppress terrorist groups; failing to deny Astervic safe havens within Vesta; failing to take active measures to deny the supply of weapons; providing funds or allowing its funds to be distributed to a terrorist group.[69]

Alternatively, customary international law with respect to the attribution of state responsibility for terrorist groups has evolved in the context of the “war on terrorism”. In response to the terrorist attacks on September 11 2001, the United States, with the tacit acquiescence or overt approval of a substantial majority of states, justified its invasion of Afghanistan on the basis of self defence.[70] There was no suggestion that the Taliban regime had ordered the attack or that the Al Qaeda operatives were de facto agents for the state of Afghanistan. Afghanistan had, however, failed to eliminate Al Qaeda. The North Atlantic Treaty Organisation invoked Article 5 of its Charter, recognising that the

[66] *Legality of the Threat or Use of Nuclear Weapons*, 1996 I.C.J., 1.

[67] Ilia Kuskuvelis, *The Method of Genetic Effectiveness and the Future of the Military Regime of Outer Space*, Space Law: Views of the Future, 97 (1988) 83.

[68] United Nations Security Council Resolution 1373, adopted 28 September 2001.

[69] *Id.*

[70] Peter Rowe “Responses to Terror” (2002) 3 Melbourne Journal of International Law 301.

terrorist incident was an armed attack attributable to a state. Other states made declarations of support. State practice can be found in this incident. Opinio juris is also found in the supportive response from other states. On this basis, Vesta is analogous to Afghanistan. Vesta failed to suppress Astervic and indirectly funded the group. Astervic remains at large and constitutes a continuing threat. Ceres was therefore justified in attacking infrastructure which might be used by the terrorists to coordinate further attacks.

B. Justification for cutting off private telecommunications under the Constitution of the International Telecommunications Union

Ceres properly concedes that an empowering provision to cut off private telecommunications under the Constitution of the International Telecommunications Union would not provide a good defence against a claim based on Article 2(4) of the United Nations Charter. However, if Vesta were to press a claim based on the illegality of cutting off telecommunications, Ceres relies on Article 34 of the Constitution as a justification for the action. Article 34 provides that:

> "1. Members reserve the right to stop the transmission of any private telegram which may appear dangerous to the security of the State ... provided that they immediately notify the office of origin of the stoppage of any such telegram or any part thereof, except when such notification may appear dangerous to the security of the State.
>
> 2. Members also reserve the right to cut off any other private telecommunications which may appear dangerous to the security of the State...."[71]

Based on the foregoing analysis under submission V(a), Ceres submits that the intercepted Vestan communications appeared dangerous to the security of Ceres and that Ceres was therefore justified in cutting off these communications by destroying the satellite which relayed them. Given the circumstances as discussed under submission V(a) above, Ceres was justified in not giving notice. Alternatively, the note verbale to the President of the United Nations Security Council constituted adequate notice of the stoppage of communications.

VII. THE ONGOING PRESENCE OF VESTAN MILITARY INSTALLATIONS ON THE MOON IS UNLAWFUL

Article IV of the Outer Space Treaty expressly demilitarises the moon. It states that:

"The establishment of military bases, installations and fortifications, the testing of any type of weapons and the conduct of military manoeuvres on celestial bodies shall be forbidden".[72]

The plain meaning of this provision is clear. The Vestan bases are military installations that have never been used for any non-military purpose. On this ground alone, Vesta's installations are manifestly unlawful. Furthermore, Article IV provides that 'the moon and other celestial bodies shall be used by all States Parties to the Treaty exclusively for peaceful purposes.'[73] Ceres submits that 'peaceful' in this context means non-military. Subject to explicit exemptions for military personnel engaged in scientific or certain purposes, Article IV bars military activities and installations on the moon. This provides a further basis for holding that the Vestan military facilities are illegal.

Ceres submits that an alternative interpretation of 'peaceful' as meaning 'non-aggressive' is, in the words of Bin Cheng, 'needless, wrong and potentially, noxious.'[74] It should be noted, however, that irrespective of the construction given to the term 'peaceful', this Court would nevertheless need to reconcile this interpretation with the subsequent sentence which explicitly bans military installations by name.

The interpretation of 'peaceful' as meaning 'non-aggressive' is needless in the sense that it deprives the article of any true purpose. Such a construction would propose in effect that the state parties agree to prohibit that which is already illegal. Aggression is unlawful both on Earth and in outer space by reason of Article 2(4) of the United Nations Charter.[75] It is superfluous to reaffirm the application of the United Nations Charter and international law because Article III acknowledges that:

"States Parties to the treaty shall carry on activities in the exploration and use of outer space, including the moon and other celestial bodies, in accordance with international law,

[71] Constitution of the International Telecommunications Union, article 34.

[72] Outer Space Treaty, *supra* note 43, Article IV.

[73] Outer Space Treaty, *supra* note 43, Article IV.

[74] Bin Cheng, *Studies in International Space Law*, (Oxford, Clarendon Press, 1997) 520.

[75] Charter of the United Nations, *supra* at n61, Article 2(4).

including the Charter of the United Nations ..."[76]

The exemption for military personnel would also be redundant since military bases would presumably be unobjectionable insofar as they were used only for 'non-aggressive' purposes.

This interpretation is also wrong because it is clearly inconsistent with the extrinsic materials relating to the drafting of the provision and the *opinio juris* of the majority of states. The primary proponent of this construction was the United States who approached the issue as a matter of national security during the Cold War.[77] In light of the facts that the United States was a minority during the drafting process and that the end of bipolar nuclear confrontation makes such a contrived approach to Article IV inappropriate, Ceres submits that this Court ought not to acknowledge such an interpretation as valid.

The extent to which defining peaceful as 'non-military' would thwart the intentions of state parties is evident when the almost identical language of the Antarctic Treaty is evaluated. Article I of the Antarctic Treaty closely mirrors Article IV(2).[78] The deployment of military bases and weapons in Antarctica would plainly be undesirable and unintended by the states parties to that treaty. The same logic and language would, however, apply equally to the Antarctica Treaty as the Outer Space Treaty. This court ought not to abandon the clear meaning of 'peaceful' as non-military in order to allow states to deploy military forces in areas specifically set aside as being 'exclusively peaceful' under the puzzling and murky guise of acting in a 'non-aggressive' manner.

Second, Ceres submits that it is not open to Vesta to terminate its adherence to the Outer Space Treaty under the Vienna Convention. Ceres submits that the only aspects of the Vienna Convention that may be relevant are the ability for a state to withdraw in the event necessity or with the occurrence of a fundamental change of circumstances. With regard to the first aspect, it is submitted that there is no state of necessity requiring a Vestan withdrawal. Even if a state of necessity did exist, ie at the time of hostilities between Ceres and Vesta, such state of necessity does not terminate a treaty, rather it exonerates a state from its responsibilities under the treaty as long as the condition of necessity exists.[79] Given that a state of hostilities no longer exists, any exoneration Vesta may have had the benefit of has long since expired, and therefore Vesta is in material breach of the Outer Space Treaty. With regard to the first aspect, it is submitted that the International Court of Justice was correct when it observed that the changed circumstances must be of such a nature that "their effect would radically transform the extent of the obligations still to be performed".[80] There are no changed circumstances that radically transform the extent of the obligations Vesta holds; namely to remove their illegal military installations from the Moon. Therefore Vesta must remove these installations forthwith.

VIII. CONCLUSION

For the reasons stated above, it is proper for the questions presented to this Court to be answered in favour of the Respondent. Accordingly, all declarations sought by the Respondent ought to be granted and the relief sought by the Applicant must be denied.

SUBMISSIONS TO THE COURT

For the foregoing reasons, the Government of Ceres, Respondent, respectfully requests the Court to adjudge and declare that:

(i) Ceres is not liable to Vesta in relation to the launch failure of BM-52.
(ii) If Ceres was liable to Vesta in relation to the launch failure of BM-52, that liability was fully extinguished by the payment of US$860 million to the government of Vesta
(iii) In any event, the heads of damage claimed by Vesta are not recoverable.
(iv) The destruction of the Vestan communications satellite system did not cause Ceres to violate any applicable international legal principles.
(v) Ceres did not contravene international law by destroying the Boznemcova.

---

[76] Outer Space Treaty, *supra* note 43, Article III.

[77] Bin Cheng, *supra* note 55, 515

[78] The Antartic Treaty, December 1 1959, 402 U.N.T.S 71, Article I(1): "Antarctica shall be used for peaceful purposes only. There shall be prohibited, *inter alia*, any measures of a military nature, such as the establishment of military bases and fortifications".

[79] *Case concerning the Gabcikovo-Nagymaros Project (Hungary v Slovakia) (Judgement)*, [1997] ICJ Reports, 58, para.101.

[80] *Id.* para.104.

(vi) The continuing presence of Vestan military facilities and installations in New Vesta is unlawful.

INTERNATIONAL INSTITUTE OF SPACE LAW
of the
INTERNATIONAL ASTRONAUTICAL FEDERATION

Standing Committee on the Status of International Agreements Relating to Activities in Outer Space

Chairman:
Andrei D. Terekhov
Senior Legal Officer
Office of Legal Affairs
United Nations

ANNUAL REPORT – 2003

Background

At the meeting of the IISL Board of Directors held at Brighton, United Kingdom, in October 1987, the Board decided to create a standing committee of the Institute to prepare and submit at each annual Colloquium a report on the status of agreements relating to activities in outer space.

Institute members who can contribute substantively to the work of the committee are invited to serve on it. Membership is open to any interested IISL member. The committee members help collect, review and verify data concerning selected space agreements. Agreements of general global applicability or regional applicability are selected for reporting. Bilateral agreements are not included in the report. In general, the agreements included in the present report, and their status, are believed to be valid as of 1 January 2003.

Coded entries are used in the table as follows:

R = ratification, accession or succession
S = signature only
D = declaration of acceptance of rights and obligations

When no entry is made in a column opposite a state's name, that state has not signed that agreement, or is not a party to it, or that state has withdrawn from the agreement. Changes from last year are highlighted by "".**

At the meeting of the IISL Board of Directors held at Paris, France, in April 1998, the Board decided that the report should also contain basic data concerning Declarations of Principles Relating to Activities in Outer Space adopted by the General Assembly of the United Nations.

COMMITTEE MEMBERSHIP

Prof. Dr. K.-H. Böckstiegel
Institut für Luft- und Weltraumrecht
University of Cologne
Albertus-Magnus-Platz 5000
Cologne, 41 GERMANY

Prof. Carl Q. Christol
1041 Anoka Place
Pacific Palisades, CA 90272
USA

Prof. Dr. Aldo Armando Cocca
Lavalle 1527, piso 10
1048 Buenos Aires
ARGENTINA

Prof. Dr. Isabella Diederiks-Verschoor
President Emeritus, IISL
Leestraat 43, 3743 EH Baarn
NETHERLANDS

Dr. Stephen E. Doyle
3431 Bridget Brae
Shingle Springs
CA 95682
USA

Dr. Eilene Galloway
4612 29th Place, NW
Washington, D.C. 20008
USA

Prof. Dr. Vladimir Kopal
IAF General Counsel
Vidlicová 2200
16000 Prague 6 - Dejvice
CZECH REPUBLIC

Prof. Francis Lyall
Department of Public Law
University of Aberdeen
Aberdeen, AB92UB
SCOTLAND

Mr. G. Lafferranderie
Legal Adviser, ESA
8-10, rue Mario Nikis
Paris 75738 FRANCE

Mrs. Tanja L. Masson-Zwaan
Van der Oudermeulenlaan 11a
2243 CR Wassenaar
NETHERLANDS

Dr. HE Qizhi
Legal Advisor
Department of Treaty & Law
Ministry of Foreign Affairs
Beijing CHINA

Mr. David Sagar
Flat 4, 51 Cadogan Gardens
London SW3 2 TH
UNITED KINGDOM

Dr. A. D. Terekhov (Chairman)
Office of Legal Affairs
Room 3430G, UN Secretariat
New York, NY 10017 USA

Mr. Leo A. Webb
4041 Valley Oaks Drive
Clinton, IA 52732-9467
USA

AGREEMENTS INCLUDED

1. **1963 NTBT** - **Treaty Banning Nuclear Weapon Tests in the Atmosphere, in Outer Space and Under Water; done at Moscow on 5 August 1963; entered into force on 10 October 1963. (14 UST 1313; TIAS 5433; 480 UNTS 43)**
http://fletcher.tufts.edu/multi/texts/BH454.txt

2. **1967 OST** - **Treaty on Principles Governing the Activities of States in the Exploration and Use of Outer Space, including the Moon and Other Celestial Bodies; done at Washington, London and Moscow on 27 January 1967; entered into force on 10 October 1967. (18 UST 2410; TIAS 6347; 610 UNTS 205)**
http://www.oosa.unvienna.org/SpaceLaw/outerspt.htm

3. **1968 ARRA** - **Agreement on the Rescue of Astronauts, the Return of Astronauts and the Return of Objects Launched into Outer Space; done at Washington, London and Moscow on 22 April 1968; entered into force on 3 December 1968. (19 UST 7570; TIAS 6599; 672 UNTS 119)**
http://www.oosa.unvienna.org/SpaceLaw/rescue.htm

4. **1972 LIAB** - **Convention on International Liability for Damage Caused by Space Objects; done at Washington, London and Moscow on 29 March 1972; entered into force on 1 September 1972. (24 UST 2389; TIAS 7762; 961 UNTS 187)**
http://fletcher.tufts.edu/multi/texts/BH595.txt

5. **1975 REG** - **Convention on Registration of Objects Launched into Outer Space; done at New York on 14 January 1975; entered into force on 15 September 1976. (28 UST 695; TIAS 8480; 1023 UNTS 15)**
http://www.oosa.unvienna.org/SORegister/regist.htm

6. **1979 MOON** - **Agreement Governing the Activities of States on the Moon and Other Celestial Bodies; done at New York on 18 December 1979; entered into force on 11 July 1984. (18 ILM 1434; UN doc. A/RES/34/68 of 14 December 1979, Annex)**
http://www.oosa.unvienna.org/SpaceLaw/moon.htm

7. **1971 ITSO** - **Agreement Relating to the International Telecommunications Satellite Organization (ITSO) with annexes; done at Washington on 20 August 1971; entered into force on 12 February 1973; amended September and October 1996, and July 2001. (23 UST 3813, 4091; TIAS 7532)**
The 1971 agreement, with annexes and Operating Agreement, may be found at–
http://fletcher.tufts.edu/multi/texts/BH585.txt

8. **1976 IMSO** - **Convention on the International Mobile Satellite Organization (IMSO) with annex; done at London on 3 September 1976; entered into force on 16 July 1979; amended December 1994 and September 1998. (31 UST 1, 135; TIAS 9605)**
The 1976 agreement, as amended 1985, with Protocol (1981), may be found at–
http://fletcher.tufts.edu/multi/texts/BH688.txt

9. 1971 INTR - Agreement on the Establishment of the "Intersputnik" International System and Organization of Space Communications; done at Moscow on 15 November 1971; entered into force on 12 July 1972. (862 UNTS 3)
http://www.intersputnik.com/doc2.shtml

10. 1976 INTC - Agreement on Cooperation in the Exploration and Use of Outer Space for Peaceful Purposes (INTERCOSMOS); done at Moscow on 13 July 1976; entered into force on 25 March 1977. (16 ILM 1)
http://www.nasda.go.jp/lib/space-law/chapter_2/2-2-2-7_e.html [Note: ***The document served from this website omits the words "and Use" in the title and is incorrectly dated "1973" instead of "1976".*****]**

11. 1976 ARBS - The Agreement of the Arab Corporation for Space Communications (ARABSAT); done at Cairo on Wednesday, 14 Rabi Al Akhar 1396 H., corresponding to April 14, 1976; entered into force on July 16, 1976. (Space Law and Related Documents, U.S. Senate, 101st Congress, 2nd Session, 395 (1990))
http://www.nasda.go.jp/lib/space-law/chapter_2/2-2-2-15/index_e.html

12. 1975 ESA - Convention for the Establishment of a European Space Agency (ESA) with annexes; done at Paris on 30 May 1975; entered into force on 30 October 1980. (14 ILM 864)
http://www.esa.int/convention/

13. 1982 EUTL - Convention Establishing the European Telecommunications Satellite Organization (EUTELSAT); done at Paris on 15 July 1982; entered into force on 1 September 1985; amended May 1999. (XI Annals of Air and Space Law 416 (1986); UK Misc. No. 4, Cmnd. 9154 (1984))
The 1982 agreement, with annexes, may be found at–
http://www.nasda.go.jp/lib/space-law/chapter_3/3-2-2-2/index_e.html

14. 1983 EUMT - Convention for the Establishment of a European Organization for the Exploitation of Meteorological Satellites (EUMETSAT); done at Geneva on 24 May 1983; entered into force on 19 June 1986. (Federal Republic of Germany Bundesgesetzblatt, Jahrgang 1987, Teil 11, p. 256 (1987). This Convention has been published in the national bulletins of the ratifying States)
http://www.nasda.go.jp/lib/space-law/chapter_3/3-2-2-6/index_e.html

15. 1974 BRUS - Convention Relating to the Distribution of Programme-carrying Signals Transmitted by Satellite; done at Brussels on 21 May 1974; entered into force on 25 August 1979. (1144 UNTS 3)
http://www.nasda.go.jp/lib/space-law/chapter_2/2-2-2-11_e.html

The texts of all the above agreements, except 1974 BRUS, 1982 EUTL and 1983 EUMT, were published in Space Law and Related Documents, U.S. Senate, 101st Congress, 2nd Session, June 1990.

Treaty Status Table as of January 1, 2003

TREATY — STATE	(1) 1963 NTBT	(2) 1967 OST	(3) 1968 ARRA	(4) 1972 LIAB	(5) 1975 REG	(6) 1979 MOON	(7) 1971 ITSO	(8) 1976 IMSO	(9) 1971 INTR	(10) 1976 INTC	(11) 1976 ARBS	(12) 1975 ESA	(13) 1982 EUTL	(14) 1983 EUMT	(15) 1974 BRUS
Afghanistan	R	R					R		R						
Albania													R		
Algeria	S	R		S			R	R			R				
Andorra													R		
Angola							R								
Antigua and Barbuda	R	R	R	R	R										
Argentina	R	R	R	R	R		R	R							S
Armenia	R						R						R		R
Australia	R	R	R	R	R	R	R	R							R
Austria	R	R	R	R	R	R	R					R	R	R	R
Azerbaijan							R						R		
Bahamas	R	R	R				R	R							
Bahrain							R	R			R				
Bangladesh	R	R					R	R							
Barbados		R	R				R								
Belarus	R	R	R	R	R			R	R				R		
Belgium	R	R	R	R	R		R	R				R	R	R	S
Benin	R	R		R			R								
Bhutan	R						R								
Bolivia	R	S	S				R								
Bosnia and Herzegovina	R		R	R			R	R					R		R
Botswana	R	S	R	R			R								
Brazil	R	R	R	R			R	R							S
Brunei Darussalam							R	R							
Bulgaria	R	R	R	R	R		R	R	R	R			R		
Burkina Faso	S	R					R								
Burundi	S	S		S	S		S								
Cambodia				S											
Cameroon	S	S	R				R	R							
Canada	R	R	R	R	R		R	R				(1)			
Cape Verde	R						R								
Central African Republic	R	S		S			R								
Chad	R						R								
Chile	R	R	R	R	R	R	R	R							
China		R	R	R	R		R	R							
Colombia	R	S	S	S			R	R							
Comoros							R	*R*							
Congo			S				R								
Costa Rica	R		S	S			R	R							R
Cote d'Ivoire	R						R								S
Croatia	R						R	R					R		R
Cuba		R	R	R	R		R	R	R	R					
Cyprus	R	R	R	R	R		R	R					R		S

Note: (1) Canada has a Cooperation Agreement with ESA, but is not a Member.

Treaty Status Table as of January 1, 2003

TREATY ---- STATE	(1) 1963 NTBT	(2) 1967 OST	(3) 1968 ARRA	(4) 1972 LIAB	(5) 1975 REG	(6) 1979 MOON	(7) 1971 ITSO	(8) 1976 IMSO	(9) 1971 INTR	(10) 1976 INTC	(11) 1976 ARBS	(12) 1975 ESA	(13) 1982 EUTL	(14) 1983 EUMT	(15) 1974 BRUS
Czech Republic	R	R	R	R	R		R	R	R	R			R		
Dem. People's Rep. of Korea							R		R						
Dem. Rep. of the Congo (formerly - Zaire)	R	S	S	S			R								
Denmark	R	R	R	R	R		R	R				R	R	R	
Djibouti											R				
Dominican Republic	R	R	S	R			R								
Ecuador	R	R	R	R			R								
Egypt	R	R	R	S			R	R			R				
El Salvador	R	R	R	S			R								
Equatorial Guinea	R	R					R								
Estonia													R		
Ethiopia	S	S					R								
Fiji	R	R	R	R			R								
Finland	R	R	R	R			R	R				R	R	R	
France		R	R	R	R	S	R	R				R	R	R	S
Gabon	R		R	R			R	R							
Gambia	R	S	R	S			R								
Georgia							R		R				R		
Germany	R	R	R	R	R		R	R	R			R	R	R	R
Ghana	R	S	S	S			R	R							
Greece	R	R	R	R	*R*		R	R					R	R	R
Guatemala	R			S		S	R								
Guinea							R								
Guinea-Bissau	R	R	R				R								
Guyana		S	R												
Haiti	S	S	S	S			R								
Holy See		S					R						R		
Honduras	R	S		S			R								
Hungary	R	R	R	R	R		R	R	R	R			R		
Iceland	R	R	R	S			R	R					R		
India	R	R	R	R	R	S	R	R	R						
Indonesia	R	S	R	R	R		R	R							
Iran (Islamic Republic of)	R	S	R	R	S		R	R							
Iraq	R	R	R	R			R	R			R				
Ireland	R	R	R	R			R					R	R	R	
Israel	R	R	R	R			R	R							S
Italy	R	R	R	R			R	R				R	R	R	R
Jamaica	R	R	S				R								R
Japan	R	R	R	R	R		R	R							
Jordan	R	S	S	S			R				R				
Kazakhstan		R	R	R	R	R	R		R				R		
Kenya	R	R		R			R	R							R
Kuwait	R	R	R	R			R	R			R				
Kyrgyzstan							R		R						
Lao People's Dem. Republic	R	R	R	R					R						

Treaty Status Table as of January 1, 2003

TREATY ---- STATE	(1) 1963 NTBT	(2) 1967 OST	(3) 1968 ARRA	(4) 1972 LIAB	(5) 1975 REG	(6) 1979 MOON	(7) 1971 ITSO	(8) 1976 IMSO	(9) 1971 INTR	(10) 1976 INTC	(11) 1976 ARBS	(12) 1975 ESA	(13) 1982 EUTL	(14) 1983 EUMT	(15) 1974 BRUS
Latvia								R					R		
Lebanon	R	R	R	S			R	R			R				S
Lesotho		S	S												
Liberia	R							R							
Libyan Arab Jamahiriya	R	R					R	R			R				
Liechtenstein				R	R		R						R		
Lithuania													R		
Luxembourg	R	S	S	R			R						R	*R*	
Madagascar	R	R	R				R								
Malawi	R						R								
Malaysia	R	S	S				R	R							
Maldives			R												
Mali	S	R		R			R								
Malta	R		S	R			R	R					R		
Marshall Islands								R							
Mauritania	R						R				R				
Mauritius	R	R	R				R	R							
Mexico	R	R	R	R	R	R	R	R							R
Micronesia (Fed. States of)							R								
Monaco			S				R	R					R		
Mongolia	R	R	R	R	R		R		R	R					
Morocco	R	R	R	R		R	R	R			R				R
Mozambique							R	R							
Myanmar	R	R	S												
Nepal	R	R	R	S			R								
Netherlands	R	R	R	R	R	R	R	R				R	R	R	
New Zealand	R	R	R	R			R	R							
Nicaragua	R	S	S	S	S		R		R						R
Niger	R	R	R	R	R		R								
Nigeria	R	R	R				R	R							
Norway	R	R	R	R	R		R	R				R	R	R	
Oman				S			R	R			R				
Pakistan	R	R	R	R	R	R	R	R							
Panama	R	S		R			R	R							R
Papua New Guinea	R	R	R	R			R								
Paraguay	S						R								
Peru	R	R	R	*R*	R	S	R	R							R
Philippines	R	S	S	S		R	R	R							
Poland	R	R	R	R	R		R	R	R	R			R		
Portugal	S	R	R				R	R				R	R	R	R
Qatar				R			R	R			R				
Republic of Korea	R	R	R	R	R		R	R							
Republic of Moldova													R		
Romania	R	R	R	R		S	R	R	R	R			R		
Russian Federation	R	R	R	R	R		R	R	R	R			R		R

Treaty Status Table as of January 1, 2003

TREATY ---- STATE	(1) 1963 NTBT	(2) 1967 OST	(3) 1968 ARRA	(4) 1972 LIAB	(5) 1975 REG	(6) 1979 MOON	(7) 1971 ITSO	(8) 1976 IMSO	(9) 1971 INTR	(10) 1976 INTC	(11) 1976 ARBS	(12) 1975 ESA	(13) 1982 EUTL	(14) 1983 EUMT	(15) 1974 BRUS
Rwanda	R	S	S	S			R								R
Samoa	R														
San Marino	R	R	R										R		
Saudi Arabia		R		R			R	R			R				
Senegal	R		S	R			R	R							S
Seychelles	R	R	R	R	R										
Sierra Leone	R	R	S	S											
Singapore	R	R	R	R	S		R	R							
Slovakia	R	R	R	R	R			R		R			R		
Slovenia	R		R	R									R		R
Somalia	S	S	S				R				R				
South Africa	R	R	R	S			R	R							
Spain	R	R	R	R	R		R	R				R	R	R	S
Sri Lanka	R	R		R			R	R							
St. Vincent and Grenadines		R	R	R	R										
Sudan	R						R				R				
Suriname	R														
Swaziland	R		R				R								
Sweden	R	R	R	R	R		R	R				R	R	R	
Switzerland	R	R	R	R	R		R	R				R	R	R	R
Syrian Arab Republic	R	R	R	R			R		R		R				
Tajikistan							R		R						
Tanzania							R	R							
Thailand	R	R	R				R								
The former Yugoslav Republic of Macedonia													R		R
Togo	R	R		R			R								*R*
Tonga	R	R	R												
Trinidad and Tobago	R	S		R			R								R
Tunisia	R	R	R	R			R	R			R				
Turkey	R	R	S				R	R					R	R	
Turkmenistan									R						
Uganda	R	R					R								
Ukraine	R	R	R	R	R			R	R				R		
United Arab Emirates		R		R	R		R	R			R				
United Kingdom	R	R	R	R	R		R	R				R	R	R	
United Rep. of Tanzania	R			S			R								
United States of America	R	R	R	R	R		R	R							R
Uruguay	R	R	R	R	R	R	R								
Uzbekistan							R								
Venezuela	R	R	S	R			R								
Viet Nam		R					R	R	R	R					
Yemen	R	R	R				R		R		R				
Yugoslavia	R	S	R	R	R		R	R					R		R
Zambia	R	R	R	R			R								
Zimbabwe							R								

Treaty Status Table as of January 1, 2003
~ Totals for 178 States ~

TREATY — STATE	(1) 1963 NTBT	(2) 1967 OST	(3) 1968 ARRA	(4) 1972 LIAB	(5) 1975 REG	(6) 1979 MOON	(7) 1971 ITSO	(8) 1976 IMSO	(9) 1971 INTR	(10) 1976 INTC	(11) 1976 ARBS	(12) 1975 ESA	(13) 1982 EUTL	(14) 1983 EUMT	(15) 1974 BRUS
"Old" Ratifications	124	97	88	81	44	10	148	86	24	10	20	15	49	17	25
"New" Ratifications				1	1			1						1	1
Total Ratifications	**124**	**97**	**88**	**82**	**45**	**10**	**148**	**87**	**24**	**10**	**20**	**15**	**49**	**18**	**26**
"Old" Signatures	10	27	24	25	4	5	1								10
"New" Signatures															
Total Signatures	**10**	**27**	**24**	**25**	**4**	**5**	**1**								**10**

~ Changes in status since the 2002 Report ~

Agreements for which status has changed:				(4) 1972 LIAB	(5) 1975 REG			(8) 1976 IMSO						(14) 1983 EUMT	(15) 1974 BRUS
Comoros							R	*R*							
Greece	R	R	R	R	*R*		R	R					R	R	R
Luxembourg	R	S	S	R			R						R	*R*	
Peru	R	R	R	*R*	R	S	R	R							R
Togo	R	R		R			R								*R*

Treaty Status Table as of January 1, 2003, for certain IGOs

TREATY *(See Note below.)* ---- ORGANIZATION	(3) 1968 ARRA	(4) 1972 LIAB	(5) 1975 REG	(6) 1979 MOON
European Space Agency (ESA)	D	D	D	
European Org. for the Exploitation of Meteorological Satellites (EUMETSAT)			D	
European Telecommunications Satellite Org. (EUTELSAT)		D		
Totals for 3 Organizations:	1	2	2	

Note: The Committee believes that only four of the agreements covered in the report (1968 ARRA, 1972 LIAB, 1975 REG and 1979 MOON) provide for a declaration of acceptance of rights and obligations ("D") by IGOs.

Declarations of Principles Relating to Activities in Outer Space adopted by the General Assembly of the United Nations

1. Declaration of Legal Principles Governing the Activities of States in the Exploration and Use of Outer Space (General Assembly resolution 1962 (XVIII)). Adopted without vote on 13 December 1963. http://www.oosa.unvienna.org/SpaceLaw/gares/html/gares_18_1962.html

2. Principles Governing the Use by States of Artificial Earth Satellites for International Direct Television Broadcasting (General Assembly resolution 37/92). http://www.un.org/documents/ga/res/37/a37r092.htm Adopted by 107 votes to 13, with 13 abstentions, on 10 December 1982 as follows (voting results are reproduced from UN document A/37/PV.100 of 17 December 1982):

   In favour: Afghanistan, Algeria, Argentina, Bahrain, Bangladesh, Barbados, Benin, Bhutan, Bolivia, Botswana, Brazil, Bulgaria, Burma, Botswana, Burundi, Byelorussian Soviet Socialist Republic, Central African Republic, Chad, Chili, China, Colombia, Comoros, Congo, Cuba, Cyprus, Czechoslovakia, Democratic Kampuchea, Democratic Yemen, Djibouti, Dominican Republic, Ecuador, Egypt, El Salvador, Ethiopia, Fiji, Gabon, Gambia, German Democratic Republic, Ghana, Guyana, Haiti, Honduras, Hungary, India, Indonesia, Iran (Islamic Republic of), Iraq, Jamaica, Jordan, Kenya, Kuwait, Lao People's Democratic Republic, Liberia, Libyan Arab Jamahiriya, Madagascar, Malaysia, Maldives, Mali, Malta, Mauritania, Mauritius, Mexico, Mongolia, Mozambique, Nepal, Nicaragua, Niger, Nigeria, Oman, Pakistan, Panama, Papua New Guinea, Peru, Philippines, Poland, Qatar, Romania, Rwanda, Sao Tome and Principe, Saudi Arabia, Senegal, Sierra Leone, Singapore, Solomon Islands, Somalia, Sri Lanka, Sudan, Suriname, Syrian Arab Republic, Thailand, Togo, Trinidad and Tobago, Tunisia, Turkey, Uganda, Ukrainian Soviet Socialist Republic, Union of Soviet Socialist Republics, United Arab Emirates, United Republic of Cameroon, United Republic of Tanzania, Upper Volta, Uruguay, Venezuela, Viet Nam, Yemen, Yugoslavia, Zaire, Zambia.

   Against: Belgium, Denmark, Germany, Federal Republic of, Iceland, Israel, Italy, Japan, Luxembourg, Netherlands, Norway, Spain, United Kingdom of Great Britain and Northern Ireland, United States of America.

   Abstaining: Australia, Austria, Canada, Finland, France, Greece, Ireland, Lebanon, Malawi, Morocco, New Zealand, Portugal, Sweden.

3. Principles Relating to Remote Sensing of the Earth from Outer Space (General Assembly resolution 41/65). Adopted without vote on 3 December 1986. http://www.un.org/documents/ga/res/41/a41r065.htm [Note: *The document served from this website omits the word "Outer" in the title.*]

4. Principles Relevant to the Use of Nuclear Power Sources in Outer Space (General Assembly resolution 47/68). Adopted without vote on 14 December 1992. http://www.un.org/documents/ga/res/47/a47r068.htm

5. Declaration on International Cooperation in the Exploration and Use of Outer Space for the Benefit and in the Interests of All States, Taking into Particular Account the Needs of Developing Countries (General Assembly resolution 51/122). Adopted without vote on 13 December 1996. http://www.un.org/documents/ga/res/51/a51r122.htm

Note: A copy of this report can be downloaded from the Institute's web site– http://www.iafastro-iisl.com/main%20pages/committee_8.htm

INTERNATIONAL INSTITUTE OF SPACE LAW
OF THE INTERNATIONAL ASTRONAUTICAL FEDERATION

INSTITUT INTERNATIONAL DE DROIT SPATIAL
DE LA FEDERATION INTERNATIONALE D' ASTRONAUTIQUE

3-5, RUE MARIO NIKIS
75015 PARIS - FRANCE

Tél. 33-1-45.67.42.60
Telefax 33-1-42.73.21.20

STATUTES

ARTICLE I

The name of the Institute shall be the International Institute of Space Law of the International Astronautical Federation.

ARTICLE II

The purposes and objectives of the Institute shall include:

(a) The providing of advice to the President of the International Astronautical Federation when requested;
(b) Cooperation with appropriate international organizations and national institutions in the field of space law;
(c) The holding of meetings, colloquia and competitions on juridical and social science aspects of space activities, thereby providing forums for individuals from different legal systems and regions of the world to engage in the free expression and exchange of ideas relevant to space law and policy;
(d) The preparation or commissioning of studies and reports;
(e) The publication of books, proceedings, reports and other papers;
(f) The granting and presentation of awards and certificates;
(g) The conduct of such other activities as may be considered desirable in fostering the development of space law and studies of legal and social science aspects of the exploration and use of outer space.

ARTICLE III

Section 1

Individuals distinguished by their contributions to or of proven interest in the field of space law or other social science aspects related to space activities, may be elected as members of the Institute by the Board of Directors upon an application recommended in each case by a Director, or by three members of the Institute.

Section 2

Corporate bodies and other institutions actively engaged or otherwise interested in the field of space law or other social science aspects related to space activities, may be elected by the Board of Directors as institutional members of the Institute upon an application recommended in each case by a Director, or by three members of the Institute. Corporate bodies and other institutions that are members of the International Astronautical Federation (IAF) may be elected as institutional members of the Institute so long as no prejudice to the IAF is thereby incurred.

October 2001

Section 3

Election to membership of the Institute shall be by a majority vote of the voting members of the Board of Directors in attendance at an annual or special meeting of the Board, or by a majority of affirmative answers of the voting members of the Board if the vote is held by mail.

ARTICLE IV

Section 1

All members of the Institute shall pay annual membership dues in accordance with the Bye-laws. These dues are expressed in terms of units.

Section 2

The Board of Directors shall establish the value of the unit in which membership dues are expressed. Alterations in the value of the unit shall take effect for each member or institutional member at the end of the period for which the relevant membership dues have been paid.

Section 3

Members of the Institute who are in default of their membership dues shall lose the right to vote in an annual or other meetings. Members of the Institute may be removed from the membership of the Institute by decision of the Board of Directors, if they are in arrears of membership dues for more than two years.

Section 4

On cause shown, the Board of Directors may reduce or remit the membership fee for a particular member.

Section 5

The Board of Directors may remove from membership of the Institute any member whom they judge to have violated the principles of the Statutes. Such decisions shall be taken by a two thirds majority vote of the voting members of the Board present at the meeting at which the decision is taken.

ARTICLE V

Section 1

An annual meeting of the Institute shall be held each year, and special meetings may also be held, at such times and places as the Board of Directors may determine.

Section 2

The Board of Directors shall submit to each annual meeting a report on the activities of the Institute. The report shall outline the events and accomplishments of the preceding year and put forward the policy and projects of the Institute for the future.

Section 3

The annual meeting shall elect from among the members of the Institute, by a majority vote of the members present, the officers and other Directors of the Board, with due regard to the provisions of Article VI, Sections 2 and 3.

ARTICLE VI

Section 1

The governing body of the Institute is the Board of Directors. The officers of the Institute are the President, two Vice-Presidents, the Secretary and the Treasurer. The President, Presidents Emeriti, the two Vice-Presidents, the Secretary, the Treasurer and fourteen other Directors shall be the voting members of the Board. Any Honorary Directors of the Institute and the Presidents of the International Astronautical Federation and of the International Academy of Astronautics ex officio shall be non-voting members of the Board of Directors.

Section 2

The Institute will seek that the membership of the Board of Directors shall reflect and represent the different regions of the world and different legal systems, due regard being paid especially to those countries in which significant space programmes or considerable efforts to develop space law have been made.

Section 3

The officers and other Directors shall be elected for a period of three years, and may be re-elected. Members of the Nomination Committee acting in accordance with the Bye-laws, and members of the Institute when electing officers and other members of the Board, shall take account of the desirability of ensuring both a continuity and an adequate rotation of membership within the Board. The election of the officers and other Directors shall be effected on the basis of the principle of progressive rotation. Each year, about one third of them shall be elected.

Section 4

In the case of a vacancy occurring in the Board of Directors between two annual meetings, the Board may appoint an acting officer or other Director to fill the vacancy until the expiry of the relevant term, subject to the approval of that appointment by the next annual meeting. If a Director is appointed as an acting officer, the Board may make a similar appointment of a new Director to fill the vacancy so caused.

Section 5

An outgoing President, who has served in that capacity over several years and has contributed substantially to the development and the activities of the Institute, may be elected for life as a President Emeritus by a majority vote of the members of the Institute present at its meeting.

Section 6

On the recommendation of the Board of Directors, persons who have made outstanding contributions to international cooperation in the peaceful uses of outer space, or to the development of space law, as well as officers and other Directors of the Institute, who have served for several succeeding terms and have contributed substantially to the work of the Institute, may be elected as Honorary Directors. They may attend meetings of the Board of Directors in a consultative capacity.

ARTICLE VII

Section 1

The President of the Institute shall guide and supervise the activities of the Institute pursuant to its Statutes and in accordance with its Bye-laws. The President shall represent the Institute in its external relations, including those with the International Astronautical Federation.

Section 2

The Board of Directors shall:

(a) Carry out the purposes and objectives of the Institute as set forth in Article II of these Statutes;
(b) Implement the resolutions and directives adopted at the annual meetings of the Institute;
(c) Create standing committees with appropriate terms of reference and powers for their functions;
(d) Create ad hoc committees and working groups for specific purposes and functions;
(e) Appoint members of the Institute to fill vacancies occurring in the membership of the Board of Directors in accordance with Art. VI (4) of these Statutes;
(f) Supervise the correspondence of the Institute and provide for the safekeeping of the archives thereof;
(g) Establish a secretariat as appropriate, designate its duties and supervise all its activities;
(h) Arrange for meetings and colloquia;
(i) Arrange for the publication of books, proceedings, reports and other papers;
(j) Make recommendations concerning the awarding of medals, certificates and prizes;
(k) Approve budgets and supervise accounts;
(l) Accept donations and legacies, and funds from private sources, and contributions from national and international organizations, governments and agencies;
(m) Approve the annual reports of the President and the Treasurer to be presented at the annual meetings of the Institute, and the annual report of the President to be presented at the plenary meeting of the General Assembly of the Federation.

Section 3

At least ten of the voting members of the Board of Directors present at its meeting, including the President or Acting President shall constitute a quorum. Where in exceptional cases a matter must be decided by mail, the same number of answers shall be required for a valid decision of the Board if a vote is held by mail.

Section 4

Decisions of the Board of Directors shall be taken, so far as possible, by consensus. Where a decision is taken by vote, Directors may cast their votes by mail or other written means on any action proposed to be taken by the Board. Except where these Statutes and relative Bye-laws provide otherwise, decisions by vote of the Board shall be valid when taken by a majority of the voting members present, or indicating their view in writing. In the case of a tie, the President shall have a casting as well as a deliberative vote.

Section 5

The ordinary affairs of the Board of Directors and of the Institute shall be conducted in accordance with the Bye-laws of the Institute. These Bye-laws shall be adopted by the Institute at an annual or special meeting by a majority vote of its members present upon a recommendation of the Board of Directors.

Section 6

The membership of standing committees, of ad hoc committees and of working groups, shall be determined by the President in consultation with the Board of Directors.

Section 7

The President, in consultation with the Board shall, by the end of April of each year, appoint the Chairman and members of the Nomination Committee responsible for nominating candidates for election as officers or other Board members whose terms of office are to begin after each annual meeting. The Committee shall be composed of not less than three, but not more than five members. The Report of the Nomination Committee shall be submitted to the President not later than one month before the annual meeting.

ARTICLE VIII

Section 1

These Statutes and Bye-laws shall be adopted at a meeting of the Board of Directors by a two-thirds majority vote of the voting members of the Board, subject to confirmation of this adoption at the next annual meeting of the Institute by a simple majority of members of the Institute present at that meeting.

Section 2

These Statutes and Bye-laws may be amended at any meeting of the Board of Directors by a two-thirds majority vote of the voting members of the Board, subject to confirmation of the amendment at the next annual meeting of the Institute by a simple majority of members of the Institute present at that meeting. All members of the Institute shall be informed of the intention to present such an amendment for confirmation at least six weeks prior to the next annual meeting.

Section 3

The Institute shall not enact Statutes or Bye-laws or amendments to either which are inconsistent with the provisions of the Constitution of the International Astronautical Federation, or its resolutions pertaining to the Institute.

BYE-LAWS

1. The President of the Institute shall preside at meetings of the Institute and of the Board of Directors. If unable to do so, the President may appoint one of the Vice-Presidents, and, if either of them is unable to do so, another Director to preside at a particular meeting. If the President is unable so to appoint or has not done so in time, a Vice-President, or if necessary another Director, appointed by a majority of the members of the Board present, shall preside and have the powers of the President for the purpose.

2. The Board of Directors shall endeavour to take decisions by consensus, but, if necessary, voting in the Board of Directors shall be by a show of hands, the President or Secretary informing the meeting of the views of those not present who have notified their view in writing on a matter. Such written views shall, wherever possible, be treated as votes on the matter under discussion.

3. The Board of Directors shall cause minutes to be kept of its meetings and of all actions taken by the Board. Such minutes shall be deposited with the Secretariat of the International Astronautical Federation and any member of the Institute in good standing may inspect them at any reasonable time.

4. A Nomination Committee, itself appointed by the President in consultation with the Board, shall make recommendations to the annual meeting as to elections of the officers and other Directors of the Board. A person may be elected to the Board of Directors even though his or her name is not included in the list of recommendations made by the Nomination Committee. The Board and members attending shall be informed of the recommendations of the Nomination Committee which shall be made available at the latest by forty-eight hours prior to the annual meeting. In making its recommendations the Nomination Committee shall have regard to the distinction of the contribution made to space law by potential nominees, as well as to the provisions of Article VI Sections 2 and 3 of the Statutes of the Institute.

5. The responsibilities of the Secretary of the Institute include:

(a) Maintaining the list of members of the Institute;
(b) Maintaining all necessary records, including financial records;
(c) Making arrangements for meetings of the Board;
(d) Taking the minutes of the meetings of the Board, and the annual and other meetings of the Institute;
(e) Depositing copies of the minutes of the Board with the International Astronautical Federation, and with the approval of the Board, making suitable arrangements for, the custody of the records of the Institute;
(f) In consultation with the Board and with the Secretariat of the International Astronautical Federation, making arrangements for the annual and other meetings of the Institute;
(g) Coordinating the Institute's involvement in the preparation of and making arrangements for any moot court or other competition involving or run by the Institute;
(h) Conducting the routine correspondence of the Institute;
(i) Communicating with members of the Institute, including preparing and seeing to the circulation of the Newsletter.

6. The responsibilities of the Treasurer of the Institute include:

(a) Ingathering membership dues and receiving donations and other monies received for or arising from the work of the Institute;
(b) Operating appropriate bank accounts on behalf of the Institute;
(c) Preparing appropriate budgets for approval by the Board;
(d) Paying bills incurred by the Institute or its officers in the carrying out of the purposes of the Institute from monies held by the Institute.

6. The President of the Institute shall refer an application for membership of the Institute to a membership committee, which he shall appoint, and the Board shall be informed of the report of that committee before it decides on the election of the applicant.

7. The Secretary of the Institute shall be informed in writing of any proposals for the amendment of the Statutes or Bye-laws of the Institute, other than those made by the Board, at least twelve weeks prior to the annual meeting, and any such proposal must be supported in writing by at least twenty individual fully paid-up members of the Institute.

8. The annual membership dues payable by an individual member of the Institute shall be one unit of contribution dues. Honorary Directors, if not otherwise members of the Institute, are exempt from the requirement to pay annual membership dues. Corporate or institutional members of the Institute shall pay three or more units of contribution dues of membership dues a year, the level of contribution being selected by the Institutional member in agreement with the Board of Directors.

9. A corporate or institutional member paying three contribution units per year has the right to nominate up to three representatives to vote in the annual meeting. Each additional contribution unit allows the institutional member to nominate one additional such representative.

10. A member of the Institute remains in good standing in the Institute provided that membership dues are not in arrear, and that a current mailing address has been received by the Secretary.

AUTHOR INDEX